ATLANTIC JEOPARDY

Book 1

PQ 17 – Convoy to Hell

Book 2

Trawlers go to War

Book 3

Night of the U-Boats

PQ 17 – Convoy to Hell

THE SURVIVORS' STORY

PQ 17 – Convoy to Hell

to Hell

THE SURVIVORS' STORY

by

PAUL LUND

of the *Lord Austin*

and

HARRY LUDLAM

W. FOULSHAM & CO. LTD.

LONDON

NEW YORK   TORONTO   SYDNEY

W. FOULSHAM & CO. LTD.
Yeovil Road, Slough, England

ATLANTIC JEOPARDY

by

PAUL LUND

and

HARRY LUDLAM

LONDON

W. FOULSHAM & CO. LTD

NEW YORK   TORONTO   SYDNEY

foulsham

Yeovil Road, Slough, Berkshire SL1 4JH

foulsham
Yeovil Road, Slough, Berkshire SL1 4JH

ISBN 0-572-01577-1

First published by W. Foulsham as PQ 17 – Convoy to Hell (1968),
Trawlers go to War (1971) and Night of the U-Boats (1973)
This Omnibus edition published 1990

Printed in Great Britain by St Edmundsbury Press Limited
Bury St Edmunds, Suffolk

To all the men who survived PQ 17
and to the memory of those who
did not, this book is dedicated.

CONTENTS

I have never been able to rejoice with my American friends on Independence Day, because July 4 is, to me, a day to hang my head in grief for all the men who lost their lives on Convoy PQ 17 and in shame at the recollection of one of the bleakest episodes in Royal Naval history, when the warships deserted the merchant ships and left them to their fate. For that, in simple terms, was what we were obliged to do.

Vice-Admiral W. D. O'Brien, C.B., D.S.C.
Commander, Far East Fleet

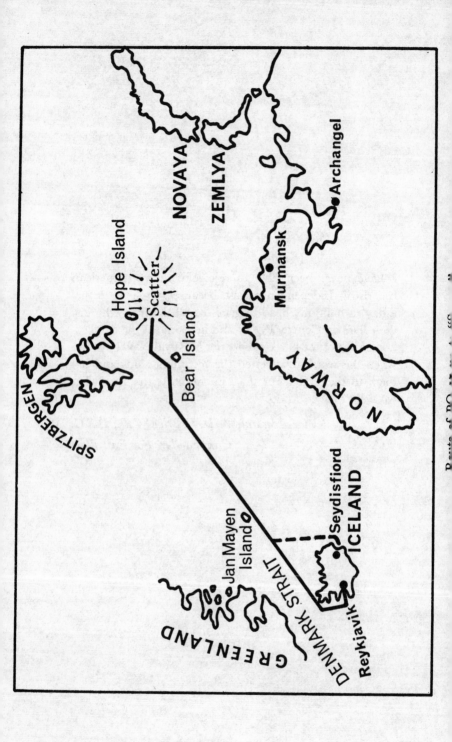

Route of PQ 17 Murmansk 653

Their bodies are laid, o'erclosed
by fitful wave and swirling tide.
No headstone but the gleam of Northern Light;
No tears shed here, only rain and spray;
No voice of pity, but that of the wheeling gull.
Their shroud the long sea grass will be,
Their plot the shifting sea bed sand.

—Third Officer Henry W. Phillips,
R.F.A. *Aldersdale*

Introduction

The Arctic Convoys

Hell below zero they called it, the men who ran the convoys to North Russia. They had other choicer descriptions, too, for the desolate Arctic regions which formed one of the most bizarre theatres of war in World War II. Here fully half the battle was fought against the elements and an icy sea that could claim a man within minutes of immersion.

In the winter it was a fight against intense cold, long hours of darkness and freezing fog, which was a constant companion until dispersed by winds that turned sharply to howling gales. Ships forging their way through dangerous loose ice and icebergs heaved and rolled while icy spray lashed across them, freezing on decks and gun mountings, striking the faces of the lookouts like whiplashes and turning them to the colour of raw steak. With the gales came hail that had the impact of tiny machine-gun bullets, and snow that piled up on deck and froze if not quickly dug away. Ice formation had to be constantly watched and kept in check, as too heavy a build-up could cause a ship to capsize in rough weather.

In midsummer, when PQ 17 sailed, the Arctic could show a very different but still treacherous face. Around the coast of Iceland you would encounter heavy seas, biting cold and dull grey skies, but as you headed north-east to pass near Jan Mayen Island, and then due east to steam north or south of Bear Island, conditions improved. There came a world where the sun shone brilliantly for twenty-four hours a day and you could feel it tanning you at 2 a.m., even with the temperature below zero—and the searching enemy could see you for twenty-four hours a day.

The ice and fog were still there, but in different forms. Away to the north was the line of the ice-barrier, dividing the blue sea from the dazzling expanse of ice that stretched away unbroken to the North Pole; in midsummer the distance from the ice-edge to the Pole was about 700 miles. There were great icebergs which sailed past majestically like multi-coloured schooners glinting in the sun, fogbanks that rose out of the sea and engulfed you in their eerie grasp. But generally it was a lighter, softer, friendlier fog than in the grim winter months, and soon you were out of its clutches and back in a world of cobalt blue sky and sea, for this was a part of the Arctic where the Gulf Stream made itself very much felt, undulating about the ocean to cause remarkable variations in sea temperature and the sudden shifting fogbanks.

The perpetual daylight made it difficult to remember whether it was 4 a.m. or 4 p.m., whether your next meal was going to be breakfast or supper; and this curious feeling of unreality was increased by the heady thinness of the air and the unusual clarity of the atmosphere, which brought a strange, dream-like quality to everything that was going on. Even the waves, dancing and sparkling, seemed to add their own hypnotic effect, and when other ships appeared to spread themselves out into the shape of islands or elongate themselves into tall trees, all length and no breadth, and when more ships sailed upside down above the horizon on a sea in the sky—then you were certain that it was indeed all a dream. Until you remembered the mirages which occurred in these regions, quite as vivid as any seen in the desert.

Such was the weird, lonely world into which sailed convoy PQ 17.

When Hitler invaded Russia on June 22, 1941 Stalin immediately appealed to Britain and America for war materials and supplies for his hard-pressed armies. A first convoy was sent to Russia in August, then in September began the long series of PQ convoys, which were planned to sail at ten-day intervals. They did not, though they still kept to a heavy schedule.

Iceland was occupied by American forces on July 7, 1941 only a fortnight after Hitler marched on Russia, and so it was from here that the PQ convoys sailed: up the west coast of Iceland, round to the north and east, past Jan Mayen Island and Bear Island, keeping far out to the northern ice-edge so as to make the greatest possible distance from the enemy's airfields in northern Norway, then into the Barents Sea and down to the Kola Inlet and the port of Murmansk—2,000 miles from Scapa Flow. The majority of ships went to Murmansk, this being the only Russian port that remained ice-free all the year, though whenever ice conditions permitted some ships sailed on a further 400 miles east to Archangel.

PQ 1, ten ships escorted by a cruiser and two destroyers, left Iceland bound for Archangel on September 28, 1941. The operation was, in the words of one who took part in it, 'a piece of cake'. More convoys followed at roughly fortnightly intervals, all similarly unmolested, until by the end of the year more than fifty merchantmen had steamed safely through.

In the early months of 1942, as successive convoys fought their way through the winter gales and blizzards, enemy resistance slowly built up. Yet when the twelve ships of PQ 12 sailed on March 1, still only one outward-bound merchantman had been lost, together with a destroyer. Then the losses mounted, though still being relatively small. PQ 12 lost one ship, the next convoy four ships, and PQ 14 one again, though on this occasion sixteen vessels had to turn back because of ice. PQ 15 of twenty-five ships, which sailed in April, lost three merchantmen; still a small total, though the Navy's losses at this date included two valuable cruisers, the *Trinidad* and the *Edinburgh*, both torpedoed.

Now it was the Arctic summer, with twenty-four hours of daylight and no darkness to give the slow-moving merchantmen and their escorts some added protection against enemy attacks. Besides the enemy planes and U-boats there was the threat from the fast, immensely powerful battleship *Tirpitz* and her consorts lurking in the Norwegian fiords. The *Tirpitz* had already made one sortie in which PQ 12 had narrowly escaped falling prey to her. But Stalin was adamant that the convoys should continue without interruption, while President Roosevelt also believed they should go on, as American merchant ships were now queueing up to make the passage. Churchill had little option but to comply with the wishes of the other two leaders and so PQ 16 of thirty-five ships, the largest convoy yet, sailed from Hvalfiord on May 21. It had seventeen close escorts plus a shadowing force of four cruisers and three destroyers which accompanied it as far as Bear Island; while to the rear cruised the battle fleet, ready to intercept *Tirpitz* should she put to sea. She did not, but during a very tough run to Murmansk PQ 16 lost seven ships, six of these from heavy attacks by enemy aircraft.

Then it was the turn of PQ 17. After PQ 16's hard experience the question was : should PQ 17 sail, or should it wait for a return of winter darkness? After the loss of the *Trinidad* and *Edinburgh* no escorting cruisers could be risked beyond Bear Island, nor could an aircraft carrier be spared for the run. And there remained the big threat from the *Tirpitz* and other German heavy ships. Strong information had been received that the enemy intended to make an all-out assault on the next convoy to sail.

Stalin, however, concerned only with his country's plight, remained blindly insistent that the convoys should continue whatever the cost, and Roosevelt concurred. Churchill was forced to make a political decision and the Admiralty, which had strongly objected to sailing the convoy in broad daylight, was obliged to follow the Government's wishes.

PQ 17's original sailing date was June 11, 1942, but because of the demands of the Malta run on fleet escorts it was postponed to June 27. At Hvalfiord then we of PQ 17 knew nothing of the higher deliberations, only that it was a long, long wait.

To Save Stalingrad

In the still, cold waters of Hvalfiord a host of merchant ships lay silently at anchor, each boldly displaying her name on large boards placed either side of her bridge. The massed scene was like the prelude to some strange regatta to be played out within sight of the snow-capped hills of the fiord, and there was the same air of quiet expectancy.

Suddenly the peace of the June day was disturbed by an urgent blinker message from one of the American ships, the *Christopher Newport*. The signal was received by the battleship U.S.S. *Washington* and soon a contingent of U.S. Marines were speeding across the fiord by motor launch to quell a 'mutiny' aboard the merchantman. They found that some of the crew had broached a shipment of Scotch whisky consigned to Admiral Stanley, the U.S. Ambassador in Moscow, and things had got out of hand, but the Marines quickly restored order.

This comic-opera incident, the first 'armed action' of PQ 17, was only one isolated symptom of the deep frustration among seamen who had made the long journey across the Atlantic only to find themselves held up at Hvalfiord for weeks, waiting for PQ 17 to sail. More than two-thirds of the convoy was to be formed of American ships; twenty-four of them, carrying massive aid from the United States for the hard-pressed Russians.

We in the small naval escorts had seen them come in. Ships like the *Alcoa Ranger* from Philadelphia, loaded with 7,000 tons of steel, armour plate, flour—and nineteen tanks lashed to her deck; the *Washington* and the *Honomu*, from the same port, loaded with ammunition, steel, foodstuffs and T.N.T., also with tanks and truck chassis stacked on deck. Tanks, too, on the *Daniel Morgan* from Baltimore, and similar cargoes and deck-loads on the remainder of the two dozen ships, all grossly overladen by normal standards; probably no ships had ever been so heavily laden before.

The majority were hard-worked vessels with names as unspectacular as their appearance. There were old Hog Islanders like the *Exford* and the *Hoosier*, with their characteristic hump-back profiles; products of the Pennsylvanian shipyard with more than twenty years of nautical miles behind them. And the *Ironclad*, a vessel so small and rusty that it was popularly wondered whether the Germans would be induced to waste an expensive torpedo on her.

There were four vessels with very proud names: *Samuel Chase*, *John Witherspoon*, *William Hooper* and *Benjamin Harrison*, names of men who signed the Declaration of Independence. But these were ships apart, the 'Ugly Ducklings' of the convoy; squat, slow Liberty ships from the quick moulds of Henry Kaiser, built at high speed in prefabricated sections and welded together instead of the traditional riveting. The seamen who sailed them did not like the Liberty ships, with their rigid construction that spelled danger in really bad seas, though these vessels went far towards saving the Atlantic lifeline.

Not all the American ships were crewed by U.S. seamen. There was, for instance, the *El Capitan* from New York, with rows of planes lashed to her decks; she flew the Panamanian flag and her gun crew of ten men were the only Americans aboard. *El Capitan* had reached Hvalfiord during the last week of May, as had most of the Americans. The prolonged delay after their Atlantic crossing had become almost unbearable for the merchant crews, being at first a tremendous let-down and then a time of tension combined with unutterable boredom, for they were confined to ship—denied permission to visit Reykjavik, the Icelandic capital, whose tempting lights could be seen not far off. Small wonder Admiral Stanley lost a little of his whisky.

The ships had made long round voyages like the *Peter Kerr*, from Portland, Oregon, whose crew, which included Second Mate William Connolly, joined her in a shipyard at New York. There the veteran freighter was fitted out with her scanty arms and armour. She loaded at New York, mainly with foodstuffs, and had her decks filled with tanks and planes. It was no secret even then where she was bound, for she had an extra steam radiator installed in each compartment, a sure sign that she was destined for North Russia.

Peter Kerr had sailed from New York on Easter Sunday, 1942, steaming alone to Halifax, Nova Scotia. There she joined a regular North Atlantic convoy and crossed to the Firth of Clyde. Then on to Loch Ewe, in western Scotland, where she joined another small convoy for Iceland; and so to Hvalfiord, where her crew were confined to ship for the entire twenty-three days they waited for PQ 17 to sail. One reason given to Second Mate Connolly and his colleagues for the ban on shore leave was that earlier crews permitted ashore had been found amusing themselves by throwing eider duck eggs at each other. As the eider duck was a valued natural resource the Icelanders had taken a poor view of such antics.

There was truth in this, though there was rather more to it, as men of the Allied forces who did get ashore, or who had the misfortune to be stationed there, could testify. The Icelanders left them in no doubt as to whether or not they were welcome. Until recently they had encountered open hostility; to go out alone after dark was to risk being beaten up with bottles and sticks. Now the resentment of the Icelanders had simmered down to more passive forms of resistance, but it was not uncommon to be spat upon when your back was turned.

This frigid reception was hardest for us to bear where it concerned the womenfolk. The fact that the Icelandic men completely ignored our presence did not worry the Allied seamen, but that the girls, those beautiful maidens with magnificent blonde hair cascading down their backs, should look over us and round us and through us—that really hurt our pride.

For the tall, willowy, elegant girls never let their eyes meet those
of a 'foreigner' for a fleeting second. In the shops, in the cafés
and in the hotels, the girls who served were coldly polite and
correct, but froze at the least sign of familiarity.

'Smashing pieces them blondes, but they don't even *see* a
bloke!' was the reproach of the British lower deck.

The Icelanders showed exceptional bitterness towards the
Americans. Among some unfortunate incidents which had not
improved the situation were cases of Icelanders, including some
children, being accidentally shot at in the vicinity of American
camps. Then, the Icelanders' craving for alcohol encouraged
'rum-running' activities from ships in Reykjavik harbour, resulting in chases and shooting by Allied and Icelandic police.
The rum bottle was the only entrée into Icelandic social life,
though other different opportunities were offered by taxi-riding
prostitutes who leaned out of the cab windows soliciting the sex-
starved seamen.

The Icelanders certainly showed no gratitude for the enormous prosperity they enjoyed as a result of the 'invasion' and
the Allied rank and file were bewildered by this attitude, looking
with mixed feelings on brilliantly lit Reyjavik, its streets busy
with large American cars, its shops full of luxury U.S. goods,
its lashings of good food, and its women dressed in Bond Street
style. Even visits to the quayside needed to be kept as short as
possible owing to the high dues charged by the Icelanders.

And so there was Hvalfiord, close by. The British sailor never
thought he might describe any place as being 'worse than Scapa
Flow', but he did so now. This Hvalfiord was a desolate place,
often swept by howling gales which tore vessels from their moorings. In winter bitter cold, and in summer, as now, just cold.
And the shore amenities: one large hut canteen selling strong
Canadian beer, where fights broke out nearly every night.

The American seamen of PQ 17 were in fact missing little,
though this did not seem so to men confined to their ships,
especially when on a glorious dawn, with the sun turning the
snow-covered mountains to a delicate pink, they could glimpse

gaily coloured Icelandic fishing boats out pulling in their catches. A people seemingly untouched by Hitler's war.

Some of the eight British merchant ships which, together with a Dutch ship and two Russian tankers, were to complete PQ 17 arrived at Hvalfiord later than the Americans, so escaping part of the frustrating waiting period. Typical among these ships was the *Earlston*, a 6,000-ton 'utility' ship only a year old, crammed with a cargo of field guns, lorries, crated Hurricane fighter planes and hundreds of tons of naval ammunition. On deck aft she carried drums of high octane fuel and toluol, the chief constituent of T.N.T., while athwartships, just forward of the bridge, was secured a naval steam pinnace or powered launch, destined for use by the Admiralty base at Archangel.

The British ships were as heavily laden as the Americans. One of them, the *Empire Tide*, was unique in that she was a CAM ship, or catapult aircraft merchantman. She carried a Hurricane fighter which could be launched into action once only, the pilot on his return having to ditch the plane into the sea after baling out by parachute, trusting to be hauled to safety from a freezing sea. *Empire Tide* had some peculiarities of construction designed to mislead the enemy, and besides her guns and barrage balloon she had the advantage of being fitted with an early type of radar for aircraft detection. Despite all the secrecy surrounding her, however, her destination had been made as obvious while loading at Newport, Mon., as had *Peter Kerr*'s at New York, many of the packages swung aboard her being clearly marked 'Admiral Dolinin—Murmansk' and 'Admiral Dolinin—Archangel'. So much for security.

Empire Tide's radar advantage was shared by *Ocean Freedom*, a new British ship rapidly built at South Portland, Mass., and, like the Liberty ships, more than half welded. *Freedom* had made her maiden voyage across the Atlantic with a cargo of steel plates, and reloaded in the U.K. with tanks, Bren gun carriers and other equipment for Russia. She then led a small convoy from Loch Ewe to Hvalfiord, with her master, Captain William Walker, as Commodore. On this trip she tasted action—of a kind. It was a standing regulation that aircraft should not approach a convoy during fog, but on this occasion an American aircraft did approach and was promptly shot down by *Freedom* and *Earlston* in mistake for a Focke-Wulf. Its crew were picked up later and Captain Walker was told to forget the unfortunate incident and not to let it affect his gunners' trigger-fingers.

Earlston's armament was typical of the merchant ships. She had twin Brownings on the 'monkey island' or gun platform above the bridge, two Oerlikons on the bridge wings, two at the after-end of the boat deck and two more forward of the poop. For further use against aircraft there were two 'pig troughs' or sets of rockets on the boat deck, and to deter U-boats, an old four-inch surface gun.

Some ships had more, some less. They carried gun crews of anything up to twelve men, in a few cases British gunners being seconded to the American ships, as with the *Olopana* from San Francisco, though the majority of U.S. ships carried their own Armed Guard unit. The one Dutch ship, *Paulus Potter*, had British gunners.

Some ships had acquired their armament very hastily; like the Hog Islander *Exford*, which had stayed at Loch Ewe just long enough to take on board two Marines and two R.N. gunners to man the 30 calibre guns still uncrated. As for the 'mutinous' *Christopher Newport*, when Lieutenant (jg) Daniel Jones, from the U.S.S. *Washington,* visited his friend the Armed Guard Officer aboard her, he was appalled to find mounted on the fantail an old four-inch gun taken from a park in Baltimore, its rifling worn practically smooth and its elevation not more than about 35 degrees. Lieutenant Jones, after seeing the other picayune weapons and quantity of ammunition with which the ship was expected to defend herself left with heavy heart and the rooted conviction that she could never survive what was in store save by a miracle.

Only a small number of the American merchant captains had first-hand knowledge of the type of seas and weather to expect. Like Captain Julius Holmgrun of the *Hoosier,* who had come out of retirement on a farm in Maine to answer the call of his

adopted country. Born in Stockholm, Sweden, Captain Holmgrun had gone to America as a young boy. Now, in his late
seventies, he was back again to the waters of his childhood.
Among the British masters with good experience of the Arctic
was Captain Stenwick of *Earlston*, a Norwegian baron now
naturalised British.

The crews of the American ships were not only totally un-
familiar with Northern waters but for many of them, boys from
all parts of the States, it was their first long voyage; for some
it was their first time at sea. There were such young men, too,
among our British merchant crews, side by side with the nucleus
of battle-scarred veterans who had acquired that quiet air of
fatalism which surrounded a man as his ship ploughed painfully
slowly through enemy infested waters.

Boys and men, too, on our naval escort vessels sharing the
long wait at Hvalfiord. There were seven of us: three minesweepers and four anti-submarine trawlers, forming a third of
the convoy's escort. By ourselves we were scarcely calculated
to deter the enemy, but the rest of the fleet escorts would be
joining us when we rounded Iceland. If the men of a 10,000-ton
merchant vessel found the small minesweepers, such as the 850-
ton *Salamander*, rather hard to accept as warships, they looked
askance on our diminutive coal-burning trawlers, whose top
speed of around ten knots was well below the flat-out capabilities
of most of the merchantmen.

Oddly enough one trawler, *Northern Gem*, was German-
built, from Bremerhaven. One of a number of German fishing
vessels given to Britain as part of reparations after World War I,
she was faster and better constructed generally than the British-
built trawlers, of which *Lord Austin* was typical. Our little
700-ton vessel looked what she was, a deep-sea fishing trawler
with single funnel, high bow and low well-deck, which in
rough weather was mostly under water. Her natural black-
and-tan colour had been Admiralty-camouflaged blue and
white to merge with the sea and ice. The merchantmen's armaments may have been a motley collection but ours were positively awe-inspiring. We carried a single four-inch surface gun,

together with an Oerlikon abaft the bridge and twin point-fives on a stern platform. Two Hotchkiss machine guns on the bridge-wings completed our guns, while on deck each side of the bridge were two depth charge throwers. Whenever we sent a depth charge over the side *Austin's* stern rose up and shuddered.

Then, set either side of the bridge were two P.A.C. rockets, similar to those carried by the merchantmen. These were rockets to which were fixed fathoms and fathoms of wire attached to a parachute, the idea being that when the rocket was fired at a diving aircraft, the plane would get entangled in the trailing wire and crash. All right on sparrows, perhaps, as someone remarked.

The most enterprising contraption of all was the Holman projector. This consisted of a stove-like pipe attached to a steam-pipe from the engine room. The man firing it built up the steam pressure and into the pipe put a tin with a lightly soldered lid, inside which was a hand grenade. The idea here was that if a plane was diving at the ship, the firer released the steam, which shot up the tin, which twisted round in mid-air and off shot the lid, the solder melted by the steam, out shot the grenade with its lever released, and the plane—if it was still there—would catch some of the shrapnel. No one did see a plane hit by one, but they had some near misses on themselves when the hand grenades fell back on the ships. The 'hot potato cart' the trawler crews called the Holman projector. Our ships shot potatoes at each other for fun; it was the contraption's safest use.

The hard core of the trawler crews was made up of naval men, fishermen and tug men of the Northern Patrol, but like the merchantmen they also carried many men absolutely raw to the sea. On *Northern Gem*, for instance, more than two-thirds of the crew were boys who had never been to sea or even seen it before they joined up. All of us, however, were fully as anxious as the merchantmen to get going. The lot of *Lord Austin* in the war so far had been mainly that of fighting heavy weather, gales, bitter cold, discomfort and soul-destroying monotony. The long months on the Northern Patrol, the long weeks in Iceland, the fogs and ice floes of a recent convoy, in all this we had not had sight or sound of the enemy. Now the prospect of meeting him face to face, of seeing some real action, however horrible and bloody, had us keyed up to a high pitch of anticipation. Some hair-raising stories of what had happened to PQ 16 had filtered back. Seven ships lost. Would it all be as terrible as others made out, or were their tales exaggerated? How would each man of us stand up to the ordeal? What would it really be like? Would we survive it?

Above all there was the strong feeling among us that at last we would be doing a worthwhile job in the war. Nothing, we were told, was of more vital importance than getting these emergency supplies through to Russia—to save Stalingrad. Without them, Russia was likely to go down to the Germans and the war might go on for ever.

Suddenly the long wait was at an end. The cruiser *London* reappeared at Hvalfiord. She had been there earlier for naval conferences, her enormous bulk dwarfing the merchant vessels and making our tiny trawlers seem like toys. *London*, the flagship of Rear-Admiral L. K. H. Hamilton, was to lead a combined British and U.S. cruiser squadron which would shadow PQ 17 to Bear Island. During the long waiting period *London* had fussed about like some mammoth nursemaid, holding conferences at Seydisfiord, Hvalfiord and Akureyri in the north; and now she was back at Hvalfiord for a final conference held in a hut ashore. Merchant gunners and some officers had received earlier briefing about the enemy's tricks in the Arctic; how the prowling U-boats were known to go under the ice to escape detection by asdic beam or depth-charge attack, or to lie in wait against an iceberg, their blue and white camouflage making them extremely difficult to detect. Now there was the actual convoy procedure to be run over for the merchant captains and officers, and there was much surprise at the presence among them of a Russian woman officer from the *Azerbaijan*, one of the two Russian tankers sailing with us.

The commanders of the naval escorts returned to ship after

their conference in good frame of mind, some very healthily fortified. As one told his whaleboat crew who collected him: 'We're going to shink shubmarines and lay the bastards we capture out on deck and shkin 'em alive!'

'Silly old runt,' commented one of the crew. 'I'd rather skin him alive any time.'

But it set the mood. At the conference one of the main speakers had been Commander J. E. ('Jack') Broome, who, in the destroyer *Keppel*, would lead the naval escorts. And he had been most optimistic in tone. The Germans, he thought, would be reluctant to attack against so strong an escort—a total of 21 warships. His destroyers had just spent a short time at sea trying out some moves in case the surface ships came our way, and it was strongly felt that the timely use of smoke and torpedoes would deter them.

Commander Broome was a well experienced convoy escort officer. He was forty years old, and a man's man if ever the Navy still bred them. In action aboard ship he could, according to members of his crew, look dog rough, sans teeth, sans cap and wearing a thick jersey; ashore, plus dentures, plus cap at a slightly Beatty angle he was a jaunty, natty, amiable figure. Everyone respected him, both for his resoluteness of character and the certain way in which he ran his ship. He held the unqualified respect and loyalty of the lower deck of *Keppel*—aboard which the rum was neat.

Nor was there anything of the remote sea commander about the leader of the merchantmen, in the British *River Afton*. Commodore John Dowding, R.N.R., just in his fifties, was a forthright man who had spent a lifetime at sea. He had served in cruisers and destroyers in World War I, and then for nearly twenty years was at sea for the Orient Line. In 1940 he had brought his crippled ship back from Dunkirk to win a D.S.O. He was quietly confident, every inch a convoy man, and the merchant captains, after patiently listening to the N.O.I.C., N.C.S.O., C.B.O. and a few more administrative officers, none of whom were coming with the convoy, were agreeably impressed when Dowding addressed them as 'Your Commodore for the trip. . . .'

The confidence of these two leaders set the good feeling of the convoy. Tactics were to be little changed from those of PQ 16. The merchantmen, together with the minesweepers and trawlers would sail up Iceland's west coast and turn northeast, where they would be joined by the balance of the escorts led by *Keppel*, sailing up from Seydisfiord. Then would commence the long haul past Bear Island into the Barents Sea. The shadowing cruiser force, comprising *London* and *Norfolk*, together with the U.S. cruisers *Wichita* and *Tuscaloosa*, and accompanied by three destroyers, would guard us against surface attack as far as Bear Island; any attack, that is, which they were capable of handling—which excluded the menacing *Tirpitz*. In any event the cruisers were not to go beyond Bear Island or the longitude of the North Cape (25 deg. E.). From this point the safety of the convoy would depend on the close escorts, together with some British and Russian submarines operating in the area. Further backing on the earlier part of the journey was to be given by a heavy force well to the rear, cruising between Scapa Flow and Spitzbergen. This, led by the Commander-in-Chief Home Fleet, Admiral Sir John Tovey, in the battleship *Duke of York* included the U.S.S. *Washington*, the aircraft carrier *Victorious*, two cruisers and fourteen destroyers. Its main function was to patrol west of Bear Island to guard the convoy against surface attack in that area. The whole operation was under Admiral Tovey's command.

And so in the afternoon of June 27, PQ 17 began its eventful journey. As the sun shone down through the thin Icelandic air the calm waters at Hvalfiord, flanked by jagged peaks, made a picture-postcard scene in which our small escort vessels circled around lazily waiting for their cue. We waited until at last the clumsy bulk of the first merchantman broke the entrance to the fiord. Slowly she lumbered past, followed by another and then another as the heavily laden vessels turned from their month long anchorages and passed in line ahead out to sea. It seemed to take hours for the procession to clear: thirty-three merchant ships, two Russian tankers and two British fleet oilers, *Gray Ranger* and *Aldersdale*, both of these rigged with a dummy funnel to make them look like merchantmen.

One by one the waiting escorts sailed out of the fiord to take up their stations. *Lord Austin*'s position being right at the stern of the convoy, we were the last to go. As we glanced back with a touch of envy at the rest of the shipping lying serenely at anchor in that desolate haven, we could imagine what the comments must be—'Thank God we're not going with that lot, poor bastards!' Hadn't we said the same thing when PQ 16 had sailed? Now it was our turn.

As soon as *Austin* passed through the mouth of the fiord into the open sea the waves rose, the wind strengthened, and our small vessel began to pitch. The sun vanished and a great greyness descended upon everything.

We began to feel the cold.

The *London* meanwhile returned to Seydisfiord, where the balance of the escorts were making ready to sail. Principal among them were two anti-aircraft ships, *Palomares* and *Pozarica*, not 'pusser' naval warships but converted merchantmen—banana boats—used in peacetime for carrying cargo and a few passengers. Now they were fitted with thousands of tons of armour plating and bristled with guns, such as the *Pozarica's* twin four-inch A/A guns and four-barrelled pom-poms; her close range arms had been newly installed. *Pozarica* was so loaded with shells that they were stacked up on the magazine deck. Deck stowage! This certainly was going to be some party.

On the messdecks of *Pozarica*, which had been busy for over a year on convoy duties in the Western Approaches, the arguments had raged: Malta or Russia, which was the lesser of the two evils? The Malta convoy was a comparatively short run. There was fierce opposition, especially in the air, but there were aircraft carriers to give some air cover. There was little let-up in the attacks after leaving Gibraltar, but there was a warm swim if you found yourself in the drink, and land was never far away. On the Russian run it was almost completely opposite.

A long journey through bleak waters, no aircraft carrier to give air cover, and very little hope of survival if it came to a swim in the icy water. Some odds.

There were four corvettes, two of them brand new and making their maiden voyages, then six destroyers led by Commander Broome in *Keppel*. These included veterans like the *Fury*, with two Russian runs behind her, but with the exception of *Offa*, a modern fleet destroyer, all were small, old-fashioned Hunt class and World War I destroyers well obsolete by this time; *Keppel* herself was known to 'leak like a sieve', her steam pipes tied up with spunyarn. There was even among them an old four-stacker American destroyer of that other war, top-heavy and awkward to handle in rough seas; this, the U.S.S. *Twiggs*, was now H.M.S. *Leamington*. She was one of fifty such ships given to the Royal Navy by America in return for a chain of bases.

A veritable jumble of old warships and conversions; nevertheless the small fleet of twelve vessels, together with two submarines—one sailing with us from Hvalfiord—would combine with our trawlers and minesweepers to present healthy opposition to any attacker.

A welcome yet sobering addition to this force at Seydisfiord were three 'Tail-end Charlies', small merchant ships whose job it would be to dog the convoy and rescue survivors of stricken ships. The *Rathlin*, *Zaafaran* and *Zamalek* were vessels of around 1,500 tons which in peacetime rarely did voyages of more than forty hours' duration, running from east coast ports to the Continent, or ploughing down from Glasgow to London. Now, fitted out with guns and medical equipment, and with a naval surgeon, sick bay attendants and gunners added to their merchant crews they were to make this marathon run over grim waters. Little *Rathlin* had been a cattle carrier and general cargo boat on a regular run from Glasgow to Ireland. Now, like the others, she had grown teeth. A four-inch gun forward, a long, thin-barrelled Bofors hurriedly installed aft, Oerlikons on her bridge and boat deck; and the Blue Ensign hoisted proudly at her stern. The lower holds of all three rescue vessels were filled with empty casks to give them greater buoyancy.

A final word among the escorts, and from captains to crew. And the repeated message now well drummed into everyone: the convoy *must* get through; it was the convoy that mattered and it was their duty to protect the merchant ships to their utmost.

In the mid-afternoon of Monday, June 29, 1942 the escorts, preceded by their submarine, slipped out of Seydisfiord past the huge bulk of the guardian *London* and headed north to join us.

That same day 'Force X' sailed from Scapa Flow. This was a dummy convoy consisting of nine assorted colliers and mine-layers, accompanied by two cruisers and five destroyers, and was designed to draw the enemy's attention away from PQ 17. It was the final part of the Admiralty's plan.

2

How Is the War?

*'I've got spurs that jingle, jangle, jingle
As I go riding merr-i-lee along . . .'*

The resonant voice was that of the lookout on our bridge, his
round, red face just visible among a heap of balaclavas, scarves
and duffle-hood. The jagged Icelandic coast was greyly discernible
on our starboard hand as the convoy wallowed its way through a
heavy swell. A little way astern of us was rolling the porpoise
shape of a submarine.

'Take good care of your baby!' the senior minesweeper flashed
us as she steamed busily down the lines of ships.

The submarine was *Lord Austin*'s special charge. We were to
keep an eye on her especially in the event of bad weather. Should
we run into fog, as was likely on this part of the voyage, perhaps coupled with drift ice, ships could easily become separated,
and whereas large merchantmen could be rounded up without
much difficulty when it cleared, the submarine would be hard to
spot—and strict W/T and R/T silence was now in force.
The surfaced submarine looked very small and helpless in com-
parison with the rest of the convoy, but she had a sting in her
and would have a say in affairs if any of the German surface
fleet showed themselves.

On this first full day at sea, June 28, the convoy had settled
to a speed of seven knots so as to accommodate the slowest
vessels. Immediately on leaving Hvalfiord we had encountered
a heavy swell, grey skies and bitter cold, and our 'baby' had a

specially rough time of it. All the merchantmen were rolling and pitching and the seamen looked with interest at the two large Russian tankers, *Azerbaijan* and *Donbass*, wondering how many women they had on board and how they were faring (nearly all the Russian ships carried women among their crews).

Already we had suffered our first casualty when the American *Richard Bland* grounded on the Icelandic coast almost as we left harbour. All the way across the Atlantic just for that! For the rest of us it was a cautious journey north, for at one point there were only four miles between the coast and the Allied minefield, and the escort vessels could never decide which was the more dangerous—hugging the cliffs or skirting the minefields.

All day the convoy wallowed along following the coastline, lashed by showers of sleet and snow. As we stared out at the bleak coast there were many of us who wondered whether some Nazi agent was even now tuning up his transmitter and preparing to tap out a message to the enemy. It was said there were spies scattered all round the coast to give information on the departure of Russian convoys and the smoke from the merchant ships and our coal-burning trawlers plumed skywards in a steady stream. There was much speculation as to how soon we would be picked up by a 'Shad', as the enemy's spotter planes were known. According to form it should be around the fourth day.

Aboard *Northern Gem* on the convoy's starboard quarter the trawler's main armament, an old four-inch gun of World War I vintage, was cleaned and traversed and the dust polished off its telescopic sights. The gunners on other ships were similarly busy.

Fog rose and persisted on and off all through the third day, June 29. Thick, dark, cold fog accompanied by heavy rain, making station-keeping a nightmare and lookout duty a freezing, soaking misery. Later we were to welcome fog, pray for it even, but not just now. At an early stage *Ocean Freedom* was groping slowly along on the inshore side, listening for sound signals, when a grey, ghostly shape slithered out of the murk close on her starboard side. Hurried action to avoid collision was taken by both ships and the merchantman and minesweeper *Salamander* glided alongside each other practically scraping the paint. As the bridges drew level an anxious voice rang out from *Salamander*: 'Where the hell do you think you're going?' From *Ocean Freedom* in an equally strained voice Captain Walker replied: 'Russia, I hope.'

Unknown to us Force X, the decoy convoy steaming boldly at sea off Norway, had become blanketed too, the fog shrouding them so completely from German reconnaissance that their attempts to lure the enemy after them were rendered quite useless.

In the fog we met heavy floes of drift-ice and though the bows of the merchantmen had been specially strengthened, their masters wondered at times whether they would be able to withstand some of the thunderous, shuddering impacts with the great floes. There was no chance of taking avoiding action owing to the poor visibility and the closeness of the ships. Consequently as we neared the northernmost point of Iceland we suffered our second early casualty when the *Exford* ran smack into ice.

It happened at 4.20 a.m. Oiler Lionel Smith had just made a round and was having coffee when he felt the ship shudder and immediately there was a 'Stop' and a 'Full Astern'—then a 'Stop' again. When no explanation came down from the bridge over the voice pipe Smith was sent up to investigate. The fog was thick and it was a lonesome sound for them to hear the ships' whistles growing fainter as the convoy pulled on ahead. Going forward Smith found the captain and mate looking over the bow, and saw that the *Exford* had hit ice jutting only some five feet out of the water, but it had bent the ship's stem and opened the forepeak, badly holing her. It was clear they would have to head back to Hvalfiord for repairs.

Exford's bosun wanted the ship to go on, even though he knew it was asking the impossible. Smith told him thoughtfully: 'This may be lucky ice...' They had always called the old *Exford* a 'lucky pile of junk'. Just how fortunate she was on this occasion they would be hearing in Iceland later, when beached there for repairs. Amazingly *Exford*'s captain broke the strict radio silence to signal *River Afton* by R/T: 'To Commodore—my bow has been damaged by ice, what are your instructions?' When, naturally, no reply came from Dowding, the captain repeated his request eight times, thereby endangering the whole convoy, before finally turning his ship back to Hvalfiord.

On June 30, our fourth day at sea, we had swung round to the far north of Iceland and reached the point in the ocean where rendezvous was to be made with the escorts sailing up from Seydisfiord. Promptly at noon they appeared: the six destroyers, another submarine, four corvettes ... and the two anti-aircraft ships, *Palomares* and *Pozarica*, looking in their peculiar camouflage like painted cardboard with no breadth at all to them, but solid enough on a closer look and heavy with A/A guns of all kinds.

What a fleet! Together with the minesweepers and trawlers it was the biggest naval escort the old hands had seen on any convoy. The new arrivals played stirring martial music over their loudspeakers as they met up with the merchantmen, whose crews cheered, waved hats and scarves and danced on deck. An enormous wave of confidence, cockiness even, swept over the vast array of ships. That so many vessels, convoy and escort, could put to sea and Hitler could do nothing to stop them, made all hearts twice as big as they really were. Across the waters sounded the throaty roars of men on the American merchantmen with their Stars and Stripes tattered from the long Atlantic voyage; now at last they were seeing evidence that the British navy could mean business.

The destroyers and corvettes quickly positioned themselves on either flank of the columns of merchantmen, with a trawler stationed forward and aft of each line of warships. *Palomares* took the starboard side of the convoy and *Pozarica* the port side, enabling the two ships to give anti-aircraft cover over the whole formation, which measured some nine miles long and five miles wide when spread out in full station. The three rescue vessels paced on each side and astern. On *Lord Austin* we now lost our 'baby' which went to join her sister submarine in the centre of the convoy, and we moved up to take the lead position on the convoy's starboard bow.

Steadily forward now through drifting, rolling banks of fog. Up starboard we lost sight of the convoy for several hours but regained contact when the fog cleared for a time. The regular pattern of convoy work asserted itself with constant gun watch, a chilling business on exposed gun platforms. It was a common sight to see our heavily muffled gun watch doing physical jerks on the barrel of the four-inch, running round and round the small platform, or practising dance steps with each other, solemnly fox-trotting and waltzing around the gun. Suddenly would come the ever welcome cry of 'Rum-O!' and up would stump another muffled figure with mugs of the life-saving spirit. The watch would drain their mugs and glow and tingle from head to toe. Never was the rum issue more appreciated.

The main duty of the trawlers was to keep asdic watch for U-boats. Asdic was like underwater radar. All day and all night the asdic set went "PING ... ping ...' the second, fainter ping being the echo from the sea-bed, and an expert operator would know from the nature of the return signal whether it was a sandy or rocky bottom. When the beam hit an under-water object the time interval between the two 'pings' indicated the distance of the object, the set also giving the bearing. Once again, the expert could tell the difference between a shoal of fish and a submarine. For four long hours at a time the asdic operator sat hunched up in his chair on the bridge listening intently to the eternal pinging note. It was said that all asdic ratings went mad in time.

If a U-boat was traced it was our drill to drop depth charges until a destroyer came up to take over the hunt. The trouble with the slow-moving trawlers was twofold: first, unless they were going at absolute maximum speed, dropping a pattern of depth charges would probably blow their stern off; and second, if they went off U-boat chasing they might never catch up with the convoy again.

Another chore of the trawlers was to urge on lagging mer-chantmen or to warn them about making too much smoke. Some

of the answers received were highly descriptive, a more repeat-
able one being: 'First we're not going fast enough, then if we
put coal on to get more speed it is too much smoke—what the
bloody hell do you want us to do, sprout wings and fly?'

A lot of smoke usually meant careless or lazy firing on the
part of the stokers; by piling on large heaps of coal instead of
just enough at a time, they could go back into the engine
room, sit down peacefully and watch the wheels go round.
Lord Austin herself drew a blast from the senior escort. We
had been belching thick black smoke from our funnel, in the
unfortunate manner of trawlers, until a long plume streamed
away behind to hang like a banner in the still air. *Keppel*
flashed an angry signal: 'Make less smoke.' The bridge passed
the rebuke down to the engine room. Back came the Chief's
voice, hoarse with indignation: 'Well, what do the bastards
want me to do—whitewash the bloody coal?'

For the lookouts, the eerie silence which prevailed in these
northern waters was at this time broken only by the occasional
clicks of Aldis lamps flashing messages to and fro between the
escorts. The destroyers were always alert for the presence of
U-boats, at this stage of the war an all too familiar and wearisome drill. The perpetual shortage of naval escorts meant that
they were hard stretched, alternating between convoys to North
Russia and those to Malta, work that brought with it a fatalistic
acceptance of losses from repeated U-boat attacks. The typical
pattern of turning over the watch on the bridge: 'Course ——,
speed ——. Usual station 2,000 yards on the port bow of ——.
I have been zig-zagging about twenty degrees either side. A
couple of ships were hit over on the far side of the convoy about
two hours ago, and someone over there has been dropping
a lot of depth charges. Otherwise nothing much is going on.
Bloody cold—as usual!'

The routine continued now, as in the destroyer *Wilton*. The
captain, depending as he had to on a handful of young and
very inexperienced officers—and he was at least three or four
years older, with a couple of years of war experience—practically
lived on the bridge; sleeping, when he could, in a deckchair

tucked in the relatively sheltered well at the forward end of
the exposed and draughty bridge, swathed in sweaters, balaclavas and blankets, only allowing himself the luxury of a nap in
his sea-cabin, one deck below, when the visibility was really
clear and things seemed quiet. He was always tired and often
bad-tempered, but his officers trusted him implicitly. For them,
too, spending long periods at action-stations, sleep was always
the most urgent need. One did not undress, things could happen
far too suddenly and quickly, but merely flopped on to the
bunk and into oblivion. It seldom lasted more than an hour
or two.

It was soon to become the same with everyone in every ship
of the convoy, this constant need for sleep, our main interest,
in fact, being in eating, sleeping and staying alive; but so far no
action-stations had been rung. How much longer would this
peaceful state of affairs continue?

Next morning, July 1, the first U-boats were sighted, surfaced
on the calm sea, and were driven off by the destroyers. But all
of us now awaited the inevitable and sure enough just after
noon it arrived, the first Shad. There was a thin mist through
which the sun was struggling to break. Alarm bells rang as the
black shape of the three-engined floatplane, a Blohm and Voss
138, loomed out of the mist, its nose tipped slightly to the water
like some ominous nose-to-sea bloodhound; as indeed it was,
for we knew that as it zoomed in and out of the fog, just out
of range of our guns, it was busily reporting back to base in
Norway details of the convoy's course, disposition and speed.

Then another U-boat alarm, and the dull rumble of depth
charges being dropped by the escorts, followed by the warning
signals of ships blowing off steam to give their positions in the
closely gathering fog. And suddenly on *Lord Austin*, still well
away up starboard, the alarm bell rang again—a surface alarm.
Our old four-inch was quickly swung round, a shell and cartridge
rammed in and the breech slammed. The fog had suddenly
lifted ahead to disclose on the horizon the shapes of several
large ships. The group seemed to include a battleship, cruisers
and destroyers. The convoy was out of sight astern; we faced

the warships alone. The same thought flashed through every man's mind: could it be the *Tirpitz*, *Hipper* and others steamed from their Norwegian lair?

W/T silence had been officially broken when the Shad appeared. Our radio operator was now ordered quickly to report the presence of unidentified warships to the senior escort over the R/T. Back came the reply: 'Go in and challenge them.'

So in sailed our gallant trawler, with her single four-inch gun trained and the signalman flashing furiously on his ten-inch lamp, to challenge the ironclads. After some anxious moments an answering flicker was seen, and a minute later came the shout of 'Friendly vessels!'

'Lucky we didn't fire first,' one of our crew ironically observed. 'We might have sunk one of our own battleships.'

As the big ships steamed away, probably unaware of the consternation they had caused, one of them blinked a message to us. 'Sorry we can't accompany,' it said—'Good luck to all'.

A nice gesture, even if it was all we ever saw of the battle fleet.

During the afternoon the fog cleared and the whole of the convoy was clearly visible. And still the Shad flew just above the horizon. These long-range planes were said to have an endurance of twenty-four hours at a stretch; they were relieved as regularly as clockwork by one of their fellows. Some tentative shots were fired at the Shad, all hopelessly wide of the mark. It was very shortly joined by other aircraft, this time torpedo-carrying Heinkel seaplanes, until eventually there were nine planes circling the convoy. A batch of them came close to the ships at the rear and there was the rattle of Bofors guns. The planes dropped their torpedoes but there were no hits. Then followed a lull with only the Shad continuing its menacing course around the horizon. The escorts' watches had now been either on duty or at action-stations for eighteen hours out of the past twenty-four.

During this time fuelling of escorts had been going on from the fleet oiler *Aldersdale*; the other oiler, *Gray Ranger*, which was destined to take up duties as station oiler in Archangel, conserving her supply. *Aldersdale* steamed at the rear of the convoy's central column. Not a happy position, for when re-fuelling ships she had to reduce speed, and by the time she had topped up a vessel she was well astern of the convoy, which left her company feeling very naked and forlorn. Captain Archibald Hobson decided to alter the routine. At the start of each operation he hoisted 'Disregard My Movements' and increased speed, hauled out of line, steamed up between the columns and when in the first line reduced speed and carried out the job. In this way when a ship had been dealt with the tanker was comfortably back in her original position. No one cared to be a straggler.

About 9 p.m. we hit more patches of fog, and the alarm bells rang again. Three torpedo-planes came in close to us and our gunners managed to fire off a few rounds. The planes vanished. Later our skipper, Lieutenant Leslie Wathen, R.N.R., saw through his glasses a U-boat surface way ahead, and one of the torpedo planes land on the water beside it. The plane took off again in a hurry when a destroyer hurried over and sprayed a pattern of depth charges over the spot where the U-boat submerged. We afterwards passed a large patch of oil and wreckage and it was considered that the attack had been suc-cessful; and yet the U-boats were wily birds, often pumping out a quantity of oil to deceive their pursuers.

Near midnight a loud crash which shook the ship like a leaf in the breeze, roused our off-watch company from their dozing and we heard something scrape its metallic way along the ship's bottom. It must have been a U-boat just below the surface but we had no time to stop to investigate; though we felt cheered by the thought that the crash must have damaged its periscope or conning tower pretty severely.

At midnight all was quiet. The convoy was now in the sea of the Midnight Sun, and the sun instead of rising and setting in the normal manner, described an irregular arc around us rather after the fashion of the Shad. The first W/T signal to the Admiralty, 'Picked up by the Shad', had been perfectly received and answered. Many a man in his mind's eye could see the heavily-braided figures in the Operations Room in London now closely following PQ 17's progress on their charts.

July 2 began pleasantly with a calm sea and the sun shining through a slight haze. But it was a deceptive scene. U-boats were about all day and the slow boom of depth charges sounded frequently as the outer escorts sought to drive them off. Destroyer *Offa* fired at extreme range on a U-boat that surfaced; she missed and it dived.

The Shad watched it all, swinging along doggedly a foot above the horizon. Close to noon it was joined by five more identical aircraft, all proceeding to circle the convoy like giant dragonflies. It was frustrating to know that they were reporting our every movement and that nothing could be done about it. Oh for an aircraft carrier—just a little one! In the afternoon the six Shads were joined by ten Heinkel 115 floatplanes, each carrying two torpedoes. It could be seen they meant business, and at 4.30 p.m. the attack came.

The Heinkels were met by a hail of fire from every ship that could draw sight on them. The German pilots were not as determined as all that and quickly retreated, most of them before having a chance to drop their torpedoes. A small group of the planes had seemed intent on laying their 'tinfish' at the *Pozarica*, on the port quarter, but they scampered off when she exploded into action. First blood, however, was drawn by the destroyer *Fury*, the Heinkel she shot down dropping to the sea on the port side ahead of the convoy. As the German crew took to their dinghies another Heinkel flew up and landing close alongside, coolly picked up its fellows. One of the escorts chased after the sitting duck but it managed to take off unscathed. A brave action by the German pilot.

During the afternoon we were treated to the unusual sight of a friendly aircraft flying over. It was a Walrus from the shadowing *London,* come to blink a message to *Keppel* to alter course more to the north, so as to increase our distance from the enemy airfields. Ships waved greeting to the Walrus. While it was still with us three more enemy planes arrived and after circling around for a time made a sudden dash at the merchantmen. They were driven off by more heavy gunfire, the Walrus getting dangerously caught up in the barrage.

A general signal was received from *Keppel* complimenting all escorts on their skill and determination in holding off the raiders, and ending: 'Keep it up, chaps!' Meanwhile the constantly shifting cruiser force steamed to within twenty miles of us, still awaiting any move by German surface vessels.

The evening brought constant alerts with the Shad still droning about the daylight sky, a dreary, monotonous, ominous sight; it was hard to drive the vision of it from one's closed eyes when trying to sleep. A destroyer called up the plane with her lamp, blinking out in German: 'Can't you go round the other way? You are making us dizzy!' To which the Shad replied: 'Anything to oblige an Englishman,' and began circling in the opposite direction. After this a regular conversation was kept up between some of the escorts and this particular aircraft, during the course of which the enemy described the dreadful fate in store for us.

At midnight we had begun to pass majestic icebergs, enormous masses of ice that would go sailing on all through the summer. They were an enchanting sight, struck by the glancing rays of the sun, but also a highly dangerous one, for at 3 a.m. *Gray Ranger* struck a small iceberg and holed her bow. She reduced speed while Chief Engineer David Hood went with Captain Gausden into the forepeak to inspect the damage. It was bad. The hole was far too big to consider temporary repairs and they feared the fore deep tank plates would not stand up to the pressure. Even so they did not relish lying so far behind the protection of the convoy, now drawn well ahead, so hurriedly steamed up to rejoin, at the same time contacting the senior escort. Instructions finally came: turn back. So at 6 p.m. *Gray Ranger* went alongside her companion oiler *Aldersdale* and handed over her special charts; she then steamed sadly back to North Shields, unmolested by the enemy, for repairs. *Aldersdale*, which was originally to have left us at the North Cape, would now continue to Archangel.

Three casualties now, though as yet none brought about by enemy action. How long before the big attack came? There was a tense air of foreboding over every ship.

The weather was much colder in this region of icebergs, one of the smaller masses of which appeared weirdly in the distance to look like an aeroplane covered in ice, but which, as *Pozarica* passed close, showed itself to be just another floating shape. An inquisitive walrus surfaced close by *Lord Austin*—a real one, not a plane. The great head with two long tusks peered at us grotesquely from a sudden wave that heaved past the ship; then just as suddenly it was gone. During the afternoon the escorts were again busy driving off U-boats, then five Heinkels approached and fired their torpedoes at us from a considerable distance without result. *Offa* beat off an attack by another aircraft.

These sporadic raids kept every nerve taut. When the shadowing cruiser force was again glimpsed mast high in the distance, their presence seemed both encouraging and fateful, for a popular theory was that they and the battle fleet, now hundreds of miles to the rear, were awaiting an appearance by the *Tirpitz*, for which we were the bait. Unknown to the mass of us was the disturbing news already received via the Admiralty that *Tirpitz* and *Hipper* had left their usual berths at Trondheim. Where they were heading was not yet known, as bad weather had hampered air reconnaissance. We pressed on, the hours of the clock now almost meaningless in the eternal daylight. Every man had only one great need: a good, sound, unbroken sleep.

Aldersdale was constantly busy refuelling escorts and now the cruiser squadron sent in U.S.S. *Rowan,* one of its two American destroyers, to top up. As she steamed over more torpedoes were sighted, their wakes perfectly visible in the clear Arctic water, and the destroyer had to dodge them. She approached us as a group of three or four planes were manoeuvring to attack the convoy from the port bow. *Rowan*'s appearance in their midst broke up their planned attack and they seemed uncertain as to whether to attack the destroyer or the convoy. *Rowan* did not allow them any time for a conference—she opened fire and sent one plane scuttling, then another, and when a third crossed her bow to starboard she tracked it with her guns. The plane did not turn for a good twenty seconds and *Rowan* got a shot right under it, setting it ablaze. The smoking plane went over in front of the convoy, followed by another, both landing. As the damaged plane sank, its survivors got away in the other aircraft before any ship could race to the spot. Another daring rescue and good luck to them; except that it meant more airmen saved to return and harry us later.

On *Rowan's* return to the cruiser squadron, *Wichita* signalled her: 'Welcome back. How is the war?'

'Mighty fine,' answered *Rowan*. 'We claim one German plane.'

With the convoy such a vast size, some of the skirmishes with enemy planes, and the torpedoes they succeeded in dropping, occurred unknown to the great number of other ships, but to those involved an encounter with a torpedo was something never to be forgotten. The quick sight of a torpedo heading for one's ship was a numbing experience that gripped the stomach hard, producing an indescribable feeling of wonder and incredulity and sheer honest fright. The fast, zig-zagging destroyers had every chance of skilfully avoiding a torpedo, but with the ponderous merchantmen and the slower escorts like the trawlers it was a hair-raising business, as exampled by an incident on *Northern Gem* after some planes had dropped their 'tinfish' well outside gun range. Coxswain Sid Kerslake was making his way to the wheelhouse when there was a shout from the point-five platform: 'Torpedo on the starboard quarter!' On sighting the torpedo's track Kerslake saw it was approaching the ship's side at an angle of 15 degrees straight for the engine room under where he was standing, rooted to the spot and heart thumping like mad. He heard the skipper's shout of 'Hard a port!' and saw with relief that the torpedo was now travelling parallel on the same course as the trawler and overtaking. More shouts: 'Steady as she goes,' and 'Bring her back,' and Kerslake saw the track of bubbles sweep under *Gem*'s bow. She had been making ten knots, her top speed, in order to close up with the convoy. What wind there was had been causing her smoke to blow 15 degrees over her starboard quarter, so that one of the planes could have crept in under cover of it before dropping the torpedo. The enemy was well versed in such tricks.

Lord Haw-Haw was broadcasting from Germany now. He could be heard regularly over the ships' radios telling PQ 17 of the dire fate that awaited it, naming individual ships and making particular threats regarding the rescue ships *Zaafaran* and *Zamalek*, which, he sneered, certainly would not get through.

These two were both German-built reparation ships, their exotic names—*Zamalek* ('Place of Kings') and *Zaafaran* ('Place of Queens') being given them by the Egyptian Mail Line. *Zamalek*, exceptionally strongly constructed, was no picture-book vessel and could always be picked out with her array of rescue rafts on deck and a large black mark amidships where there were overflows of oil on the boat deck every few months. On this trip she was carrying on board a naval commander, an official observer for the Admiralty briefed to find out why so many warships were being lost on the Russian run. He had an early taste of action during this day's brief raids when a marauding Shad accorded *Zamalek* the doubtful honour of being the first ship in the convoy to be attacked by machine-gun fire. The plane, passing overhead, raked the rescue ship with bullets. One bullet passed through the commander's duffle coat and in ducking out of the way of more he sprained an ankle. He was lucky. One of *Zamalek's* gunners was badly injured by a splinter from a gun casing entering his eye.

As midnight passed and ushered in July 4 there was a temporary calm as we steamed to the north of Bear Island. Aboard *Palomares* Signalman Barron Taylor had just taken over watch and the scene from the bridge was an unusual one. The convoy was visible in all directions but the sky was blotted out by a mist that hung in the air just above mast height, giving, as was thought, good protection against discovery from the air. As Taylor stood scanning the ships sailing quietly on in a smooth sea he heard what he thought was the noise of an aircraft's engines. He reported this to the officer of the watch, and while waiting for the captain to come up to the bridge everyone listened out. Taylor thought he heard the noise again very faintly but no one else did, and he began to fear what the captain would say had he been called up on a false alarm. But to Taylor's relief, just as the captain got to the bridge the sound of an aircraft reached the ears of all assembled there.

As they strained to detect from which direction it was coming there was hope that the plane would fail to make contact because of the thick mist, though it was now very close on the starboard beam. Suddenly the plane dived through the mist at the edge of the convoy and before any guns could be brought to bear on it, dropped a torpedo, pulled back into the mist and was lost. Taylor ran to the ship's siren and sounded six short blasts to warn the merchantmen, as *Palomares* took swift action to avoid the torpedo. It passed within yards of the ackack ship's bows but went straight on for a merchant ship on her port side.

It was 2.30 a.m. The menaced ship was the luckless *Christopher Newport*. Her seamen gun-loaders and others near the gun-pits panicked and yelled at Seaman-Gunner Hugh Wright to run for safety as they scrambled down the ladder on the after end of the flying bridge, heading for the lifeboats on the port side. But Wright stuck to his post. Opening fire in the water just ahead of the torpedo wake he continued firing and changing the pans of his 30 calibre gun as fast as he emptied them. He kept up a cool and accurate fire, streaming oaths at the ineffectiveness of his gun, until the torpedo passed out of sight under the starboard boats which were swung out, and struck the ship, when he was blown off the flying bridge down two decks to the boat deck, spraining his ankle and being knocked unconscious.

The torpedo struck *Christopher Newport* squarely amidships where the firemen, oilers and a second engineer were standing

their early watch. Thick black smoke rose from her after the
explosion, her engines stopped and she swung broadside on to
the convoy, *Empire Tide* having to take swift avoiding action
to get clear of her.

It was a pitiful, sobering sight to see the huge vessel fall back
maimed and helpless. It had all been so fast and totally unexpected. *Zamalek* was quickly on the scene to rescue the crew
and *Zaafaran* also took aboard some survivors, but to the
watchers on the *Peter Kerr*, immediately to starboard, the ship
presented a smoking scene of utter chaos as she was abandoned.
One end of each boat on her side towards *Peter Kerr* was
dropped completely and each boat was hanging on one fall
as long as they could see her.

Christopher Newport's captain came aboard *Zamalek* carrying
a revolver which he insisted he must keep as he had such a
mixed crew. The rescue ship's captain quietly relieved him of
the gun.

Destroyer *Offa* meantime had been contending with another enemy raider. Afterwards the crippled *Newport*, a danger
to navigation and a possible prize for the enemy, was torpedoed
by one of our submarines. There was a big explosion but she
still took twenty minutes to sink to the bottom with her precious
war cargo.

The rest of the early morning passed in ominous quiet. Four
planes hovered, seemingly motionless, over the horizon, but
they were now too familiar a sight to arouse much interest.
We were passing far to the north of Bear Island, the stark piece
of land visited in normal times only by deep-sea fishermen,
whose tales of incredible hardships were remembered at this
moment by many men; now this island, unseen in the far
distance, was the most dangerous part of the Arctic run, being
the nearest land on a straight flight out from the German air
bases. We awaited fresh events with keyed up expectancy.

In this action area a man's thoughts turned all the more
keenly to his own personal safety, which basically concerned the
clothes he wore. Should he continue to wear all his thick,
heavy gear—or lighten himself, with the risk of being frozen

stiff? Heavy clothing could soon drag a man down in the sea, but on a long watch on an exposed gun platform he had to muffle up or freeze. What many did was to compromise by leaving off their seaboots and wearing thick stockings and gym-shoes. If sunk or blown out to sea they had a fair chance of pulling off their duffle coats, scarves, balaclavas and the rest in order to fight their way to a rescue net, but seaboots were impossible to remove and would drag a man down into the icy depths.

In such a tense frame of mind many of us in the British ships were far from happy to see the next astonishing sight of all the American vessels hauling down their Stars and Stripes from the jack staff. Had they gone mad? The answer came two minutes later when they hoisted their colours once more—brand new Stars and Stripes that seemed ten times the size of the old Atlantic-blown ones they replaced. Of course. If was the Fourth of July—Independence Day. A splendidly defiant gesture in the face of the enemy. The loud sound of music came from some of the American ships and their crews could be seen dancing around on deck; not this time simply as an exercise against the cold.

Over in the cruiser squadron to starboard *Tuscaloosa* and *Wichita* lowered their normal cruising ensigns and hoisted large ceremonial flags, and there was a flutter of messages exchanged. Admiral Hamilton sent the American cruisers and destroyers in his force: 'On the occasion of your great anniversary it seems most uncivil to make you keep station at all, but even the Freedom of the Seas can be read in two ways. It is a privilege for us all to have you with us and I wish you all the best of hunting.'

U.S.S. *Wichita* replied: 'It is a great privilege to be here today with you in furtherance of the ideals which July 4th has always represented to us and we are particularly happy to be a por-tion of your command. Celebration of this holiday always re-quired large fireworks displays. I trust you will not disappoint us.'

The British cruiser *Norfolk* joined in, sending *Wichita*: 'Many happy returns of the day. The United States is the only country with a known birthday.' To which *Wichita* answered: 'Thank you. We think you should celebrate Mother's Day.'

Celebrations, or at least fireworks, there very soon would be.

3

Scatter!

It was a cold but a glorious morning, this Fourth of July. The sun now shone brilliantly from a clear blue sky on to an equally blue, sparkling sea as calm as a millpond. The cruiser force had moved in closer and could be seen a few miles ahead on our starboard hand, the four cruisers and their three attendant destroyers with a Walrus spotter plane floating lazily above. Our little trawler was the ship nearest to them, steaming up ahead on the convoy's starboard bow. It was from the starboard—the south—that more enemy aircraft would come, flying out from the North Cape, and anxious eyes watched the sky.

The calm of the sea seemed to be reflected in the orderliness of the convoy. The merchant ships were now steaming in four long lines abreast with the two ack-ack ships among them and the remainder of the escorts deployed on either flank, the little specks of the two submarines lying astern of the freighters; but hanging low on the horizon ahead and astern were two Shads.

After a long, uneasy interval these Shads were joined by Junkers 88 bombers, one or two at a time, like vultures gathering for the kill; until there were planes droning menacingly all around us.

The cruisers' Walrus made a hasty landing. Two spotter aircraft from the American cruisers, out on anti-submarine patrol, also returned to ship after a brief encounter with a Shad; they were no match for the pugnacious and far superior enemy aircraft.

Then as the afternoon wore on the Junkers 88s began to make quick tip-and-run attacks, dropping their bombs without success but keeping the convoy's gunners busy, the deep boop-boop-boop of the multiple pom-poms mingling with the more staccato crackle of the Bofors and Oerlikons from the merchant ships under attack. There was a low mist back now and the planes could often be heard but not seen.

Other enemy aircraft appeared, among them Heinkels and a Focke-Wulf or two; but still no concentrated attack was attempted. In the late afternoon when things seemed to have quietened, the U.S. destroyer *Wainwright* steamed over from the cruiser force to refuel from *Aldersdale*. Shortly after five o'clock she was halfway through the convoy on her way to the tanker when six Heinkels were seen flying in from the port side. *Wainwright*'s Captain 'Don' Moon closed the planes to see if he could get within firing range—the destroyer's five-inch guns had a maximum range of about 12,000 yards—but when she did fire the splashes fell 500 yards short. Captain Moon moved in still closer and fired a few more rounds, but they were still short about the same distance. The German pilots undoubtedly knew the ship's gun range but at least she had given them to understand that she was ready and willing.

All this time the merchant ships and escorts had blazed away and been joined in the barrage by *London*, which opened fire at long range with her big guns. A total of twelve Heinkels made the raid, circling round and dropping torpedoes, but all without success. They continued to circle the convoy for a time and then attacked some of the escorts but retreated in the face of more heavy gunfire. So that by the end of the afternoon all we had suffered in the various attacks of the day was a little superficial damage to various ships, and some of this from our own over-enthusiastic gunners.

There followed another lull, during which at six o'clock U.S.S. *Wainwright* finally made contact with *Aldersdale* and started refuelling. A misty overcast now hung low in the sky on the convoy's starboard side, so that while some ships on the port side, looking north towards the ice-barrier, could still see bright sun in a blue sky, many of those to starboard saw only a muffled grey ceiling. But still at lower level beneath the overcast visibility was remarkably clear and sharp, and the sparkling sea as smooth as glass.

An Admiralty signal had been received warning that an unspecified number of aircraft had left Norway and could be expected within the hour. It presaged the big attack we all knew must come; and sure enough it came almost on time.

The ack-ack ships' radar picked up approaching aircraft and alerted the convoy; on *Lord Austin* we received an R/T message that twenty-five planes were flying in at a distance of thirty miles; these in addition to the other planes still circling overhead and obviously waiting to join the mass attack. *River Afton* hoisted signal 'JG'—which meant 'Man the guns and prepare for instant action'. Those escorts with the greatest anti-aircraft power closed their ranks to give maximum barrage against the raiders; every gun on every ship was closed up in readiness, making a formidable array of fire power with the two ack-ack ships as the spearhead.

It was 6.22 p.m. as *Wainwright,* still fuelling from the tanker, received her first report of nineteen low-flying aircraft bearing towards the convoy. Captain Moon immediately cast off fuelling lines and steamed at emergency full speed to place his ship between the planes and the convoy. As he did so one of the aircraft circling overhead made a brisk attempt to put the destroyer out of action. Its engines were heard off her starboard quarter, just above the overcast. Captain Moon went to the starboard wing of the bridge, listened for a moment and quickly gave the order to the helmsman for hard right rudder. Seconds afterwards three explosive fountains of water shot up in the air 100 yards off *Wainwright*'s port bow, dead on her former course. The unseen bomber had laid its eggs well; Captain Moon's manoeuvre undoubtedly saved his ship.

Another plane made a similar swoop on *Keppel* but she too escaped, the bomb bursting in the sea less than 100 yards astern.

Aboard *Pozarica* A/B William Mayne suddenly spotted from his action station on the after deck a great number of seaplanes

which appeared to have landed on the sea about six miles astern
of the convoy. It could have been a refraction of light, but they
seemed to be stationary, almost to be holding a conference.
Then one plane appeared to take off and others follow. From
the bridge of destroyer *Offa* the enemy aircraft were seen to
suddenly lift above the whole arc of the southern horizon like
a swarm of mosquitoes.

The tension had mounted on *Palomares* as her radar picked
up the mass of planes flying in. 'Ten enemy aircraft
approaching!' reported the gunnery officer, but almost immediately this was amended to 'Twenty aircraft ... Thirty ...' On
the bridge Sub-Lieutenant Leslie Clements, the ship's radar
officer, counted up to an astonishing 42 planes as they came
up on the starboard side with the leading plane away on her
bow. There may have been one or two more but at that
moment they turned in to attack and Clements stopped counting to hurry below and watch them on the gunnery radar
screen. There were bunches of echoes on the screen and he
stood with knees bent holding on to the transmitter frame
as he waited for a torpedo to hit; he was so sure that one must
hit out of all those planes.

At the radar screen in destroyer *Leamington* A/B Oswald
Tranter could scarcely keep pace. 'Twelve airpedoes approaching, bearing ... Twenty airpedoes approaching, bearing ...
Thirty-five airpedoes approaching, bearing ...' The screen
was one whole mass of contacts and he could no longer
hear himself shouting his readings up to the bridge as all hell
was let loose on board.

Up ahead on the convoy's starboard bow we looked back
from *Lord Austin* to see the whole broad sweep of the action
as the combined flock of Heinkel 111s and torpedo-carrying
Junkers 88s launched their attack. There was a shout from our
lookout: 'Look, there's one of the bastards!'

A little black dot was racing for the convoy, skimming the
surface of the smooth sea like a water-beetle. For a moment there
was silence, then a barrage of fire was let loose on the lead
flier. Flying straight on unheeding through the bursting shells

the plane came upon the convoy from the rear, a spout of water rising near the two submarines as it gave them brief attention before making for the merchantmen between the lines of warships. As the plane banked across the bows of *Pozarica* the pilot was seen to put up his hand, as if to tell them 'You are going up!' In the terrific barrage of close-range anti-aircraft fire *Pozarica*'s pom-pom shells appeared to burst on the sides of the merchantmen as well as hitting this daring floatplane. As it banked away it was hit by shells from the ack-ack ship's starboard pom-pom and a small fire started just in front of the tailplane.

Chief Engineer William Brown of *Aldersdale* had kept his binoculars trained on the plane as it flew in close. 'I could see right into the perspex-covered cockpit. With tracer bullets ripping the plane from all angles the cockpit was a mass of flames and inside were five men, four of them laid around either dead or dying, and a fifth, the pilot, swaying but still upright. I saw him reach out, touch something, and a moment after I saw the torpedoes fall and the pilot drop . . .' The fire spread rapidly as the plane crossed *Pozarica*'s bows and it dipped, recovered, then dipped again and nose-dived into the sea. A splash, followed by a blinding flash of flame shooting high into the air, a great cloud of smoke, and with the blazing cockpit still fiercely burning the plane sank slowly below the surface. When *Pozarica* passed by all that could be seen was a large oily spot on the water with a flame flickering in the centre. It had been an awe-inspiring display of suicidal courage and a successful one, for the pilot's resolutely planted torpedoes had leapt, skimmed and rushed the water to the merchant ships, striking the British *Navarino* with a terrific explosion. She reeled from the shock, smoke pouring heavily from her.

More planes were upon the convoy almost immediately. Like their late leader they came in so low that they seemed to be touching the sea, little winged insects growing bigger and more menacing every second, until suddenly they were blotted out by a black wall of bursting shells.

As the deafening roar of the barrage went up there was a

tremendous explosion heard even above it, and to those watching from the merchantmen it seemed that *Wainwright* had blown up. In fact the destroyer had opened up with all of her five-inch guns, seeming to leave the water in an eruption of fire as her semi-automatic main battery let loose. Two planes went down quickly one after the other before her devastating initial salvoes and could be seen speedily sinking with their tailfins high in the air, a large black swastika on the tail. Yellow liferafts were quickly in the water beside downed planes with at least one man in each. At close range *Wainwright*, acrid smoke from burning powder and flying cork filling the air around her, opened up with her 20-millimetre guns, spraying the heavy bullets over the whole area. Her five-inch guns never stopped firing even when the planes were within 100 yards of her. The shells exploded when about 25 or 30 feet from the planes and one that burst under the port wing of a Heinkel nearly turned it over, but incredibly the pilot managed to level off and release two small, fat, chubby torpedoes that hit the water, bucked twice and then submerged on their course to the convoy.

By this time *Wainwright* had steamed right into the centre of the planes' course and they split up, some going astern of the destroyer and some ahead. At least three more planes were downed in the general barrage and some were smoking as they dived by her, one flying across the bow only a few feet away— its pilot could be seen gritting his teeth as the destroyer's 20-millimetre gunner fired directly into the Heinkel's belly as it passed over.

The fact that the German torpedo-planes had had to get under the low overhang of clouds to make their attack was an undoubted advantage to us as it left them wide open to the warships' tremendous fire power, the two ack-ack ships in particular putting up a great curtain of fire. The din was indescribable. It seemed nothing could live in that closely-knit mass of high-explosive, yet emerging from it the remainder of the planes were now weaving, dodging and turning like a flock of black crows scared by a shotgun. Some made resolutely for their

targets, others hesitated, wavered and turned to port and starboard, trying to fly round the intense barrage to attack the
convoy from front and rear. They flew up and down
the lines of ships so close that the pilots and navigators could
be clearly seen in the cockpits. Seamen used to looking up at
aircraft found themselves fantastically looking *down* on the
planes as they raced in, so low and close that it seemed they
could be hit down with a sling-shot.

The sea became alive with torpedoes, the water criss-crossing
with them as they snaked through the merchantmen. Messages
flew to and fro on the R/T—'My God, one's coming straight
at us!' ... 'Look out, *Bellingham,* there are two heading right
for you! ...'

The swooping, swerving planes were coming in from all
sides now, often narrowly missing each other. The ear-shattering
roar of the guns continued; cockpits were seen to glow red and
incandescent orange balls to float down to the sea or explode
violently in mid-air. As soon as the planes had dropped their
two torpedoes they went streaking out of the barrage like bats
out of hell.

It was inevitable that some torpedoes should find their mark.
Three planes swooped close to the brand new Liberty ship
William Hooper, heavy in the water with her trucks and tanks
stacked on deck. She blasted off with her three-inch and four-
inch guns and such of her machine-guns as could be brought
to bear, setting the port engine of one plane on fire and registering a direct hit with a three-inch shell on the starboard wing of
another. But the third plane, coming to within 800 feet of the
ship coolly released two torpedoes point-blank. *William Hooper*
desperately made hard left rudder and avoided one of them,
but the other scored a hit on her starboard side direct in the
main engine room, actually penetrating to the engine room
before exploding and blowing up the engines and steering gear.
Three men in the engine room were killed; fire broke out and
flooding began at once. Three seamen and four of the ship's
gun crew immediately jumped overboard and the captain per-

sonally had to prevent the lifeboats being lowered before the ship lost way.

Next a torpedo which missed *Aldersdale*'s stern by less than 20 feet struck the Russian tanker *Azerbaijan* in the tank just forward of the engine room, blowing a great gaping hole in her. She veered wildly to starboard and once again *Empire Tide* narrowly escaped a collision as the tanker only just cleared her stern, a fountain of oil shooting up from the stricken vessel as though from a hose as she belched black smoke which towered mountainously to the sky and poured from both sides of her. A bridge gunner on destroyer *Ledbury* only had time for a short burst as the torpedo-bomber passed over but he was right on target, and one of the last split-second glimpses of *Azerbaijan* before she dropped back ablaze was that of one of the women crew rushing to the aft machine-gun to join in firing furiously at the retreating plane, which crashed to the sea farther on down the line of ships.

As the tanker was hit there was a shout down the voice pipe in minesweeper *Halcyon*: 'Sparks, get yourself on top it's just like the bloody pictures, there's a tanker standing on end!' At this moment it was still not realized that this was an encounter with death. Rushing on deck Telegraphist J. A. Hart looked over the minesweeper's side to the blue-rinsed sea which in a strange flashback brought back memories of his mother's 'blue bag' on washing day. Now already marring the blue was wreckage, and lifeboats, and seamen struggling for survival in fuel oil.

In the confusion with the torpedo-planes flying so low the merchantmen had to contend with the added danger of ship sweeping ship with the crossfire from their own guns, the mast of one vessel at least being brought down in this way. *Silver Sword*, last in one of the lines of ships, took a four-inch shell in her starboard bow fired from another U.S. merchantman, though it luckily failed to explode and remained embedded in her cargo in number one hold.

The American ships on *Empire Tide*'s port side had begun firing when the planes were well astern of the convoy and kept tracking and depressing their machine-guns until they smothered the British ship in a hail of bullets; her rigging was shot away, her boat decks riddled and the smoke floats under her 12-pounder platform were ripped by a stream of lead which, had it been two inches higher, would have smashed the legs of the gun crew; as it was one of the gunners on the monkey island had just set foot on the ladder to his gun-pit when he was cut down by a ricocheting point-five bullet which shattered his thigh bone. However in the melee *Empire Tide's* gunners succeeded in helping to shoot down two torpedo-bombers, bursting a 12-pound shell right on the nose of one of them.

On *Ocean Freedom* as A/LS Gunner Jimmy Gordon was making a quick run round the different gun-pits to see that all was well Captain Walker looked to the top of the wheel-house where Gordon operated his own pet gun, a twin-barrelled quick-firing Colt nicknamed 'Wimpey'. Seeing the gun un-manned with a diving Heinkel apparently picking out *Freedom* for a raid, Captain Walker scrambled up to try and bring 'Wimpey' to bear on the menacing aircraft. Just then Gordon came dashing up to take over the gun, and in turning quickly away Captain Walker caught his foot on the lanyard of one of the P.A.C rockets—and triggered it off. The captain got a terrific fright as the rocket went 'swoosh' right alongside him, zooming up with its fathoms of wire attached. The plane was now right overhead and the rocket made straight for it. Off came the Heinkel's port wing clean as a whistle, to float gracefully down alongside the ship like a piece of paper. The plane burst into flames and crashed into the sea a few hundred yards ahead. A great cheer went up from all on board. Through the din Gunner Gordon told the captain: 'It's my wedding anniversary today...' Replied Captain Walker: 'Count yourself honoured —you've had more than a twenty-one gun salute!'

Curses rent the air on *Dianella* as all her A/A guns jammed. The corvette's four-inch was brought to its lowest depression and as planes flew past it fired—and blew off the door of the wheelhouse. More curses. The captain ordered cease fire, they were doing more damage than the Germans.

One of the quietest of dramas was played out in *Zamalek*. Just as the planes attacked, Surgeon-Lieutenant Norman McCallum had begun a difficult operation on the ship's gunner badly wounded by a splinter in the temple and eye the previous day. Amid the great barrage as *Zamalek* ploughed steadily on with her guns roaring overhead, Surgeon McCallum worked on calmly and methodically as if in the quiet of a hospital ashore. Though his medical orderly's hands were trembling, as was the ship, Surgeon McCallum began to stitch the wound but was deterred for a moment in his task owing to the heaving ship and had to steady himself by the belt attached to the operating table. The delicate operation on the gunner was efficiently completed even as the ship was wheeling to rescue survivors. Coming up on deck the M.O. saw the rigging in tatters owing to the fire from the point-five forward during the attack, and the ship's barrage balloon had disappeared.

Over in the cruiser force they watched the battle from less than 10,000 yards away, still keeping to instructions and staying out of range of concentrated attack and the constant U-boat danger—waiting for the surface situation to be clarified by the Admiralty. All fretted at their inability to help as they gazed on a sky packed with brown and black blotches of bursting shells. *London* and *Norfolk* had set up a long-range barrage, engaging the enemy formations briefly as they flew past, though the aircraft paid little heed to the cruiser squadron and headed straight for their primary target, the convoy. The fact that *London* managed to get one plane just as it was going over the horizon was poor consolation. For the American cruisers it was even worse, not being able to join in the long-range shooting at all as their five-inch shells were not self-destructive but of the impact-only type, requiring a direct hit.

On *Wichita*'s bridge they listened in admiration to a running account of the various actions given by R/T from one of the convoy escorts. Calmly the voice coming over the monitor from the thick of the fighting described exploding ships, planes and torpedo bearings. It was a grandstand seat with immunity, and a distressing one, as the steady voice from the convoy continued. But they were 'doing fine', it said.

When on *Wichita* they saw two enemy planes come down and burst into huge sheets of flame as they hit the sea, everyone cheered 'as if we were in New York watching "dem bums" from Brooklyn.' From the cruiser's bridge Signalman G. Edward Young through his glasses watched a Blohm and Voss plummet to the sea. It managed to pull out and land on its floats near the convoy's flank. All ships in the vicinity concentrated a withering fire on the plane and it seemed incredible that it was not destroyed immediately; but more incredible another Blohm and Voss set down alongside the damaged plane, took off its crew and flew off unscathed.

On *Lord Austin* over our hail of fire we saw another plane land to pick up a pilot who had baled out and was in his dinghy. A destroyer dashed towards them but the plane got away. A surfaced U-boat which seemed to be filming the action picked up another ditched pilot and quickly submerged.

Then as suddenly as it had begun, the tumultuous thunder of explosive subsided and there was a heavy silence broken only by intermittent firing at the several reconnaissance and rescue planes which remained still circling after the departure of the torpedo-bombers. The convoy steamed on still in surprisingly orderly formation after an action which seemed to have lasted for hours but in reality was all over in the space of a few minutes.

Behind was a scene of devastation, the sea covered with patches of burning fuel oil, with here and there a ship's lifeboat and pieces of shot-down bombers. Far astern a small group of German fliers were adrift in their inflated doughnut with above them, slowly descending, a red distress flare suspended by its tiny parachute. There were also pilots standing on the wings of downed planes, waiting to be picked up by the daring rescue aircraft.

On *Lord Middleton* when a lookout reported an object in the water off the port bow the trawler steamed to investigate, closing up her four-inch gun. She was about 1,500 yards off when it was seen to be another German seaplane landed to pick up a ditched crew. *Lord Middleton* opened fire. The fall of shot was very close but it was the only shot she made, for after it the old gun just 'sat back', its recoil system broken down, while the enemy plane took off with its rescued crew right before their eyes. Good luck to them, it took some nerve. It was a few hours before the trawler got her ancient gun working again.

There were British and American seamen in the water, too, and some were fired on by an enemy plane, though this in turn fell a victim to one of the corvettes. Other aircraft gunned the rescue ships.

Our three stricken vessels had dropped well astern and around them now fussed the destroyers and corvettes. *Navarino* and *William Hooper* were both listing and smoking as *Rathlin* moved slowly through blazing wreckage, her nets and scrambling lines out to pick up men struggling in the icy water. Among those she dragged to safety were some who were just able to make it over the side before breathing their last on her crowded little deck, though she saved more than sixty men from the *William Hooper*. Some survivors of *Navarino* were taken aboard by *Zaafaran*.

Among the rescued was a bemused Filipino who had been sitting on a crate on deck when his ship was torpedoed. All he could say when picked up was: 'I go up, I come down. As I come down I see aeroplane go under me!'

It had seemed that *Azerbaijan* as she disappeared under her funeral pall of smoke, was done for, but now came a shout from the bridge of destroyer *Ledbury*: 'Good Christ, the women are putting the fire out!' The women crew certainly showed great resourcefulness, though some of their male companions were not made of such stern stuff. Four of them along with a Commissar quickly abandoned ship in a lifeboat and were picked up by *Zamalek*, while watchers from *Aldersdale* also saw the tanker lose a boatload of crew when the boat's forward fall was slipped before the after one; the way on the ship towed the boat under and the occupants were flung into the sea.

Zaafaran rescued some Russians who seemed to have been blown or jumped overboard. One was badly injured in the legs and as the sea around was covered with linseed oil they had much difficulty in scrambling him aboard, willing hands constantly slipping from the oil.

More seamen of *Azerbaijan* had tumbled into a lifeboat and were starting to pull away when suddenly a machine-gun began spraying bullets in the water all round the boat. The gunner was a woman, and another woman with a loud-hailer was shouting at them and waving her arm for them to come back. The rowers stopped, there was another burst from the machine-gunner, and back they came and climbed aboard—and stayed to help the women fight the fires. *Azerbaijan*'s cargo was mainly less inflammable linseed oil, not petrol, and it was this that had spouted skywards. So with his 'volunteers' the tanker's captain was able to save his ship. After a time the rear ships of the convoy saw to their amazement that she was free of her great column of smoke and moving again; as her top speed was 15 knots she was able to make a good effort and catch us up. The captain had won through but at a cost, for an early fatal casualty had been the ship's radio operator—his wife.

On the *Donbass*, the other Russian tanker, the women crew waved cheerfully to the escorts. Young women and middle-aged, like the large, plump one in a long dark skirt covered with a sacking apron down to her big boots, her crowning glory a cloth cap. Haunting figures like this would live long in memory.

Ledbury and *Offa* pulled out to drive off a new threat by the U-boats. *Offa* had accounted for one torpedo-bomber. It was on this ship that, while waiting for the Heinkels to come within range after the early alert, the captain of her 'X' gun, Leading Seaman Tommy Ferns, marched his crew round the gun with broomsticks at the slope to the strains of 'Colonel Bogey' coming over the ship's loudspeakers.

Twelve enemy planes had been destroyed for certain—had been seen to sink. There were probably more, and in addition many had been seen to be so heavily damaged that they were unlikely to survive the return flight to Norway. Even so, our claims were conservative. *Wainwright* claimed only one plane that was definitely seen to sink, reports of three others downed having yet to be verified by her captain. She left us to return to the cruiser squadron amid rousing cheers from the merchant ships nearest to her and with a congratulatory signal on her fine shooting from *Pozarica*, to whom she replied: 'Thank you—we are enjoying the celebrations.' She signalled briefly to *Wichita* later: 'We have had the fireworks we were talking about . . .'

It was astonishing that the enemy's mass of torpedoes had not achieved more hits. This owed much to good luck but also to the skill of some merchant masters, as well as the alert escorts. Many were the narrow escapes. *Offa* skilfully avoided three torpedoes, while on *Palomares*, which had met the full force of the attack on the starboard side, such incidents as when a torpedo was seen running alongside the ack-ack ship never left the memory of her company, for clearly it would have had the ship's name on it but for the captain's astute seamanship. Aboard her sister ship, *Pozarica*, it was almost impossible to walk along the upper deck for empty shell cases. As an indication of how her crew had worked in the heat of the battle, when O/D Charles Gooch ran to his action-station—taking the four-inch fixed shells from the cradle and pushing them up the chute to the gun-deck—he was muffled in the clothes he had been wearing on bridge lookout; thick jumper, overcoat, duffle coat and boots, and a long scarf wrapped several times round his head. When the action ended he was stripped to the waist and in stockinged feet.

Casualties on the escorts included some more unfortunate results of the heavy crossfire, as on the corvette *Poppy*, whose four-inch gun trainer got a machine-gun bullet in his buttock from the wildly firing destroyer *Leamington* on her port beam. The injured gunner, however, showed the neat round hole afterwards, seemingly quite unperturbed about the whole thing. *Poppy* had several brushes with torpedoes. During one hectic moment Sub-Lieutenant Denis Brooke, at his action station aft by the pom-pom, alerted the gunner to a torpedo emerging from under the ship's port side and the gunner tracked it towards the merchantmen. There was a small explosion and he may have upset its course. Generally the torpedoes ran deep for the heavily-laden merchant ships, so passing harmlessly under the small vessels.

Keppel experienced her closest shave just after the leader of the enemy aircraft had crashed not far off her stern. Men still gazing at the spot where the Heinkel had nose-dived were suddenly aware of a dead straight line in the calm sea streaking right for where they were standing, directly above the ship's ammunition store. In a semi-trance they merely stood and gaped, and all A/B Harold Williams could think of in a detached kind of way was how many pieces he would be blown into. But before any panic could spread the ship's stern veered smartly to starboard and the danger was averted. The incident rated one brief sentence in the log: 'Torpedo passed astern of *Keppel*.'

As our last bullet was fired on *Lord Austin* the skipper came down from the bridge his blue eyes blazing with excitement, his short greyish beard bristling.

'Well,' he said to us in a voice cracked with shouting, 'that was a good bit of action, wasn't it?'

A good bit of action it certainly was and the first real taste of it for many of us. Inevitably, as on other ships, we now suffered from reaction. Although some of us had leapt and cheered as planes had gone flaming down into the sea, now they remembered that there had been men inside those orange balls. Enemies, fanatical Nazis out to destroy us. But at the same time they had been men, and brave men at that.

We steamed on now in perfect formation, leaving *William Hooper* and *Navarino* to be sunk within the hour by the escorts. Three merchantmen now lost, but we had beaten off the enemy's first great air attack. Would there be another? And what of the U-boats, so far held at bay by the destroyers? We still had four or five days to go and there were mixed feelings about our chances of getting through, the chief concern being our stocks of ammunition. We had expended quite a bit of it; if there were more heavy attacks how long could we last out?

For Commander Broome as he steamed *Keppel* through the convoy it was 'a tonic' to see the ships 'all in station and looking prouder than ever. I think we all felt that the enemy had realised that PQ 17 meant business and that feeling did us good.' In his diary the commander wrote that he thought PQ 17 could get anywhere as long as the ammunition *did* last out. This feeling was shared by Commodore Dowding, so it was with the high confidence of our two leaders that we steamed on into the Barents Sea.

Keppel signalled *Empire Tide*: 'Can you kill shadower?' The CAM ship apparently did not receive the message for she did not fly off her Hurricane, but in any case the evening sky was soon clear of all but a few white clouds, the Shads seeming to have gone. But while the lookouts scanned a cold quiet sea there was intense activity in the radio cabins.

It was clear to the telegraphists in the escorts that something was in the wind when most of the W/T signals now received from the Admiralty bore the prefix OU—'Most Immediate'—which was used only in cases of the utmost urgency.

The first signal, addressed to the nearby cruisers, had an ominous ring to it: *'Most Immediate. Cruiser force withdraw to westward at high speed.'*

Admiral Hamilton's cruisers were in any case to have withdrawn shortly as originally agreed, they were not to be risked in the U-boat infested Barents Sea. But for the Admiralty now to order their withdrawal *at high speed* seemed to indicate only one thing: that the 'missing' German surface ships had now been located by Allied reconnaissance and there was an immediate threat to the cruisers. Admiral Hamilton had earlier received a message ordering him to remain with the convoy pending receipt of further information; now this urgent signal seemed to confirm the worst fears.

Twelve minutes later there came a second signal this time addressed to Commander Broome: *'Immediate. Owing to threat from surface ships convoy is to disperse and proceed to Russian ports.'*

The shock of this had scarcely registered before there was a third signal, timed thirteen minutes after the other: *'Most Immediate. Convoy is to scatter.'*

As Commander Broome describes it: 'This one was lethal, it exploded in my hand.' If any lingering doubt had remained this last despairing signal dispelled it—the cruisers were threatened, but so was the convoy itself. *Tirpitz!* The battleship must be on her way—only she could have precipitated such a complete and utter panic order by the Admiralty. For our merchant ships to disperse was one thing, and bad enough, but to *scatter.* In dispersing, the ships of a convoy were required to abandon formation and make their way to port at top speed. As all our ships were bound for Archangel, some projected calls at Murmansk having been cancelled, they would have been bound to keep in some company and therefore retain the chance, however slight, of safety in numbers; but in scattering they would 'star' off north, east and south, each ship being entirely on her own.

It was an appalling situation. Bad enough for Admiral Hamilton and Commander Broome, who had to obey orders, much as they disliked them, in the belief that the Admiralty obviously was in possession of vital information not known to its commanders at sea, and which precluded their being alerted and left to make their own decisions on the spot. Bad enough for those few officers and men of the naval escorts who could grasp a little at the reasons for the urgent signals. But what of the merchantmen, who would see only the Navy abandoning them to their fate? What of the pledge of we escorts to protect the merchantmen at all costs, a pledge never broken in naval history?

All at once the outer escorts were closing in with flags hoisted and Aldis lamps flashing as for a short time the other ships were left wondering what on earth was happening.

At 8.32 p.m. *Keppel* signalled: *'All convoy scatter and proceed to Russian ports. Escorts—negative destroyers—proceed independently to Archangel. Destroyers join Keppel.'* The instruction came as such a tremendous shock to Commodore Dowding that he twice asked for it to be repeated. When he finally hoisted the two-letter flag signal on *River Afton*—it was No. 8 Pennant meaning 'Scatter and proceed at your utmost speed'—his own utter astonishment and dismay was matched by the incredulity of the merchant masters, who could not believe their eyes. If there had been ears in London and Washington D.C. attuned to the blistering remarks on those ships they would have burned and dropped in the split of a second. At that moment the merchant seamen felt, all of them, like the proverbial sacrificial lamb. It seemed incredible that they should be left to their own devices.

When the radio operator on the old World War I S.S. *Washington* came up to the bridge reporting he had intercepted messages that the convoy's protecting fleet and escorts were to withdraw, and that there was a wild rumour that the *Tirpitz* and her consorts were on the prowl to intercept the convoy, Captain Julius Richter refused to believe it. 'I thought these messages were only scuttlebut rumours or some hoax message the Germans were sending out to decoy the escorts away from the convoy.' But what began as rumour soon turned out to be fact as the signal was hoisted on *River Afton*. 'I called my naval gunnery officer and ships' officers to the bridge to tell them of the fateful message and what to expect from here on. As we were discussing our hopeless situation there unfolded before our eyes one of the greatest naval tragedies of the war as the escorts one by one withdrew.'

On *Lord Austin* too, still up starboard, when a signalman reported the flag hoist signal to scatter our skipper refused to believe it. 'Don't be a bloody fool!' he said—'Get the proper signal on the lamp!' The signalman did so, and that was it. PQ 17 had ceased to exist.

In spite of the totally unbelievable situation the merchant masters responded as one and their ships accordingly broke formation and spread out over the calm waters; from our position on the starboard flank we saw the whole vast array of vessels gradually melting away on all sides. *Keppel*'s final signal to the Commodore was: 'Sorry to leave you like this. Looks like being a bloody business. Goodbye and good luck.' She had hoisted the signal CHARLIE-MIKE ('Join Me') for the other five destroyers to follow her in line towards the enemy—Commander Broome believed that action was imminent. 'No enemy warships were in sight but in my hand I held the assurance of the First Sea Lord that they soon would be. Having made certain that the Commodore saw the situation as I did, my next instinctive step was to place myself and my destroyers under the order of the cruiser admiral...

'As we steamed through the convoy and down its wake for the last time, our guns, torpedo tubes, smoke floats and all were being manned and checked, for there was no doubt in our minds that we were moving out to fight. My impression was that the fogbank to the westward which the cruisers were approaching was probably where the enemy was hiding...'

Captain Hobson of *Aldersdale* tried to contact the Commodore or *Keppel* to ask whether or not he should join up with the escorts, but he was unsuccessful. So the tanker struck out on her own, an extremely hazardous business with her load. During the battle with the torpedo-bombers her gunners had earned a signal from the Commodore: 'Damn good shooting—keep it up!' They would have exacting need of their guns now. Our two submarines had already been instructed by *Keppel* to act independently.

The cruisers had turned quickly to westward, passing the splintering convoy at a swift 25 knots. Their departure was so abrupt that a Walrus catapulted off half an hour before returned from patrol to find its mother ship gone. Efforts to recall the plane had been unsuccessful. It was action-stations on *Palomares*, then still in company with a few other ships as the Walrus approached, for they had already suffered the attention of a loitering Shad which had returned in time to see the break-up of the convoy. The Walrus tried to contact *Palomares* by its lamp. As it circled round it was suddenly realized that the Shad was closing in with the intention of making a kill, and the Walrus was to be its victim.

Palomares opened fire but the Walrus, in trying to evade the enemy, flew right into the line of sight and only a prompt 'Cease fire!' from the bridge saved a calamity. The Shad beat a hasty retreat out of range and the Walrus was then able to exchange messages. It had not enough fuel to follow on after the cruisers so it landed on the sea alongside *Palomares*, the crew being hauled aboard and the aircraft taken in tow. It was a strange sight to see the ack-ack ship steaming on with the tiny plane bobbing along behind. *Palomares* had been on the starboard side of the convoy and so steamed south-east, while *Pozarica* headed north. As we and all the other close escorts now drew away in the silent sea dotted with icebergs, the six destroyers steamed from us at full speed in line ahead.

Aboard *Keppel* Commander Broome addressed the ship's company. No one wanted to leave the merchant ships, he said, but the Admiralty had received information that the *Tirpitz* had left Trondheim with her escorts. The battleship, with her superior fire power, could stand off and pick off every ship as long as her ammunition lasted. The job of the screening force of cruisers and destroyers was to proceed at full speed to intercept her. Similarly Admiral Hamilton in *London*, as the cruisers raced quickly westward, broadcast to the ship's company about the order to scatter. The *Tirpitz*, *Hipper* and several destroyers had left Trondheim Fiord, he said, and were possibly converging on the convoy; *London* made immediate preparations for surface action.

In all the destroyers in *Keppel*'s flotilla they had gone to action-stations and put on their tin hats, quite certain that they were about to be committed to a bloody death-or-glory action with heavy surface units; in the tense atmosphere aboard *Fury* the medical officer quietly laid out all his instruments and dressings in the sick bay. After a time, however, when still no enemy mastheads appeared on the horizon, there was the growing realization that they might not after all be racing to meet a German fleet but were simply carrying out a tactical with-

drawal. It was a shocking situation, all those defenceless merchant ships left behind to fend for themselves ...

All on the bridge of *Offa* had seen the agony in the captain's
face as he sent 'God be with you' to one of the ack-ack ships.
Soon an animated argument began on the bridge. First
Lieutenant W. D. O'Brien: 'The captain (Lieut. Cdr. Alastair
Ewing), the navigating officer (Lieut. David Unwin), myself
and several others all expressed in various degrees the horror we
felt at what we had been told to do. "We *can't* do this ... We
can't leave the convoy ..." Yet we were doing so. Someone
argued, reasonably, that *Tirpitz* must be just over the horizon;
yet she did not appear. Then we discussed at length the desir-
ability of having a 'breakdown', stopping the ship, waiting for
the others to disappear over the horizon and then turning round
to rejoin the convoy. We very, very nearly did this. To this
day I blame myself for not pressing this policy more forcefully
to my captain, but always we came back to the belief that we
could not be doing what we were doing without a purpose and
that soon something more would be told to us and the enemy
would appear. Nothing more was told to us, no enemy appeared,
and the distance between us and the convoy opened steadily.
Our instinct that we should turn back was right, it was a
moment to disobey; there must always be a sense of shame
that we did not do so'.

The destroyers and cruisers continued a nightmare dash at
high speed through fog and a sea scattered with icebergs. The
faster ships zig-zagged as a precaution against U-boats, but
those like *Wilton*, with the limited speed of an old Hunt class
destroyer, went flat out on a steady course and still barely
managed to keep up. At one stage *Wilton* received an ironic
signal from one of the cruisers: 'Don't rupture yourselves!' A
sister destroyer signalled her in commiseration: 'I feel like a
bloody Italian!' It summed up the feelings of them all.

After some hours of this tearing along, destroyer *Ledbury*
asked permission to ease down as the pace was threatening her
boilers and joints were leaking. At this time there was poor
visibility and a good deal of floating ice about. On the bridge

peering into the murk, the lookouts began to imagine seeing ships and icebergs everywhere and nerves were on edge. The squadron still kept tight formation, each ship towing a fog-buoy astern to avert collision. Even so, the lookout astern on *Keppel*, suddenly hearing many more voices than usual, lowered the binoculars with which he had been trying to peer into the mist just in time to see a blacker wall than the fog closing in on the destroyer. Very quickly it proved to be the port side of a much larger vessel and only a matter of feet away. The great ship drew away with the same speed as she had approached, the air then filling with the discordant music of sirens. Only by a fraction had *London* escaped sending *Keppel* to the bottom.

As the fast run of the cruiser squadron continued the most melancholy aspect of it all was the plaintive signals that began to come in from the scattered merchant ships, many miles to the east ... 'We are being bombed ... We are under attack by U-boats ...' The despairing messages made the destroyer men especially sick at heart, for theirs were no big ships to be protected at all costs, like the cruisers, from a damaging torpedo, and they could have given full fight to the U-boats. It was now clear that *Tirpitz* had not steamed to attack the convoy, so what had gone wrong?

Commander Broome had signalled to the admiral that he was ready and willing to go back, but it was too late.

Admiral Hamilton signalled all ships: 'I know you will all be feeling as distressed as we are to leave that fine collection of ships to find their own way to harbour. The enemy under cover of his shore-based aircraft, has succeeded in concentrating a vastly superior force in this area. We were therefore ordered to withdraw. We are all sorry that the great work of the close escort (the destroyers) could not be completed. I am sure we shall all have a chance of settling this score with the enemy soon.'

Aboard U.S.S. *Wainwright* feeling was very strong. There was no mincing words, they had flatly deserted the convoy. Even when the destroyer on her return to Hvalfiord would be credited with seven aircraft and proudly paint seven swastikas on her

stack, still it would have a hollow ring. On U.S.S. *Wichita,* with
feeling running equally high, they marshalled such facts as
were known from all the reports and signals received, and
made effort to find hopeful conclusion from them. A summary
was quickly put together and printed in the ship's paper as
the cruiser sped westward. The paper was dated July 5, 1942
and within twenty-four hours of the fateful 'Scatter' signal it was
being read by all on board. It explained:

'Cruiser Squadron One, consisting of U.S.S. *Wichita,* U.S.S.
Tuscaloosa, H.M.S. *Norfolk* and H.M.S. *London,* under immediate command of Admiral Hamilton, was ordered to patrol
an area adjacent to PQ 17 and to act as a covering force in the
event of a surprise attack by enemy surface units. Our instructions
were explicit. We were not to go beyond Bear Island unless an
enemy threat was imminent and then under no conditions to go
beyond 25 degrees east longitude. The convoy had been sighted
early by a Nazi patrol plane, and subsequent intelligence from
Headquarters suspected that the enemy had, indeed, been moving
ships and planes northward. After all, the last few convoys had
been far too successful for his taste and it was not likely that he
would sit down and let things go on that way. Reconnaissance
of German bases had failed for several days because of thick
weather, but about three days ago the RAF reported that all of
the main Nazi naval units had left their ports and were presumably sliding northward up the Norwegian coastline with heavy
air protection.

'Admiral Hamilton, hoping that we might be able to "take a
crack" at some of the Nazi pocket battleships, kept covering PQ 17
several degrees beyond the ultimate line specified in our original
instructions. The convoy was told to take advantage of the heavy
mists by steering a course a great deal farther north than expected.
Much to their surprise we were still covering them at a position
nearly 30 degrees east longitude.

'When attacks by enemy aircraft began everyone in the squadron
wanted to join in the fight and help them out. But our mission
was clearly specified and were we to rush in and be anti-aircraft
ships we would leave ourselves open for a lucky torpedo or bomb
hit—thereby crippling our strength for any full scale naval engagement.

'It would have been a gallant but strategically foolhardy gesture. After all, the convoy was well supplied with local escorts equipped for defence against air or torpedo attacks. Another materialistic consideration was that the damaging of one cruiser is more serious than the loss of a dozen fully loaded merchant ships. The ships and their cargo can be manufactured in a few months. Highly complex mechanisms, such as modern naval craft, take a good two years and a fortune to build. The recent loss on Russian convoys of the cruisers *Edinburgh* and *Trinidad*, due to their anxiety to "mix it" at the wrong time, definitely decided the High Command not to place other forces in a similar predicament where without fighter protection they would be victims of enemy bombers.'

After briefly describing events of July 4, including the torpedo-bombers' attack, *Wichita*'s paper continued:

'And then the big news broke. Allied Intelligence reports had confirmed our suspicions. In fact, the situation was worse than we expected. All of the main heavy units of the German fleet had crept through the fog to the northern tip of Norway. They were reinforced by the addition of hundreds of shore-based planes moved up specially for this operation. A fresh squadron of U-boats was also underway. Already we had gone far beyond the limits of where we could meet the enemy on even terms and where our farthest point east was to be. Now he had the unlimited help of bombers and torpedo-planes operating from nearby bases. We, for our part, had no means of combatting this combined attack and the Russians were still too far away to be of assistance. A new full scale attack was being launched, so the convoy was ordered to disperse and, by various routes, make for Russian ports. As they proceeded Russian ships and aircraft would give them what protection they could.

'Our main battle fleet was still some ways away and despite the fact that there was a carrier with them our combined forces could not combat the preponderance of air, surface and undersea power which could be thrown at us. The German ships could operate far enough off from shore to carry on a surface battle while at the same time be close enough to have an umbrella of fighter planes hovering over them the whole time. One of the first lessons of military strategy is "always, if you can, meet your enemy on ground of your own choosing and be able to concentrate superior forces at his weakest point". If this is impossible then the next lesson is to retire until trapped and have to slug it out, but we were lucky enough to avoid that disastrous alternative. . . .'

And finally, after reiterating Admiral Hamilton's signal: '. . . I am sure we shall all have a chance of settling this score with the enemy soon . . .' *Wichita*'s paper concluded:

'We, too, are sure. None of us likes the feeling of seeming to run away but it must be remembered that we are in possession of only limited information. No one can accuse us of ever having a faint heart. The *Wainwright* and the *Rowan* showed that. And what they gave them is only a taste of what is coming. Nor can anyone say the British lack guts. After all, they have been fighting this war for nearly three years. For one whole year they fought it alone, without allies, without a trained army and without equipment, their fleet spread thin around the seven seas of the world. Anyone who has seen the people of London, of Liverpool, Bristol, Portsmouth, Coventry or Southampton can testify as to their worth. Anyone who has seen the Commandos in action, was at Dunkirk, or at Malta, would be a good witness. No, we are kin-folk and allies in more ways than one. Our combined spirit and purpose will certainly triumph. Our force in going beyond its designated turning point in attempting to lure the enemy fleet towards us did its share. We all would like to have done more. But war takes a lot of patience and broad thinking as well as action and courage. We've only been at this game for seven months. We're fresh and all we need is the chance—and we may be surprised at how soon that chance comes. In the words of a Signalman 2nd Class : "We'll get those sons of bitches yet, by God !" And so we will !

'The ship is now proceeding SW to Hvalfiord, Iceland.'

Far behind them, scattering in all directions in the Barents Sea, were our thirty-one merchant ships and tankers, and the escorts too, for it was every ship for herself now.

Already, after the first bewilderment and anger the recriminations had begun, the feeling that was to come down through the years; the feeling that we had been used as a piece of cheese for the German mouse. But in the dying hours of Independence Day there was above all a sense of horror and fear— a fear that no man who survived would be ashamed to confess.

4

Black Sunday

With the threat of German surface raiders appearing over the horizon at any moment the only scant hope of safety for any ship lay in instant flight.

Some among the escorts did consider pairing off. Like the corvette *Poppy*, which had been on the convoy's starboard hand. She picked her way through the dispersing ships and sought out her fellow 'new boy', *Lotus*, on the port side, but before any mutual tactics could be agreed between them *Pozarica* asked the corvettes to screen her. The ack-ack ship had only a defensive asdic set and her commander was apparently thinking of the menacing U-boats in the vicinity. So *Poppy*, *Lotus* and *La Malouine*, which flew the French flag as well as the British ensign, but whose crew were all R.N., joined *Pozarica* in heading north-east for the ice-barrier—with many an apprehensive glance cast towards the glaring south-western horizon. A Shad followed the hurrying group and was there to see them meet up with *Rathlin*, carrying her load of more than 60 survivors. The little rescue ship strained to her top speed of 12 knots to keep in company, black smoke belching from her funnel as the stokehold gang toiled with their shovels.

Minesweeper *Halcyon* struck north for the icefield, while the other two sweepers, *Salamander* and *Britomart* aimed south-east along with *Palomares* and the remaining corvette, *Dianella*. This left only we four trawlers, the slowest ships in the convoy and the ones with the poorest chance of reaching safety. *River Afton* and trawler *Ayrshire* both signalled our skipper asking if we would join them, but with the orders for the escorts to proceed 'independently' our skipper declined. So *Ayrshire* went off for the north. Our skipper would have liked to have gone with her but eventually *Lord Middleton's* captain, being the senior officer, took command of the remaining trawlers and so in line ahead with *Middleton* and *Northern Gem* we steamed northeast at our best speed to find the ice-edge. Still scattered about in the distance were some of the merchantmen, though the majority had by now vanished from our view, some heading direct for the northern ice, to gain protection from the U-boats on one side at least, others turning to make a dash eastwards. An added difficulty for many of them now was that of actually keeping to a true course. In convoy their course had been set by the naval vessels, which were equipped with non-magnetic gyro compasses. Many of the merchantmen had only magnetic compasses, which were of little use in these latitudes; the farther north they ran, the more the variation of the earth's magnetic force pulled their compasses off, until it was near hopeless to try and make a true course.

So July 4 reached its incredible end, and as we trawlers punished our boilers in all-out flight the merchant ships we had been forced to abandon sailed alone to their various fates. There was for them all a brief, unnerving period of quiet as the surprised and jubilant enemy aircraft and U-boats mustered for the kill; then began the long, tragic hours of July 5—Black Sunday.

The first to fall victim to the U-boats was, bitterly enough, an American vessel making her second bid to reach Russia. The S.S. *Carlton* had been on PQ 16. Four days out from Iceland on this convoy she was damaged by a near miss during a dive-bomber attack and had to be towed back to Hvalfiord by a trawler. Now, in the early hours of Sunday morning, some seven hours after scattering, she was quite alone on a calm sea, pushing along at her best of nearly 12 knots under some thinly protective patches of haze as her master endeavoured to hold her on a steady course ESE for the White Sea.

Her five lookouts were given no warning of the U-boat stalking them. At 5.10 a.m. a torpedo struck her on the starboard side amidships, penetrating one of the two deeptanks containing 5,000 barrels of Navy Special, which ignited by the explosion quickly spread fire over a wide area. A sheet of flame leapt from the engine room and a column of water thrown up from starboard, together with oil from the deeptanks, descended on the midship housing; the two starboard lifeboats were hurtled on to the well deck; hatch covers were blown off and cargo—flour—thrown up on deck. Partitions in the living quarters amidships collapsed and the gun turrets on the poop deck buckled.

There was immediate flooding of the engine room, where the explosion killed two men. With no one left to control the engines the propeller continued to turn for several minutes until the fireroom was flooded. All power was off and the emergency radio transmitter was smashed. The ship's gunners, having no sight of the attacker, quickly abandoned ship along with the others on orders of the captain, who saw that his ship was sinking rapidly and feared that the 200 tons of T.N.T. she was carrying might explode any second. Seamen slid down ropes or jumped into the sea, swimming to the four liferafts and one remaining lifeboat—another had been lost in a storm. All thirty-two surviving crew and eleven Armed Guards managed to scramble or be pulled from the sea.

Carlton settled rapidly on an even keel and sank in twelve minutes. The U-boat surfaced and watched her last dying moments but made no attempt to communicate with the survivors, disappearing from sight inside half an hour and leaving them alone on the icy expanse of the Barents Sea.

To the north of *Carlton* and within an hour of her sinking, the British *Empire Byron* was struck by a torpedo amidships. Ship's carpenter Frederick Cooper rushed on deck to find it a shambles, with wreckage strewn all about. Motor trucks the ship had been carrying were no longer to be seen—they had been blown sky-high.

The ship, which had been making a hard eleven knots, was hit in number three hold under the gunners' messdeck. One gunner had just taken his watchmates a mug of cocoa each and gone back below to the messdeck to replace his mug when the explosion struck under his feet and killed him. It shifted two big central cases containing aircraft which slid across and pinned six gunners against the ship's starboard side. When Captain John Wharton quickly gave the order to abandon ship Frederick Cooper ran aft to launch the remaining two liferafts. As he did so he heard the continued screams for help in number three hatch. The companion ladder had been blown up, so he lowered a rope and climbed down. Tanks and lorries running wild had now stove in all the accommodation and bodies were floating around in four feet of water, as the ship's stern was already well under water. Cooper managed to drag four dazed men to the companion, climb up the rope and heave each of them up after him. He went back a fifth time and tried to free the gunners pinned against the ship's side, as others had tried to do by desperately stripping the hatch, but to no avail. He took the hands of one man who was trapped by the legs. The terrified man kept shouting: 'For Christ's sake, don't leave me Chippy, chop my bastard legs off . . .' But the water crept higher and higher until Cooper could feel the trapped man's life ebbing away in his hand-grasp. He could do no more. As he climbed the rope for the last time tears were streaming down his face.

He quickly put life-jackets on the four men he had rescued and rolled them into the sea to be picked up later. Then, the last man to leave the ship, he dived over the side and swam hard for nearly half a mile to reach the ship's jollyboat which was floating empty.

Ten men went down with the *Empire Byron*, which sank in twenty minutes, stern first and flag flying. Besides those killed and trapped, another man lost was one who on reaching the lifeboat station said he had forgotten his bankbook and must go back for it. He was never seen again. Nor was an exhausted fireman who, after being woken up by the crew, simply turned over and went back to sleep, and in the confusion was forgotten.

Two lifeboats got away safely, though one of the forward liferafts was smashed up against the ship's side before the painter could be cast loose. In the jollyboat Frederick Cooper picked up several of his shipmates from the sea.

The U-boat surfaced and after circling the wreck came to them out of the mist and handed over the third engineer whom they had picked up out of the sea. The U-boat commander asked the name of the ship, her destination and cargo, and for her captain, but was told the last they had seen of him was on the bridge. In fact he was in one of the lifeboats but had stuffed his uniform coat under the seats. The U-boat took prisoner instead an Army captain who had been going to Russia to instruct the Russians in the use of the tanks *Empire Byron* carried. Then, while cameras on the U-boat recorded the scene, the commander handed them sausages, black bread and cognac, and gave them a course to steer by. He expressed his regret at having to sink their ship, wished them a safe passage and had his men give a salute—the British salute—before the U-boat drew away and submerged.

Now there was a new wave of enemy aircraft over the southern horizon and their first victim was the *Peter Kerr,* which had 'starred' to the south. Her master, Captain W. A. Butler, had elected to continue on a rhumb line course for the White Sea, and in fact she was the most southerly placed of all the merchantmen and so the first to fall foul of the planes. In the late hours of Sunday morning three Junkers 88s swooped to attack. *Peter Kerr* fought back, but though the tracer bullets from her small anti-aircraft guns were seen to hit the planes they made little impression. After some near misses one plane finally succeeded in dropping three bombs into the hatch between the bridge and engine room. The explosions rocked the freighter, setting her quickly ablaze, and with all the fire-fighting lines ruptured they had no chance of saving her. Captain Butler gave the order to abandon ship and two lifeboats were launched without difficulty on the glassy smooth sea.

'Thank God I've got my good leg on!' exclaimed Chief Engineer Herbert Burkhead as he dropped into a lifeboat; he wore a wooden leg and always carried a spare, but one was his favourite.

The attacking planes circled the boats and as one passed over them very low an engine backfired. A fireman thought they were being strafed and leaped over the side. But the pilots were simply taking pictures, and when they had done so flew off with a jubilant wave.

No one among *Peter Kerr*'s 36 crew and twelve gunners was even slightly injured. They saw two vessels to the north under attack and decided that any return to their blazing ship would be extremely foolhardy; but she was settling in the water as they pulled away.

More U-boats were joining the kill now. Some miles to the north the *Honomu* was steaming flat-out at nearly 11 knots when, unseen by her ten lookouts, a torpedo struck her on the starboard side. The explosion completely demolished the fireroom, shutting off all power, and blasting the radio out of commission. The ship began to settle immediately, and with still no sign of her attacker her guns were useless. Nearly forty of her company abandoned ship in good order but another nineteen men were unaccounted for, most believed killed either by the first torpedo or the second which struck her port side shortly afterwards. The ship sank rapidly, disappearing by the stern in ten minutes.

Soon after she had gone two U-boats surfaced close to the wreckage while another broke the water about a quarter of a mile away. The U-boat which approached the lifeboat and rafts had a victory 'V' over three dice painted on its conning tower. Its commander ordered *Honomu*'s captain aboard and he was taken prisoner; the survivors were then asked if they had sufficient drinking water and were given some canned meat and bread. They were bound to be picked up in a few days said the Germans magnanimously. Then the three U-boats made off to the east.

It was to the east of *Honomu* that *Fairfield City* and *Daniel Morgan* were now both subjected to heavy attacks by the continuing wave of dive-bombers and other aircraft. Junkers 88s soon stopped *Fairfield City*, rocking her with several near misses and two direct hits; and her crew abandoned, pulling away from the ship as she quickly settled in the water.

Three miles away *Daniel Morgan* retaliated strongly, fighting off her attackers for more than two hours. Her captain had set course for the islands of Novaya Zemlya, far across the Barents Sea. Now she was making a valiant 13 knots and zig-zagging so as to give a broadside rather than a fore and aft target for the dive-bombers as Heinkel 115s, Junkers 88s and Shads all joined in the running attack. Her guns blazed away continuously, disabling two Junkers 88s which landed in the water some distance from the ship while another flew off with black smoke pouring from it. The dive-bombers dropped an astonishing eighty bombs of which thirty were near misses, but then came three direct hits which badly damaged and flooded two of the ship's holds, finally slowing her down. As she lost speed a torpedo struck her cruelly on the starboard side, stopping the engines and wrecking the steering gear. The ship's three-inch gun had jammed through overheating and her ammunition was almost spent. It was the end.

So far in her desperate battle there had been only one casualty, a seaman killed in one of the bomb explosions, but as all hands now abandoned ship in the lifeboats two men were drowned when a boat capsized.

Daniel Morgan sank by the stern. Soon afterwards a U-boat surfaced and approached the lifeboats, demanding her name, tonnage and cargo. *Daniel Morgan*'s captain gave false answers. One of the Germans took photographs of the survivors and they were then ordered to follow the U-boat. This they did, pulling behind it for about an hour and a half in a southerly direction, when suddenly the U-boat made off at full speed.

The survivors carried on, resigned now to a despairingly long, cold haul to land, when over the horizon a few hours later came a surprise rescuer, the tanker *Donbass*. Though utterly exhausted, *Daniel Morgan*'s gunners volunteered to man the Russians' forward gun and shortly afterwards scored a direct hit on a diving Junkers 88, also beating off attacks by two others.

But all day long the quick slaughter of ships went on.

Four vessels came in sight of each other as they steamed eastwards— *Aldersdale, Zaafaran, Ocean Freedom* and *Salamander*. The tanker had been shadowed for hours by a lone bomber circling in a bright clear sky, too bright, and they were glad to find some cloud cover and at the same time close up a little with *Salamander* and *Ocean Freedom*. Among most of *Aldersdale*'s company there was no real feeling, just a weariness, a loneliness and a fatalism of 'let it happen soon and get it over with'. It seemed impossible that any merchant ship could escape and Captain Hobson's decision to head for Novaya Zemlya was regarded as being only a gesture in the direction of safety. Nevertheless her gunners were prepared to give as good as they got.

Zaafaran, carrying her survivors from the previous day's battle with the torpedo-bombers had pushed on at speed when warned by an escort that the German heavy ships were believed to be only thirty miles away. Captain Owen Morris of *Zamalek* had invited *Zaafaran*'s Captain Charles McGowan to steam in company with him, but there was a certain rivalry between the two rescue ships, especially between the masters, and Captain McGowan had refused. *Zaafaran*'s flat-out speed was a good half a knot more than *Zamalek*'s so she was able to draw well ahead. Her crew were well thankful, as they cursed *Zamalek* for the heavy smoke she made; in the absence of any wind the betraying black cloud hung above her like an inviting signal in the sky. Besides, on the radio she was the target for some of Lord Haw-Haw's direst threats. So *Zaafaran* sped on, though as she did so ship's carpenter James Ramsay brought out a bottle of whisky he had been saving to take home. Being a good Scotsman he could not bear to lose it if they did have to go over the side, so in the early hours he killed it with some of the gunners.

Now it was late morning as a number of marauding planes descended on the four ships.

Three Junkers 88s swooped down to bomb *Aldersdale*. One was successful. Gunner Thomas Urwin as he blazed away with his Oerlikon saw the grey eggs drop just off the port side beam. They exploded near and under the ship's stern, splitting her engines right across. The after flying bridge buckled, the pump room flooded, steam poured from the engine skylight and the stink of oil and petrol was everywhere. One of the junior engineers, answering an anxious call from the bridge as to whether anyone was hurt replied: 'Hell, what colour's blood?'

With the tanker immobilized and rescue close at hand, Captain Hobson decided to abandon ship. One of the emergency duties of Third Officer Henry Phillips was to dump the ship's weighted confidential books and papers. On going into the chartroom he found the navigator, Charlie Cairns, almost in tears. It was chaos. Newly-corrected charts, coloured inks, glue and other cartographical debris lay all over the deck. Cairns' comments on the wasted efforts were lurid. On reaching the lifeboat station later Phillips found that both boats had cast off leaving about six of them on board, each boat assuming that they were in the other one. There was the captain, the chief officer, the chief engineer, Phillips and two others. Making their way aft they launched the jollyboat—after first seeing off some of the captain's rum.

All were soon picked up by *Salamander*. Before leaving, Gunner Urwin and his colleagues took the Oerlikons off the mountings, their barrels red hot, and these were slung over to the minesweeper.

Aboard *Salamander* Captain Hobson and Lieutenant Mottram, her commander, talked over the situation and decided to try and tow the tanker, but just as efforts were being made to fix up a tow, *Salamander* received orders to proceed with all speed. Captain Hobson was given five minutes to decide whether to return to his ship or remain with the sweeper. Reluctantly he chose to stay and so it was decided to try and sink the tanker by gunfire. The result was as hilarious as it was

sad. The first shell from *Salamander*'s four-inch took some of
her stanchions and wires away; when the order was given to
elevate the gun it rose to its maximum and the breech block
fell off. So it was decided to set the tanker ablaze by firing
incendiary bullets into the pumproom to explode her aviation
spirit, but the bullets simply rebounded off her shell plating;
fortunately, some thought, for she might have taken them all
with her in the resultant explosion. Finally some depth charges
were heaved at her engine room plating. Three or four charges
were sent over but still she did not sink, though as they drew
away *Aldersdale*'s stern was well down and her fore-foot clear
of the water.

The other ships in the group had managed to fight off the
aircraft, but not for long. *Ocean Freedom* and *Zaafaran* had
each pulled away on their own and now a single determined
plane dived on *Zaafaran* and dropped three bombs in a perfect
straddle. The middle bomb was either a very near miss on the
starboard side amidships or else it struck under the waterline;
after the shock of the explosion the rescue ship was quickly
down by the stern, her engines stopped and covered with steam.

Carpenter Ramsay, his left hand badly gashed in the explosion,
made for the boat deck where some frightened passenger survivors had the jollyboat swung out. Tough Captain McGowan
threatened them and ordered them out of it. However, the
boat was lowered and Ramsay and a deck-hand tried to lower
the heavier boats. None of the lifeboats had ever been swung
out before. The jollyboat was on the ordinary swing-out davits,
but the others were on heavy patent wind-out davits and were
still resting on the chocks. After winding for some time Ramsay
and his helper discovered that the davits had burst through
the deck and the boats could not be got away. Ramsay ran to
the boats on the starboard side and found that exactly the same
thing had happened there.

By this time *Zaafaran* was pretty far down in the water and
Captain McGowan shouted for Ramsay to look after himself.
The carpenter ran forward and released the raft on the port
side, which was immediately crowded, so he crossed to the other

side and went over into the water. He swam to a raft which kept overturning; it was for ten men and there were more than twenty scrambling for places. Ramsay hung on to the side of the raft with the others and as they slowly drifted clear of the ship *Zaafaran* suddenly upended and went down stern first.

It had all happened in four minutes.

Surprisingly the sea was quite warm, one of the quirks of the Gulf Stream. Ramsay and his shipmates managed to reach two rafts and scramble aboard. By this time it had become foggy, and with no other ship in sight the outlook was miserable. But after drifting for some three or more anxious hours they sighted *Salamander* far off. Then along came the smoke-making *Zamalek*. The ship they had cursed they now blessed—once they had got over their initial shock. For it was strange to board a ship which, according to one of the last broadcasts of Lord Haw-Haw over *Zaafaran's* radio, was among those already sunk.

On counting heads it was found that luckily only one man had been lost, a D.E.M.S. gunner. There followed a brief clash on *Zamalek* when Captain McGowan, who was the senior of the two masters, went up on the bridge with the idea of taking charge. He was put smartly in his place by Captain Morris, who, though not physically a big man, had the courage of a lion. Captain McGowan went below and brooded for the rest of the voyage. But he had had to swallow quite a lot in losing his ship and being rescued by his slower rival. As for Captain Morris, he had already had some arguments over tactics with his own naval gunnery officer, who at times seemed to think *he* was running the ship. Captain Morris gave the officer short thrift— after the scatter order the navy stank in the nostrils of the rescue ship's company.

Up in the north, towards the ice-barrier, steamed the *Earlston*, alone now, though in the early morning her crew had glimpsed the quick end of *Empire Byron* not far off. After scattering *Earlston* had turned all steam off the winches to get maximum pressure on her engines and succeeded in pushing up her speed to nearly 14 knots; in the words of one of her company she 'got a wiggle on'. A few hours after *Empire Byron* had gone, when *Earlston*'s crew had just sat down to their Sunday dinner, the alarm bells rang. Five torpedo planes were flying in on the port bow. The ship's old four-inch opened up at long range and planted its second shell right under the nose of one plane, which swerved and shuddered but dropped a torpedo that streamed straight for the ship. The command 'Hard a port!' rang out and the ship began to swing, agonizingly slowly ... But they made it, escaping the torpedo by just 20 feet—it shot on parallel to them along the ship's side. The planes flew off, the damaged one lagging behind the others very low on the water, but now two U-boats were sighted astern. The four-inch crew opened up again but had to stop firing when the U-boats manoeuvred between two lifeboats of survivors from another ship. Then eight Junkers 88s droned in on the starboard beam and one peeled off to attack.

'Here he comes!' came the shout from the monkey island— 'Right out of the sun!' For a few seconds all was quiet, then every small arm on the ship burst into explosive action. Down came the plane, closer and closer—would it never pull out? They saw the bomb doors open and the bombs float out, the fins swaying about as they whistled down. One bomb fell to port, the other to starboard; there was a great splash and water burst over the ship, but she was not hit. The Junkers, however, never came out of its dive, smacking down into the sea on the port side. A second bomber flew in—though not so low—to drop its bombs feet ahead of the ship and sheer smartly away. But still the ship steamed on unhurt. Then a third plane, two more bombs, and still no damage. From then on *Earlston*'s gunners had no time to count; they loaded and fired as fast as they could as the other planes came in and more bombs straddled the ship.

Then came the unlucky one. It was either a hit or a very near miss, the force of it lifting *Earlston* right out of the water. All the pipes in the engine room were fractured, the pumps blown off their bed-plates, and the whole engine seemed to have shifted nine inches across the engine room, which flooded fast. There was nothing more they could do, no use remaining aboard; with no power the ship was a sitting duck and the best way of saving the lives of her crew was to take to the boats. At 3.10 p.m., three hours and ten minutes after the alarm bells had rung for the final action of S.S. *Earlston,* Captain Stenwick ordered abandon ship.

The first thought of Lance Bombardier Richard Crossley on leaving his gun station was to grab some warm clothing, and he hurried below and seized his Army issue sheepskin jerkin, together with half a pound of tobacco which he had been saving to take home for his father. He then ran back to help get the lifeboats over the side. There were two, plus a dinghy and a raft. The dinghy was holed and started to sink, but all the ship's company got safely away, though the planes deliberately fired on them as they were getting into the boats. Besides the ship's crew and gunners there were five passengers: a Ministry of Supply man bound for Russia, another civil servant and three Russian seamen whose ship had been sunk.

The planes continued to circle the lifeboats and also made another run over the ship, but without dropping more bombs. Then four U-boats surfaced: two within 200 yards of each other, another half a mile away and the fourth a mile distant. Now they knew that the best decision had been made; had they not taken to the boats, more likely there would have been no boats to take to. The three nearest U-boats formed a triangle around the two lifeboats. The commander of one ordered the boat containing Norwegian-born Captain Stenwick to come alongside, and he was taken aboard. He appealed for help for his crew but it was refused. A final 'Cheerio!' and he was gone. When the crew asked for a course to steer by the U-boat commander replied coldly: 'We are all at war—just find your own way!'

Three torpedoes were now fired at the helpless ship, which lay absolutely still and broken on the calm sea. Two missed and the third struck her amidships, but still did not sink her. The U-boats submerged. The Junkers 88s were still about and one flew very low over the boats, as if to machine-gun them, but instead it gave a brief victory roll and flew off. The lifeboats joined up and pulled away together. Now the planes resumed attacks on the crippled ship, flying down almost to masthead height before releasing their bombs, yet still unable to hit her. Finally one succeeded in dropping a bomb in *Earlston's* number one hold where the naval ammunition was stored. There was an enormous dirty blue flash as the ship went up like a firework, the whole fore-end blowing to bits and the naval pinnace across her deck disintegrating in mid-air. All the survivors saw of the rest of the ship was the stern as it rose out of the water and turned over, disappearing beneath the surface. This was at 4.30 p.m.

To the east, just as *Earlston* was abandoned, the American *Pankraft,* a very old West Coast freighter, was also steaming hard alone at a manful ten knots when seven Junkers 88s swept towards her out of the sun. Three Junkers attacked the ship, keeping out of range of her fast firing machine-guns, and dropped nine bombs. Six of these fell wide, but of the other stick of three one bomb dropped directly on number three hold amidships between the bridge and the crew's quarters. Fortunately it landed in a large pile of bagged coal stacked on top of the hatch cover, and this took the main force of the explosion. But the other two bombs were near-misses which buckled the ship's plates; her oil and steam connections were ruptured, the engine room began taking water and the engines were stopped.

The main transmitter went dead and the captain could not order abandon ship over the loudspeaker system. Radioman J. E. Blackwell left the radio shack to find that all the lifeboats had been lowered and had pulled away some 25 yards or more, except one which still had the painter line tied to the ship but had drifted some eight feet away. He went back into the shack for the other operator and they climbed down the sea-ladder and pulled themselves through the water by the painter line to be hauled into the waiting lifeboat.

The captain was already in one of the other lifeboats. To the intense anger of the crew he and the chief officer had been among the first to leave. Some men believed that the damage to the ship could be repaired, enabling her to continue; they afterwards accused the captain and chief officer of being generally incompetent in handling the ship. The captain had disposed of all his American confidential papers but in his haste to abandon ship all the British papers were left on board.

In the general confusion the second mate had stepped forward and taken the responsibility for seeing all the ship's company safely away. Radioman Blackwell and his colleague believed themselves to be the last to leave, but after their lifeboat had pulled nearly a mile away they could see there were still three men on the ship. One jumped and fell into the water, another went forward and released a liferaft, while the other seaman, who was badly wounded, fell off the sea-ladder into the water and died a few minutes after the lifeboat returned to pick him up. They also recovered the body of one of the other men—the second mate: he was about sixty years old and seemed to have died of a heart attack as there were no wounds on him when they picked him out of the water. His tragic death increased the crew's bitterness towards the captain as they pulled grimly away from the ancient freighter, now motionless but still well afloat on the smooth sea, the planes circling them apparently taking photographs.

Captain Richter of the *Washington* had pushed his vintage freighter to her top speed of ten knots, heading north-east for Novaya Zemlya. Heavy ice forced him to take a more southerly course than he wished, as it brought them ever closer to the enemy planes, but to his relief the ship eventually ran into fog. Taking full advantage of this he forged ahead with every ounce of steam, but as the day wore on the fog lifted, the sun came out brightly and suddenly out of low cloud a lone dive-bomber dived on the ship. Fortunately its bombs fell some distance from her.

As the horizon cleared, other ships could be seen struggling along. Captain Richter closed in on the two nearest vessels and signalled them, suggesting they should join together to afford mutual protection against aircraft. The two ships, the British

Bolton Castle and the Dutch *Paulus Potter* readily agreed. *Bolton Castle* was fortunate in having aboard four Russian survivors from an earlier convoy, one of them a navigation officer who knew the Arctic well; he had given the British captain instructions on how to get right up into the ice and steam north of Novaya Zemlya, coming down on the eastern side of the islands through the Kara Sea.

As the three ships sailed on together appeals kept coming over the radio from other vessels being attacked—calls for help that never came. It was mid-afternoon when a bomber swooped down just out of reach of the three ships' combined guns to release its screeching load of bombs. *Washington* shook and trembled from a near miss. Within minutes of the lone plane completing its mission they were again attacked by a group of six or seven planes coming in low to drop their bombs and machine-gun the decks.

Aboard *Bolton Castle* the crew's tea was laid ready on the galley tables: cold meats, salads, fruits, cakes and pastries. Often during the next long days in an open lifeboat Chief Cook Leonard Osmundsen was to think longingly of all that food. Most of the ship's gunners were busy firing at circling Focke-Wulfs and Shads when out of the blue in a straight dive came a Stuka to straddle the ship from port to starboard, obtaining a direct hit. The whole top part of the ship just forward of the bridge was torn apart, a gunner on the bridge being hurled into the sea by the blast. To those on the *Washington* it seemed that the British ship virtually disintegrated. Amazingly the ammunition she was carrying did not explode.

Cook Osmundsen dashed out on deck to the nearest lifeboat station where the seamen were already lowering the boats. Though the ship was listing heavily to starboard they managed to get two lifeboats away and begin pulling like blazes away from the rapidly sinking ship. Miraculously there were no casualties. Even the gunner blown overboard was pulled from the water after a few minutes and, though in very bad shape, suffering from cold and exposure, was later brought round in one of the lifeboats.

For thirty-six hours *Bolton Castle*'s tireless gunners had kept the enemy aircraft at bay. Now the stricken freighter died in five minutes. Suddenly she lifted herself out of the water and began to slide under, stern first, the red duster still flying as she slipped below the surface.

A plane swooped over the lifeboats and gave them a burst of machine-gun fire but no one was hit. Then other aircraft flew in low and it was realized they were taking photographs. As they flew off one pilot waved his hand as if showing the survivors which way to sail, but in that direction lay Norway and a prison camp, so they decided to strike due east. After collecting all the bits and pieces floating around that might come in useful, they discarded a third lifeboat, sharing out its rations between the captain's motor boat and the sailboat. Then, the power boat towing the other they pulled away from the scene.

Scarcely had *Bolton Castle* been hit before it was the turn of the *Paulus Potter*. Her British gunners kept the attacking planes at bay until for a third time a stick of bombs dropped close to the ship. All the earlier near misses had sprung her plates and shifted her engines, now these last bombs, narrowly missing the four-inch gun platform, blew the ship's rudder off and damaged her propeller. The captain ordered abandon ship, but Gunner David Richards and his comrades, having a shell in the breech of the four-inch, continued firing at an aircraft flying astern. The plane lost height and dropped its bombs in the sea.

The four gunners were the last into the lifeboats along with the captain and second mate. The planes continued to spray *Paulus Potter* with machine-gun fire but did not attack the four life-boats, and when they had flown off the motor boat took the other three boats in tow away from the helpless, burning ship.

And then it was *Washington*'s turn. More bombers appeared overhead and attacked her in force, dive-bombing and strafing the decks packed with tanks and truck chassis. The ship's small guns blazed away with no effect and finally a stick of bombs exploded close on the starboard side, fracturing her side plates; she listed heavily, taking in water, while the deck cargo burst into flames from incendiary shellfire. Another stick of bombs astern disabled the steering gear; Captain Richter ordered abandon ship.

The entire crew got safely away in two lifeboats while the bombers continued to rake the ship with machine-gun fire. Because of the high danger of the fire spreading to the 500 tons of T.N.T. stowed under her deck the boats pulled away from the fiercely burning ship with all speed. Soon afterwards four bombers circled low over the boats, but only to take more pictures. The pilots waved as they flew off, leaving *Washington*'s survivors to take the oars for the long, daunting pull of some 360 miles to Novaya Zemlya.

Only hours later the S.S. *Olopana* steamed up and came upon the lifeboats from the three ships. She slowed and stopped. *Olopana* had been lucky so far, though her master, Captain Stone, was doubtful of his luck holding out much longer. Captain Richter boarded her by jacob's ladder and was asked if any of his crew wished to join *Olopana* and take a chance with her, but when he returned to his lifeboat and put it to the men their answer was firm. 'I hollered back to Captain Stone on the bridge: "We are not coming aboard as my crew feel safer in the lifeboats. Wish you luck. Be on your way!"'

And so it was with the survivors of *Bolton Castle* and *Paulus Potter,* who also chose to remain in their lifeboats, more willing to fight the open sea rather than board a ship which they believed to be doomed. During these exchanges a panic started when there were sudden cries that the bombers were returning. Some of *Olopana's* crew took to the boats and lay off, while the rest of the crew, her master, and all the gunners stayed aboard. It proved a false alarm. The tiny specks of 'enemy aircraft' spotted on the horizon turned out to be nothing more than a flock of birds. The *Olopana men* returned to their ship, handed out cigarettes and loaves of bread to the lifeboats and steamed on their way.

Many miles to the south-east a U-boat was claiming the enemy's last victim of the day—the Commodore's ship. *River Afton* was steaming for Novaya Zemlya when, totally without warning, a torpedo struck her in the port quarter engine room. The time was 8.15 p.m. A/B W. N. Marsh should have finished his four-hour watch at 8 p.m. but the crew were having to double-up, so his watch carried on. He had just returned to the gun-box when the torpedo hit the ship. He ducked into the box at the explosion and on lifting his head again all he could see was a hole where the ship's stern had been. The port lifeboat had vanished and so had the three or four gunners operating the four-inch gun; they were never seen again.

Marsh and his shipmate Gilbert White, both Newfound-landers, ran to their emergency stations, Marsh to help lower the starboard lifeboat, White to release the rafts, a cool-headed action to which many men subsequently owed their lives. It took an effort to lower the lifeboat as the warps were covered with debris, and when they got into the boat it capsized with the speed the ship was still going. Nearly twenty men were trapped under the boat and drowned, Marsh diving over the side just in time and swimming to one of the rafts. Three other men, one a badly injured fireman, struggled through the water to join him.

A second torpedo had crashed into the engine room as the boats were being lowered. A/B Adam O'Hagan rushed to lower the jollyboat, on the second mate's orders, but this too capsized because the ship was still making way. O'Hagan got away with others on a raft, among those not so fortunate was the chief mate.

The U-boat manoeuvred and sent a third torpedo crashing into the stricken ship's starboard side. Only then did Commodore Dowding abandon her, one of the last men to leave. He found safety on a raft along with two seamen.

The surfaced U-boat moved alongside A/B Marsh's raft and ordered one of the four men to come aboard and give particulars of *River Afton's* cargo. The commander then handed them some wine and bread and took photographs. He told them to steer due east 200 miles to land—Novaya Zemlya. They asked if he would take the injured fireman aboard but he replied he was sorry, he was "full up".

Later Marsh and his comrades were joined by another raft
and the refloated jollyboat, in which were the ship's master,
Captain Charlton, and another officer; the two had a struggle
to keep the little boat afloat. All around now in the rising mist
was wreckage and rafts with men clinging to them, and here
and there the floating bodies of the dead.

Fourteen ships gone in one black day. It was a fantastic
figure. With the three ships sunk earlier, PQ 17's losses now
equalled the entire losses of all the previous sixteen convoys to
Russia. But the holocaust was not over yet.

5

Flight to Funk Creek

In the afternoon of Sunday, as *Pozarica* together with her attendant corvettes and *Rathlin* steamed eastwards alongside the ice-edge a Junkers 88 flew in to keep company with their shadowing Blohm and Voss but did not attack. As more and more harrowing signals came in from the dying merchant ships *Poppy* and *Lotus* both sought permission to turn back to the aid of survivors but *Poppy*'s request could not be agreed. Some of her company were very bitter about this and tried to urge their commander (Lieut. N. K. Boyd, R.N.R.) still to turn his ship, but he was a lieutenant with his first command and in no position to disregard a four-ring captain R.N. Feeling was so strong among some of *Poppy*'s officers that they accused *Pozarica*'s captain of saving his own skin before that of the con-voy—unjustly so. For when tempers cooled, his position could be seen too: with some 300 souls on board a converted banana boat it would be foolhardy to break up the defensive unit formed by her A/A guns combined with the anti-submarine po-tential of the corvettes; each without the other stood a lesser chance of survival. However it was not unreasonable for one corvette to go and *Lotus*'s commander (Lieut. H. J. Hall, R.N.R.), as a senior escort officer was in a stronger position than the others; and so he took his corvette back apparently into the jaws of the approaching enemy battleships, to effect what rescue work he could.

Lotus had not been gone very long before *Pozarica* picked up a stark warning signal from the Admiralty: 'Most likely time of enemy surface attack now tonight 5th/6th or early tomorrow morning July 6th. . . .'

Pozarica's Captain Lawford explained the position to the corvette commanders and *Rathlin*'s master by loud-hailer. It was clear now that they could not attempt a direct descent to the White Sea but would have to continue skirting the ice-barrier and make for Novaya Zemlya, perhaps finding a refuge in the narrow Matochkin Strait which divided the two islands. Behind this plan was the resolution that if, on arrival there, it was found impossible for the ships to continue south to the White Sea, then their companies might have to consider going ashore and making their way south overland.

At 6 p.m. *Pozarica's* captain told his ship's company all that was known. If they met up with the enemy destroyers, he said, they stood a chance of fighting them, but they could have little hope of out-gunning the battleships and once they engaged them, as they should, it would be 'Goodnight'. Laughter at this hid the very real fears of the company. The captain ended by telling them all to get as much sleep as possible and to seek peace with their Maker.

The four ships now steamed on spaced out in line ahead, a formation adopted to deceive the enemy into believing from their silhouettes that they were actually a more impressive force. Scarcely an hour after the captain's speech *Pozarica* intercepted another signal and the good news was piped over the ship's loudspeakers—the Russian submarine *Red Star* had claimed two hits on *Tirpitz,* which had slowed speed with all the other German units closing around her. There were big cheers. But as the hours went by without confirmation of this signal there were many who spent their time on the after-deck looking for the signs of ships appearing astern over the horizon. When two masts did appear there was a general alert followed by an anxious interval until the lookouts identified the vessel. It was the *Samuel Chase*. When close enough she signalled: could she join them?

Five now, steaming somewhere north of the 77th parallel

bound for unknown Novaya Zemlya. As the ships steamed along-side the ice-edge there came a brush with a U-boat which had been stalking *Samuel Chase*. A torpedo was seen approaching the merchantman from her seaward side. She managed to avoid it and it struck home upon the ice wall and exploded, bringing down masses of ice. *Poppy* fruitlessly chased the U-boat under the ice with shells from her four-inch, which fell short. Eventually *Rathlin* found the pace of the other ships too much for her and dropped astern.

Far from the *Pozarica* company we three trawlers—*Austin, Middleton* and *Gem*—had forged our slow way ahead, hearing an occasional dull, rumbling explosion in the distance followed by a rising cloud of black smoke. On *Gem* their two lifeboats were slung out ready for a quick getaway; with the sea calm and little rolling movement in the ship it was possible to lower them almost level with the ship's rail. They were packed with extra food, clothing, blankets, water and rum, guns and ammu-nition, tobacco and cigarettes. Each man put on extra clothing and made sure his lifebelt was on him or close at hand. One seaman packed a suitcase. Old Frampton, *Gem*'s second engi-neer, who had been recalled to service after being pensioned off and now found himself in this predicament in a ship that was hardly pusser's Navy as he had known it all his life, had his pension book and other private papers hung from his neck in an oilskin bag under his vest.

Middleton and ourselves also loaded our smallboats with extra stores and readied them for instant lowering, while on each ship confidential books were put in weighted bags.

On nearing the edge of the icefield we had to skirt carefully round huge sheets of ice from which the glare of the sun was so dazzling that it hurt the eyes. Soon after we had passed an enor-mous iceberg the alarm bells shrilled when three aircraft were sighted flying towards us, but they paid us no heed, making for a merchantman far away on the horizon. We had been bom-barded by distress calls from the merchant ships and the ship ahead, it was reckoned, must be the *Pankraft* whose signal we had just received. Other Junkers 88s were seen flying in to the

kill and as the merchantman lay motionless beam-on to us, a
spiral of smoke curling up from her, we could see the planes
attacking from very low level and the sticks of bombs falling
around the ship one after the other. When some of the planes
had done, back they droned. Would they now attack us? One of
our signalmen stood alert on deck with the bag containing the
thick, heavy red Fleet codebooks, ready to plunge it over the
side if the planes descended.

'No, not yet!' came the caution from the bridge. 'Not yet. . . .'

The planes arrived, flying high above us. But no bombs were
dropped and they flew on apparently taking little notice of our
slow moving vessels. Around *Pankraft* now, still with planes
circling, were scattered little blobs on the ocean. They could have
been U-boats or seaplanes landed with the intention of capturing the ship, so we proceeded warily, but no, they were lifeboats, and as we came nearer they turned about and pulled in
our direction.

Our skipper signalled *Lord Middleton* that if we picked up
the survivors she could sink the crippled ship, but there was no
answer, and then *Middleton* signalled for us all to alter course
almost to reverse. Our skipper, considerably surprised and
aware of our duty to go straight to the aid of the merchant seamen signalled *Gem's* commander, asking if he would disregard
the order and come with us to the rescue. But *Gem* replied that
she was bound to obey the senior officer, and so all three trawlers turned off and made for a sheltering fogbank. But it was
too much for our skipper who boldly turned again and steamed
for the *Pankraft* alone, presenting a perfect target as we steamed
to within two miles of the merchantman. The planes, which had
apparently used all their bombs, started machine-gunning the
ship—we could see it all quite clearly. The bombers ceased
their machine-gunning and came for us, but, unbelievably, they
passed overhead without opening fire.

We were joined eventually by *Middleton* and *Gem*, but just
as we neared the lifeboats they suddenly turned and pulled
furiously away from us. Then fast into sight came *Lotus*, heading
straight for the stricken freighter. Her lamp blinked as she swept

by: she would take care of the survivors—we were to keep going like hell's delight in an easterly direction, as according to an Admiralty signal a strong force of enemy vessels including the *Tirpitz* was following at 25 knots. It was the first we had heard about this, our W/T reception from the Admiralty being so poor.

It was only afterwards that we learned the reason for the curious behaviour of the lifeboats in turning away from us. They were unable to make out our signals and thought we were a U-boat about to torpedo the *Pankraft*. Then when *Lotus* arrived and they saw our guns apparently trained on each other they thought they were going to be caught up in open lifeboats in the middle of a naval gun battle!

Lotus began to pump shells into the motionless *Pankraft* which was soon burning fiercely. In a very short space of time *Lotus* had all the survivors safely aboard, then she overtook us again at a cool 18 knots—almost double our speed. She signalled: '*Pankraft* went up—bigger and better bangs all the time! Clear area with all despatch—two enemy capital ships and eight destroyers nearer and still approaching. Good luck, Harry Tate's navy!'

We needed no second bidding to get a move on. Three extra men were put in the stokehold and for the next hours the sound of shovels clinking with a new urgency as they heaped coal on the fires was ever in our ears; our safety valve was screwed down and we were going all out, the engines crashing away as if they must fall through the bottom of the ship, smoke pouring from our stack in gigantic clouds and the stench of steam reeking through the vessel, the Chief threatening to 'blow the bugger up any minute'. She was doing a fantastic $11\frac{1}{2}$ to 12 knots, more than she had ever done before in her whole existence. But the engines could not stand that violent treatment for too long.

As we pushed on into the early hours of the next day, July 6, the stubborn, buffeting ice and intermittent fog occasionally separated us from the other trawlers but our mutual plan had now been made: we were to aim for remote Matochkin Strait, anchor there under the cliffs, put out our fires and lie low till the enemy's assaults had subsided. If necessary we would leave the ships and try to make it on foot over the land and ice until we reached a settlement. Not an attractive prospect, but better than the possibility of freezing to death in an open boat.

At intervals more planes flew near, sometimes diving to take a look at us before going on—it was really rather slighting to our dignity as warships, this contemptuous indifference to our presence. Even so our main fear was that German H.Q. would become so tired of getting reports of three trawlers that a force would be sent to finish us off.

Aboard *Middleton* as she steamed temporarily alone there was a shout from one of the lookouts: 'Enemy aircraft!' The plane, he reported, was signalling the ship by lamp. The captain and a signalman were called and right enough the flashing signals continued.

'What the hell does he want?' asked the captain. The signalman studied the high flying aircraft. 'Sorry, sir,' he said, 'I can't make it out. He must be talking German.'

'In that case,' said the captain, 'he is not signalling to us but to someone over the horizon—surface craft! Bosun, turn out the lifeboats, get the codebooks ready for dumping and tell the crew to be ready to abandon ship at short notice!'

It was some time before the truth of the anxious situation dawned on them: the mysterious 'signals' were being caused by the sun striking the perspex dome of the enemy scout plane. Red faces all round.

Four bombers circled *Austin* later when we too were alone but they did not attack, obviously looking for bigger game. But after the relief of their passing our spirits dropped to zero when a W/T message from the Admiralty reported the position of three enemy destroyers between us and Novaya Zemlya. Would we, *could* we escape them and get through? We were still steaming flat out with the ship shaking so much it seemed that the boilers *must* explode. Sparks and clouds of heavy smoke belched from the funnel, covering us as effectively as any smoke screen.

At last, at the glad hour of 7.50 p.m. on July 6 we sighted land—and three hours later reached the rocky coast of Novaya

Zemlya's north island. By this time our Chief was insisting that if he did not 'blow his tubes' the boilers would burst, so the ship was stopped for this to be done. The waiting period was an eerie and nerve-racking experience for us all, the ship lying practically motionless, cloaked in a silence one could almost feel, broken only occasionally as the helmsman made a wheel adjustment, and from time to time by the sound of hammering from the bowels of the ship as the engine room staff worked at their repairs, a disturbing noise which one felt must be carrying through the water to the eager listening equipment of some underwater prowler. To cap it all it was discovered that we had halted in approximately the same position as the three enemy destroyers reported earlier!

Our skipper held a pow-wow with *Middleton* and *Gem* over the loud-hailers. Then thankfully we were under way again, taking the lead from the other two trawlers as we steamed south along the rugged, uninviting coast searching for Matochkin Strait —a name as unknown to us as the land at which we were now looking, a God-forsaken island no one in their lives had even noticed on the map before. We found an opening which seemed likely to be the place we wanted, but whereas our inadequate charts, dated 1904, showed only one landmark, a light on a wooden tower on the cliffs, here were two 'towers'. There was no sign of life—and no knowing what we may find. Just then over *Gem*'s loud-hailer came news of a W/T signal warning of an enemy force operating only ten miles away—almost in sight of us. All three of us quickly crammed on steam.

Another more up to date chart had been discovered and our skipper signalled *Lord Middleton*, as senior ship, to lead us in past the headland of rock which had to be Matochkin, but *Middleton* replied—twice—that we should lead, and to make sure of this abruptly steamed off down the coast. The reason for her odd behaviour, as we discovered later, was that she had thrown overboard all her codebooks and so would not be able to answer a challenge from another ship.

So *Lord Austin* went in with all guns manned. From behind the rock a light suddenly flickered out—'What ship?'

It was *Poppy* guarding the entrance to the Strait. We were safe.

We realized for the first time what a wonderful morning it was. At 2 a.m. on July 7 the sun was so strong that it burned our faces, but this trick of Arctic time no longer registered; in the past hectic days many of us had given up trying to keep track of the clock, the actual hours being merely figures for the log. Up forward on *Austin* a seaman was taking soundings in the twisting entrance to the Strait with a lead-line and the help, or hindrance, of half a dozen supporters. His soft Scots tones floated back to us: 'It's nay bother, nay bother at all. . . .' The whole ship's company was up on deck. Signals flickered like summer lightning between us and *Poppy*, something like this:

'What kind of a time have you had?'

'Pretty bloody. How about you?'

'Much the same. This looks better, though.'

'Yes, it's quite snug here.'

Then we were round the bend and the sparkling morning took on a new glory, for the most cheering sight met our eyes. Lying peacefully at anchor in the midst of a small natural harbour were no fewer than a dozen other ships from the convoy. *Palomares, Pozarica,* all three minesweepers—*Halcyon, Salamander, Britomart,* together with *La Malouine* and *Zamalek.* But only five merchant ships—*Ocean Freedom, Samuel Chase, Hoosier, El Capitan* and *Benjamin Harrison.* Were these all that were left?

As we passed by the ack-ack ships there was a shout from one of them: 'My word, you won't arf cop it—you're adrift to hell! What have you been doing—fishing?'

Minutes later our anchor rattled out of the hawse-pipe and by those not on watch there was a general movement below, bunkwards, as all at once the desire for sleep became overpowering.

Palomares had been first to reach Matochkin. She had made most of the early part of the journey on her own, still towing the Walrus. There was quite a scare when the lookout in her crow's nest saw a ship coming up astern—a warrant officer gunner who was sent up the mast to check reported it was definitely a warship. All thought the enemy had finally caught up with them and there was a tense interval before the ship approaching began to signal. It was *Salamander,* with her four-inch gun jammed, asking: could she stay in company? Finally there were three or four of them all heading for the Strait.

As *Palomares* steamed close to Matochkin her navigator found there was a mistake on his chart—the height of a mountain shown was too great by an extra nought. It was just another example of the inadequacy of the charts for this region of the Arctic which no one had anticipated using, and explained why they could not get a range on their radar. The ack-ack ship cautiously sailed into the Strait and, turning the corner out of sight from the open sea, anchored where she could cover the opening at short range, bringing up armour-piercing shells for ready use should the enemy close in. And then the other ships arrived.

The stoic inhabitants of a small Russian settlement on the shore of the south island showed little surprise at the invasion. The settlement was simply a collection of austere wooden buildings, the occupants roughly clad traders and hunters with their womenfolk, children and hunting dogs. A trading ship flying the Soviet flag was moored alongside a small jetty and some of the British ships as they arrived were 'inspected' by a Russian naval officer, a bizarre figure in a long black overcoat who cruised the Strait in a little motor-powered fishing boat with a machine-gun mounted in the bows. He spoke no English but was affable enough over the odd whisky and was pleased by such courtesies as *Britomart* hoisting the Russian flag. His one-man crew, a Russian sailor, was similarly made happy by the British sailors over an exchange of cigarettes.

After *Palomares* had come the first merchantmen, *El Capitan* and *Benjamin Harrison,* followed by *Salamander* with *Ocean Freedom,* then *Hoosier, Zamalek* and the *Pozarica* group, the radar operators on *Palomares* picking up *Pozarica*'s radar long before they saw her.

Like the naval craft, the merchant skippers had made for Novaya Zemlya with various emergency plans. *Hoosier,* heading north, had several times become stuck in the icefields, though thankfully running into sheltering snowstorms and fog. She had met up in the ice floes with other ships, but then lost them. Her captain had aimed to anchor in the Strait and send a radio message for rescue. *El Capitan's* master too had hoped to find an inlet in which to lie up for about a week before attempting to cross to the entrance to the White Sea. The Panamanian freighter had got through by seeking every bank of fog and altering her course frequently to avoid the danger areas as the distress signals came in from ships being attacked.

A new strength and optimism was found in our reformed numbers and a further triumph was when, shortly after the arrival of our three trawlers, *Lotus* steamed in carrying more than eighty survivors—her decks teemed with heads. There were great cheers as she came slowly into the Strait, the rescued men waving. Hours after rescuing the *Pankraft's* crew and shelling the ship the gallant little corvette had come upon wreckage, floating corpses and the half-frozen survivors of *River Afton* on their rafts—the grim ordeal of these men had lasted for five hours.

The survivors were spread among the bigger ships, where they were made welcome to occupy any space aboard; they had lost everything and a dry billet and food seemed little enough to offer them after having to abandon them out in the icy sea. Aboard *Pozarica* the survivors won instant fellowship as they volunteered for the various action-stations. Like the full-blooded American Indian from *Pankraft,* called 'Cherokee' by his mates, who opted to help as a machine-gun loader and became in some ways more efficient than his opposite number. *Salamander* also distributed some of the survivors she was carrying.

Except for the missing trawler *Ayrshire* and corvette *Dianella,* all of the escorts were now present, a total of eleven of us to shepherd the five remaining merchant vessels and the rescue ship, and so all thoughts of abandoning ship and making a long march overland were quietly let drop. So was the idea of waiting in the Strait for a few days until the enemy had withdrawn. Bottled up as we were, with no room to manoeuvre against raiding aircraft, and with the possibility of U-boats gathering off the entrance to pounce whenever we left, there seemed to be no alternative but to quit the Strait as soon as possible. On *Palomares* they had seen an enemy plane searching for us—it was glimpsed between the two hills at the mouth of the Strait for a few seconds, but fortunately did not see the ships.

Our depleted stocks of ammunition were another factor in deciding on a quick dash to the White Sea. Most of our ships were in a similar position to *Halcyon*, who at the time the convoy broke up had used up nearly half of her four-inch shells. She had reached Matochkin with very little fuel left, and was by no means alone in this.

At 11 a.m., not many hours after our own arrival, a conference of captains was held aboard *Palomares* to plan a course of action to get the small group of ships to the White Sea and Archangel. At this talk someone did still suggest scuttling the ships and living ashore, but the idea was passed over as if unheard. *Palomares* got a message through to the Senior Naval Officer North Russia, and in reply was given a course to follow to reach Archangel. The messages were passed via the radio station ashore, so as to avoid using ships' radios which might be detected by the Germans.

It was decided to sail at 6 p.m. On *Austin* there were new orders being shouted: 'Stand by to heave in! We're going to coal!' For men whose eyes had scarcely had time to close it took a superhuman effort to bring their bodies on their feet again but somehow it was done and our tired company cursed and shoved each other up the ladder. We went alongside the coal-burning *Ocean Freedom* and soon the bags were coming over the side and we were exchanging yarns with her crew and throwing them cigarettes and tobacco, for the merchant seamen had completely run out of stock.

It was either in Captain Walker's dayroom on *Freedom* or in the wardroom of *Austin* that a new, explicit name was coined for Matochkin Strait. It was 'Funk Creek.'

In our exhausted state we had only managed to haul ten tons of coal over from *Freedom* before sailing time; we might just make Archangel on our supply. The Walrus which *Palomares* had towed for hundreds of miles was hoisted to the deck of *Freedom,* which was appointed lead ship of our reformed convoy of seventeen ships. The plan was to steam south hugging the coast of Novaya Zemlya, so as to have open water and the U-boats only on our starboard side, then on south towards the Russian coast, turning back west to approach the entrance to the White Sea.

Promptly on time we weaved out of Funk Creek into a shrouding mist, *Lord Austin* bringing up the rear and so being the last vessel to leave our brief bolthole.

In the meantime, far from the sheltering crags of Matochkin, the great slaughter had gone on. Even as our various ships had been converging on the Strait the previous day, July 6, the enemy aircraft had found another easy kill. The *Pan Atlantic* from Mobile had taken a south-easterly course which led her below Matochkin on a push to the White Sea, hoping to meet up with Russian air support on the way. But as she steamed along the patrolling bombers had found their prey and flew in to the attack. *Pan Atlantic* received at least one direct hit and was quickly ablaze, sinking within minutes. Several men were lost, among them the chief engineer. As the ship was abandoned young Third Engineer Richard Tallon, finding one of his shipmates without a lifejacket, immediately took off his own and handed it to the man, with the light quip that back home he had swum the Mobile River, so why not the Barents Sea? The gallant lad was never seen again.

In the early hours of the following day, at the precise moment that we trawlers were entering Matochkin, the killing began all over again, the aircrafts' grim work now being taken over by the U-boats which had raced for Novaya Zemlya to head off other merchantmen fleeing there.

At 2 a.m. on July 7 the British S.S. *Hartlebury* was steaming alone towards Novaya Zemlya's south island. She was as yet unscathed and alert with many lookouts, but the end came very suddenly when two torpedoes rocked the ship. Gunner Arthur Carter was off-watch and asleep when the torpedoes struck. The first thing he saw on opening his eyes was a spread of flames coming through a bulkhead. He was dressed only in Army trousers, shirt and pullover, with socks and seaboot stockings on his feet, and as he leaped up to dash on deck the first thing on his mind was his lifebelt—he *had* to have it. He found it, grabbed it up and ran, but three times he had to rush back when it caught between the hand-rail on the bulkhead and was torn from his grasp. When he finally reached the deck *Hartlebury* was listing and at an angle of 45 degrees. As everyone automatically took up their allotted stations for abandoning ship Carter saw that his closest ship-mate, a gunner who had been on watch, was very dazed though he did not appear to have been hit.

The debris-strewn deck was covered with what appeared to be flour and water mixed, so slippery that men could not keep their feet. Some seamen launching a lifeboat were halfway through the job when the bow went straight down and the boat just hung there. In a confusion of shouting another boat was quickly lowered and landed perfectly on the water—but there was no plug in the bottom and by the time a man had scrambled down the rope the boat was flooded.

The ship was still moving. Carter saw the liferaft on the for-ward rigging being cut free and as it came sliding down the side of the ship he somehow scrambled on to it—just how he could never remember. As they paddled away from the ship a third torpedo struck her in the engine room, and with a tremendous explosion the two ends of *Hartlebury* stood straight up in the sea then quickly disappeared.

There were thirteen men on Carter's raft, one of them the first mate. Carter was relieved to see that the dazed gunner had managed to get to another raft, but he heard afterwards that his friend and a seaman both died on the raft and were buried at sea.

The U-boat surfaced a short time after *Hartlebury* sank. There was quite a crowd on the conning tower and two men pointed machine-guns at the rafts. It was a bad scare for the Britishers, who remembered recent newspaper headlines that all ships' survivors were being shot, especially the gunners. It was from this moment, Carter was convinced, that his auburn hair began to turn white.

The U-boat, a wolf's head on its conning tower, closed in on his raft of thirteen men, and three officers in turn addressed them in English.

'What ship are you? Where were you bound? What do you want to go to Russia for—you are not Bolsheviks, are you?'

One officer told them in which direction land lay. He asked if they had a compass (they had) and apologized for not taking any prisoners as he was already full. The survivors were then thrown two bottles of Schnapps and seven loaves, motion pictures were taken of them and the U-boat moved off.

It was the first mate who saved the thirteen men, many of them thinly clad. In the raft's locker were two sheets of canvas. One of these he folded in two lengthways and put round them all, the other he stretched completely over them, so that they were in a canvas igloo. He then kept everyone awake, talking, singing and moving their limbs as best they could as the raft drifted on.

At this time, well to the south, the *Alcoa Ranger* from Philadelphia was making a good 13 knots on an easterly course which would have brought her below the southern tip of Novaya Zemlya. Although attacked earlier by planes she had escaped damage, and now, as she steamed along in clear weather there seemed nothing to threaten her passage on a quiet, calm sea. Then two enemy scout planes suddenly appeared. When one closed in and circled the ship but without attacking, *Alcoa Ranger*'s master, convinced that they were cornered at last, surprisingly gave the order to display international flags meaning 'Unconditional surrender', and called for the Stars and Stripes to be struck and the ship abandoned. But the second mate promptly took command and asked for volunteers to sail the ship on, at which the master changed his mind, ordered the flag to be hoisted again and the guns manned, and took charge once more.

Then without warning a shadowing U-boat struck. At 8.30 a.m. a torpedo exploded on the vessel's starboard side, opening a large hole which caused her to list heavily. The ship was immediately reversed to kill speed and her engines secured; distress signals were sent and the ship's papers dropped overboard in an iron box. All hands then abandoned ship. To the intense anger of the crew the master gave no leadership at all in handling the lifeboats, but in spite of this all managed to get away safely. The U-boat, an unusually big one, surfaced and began to shell the freighter. The survivors counted more than sixty shells explode on contact with the ship—it seemed that the U-boat's gunners had been given their heads for a leisurely round of target practice. *Alcoa Ranger* went down by the bows three hours later at 11.30 a.m.—just as our captains at Matochkin were holding their conference.

The U-boat came alongside the master's lifeboat and its commander asked in broken English the name of the ship, her destination and cargo. Many pictures were taken of the survivors. They were told the direction of land and asked whether they had sufficient provisions, after which the U-boat quickly moved off south.

There followed a quiet few hours now, but the U-boats operating off the island coast were by no means through. Already, steaming on a fatal course which would bring her into the region of *Alcoa Ranger*'s death throes was the Liberty ship with the proud name of *John Witherspoon*. She had scattered north and east to seek some refuge along the shore of Novaya Zemlya; north and east, that is, largely by guesswork, for there were times at the wheel when A/B Ferocious O'Flaherty saw the magnetic compass fluctuate by as much as 70 and 80 degrees. They had only to glance astern to see that the ship's wake was meandering all over the ocean.

O'Flaherty asked the first mate: 'Do you think it will do any good if I keep looking aft to try and compensate for this?'

'Ah, what's the use,' was the mate's dry reply—'we'll never reach Russia anyway.'

After a time he noticed that O'Flaherty was holding a course on something straight ahead. He asked O'Flaherty what it was.

'A cloud,' said O'Flaherty.

'Whoever heard of steering by a cloud?'

'Well,' said O'Flaherty, 'take a look aft. The ship's wake is a lot straighter than it has been.'

It was enough for the mate, who decided he had important papers to attend to. With time to plot the arc of the sun they could have made a fair course, but all felt sure that time was short and none of the officers had the heart for it. German scout planes were on the horizon for a very long time and never had they realized how much a gliding seagull could look like an approaching enemy aircraft. All hands reacted the same way to the harmless seagulls—they cursed the birds roundly. But *John Witherspoon* finally escaped from the hunting planes and in fact it was when the aircraft disappeared and she was sailing alone beneath an empty sky that everyone sensed danger to be the more imminent. All felt that a U-boat attack must come, and with nerves ragged from the constant harassment of the past three days many even looked forward to the tranquillity of bobbing around in a lifeboat.

When the attack did come on the afternoon of July 7 there was no prior hint of it. At 4.15 p.m. a torpedo struck number three hold on the starboard side and sent the Liberty ship far over on her port, scattering equipment and men. She flopped back to starboard with a heavy list and lying with her starboard main deck awash, started to turn in short circles like a wounded bird. The torpedo might have blown her completely in two had it not been for the cargo of truck tyres in number three hatch which absorbed a great deal of the shock, many tyres floating out of the hole made by the explosion.

All hands had been so on edge that they were in action before the officer of the watch got his hand to the alarm bell. The after gun crew fired only one shot at an object over which they heatedly disagreed was a U-boat; it was all they had time for before the steep list of the ship made their gun and the forward gun useless. The two lifeboats on the starboard boat deck were hanging from their davits, one in pieces and the other doubtful, and as all were certain that the U-boat would send another torpedo into the ship from the port side where the two remaining boats hung they acted quickly, all the company converging on the two lifeboats except the captain, who remained on a wing of the bridge. A raft was also launched from its cradle in the shrouds.

O'Flaherty and another seaman, who were below when the torpedo struck, were both without jackets when they hit the cold air on the boat deck. It would take a few minutes to swing out the boats and that was all O'Flaherty needed to run back to his room on the deck below. The law of salvage was in order and one could grab the nearest jacket, but someone had already observed that law in passing and the most valuable object in O'Flaherty's room was gone. He went back up to the boat deck so fast that reasoning had not caught up with him; that was, to gain a garment in the same way that he had lost his own. Back down again, in and out of rooms—nothing. By now he was flying. He had to go up on the boat deck again to check how many seconds he had left.

The jarring experience of breaking a routine to abandon ship frequently made men act without reason but still the crew looked askance at him, for he had been running up and down the ladder with no obvious purpose. For a third time he turned and bounded down the ladder, to the port side this time, and grabbed a jacket lying on a bunk. No seaman ever went up a ladder so fast after that, only his toes touching metal as he flashed back to the boat deck and tumbled into the last boat as the men on the falls prepared to lower.

The captain had come down from the bridge but remained on deck, motioning to them to shove off. Just then an engineer and oiler wandered out of the midship house apparently stunned. In the confusion the lifeboat was released from the ship's side and the two men on the falls had to drop into the water. The oiler, suddenly coming to life, ran to a raft and released it; then he and the engineer grabbed the captain and forced him over the side on to it.

One of the two men on the boat-falls who had dropped into the water was knocked unconscious by the shock of plunging into the cold sea and the men in the lifeboat grabbed their oars and went after him, while the other boat, drifting down wind, intercepted his partner; but the first man was lost. The lifeboat, buffeted by the waves, was unable to save him. He showed no sign of life as the seas pushed him farther away until they lost sight of him in the streaming grey waves.

The ship was still turning in short circles. When, as anticipated, a second torpedo was fired at her the men in the nearest lifeboat could feel the hiss of it through the bottom of the boat as it bore for the ship and hit with a thud into number three hatch again, but on the port side this time. *John Witherspoon* did not even have the dignity to go down in one piece but ripped herself completely open around the hull like a tin can until the bow and stern almost met, then plunged like a stone.

The U-boat surfaced, a wolf's head on its conning tower, and a gun was trained on the survivors while a camera took pictures. Then the commander asked in good English: 'Is anybody hurt?' 'No,' said their radio operator. 'Do you need any food or water?' 'No.' 'How many tons of cargo did you have aboard?' 'I don't know.'

The German commander, undeterred, produced a sheet of paper and told them exactly how many tons their ship had carried. 'Where is your captain? he asked.

'We don't know.'

In fact the captain had shifted from the raft and was lying in the bottom of the second boat, so as to avoid capture. None of the other ship's officers wore uniformed clothing. The U-boat commander studied the survivors while his craft drifted some fifty feet away from them. Then with a point of his hand he told them 'Land is over that way,' gave a wave and started down the hatch. They waved back and watched the U-boat slowly submerge.

At this time, with the excitement of the sinking over and their ship gone, the men in the boats began to realize the cold and the loneliness of the sea around them. As they pulled away, the one a sailboat, the other a motor boat, the final drama of that day was drawing to a close some miles to the north, almost in the path of our reformed convoy now steaming out from Matochkin Strait.

The *Olopana,* after being rejected as a rescue ship by survivors of *Washington, Bolton Castle* and *Paulus Potter* had continued on for hundreds of miles until she was almost within striking distance of the coast of Novaya Zemlya's south island. Her journey had not been uneventful. At an early stage, when the crew panicked and made to abandon ship, Captain Stone calmly discussed the situation with the British gunners. Their firm answer was that it was their duty to stand fast at the guns until the ship was put out of action. This quietened the panic and generally restored morale. The gunners arranged with the captain that if the ship was attacked from the air they would stay aboard while her two lifeboats pulled away and light a smoke float on deck to pretend that the ship had been hit. It seemed much their best course after finding that their machine-gun bullets and tracers simply bounced off attacking planes. The smoke float ruse worked well the first time it was tried, and on the afternoon of July 7, after fighting off an attack by a Heinkel bomber, they let off another float on the forecastle head. The plane must have thought they were hit for it never returned, but *Olopana's* radio officer heard the pilot transmitting to a U-boat. After that the end was not long in coming. At 10.55 p.m. a torpedo struck the ship on the starboard side, killing all the kanakas in the boiler room. Some seamen and a gunner were also lost.

Gunner Edward Hennessey was asleep in the radio room when the torpedo hit; he had come off watch and the radio room was the nearest position to his gun station. He rushed on deck to find utter chaos. The explosion had flung the starboard lifeboat on to the deck, smashing it to bits. He looked over the rail where the torpedo had entered but could see nothing but clouds of steam. He then looked down to the engine room but could not see in there either for the billowing steam. In a panic someone let go the forward falls of the port lifeboat and it was swept away. A raft too was lost, but all the survivors managed to get away on the remaining three rafts.

The U-boat surfaced—a wolf's head emblem again—and shelled the reeling ship for fifteen minutes. When it had finished *Olopana* was well on fire and sinking by the stern, clouds of yellow smoke rising from the smashed and holed drums of chemicals stacked on her foredeck.

The U-boat came alongside the rafts and again the questions were asked: 'Are you Bolsheviks? No? Then why are you helping Russia?' The commander asked if they had enough food, pointed out the direction of land and told them boastfully: 'The ships of your convoy are all at the bottom of the sea!'

It was a sickening parting shot for the survivors to stomach, that lonely midnight on the Barents Sea. In fact *Olopana* was the twenty-second ship to die; but she was still not the last.

6

Bloody Marvellous

Our reformed convoy as it steamed into the mist outside Funk Creek was quickly spotted by a lurking U-boat. *Austin* being the last ship out of the narrow Strait we had a good sight of the enemy craft surfaced not many miles off. When one of the corvettes opened fire it submerged quite leisurely. There were reports of more U-boats in the vicinity and these now were our main danger, for word had reached us that the enemy's big ships had returned to anchor in Norway.

The mist turned to fog, our oldest enemy becoming once again our firmest friend; if this kept up all the way we might manage the rest of our journey unmolested. Before midnight the fog cleared for a while then came down thicker than ever, making near collisions frequent—we just missed hitting *Zamalek* by a coat of paint. *Benjamin Harrison* lost touch completely and her skipper, after trying for twelve hours to find the convoy, turned back for the Strait, not caring to fumble through alone.

By next morning, July 8, the fog had improved and was exactly as we wanted it; just enough visibility to keep contact with each other, but enough of a blanket to make us invisible from the air. We sent up a prayer to the God of Fogs to keep it just like that. Now that the immediate danger had passed each man found himself again suffering from an intense craving for sleep. The odd three hours here and there merely seemed to aggravate the complaint; about three days would have been nearer the mark. On the wheel, staring into the bright, hypnotic square of light in which the block markings of the compass card turned and swam before the eyes, it required all one's will-power not to drop off.

In the afternoon the fog became thick and heavy, and there was a new chill in the air. Sirens hooted and we slowed just in time to avoid ramming the ship ahead, from which came the cry: 'Look out! Bad ice coming!' In a few minutes we were in the midst of pack-ice which grew thicker as we advanced. Soon every vessel was juggling and dodging to turn round and get out before it was too late and they were gripped fast—a chorus of sirens blared out. We on *Austin* had a bad scare when a huge merchantman loomed out of the fog right across our bows. There was no room to manoeuvre so we quickly stopped engines. Then a warning shout from the lookout: we were drift-ing stern first on to the grandfather of all ice-blocks. *Austin* was rising and falling in the swell and if she touched that mammoth chunk it would slice off her propeller and rudder. We were saved by the alertness of Signalman Gordon Hooper who seized his lamp and flashed urgent SOS's to the other ship, which, quickly understanding the danger, sheered off and allowed us to restart our engines in the very nick of time.

Lord Middleton had a similarly alarming experience. Com-pletely surrounded by ice she kept going at about six knots, for to stop would have been crazy, when suddenly the alarm bells went and everyone rushed on deck as a 10,000-ton merchant-man loomed up in the greyness. Neither ship could stop or go astern as the ice would have smashed their propellers, nor could they turn to port or starboard because of the ice packed all around. The trawler's two smallboats were quickly over the side and the crew all ready to leave ship when the merchant skipper acted. He increased speed, hoping that with her greater speed the freighter would pass the collision point before the trawler reached it. What a fine decision it was, for as the merchantman passed dead ahead of *Middleton* there was scarcely a couple of yards between them. Had she hit the little trawler she would have turned her over and gone on without a scratch.

The struggling ships tried to maintain contact by fog-horns and over the R/T. It was here, probably, that we gave away our whereabouts to the listening enemy. As *Lord Austin* retraced passage we kept running into new icefields. We took turns as lookout right up in the bows and assisted by our sleepless state, in the murky greyness the ice took on some queer shapes and likenesses. Sometimes a lookout would swear to having seen a U-boat ahead, while once an 'E-boat' was reported heading straight for us. It had become bitterly cold but it was vital to keep contact with the main body of ships; to become detached here would be grim indeed. A signal was intercepted warning of an enemy warship in the neighbourhood. Added to it all was our coal worries, for all this going back and dodging around was eating into our scanty stock. Would we *ever* reach Russia?

All the other fifteen ships were busy fighting their own battles with the ice. Among the merchant vessels *El Capitan* and *Samuel Chase* won clear, but *Hoosier* was completely lost. When eventually she sighted land Captain Holmgrun went in close to shore and signalled, but there was no reply. Then men were seen walking about the lonely shore—a part of Novaya Zemlya. The captain landed and conducted a conversation in sign language, after which he was able to return to his ship and set a course to catch up with the others.

It was our friends on *Ocean Freedom* who suffered most in the chaotic conditions. She had earlier been in company with *Northern Gem*, the trawler keeping station on her port bow; though as one of *Gem's* crew laconically observed: 'There's no bloody freedom in *this* ocean. . . .' When they first came out of the fog the two vessels were still together but with no other ships in sight; it was a lonely and weird position with the ever-present feeling that they were being watched. When the two skippers saw a new bank of fog on the port bow they both ran for it as fast as they could go. Then the ice. As *Freedom* steamed at much reduced speed, skirting the ice as best as she could in the fog, it was more trying to the nerves of the crew than any of the previous action had been. In no time she seemed to be entirely hemmed in. Floundering around like a man in a maze seeking a way out, she came across *Gem* again, now stuck fast in the ice. With her greater size and weight the merchant ship broke the trawler out, clearing herself at the same time. Being then more or less in clear water Captain Walker decided to crack on speed, taking the lead from *Gem* in case they should encounter more ice. They very soon did. Still in heavy fog *Freedom* ran full tilt into thick pack-ice. Fortunately the trawler was not astern or she would have run into her back; instead *Gem* ran up alongside, rising on top of the ice almost to her foremast. She went astern and stopped while Coxswain Kerslake went anxiously to inspect the forepeak. It was snuff dry, with not a sign of water or damage. The old girl had brought them through again; they certainly had built her well in Bremerhaven.

But on *Freedom* it was a different picture. After taking the full impact of the ice her stem was gone from the waterline down, the frames and plates along each side were buckled and twisted, and the forepeak flooded immediately. The chief officer and carpenter anxiously inspected the damage and number one hailed the bridge: 'The forepeak is open to the sea! Abaft the collision bulkhead she's tight—try going ahead....' Captain Walker eased the ship forward, gradually building up speed. Then another hail: 'She's still holding—give her the works!'

And so as the fog began to clear the two ships piled on steam in an effort to catch up with us, *Freedom*'s speed being retarded by her mangled bow but still enough for her to keep one step ahead of *Gem*.

In fog up ahead *Palomares* had her hectic moments. She was steaming along with *Pozarica* immediately astern when she hit a barrier of ice head-on, giving the men in the forward mess-decks a nasty shock—the noise was so thunderous below decks that there was a general scramble aft before it became clear that the enemy had not in fact scored a direct hit. But *Palomares* was well and truly stuck in the ice and it was only after a great amount of strain on the engines that she eventually freed herself from a very precarious position. There were many bitter comments about the Russians having given them a route that led straight into the ice. *Pozarica* took quick evasive action, only narrowly escaping ramming her sister ship, and as she continued slowly on O/D Gooch was on the upper deck off-duty, looking over the side and peering into the fog when suddenly the bows of *El Capitan* loomed up so close he could have touched her with his hand; but here again *Pozarica* was lucky and did not collide. Then in a sudden break in the fog, almost under the ack-ack ship's bows was a lifeboat with a red sail up and men shouting and calling as they were spotted by the careering ships. The lifeboat held nineteen men of the *John Witherspoon*, many of them frostbitten and all in a very weak state as they were picked up by *El Capitan*.

All ships now were retreating westwards from the pack-ice which was obviously sweeping round the southern tip of Novaya Zemlya. We would have to steam back westwards for many miles before being able to turn south again for a last push down to the entrance to the White Sea. And so our confused and disintegrated convoy stumbled along, skirting the ice on the port side and praying for an end of it.

The early hours of July 9 brought us a clear sea with the fog considerably lessened and just thick enough to give us adequate cover. On *Austin* we passed over a huge patch of oil, the sombre marker of a recently sunk merchantman. Then the fog lifted completely and, like all the scattered ships, we were looking out for our companions. Surprisingly a strong nucleus of the convoy had kept within fair distance of one another and we very shortly found ourselves in company with both ack-ack ships and all three corvettes, together with *Lord Middleton* and *Britomart*, and *Hoosier*, *El Capitan* and *Zamalek*.

Soon out to port could be seen a few black specks, and *La Malouine* raced over to what proved to be two lifeboats of survivors from *Pan Atlantic*, others of whom had been picked up earlier by *Pozarica*. Throughout the day, during which we finally left the ice and swung south, the corvettes were kept busy dropping depth charges against shadowing U-boats. We began to pass occasional logs floating in the sea, a comforting indication that we were now approaching Russia, if still with

Route of "Lord Austin," after "Scatter"

quite a distance to go. Any moment we hoped to see a squadron
of Red Air Force planes come into view; but when during the
afternoon two planes were sighted, they were not Soviets. Like
giant dragon-flies they hovered just above the horizon; we had
seen planes like them somewhere before. One a Blohm and Voss,
the other a Heinkel 115, they flew round the convoy in opposite
directions, meeting each other as they passed on ominous patrol
busily reporting back to base and to the U-boats. Almost at the
same time a U-boat surfaced some miles off, scrutinized the convoy and then quickly dived. The game was about to begin all
over again.

It did so in the late evening, when the lead ships of our sorry
remnants of PQ 17 were approaching to within about eighty
miles of the Russian coast. Aboard *Palomares* the radar gave
the first warning of approaching aircraft when they were some
seventy miles away. Long blasts on the ack-ack ship's sirens
were followed by a hoist of flags, and as the other vessels were
alerted the radio operators on each and every naval ship broke
silence and made frantic efforts to contact the signal stations at
Archangel and Murmansk with an appeal for fighter protection.
On *Palomares* they called up in code, R/T and plain language,
in English and Russian, on several wavelengths, but to all the
urgent messages there was no answer. Whether there was something wrong with the wavelengths or they were being jammed
by the Germans it was impossible to guess. But the plain fact was
that our operators could not get through and we badly needed
air support quickly.

On *Lord Austin,* haggard-eyed, we searched the horizon. We
had not long to wait. Soon five tiny specks were seen flying very
high. Round went our guns, but the planes were much too high
for them. Boomp! Boomp! Boomp! went the high-angle four-
inches of the ack-acks—how we wished we had such a gun. Puffs
of black smoke appeared in the path of the raiders, but those
five planes did not swerve from their course. Straight on they
flew, and then when they were quite near, broke formation to
come in from different points.

We saw one plane put its nose down for a dive and three

spouts of water rose into the air off our port bow. There was no sound, only a massive shudder through the ship's hull. Now another five specks were coming in from a different quarter; then more, and still more, always in fives. They picked their targets and dived, though never very low. From each plane three bombs floated down, like large silver Indian clubs, slowly at first, then faster and faster as they came nearer. Almost halfway down it was possible to decide which ship was their target. We would wait, holding our breath, until three great waterspouts mushroomed up, completely hiding the marked ship. Then the curtain of water would drop and there would be the vessel still sailing steadily on course, her decks lined with men soaked to the skin by the mighty splash.

Pozarica heeled over from the force of three bombs, turned a complete circle to port and stopped dead. She signalled : 'Three very near misses but we think we are O.K.' *Palomares* steamed over at a furious pace to check on her sister ship. She came up to cross our bows fast, a voice on her bridge crackling harshly through the loud-hailer : 'Ahoy, *Lord Austin*—take care! We are coming through you all !' There was a heart-stopping moment as she loomed high above us—we slowed and turned hard to starboard as the ack-ack surged past with no more than twenty feet between us. She swept by still firing and a plane that dropped a stick of bombs at her missed. Instead the whistling explosives came for us, the slower ship. Two bombs hit the sea on either side of us ahead, the third came wobbling down straight for our deck. Our junior "sparks", Telegraphist Johnny Rose, well captured the tension of the fleeting seconds before it descended. He wrote in his diary :

'We saw the bomb get bigger and bigger, and I remember thinking that if I continued to look up into the air, my mouth would be dragged open and the bomb would fall right into it— it was surprising how smartly I snapped my jaws together. . . .

'George was standing by my side, looking up—his boiling hot mug of cocoa tilting over, its contents dribbling and splashing down his chest and stomach and legs, soaking into his clothes unnoticed (he showed me the scalds afterwards but said he hadn't felt them). Jock had a lump of corned dog in his great fist, which he was squeezing until it oozed between his fingers. The oaths he was muttering were sweet to hear. Jim Morris, the only one who seemed unperturbed, had seen the bomb but had turned away to make a lightning sketch of others falling alongside the *Lotus*. The coxswain behind me was straining his ears to hear the orders from the bridge—already he had the wheel hard to port, and the old tub was answering painfully slowly. Johnny was there on the Lewis, one eye on his Junkers target, the other on the whistling missile; sweat ran down his face but he was still firing, as were the two men on the twin point-five platform, sending streams of bullets towards the planes. The skipper was yelling again and again : "Keep her hard to port!" and watching the bows shudder slowly round. The four-inch gun crew on their platform could do nothing—they simply stood there waiting for the inevitable, not knowing whether to crouch or stay as they were. Ron, on the bridge, clutched at the loose halyard ends, saying the word "Jesus" over and over again to himself. My knees felt like jelly, my stomach had shrunk into a tight ball of painful gristle. My head thudded and ached and I couldn't look upwards any longer. . . .'

The scream of the bomb became almost ear-splitting. Then, after what seemed an eternity, it was down and smacking into the sea just off our bow, sending up a giant waterspout which doused the ship and all of us in its icy wave. Surprisingly it had not exploded; had it done so our bows would have been smashed in. But if our skipper had not turned to port split seconds earlier the bomb, whether it exploded or not, could have hit the magazine and taken us all to the bottom.

Pozarica was soon under way again and *Palomares,* firing fiercely as ever, returned through the ships to take up her former position.

Shrapnel fell like snowflakes in the heavy barrage as every vessel began a new fight for life. The attack had begun at 9 p.m. After only fifteen minutes *Hoosier* was abruptly out of the battle. A V-shaped formation of bombers went for her, flying so high that her small guns were useless, then peeling off to dive and loose their bombs. Finally a stick of three fell just short of the ship's number three lifeboat, passing under the freighter and exploding, lifting her completely out of the water. Her steam turbine main engine jarred back on its foundation, jammed and would not run; all steam gauges and small steam lines were broken, and the fuel oil pump was knocked off its base. The chief engineer told Captain Holmgrun that the ship was unable to run and reluctantly the master gave orders to abandon. Bombs were still dropping as the crew went over the side into the lifeboats. There was no panic, though three men who finally cracked-up under the strain had to be helped over by the others.

As *Hoosier* swung out of line and drifted astern with steam pouring from her we saw *Poppy* race to her aid and help aboard the survivors as they rowed over in their boats crammed with luggage and provisions. When the steam cloud had cleared *Poppy*'s commander tried to persuade *Hoosier*'s master to return to his ship and see if the engine would run, but Captain Holmgrun said this was impossible. So to avoid leaving such a costly prize to drift, possibly to the enemy held coast of Finland, Sub-Lieutenant Brooke was ordered to sink her with *Poppy*'s four-inch. He was told where *Hoosier*'s tons of ammunition were stored, but though they put more than thirty shells into the freighter, peppering the hull and setting a fire burning inside her, they got no spectacular results, and left *Hoosier* settling slowly in the water.

More high level bombers now came over near *Poppy*, one of which Brooke thought was low enough to have a crack at. 'I suppose the bombardment of *Hoosier* had perhaps gone to my head a bit, for I omitted to ask the captain's permission to open fire. I didn't get the gun trainer or layer to use sights but merely got them to raise the old four-inch with such unnautical expressions as "Up a bit ... Right a bit ... Fire!" By this time the mouth of the barrel was near the wing of the bridge and the captain and company were as shattered as some of the canvas screens by the blast. It was nothing to the blast which poured down on me afterwards from the captain wanting to know what the bloody hell I was up to. With some satisfaction I saw the shell explode in front of the bomber which sharply altered course away; I pointed this out to the captain who was not impressed and merely called it a waste of valuable ammunition on aircraft which had obviously dropped their bombs. ... Suitably abashed I watched the next wave of bombers course slowly over with *Poppy* holding a steady course at full speed. Fascinated I saw a single stick of three bombs fall from one aircraft and produce towering geysers of water on our port bow near enough to wet the foredeck. I didn't dare look the captain in the face.'

When *Poppy* finally caught up with us the convoy was still under continuous attack and *Hoosier*'s gunnery officer and his men asked what they could do to help the corvette's crew. They were gratefully allocated to ammunition hoists and gun-loading. Many of the seamen however, though they had not wetted their feet crossing to *Poppy*, acted the part of survivors to the full for the rest of the voyage, putting quite a strain on Anglo-American relations. Admittedly they had brought with them some welcome supplies of tinned food, but members of *Poppy*'s company even had to stop some of them, before they finally left the ship, throwing what was left overboard rather than leave it behind for the naval men. The seeds of misunderstanding were already germinating.

Hoosier died at five minutes past 1 a.m. on July 10, three hours after she had been abandoned. There were two terrific explosions and *Poppy*'s commander came down from the bridge to tell Captain Holmgrun: 'Your ship has exploded twice and is now sinking.'

'God bless her,' replied the master. 'May she rest in peace.' All his crew admired the old man for the way in which he had stood up under the strain while younger men were breaking.

During all this time the bombing had continued, hour after hour, with short intervals as some planes withdrew and others arrived to take their place. Men on the guns just had time between attacks to replace new belts and pans of ammunition, light up a cigarette, take a few puffs, and then—tin hats on, cigarettes out, and back to their guns to meet the next oncoming group of bombers. The planes delivered their attacks in long, dodging 85 deg. dives, the majority of them Junkers 88s, though there were also some Heinkel 115s. During one lull a U-boat contact was reported and away went *Lotus* to drop venomous 'ash-cans' over the spot. Then fresh quintettes of planes were approaching and whether by accident or design they made the corvette their target. We saw stick after stick of bombs fall around her as she writhed and dodged; it seemed she must be hit, so close did they fall. But no. As the last trio of waterspouts subsided, there she was still in one piece and still under way. A stout little ship, that corvette.

A boatload of exhausted survivors from *John Witherspoon* picked up by *La Malouine* saw how that corvette similarly dodged the bombers. A/B O'Flaherty: 'An officer lay on his back just forward of the wheelhouse and dead centre of the ship, focusing his binoculars on the underside of each plane as it dipped down to release its bombs. If a bomb disappeared from his view he said nothing; if it remained in view it meant that it was heading for us, and he would order the helmsman to turn either way without taking his eyes away from his line of vision. This method avoided the error of zigging when you should be zagging. It was very tiresome on the eyes, calling for frequent change of watchers. It was also a strain on the animal instinct to evade, until you drew an imaginary line from the centre of the ship to the belly of the plane and realized that the blighters were right. All the same, it was a weird experience to be sailing along on a straight course while bombs dropped around us, being averted by a combination of drift, speed and the coolness of the men on the corvette.'

From *Austin* we saw *Lord Middleton*'s narrow escape. She was lying astern of us when three bombers came in close, one right over her, and nine bombs fell each side and astern, the nearest only feet away. All we could see was one huge spout of water, yet *Middleton* rode through magnificently.

One of the greatest surprises was how *Zamalek* managed to keep going, for she could scarcely be seen for the great eruptions of water around her. She was specially singled out for attack and only by a miracle and the expert handling of Captain Morris was she saved from going down with heavy loss of life. She was crowded with more than 200 survivors and all the officers and crew were sharing their cabins and mess-space—the chief engineer alone had eight 'guests' in his cabin—and food was running very short. Kept very secret from the survivors was the fact that she carried sixty tons of depth charges for use by Russian-based aircraft—plus several hundred gallons of petrol for the launch carried on deck. As the bombs rained down the fuel pipes in her engine room were fractured and a generator put out of action; Chief Engineer A. S. Dawson was alone at his post in the engine room, the others being at stations on deck, when suddenly all the lights in the ship went out. Calmly he told the bridge of his plight and several engineer-survivors, including *Zaafaran's* Chief Engineer Miller, went below to help him right the main switch and fuse.

From *Austin* we saw a plane turn away smoking and try to make altitude. It failed, and as its pilot and gunner parachuted down to the sea near *Zamalek* she was alerted. 'Well,' she started to reply, 'if the Bosche behave...' Then she was straddled again by near misses. When she emerged from the splashes she was still flashing: '... I was about to say before being so rudely interrupted that if the Bosche behave I will go back for them, but now following this little packet from the Fatherland, if they haven't frozen to death in this water they can either start swimming or bloody well tread water....'

As the bombing continued some planes dropped parachute mines ahead of the convoy and a sweeper went ahead to clear a passage through them. The escorts' radio operators made more efforts to contact the Russian signal stations, but again without result.

During one of the earlier brief spells between the waves of attackers someone on *Palomares* saw blood running down the mast on to the deck and remembered that the lookout was still up in the crow's nest, not having had time to get down before the first bombers were upon them. As all eyes gazed upwards the man was seen hanging perilously over the edge of the nest and there was an ominous hole visible at the bottom of it. He had been hit by a low-angled shot from one of the other escorts. A rope was specially rigged and when brought down he was found to have lost a lot of blood and a large part of his backside. This was sewn up by the ship's doctor and remarkably after being in hospital in Archangel, the sailor was left with only a pronounced limp.

Pozarica's guns were loaded and fired over and over again until everyone became insensitive to the noise. The decks cluttered up with empty shell cases, the gun barrels grew hot and the paint peeled off in large flakes; in between attacks the guns were trained into the wind to let the icy air flow through and cool them down. At one of the twin Lewis guns, where the rejected cartridge cases had become waist high, A/B Mayne and 'Cherokee' had just reloaded for A/B Taffy Cooke when Mayne caught sight of a Heinkel 115 flying in just above the waves with the obvious intent of loosing its two torpedoes at the ack-ack ship. Mayne signalled to Cooke, who opened fire. The gunner gave the aircraft the two magazines full, 90 rounds in all, and the three men saw the Heinkel drop to the sea and sink fast from the weight of its torpedoes. Cooke undoubtedly saved the ship, the other guns being too busy with the aircraft overhead. His action was accomplished under desperate conditions of blast from the four-inch gun muzzles just above their heads. When Leading Seaman Berry reported Cooke's feat to the bridge he got the typical naval reply: 'Very good.'

On *Austin* because of the planes flying so high we could not fire our four-inch very often, and our gunner grumbled and swore as the gun was trained first from one side and then the other. When a Junkers 88 swooped low enough for us to get in a burst with the point-five we saw that its wings were tipped with yellow—the mark of one of Goering's special squadrons. Crack pilots they may have been, but fortunately they lacked the daredevil courage of the torpedo-bombers of Independence Day. They pulled out of their dives at about 500 feet to release their load. Having dropped its load a plane would contine to make feint attacks to draw the convoy's fire from the real attackers.

As the bombs came down the fish went up, dropping back on to the sea dead and stunned by the explosions until the water was covered with them; good fresh fish—even in mid-action our hungry stomachs protested at the sight of all that food going begging.

Now *El Capitan* with her deckload of aircraft was running the gauntlet. At the same time another plane dived for us and again it seemed we were done for, but either the pilot decided against wasting his cargo on such small fry or the bombs jammed in their racks, for he peeled off and we turned our attention once more to *El Capitan*. Up went the waterspouts, but always she reappeared. Suddenly the planes were making off, but to our dismay we saw the merchantman was losing way and we were signalled at once by *Palomares*.

'Out scramble nets!' ordered our skipper. 'Stand by to pick up survivors!'

Early in the bombing three bombs had fallen astern of *El Capitan*. Her after peak, also the gun crew's quarters, had begun taking water, but the situation was not critical and she had survived many more attacks only to be crippled now in the last gasp of more than seven hours' continuous bombing, for it was 5.30 a.m. on July 10 when three bombs landed within twenty feet of the ship on the starboard side, blowing in the sea valves and bursting fuel and water pipes to the main engines. The starboard side of the engine room was completed wrecked and two holds began taking water.

The boats were lowered from the helpless merchantman and men tumbled into them to start rowing towards us. Our skipper bellowed over the loud-hailer: 'Bring some guns if you can!' at which they paused to dismantle the lighter machine-guns.

We helped them aboard without ceremony, grabbing outstretched hands to drag them quickly over the side on to the deck, and let all but one of their boats drift away. Our decks were now very crowded. Then the order: 'Stand by the four-inch crew!'

El Capitan's old captain, a Norwegian, warned us not to hit her in number two hold as it was full of T.N.T. and we would all go to Kingdom Come. He stood on our bridge with tears in his eyes as the shells crashed into his ship; at only a cable distant it was impossible to miss. Our own feelings were pretty mixed when he told us his fridges were still stuffed with turkeys and other delights for Independence Day, for by this time our rations were very meagre. Six hits below the waterline and three holds flooding, it would not be long before the huge vessel passed below the surface. We had no means of knowing it then but she was the twenty-fourth ship to die. Her machine-guns were fixed to the sides of our bridge and the revolvers with which her gunners were armed were taken in charge by our skipper, who did not like the idea of having any armed men in his ship.

During the rescue operation and shelling the bombers had left us alone, but now they returned for another fling at the settling *El Capitan* and at us, *Austin* shaking alarmingly from more near misses. With our condenser badly damaged and plates buckled it would not have taken very much more to put us under, but they eventually drew off and left us suddenly gazing, rather bemused, at an empty sky.

We had a senior asdic rating who, early in the voyage had been found by the skipper sleeping behind the funnel—having been torpedoed he had sworn never to sleep below decks again. But he was a good hand and the skipper fixed him up a cabin in a passage off the deck. Now as we all relaxed he approached the skipper. 'Sir,' he said warmly, 'I thank you—you were bloody marvellous!'

By this time the convoy was almost out of sight on the horizon and we made gruelling speed to catch up. Fortunately they slowed and waited for us, and for the gallant *Zamalek*. *Pozarica*'s captain took his ship in as close as possible to *Zamalek* and all aboard raised a cheer to the rescue ship, from whose crowded decks the answering cheers rang back; a strange, moving incident in that desolate sea.

Soon after we rejoined the convoy the aircraft warning was sounded as a little speck was seen far ahead. All thought it must be another German plane coming in to assess the results of the long raid, but then it was dropping flares, a green and a red, and the convoy was sending up answering flares. As the aircraft came nearer we could make it out to be an antiquated flying boat with a pusher screw. It was friendly! It was Russian! Everyone waved and cheered and capered wildly about —except for the Walrus from the cruisers it was the first friendly aircraft we had seen since leaving Iceland. The flying boat flew low over us, the pilot returning our greetings, then it turned and flew off. Surely it would not be long now before we had some fighter support.

Some miles away from us, however, the *Samuel Chase* was in serious difficulty. Just after passing Cape Kanin, *Halcyon* came upon her drifting helplessly. Her master signalled: 'Two direct hits, three near misses, main steam line broken. Shall we abandon ship?' *Halcyon's* captain determined to try to save the situation. He replied: 'Do not abandon ship—we will take you in tow.' There then followed a very fine piece of seamanship. The minesweeper had reciprocating engines, which enabled her to pull a considerable weight. Very efficiently a strong tow was shot over to *Samuel Chase* and *Halcyon* gradually increased engine revolutions and both screws began to thrust; the merchantman began to move. The two vessels made a steady five knots south to the White Sea, ready to cut clear if they should be attacked, until after some hours the Americans, fired no doubt by the example of the little 1,000-ton sweeper, managed to get their engines going again and finish the journey under their own steam. In recognition of *Halcyon's* assistance the master of the *Samuel Chase* asked that the minesweeper be allowed to escort him to harbour, which she did.

On *Austin* we had turned to looking after our guests from *El Capitan*. They were men of mixed nationalities, Americans from both north and south, and Argentines, Poles, English and Chinese. Besides her crew there were the survivors from the *John Witherspoon* she had been carrying, some of these suffering badly from frostbitten hands and feet, with the threat of gangrene setting in. All were given a double tot of rum and then began the problem of feeding and finding sleeping room for eighty-nine extra bodies. The Chinese were very helpful, offering to give a hand in the mess and the galley, and refusing to sleep anywhere but under the whaleback on deck.

The survivors as a whole were quite cool, cheerful and fatalistic, though inevitably, once all danger had receded, there were grouses about the crowded conditions in a ship with accommodation for fifty officers and men which now had to carry 140. We had to improvise nine sittings for meals—the galley never stopped—and there was a desperate shortage of cutlery. The white Americans did not like eating or even mixing with the coloured seamen and in the confined space quarrels sprang up between them. Men flopped down to sleep everywhere, on the floors of messdeck, wardroom, and along the corridors all over the ship; those who could not find space below had to sleep on the open deck. Some survivors had no compunction about taking a crew member's bunk while he was on watch and refusing to get out of it afterwards. They were used to a considerable standard of luxury on their merchant ships and found it hard to come down to the spartan conditions of a trawler. Not least the sanitary arrangements. There were just two lavatories or 'heads' for our crew, and these were nerve-racking places to perform in at the best of times. The situation now was chaotic, and the sight of bare bottoms sticking out over the side all over the ship became a familiar one. The only newcomers happily unaffected were the stoker survivors, who, joining their brethren below, followed the long-standing tradition of employing the shovels which were put into the furnace.

Far behind us as we raced for the White Sea the damaged *Ocean Freedom,* with *Northern Gem,* was straining every nut and bolt to catch up. Eventually, from about eight miles astern, she sighted our depleted group and made still greater effort to reach us, but when about three miles from Cape Kanin she was attacked by several aircraft. There were only about eight or nine planes but to Captain Walker and his company it seemed like the entire Luftwaffe, as they gave *Freedom* their undivided attention. Time and again she was straddled by bombs, shivering and shuddering under the storming attack. Her gyro compass and bridge instruments were shattered, the magnetic compass blown out of its gimbals, the plates along both sides of the ship further buckled by the bomb explosions. Huge columns of water boiled up each side of the ship and enveloped her; as the water cascaded down it was like coming up to the surface from a great depth, only to be enveloped again and again. The bridge was awash and gunners were totally submerged and washed out of their gun-pits, only to scramble back again, numbed and soaked to the skin but their trigger-fingers still working.

Still the planes could not plant one bomb directly on her, hampered in their efforts by those resolute trigger-fingers. On *Gem*, too, everything the trawler had was saying its piece and adding to the din. Then suddenly the planes were gone, leaving *Freedom* practically out of ammunition and her decks covered with empty shell cases but still, incredibly, intact and gamely steaming, her only bad casualty being a gunner hurled from his platform on to a hatch, injuring his spine.

Far ahead of *Freedom* our group had at last sighted the coast on our port hand. The last hours of July 10 had seen a queer phenomenon of sunset and sunrise at the same time, now it was a dazzling morning of July 11, during which more survivors in open boats were spotted and picked up, again some badly frostbitten. The sea was glassy and there was a striking mirage. The ships ahead were elongated into tall, slender trees, their smoke taking the place of branches, and those which were beam-on to us became as great square islands, while the hills ahead seemed to be chasing each other madly across the landscape. At first we thought the strain had been too much for us, that we were seeing things, but after a time we became accustomed to it, though the lookouts kept reporting our own ships as submarine periscopes.

After nosing into one of the little harbours at the entrance to the White Sea for a brief spell we steamed on together into the White Sea and were met by Russian armed trawlers and wood-burning destroyers painted in fantastic camouflage. Father into the White Sea we were passed by two British minesweepers with their magnetic sweeps out, combing for enemy-laid mines. It was a comforting sight to see these several vessels. We discovered that the sea, in spite of its name, was a dirty brown colour, with logs floating everywhere.

During the afternoon two Junkers 88s swept out of the clouds to drop a stick of bombs each. One of the sticks fell about 100 feet off *Pozarica*'s starboard quarter, giving them quite a shock. But it was the enemy's last fling.

Some of the stragglers now came up over the horizon and joined us, including the indomitable *Ocean Freedom,* and we pressed on down the White Sea without further incident.

That night as the sun, an enormous quivering red ball, dropped to the horizon the whole sea between skyline and ship became a blood-red corridor as though on fire. Around the molten glow was a deepening dusk which lasted for ten minutes before the sun reappeared over the horizon; it was the nearest approach to darkness that we had had for about ten days.

The morning of Sunday, July 12, broke cloudy with a drizzle as *Austin*'s bows cleaved the water, throwing up a muddy-brown wave; the rain ceased, the clouds cleared, and the sun shone strongly as we dropped anchor off the mouth of the North Dvina River which led to Archangel. 'Oh, what a wonderful night we've had tonight' played over *Pozarica*'s loudspeakers. *Palomares* checked the number of survivors on board each vessel; one alone had more than 300 and the total approached the thousand mark. One thousand men without their ships— what a desperately broken and miserable fleet we were.

The pilot boat arrived and we had our first sight of the Russians. A smart naval officer boarded *Austin* and had a rather involved conversation with our skipper, who refused to go further until the men suffering from frostbite were transferred to a ship where proper medical attention was available. This done, our pilot came aboard and we set off up the river, which twisted and turned like a snake. Tired though we were, every man was on deck to take his first look at the land of the Soviet Union. There were logs everywhere, in the river and piled high on the banks; women working among them laughed and waved as we passed, as did other women from the doors and windows of their wooden dwellings. Passing boats dipped their flags and the crews waved. In spite of the poverty of our numbers we were getting a royal welcome.

There were sandy beaches and behind them splashes of green in the shape of plantations of young trees, while still farther back from the river stretched great pine forests. Immense barges, larger than anything of the kind we had ever seen, swept past us. They had full size wooden houses built on them, and spacious decks; some even were topped by windmills. All dipped their red flags showing the hammer and sickle.

Pozarica ran on to a sandbank and stuck fast. Hands were made to jump up and down on the forecastle but they could not shift her and so she had to wait there several hours for high tide. It seemed a mortifying finish to her journey as we all steamed past her to our respective wharfs a few miles from Archangel. *Austin* came alongside a wooden quay at the village of Maimaksa, where to our great relief our survivors were transferred to a larger ship to continue to Archangel. As soon as we tied up children swarmed on to the jetty offering to barter elaborate badges and emblems for cigarettes, chocolate or soap, and they were joined by old women begging for bread.

After a few hours we moved on to moor at a huge wooden quay—it was said the Russians had built it in two weeks—at a village on the opposite side of the river to Archangel. Here we met up with others of our convoy and swopped experiences. The bits and pieces were put together and the full extent of the catastrophe began to take shape. At 10 a.m. next day, July 13, the survivors were 'counted off' on the jetty, a long business, and a 'missing list' compiled, after which several of the escorts prepared to steam back at once to the Barents Sea to begin a rescue search.

There was good news of *Dianella*, who had won through on her own, unscathed. After scattering the corvette had cracked on at full speed for Archangel. On reaching the White Sea she was challenged by three Russian torpedo boats and quickly ran up a couple of Union Jacks to assure them of her identity;

she then hurried on and was the first ship among us to reach
Archangel—and the first out again to begin rescue work.

Better news still brought our total of merchant ships safe to
four, together with the reappearance of plucky *Rathlin*. She, it
turned out, had arrived at Archangel before us almost on her last
scrap of coal—and she had a rousing tale to tell. After slipping
back from the *Pozarica* group, up north in the ice, Captain
Augustus Banning had pushed his ship on alone, thrusting right
up alongside the polar icefield until, off Cape Zhelaniya, the
most northerly tip of Novaya Zemlya, she reached a point
78 deg. 45 min. N—some 700 nautical miles from the Pole and
a record high for any British ship this century. Turning south
and steaming along the coast of Novaya Zemlya she had then
met up with the American *Bellingham*.

Bellingham had had a remarkably lucky escape from an enemy
plane. The aircraft circled the ship several times and finally
started in from her stern for the kill. At that moment a fogbank
loomed and Captain Mortenson ran his ship hard into it. The
confused plane released its bombs on an iceberg off *Bellingham's*
starboard side, blowing it apart; but the ship was safe.

And so on July 8, while we in the reformed convoy were steaming from Funk Creek, *Rathlin* and *Bellingham* had forged ahead
and were moving through broken ice near to the approaches
to the White Sea. The rescue ship, with her companion about
500 yards astern, was going flat out at a punishing 12 knots
when suddenly the morning calm was broken by the heavy
drone of an aircraft. It was a Focke-Wulf Condor—a long
distance convoy raider—out on morning patrol from Petsamo
base in Finland. Flying out of the morning mist it swooped in
a long shallow dive over the two ships, releasing three heavy
calibre bombs which fortunately were all near misses. But it
then turned to make another run in, this time at almost masthead height.

All knew that if the plane got them now it was God help
them, for *Rathlin* carried a staggering 240 men—many of them
survivors so shaken up with their recent immersion in an ice-
packed sea that they refused to go below and spent their time

huddled round the funnel casing on deck. The ship had not
enough lifeboats or rafts to accommodate half their number.
As the Condor passed over, its rear gunner opened up with
cannon fire at *Bellingham* whose funnel and superstructure were
riddled like a soup strainer. *Rathlin*'s stern gun crew replied
with their new rapid-firing Bofors, and to much amazement got
the plane with their first few rounds. The Condor sheered off
to port and at first a dull red glow was seen in the forward cockpit, then seconds later the whole of its fuselage burst into bright
orange flame and it staggered and crashed into a dead flat sea
about a quarter of a mile away, the wreckage still burning
fiercely.

Rathlin's rescue launch was soon away but as they approached
the plane it slowly sank and all that was left were scattered
papers and burning bits and pieces over a wide area. Out of the
aircraft's probable crew of seven all that was seen were two
lifeless bodies floating face downwards, the early morning sun
glinting on their half-opened parachutes. The launch turned
back and *Rathlin* quickly resumed her course, as the Condor
had been sending out radio messages before the attack and
more planes might even now be on the way. But no other aircraft did appear. The two ships safely entered the White Sea,
where they were met by an ancient Russian destroyer, and
subsequently arrived at the mouth of the North Dvina two days
before us. There they found a third ship waiting for the pilot—
the Russian tanker *Donbass*. She had won through on her own
despite a torpedo hole torn in her bows into which the sea
poured in and out like some fantastic Fingal's Cave. Her survival owed much to the efforts of *Daniel Morgan*'s gunners; a
high-ranking Commissar was sent to thank them personally for
all they had done.

Lord Haw-Haw's message on the radio now was one of complete triumph: 'Mr Churchill, you have not told the British
people the truth about your latest convoy to Russia. I will tell
you the truth. The whole of that convoy has gone to the bottom, not one of your merchant ships has reached Russia!' A

communique put out by the German High Command was only slightly more temperate. This claimed that one U.S. cruiser and twenty-eight merchant ships had been sunk and ten other vessels damaged, while a number of American seamen had been rescued and taken prisoner.

What the Germans sank for a cruiser we never did find out, but the picture on the naval side at Archangel was one that did nothing to improve the feelings now boiling up among many American survivors. Twelve of the thirteen escort ships had arrived safely—the only vessel not accounted for was trawler *Ayrshire*. Against this we had with us only four out of thirty-three merchantmen—*Ocean Freedom, Samuel Chase, Bellingham* and *Donbass*; together with two rescue ships.

What of the rest? Soon word arrived that some ships had successfully reached Novaya Zemlya, and on July 16, four days after our arrival, Commodore Dowding set off in *Poppy*, accompanied by *Lotus* and *La Malouine*, to salvage what he could of his ravaged convoy. Meantime on *Austin* we began to coal up, a lengthy job, in preparation for patrol duties.

7

Snatched From the Sea

Although desperately short of medical facilities the Russians gave our host of survivors what ready hospital treatment and comfort they could. There were many bad cases of exposure and frostbite, and more to come, resulting in amputations, but for the majority of the survivors their main need was sleep and treatment to regain the full use of their limbs; after this they were billeted out in public buildings all over the town.

Ferocious O'Flaherty, of *John Witherspoon*: 'We were delivered to hospital, a plain one-storey building with a statue of Lenin in front, where the nurses put us to bed and began pill medication. We all had partly frozen feet. For eleven days and nights I could not sleep soundly. If I moved my feet suddenly, even the touch of the blankets would awaken me. The rest of our boat's crew were in a similar condition. Each night a nurse would make the rounds with pills, saying 'Schleep—schleep. . . .' The beds had no springs and the mattresses felt like straw, but we were grateful to the staff for they were doing the best that could be managed with what was on hand. We did not expect the doctors to have time for us as they were too busy with more serious cases of frozen limbs—one young merchant seaman lost both feet, one hand and part of the other.

'After eleven days and nights of this a friend and myself were able to hobble outside. We were the only two who recovered this fast; others of our boat's crew were still hobbling weeks later and one man had to be carried about. This after 72 hours in an open lifeboat.'

The reception of some of the survivors was not without humour, such as experienced by Third Officer Phillips of *Aldersdale,* who was one of those marshalled into a large hall which formed part of a hospital:

'From the collection room we were ushered at about six at a time into a reception room. Ranged across one end of the room was a row of trestle tables and seated behind these, like wizened oranges, were half a dozen elderly Russian matrons, who obviously spoke no English. Through sign language we understood that we were to strip to an undefined limit. In front of each woman was a notebook, and as we removed each garment, giving the name in English, it was written down phonetically in Russian. Eventually we arrived at underpants and vests, short, tall, paunchy and thin, faced by six near hysterically hilarious nurses and the dilemma of how far to go. After much discussion we reduced to the buff and made our way through an adjoining door to an enormous shower-room. The showers were set high up and were controlled by a small boy. After setting the temperature some muscular nurses came in and proceeded to scrub us with an ersatz loofah on the end of a short stick, the more masculine-looking of us being singled out for some special female comments—earthy Russian type. From here we were issued with white pyjamas which were our uniform for a long time. We walked, talked, danced and even slept in the damn things.

'The hospital was fairly comfortable and the food plain and monotonous. Porridge formed the staple vegetable; we even had it with meat and gravy. The staff, being female, were hotly pursued by the more virile survivors, with varying degrees of success. Little English was spoken, though the resident medical officer was a handsome woman who spoke English with a Home Counties accent—and she had never been out of Russia in her life. She was a tower of strength to us.'

Gunner Urwin of *Aldersdale,* one of those lucky ones who simply needed three days rest, went out on to the green outside the hospital and saw some of the staff cutting off the lawn what looked like dandelion leaves. 'We asked in our sign language and pidgin English what they were for and the answer was *'Soupo korosh'*—meaning soup was good when laced with rabbit meat (but no rabbit). Dinner was boiled wheat with two meat-cube sized pieces of yak which seemed to have died of old age.'

Hospital life for Third Officer Phillips' group came to an end. 'We were given back our clothes in a typically Russian method. The ceremony was a shambles and took place in the same room where we had stripped off before our giggling audience. The doors of the room opened and before us on the floor lay a mound of miscellaneous clothing—our clothes. The ensuing chaos was hilarious and pathetic, but after scrabbling and bartering we ended up decently, if ridiculously dressed. At least the pyjamas returned to their original purpose. I had managed to preserve my blue Burberry and guarded it with my life. It had served as dressing gown, overcoat and raincoat.

'We transferred from our pleasant hospital to the Intourist Hotel. Top floor, six to a room, one bulb at the foot of the next floor up as lighting, sparse beds and close neighbours in the form of voracious bed-bugs. It was not until we turned in and extinguished the solitary distant bulb that they visited us for supper. Not just a family but the whole generation from Peter the Great. Next day we attempted to smoke them out with paraffin wads and merely succeeded in almost setting fire to the hotel. Eventually a naval debugging squad sprayed the room but I never slept there again, bunking in a room on the floor below which was occupied by R.A.F. personnel.'

It says much for the majority of survivors that they were able to hold on to a good sense of humour, especially those from the open boats, for they were far worse off than us. They were men without ships, with only the clothes they stood up in, and though our own food situation rapidly became critical they were on poorer rations even than ourselves.

Our own first impression of the Archangel area was that quayside swarming with children who offered an amazing variety of souvenir badges. They were a lively, talkative crowd of young-sters, dressed in a patchwork of clothing, who were to dog us throughout our stay. They had badges to commemorate everything and everyone; the Russian army, navy and air force, all branches of the civil defence, and for shooting, athletics, agriculture, doctors, nurses, Commissars, inspectors, drivers, civil aviation. All the badges seemed well made with enamelled designs and the price, in cigarettes or chocolate, varied according to the class of the emblem. A common Red Star could be had for two or three cigarettes, but a comprehensive air-raid model, showing aircraft, searchlight, ack-ack gun, gas-mask and all, might cost ten cigarettes. A brisk trade was done at first, for we were well stocked with the necessary currency, but later on it was to become a problem whether to smoke our slender ration and eat the 'nutty', or to barter for more souvenirs.

And there were the old women, pinched and poverty-stricken, begging for food. On the first morning after we docked we threw our stale bread over the side of *Lord Austin* as usual only to see these women produce long fishing nets, fish out the bread pieces, dry them in the sun and eat them. After this incident we were warned not to throw any food into the river, which brought about a difficult situation when the Russians, knowing that we were short of food, generously offered us some yak meat, all they could spare from their own scanty resources. Two carcasses were carried aboard—rather blue-looking and with a distinct odour about them—and hung up in the meat safe. After our first meal from them the unanimous decision was that it would be better to remain hungry.

Next day the gift carcasses were seen to have certain signs of life in them, and the problem of their disposal arose. It would have been discourteous and ungrateful to return them to the Russians, nor could they now be ditched over the side. So it was decided to burn them in the stokehold. Two men were detailed for the job—one insisted on wearing his gas-mask. They lugged the carcasses along the deck and lowered them into the stokehold by means of the ash-shute. But they had reckoned without our chief engineer. Refusing to have them anywhere near his domain, he hoisted the yak up the chute again. It took much coaxing and persuasion on the part of the duty officer before the Chief would relent and let the carcasses be cremated in his fires.

The quay hummed with activity as our pitifully few merchant ships were unloaded. Women of middle-age, hardy and strong, did the bulk of the work while green-capped Commissars with revolvers in their belts paced the closely-guarded quayside. It was said these Commissars had discovered a Russian stowaway in a ship about to sail back for Britain and had shot him on the spot. As they did an unfortunate stevedore who pocketed a tin of peaches.

We moved up river and began coaling from *Ocean Freedom*. It was a long, arduous job bagging the coal in the merchant-man's hold and slinging it over to our decks. It was heat-wave weather now—surprising, considering that we were so close to the Arctic Circle—and there were mosquitoes; thousands of them. They were not malarial, but all the same they raised a nasty lump. At night it was too hot to keep the hatches closed, and the mosquitoes came down and bombed us in our bunks. We would almost have preferred Junkers 88s. One had the choice of either sticking one's head under the blankets and being suffocated, or keeping it out and being bitten; there were no nets to be had. For some protection during his watch the quarter-master carried a paraffin-soaked rag on the end of a stick which he waved around his head.

The ships from our convoy, and some merchantmen still remaining from the previous convoy, were scattered about the Archangel area at wharfs and jetties along the Dvina and in small creeks running from it. Most berths were well supplied with sentries and guards, and had high wooden towers in which women with machine-guns were stationed. At the bigger wharfs it was impossible to get out of the jetty area without passing a guardhouse and having to identify one's-self to the very suspicious and often deliberately obstructive guards, but at the smaller quays there might be only a few sentries strolling about the jetty area and it was possible to leave ship and wander into the countryside and round the villages without check, returning in the same way. And so, while coaling from *Freedom*, we made our way into a village nearby. We found the villagers, almost all women, very hospitable. They waved from the windows of their large communal dwellings, invited us in and produced tea from a samovar or a bottle of vodka—some thought we might need more than vodka and were willing to oblige.

The effects of the vodka could be disastrous on those not accustomed to its potency. Some men heeded the warnings to treat it with respect; others did not, to their cost. Bottles of it were offered in barter by the ubiquitous badge-toting children, and while some of this was genuine, some was merely a hooch concocted of wood-alcohol. Two Americans died after drinking the stuff—it paid to be careful.

The children followed us everywhere—'Give me smokum, Comerad.' Then, when refused, pointing to the half smoked cigarette in one's mouth: 'Little smokum, Comerad—give me little smokum!' And there were the knowing ones, tiny tots some of them, who had 'beeg sister—beeg sister very nice.'

Archangel itself, reached by ferry across the river from us, was a sprawling timber town, the few tall cement buildings in the centre standing like islands among a mass of wooden houses and buildings. There was a general air of shabbiness and dilapidation about the town, even the new cement buildings showing quick signs of decay, with large cavities in the sides where the improperly bonded cement had fallen to the streets.

Never had any of us seen so much concentrated wood. The streets themselves were laid with timber to resist the hard winters, with raised wooden sidewalks which needed repair. Above it all was a peculiar stench, for the sewers were open and primitive, and this combined with the smell of pine to make a sickly odour hanging over the ancient town. Outside the town the flat 'countryside' was covered with a deep layer of sawdust into which one's feet sank, and way beyond this stretched vast forests that seemed to go on for ever. Easy to see why the port was one of the largest timber centres in the world.

Most naval and merchant personnel found the townspeople friendly, hospitable and full of humour, though with a natural suspicion of Allied officers, as they had of their Commissars; they only really loosened up with the rank and file. There was no spying on us by the authorities but there were many regulations to observe. We made allowances for many of the things we found odd; it would have been unfair to judge the Soviet Union from the conditions of life prevailing in a remote port in the summer of 1942, when the Russian armies had their backs to the wall. The battle for Stalingrad was still at its height; the Germans were advancing through the Caucusus, menacing the oilfields. If Baku was taken the Soviet would be doomed, for from where else could they obtain their oil supplies? Certainly not by the Arctic route. The amount which had arrived with us would hardly keep the war going for half an hour. If convoys were arriving every week that would be another matter, but the agreement had of necessity slipped to one a month, and after the disaster of PQ 17 it seemed doubtful whether any further convoys could be risked until a reasonable period of darkness was present to provide cover.

There were some Russians who could not believe that P.Q. 17 had started out with as many ships as was claimed. Small wonder. Looking at the sad remains of our merchant armada we found it hard to believe ourselves. Yet the bedraggled, exhausted and frostbitten survivors still coming in provided the bitter testimony.

The courtesies of the citizens took by surprise the many men among us who had arrived heavily prejudiced against the Russians, imagining them to be little better than the Nazis. Not the least the merchant seamen, for whom to find flags flying in their honour was a totally unknown experience. It was impressed upon them by the Russians that they were the guests of the Soviet Government for their attempt to help Russia with supplies. In many little ways the courtesies were extended. Both naval and merchant men were, for instance, given the 'freedom' of Archangel's single-deck trams. On these trams there was no nonsense about carrying a certain number of passengers, everyone who could obtain a fingerhold was carried. The smell inside them was unspeakable. Only the wounded and pregnant women were allowed to ride out front with the woman driver, but as visitors we were permitted to do the same and were not asked to pay, though most of us did. In the 'kinemas' we were speedily taken to the front rows—an alarming experience for some. Signalman Douglas Blamey, of *Palomares*: 'Looking for local experience we entered a kinema. It was late as we bought our tickets and went through to the gallery. A heavy Russian period drama was in progress. As we got inside and groped for the nearest seat to the back we suddenly found hands grabbing for us and were pushed and lifted towards the front of the gallery. For one horrible moment we feared their object was to throw us down into the stalls, but they only meant us to have the position of honour in the front row!'

On every hand were the stark reminders of the plight of the Soviet at war. Outside one shop we saw a long queue of women, queueing not for food or cigarettes but to buy copies of a poster showing a Russian woman and her child shrinking from a German bayonet. Where else would one find people queueing to buy a war poster? Was it compulsion or national patriotism? We never knew the answer.

As for food, there were the poignant scenes as women stood in long patient queues outside the various communal food kitchens, one at least set up inside an old and beautiful church. The women carried contraptions like three-tiered cakestands on which they collected their strict ration: one tier for soup, another for black bread, and the third for a morsel of yak or similar meat. Their daily ration would hardly make one English meal even in wartime, and on one day of the week they had to give up their rations for the Red Army. Poor devils, no wonder they looked hungry, and yet in spite of their privations they remained mostly friendly and cheerful. Platoons of men and women soldiers sang magnificently as they marched, their voices rising high above the eternal wood piles near the quays.

Because of the distance to Archangel from the various quays, and the difficulties of travel, and later because of our dwindling cash and supply of goods to barter, visits to Archangel were for most of us infrequent. The children who pursued us from ship to shore seemed to have a never ending supply of rouble notes, probably because in this country of grim scarcity there were few necessities that could be bought. They offered the notes in exchange for cigarettes, chocolate and soap. The barter price of a

two-ounce bar of chocolate became accepted at 30 roubles—
nearly 30 shillings—though a bar in a red wrapper could
fetch 40. Similarly, cigarettes would produce 40 roubles a packet,
but in a red packet would be worth 50. There were smiles over
these 'Red' Russians. But as we had no means of changing our
sterling, it gave us currency.

When we could afford it we could buy food at the International Club in Archangel, which was used also by the more
privileged classes of Russians, high-level citizens graded by
their importance to the State. The club was well run and, like an
oasis in a desert of want, provided fairly good meals to supplement our own spartan rations. Here the waitresses seemed to
regard their job as the best fun in the world, taking a gleeful
delight in saying 'feenish' to the dishes that were off. The girls
who came into the club were attractive and nicely turned out
in summer dresses, in sharp contrast to the other womenfolk
who were poor and shabby, though we were shocked at first
when some of these pretty girls smiled and showed three or four
gruesome metal teeth; the dentures of both men and women
were made of some sort of metal, presumably a wartime measure.

Dances, concerts and sing-songs were put on in the club by
the Russian and Allied forces; but all this was when we could
leave our ships and had roubles won by bartering to spend. For
the most part it was a tedious life that now began.

During our first days in port, the final dramas of PQ 17 were
being enacted on the bleak Barents Sea. Reports came through
of a lifeboat from *Alcoa Ranger* making land at remote Cape
Kanin, followed by news of other men from ships sunk on Black
Sunday.

Like the survivors of *Peter Kerr*. For two days in dead calm
weather her two lifeboats had been able to make some headway with the oars, then a wind came up which enabled them to
make good time sailing. They covered 360 miles in seven and a
half days. Second Mate William Connolly had saved his sextant
and chronometer and so was able to navigate his boat of twenty-

four men adequately from a chart which had been put ready in it.

'On leaving the ship the rudder in our boat was broken and we had to steer the whole time with a sweep oar. I was fortunate to be one of the three chosen for this job and by virtue of the extra exercise it afforded we three were the only ones who did not suffer some degree of immersion foot after getting ashore.

'Landfall was made a short distance east of Murmansk and when we were about a mile offshore a Russian torpedo boat came alongside with its machine-guns trained on us. After satisfying themselves of our identity they took us in tow and into a nearby submarine base. From there we went on to a hospital where we were all given clean, comfortable bunks. Fortunately no one was in need of medical care but all relished getting a good sleep.

'After a day or two in the hospital we were brought to a nearby barracks for further rest. Most of the soldiers here were Lapp women and they paid no attention whatsoever to us. There was some air action near the barracks but apparently it was not the specific target. After about a week here we were taken to Murmansk where about the only evidence of a city once having been there were the chimneys that remained—all else seemed burned out. Here we were put on an old woodburning train for Archangel.'

After travelling three days north from Archangel *Dianella* picked up the two boatloads of survivors from *Empire Byron* off Novaya Zemlya. By this time most of the seamen's minds were wandering, seeing imaginary clear water and ships. Among them were two young apprentices, aged fifteen and sixteen, both of whom lost toes and one a foot from frostbite. In the jollyboat after the sinking Carpenter Frederick Cooper had rescued the ship's young third radio operator, Dick Phillips. Bravely this lad had gone back for the radio receiver after first handing the others the transmitting set, and with the lifeboats then gone he had jumped into the sea. The exposure killed him, on this his first voyage. Dick died in Cooper's arms and was buried at sea (he was awarded a posthumous George Medal). Also among the survivors was a badly injured gunner and a fireman who had had his finger nearly torn off while leaving the sinking ship; this man never complained at any time, though he must have suffered agonies from the salt water getting to his bandaged wound. The finger was amputated in Russia.

A/B Walter Shepherd was in one of the lifeboats. 'The second mate organized singing and guessing games but after the second day nobody wanted to know. The third engineer started drinking salt water and turned very bad-tempered. He was warned that if he did not stop he would be tied down, but it had no effect. Our ration every six hours consisted of two ounces of water, two Horlicks tablets and two small biscuits. Since that time I can't bear to see a tap dripping. We rigged the sails but there was very little breeze. We also shipped the oars, but this was more to keep the blood circulating than anything else. In the end we were too cold and exhausted to do that even. We took turns rubbing each other's feet with whale oil.

' "Planes" were sighted at intervals but all turned out to be seagulls. As time wore on the snarl set in. Tempers were frayed and arguments arose which were quickly quelled by the captain. Suddenly someone shouted: "A ship–look!" "Another iceberg more likely," said someone else. But it was *Dianella*. She signalled us: "I will circle round you twice. If I get a ping I'm away. If not, come alongside as quickly as possible and lose no time—you may be a decoy." They put scramble nets over the side and we watched with anxious eyes as they circled us, wondering if a U-boat was lying waiting. But in less than 15 minutes we were all aboard, the two lifeboats bobbing about in our wake. I and several others collapsed on deck and we were helped below. We were given a plate of hot soup and twenty cigarettes. The sailors gave up their bunks for us for 24 hours, and then we slept anywhere we could find. The sailors had not much food but they shared it.

'We were aboard for six days looking for an American ship which was in difficulty among the ice, but did not find her.'

One of the most dramatic rescues was made high up in the Barents Sea by *Salamander* and *Halcyon*, along with a third minesweeper, *Hazard*. A Russian Catalina out on patrol had

spotted three rafts and radioed back their position with an estimate of the direction in which they would drift. The three
sweepers were sent out from Archangel to find them. They were
given nine days for the search as they were needed for minesweeping work. This gave them three days to reach the area,
three days to look for the rafts, and three days to return.

On reaching the area of search the three ships found perfect
weather but the first twenty-four hours of vigilance slipped
fruitlessly by and everyone was beginning to feel disheartened.
'What sort of a fool's errand is this?' was the question asked
on *Halcyon*. Every man was badly strained and tired after the
activities of the past two weeks; no one had had more than
four hours sleep for what seemed years. However, they were
fortunate in having absolute quiet for their search on the sunlit sea, for no U-boat echoed on the asdics, no bomber marred the
blue sky. As they got back into regular routine men's spirits rose
and they began to take an interest.

In the afternoon that began the third day of the box search
the atmosphere was tense. The night hours passed quietly, the
sun just on the horizon shedding on the ripples of the sea a path
of crinkling liquid gold. It was an eerie scene, and there was a
sudden inexplicable feeling that perhaps they might find the lost
seamen after all. This despite the fact that the survivors had been
afloat for thirteen days, and the minesweepers were only going
on calculations made a week before by the Russian pilot. Though
they were tackling the impossible, excitement mounted and
hopes rose as the time grew shorter.

But at 7.30 a.m. the black Arctic fog descended. This seemed
the end. Their time was up at noon and they were helpless in
the fog. All they could do now was to feel their way and hope.
At 8.15 a.m. on *Halcyon* there was the usual anti-freeze routine
on the guns, a few test rounds being fired by each. Now, all
those not on watch-below came and stood shivering on the upper
deck, either cursing the fog or silently praying for it to rise.
Sometimes it would lift just enough to let them see *Salamander*,
but not *Hazard*, which lay 200 yards farther off. At 11 a.m.
the coxswain served the rum and all went below for their tot,

then returned. There was no argument or lively banter as usual, just a strained silence.

Halcyon's captain had ordered the Very pistols fired. He now sent the signal for the last lap. For this last half hour everyone lined the rails, watching, waiting, praying; and at a quarter to twelve, just fifteen minutes to go, a miracle happened. The fog lifted. First they saw *Salamander*, and then *Hazard's* ghostly shape appeared. A faint cheer sounded—or was it their over-stretched imagination? No, it was not, for right between each ship was a raft crammed with men waving weakly. They began to shout: 'God Save the King!—We knew you would save us.' They had heard the gunfire and paddled wearily towards it.

The sweepers dropped their scrambling nets. On *Salamander* a seaman missed with his first attempt to throw a line to one of the rafts. 'Limey,' said a cracked and dry voice, 'I have been on this raft for thirteen days and would do better than that!' After taking thirteen men from one raft—there were more than thirty survivors in all from *S.S. Honomu*—*Salamander* moved off to drop depth charges in case a U-boat was near. Aboard *Halcyon* the survivors were too weak, and their feet too swollen, to stand, but otherwise they were in surprisingly good shape; from the first day they had taken turns at four hours on the paddles and four off, and during the off period had washed their deadening feet with salt water. Only a coloured seaman who would not do this later lost part of a foot with frostbite. The U-boat which sank *Honomu* had surfaced again on the third and sixth days of their ordeal, giving them more water. Every man among them now repeated the same vow: 'If I get back to the States I'll never go to sea again.'

Yet other Black Sunday survivors got through to the Russian mainland, among them a boat from the *Bolton Castle*. They had started out with sufficient water for about an egg-cup full twice a day, and for food, two Horlicks malted milk tablets twice daily, with a two-inch square ship's biscuit once a day and a tea-spoonful of condensed milk. They had a dozen small tins of corned beef but decided to conserve these until later.

The sea got rougher and they were baling out continuously.

Six Arab firemen among them suffered badly from frostbite. Because of their religion they could not make water in front of the rest of the company and the situation so worsened that one pulled a knife on a young apprentice. After that the Arabs were searched and their knives taken off them, and when they wanted to urinate the rest of the boat's company had to turn their backs to them. As one man aboard remarked: 'Anything for a quiet life!'

On the fifth day the corned beef was opened; the condensed milk was finished and the water reduced to one egg-cup full a day. They sighted another lifeboat and pulled wearily over to it. It was an American boat, empty, but inside it they found a carton of American cigarettes; they had been sharing what few smokes they had. But the situation now looked pretty sick and hopes were dwindling. Suddenly on the seventh day they saw what they thought was a ship coming up astern. Excitedly they threw flares into the sea, sending up thick clouds of red smoke, but when the ship was only three miles off she suddenly disappeared. They could hardly believe their ill fortune. That night brought heavy seas and bitter cold. On the morning of the eighth day still nothing could be seen, but they could hear distinctly the thud of a ship's engine. It was the motor of a Russian submarine beneath them—the 'ship' they had seen the previous day —and soon in answer to its radioed messages there arrived a Russian trawler.

Chief Cook Osmundsen: 'We were given a good reception by the Russian crew—a slice of sausage and a glass of vodka which knocked several of us out cold.' After eighteen hours' steaming they were into the Kola Inlet leading to Murmansk. 'What a sight! The harbour was literally crowded with sunken ships with funnels and masts sticking out of the water everywhere.' There, too, they saw the two Polish submarines from the convoy. 'Nothing could be done for us so we were taken by lorry to hospital in Polyarno. The doctors and nurses there were wonderful to us. I remember being given a mug of hot coffee with plenty of milk and, having finished it, asking for another. The nurse actually ran to get it. Nothing was too much trouble for them.'

The men made good recoveries and it was decided because of enemy bombing that they should go to a rest camp in the forest country. 'A long journey by lorry to get there and we were billeted in a long, narrow shed with shelves like the racks on railway carriages but made of wood, and we were issued with a blanket and straw mattress. We had to sleep on these shelves side by side. Sometimes two mattresses were put together for three men, as there were not enough to go round. The food was awful, the main meal a sort of stew with everything one could think of in it except meat: fish heads, beetroot and so on. After a week there it was decided to take us to Archangel, a five-day railway journey around the White Sea coast. On arrival at Archangel we were put up in a schoolhouse. The accommodation was very good indeed and so was the food, except for the black bread. Again, everyone was kind.'

The two lifeboats from *Earlston*, sunk to the south of *Bolton Castle*, lost each other in thick fog but afterwards met up again. At midday on July 6 both were rowing steadily and holding a rousing sing-song as they pulled at the heavy boats. But then one boat slipped away, leaving the other to forge on through a choppy sea. In this boat of thirty-three men, who hoped to reach Murmansk, was Stoker A. J. Robinson. 'I must take off my hat to the chief steward. He had put three bottles of brandy and some cigarettes in the boat so we had a little tot every morning, a godsend.' But it was a big blow when they found that the boat's 20-gallon tank of drinking water had burst; they had to go very sparingly with the little that was left.

In command of the boat was Second Officer David Evans, who showed exceptional resourcefulness in keeping the boat on course, and when he had to give in to exhaustion Cadet Andrew Watt, just nineteen, took over for a spell. Watt also kept a pencilled 'log' on a single sheet of notepaper. Spirits were still high on the fourth day when he noted: 'July 9, noon. North-easterly breeze; running free due south. Great excitement, sighted two objects astern on horizon, rising fast. What are they? Everyone speculating. . . .' They thought it was a rescue ship, but to their disappointment it was only a motor boat from the *Bolton Castle* pulling another boat behind it. They too were hoping to make Murmansk, and courses were checked and a few words exchanged between the parties before each continued on their separate ways. When the wind became stronger *Earlston*'s boat made such good headway by sail that it overtook the other boats —giving them a cheer as it passed by. But the sea became very rough and the boat was tossed about like a cork in a basin.

On the fifth day three men were suffering badly with swollen legs, next day three more. Stoker Robinson rubbed the feet of every man in whale and vegetable oil three times a day. 'I praise the three able seamen who steered the boat for seven days. We could not have gone on much longer without casualties as some men had begun to drink sea water.' On the seventh day— Sunday again, July 12—Cadet Watt noted in his log: '5 a.m. Land sighted fine on port bow—Thank God! we all say. . . .' And at noon: 'Volunteers for oars to help make bay.'

Stoker Robinson: 'We were all very weak. We came to a little beach and were approached by soldiers—we had landed on the Rybachi Peninsula, right in the Russian front line against the Finns. Among us was a man who could speak Russian, a Government passenger on *Earlston*, and so he could explain who we were. I thought I was in fair shape and was second out of the boat, but found I just could not stand up. Others fell down around me. The soldiers carried the rest of the men out of the boat and sat them down. They gave us a sip of water—I could have drunk a gallon. We were then put in lorries and taken to a dugout where we had a hot drink, some bread and jam, and a shave. We had to get out quickly as they were expecting a big push at any moment.'

They were taken by lorry to a front line hospital. The log entry: 'On arrival, casualties attended to and put to bed, others bathed and given meal (excellent fish and macaroni, coffee, bread and butter). Oh boy, wasn't it good!' Next day they were taken by lorry and ship to hospital at Polyarno, where they stayed for three days, followed by a period in a rest camp before joining a train for Archangel.

Earlston's other lifeboat was by no means as fortunate. After having to force its way through large pans of pack-ice it encountered a sea of dangerous proportions in which large floating baulks of redwood were a danger. In this boat was Lance Bombardier Crossley.

'The wind and seas eventually dropped late on the third day or early on the fourth, and we began to row. Several of the crew suffered from exposure. One old A/B, Paddy Murphy, swore he could see "some lovely big red buses" when we were in the crests of the waves. A pity they did not come up, I would have enjoyed getting one to King's Cross. Later this old chap died after operations to his feet, which became gangrenous. Some others of the crew also lost parts of their feet.

'We just rowed and rowed, never seeing another human being for ten days. I learned a lot about gulls and fulmars and puffins, and we got tangled up in a school of whales. I can vouch that at least one whale had a helluva bad case of halitosis—it surfaced about six feet from us and exhaled over the boat.

'On the tenth day we sighted a plane. It flew over us once. We also sighted a mountainous coast. A small motor boat was seen, but we were too far away to make contact. The first mate was noisily certain that he had made a landfall in Russia, and when another fishing boat came out he sent our English-speaking Russian forward to speak to the boatman. After the first hail the Russian turned sadly round, spread out his hands and said: "He is not Russian". The bosun, a former Dane, growled: "He is Norwegian." The fisherman guided us through an intricate passage to a small cove near the North Cape. I carried a little Scots seaman up the cliff to the house of the fisherman, whose wife was very kind to us, bathing the feet of the worst frostbitten and giving us soup. Those of us who could stand and walk went outside to lie down to sleep in the sun. Gunner Officer Lieutenant Hough, Gunner Kidd and myself decided to make a break for Sweden (a stupid idea we learned afterwards), but while we were asleep the first mate, being nervous of German

reaction to an escape, sent the bosun to a nearby lighthouse to
report our landing. I was awakened by a German boot under
my backside and a voice saying 'Raus, raus!'

'We were taken from there to Nordkyn, and eventually to
Wilhelmshaven. I was interrogated by an extremely good looking
elderly German speaking perfect English. He wanted to know
all about our guns and the rest, but I repeated that I would only
give my rank, name and number. When he asked where I came
from I said "Hull" and he replied: "Don't you mean Kingston-
upon-Hull?" which of course is the full name of my native city,
though hardly anyone uses it. He then said: "Tell me, does
Queen Victoria still watch the people going to the lavatories in
the square?" This was a reference to the fact that underground
conveniences were built on the spot formerly occupied by her
statue, and they replaced the dear old Queen on top of them.
He evidently knew Hull! He sent me for three weeks' solitary for
my non-co-operation, telling me that they knew all they wanted
to know already, just wanted my confirmation. When the Germans left our camp at the end of the war this man was found
hiding in a barn nearby by one of my pals, who was undecided
whether to kill him or not. He didn't.'

The unluckiest ones of all were the crew of the *Carlton*. Not
only was this American merchantman the first ship to die on
Black Sunday, but every surviving member of her company fell
into enemy hands, so substantiating part of the claim of the
boastful German communique we heard at Archangel. Six hours
after *Carlton* was sunk at 5.22 a.m. on July 5, as the lifeboat
and rafts were trying to pull away from the scene, an enemy
seaplane landed on the water and picked up two survivors.
Shortly afterwards a flying boat descended and took aboard
nine gunners and a seaman. In the evening another flying boat
picked up twelve more men and handed out rocket flares. Early
next morning a seaplane picked up another two men; all were
flown to Norway.

The seventeen remaining survivors transferred to the one lifeboat and cut the rafts adrift. The second mate, who had clung
on to a sextant and charts, set a course for the nearest Russian

territory. On the fourth day after the sinking a British plane dropped them a rubber life-suit and some canned food; then on the eighth day a surfaced U-boat came alongside. The young commander, who said he had lived on the U.S. west coast for some time, apologized for not taking them aboard as he was "still outbound on patrol." He offered medical aid, which was refused as not being needed, and gave them a compass, charts, position, time, and course and distance to the Norwegian coast. He also handed them water, biscuits, cigarettes and blankets—most of the goods being of U.S. manufacture—and told them that forty-two U-boats were hunting the scattered ships.

On the thirteenth day the first assistant engineer died of exposure and reluctantly the lifeboat's course was set for Norway. Six days later, in a very distressed condition, they made landfall near the North Cape and their war was over.

There remained those ships and lifeboats which had managed to struggle through to Novaya Zemlya. How many? Commodore Dowding's little rescue fleet was soon to find out. In these adventures *Empire Tide*, one of the only two British merchantmen to survive, figured largely, and it is her story that follows.

8

Full Ahead on a Prayer

When the signal had come for PQ 17 to scatter *Empire Tide* was steaming along in her position in the middle of the convoy. After their first shocked disbelief at the incredible order, her captain and chief officer held hurried consultation and decided to remain right on course, letting the other ships draw away from *Tide*. Captain Frank Harvey rang 'Full Ahead!'

Treatment for their gunner wounded in the torpedo-bomber battle earlier now was a problem. Chief Officer George Leech: 'I had a look at his leg and was appalled by the wound. The bullet must have been spinning, making an entry hole an inch round and an exit hole which was a gaping wound about nine inches across. I spoke urgently to the captain, as it was more than we could handle. We called up an American destroyer by Aldis lamp and asked if she would take the injured man. But they had their orders, and the reply was: "Sorry, we are unable to help you." And off she went with the others. All we could do was to apply dressings and make the man as comfortable as possible.

'We kept going on our course of 020 deg. (True) at about 13 knots and shortly before midnight came to the edge of the icepack, which was solid as far as the eye could see on our port bow. We altered course slightly to clear the ice sticking out ahead of us, then resumed our former course when the ice-edge curved away again to the north-east. We next ran into fog. The captain and I discussed which was the better course of action—to slow down in the fog or, regardless of risk, keep going at full speed to get as far away as possible from the searching enemy. Our decision was to keep going and pray!'

And so *Empire Tide* made swift and hazardous passage through the fog. Large ice floes and icebergs loomed dangerously around her, 'but we were pretty desperate by this time. It was not long before SOS messages began to come in as one ship after another was attacked and sunk. One message in particular I cannot forget. It was from the *Earlston* and said: "Am being attacked by seven dive-bombers and three U-boats—have repulsed them so far." I think this deserves to rank with Nelson's "Engage the enemy more closely".'

Empire Tide's Hurricane fighter was now more than ever their greatest asset, an evident deterrent to the enemy planes.

'The firing point for the catapult was in the carpenter's shop forward. It was the chief officer's job to actually fire the catapult rockets when the aircraft was launched, and before this was done a special "link" connector had to be fitted into the circuit. This was always kept padlocked to the bulkhead beside the firing switch. I had to keep the key constantly with me, and could not hand it to anyone except the two R.A.F. officers we carried. It was returned to me as soon as the periodical checks of the circuit were made.

'From the start of the convoy this key haunted my dreams; I lived in fear that action-stations would be sounded and that after rushing to the firing position I would find I had lost the key. The first two days after scattering brought continuous alarms—time after time when the weather cleared we sighted single aircraft approaching, and immediately action-stations was sounded the R.A.F. pilot and myself would make all speed for the Hurricane and firing point respectively. From the bridge to the fore well-deck there were three ladders and we learned very quickly how to slide down the handrails without one's feet touching a step, making the foredeck from the bridge in about ten seconds. The pilot would start the Hurricane, I would unlock the "link" and plug it in (thanking God I had not mislaid the key) and stand by to bang-off if we got the green flag from the bridge. On each occasion, however, the enemy was obviously discouraged and kept his distance on sighting the Hurricane on the catapult.'

Stowed away 'tween decks was *Empire Tide*'s 'secret weapon'. Someone's bright idea at Hvalfiord had been that she should carry a mock Hurricane fighter, so that if the real plane was fired off the dummy could replace it on the catapult and so deter other bombers. As it happened this dummy aircraft, made of wood and canvas and painted in regulation colours, was never needed and ultimately disintegrated.

Empire Tide was one of the few ships to have a gyro compass which could take over as her magnetic compasses lost almost all their directive force. She continued hard on course until reaching 78 deg. N., when it was decided to turn and make for the coast of Novaya Zemlya. They sighted the coast early next morning, July 6, and it was at this point that *Empire Tide* took a very different line of action from most of the other ships which managed to reach the island—her captain decided to keep well clear of Matochkin Strait.

Chief Officer Leech: 'We thought that if a concentration of surviving ships were anchored there it would be too good a target for the enemy. Luckily we had the Admiralty chart, "Anchorages on the Coast of Novaya Zemlya", and some way south of Matochkin was shown a small anchorage in a bay, the entrance to which was partially obstructed by a reef marked "Extending 1935". We decided to take a chance and anchor there for a few hours so that all hands could have a break from action-stations. We approached the bay cautiously at a very slow speed, taking cross bearings by gyro, when suddenly the ship shuddered and came to a standstill—we were on the reef. At that very moment the lookout aft sighted an aircraft some distance south of us flying towards the land—it disappeared behind the hills as we sounded action-stations again.

'Careful checking of our position showed that according to the chart we *should* have been in $17\frac{1}{2}$ fathoms of water, but the fact remained that, looking over the bow, the reef with all its colours and waving weeds could easily be seen.'

They had to pump all available water and oil overboard, shift cargo and all hands go aft as the main engine was run full astern, but it was an agonizing seven hours before the ship finally came off the reef at high tide, as a result of the persistent efforts of Chief Engineer Hughes. The fact that her forepeak was filled with concrete saved the ship's bows from being ripped open. Once off the reef they could see daylight through the bottom of the forepeak and tried unsuccessfully to plug it, but they were in no immediate danger, the bulkhead being strong and well shored up for ice.

Thankfully during these pretty hopeless hours there had been no return of the mystery aircraft. Captain Harvey, having had enough of improperly charted anchorages now decided to steam on boldly down the coast and risk an all-out dash to the White Sea. By next morning, July 7, they had forged on without further incident well down the coast of Novaya Zemlya's south island when they sighted a ship ahead. She appeared to be another merchant survivor from the convoy and by 8 a.m. they were slowly gaining on her.

Chief Officer Leech: 'The captain and myself had been continuously on the bridge for the past nine days, taking only occasional sit-down seats in the chartroom, and now with the weather fine, the sea smooth and all seemingly peaceful, Captain Harvey suggested I should go down to his cabin for a quick wash and breakfast, then relieve him to do the same. But I had only been down five minutes when I got an urgent message to return to the bridge. The captain asked me to take a good look at the other ship now about six miles ahead; she had turned broadside on to us and he thought she looked a bit odd. I took the telescope and saw at once that she was down by the head, apparently sinking (we discovered afterwards that she was the *Alcoa Ranger*). I then spotted close to the ship three U-boats on the surface—and the white bow wave from one of them as it made full speed towards us. We immediately went hard-a-port and showed our stern—we thought that if they came close enough we could make use of our twelve-pounder aft. As we steamed back north at full speed the problem now was where to go!'

They again studied the Admiralty chart and decided to try and enter Moller Bay, well south of Matochkin.

'We gathered from the chart that there was a small Russian settlement there called Mali Karmakulski Stansovische, and it looked as if there was just sufficient room in the bay for the ship to swing to anchor, though the entrance to it was extremely difficult, quite narrow with a right-angled turn to be made. But Captain Harvey said he would sooner put the ship ashore trying to escape rather than be sunk by the enemy, and I agreed. So a few hours later we reached the approach to the bay, and with the bosun up forward with the leadline, made the turn successfully and anchored right up in the middle.'

A launch came out from the settlement carrying some officials, but there was no difficulty in *Empire Tide* identifying herself for among her passengers was a Russian naval officer who spoke perfect English. There were about fifty people in the settlement, families who made a living by hunting and collecting duck eggs which they sent to the mainland. They were a hospitable crowd and agreed to radio Archangel and report the ship's arrival, also asking for medical help for the wounded gunner. Unless enemy aircraft found them now, *Empire Tide*'s company of sixty-six were safe for a while.

Farther south down the coast two lifeboats of men from *Olopana* had stumbled ashore, the survivors in one of them luckily finding a tiny Russian trading post. The other contingent, beaching more to the north, found an open timber lighthouse in which they sheltered. They had not been there long when to their surprise they awoke from exhausted sleep to see a ship stranded offshore. She was the *Winston Salem*. The American vessel had withstood several enemy attacks only to run hard aground on a sandbank while pulling in close to the island coast in the thick weather. Soon some of her crew came ashore with tins of food and boat stores, and the fortunate men from *Olopana* were taken aboard and given a chicken dinner and some warm clothing.

Winston Salem could not be kedged off the sandbank and her

crew, fearing air attack, decided to set up permanent camp on
the beach for safety. They were unloading more stores on to the
beach when a plane came over and caused high panic, the ship's
gunners having dismantled her light guns, but it was only a Russian Catalina. Flying low it dropped a note to say it had picked
up other *Olopana* survivors and would return. After some time
it did so, flying more *Olopana* men up to the *Empire Tide* in
Moller Bay.

Winston Salem remained stuck fast, though her misfortune
proved a godsend to others. First, some men from the torpedoed
Hartlebury. The thirteen men on Gunner Arthur Carter's raft,
shielding themselves from the cold with a canvas screen, had
paddled for two and a half days on a desolate sea before sighting
a lifeboat ahead.

'It was the captain's lifeboat from our own ship. In it there
had originally been thirteen men, but eight had died before we
reached her and been put over the side. A ninth man had just
died but no one had the strength to haul him over the side until
we got into the boat. He was a big, blond Swede. In dying he
had slid between the seats and we had the devil of a job to free
him. I'm afraid there was no ceremony, just over the side; I
remember the great big hole he made in the sea. We all got into
the boat with the remaining four men, abandoned the raft and
set sail.

'The first mate from our raft was the only officer in the boat
and despite an injured arm he *was* good. Half the crew were
put to rowing, the other half rubbing the feet of the rowers. It
was awkward but we did our best, and what was important, we
were all kept moving. After half a day in the boat we sighted
Novaya Zemlya and eventually reached the shore. First thing
we did on landing was to make a fire to dry ourselves out, then
the mate split us into two groups, one to search for wood or
anything burnable to keep the fire going, the other to look for
anything eatable. Two birds were caught and a few birds' eggs
found. The birds were obviously not afraid of us—they just sat
there and let us take them. Their feathers seemed to come off as
a kind of skin, but they were birds all right. We made a stew,

filling a biscuit tin with snow and putting bits of the birds in when it melted. We also made a tent from the lifeboat sails.

'While our scavenging parties were out we left three men by the fire. One was a young seaman with frostbite in both feet; we had nothing and could do nothing except try to comfort him. However, while he was alone for a short time this lad put his feet in the fire—to warm them, he said, and when we returned to camp they looked terrible, like two big balloons of raw meat. Later he had both legs amputated in Archangel.

'Our parties worked away from the fire in ever widening circles, and the wider we got the higher we got, which is how we came to see a column of smoke rising a long way off. It *had* to be a ship, so we decided to row along the coast to her. This meant crossing a large bay and rounding a headland, and in the event the tide was too strong for us, but the ship saw our difficulty and sent a lifeboat to help. And so we found the *Winston Salem* aground—and they certainly made us welcome. As we got up the rope ladders and over the side, one of the crew was calling "Coffee this side, tea over there!" In a big saloon were two long tables heaped with eatables, a coffee urn on one table and tea on the other. The ship seemed crammed already with survivors. Her crew scrounged us some clothes; how they had anything left surprised me, as the ship was so packed we had to go ashore again. But camping preparations had been under way for some time and all sorts of stores had been put ashore including tents and plenty of blankets, while cases of eggs had been buried in the snow. Three cooks stood on the beach, each with a tin barrel made into a makeshift stove. They were cooking flapjacks, which smelt great, and there was a large tin of molasses. It was a case of help yourself—you just joined the queue, anyone, and went round until you had had enough.

'After living with the Americans for five days we were sighted by a Russian Catalina, which dropped a message to say that help was coming.'

And still more men came in from the sea to the *Winston Salem*.

In the early stages of their long haul across the Barents Sea the two lifeboats of survivors from S.S. *Washington,* rowing through heavy ice floes, icebergs and fog suddenly came upon a motionless ship smoking and burning fiercely. They pulled close and read the name on the stern—*Pankraft*. Knowing that the fire must eventually reach the abandoned ship's cargo of explosives they rowed quickly away and stayed on course for Novaya Zemlya. Limbs were cramped, numb and sore by now, but nothing could be done about this except for the men to take regular exercise at rowing. Captain Richter:

'We were not only plagued with cold weather and ice but came upon a school of whales who insisted on being playful and swam dangerously close to the boats, following along with us for hours. Luck was with us that they did not venture to dive under and capsize the boats. When the weather occasionally changed we took full advantage of favourable winds and hoisted sail, giving the crew a rest from rowing and some much needed sleep under what little cover the lifeboats afforded.

'We kept close count of the lapsing days by our watches. On the tenth day the weather cleared and we were joyfully rewarded for our efforts when ahead on the horizon there loomed the white snow-capped mountains of Novaya Zemlya—it gave us all renewed hope and courage. As land was still a good day's rowing away the crews of both boats now set to with renewed vigour and we found a favourable landing cove along the beach. By dead reckoning I estimated we had landed just south of Matochkin Strait. The coast was uninhabited, desolate and barren.

'The crew were soon busy building huge bonfires from logs and driftwood, and we lay down to sleep and rest near the fires. Some men suffering from frostbite gained a little relief after vigorous exercise. Sea birds, ducks and geese were plentiful and with good revolver marksmanship the crew managed to bag some much needed food. While we were camped on the beach enemy reconnaissance planes circled the area to investigate, apparently attracted by our bonfires and smoke, but they did not bother us in any way. After three days of recuperation on the beach we broke camp and took to the lifeboats again. Keeping close to the shore we headed south, hoping to find a Russian fishing village, but we ran into dense fog and with a stiff in-shore breeze it took our utmost efforts to keep the lifeboats from being blown ashore against the rocks. Next day the wind sub-sided and as the weather cleared we saw two other lifeboats ahead. They were from the Dutch *Paulus Potter*. The captain and some of the crew were suffering from severe frostbite, unable to walk and badly needing medical aid. The boats' joined up with us and we carried on rowing southward together. Some time the following day, through the light fog and haze, we sighted a ship close in to the beach and pulling to her we found she was the *Winston Salem*, hard aground. Soon we were aboard and being treated to our first hot coffee since abandoning the S.S. *Washington. . . .'*

Winston Salem's captain was now awaiting a favourable high tide and the promised assistance of two Russian tugs to pull his vessel free. He had learned of *Empire Tide's* safe anchorage to the north and was expecting two Russian trawlers to pass by *Salem*; these were persuaded to take the *Washington* and *Paulus Potter* men and others up to the British ship.

So it was that one of the trawlers steamed into Moller Bay carrying well over a hundred American, British and Dutch survivors, including some from *Alcoa Ranger*, and towing five lifeboats. What with other men flown in by the Catalina the CAM ship was now crowded to capacity and hard put to stretching out her fast diminishing food stocks to provide rations for more than two hundred men; she had only been stored up with three months' supplies for her crew and had been obliged to dig well into these while waiting a month at Hvalfiord for the convoy to sail. To eke out the rations some American sur-vivors went ashore and caught ducks. There were thousands of the birds and unsuspecting victims were caught quite easily while nesting by means of a long noose on the end of a pole. The birds, which had a distinctly fishy flavour, were scarcely a delicacy, but they made a change from beans and spam. Other Americans went off in a small sailing boat to the *Winston Salem*, returning two days later with a thousand tins of spam and fourteen bags of brown pinto beans. Oddly enough most men seemed to thrive on the weird diet, putting on weight.

The ship kept constant gun-watch, some survivors also taking a turn to ease the hours of the crew. Twice enemy planes flew over the little bay and although they did not attack, most of the American survivors decided it was too dangerous to stay on board ship and so went off and camped ashore. The very ill were cared for in the settlement's small hut hospital, help for them arriving eventually in the form of a Russian Catalina. Everything moveable, including guns, had been taken out of the plane to make more room for the casualties, and some of the worst cases were loaded on and flown off under the care of a woman doctor.

Besides the low food stocks shortage of water now became a worry, and with the ship's tanks running perilously low Bosun Bill Medhurst, with the aid of the ship's carpenter, decided to try tapping a stream that ran down into the sea. 'I built a dam of sorts, inserting a five-gallon oil can to which we had fixed a fire hose. We then ran the hose down to a steel lifeboat which had been well scrubbed out, filled the boat with the crystal clear water and rowed it back to the ship to be pumped up by a fire pump. We had two days of this, two very uncomfortable days; it was no fun rowing a boat with icy water lapping one's behind!'

But it helped to top up the ship's freshwater tanks and it was at this moment in their long, frustrating wait at Moller Bay that suddenly one afternoon *La Malouine* appeared at the narrow entrance, asked how the hell *Empire Tide* had got into the the bay and said she would be back in the morning to escort her to join a convoy to Archangel.

Bosun Medhurst: 'Never was the sight of a warship more welcome! Away went the feeling of being abandoned and there was jubilation throughout the ship. Back came the men who had been living ashore to be housed in one of our 'tween decks. We collected all the lifeboats, hoisted them up to the rail level, leaving them hanging secured that way, hoisted anchor and away we went. Imagine our surprise when we got outside to find five other ships waiting. The naval vessels had rounded them up from farther along the coast. Some were a peculiar sight for they had splashed whitewash and white paint all over themselves from truck to water's edge. This camouflage may have helped them when they were anchored against the ice but at sea they stuck out like a sore thumb and they were asked to get the paint off quickly, though they could not really do much before we sailed.'

The strange white ships were the Americans *Silver Sword, Troubadour* and *Ironclad,* led by trawler *Ayrshire.* Their high adventure began up in the northern ice to which all had steamed after scattering. *Ayrshire,* commanded by Lieutenant Leo J. A. Gradwell, R.N.V.R., first headed north-west to Hope Island, but on meeting ice struck out north for the barrier edge. First Lieutenant Richard Elsden: 'After scatter we spliced the mainbrace, got the cook to make heaps of corned beef sandwiches, got up all the four-inch ammunition and stacked it around the gun. We then fixed depth charges and oil drums together with wire, setting the charges to go off at 50 to 60 feet below the surface, the idea being that if we could get under *Tirpitz*'s bows we would drop the things and they would go off like mines under her. All this helped to keep up morale.'

Soon, like bees round a honey-pot, the three merchantmen joined the little trawler, each anxious for naval support, and *Ayrshire* took them under her wing. Second Mate John Behnken of *Silver Sword:* 'On scattering we headed due north at our full speed of nine knots and after about twelve hours' steaming reached the icefield, where we joined *Troubadour, Ironclad* and the trawler. *Ayrshire*'s commander suggested that our four vessels should form a sort of square to give us the maximum defence against attack. It was then decided to steam right up into the ice as far as we could go.'

Captain George Salveson's *Troubadour,* with her strong ice-breaking bows, led the ships slowly into the icefield at 3½ knots until they had pushed twenty miles into it and were firmly entrenched with no open water visible on any side. First Lieutenant Elsden walked over the ice to the merchant ships to see how they were fixed for stores and ammunition. On one ship it struck him that the grey decks and cargo must stand out alarmingly from the air so he asked if they had much white paint, found they had, and suggested they should splash it all over the decks and cargo as fast as possible. On returning to *Ayrshire* he told Lieutenant Gradwell of his idea and Gradwell agreed that all ships should apply the same camouflage—on decks, cargo and starboard side only, as *Ayrshire*'s officers guessed that the Germans, with their work-to-rule methods, would not go north of them and sight their port sides.

Second Mate Behnken: 'On *Silver Sword* we painted the masts, most of the superstructure and the hull, then spread white bed linen over the whole of our deck cargo and the hatches. In the flat calm we had no need to secure the linen and there was an abundance of it, as there was of white paint, though we were short of everything else, including food. But the morale of our crew was always good, which may have been partly due to the fact that they were kept so busy.'

It was also decided that the merchant crews should sponge the grease from inside the gun barrels of the tanks carried on deck, and ready them for firing, breaking open the crates of tank ammunition. Some tanks were raised on the outboard sides to give the guns more elevation.

And so for the next two days, as SOS messages came in from the other ships being attacked all over the Barents Sea, the four vessels remained safely hidden in the ice, First Lieutenant Elsden frequently walking over to check that all was well on the merchantmen. Once they heard the reverberations in the ice as a ship was bombed just off the ice-barrier to the south—probably *Pankraft*—and *Ayrshire*'s officers discussed whether they should steam out and help, but they decided this would only give away the position of their three charges; so they stayed.

When the situation seemed to have quietened, the four ships broke out of the ice and steamed east alongside the barrier edge. Searching aircraft flew over them but thanks to a comforting fog the ships were not spotted and eventually reached the north island of Novaya Zemlya. They went into a bay some fifty miles north of Matochkin, where, as they lay up for twenty-four hours, *Ayrshire* took in fresh water from *Silver Sword*. They then steamed on to find Matochkin. *Ironclad* ran aground on the coast but *Ayrshire* managed to tow her off and at last on July 11 all reached the Strait.

Not knowing what their reception might be, *Ayrshire* sent a heavily-armed party in a whaleboat to contact the settlement. They included a man who spoke Polish; but in spite of his efforts, along with sign language, the Russians at first refused to radio another message to Archangel, though later they agreed to do so. Some measure of the heartfelt gratitude of the three merchant ships towards *Ayrshire* was when *Troubadour,* towering high above the trawler, showered her foc'sle with packets of cigarettes and chocolate—and presented her officers with a brand new coffee percolator.

In the Strait *Ayrshire* and her brood found the *Benjamin Harrison* and the damaged *Azerbaijan,* so all together formed quite a refugee fleet. *Ayrshire,* steaming a long way up the narrow Strait, found another tiny settlement, where she anchored. A Russian armed trawler appeared and the two ships tied up together, looking very much like twins. The Russian crew proved very friendly.

One small bedraggled party of survivors were especially glad of the late arrivals at Matochkin. These were more men of the *Paulus Potter,* who had struggled along the coast until coming to a small Russian weather station; the Russians, after feeding them with salmon and black bread, took them up the Strait to join *Silver Sword.*

Commodore Dowding's rescuing corvettes arrived at Matochkin on July 20. A Russian icebreaker, the *Murman,* had now joined the ships there and Dowding decided to lead the return convoy in her, as she would be able to force a passage if they encountered strong ice. All ships headed south at once and it was as well they did, for the next day a U-boat arrived at the Strait and, thwarted at everyone having flown, shelled the settlement.

The convoy, after picking up *Empire Tide,* went on to the *Winston Salem* but had to leave her, for she was still firmly aground, with two Russian tugs standing by. Then on south-wards towards the Russian coast. . . .

Pozarica and other escorts went out from Archangel to meet the remnant convoy as it approached the White Sea, but except for some U-boat alarms, what could have been the most dangerous journey of all was entirely uneventful. There was, however, one disconcerting incident involving the *Murman*. When the U-boat alarm was given the icebreaker, much to the astonishment and anger of Commodore Dowding, instantly cracked on speed and high-tailed it away from the slow moving convoy, returning only when the danger had passed.

We saw them come into Archangel late on July 24, the incongruous sight of *Ayrshire* leading her three merchantmen, all still coloured a dazzling white. The battered *Winston Salem* lumbered in four days later, her final rescue from the sand-bank being achieved as a result of the efforts of the U.S. Naval Attaché in Archangel, Commander Sam Frankel, who flew out to her in a Catalina. *Salem*'s captain suffered a nervous break-down.

And now came the reckoning. A total of twenty-two merchantmen had been lost: fifteen American, six British and one Dutch—plus a rescue ship and a British fleet tanker. Twenty-four ships, together with equipment and supplies enough for a whole vast army lay at the bottom of the Barents Sea. So far as was yet known, some three hundred men had died or were missing, or had been taken prisoner; two captains at least had been captured and two others had died. The marvel of the disaster was that the loss of life had not been far greater, but there were many broken men, more yet who would die as a result of their ordeal, many who would lose limbs or parts of them; some, paralyzed from the waist down, who had to be carried everywhere.

All this, yet the *Tirpitz*, the menace from which we had so desperately fled, had never at any time proved more than a threat on a signal pad.

9

The Hungry Wait

The massacre of PQ 17 caused the Admiralty first to postpone and then to cancel the sailing date of the next convoy, PQ 18, which had originally been expected to leave Iceland towards the end of July. It was decided that PQ 18 could not run the same risks as ourselves and would have to wait until an aircraft carrier escort could be spared or winter darkness returned; or both.

At Archangel we knew nothing of these discussions going on behind the scenes more than 2,000 miles away. We anticipated being at Archangel for not more than two weeks—our supplies had been geared to this plan. Instead, as the days and weeks dragged by, what had been an interesting experience, meeting the Russians, turned to a time of extreme boredom and frustration as we waited impatiently for the return home. We knew that PQ 18 must sail first as it was the practice for each return convoy to cross the outward bound one.

Some escorts kept busy with turns of sea duty, but the trawlers generally remained idle. A projected Barents Sea patrol for *Lord Austin* did not materialize; the corvettes did it instead, for as there was an acute shortage of coal in Russia it was thought best that we should hold on to our small supplies for the eventual homeward run. And so after a much needed refit, continual topping up of coal and painting ship became the daily duty.

Life was not helped by the suspicious Russian guards on the

jetties who caused many upsets among the Allied seamen. When *Empire Tide* got to her unloading berth the spare lifeboats she carried had to be put in the water and tied to the quay. After unloading she shifted half a mile to a new berth, and Bosun Medhurst took four men along the quay to collect the boats, but they were confronted by two guards with tommy guns. Every time the seamen attempted to man the boats the guns were pushed in their way, so they finally had to leave them.

The guards seemed to object to any contact between our various ships. A whaleboat from *Palomares* went upriver to collect some tinned corn from a merchantman to supplement the wardroom stores. On its return the crew were not allowed out of the boat until an interpreter was called and explained their 'indiscreet behaviour'. The petty incidents, all too numerous, were made more difficult by the language barrier. A Russian woman sentry wanted to bayonet the number one of a corvette who tried to get ashore. A gunnery officer of *Palomares* was arrested and held prisoner for a night because he went near some guns carrying a small suitcase—inside the case was a pair of shoes he had been trying to get mended. Signalman Blamey from the same ship was refused exit from the jetty simply because he was carrying a book. It happened to be the life of Cecil Rhodes of all things, and despite its being bound in red the zealous sentry treated it with great suspicion. Once Blamey had given the book to a colleague to take back to the ship all was well and he was allowed to pass.

Ashore, authority ruled everywhere. We saw the deference paid to the green-capped Commissars; old men, women and children, all that seemed left of the civilian population, stepped off the wooden pavements when these officials walked by. But there was no giving way when green caps and Allied blue caps edged past each other *on* the planks.

In the hot weather it was impossible to quench one's thirst when ashore. Beer was unobtainable, the water not fit for drinking without first boiling, vodka was definitely not a thirst-quencher—and the Russian tea simply made one more thirsty. Men actually returned to their ships long before they needed to, just to be in time for the evening cup of char. Surgeon-Lieutenant McCallum raised cheers on *Zamalek* when he managed to distill some beer and spirits from the barley and yeast they could spare.

The combination of lack of mail, growing shortage of food, the surfeit of heat, mosquitoes and coaling was beginning to tell and brought morale to a new low level; the defaulters' tables were well attended. In every ship the unchanging diet of corned beef in all its various forms—cooked, souped, sandwiched, or served just as it was; the watery stews with their 'find-the-meat' quiz; the everlasting starchy rice, which gave the men diarrhoea; all added to the general gloom, and no man thought he would ever be able to look a rice pudding in the face again. If only there had been some potatoes and green vegetables to vary the meagre rations, but all that was offered in lieu of greens were tiny pills to prevent an outbreak of scurvy.

Three minesweepers which had been in Russian waters for six months should also have gone back to Britain with us and they were perilously low in stores. *Pozarica* helped them out, as she did other ships, and her own company found themselves eventually living on hard-tack—corned beef and biscuits. They notched the date, August 5. A/B Walter Edgley: 'Biscuits, too, were gradually reduced in quantity until four biscuits a day was each man's ration. There was no bread, and tea was an interesting meal with everyone nibbling at their biscuit or biscuits.'

Poppy, doing constant patrols and rescue work, had no bread or meat and her crew also had to live on hard-tack. The Russians did give them dried fish but it was so hard they could not eat it. So on patrol they exploded depth charges to kill fresh fish, much to their mortification on one occasion raising only three fish with one hopeful charge.

We found the Russian bread salty, sour and uneatable, so on *Austin* our cook was forced to bake every day, despite his strong protestations that he had never been taught how. The daily bread ration, so long as it lasted, was two rounds per man, and woe betide the messman who did not cut those rounds in equal thickness. On *Salamander,* in response to desperate appeals, their assistant cook said he could bake; but he forgot to add the yeast, and each mess was served with a loaf of bread like a brick. Stoker Thomas McClements: 'A scouse seaman came to the rescue. He had done a bit in a bakehouse as a lad. His effort turned out a treat. There were two D.S.M.'s sent to the ship for her part played in the convoy, one for the officers, one for the crew. We voted unanimously for this chap to receive the crew's medal—we should have been lost without his knowledge.'

Coxswain Kerslake of *Northern Gem* had to make the ferry trip to Archangel almost every day to try to forage food. 'We were down to tea with no milk and sugar, hard biscuits and pusser's peas. We had flour but no yeast, so we could not bake bread. I never had any success with either British or Russians in Archangel, so we eventually pulled a whaleboat up and down the Dvina, calling on any merchant ship we saw, begging what we could here and there; and luckily from an American ship we managed to get some yeast. What a joy to taste fresh bread again!'

One afternoon with great ceremony two Russians brought a sack of green vegetables on board *Gem* and excitedly her crew looked forward to fresh cooked greens with the next day's dinner. 'Alas, after half an hour the Russians were back, this time with a guard, and said they had put the sack on the wrong ship, and that it should have gone to one of the minesweepers which had been working from Archangel for so long. We thought it rather funny, but our mouths were watering all the same.'

There was another comedy later on, and with a better finish to it. News came through of the Canadians' landing at Dieppe. The delighted Russians thought this was the 'second front' they had all been waiting for, and to *Palomares* a deputation appeared with a gift of yak meat, while two other Russians boarded *Pozarica* importantly with a sack of cabbages. Next day when the news came that the Dieppe forces were being evacuated the Russians reappeared for their yak and cabbages, explaining they had been delivered by mistake and should have gone to Russian ships farther along the quay. They were out of luck—both meat and greens had been speedily disposed of!

Of course our privations were small compared to those the Russians themselves were enduring. An example of this was when on *Austin* we had the small job of running some stores from one place to another along the river. Among the stores were some barrels of flour. The working party of Russians looked very emaciated—perhaps they were political prisoners. The barrels were of poor quality and when they had been hoisted aboard there was a mound of flour left on the jetty. As soon as the armed guard had driven away in their lorry and we had cast off, the poor devils in the working party threw themselves on the mound and stuffed the flour into their mouths as fast as they could. What they could not eat then they pushed into the pockets of their tunics. We wondered what the guards would have done if they had seen them at it. Would they have been shot out of hand, as had happened to others caught pocketing food on the quays?

Three of the navy's fastest destroyers arrived from home. The *Martin*, *Marne* and *Middleton* had made a quick, dangerous dash across the Barents Sea packed jam-full with ammunition, stacked out with four-inch shells even on the upper deck. This ammunition, with gun barrels to replace those on which the rifling had gone, was badly needed by the ack-ack ships for the return journey. The destroyers also brought medical supplies and some stores, though these did little to alleviate our food problems. After the first flutter at the destroyers' arrival, which it was hoped was a sign of our early return, it was soon evident that this was not to be and the tedium of life on the Dvina resumed.

One day, to the accompaniment of great cheers from the banks, the huge Russian submarine *Red Star* glided up river. This was the vessel said to have put two torpedoes into the *Tirpitz*, a claim later rejected by the Admiralty. Two Russian destroyers, their multi-coloured camouflage laid on in cubist designs, anchored near to *Austin*'s berth. They bristled with ack-ack guns, the odd layout of which gave one the impression that these had simply been wheeled aboard and left on deck. All the same, the ships had a very businesslike air about them; like the Russian trawlers, whose ack-ack armament put us to shame.

Admiral Stefanov, the Russian C-in-C of the White Sea Fleet went by in his ultra-modern launch, a be-flagged vessel with burnished brass gleaming against a background of shining white. The funnel was its crowning glory; wide and oval-shaped, it leaned back at an incredible angle. Stefanov inspected *Pozarica*'s company. An old man but very firm, he made a powerful speech with much hand waving. They would be returning home and coming east again with more supplies for the glorious Red Army, he told them through his interpreter. 'See to it that you have an aircraft carrier with your convoy to protect it. . . .'

The British admiral who accompanied Stefanov told the company they were not forgotten, a sentiment received rather dubiously by us all. When, just before the Dieppe landing, Churchill visited Moscow it was hoped there might be an improvement in our beggarly situation, but nothing happened. The state of the war still remained critical for our hosts. We were relieved to hear that on the Murmansk front things remained static, but elsewhere the Russians were hard-pressed. One strong rumour which caused a near-panic for a time was that Russia had capitulated, and that we should have to look slippy to get out before the Germans arrived.

By this time, with the object of keeping us all active, an orgy of sport had begun. Before we had played nothing, now we played everything. We found ourselves down for soccer after dinner; and after tea, rugger, cricket or a weird form of hockey, using a wooden square puck, all played on the wooden-planked quay. In the evening there was shooting and boat-pulling, and sessions of swimming in the log-laden Dvina, with the added excitement of trying to miss the submerged logs as you dived in. There was, besides, a Russian Army assault course near the ships and the Russians had no objection to some of the sailors joining them on it. The Russian recruits here were a ragged bunch, their ages ranging from sixteen to sixty, but all held themselves well

and sang roundly on the march, though with strangely emotion-
less faces.

There was at first a certain enthusiasm for the various sports,
but as the days went by it became too much of a good thing;
and because of our diet we found we were none too fit. For
Lord Austin the situation was saved by our moving to another
berth, where sports broke out again but in a much milder and
more enjoyable form. More importantly, when it was decided to
row our contesting teams over to a nearby island to play their
fixtures we had the extreme good luck of being able to obtain
some potatoes, our first for many weeks. They cost us nearly all
our spare woollen comforts in barter, but we could have assured
the knitters they had never been put to better use.

Others made their own luck. Sub-Lieutenant Brooke of *Poppy* :

'Our Number One mounted an expedition to get some potatoes and one night several officers from the corvettes, clad in
dark jerseys and gymshoes, rowed downstream with muffled
oars to a field alongside the river which we had previously recon-
noitred. We knew it contained potatoes, and that it was guarded
by armed sentries who patrolled the dykes which kept the river
out. Choosing our time carefully, we crawled over the dyke
and down in among the potato plants; then, keeping flat on our
stomachs, we wriggled down the rows, burrowing in with our
hands to get the potatoes without disturbing the plants. We
stayed as long as we dared, then scurried back to the boat with
our spoils in a sack. It was not a great quantity of vegetables but
Queen Elizabeth couldn't have enjoyed Raleigh's potatoes more.'

One mess on *Pozarica,* after many weeks, also managed to
get a brief taste of the now highly prized and almost non-
existent vegetable. By scraping the barrel absolutely they gathered
together sufficient cigarettes and chocolate from their small ration
to barter for enough potatoes to give them a couple of expensive
but glorious meals.

Meanwhile many of the survivors billeted in Archangel were
living on black bread, grass soup and barley, and, where fortunate, the inevitable corned beef. They were given Russian
tobacco too, when available, though they found this to be like

birdseed and it would not roll. But at least it burned—using newspaper and toilet rolls for cigarette papers—and was better than the dried tea leaves which some men were reduced to smoking. The American survivors in particular found it hard to adjust themselves to the spartan food and conditions, only the Chinese seamen fully retaining their poise and manners. The survivors who were not hospitalized had little to do with their time except to sit in the International Club or find themselves girl friends, and many found regular sleeping partners, as did some naval officers who 'went native' and lived with girls ashore. For the naval men generally this other side of life varied from a number of steady romantic partnerships with Russian girls to such pathetic episodes as that involving a Russian woman who came down to one of the jetties every night. Aged about sixty, her face lined and worn, she stood in a little alcove in the logs where she received her customers. All she asked by way of payment was a few squares of chocolate or two or three cigarettes.

The American survivors, understandably restless and impatient, and with the disaster of PQ 17 festering ever more strongly among them, sent representatives to the U.S. Naval Attaché in Archangel, Commander Frankel, demanding better living conditions and a decision on when they would be going back to the States, but there was little he could do on that score. He did, however, hold meetings to tell them of the war's progress. At one of these meetings they learned that the enemy had known the name and details of every ship of the convoy. Furthermore, it was claimed that in one instance the crew of an enemy seaplane had landed and boarded an abandoned ship (long afterwards a U-boat commander also claimed to have boarded the *Paulus Potter,* which for a whole week drifted through the ice floes like a phantom ship, and found her secret codebooks together with a complete list of the ships in the convoy).

Since our arrival Archangel had been remarkably free from the attentions of the Luftwaffe, but as short periods of darkness in the night hours returned, the enemy resumed his bombing attacks. We had often wondered what the result might be of a full-scale incendiary attack on this city of wood—where it seemed just by shaking hands with its people you risked getting a splinter in your palm. Even the high air-raid towers from which women kept watch were built of timber, and the fire-fighting apparatus we had seen looked as if it had strayed from the set of an old comic film.

But although the first raid lasted for five hours and huge fires were started, the town was not burnt out. It was sheer man and woman power that saved it, and the closeness of the river. Everyone not actually bed-ridden turned out to lend a hand. No one sheltered, for the simple reason that there *were* no shelters. Hundreds of troops were brought in by ferry and tram from the surrounding villages, and the women worked alongside the men as Russian women always do. Next day Archangel looked very much like its usual self. A second big raid again produced great fires, and we had to keep our hoses going to protect the decks and the adjoining quay; yet the result was much the same. Some fires burned for two days after, but the actual amount of damage was surprisingly well contained. The methods of ensuring this were ruthless; to stop fires spreading all intervening obstacles were systematically demolished. On one occasion this brought an unwelcome surprise for some of the Allied survivors who willingly pitched in with the Russian fire-fighters.

Third Officer Phillips of *Aldersdale*: 'One particular hut was on a piece of waste ground between two blazing rows of houses. Harries, our chief sparks, and myself recruited some Russians and armed ourselves with a telegraph pole. Harries, being the heftiest, took the leading end of the battering ram, and I the rear, with some Russian volunteers between us. With a whooroo we charged the offending hut, with a view to immediate demolition. Unfortunately the side which presented itself to our assault was the opening one, and as the butt struck the door it flew open and Harries swept inside followed by two of the Russians. A blasphemous yell, silence, and then the emergence of three dripping figures. It had been the communal loo for the surrounding houses. It took hours of nakedness on the banks of the Dvina to get rid of the debris and smell.'

Big news came at last with the arrival at Murmansk of U.S.S. *Tuscaloosa*. The fast cruiser had steamed from the Clyde with three destroyers, all carrying stores, and *Tuscaloosa* also brought a medical unit which, because of the Russians' severe shortage of medical supplies, was aimed to establish a base hospital to look after convoy survivors. 'Operation Dudley' this unit was called, but it was a flop. The Russians, for vague reasons of suspicion, jealousy and pride, refused to allow the unit to land on the ridiculous grounds that the men did not have a visa. The unit was finally put aboard *Zamalek,* but the medical men wanted to return home with naval ships, and so all except one sick berth petty officer quit the rescue ship, taking their stores with them. This was a blow for Surgeon-Lieutenant McCallum, who could well have done with the men and their help on the return journey later.

However, *Tuscaloosa*'s mission was also one of repatriation, and she brought blessed earlier release for many survivors, who were taken to Murmansk to join her. Twelve fortunate American merchant crews were taken aboard after the survivors had drawn lots. Among the crews taken from Archangel by a destroyer were those from the *Washington*, who left three men behind in hospital, and the *John Witherspoon*. Ferocious O'Flaherty:

'I never knew that an American destroyer could look so beautiful until we saw her swing round a jetty towards us. This was the first we had seen of the U.S. Navy since they had left us in the Barents Sea. They tied up just long enough to drop a board across the dock while we scurried over it; we were told that another destroyer had gone before us with the litter cases.

'Before long we were swinging round into the harbour of Murmansk. Here we saw more naval ships. All but one were at anchor, with *Tuscaloosa* dominating the scene as the largest. They did look good to us. We had been on the run from the Germans for so long that it was encouraging to see the ships feeling safe enough to lie at anchor.

'Going aboard *Tuscaloosa* was like entering a luxury hotel after the plain fare at Archangel. Plenty of sailors were on hand to help carry the weak and limbless aboard. Even those of us who were ambulant were apologetically offered help. We knew that this ship was among those which had to obey the order to leave us, and accepted the regret that was so obvious in their faces. . . .'

The Germans broadcast the news of *Tuscaloosa*'s mission to Murmansk; how many men she was repatriating and where she was bound. This precise knowledge of Allied ship movements no longer caused any surprise. Nor was there any substantial fear that *Tuscaloosa* would be attacked in her mercy work, for it was the merchant ships laden with war materials that remained the enemy's prime target. Nevertheless, Shads followed the cruiser and her destroyer escorts across the Barents Sea, and bombers also appeared, though they kept their distance.

And so in this last week of August, with *Tuscaloosa* gone, still we were stranded impatiently at Archangel, along with the hundreds of remaining survivors. Rumours began to circulate about our impending return and we hoped devoutly that they were genuine, for we did not want to remain to be frozen up for the winter, as had more than one Allied ship the previous year. With the last blaze of hot summer upon the wooden city, the river still flooding and ebbing fast with the tide, the bright cotton frocks of the girls, and the insatiable mosquitoes, it required a strong effort of the imagination to picture the scene blanketed in snow and ice, the river stilled to a frozen sheet of ice across which people walked. But the sight of skis and sleighs left lying about, the immensely thick jackets and trousers worn for working dress, the double thickness of walls and windows of all buildings, and the way in which the faces of the people clouded over when they spoke of the coming 'vinter'; all these things made one realize that the smiling summer face must soon give way to the hard, grim and bitter visage of the Arctic winter.

Another constant reminder came from the orphaned children living among the logs on the quay, who begged and wheedled from us every spare piece of woollen clothing. Some of these children were 'adopted' by the ships, fed and clothed by them. *Lord Austin* had two, Nina and Freddie—at least he told us this was his name. They were bright, intelligent children but much older in mind than their English counterparts.

Nina was a very composed and self-possessed little girl with a look in her dark eyes which made you feel she was always laughing at you. Freddie was talkative.

'Comerad Pa-ule, you have the woolly for Freddie—scarf, cap, sock, jersey?'

'But it's too hot for woollies, Freddie.'

'Da, da, but ven the vinter he comes . . . Brrrrr!'

He would stamp his feet and huddle up, shivering. He was difficult to resist until we found that he had already obtained enough woollens to clothe about ten children for the 'vinter'.

Nina and Freddie were fed by our crew and given baths in the engine room when the Chief was absent. Alf, one of the stokers, became their foster-father. The skipper refused to allow them to sleep aboard so we used to smuggle them over after dark. We all became very attached to them.

Dianella 'adopted' a seven-year-old called Woolfga. They re-named him Vodka, made him a little P.O.'s suit with the proper badges, and a hammock, and gave him a bosun's whistle so that he could go around the corvette in high glee piping the routine. He always ate with the crew. Before we left, *Dianella* made many efforts to adopt Vodka officially, but all in vain.

By the end of August morale reached its lowest point. Sports and practically all activities had long collapsed; even the sailors' saving pastime, tombola, which had been played from ship to ship, came to an end when the supplies of tombola tickets ran out. Everything had lost its shine. Visits to Archangel had long stopped, and there were fewer calls to the Intourist Club in the local village, the 'Welcome Inn' where officers and ratings drank together with no distinction of rank. Tempers had short-ened and needed the merest spark to explode. Then on August 28, a date few men there were likely to forget, a mine-sweeper near us flashed the electrifying signal: 'Come over if you want your mail!' There was none of the usual struggle to find a boat's crew. On *Austin* as in all ships that day, hours were spent reading and re-reading the first letters to reach us since leaving Iceland, and we blessed the girls' school which had adopted our little ship, for they had sent us a parcel of 2,000 cigarettes.

Ashore there were some poignant scenes as the survivors also received their mail, some of the frostbitten eagerly crawling for it on their hands and knees.

At last some supplies of food and NAAFI goods were circulated, and as the food improved, however slightly, so did men's spirits. Until finally there came the best news of all: our return convoy, QP 14, would soon be under way, for PQ 18 had sailed from Loch Ewe in Scotland on September 2. With an *aircraft carrier* among its heavy escorts.

The escort ships did some quick stock-taking and pooled their resources of stores and ammunition; some depth charges to that ship, some four-inch shells to the other, a few tins of milk and beef, and a bag or two of rice changed hands. For the hungry coal-burning trawlers it was time for a massive coal-up, and a bizarre one it turned out to be, without any of the crews dirtying their hands. Sturdy Amazons armed with shovels came aboard and trimmed the coal in the bunkers as it shot down the long chutes. Our skipper, his chivalry roused, sent a working party to help, but it was quickly made clear to us that we were not wanted, the laughing women merely pinching the Chief's backside and getting on with the job. On *Lord Middleton* they had quite an argument before it was made clear that the girls had been ordered to trim the coal—they had been sent from camp to work the ship for an extra couple of roubles. So *Middleton*'s men let the girls get on with it, rustling up a pot of soup for them; the girls were so hungry it seemed they might eat the pots and spoons too. The Russian coal was very poor stuff, almost dust and earth, and there were grave doubts whether it would keep the trawlers going at decent enough speed to keep up with the convoy; but all of us were determined to get the ships through if it meant doing shiftwork down the stokehold to keep the kettle boiling. The alternative, it was rumoured, was for the trawlers to be left to freeze into the ice for the winter and for us to be drafted into the Russian Army to fight on the

Murmansk front. We would get those ships home if we had to get out and push!

Final confirmation that we *would* be making the journey came when *Austin* was ordered to take on her quota of survivors, each ship of the return convoy having to carry a certain number. Many American seamen complained bitterly about returning in the small naval vessels, arguing that according to their articles they should be repatriated in a large liner or cruiser. They were bluntly told that they could take it or leave it; if they decided to stay they might have to remain till next spring. They took it. A great number of merchant men, both British and American, flatly refused to return in the merchant ships, so all the naval escorts were well loaded up. Our quota was fifteen men.

Under great secrecy *Austin* picked up her survivors at 3 a.m. from a deserted quayside. It was hard to part from Nina and Freddie but it had to be done, and they were in tears when they left. They and all the other adopted orphans went off to tell their friends about it. Consequently the whole of Archangel very soon knew that we were about to depart. So much for secrecy.

The ships' officers held a grand farewell party and got gloriously tight, one captain nearly following the steward into the river when returning aboard.

Sailing date was September 13. The previous day a rating of *La Malouine* broke his leg playing football and was treated on board *Zamalek*. Surgeon-Lieutenant McCallum: 'He was put in a plaster and a walking metal calliper splint applied to make him mobile. I told him it would keep him upright in the water anyhow, and he wryly replied, "Yes, but at what depth?" '

Zamalek's last passenger aboard was an American seaman from the *Samuel Chase*. This man had swum ashore as soon as his ship arrived in Russia and had been detained in a mental hospital. For the return convoy he was sent over to *Northern Gem*, but before *Gem* reached the point of convoy assembly the man had twice tried to jump over the trawler's side and had to be restrained and carried below by force. He would neither eat nor drink, and thought anyone offering him food was trying to poison him. If *Gem* got into action they could ill afford a rating to watch the man so they asked for his transfer to one of the other ships. And so he was taken to *Zamalek,* where surprisingly he rallied and proved a great help on board.

Left behind us at Archangel was the Walrus that *Palomares* towed half across the Barents Sea. Its radar set removed, it had finally been abandoned. Not before our Russian hosts had laid strong claim to it, as part compensation for our having failed to deliver 87 of the Spitfires expected from PQ 17. Another, more enterprising group of Russians, offered to buy it.

As *Austin* drew away from the quayside at Maimaksa a Russian rowing boat passed us slowly, struggling against the fast-flowing tide, a woman at the oars while two men reclined at ease in the stern sheets.

'*Do svidania,* Russia!'

10

The Final Toll

Sunday, September 13. It was a day of cold and wind and drizzle, with the first hard touch of winter upon it. But a glad day, as we steamed from Archangel after our enforced stay of two long months. Not even the prospect of bitter weather and more fierce battles with the Luftwaffe and U-boats in the next two weeks could mar our eager anticipation of home leave—for those who lived to enjoy it. Better to face the risk than to lie and rot in what had become a wooden prison.

QP 14's sixteen merchant ships included surviving vessels of PQ 17 together with others which had been awaiting a return convoy. They were mostly sailing light, though several carried exchange cargoes—and wood! One British ship, *Ocean Voice*, surprisingly had women and children among her passengers, the families of a Russian trade delegation to Britain; only Russian women would have contemplated making such a dangerous journey, and only Russian men let them. *Ocean Voice* had been the Commodore's ship of PQ 16. On that convoy she had had a great hole torn in her side by enemy bombs, but she had doused the fires and fought through. Now she was trim again and once more chosen as the lead ship, with Commodore John Dowding aboard. The convoy as it progressed settled into two columns with *Voice* leading one column and our friends on *Ocean Freedom* leading the other, with Captain Walker as Vice-Commodore.

Most of the other PQ 17 escorts were with us again; the ack-ack ships, the corvettes, our sister trawlers and the two rescue ships. There were, besides, two destroyers and three minesweepers new to us. The number of escorts, in fact, fully equalled the merchantmen, and soon we expected to have many more when warships from the approaching convoy PQ 18 would transfer to us after seeing their charges safely on the last lap to Russia.

The White Sea was unpleasantly choppy and the coal piled up on *Lord Austin*'s decks shifted dangerously. As we steamed north into the Barents Sea our only enemy was the weather; after our long spell of Russian summer it was hard to be flung back into severe Arctic conditions once more. Even harder for some of the lightly-loaded merchantmen tossing high in the water.

It seemed strange that these harsh waters could produce such an awe-inspiring spectacle as the aurora borealis or northern lights. The first hesitating white fingers would come groping over the horizon and then like giant searchlights stretch and stretch up in the sky, while smaller branches grew out from them and criss-crossed each other until the whole of the heavens was cut up into geometrical designs by their beams, sometimes achieving a display of the most marvellous colours. Many a sailor was held fascinated by the sight during the long night watches.

It was during a snowstorm and aurora borealis on our first night out of the White Sea that the *Winston Salem* ran into trouble. After her rough grounding on Novaya Zemlya she was now literally floating on her tank tops and during the lights her magnetic compass actually spun—she had no gyro—and she lost the convoy. All her master could do was to aim north and attempt to follow the stragglers' route along the edge of the icefields.

Soon afterwards the ancient coal-burning *Ironclad* was lagging badly. Escorts went back and fussed round her continually, but it was no use; she could not make any more knots. The convoy would slow down for an hour or two, then go on again at its normal speed and leave the lagging ship astern. At last it was decided that she must be left, and a minesweeper was detailed off to be her own special escort.

For the rest of us the first three days were fairly uneventful. Through the sub-zero weather, with its gales, snowstorms and black fog we did at least have the company of some friendly aircraft, first R.A.F. Hurricanes, and then Russian seaplanes and Catalinas. Now and then a Junkers 88 appeared, shadowing us from afar, but they gave no trouble and sheered off after gunfire from the escorts.

September 15 was a bleak day for *Pozarica's* company. On this date, in the bitter weather, the poor devils drank the last of their rum supply. We were lucky that our own stock, admittedly a weird mixture of rum and vodka, promised with care to last the journey. The first of *our* troubles concerned our batch of survivors. When they found themselves included in the watch-bill —the stokers to the stokehold, the seamen to the lookout and wheel—a deputation was sent to explain to our ignorant skipper that, under their articles, they were to be transported home as *passengers*. The skipper refused to see the deputation, informing them that under his own articles, in this ship every able-bodied man had to lend a hand in some way. When they then sent a message to him refusing to do any watches, the reply was brief and blunt: no watches, no meals. At this the belligerent 'strike' leader washed his hands of the whole business, declaring that no one was going to make him work against his will, and turned into his hammock, where he remained on the pretext of being ill. Of course, he got his food.

Our other fourteen 'guests', six of them coloured men, were a mixed bunch. Only three had been to sea before, while two others were cowboys who had never even seen the sea before PQ 17. A burly stoker who had served since the days of sail looked upon his fellows with undisguised contempt. He would sit round the fire with our crew and say loudly in presence of the others: 'Of course, they're just a bunch of cream puffs, this lot. I wouldn't have them sailing with me at any price. I like men—not puffs. But these are cream puffs, all right....'

Another old hand among them was a ship's carpenter, and he became their new leader and spokesman. This man could do any sort of job well and was willing to lend a hand anywhere above or below decks. He handled his crowd with tact and understanding and we found him a good companion either in the mess or on watch, for he combined unruffled good temper with a deep sense of humour.

One of the lighter moments during this quiet period was when some of the escorts began passing messages—firing them across by Costin gun or similar line-throwing apparatus. A minesweeper came up close on our starboard beam and fired her gun. The line which it shot, swept by the wind, caught round the firing lanyard of one of the PAC rockets on our bridge. The rocket, still tightly encased in its canvas covering, was triggered off. It staggered drunkenly out of its mounting and, belching flame and smoke, sailed horizontally straight for the sweeper. There were two sailors on her after gun platform and their mouths opened wide as this flaming comet bore down on them, landing plumb in the platform among all the ready-to-use shells. In an instant the two men were furiously ditching everything— rocket, shells, burning canvas and almost themselves.

An officer who took charge of the fire-fighting called across to us in one of those tired, naval sort of voices: 'Your aim is damn good, old boy!'

After all this the message was not for us—it was addressed to *Poppy*. Our skipper grabbed his loud-hailer and bawled at the other ship:

'I'm afraid you've given us the wrong message. We've got *Poppy*'s copy and *Poppy* must have our copy. We will send back *Poppy*'s copy for *Poppy* and *Poppy* will give your our copy. Stand by for *Poppy*'s copy!'

He had to repeat this twice until he was saying 'Copy's Poppy.' It was hysterically funny.

On September 16, our fourth day out, the convoy, now far up in the Barents Sea, ploughed on through heavy snowstorms and rolling banks of fog, passing many great icebergs. We were due to meet our big escorts after they detached from PQ 18 the next morning, and sure enough at midnight a white rocket was seen in the distance. In the early hours of the 17th they joined us, a formidable force led by Rear-Admiral Robert Burnett in the cruiser *Scylla*. There were no fewer than seventeen destroyers, which gave us a total of almost forty warships escorting the remaining fourteen merchantmen. But we had no eyes for the destroyers or the rest; it was one other vessel in that immense force that every man on QP 14 strained his eyes to see, and suddenly there she was, just over the horizon, looking exactly like a pudding basin; the aircraft carrier *Avenger*. Ugly she might be, this small 'Woolworth' carrier—the wags remarked that you had only to put a couple of taps on her and you had a bath. But to men chased, bombed and torpedoed over the length and breadth of the Barents Sea, the sight of her was pure joy. It was fascinating to watch the little black beetles crawling along her deck. So slow did they seem from a distance that one felt they must tip over into the sea. But no, each plane rose resolutely into the air, circled the mother ship and set course to the southward on patrol. It was odd to see them signalling to the carrier—the flash of its Aldis lamp seeming bigger than the plane itself, and giving the impression of a major twinkling star.

These reconnaissance planes were the reliable old string-bag Swordfish biplanes, but huddled together on the stern of the pudding basin was a wicked looking clump of fighters of the Sea-Hurricane type, specially designed for aircraft carrier use. It was the first time that many of us had seen anything resembling a Hurricane or Spitfire being sea-borne, and it gave us a feeling of tremendous confidence. *Avenger* took up station right in the centre of the convoy—another new departure in tactics which gave her maximum protection from torpedoes. But it was nerve-racking for the ships near to her when, in a terrific burst of speed, she turned into the wind to fly off her planes.

We had already had a number of U-boat alarms and depth charges had been dropped. The effect of these depth charge explosions on our survivors in *Austin* was alarming: most leapt immediately from their bunks in a state of near-panic. There were similar scenes in other escort vessels and on *Zamalek* every action-stations alarm created a special problem. The ship's hospital was full of sick members of the Dutch crew of the *Paulus Potter*, many suffering badly from frostbite and still losing toes and fingers. They were all huge men, and all had to be carried up on deck at an alarm—and carried back down afterwards.

The temperature dropped steadily and heavy snow continued to fall. We now had with us two fleet-oilers, who spent their time refuelling the warships which had come all the way from the U.K. without touching land. One of the oilers was an old friend of PQ 17, *Gray Ranger*, which had been forced to turn back when damaged by ice.

The convoy now kept up a fairly good speed of around eight knots and eventually we were in the region of Bear Island, scene of the big attack on our outward run. The Sword-fish, continually scouting for U-boats, could not stop us from being found by a shadowing Blohm and Voss. Destroyers in the vicinity had a few bangs at it, but it kept prudently just outside range. It was joined by two more, and for hours they dogged us. *Avenger* flew off more planes and a game of hide-and-seek developed. It was strange to see our planes on one side of the convoy and the enemy's on the other. But these Shads were very wary, and every time the carrier's planes went after them they carried out a great sweep to the opposite side of the con-voy. The sight of these skirmishing enemy planes was a rude eye-opener for a member of a Russian delegation being carried on *Ayrshire*; he had been supremely convinced that there was really no war going on outside the Soviet Union and that all planes were 'Americansky'.

Still no big air attack came, and the shadowers departed.

Next morning, September 19, the sun shone for the first time for many days and reflected in its rays we saw ahead what at first appeared to be another large iceberg, but it was land— Spitzbergen. That morning too one of our lost merchantmen unexpectedly returned to the fold. The *Winston Salem* had cracked on alone alongside the polar ice-edge and, during the black of night, had run right across our convoy. Now as we steamed along Spitzbergen's coastline another fleet-oiler came out to join us, bringing extra fuel. Still keeping close to the coast the convoy turned northward. This was a ruse to deceive the enemy, and to put more miles between us and the North Cape airfields. After some hours we turned southwest again and were on our last long lap to Iceland.

The U-boats were still kept at bay by the outer escorts and the Shads had not reappeared; hopes were high that we would now shepherd all the ships safely home.

Next day, September 20, was Sunday again—and another Black Sunday it turned out to be. Just before 5.30 a.m. watchers on *Ayrshire* saw what seemed to be waves breaking on an oddly disturbed sea. They were puzzling over the curious looking waves when a series of explosions rocked the minesweeper *Leda*, steaming astern of the convoy. She had been torpedoed and was very quickly in serious trouble.

Northern Gem, steaming two miles astern of the convoy, was stationed about one and a half miles on *Leda's* port beam. When a muffled explosion was heard and flames were seen belching from *Leda's* funnel Skipper-Lieutenant Mullender immediately rang full ahead. 'I brought *Gem* hard-a-starboard, intending to put her alongside *Leda's* starboard, weather side. When we got within 250 yards of the sweeper I could see many of her company scrambling to the forecastle head—she was well afire amidships and threatened to break in two. I ordered my crew to get our port boat inboard so that we didn't smash it as we went alongside—I thought we might well be in need of it before we got home. Then, on looking back at *Leda* I saw an officer dive overboard to swim to us. By hell, he was getting along! But it was the worst thing he could have done, as suddenly other men started jumping and sliding into the sea off her foredeck and leaping through the torpedo hole in her side. I had to stop *Gem* fifty yards off the sweeper's bow or we would have drowned them between the two ships. I ordered our boat lowered to pick the men up out of the water, but it was a hell of a job to hold them as by this time they were covered with oil which had poured from the torpedoed ship. Other survivors were all around on rafts and clinging to our side nets.

'A trawler which steamed down between us and *Leda* ran over six men on a raft, one of them I think being *Leda's* doctor. I saw

all six men go under the trawler's bottom. *Leda* turned turtle
and the last I saw of her captain he was sitting on the ship's bottom,
or what was left of it. I think he was saved.

'A destroyer steamed over and ordered me to leave the men in
the water and get back to the convoy. I told her to go to hell. Her
captain was right in one respect, because if we too had been
torpedoed while we lay there many more men would have died,
but in the circumstances such a chance had to be taken. If only
Leda's company had waited until we had got alongside no doubt
we could have saved more....' As it was *Gem* pulled seventy
men from the sea, but others were doomed.

Aboard *Ayrshire*, which had no scramble nets or rope ladders, Sub-Lieutenant John Aylard and others hung over the ship's
side with someone holding their feet, grabbing the hands of men
in the sea and trying to pull them on board, but in many cases
owing to the oil everywhere the hands of the struggling men
slipped from their grasp and the men were swept away and
drowned. Cruelly among them were six survivors of *River Afton*
which *Leda* had been bringing home. Others saved from the
sea died shortly after rescue. It was a savage blow.

Now the shadowers were ominously in the sky again, and
throughout the rest of the day there were U-boat and aircraft
alarms. *Avenger's* planes were up all the time, but still those
vultures hovered on the horizon. Shortly after 5 p.m. *Austin* shivered and trembled as if a depth charge had exploded beneath
the surface. We were keeping station on the convoy's starboard
quarter and looked across to the ships about a mile away. We
saw a giant waterspout rising by the bow of PQ 17's *Silver Sword,*
silver in colour as well as name and loaded on her decks with
logs. As we stared at each other wonderingly, *Austin* shivered
again and a second waterspout leapt up near *Sword's* amidships.

'Can they be bombing her?' someone asked, glancing skywards.
But before he had finished speaking there was a third shudder
and a great red glow appeared at *Sword's* stern. Suddenly we
knew the answer—torpedoes again. She had been tin-fished
three times. She still seemed to be steaming tranquilly along and
and for a moment we thought she was not seriously harmed. But

then she slowly lost way. Two escorts made for her and soon all three ships were left far astern.

The three torpedoes had smashed the crew's quarters on *Sword* both forward and aft. There would have been a grave loss of life but for the fact that practically all hands were amidships for their evening meal. One man in the quarters aft was fatally injured, dying during the night after rescue. The merchantman, her propeller blown off but still not sinking, was shelled and sunk by an escort.

After this second attack the U-boat hunt was on with a vengeance. For two hours the crashes and rumbles sounded, then suddenly *Somali*, one of the hunting destroyers, was brought up dead in her tracks by a torpedo which smacked into her engine room, killing five men and injuring others. There she lay in a pall of smoke, with rescuers quickly around her. Her damage was crippling but not fatal and it was decided to try to take her in tow. *Lord Middleton* went alongside to help. Asdic operator Arthur Jones:

'We started taking off any easily removable stores and personal belongings that could be got at by her crew, then everything movable such as shells, ammunition boxes and depth charges—deprimed, we hoped—were seized and flung over the side in an effort to lighten her. We were alongside her for about twenty minutes when suddenly one of the aft engine room hatches was flung over and out came one of the engine room crew. Whether he was injured I don't know, as he went over to the other side and boarded another rescue ship which had pulled alongside.'

A skeleton crew was left on board *Somali* and she was taken in tow by a sister ship, *Ashanti*, with three more destroyers forming an escort. Ironically by rights the torpedo should have been *Ashanti*'s, as she had just changed stations with *Somali* before the attack.

Nerves were stretched taut now. Three ships torpedoed in a day without any warning from the asdics. The crowning blow was that our sheet anchor, the aircraft carrier, with her attendant destroyers had withdrawn to leave us in the middle of the

U-boat hunt, as had the cruiser *Scylla*. Once again there was that horrible feeling that we were being deserted in our hour of need, and the comments in many of the remaining ships were caustic and vivid. We did not know then the explanations for the withdrawal: that *Avenger*'s Swordfish pilots, constantly on the go since the start of PQ 18, were about at the end of their tether, and that as we were now beyond the danger point of massed air attack it was felt they could be rested and the valuable carrier removed from the area of U-boat attack around the slow-moving convoy. Similarly it could have been inviting fate for the cruiser to remain as a U-boat target. Yet these decisions of Admiral Burnett could not be appreciated at the time; all we and our long-suffering survivors could see was the sight of the heavy ships once again vanishing rapidly over the horizon.

Admiral Burnett transferred to one of the remaining destroyers. He had asked for air cover from Coastal Command, and eyes now watched the sky for the expected arrival of friendly planes. As darkness descended the tension increased; in the dark especially it was not a pleasant feeling to know that you were being hunted by a U-boat pack.

The morning of September 21 came with us still being dogged by the Shads, but then arrived a single Catalina. It flew in and, after contacting the Commodore by lamp, went off on anti-submarine patrol. Two hours later it returned across the front of the convoy, slowly losing altitude, and landed on the water about a mile ahead. It was soon obvious that it was sinking. The tail rose and its crew of five scrambled out on to the wing, to be taken off by a boat hurriedly sent out by a destroyer. We learned that the Catalina had sighted and attacked a U-boat, only to be hit itself. So much for our air cover.

Soon afterwards—11.15 a.m.—a periscope crossed only 200 yards from *Pozarica*'s bows. The depth charges thumped all day until darkness came again, the convoy proceeding in uniform slowness at only five knots, with *Somali* struggling along under tow astern. The situation could not last, nor did it. The dawn of September 22 broke with a calm sea and the sky clear even of Shads. One of the destroyers now left us, taking Admiral Burnett off to rejoin *Scylla*. Scarcely had she gone when on *Austin*, shortly after 6 a.m., we felt the familiar shudder and eyes turned instantly towards the main body of ships. A waterspout was rising beside a big merchantman. In quick succession five more vibrations were felt, the eruptions of water rising so fast that we could not distinguish which ships were being attacked. The action bell rang and some among our survivors shot out of the messdeck hatch like demons in a pantomime. One of the ack-ack ships put on a sprint and raced up the line, but we greatly feared that her twin had received one of the 'fish'. It would be damnable luck, now that we were so near, if these two stalwarts did not get home together. But it was not the ack-ack after all; it was her closest neighbour, the *Ocean Voice*, leading the port column. Once again Commodore Dowding felt his ship explode beneath him.

A U-boat well out on the starboard bow had fired at the convoy. *Ocean Freedom*, leading the starboard column, was just slightly astern of position, so that the first torpedo streaked across her bow and shot over to *Voice*, leaping from the water and striking the ship's bow with a tremendous flash and explosion. Three days out a baby had been born to one of the Russian wives on *Voice*, and when the torpedo struck the baby was hurriedly put in a suitcase for safety. But then a second torpedo struck, also near the bow, collapsing the passengers' temporary accommodation, and the suitcase was lost. Several survivors afterwards told how they saw the baby floating in and out through the hole torn in *Ocean Voice*. The ship did not sink but was entirely disabled and *Zamalek* steamed over to the rescue.

Meanwhile other torpedoes had hit *Gray Ranger* and the American *Bellingham*.

Palomares had a narrow escape as *Ranger* was hit. The officer of the watch, sensing an emergency, rang down for full speed ahead, and as the ack-ack ship picked up speed a torpedo scraped under her stern so close that the men in the engine room heard the noise of it. *Ranger* was struck aft, the torpedo tearing through her buoyancy tanks into her engine room, killing three men. Three deck ratings were also lost; in the explosion a figure

like a film dummy was seen to cartwheel into the air from the
bridge. Then *Bellingham* reeled from an explosion which shivered her great bulk and her stern began to settle. We were
quickly signalled to stand by her. Already boats and rafts were
pulling away from the sinking ship and the sea was dotted with
floating wreckage. We stopped engines and the survivors made a
bee-line for us; in a few moments we were helping them over the
side.

'Thanks, fellers,' said one of them. 'Say, this is becoming quite
a habit with me—it's my fifth time since we left Iceland.'

Luckily there were no injured among them and only one
man was reported missing. While we were helping them aboard
and hauling up the very welcome boxes of food they grabbed
before leaving, *Bellingham* rose high above us, half the huge ship
thrusting up out of the water at an angle of sixty degrees. It was
an awe-inspiring sight from such close range; there was a
certain majesty and grandeur about this monster in her death
throes. Scarcely two or three minutes later she had gone, leaving
behind her a vortex of whirling wreckage with calcium flares
burning, the funeral pyre of the last luckless PQ 17 merchantman to die. Our rescue work lasted about half an hour and
with engines stopped, the convoy disappearing ahead and the
unseen U-boats near at hand, we were the perfect target. It was
the longest half-hour we could ever remember.

When *Ocean Voice* was hit Captain Walker, Vice-Commodore in *Ocean Freedom,* took over as lead ship of the convoy—'I can still see Commodore Dowding shaking his fist at me
from the bridge as I broke my Commodore's pennant.' *Zamalek*
picked up most of the Russians, also the women and children, for
whom the crowded rescue ship rigged up special accommodation.
Apart from the distressed mother who had lost her baby, and
another woman with a fractured leg, injuries were slight. *Voice's*
crew were taken off by the minesweeper *Seagull* in which Dowding finished his passage at the tail end of the convoy. Captain
Walker: 'Later the Commodore made a couple of attempts to
board us from the *Seagull* but the sea was too rough. I reckon
it could have been done had I broken formation and hove-to,

but he wouldn't have that. Thinking of the ships rather than his own gratification, I guess.'

Voice was sunk by one of the escorts.

Gray Ranger's engine room was extensively damaged and flooded, and her survivors were quickly ordered to abandon ship. The majority got away by the port motor boat and were picked up by *Northern Gem*, a few others being rescued by *Rathlin*. A junior engineer who had jumped overboard from the tanker's stern was thrown a line by one of the rescue vessels which fortunately caught him by the wrist, but the ship was unable to stop and they pulled him a full mile and a half through the water before managing to drag him aboard half drowned. He was only twenty years old—not many older men would have survived that terrible ordeal in the icy sea.

Ranger was almost out of oil but she could not be towed and it was undesirable to chance leaving her for the Germans, so she too was finished off by an escort. Such was her sturdy construction that it took thirty minutes' shelling to dispose of her.

And then it was all over. When no more attacks came we on *Austin* turned to looking after our fifty-odd new survivors and their pets, a cat and a Husky puppy. The desperate problems of sleeping and feeding everyone came up again, though *Northern Gem* was in a far worse position than ourselves. Carrying men from *Leda*, *Ranger* and now a quota from *Bellingham* as well, they had scarcely room to turn, and their meagre rations of corned beef, biscuits and tea shrank alarmingly before they reached port, despite a small extra supply begged from a destroyer. And *Rathlin*. She now had some 200 men aboard besides her crew, and with many of the survivors suffering from nervous shock and refusing to go below deck, she was in a highly dangerous plight, jam-packed like some river excursion steamer.

For the remainder of that day and into the night, as two Focke-Wulf Condors arrived to shadow us, the convoy steamed doggedly on. Action-stations came again at dawn and we zig-zagged furiously for two hours, still with a Condor shadowing us. Where *were* our planes? But as we neared the safety of our own minefields no further attacks came. In the afternoon, after rolling in a heavy swell, we sighted Iceland, but for some reason plans had been changed and most ships now were to run for Loch Ewe. For the rest of that day and the next the sea took over where the U-boats had left off. A blizzard enveloped us and the wind increased to gale force, during the height of which, on *Austin,* we had to swing the smallboats inboard. Steering was near impossible.

'Sing out when you're on,' came Number One's voice from the bridge.

'She's swinging twenty degrees either side,' replied the helmsman.

'Then sing out as she whizzes past,' was the dry comment.

In the blinding gale we feared for the crowded *Rathlin,* rolling over almost to her beam ends; she left us to call at Seydisfiord for emergency supplies, then followed on. The long-suffering *Winston Salem* dropped astern with rudder trouble.

Every ship took an alarming battering from that storm, *Dianella* suffering her worst moment of the entire voyage. A/B Kenneth Richards: 'We caught a sea on the port side and heeled over. I was on my seat in the bridge-hut, and what angle we were at I couldn't say, but I was in a position looking down at the sea and it seemed like an eternity. The voice of the First Officer was heard calling to the helmsman: "Whatever you do, don't touch the wheel!" The scuppers on the starboard side had stuck and the waist was full of water, but somehow she righted herself, and thank God she did!'

The gale abated and in the sudden new calm we passed schools of porpoise and floating mines, while belatedly here and there in the sky were Fortresses, Sunderlands and Whitleys. The destroyers now left us and we were picked up by a coastal escort. A signal to Captain Walker: *'To Ocean Freedom from Seagull: lead on and take them home. Sorry not to be with you at the end. Pass to all ships well done.—Dowding.'*

We sighted the Butt of Lewis. Over the radio the BBC informed us that our return convoy had 'arrived safely'. But behind us had occurred the final tragedy.

Somali had struggled along painfully slowly under tow by *Ashanti*, constantly pumping out the sea that threatened to flood her. She was kept going by her skeleton crew of eighty men, and though her boats had been destroyed there were rafts enough for them all in an emergency. Then came the fierce gale, and, in the darkness of the night, the end of her tortuous journey. Fortunately as the towing became more dangerous all hands had been ordered to stay above deck. Arthur Jones of *Lord Middleton*:

'Her forward light was seen to be behaving queerly, seesawing to and fro at a mad angle, then suddenly the towline parted and at the same time there was a great noise of rending metal as the destroyer broke in half and the two ends of the ship fell apart. She went down very quickly. With the heavy sea that was running our skipper decided to lay off astern, knowing that the men we saw jumping overboard would be swept down towards us. We were able to rescue a few, but owing to the fast waters others were swept right past us and so to their deaths; I'm afraid the poor souls had no chance at all.'

Among those miraculously dragged from the sea was *Somali's* captain, who was floating unconscious when found by the searching *Ashanti*. But more than forty men of *Somali* died, including some who were hauled from the freezing water too late. Like her chief yeoman of signals, who died on *Middleton* shortly after rescue; he was buried at sea off Seydisfiord, almost at journey's end.

September 26, 1942. We berthed at Loch Ewe. *Winston Salem* limped in the following day and we heard later that *Ironclad* had managed to get to Spitzbergen, afterwards coming on to the U.K. So the bald figures were: two British and five American ships, the only surviving merchantmen of PQ 17. These and the two rescue ships; and the two battered and holed Russian tankers that had made it to Archangel. What a sorry tale to tell.

For the thousand survivors we had brought home (a number of men died on the journey) there was one more short voyage, by mailboat to a civic reception and lunch in Glasgow, and then, for many, comfortable billets until they were fit to join other ships and the Americans to make passage home across the Atlantic.

For all men it was a matter of closed lips. Official security. Despite heavy German propaganda and a hundred twisted rumours—besides a truer common knowledge already spreading to many parts of the world as the survivors went home—there was not a communique, not a statement, nothing. So the bitterness was carried home in Britain and the U.S.; the heavy charge of desertion by the Royal Navy following a panic order from the Admiralty unparalleled in the history of the sea.

We took home our memories. Like Surgeon-Lieutenant McCallum of *Zamalek*, who for a long time afterwards, every time he closed his eyes would see a Blohm and Voss circling the convoy low on the horizon; an experience common to many of us. Like Chief Engineer Dawson of the same ship, who when he landed had lost two stone in weight and looked like a scarecrow, and who could never erase from his ears the noise of the bombs and the cries of those being rescued. And like Gunner Herbert Wharmby of *Ocean Freedom*, who every night from that year to this has said a prayer thanking God he was saved.

Aboard *Palomares* as she steamed down to Belfast they heard the news given over the radio that another convoy had fought its way through to Russia, thanks to the help of the R.A.F. No sooner was it said than the men on the messdecks let out a bellow of rage which could be heard the length and breadth of the ship.

It was to be a lasting anger shared by us all.

II

Whose Fault?

Even after the catastrophe, after everything, PQ 17 might have slipped into history as another tragic episode of the war; the worst convoy disaster suffered by the Allies, but one from which the lesson was quickly learned and its destruction avenged as more convoys went on to battle their way through to Russia.

Instead, because of the great blanket of secrecy spread over PQ 17's fate and the blunder that had brought it about, it was not like that at all.

On the day we berthed at Loch Ewe—September 26, 1942—we read in the morning papers a very long and glowing Admiralty communique telling of the great battle of PQ 18 in which 40 enemy planes had been destroyed, with the majority of ships arriving safely at their destination. At the end of this communique were four short paragraphs noting the passage of QP 14. These recorded 'some losses among the ships' and briefly announced the sinkings of H.M.S. *Leda* and H.M.S. *Somali*.

Nothing about PQ 17. Nor had there been any mention of the convoy in our absence, other than the appearance of a few photographs released to the newspapers on August 4. These were scenes of the battle with the torpedo-bombers on Independence Day exactly a month before—described as 'one of the biggest convoy battles at sea' by a 'huge United Nations convoy'. An example of the censored reports accompanying the photographs is this from the *Daily Herald*:

'These dramatic pictures show a German air attack by torpedo planes on a convoy to Russia. The ships were taking the Arctic route early last month, when darkness never really sets in, and the visibility helped the enemy. But in spite of repeated attacks, the convoy, with its badly needed war cargoes, got through. . . .'

Yet when this was published, German statements about the mass sinkings, naming individual ships, had already been well circulated among the neutral world. So had some of the many propaganda pictures taken by the planes and U-boats, showing sinking ships and hapless survivors.

In America on this same day, August 4, *Life* magazine published a big spread of photographs of the Independence Day battle taken by a staff man who had travelled in U.S.S. *Wainwright*—unnamed but described as 'one of the U.S. warships guarding the great train of United Nations ships'. *Life* was not as heavily censored as the British newspapers. It reported: 'The Germans broadcast first that they had sunk a U.S. cruiser and 28 merchant ships in the "greatest catastrophe" of the sea war. They claimed planes had destroyed 122,000 tons, U-boats another 70,000 tons. Their next claim added four more cargo vessels; their next, three more. On July 9, the Russians announced that the convoy had "arrived safely in a Russian Arctic port". It had taken losses, but it had delivered a huge mass of American and British planes, tanks, guns, food, medicine and wartime tools to the hard pressed Russians. It had done its part in the long delivery line from factory to the fighting front.'

Actual Allied losses had not yet been announced, *Life* added, but they were 'certainly a great deal smaller than the extravagant claims of the Germans'.

The Admiralty, however, remained silent. A few months later, in the spring of 1943, Lord Winster, a naval officer, caused a stir when in the House of Lords he demanded a statement about what he described as 'the worst voyage in the world'. The *Daily Express* reported next day: 'Lord Winster disclosed that in one convoy to Arctic Russia we lost 34 out of 38 ships. He was apparently referring to the worst Allied convoy disaster of the war, at the beginning of last July. The enemy claimed annihilation of an entire convoy carrying more than 250,000 tons of planes, tanks, munitions and food. Official German reports claimed that 19 merchant ships were destroyed by bombers and nine by U-boats off Spitzbergen. All the other ships were said to be destroyed "in a pursuit battle" a day or two later as they neared their destination in the Barents Sea.

'What happened was that after incessant air attack and severe losses on July 2, the convoy turned north—evading a German battle squadron, including the *Tirpitz*—and was again attacked by bombers as it neared Archangel. U-boats finished off damaged stragglers. Only four merchant ships survived.'

Now the facts about the convoy were truly getting out of hand, but still the Admiralty maintained its silence. A few months later Admiral of the Fleet Sir Dudley Pound, First Sea Lord and Chief of the Naval Staff, resigned because of illness. He died the same year. But even on his death there was no mention of PQ 17, the conduct of which had been his ultimate responsibility.

The silence continued for two more years, until February, 1945. In this month the Swedish-American exchange ship *Gripsholm* arrived at New York with the first group of American merchant seamen to come home after up to three years in a German prison camp. Among them were twenty-five survivors of PQ 17, bearing bitter memories of the loss of their ships which, they told the welcoming city, had resulted when a heavy naval escort, including destroyers and cruisers, had abandoned them to the mercy of enemy planes and U-boats when lured off in a wild goose chase after German battleships. Especially bitter were men from the *Carlton* and *Honomu*, who poured out stories of their ordeal to an astounded city gathering. All but four of the thirty-eight merchant ships were sunk, the seamen said. Some heatedly charged the Royal Navy with cowardice—'The limey navy just turned and ran'.

The U.S. newspapers headlined these shock reports about a convoy which had been predominantly American. The U.S. Navy Department declined to comment, so the spotlight fell on the

Admiralty. The *New York Times* checked and reported: 'The story was ignored officially by the Admiralty but naval officers described it unofficially as "arrant nonsense" . . . In a case like that, the practice when attacked has been to disperse the convoy while escort vessels try to break up the attack, officers pointed out.'

For two days, while resentment boiled, the Admiralty did nothing. Then, 'in order to correct erroneous reports recently circulated', it issued a statement. This consisted of a brief account of the movements of battle fleet, cruisers and escorts. It gave the correct number of ships in the convoy and those lost, but incorrectly sank five of them in the Independence Day battle. It did not dwell on the scatter order but said that 'for several hours' after the battle with the torpedo-bombers 'the convoy proceeded on its way without further interference. Later, when in a position due north of the North Cape, an attack by the enemy surface ships seemed imminent and the convoy was ordered to scatter. The six destroyers joined the First Cruiser Squadron to form a balanced striking force. An anxious 24 hours followed, but no surface attack developed on the scattered ships, this project apparently having been abandoned as a result of the dispersion.'

The last observation may be considered something of a classic, seeing that in those 24 hours, as a result of the swooping planes and U-boats, fourteen ships were already at the bottom of the sea or fast on their way there.

In conclusion the statement emphasized: 'During the past 42 months our Russian ally has safely received no less than 91.6 per cent of the vast amount of war supplies shipped by the northern route, the great proportion of which have been conveyed under British escort.'

The *New York Times*, which in common with other American newspapers repeated the statement without comment, observed in passing: 'Out of the dark past now fading in a brighter light the British Admiralty reveals some shocking figures. . . . Only now do we realize what dreadful losses we were taking then.'

Then again, silence. Nearly two more years went by with

still not the slightest admission of an error in the conduct of the convoy. Then in October, 1946, the Russian newspaper *Red Fleet*, official organ of the Soviet naval forces, published two hard-hitting articles written by Captain of the Second Rank V. Andreyev, of the Soviet Navy. Entitled 'Lessons of One Convoy', they ran the whole gamut of criticism against the Admiralty and openly condemned the order to scatter as being given without necessity. Andreyev said : 'The main motive for the dispersal apparently was the confusion of the English command, exaggerated fear of the German ships, fear of "losses" in battleships which supposedly "could have" taken place.' There was a tradition, said the captain, that ships under escort must be defended. 'In this case the tradition was disregarded, and as a result, after dispersal, when the transports were defenceless, the convoy suffered its heaviest losses.' The order to scatter was given 'when the enemy ships supposedly threatening it were 300 miles away'.

Andreyev further charged that the Admiralty did not take the organization of the convoy 'seriously enough'; its departure was widely known in Reykjavik and enabled the enemy to prepare his attack. It was insufficiently defended and should have had an aircraft carrier (the captain of the *Donbass* had told of seeing only one British plane—the Walrus); also, 'irresponsibility and panic' reigned among British and American merchant crews and ships were deserted after suffering only 'negligible damage'.

Andreyev went into a wealth of detail, and unsoundly based as were the bulk of his assertions—he blamed the scatter order on the convoy Commodore and the escort commander—he had certainly done his homework, giving the correct number of ships and sinkings, the dismal total of merchantmen that eventually reached Archangel—eleven, including the two damaged Russian tankers—and citing the reply given to the master of the holed *Azerbaijan* when he appealed to a destroyer for help : 'Convoy will not reform. Save yourselves independently. Advise keep to north as far as ice permits. Good luck.'

The fullest disclosure of Captain Andreyev's articles was made by the *New York Times*. Uproar followed in Britain. Mr Anthony Eden, the wartime Foreign Secretary, publicly declared: 'Any fair-minded ally would have taken the Admiralty's detailed statement issued last year into account in passing judgment on this most daring and hazardous operation. It has, in fact, been completely ignored. ... It seems to me, to say the least of it, ungracious that our ally should single out the fate of one convoy for remonstrance.'

In the House of Commons, M.P.s voiced 'the burning indignation felt by all Britons' over Andreyev's 'outrageous' statements. The Secretary to the Admiralty, Mr John Dugdale, said the account had been read with considerable feeling since it impugned 'not merely the naval tactics of the convoy but also the courage of the British and American seamen who took part in it'. He assured M.P.s that a further Admiralty statement would be given publicity not only in Britain but abroad.

This statement, reiterating the outstanding success of the forty Arctic convoys, explained that it would have been inviting disaster for escorts to detach and stand by disabled ships; the only course in the circumstances was to take off the crews and sink the vessels. As for the scatter order, the statement repeated that north of the North Cape 'an attack by surface vessels seemed imminent'. The convoy was too far to the eastward for Admiral Tovey's battle fleet to give support, so the Admiralty ordered the convoy to scatter and the cruisers and destroyers to withdraw to form a balanced striking force to divert the enemy —'This is the recognized form of defence in such extreme circumstances. In any event, the action of the escort and the scattering of the convoy achieved its primary object, and the enemy heavy ships withdrew and thereby the convoy avoided annihilation.'

So the action was, in fact, successful? Another observation for the history books.

However, in *Pravda* a day later there appeared a handsome retraction. The Soviet State and public opinion appreciated the skill and 'indisputable courage' of the United States and British navies in convoy work, it said, 'and this appreciation found concrete expression in the decoration of British and American sailors'. Captain Andreyev's articles were 'clearly unsuccessful'. He had chosen the wrong approach; instead of studying the experience of many operations he had made 'a generalization on the basis of one isolated operation, and that an unsuccessful one'. *Red Fleet* also published *Pravda*'s rebuke in full, but added the protest that foreign commentators had exploited the captain's statement 'for the purposes of an anti-Soviet campaign'.

And that was that. There the matter was left for another four years, until in October, 1950 the Admiralty finally released Admiral Tovey's despatches on the Russian convoys for publication as a supplement to the *London Gazette*. The Press flew to them, for they presented a very different picture from all that had gone before. They revealed how the C-in-C Home Fleet had repeatedly asked for better escorts, and for a reduction of the convoys in the early summer until the ice barrier had receded north. They told of his many requests to the Russians for help over the last part of the journey, requests that had met with almost negligible response, the Russians calling for still greater efforts while doing little to help. Promised Russian bombing attacks on the Norwegian airfields had not materialized. Every other page of the despatches held some brief reference to the lack of co-operation from the Kremlin.

And then for some details of what the Press now described as 'the notorious PQ 17 disaster', a story on which, the *Daily Express* said, 'for eight years Admiral Tovey has kept silence, though accused in Parliament of withdrawing the destroyer escort from the convoy to protect his battle squadron'.

The battle fleet's movements were at last made fully clear. It had cruised to the west in an area bounded roughly by Jan Mayen, Spitzbergen and Bear Island, where Admiral Tovey considered *Tirpitz* would be most likely to attack. When Naval Intelligence suggested earlier that the enemy surface raiders planned to attack *east* of Bear Island, the C-in-C had suggested to the Admiralty that on reaching the longitude of 10 E., the convoy should turn back for 12-18 hours (if the *Tirpitz* did sail) so as to lure the enemy back into his range. This suggestion was not approved. Therefore he could do no more than patrol his own area.

Following the report on July 3, of *Tirpitz* and *Hipper* having left Trondheim, Admiral Hamilton decided to continue sailing his cruiser force east of Bear Island. The same day, when air reconnaissance showed the ice barrier had receded north, the Admiralty suggested to *Keppel* that the convoy should pass at least 50 miles north of Bear Island, but Commander Broome preferred to stay in low visibility on the original route and make ground eastwards. Admiral Hamilton, deciding that a more northerly route was necessary then closed the convoy and ordered Commander Broome to alter course to pass 70 miles north of Bear Island, and later to open 400 miles from the enemy airfields.

At noon on July 4, the Admiralty gave Admiral Hamilton permission to take his cruisers beyond 25 deg. E. if the occasion demanded, or unless contrary orders were received from the C-in-C. Admiral Tovey : 'This was a reversal of the policy agreed between the Admiralty and myself. As no information I had justified this change, I ordered Hamilton to withdraw when the convoy was east of 25 deg. E. or earlier, unless the Admiralty could assure him that the *Tirpitz* would not be met.' Seven hours later the Admiralty signalled Admiral Hamilton that further information was expected shortly and he was to stay with the convoy pending further instructions. Then, two hours later, came the three fateful signals, all sent over the C-in-C's head.

The last signal was sent as a correction of the technical wording from 'disperse' to 'scatter', but this was not known at the time. And so it was taken by Admiral Hamilton and Commander Broome that the *Tirpitz* was chasing, hence Commander Broome's action in turning his destroyers to the fight.

At 5 p.m. on July 5, the Russian submarine *Red Star* reported the *Tirpitz* and her consorts outward bound from North Cape. Three and a half hours later she was reported by another submarine, but soon afterwards the enemy ships abandoned their enterprise and returned to harbour 'for reasons not known'.

During the night of 5/6 July, the Admiralty signalled Admiral Tovey three times suggesting that if the battle fleet was sighted steaming east it might make *Tirpitz* reluctant to go as far as the convoy; *Red Star* might have damaged her and there would be a chance for the planes of *Victorious* to attack her. Admiral Tovey thought this unlikely, but at 6.45 a.m. on July 6, his destroyers having refuelled, he did alter course back to the north-east, and when an hour later an enemy plane passed over above the clouds he tried to attract its attention with gunfire and fighters, but without success. Later that morning he was joined by the cruiser force, and as the weather was unfavourable for air reconnaissance he reversed to the south-west and the ships returned to harbour.

There it was, all concisely explained. But who in particular was behind the Admiralty orders clashing with and overruling those of its Commander-in-Chief? Whose final decision caused the three fatal signals to be sent? *Whose order was it that scattered the convoy, and on what grounds?* Admiral Tovey would not comment to questioning newspapermen. He said: 'There are a great many things that I could say. But perhaps I had better not.'

For seven more years the official silence continued. Then in 1957, fifteen long years after that melancholy Fourth of July, years during which the bitterness had spread and rooted and a ghost had risen which would never be laid, the truth finally emerged. In the second volume of *The War At Sea* (H.M.S.O.) the official naval historian, Captain S. W. Roskill, revealed that the man responsible for repeatedly overruling Admiral Tovey and giving the crucial order to scatter was the First Sea Lord, Admiral of the Fleet Sir Dudley Pound.

For the first time it was admitted, officially and publicly, that the order was a grievous error and should never have been made.

To the men of the convoy the name of the First Sea Lord was

scarcely known. Unlike the leaders of the other two Services
he remained a vague, shadowy figure, masked by the authority
of the Admiralty. This although he had been First Sea Lord
since the outbreak of war.

What kind of man was he? He was sixty-four, with a considerable naval record which included distinguished service in
the Battle of Jutland in World War I; and yet he never became
known to any popular degree among R.N. personnel. One of the
very few attempts to give a personal pen portrait of him was
made by a *Daily Mail* writer just before the First Sea Lord's
death, which occurred on Trafalgar Day, 1943 shortly after
the death of his wife.

'Night after night this man, who held down Britain's most
exacting job during the four most exacting years history has
produced, would telephone his wife. "I am sorry," he would say,
"but I shall not be able to get home." "I understand," Lady
Pound would reply.

'The Pounds lived in a six-guineas a week furnished flat in
Hornton Street, Kensington, W. But after the war was declared
Sir Dudley kept what amounted to a 24-hours watch at the
Admiralty. Fifty yards from his big, bare office, hung with
charts, was an equally bare bedroom, its cream-coloured walls
relieved with green painted woodwork. Its austere iron bed-
stead and straw mattress were the only pieces of furniture to
indicate its use. Even the mahogany chest of drawers was
covered in rolled-up signal pads and an assortment of books
ranging from the Navy List to signal codes.

'In these monkish surroundings Sir Dudley Pound was always
on duty. An action in the darkness of the Channel would mean
he had to be called from bed. The fortunes of a convoy for
Archangel would keep him as busy by night as by day. In his
dressing-gown he would go to his office to plunge into vital
consultations, urgent telephone calls, and decisions which
finished only with the final dictation of the signals of instruction. On other nights he would retire to his bedroom fully
dressed, knowing that in an hour or two he would have to
return to the duties at which no man could relieve him.

'When Lady Pound's health began to fail he tried to get back to his flat in the evenings. But only on an average of four times a year did he manage to get home. So he set aside his lunch hour to be with her. He never went out to lunch—always he journeyed to the Kensington flat on the second floor. He could never stay longer than just an hour. Then he turned back to his work again.'

Admiral Pound had been bitterly criticized in the Commons late in 1940 for the way in which the Admiralty was conducting its higher operations. It was not the only time he was under fire, yet he weathered the storm created by his opponents to be generally credited with pulling the Royal Navy through the dark days of early wartime. His particular failing, as testified to by officers who worked closely with him, was a tendency to retain too much personal control and not delegate powers sufficiently to his commanders. In the words of the official historian 'he was too inclined to try and control squadrons and fleets either from the bridge of his flagship or from Whitehall'. His intervention in the conduct of fleet operations was 'excessive'.

The Admiralty was strongly against sending through PQ 17 in the round-the-clock Arctic daylight. When Naval Intelligence reported the enemy's intention to launch an all-out assault on the convoy with planes, U-boats and surface vessels, losses seemed bound to be heavy, and Admiral Pound believed the biggest threat to be that of attack by the *Tirpitz* and her consorts. He had some two weeks to dwell on this before the convoy sailed, and as it transpired, his order for the ships to scatter was not only a very carefully considered personal order but a fully premeditated one. Vice-Admiral B. B. Schofield, who worked on the organization of the Russian convoys, has recently made this perfectly clear. In his book *The Russian Convoys* (Batsford, 1964), which brilliantly covers the operations of all the convoys and the strategies of the opposing sides, Admiral Schofield reveals :

'When Admiral Tovey learned that PQ 17, like the previous convoy, was to consist of 35 ships, he suggested to the First Sea Lord that it should be run in two sections, as he still adhered to his opinion that large convoys were undesirable. It was during an unrecorded telephone conversation between them on this point that Admiral Tovey first learned that Admiral Pound had it in mind to order the convoy to scatter should it be assailed in the Barents Sea by a powerful German surface force which included the *Tirpitz*. The order to a convoy to scatter is an accepted naval principle in ocean warfare where a group of merchant ships is attacked by an enemy surface force greatly superior to that escorting it. It had been used successfully when a 37-ship convoy escorted only by the armed merchant cruiser *Jervis Bay* was attacked by the pocket battleship *Scheer* in mid-Atlantic, but the circumstances were entirely different in the Barents Sea, where lack of sea-room caused by the pack-ice to the north prevented ships from escaping out of range of German shore-based aircraft. Moreover, experience had shown that mutual support was essential in the face of both air and U-boat attack, so that from every point of view Admiral Pound's suggestion came as a profound shock to Admiral Tovey.'

On July 3, came the report of *Tirpitz* and *Hipper* having left Trondheim. Though bad weather hampered further reconnaissance the Admiralty was practically certain, late on July 4, that the pair had sailed up to join the *Scheer* at Altenfiord, near the North Cape, and perhaps even then were sailing north-east to attack the convoy. Admiral Tovey's battle fleet, some 350 miles to the rear, could have been ordered to steam eastwards to the convoy, but apart from the time lag, that move would have pitted its single aircraft carrier against an overwhelming mass of German planes. As for the cruisers, these were considered to be no match for the enemy battleships. Admiral Schofield:

'It is evident that the threat of attack by the *Tirpitz* was uppermost in the mind of the First Sea Lord. . . . Bad weather might save the convoy from air attack, the perpetual daylight was a hindrance to the U-boats, but only fog could prevent an attack by the surface ships. As already mentioned, he had turned the situation over in his mind long before it actually happened, and reached the conclusion that scattering the convoy was, in the circumstances, the right solution. Although the general feeling of the conference over which he was now presiding was against such action, the arguments advanced were not such as to cause him to change his opinion. When everyone present had had his say, he closed his eyes for a moment while he made up his mind, then turning to the Director of the Signal Division he said: "Tell the cruisers to withdraw to the west at high speed, and the convoy to disperse." In the whole of his long and distinguished career Admiral Pound could never have been called upon to make a more fateful decision.'

In fact at the moment the signal was sent, in the late evening of July 4, *Tirpitz* and the others were still in harbour at Altenfiord. *They did not sail till noon the next day.*

It is now commonly admitted that the scatter order was premature. Why Admiral Pound acted so precipitously on the limited intelligence at hand, without waiting for further confirmation of the *Tirpitz's* movements, is doubly puzzling, for clearly the moment the merchant ships scattered they were a prey to the planes and U-boats and quick and heavy losses were bound to result. Why then deliberately imperil them before the danger from the enemy surface ships was more firmly established? Intelligence, as every Serviceman knows, is an important aid to operations but never a deciding factor—and certainly not while the minimum of doubt remains. It is valid here to note the reported view of Vice-Admiral Sir Norman Denning, one of the founders of the Naval Intelligence Division. The *Sunday Telegraph* of August, 1965 stated: 'It was Denning who developed the technique of tracking and identifying the German surface raiders sent to various parts of the world, in a manner which led to the destruction of most of them, including the *Graf Spee*. If his advice had been taken, the disastrous order from Sir Dudley Pound to the Russia-bound convoy PQ 17—to scatter before imminent U-boat and surface attack—would not have gone out.'

But it did go out, thereby setting off a chain reaction which could not have been halted. All ships acted expressly to orders, and in the case of the escorts, according to correct naval procedure.

One of the most poignant features brought out during research for this book has been the agony which the men of the
destroyers have borne all these years; a deep-rooted feeling which
goes much further than the first anger at the shallow smears of
'cowardice' and 'betrayal'. Turning away from the convoy, as
they had to, went right against the grain; their every instinct
was to protect the merchantmen, and in fact as they turned to
face the enemy expected on the horizon, this is what they were
convinced they were doing. The moment of horror when harsh
realization came has moved men who helped with this book even
to offer the later war record of themselves and their ships, and
that of the Navy's destroyer service as a whole, as some measure
of 'atonement' for that bleak day.

Commander Broome (now Captain Broome, R.N., Retd.)
has recently crystallized the feelings of all in his flotilla when the
enemy warships did not, after all, appear. 'Our rapidly increasing distance from the convoy began to infuse unpleasant doubts.
Was this situation getting unreal? Were we part of any plan at
all? A mathematical fact, striking colder than the freezing Arctic
fog, slowly registered that as far as the convoy was concerned,
we had passed the point of no return from the fuel angle. From
then on, uncertainty nagged and grew, ending in a moment I am
not likely to forget, when the first pitiable cry for help came
limping through from a merchantman who was being attacked
by U-boat and plane. Something had gone hopelessly wrong. A
trust we had believed in implicitly had let us down flat. I signalled to the admiral that I was ready and willing to go back, but
it was too late.'

As the details of PQ 17 have emerged, various 'inquests' on its
fate have been conducted by people who were not involved. The
escort commander's blunt comments on these are wholly sub-
scribed to by the authors.

'A lot of whitewash and criticism has followed in the wake of
this disaster, with the whitewash mainly confined to the end of
the story carrying the Top Brass. Historians, factual and fic-
tional, still cash in by keeping the pot on the boil, but as one
of the few remaining central figures I have never been able to

see anything controversial about it. PQ 17 was just another splendid convoy, ploughing along with no claim whatever to history or fiction until those signals arrived from the Admiralty. The order given in the final signal either had to be obeyed or ignored. To my dying regret, I obeyed it. Having done so, it triggered off a sequence of events which, as Admiral Tovey agreed later, were inevitable by accepted naval procedure. Eleven ships reached Archangel. What the results would have been had the order to scatter not been given, no one knows. But with the *Tirpitz* and her consorts then almost regarded as "sacred cows", the results could hardly have been worse. The responsibility for what actually did happen must therefore for ever rest on the shoulders of the man who gave that order and his advisers.'

Equally forthright are the views of an officer serving in *Keppel's* flotilla: Lieutenant W. D. O'Brien, now a Vice-Admiral and Commander, Far East Fleet. It will be remembered how his ship, *Offa,* 'very, very nearly' turned and went back to rejoin the convoy. Now Admiral O'Brien has this to say:

'I have never been able to rejoice with my American friends on Independence Day, because 4th July is, to me, a day to hang my head in grief for all the men who lost their lives on convoy PQ 17 and in shame at the recollection of one of the bleakest episodes in Royal Naval history, when the warships deserted the merchant ships and left them to their fate. For that, in simple terms, was what we were obliged to do.

'To me, PQ 17 provides the classic lesson, and goodness knows it was not a new lesson, of the dangers that attend a military enterprise when the central authority—in this case the Admiralty—takes over control of the tactical moves of ships from the commanders on the spot. In PQ 17 this error was compounded by the Admiralty passing no information to those commanders on either the intelligence or the reasoning which led to the release of the three dramatic signals.

'I am not, and never have been, in any doubt that these three signals were wrong in principle and wrong in fact. The Commander-in-Chief, Home Fleet was responsible for the planning and passage of PQ 17; Admiral Hamilton, with a U.S./U.K.

cruiser force of considerable power, was given responsibility by
him for covering the convoy against surface attack; Commander
Broome was likewise charged with the duty of close escort to the
convoy. The proper proceeding was to give these senior officers
all the intelligence available and leave the tactical decisions to
them. They were wholly deprived of this right and placed in
the humiliating position of being ordered to desert a convoy without having the information which would allow them to judge
whether this horrifying sacrifice was justified or not.

'I do not think I am making this serious judgment wholly
with hindsight. There could be no doubt what the fate of the
ships of the convoy would be, single defenceless targets on a flat
calm sea in the seemingly eternal daylight. To order this was
wholly contrary to the principle, firmly in my mind at that time,
that the best defensive posture against all forms of attack, submarine, air or surface, was for a convoy to remain concentrated and for it to be scattered only when under *actual* attack by
overwhelming surface forces.'

The feeling in the cruiser force was fully as strong as
that among the men of the destroyers. An observer aboard
USS *Wichita* was Lieutenant Douglas Fairbanks, USNR (now
Captain, Retd.), who, as a member of the staff of Rear-Admiral Robert C. Giffen in the flagship USS *Washington,* had been
sent to the cruiser on temporary assignment. He was afterwards
commissioned to write an official account of the action. Captain
Fairbanks says regarding the cruisers' withdrawal and the
order for the convoy to scatter:

'Our reaction was one of stunned shock. We felt there must
have been some error in transmitting the signal.

'The Americans were particularly bitter, cursing the British
for what they believed to be running away in the face of a good
battle which we had a chance of surviving. We resented leaving
the defenceless merchant ships to straggle at nine and ten knots
through icy water which we knew from experience would not
permit survival for more than a very limited time. Two of our
Wichita observation pilots had already died before we could fish
them out of the drink. Our anger was made more intense by the

philosophic and good-natured spirit in which the merchant ships received the order and saw us turn tail. Only when we were clear of the immediate battle and steaming back in line ahead for Scapa Flow were we able to compare notes with the British cruisers, and found that they were as bitter and angry as we were.

'I recall an exchange of signals between *London* and *Wichita* in which we were informed that the Germans had claimed us as sunk and that therefore we must be a ghost ship. Captain Hill replied: "We are so numb we cannot tell but feel positions must be reversed as we have been attending your wake all day."

'In the officers' mess at Scapa, after rather too many beakers, there was much mutual recrimination and many hard words were passed. These were finally resolved in cursing the Admiralty and their inability to judge a tactical situation from a lot of pins on a board more than a thousand miles away. It was considered to be a pusillanimous defeat and a shocking error of judgment.'

The full irony of PQ 17 is not even in the fact that the *Tirpitz* did not sail until fifteen hours after Admiral Pound's order to scatter was given; it is in the later knowledge that had the British and American forces mounted a firmly threatening opposition to her she most certainly would not have left harbour at all. For the Admiralty's concern for its heavy ships was far surpassed by Hitler's own worries over keeping his remaining capital ships intact. His fear for them was such that he had strictly ordered his naval commanders that the ships were not to be risked even against an *equal* force, but only when they had definite superiority. Had the Allies known of this, the chess of naval strategy could have been played vastly differently.

There are no mysteries about the German plans, which in recent years have all been made clear. A combined attack on the convoy had been agreed. The project was called *Roessel-sprung* ('Knight's Move'). The *Tirpitz*, cruiser *Hipper* and pocket battleships *Lutzow* and *Scheer,* together with ten destroyers, were to strike out and engage both the close escorts and the convoy—but they were to complete the action before the British battle fleet could intervene. The surface ships were to operate backed by a strong U-boat force and crack air squad-

rons brought up from Sicily to reinforce the Norwegian and
Finnish air bases.

In the event *Lutzo*w grounded while leaving harbour and
three destroyers also ran ashore. *Tirpitz, Hipper, Scheer* and
the remaining destroyers did sail from Altenfiord but not until
noon on July 5, and even then, although the enemy was aware
of the withdrawal of Admiral Hamilton's cruisers, the heavy
ships were only to make a quick strike and run, so as to avoid
a clash with the far off British battle fleet should it steam to the
attack, or with the planes from its carrier. The threat from
Victorious's planes was much on Hitler's mind and largely accounted for his delay in sanctioning the sailing of the *Tirpitz*.
This is addition to the cruisers *London* and *Norfolk* having
been reported by German planes as 'aircraft carriers'. In the late
evening of July 5, when the success of the German planes and
U-boats became known, *Tirpitz* was recalled, and at 9.30 p.m.
she turned back. The two torpedo hits claimed by *Red Star*
were not hits at all and had no bearing on the battleship's withdrawal.

The continuing arguments over the strategy of PQ 17 will echo
in the wardrooms long after the lifetimes of the men who sailed
on the convoy. They are full of 'ifs'. If the convoy had not
been prematurely scattered, what then?

On the British side it was considered that Admiral Tovey's
battle fleet could only take on an enemy fleet in open sea where
the Germans had no land-based air support. The loss of *Prince
of Wales* and *Repulse* had shown that determined planes alone
could sink capital ships, so it was thought folly to risk heavy force
against heavy force with the enemy's advantage of several
hundred land-based planes, besides the U-boats. Only if the
Tirpitz force came west and passed out of range of their air
support would the British have the advantage with two battleships plus the *Victorious*'s planes.

Admiral Tovey's two plans, the first to sail the convoy in two
parts at intervals, the second to turn the convoy back for 12-18
hours to lure the enemy forward to his area, were both rejected

by the Admiralty as having serious snags. In the first case the enemy could have attacked each part convoy as heavily as the whole; in the second, the convoy would have had to steam twice through a very dangerous zone—and the Germans, being only interested in *preventing supplies from reaching Russia* would scarcely have been fools enough to follow it back westward into the jaws of the British heavy force, which they knew to be somewhere in that area. Instead they could afford to wait until the convoy returned to the Barents Sea.

Admiral Pound's chief concern, in the event of the *Tirpitz* sailing, appeared to be that of saving valuable warships, letting the merchantmen fend for themselves.

The authors do not set themselves up as naval strategists, but the facts are there. It is an imponderable how the convoy would have fared had it been dispersed later, when attack really was imminent, though certainly by then, late on July 5, the ships would have been a day closer both to the Russian coast and to Novaya Zemlya.

But another major point arises, one made very clear by the great number of naval escort men who contributed to this book. This is that if PQ 17 had gone on as a convoy, and if the enemy could have mounted a series of attacks like that of Independence Day, ammunition must have run out on some ships and run very low on others, with the inevitable consequence that the merchantmen would have been left undefended just the same. It now seems unlikely that such overwhelming attacks would have been made, but the fine balance of the argument must rest on the fact that several of the escorts, on reaching Archangel, were down almost to their last shell. Had the fleeing ships met any of the 'enemy vessels' continually reported by Admiralty signals there would have been a different tale to tell. These curious signals, several of them intercepted by *Lord Austin*'s limited radio equipment, remain a mystery. None of the 'warships' reported so dramatically was ever seen, though it will be remembered that on one occasion *Austin* passed over the exact position of a reported enemy group.

All considerations, however, do not detract from the main

issue, which is that the convoy was scattered prematurely and entirely above the heads of the three commanders at sea. With this firmly established, it becomes a matter of how far some writers would wish to drive a man deeper into the grave. On a second count there is the absolute folly of the Admiralty maintaining for years a secrecy which has matched the operation itself in its resultant misery, for the admissions of error came too late to repair the hurt caused at the time, and they have not been sufficiently widely made known. Survivors of the convoy, their families and friends, and others not involved with the action yet strangely gripped by its despairing mysteries, have repeated to the authors the same plaintive questions. What *really* happened? And why? *Why?*

In America particularly, merchant seamen of the convoy have through the years seen various writings appear and observed sadly the way in which, from time to time, higher controversies have been conducted, their lost ships being swallowed up among brief statistics, their fate never fully told. They have read pulp stories of ships 'tossing and heaving their way through sheeting blizzards and pitch darkness' in the middle of the Arctic summer, and similar tales so very far removed from reality that they would be laughable were they not an insult to those who sailed. Stories, even, describing a great enemy feat of arms.

The enemy's exuberance at his 'victory' over the scattered merchant vessels is something which has stuck in the craw of the surviving crews. As one man twice torpedoed sums it up: 'They were virtually handed a licence to bomb, torpedo and photograph us, then shoot off home to photograph themselves putting on their medals!' Which in essence is true. Seldom can so much film footage have been taken of a single action at sea, all from an enemy standpoint and reaping a rich harvest in propaganda. These pictures have, in the years since, provoked many a hollow laugh. For the enemy's action to be taken as any special feat of arms is to border on the ridiculous. Such incidents as four U-boats stalking one ill-armed merchant ship; of a U-boat taking three torpedoes to register a hit on a motionless vessel; of combined U-boat and aircraft assaults in some cases beaten off

for hours by a single merchantman; of planes dropping a fantastic number of bombs in crazy effort to obtain a direct hit;
these are scarcely stories of skill and courage. In the major
actions, the torpedo-bomber battle of Independence Day alone
can be recognized in part as a spirited assault. In part because
although the daring of the squadron leader is unquestioned, the
bulk of the other planes could well have done more. As the
Life photographer with U.S.S. *Wainwright* commented in his
article at the time: 'The Americans watched with interest the
way the pilots of the German torpedo planes drove home the
attack. Only the squadron leader of a Nazi formation of seven
planes dove in through the A/A fire, and won the admiration of
his enemies. The other German pilots veered off, fudged their
run and dropped their torpedoes at random. It was a far cry
from the way the American and Japanese torpedo planes have
been fighting in the Pacific. After two-and-a-half years of it,
the Germans seemed to have lost some of their determination.'

The seven hours' bombing of the remnant convoy on its way
from Matochkin Strait to the White Sea is an especially dismal
statistic for the enemy, if one for obvious reasons happily recorded here. In all that rain and hail of bombs only two vessels
were lost, and both of these shelled and sunk by the escorts after
damage from near-misses. This appalling marksmanship of the
enemy bombers was a consistent feature, their inability to hit
even a near-defenceless merchantman having been repeated time
and again in the survivors' stories.

As for the U-boats, before scatter they had not sunk a ship or
penetrated the escort screen. Even during the attack by torpedo-
bombers, when the escorts were busy with the planes, they did
not move in to attack. The only ships sunk by U-boats were
'sitting duck' merchantmen without asdics, and often it took
three U-boats to sink a ship. No wonder Allied seamen have
smiled at pictures of the U-boat crews being pinned with their
medals. The poor showing of the enemy planes and U-boats is an
important point to be considered against the Admiralty's re-
luctance to risk the battle fleet east of Bear Island; when, according to some senior British and American officers who were

with the fleet, the battleships U.S.S. *Washington* and H.M.S. *Duke of York* could well have handled the *Tirpitz* in a show-down.

The plain fact is that by the book, following the scatter order, not a ship of PQ 17 should have survived. Had the enemy kept to his original plan and the planes, U-boats and surface craft attacked in a more aggressive manner PQ 17 would have been totally destroyed as prophesied by Lord Haw-Haw. It was no idle comment made by Admiral Pound that, had he such forces as the enemy commanded, and the positions been reversed, he could have stopped all Arctic convoys completely.

The finale to PQ 17 is the story of the return convoy, which with more determined efforts by the U-boats saw two of the surviving American merchantmen go down, along with the lead British ship, a tanker, minesweeper and a destroyer. Six losses, when the merchantmen were outnumbered more than two to one by their escorts. About QP 14 Admiral O'Brien has some further strong words to say:

'I have always had one major criticism of its conduct—applicable to PQ 18 and QP 14. A special screening formation was produced for the escorts and this formation was stuck to without alteration from the start of PQ 18 to the end of QP 14. I thought it more suitable for a fleet than a convoy, i.e. a formation with a greater speed of advance than eight knots, but I expect this is arguable. What is not arguable to my mind, is that when under continuous enemy surveillance (as we were) one must employ a flexible system of screening which can be, and should be, varied at frequent intervals. This was never done and the pattern of sinkings by submarine attack indicated clearly that the Germans worked out a method of penetrating this screen and proceeded to do so with dreadful regularity. One must not help the U-boat—how can one help him more than by presenting him with exactly the same screen formation day after day?

'I remember feeling much sympathy with the ships who found themselves at the rear of the convoy because, it seemed to me, they were the next victims of the inevitable attacks being successfully launched from the quarters of the convoy. And very often they were.'

At this space of years one cannot look back at PQ 17 without the feeling that it was doomed from the start, and that presentiments at the time were spelled out in full. Yet one can see the many small miracles that attended it, for it is remarkable that the actual loss of life was kept so small.

But what a fiasco. The remnants of the great United Nations convoy to save Stalingrad got through, in the end, with a puny load of supplies. Yet the Russians, in spite of this failure and the long, long wait for the next convoy, did not collapse. Not only did they hold out during this time but before long they drove the enemy back. A fortunate set of circumstances, but for us the final irony.

How different PQ 18. The 'Woolworth' carrier, cruiser cover and plenty of fighting destroyers all the way. Film and newsreels, the whole operation well publicized. From now on, convoys would have much-needed air cover.

Maybe PQ 17 did not sail in vain.

And *Lord Austin?* After QP 14 she joined Western Approaches Command at Liverpool for a short spell of escort duties. Then the old Admiral, C-in-C Northern Ireland, told her company almost with tears in his eyes that she was required for Arctic service again, but not from Iceland this time. Now convoys were sailing from Loch Ewe, because German agents were active in Iceland.

Austin sailed with a convoy in the spring of 1943 in some of the worst weather encountered on the Russian run, fierce gales and mountainous seas which swamped the accompanying *Lord Middleton* so that she had to turn back. But enemy activity was negligible and Murmansk was reached without mishap. *Austin* stayed in Russia for some months, working with minesweepers, then back to the U.K. for more escort duties.

Hours after D-day she escorted a convoy to Normandy. She was making an asdic patrol round the anchorage off the French coast when she set off an acoustic mine over which several ships had already passed unscathed. It broke her at once and she sank quickly, taking some of her company with her.

Such was the sad end of the gallant little trawler, one of the only two British warships to be sunk during that particular operation.

> *'My word, you won't arf cop it. . . . What*
> *have you been doing—fishing?'*

ACKNOWLEDGMENTS

The authors are grateful to the following merchant survivors and naval veterans of PQ 17 who unstintingly gave their time to help in the making of this book, often providing diaries and papers together with their first-hand reports. Names are given alphabetically, with rank held at the time; decorations are those awarded for service on the convoy.

AMERICAN MERCHANTMEN

BELLINGHAM: A/B Harold D. Lunt.

CHRISTOPHER NEWPORT: Lieutenant (jg) Peter M. Coy, USNR, Armed Guard Officer.

EL CAPITAN: Lieutenant (jg) Louis D. Marks, USNR, Armed Guard Officer.

EXFORD: Oiler Lionel W. Smith.

HOOSIER: First Assistant Engineer Willard L. Davis.

JOHN WITHERSPOON: A/B Ferocious O'Flaherty (with many thanks for permission to refer to and quote from his book 'Abandoned Convoy').

OLOPANA: Gunner Edward Hennessey, BEM.

PANKRAFT: Radioman J. E. Blackwell, USN.

PETER KERR: Second Mate William P. Connolly.

SILVER SWORD: Second Mate John Behnken.

WASHINGTON: Captain Julius Richter.

Also the response and help of: Mrs. Anne T. Hill (*Pan Atlantic*); Gunner Arthur McDonald, Jr. (*Washington*); Oiler W. C. Stackhouse (*Alcoa Ranger*).

In addition the authors acknowledge the invaluable assistance of the U.S. Navy Department (Captain F. Kent Loomis, USN, Retd., Assistant Director of Naval History) in providing official survivor reports of the following ships: *Alcoa Ranger, Carlton, Daniel Morgan, El Capitan, Honomu, John Witherspoon, Pankraft, Washington, William Hooper*.

BRITISH MERCHANTMEN

BOLTON CASTLE: Cook George Duncan; Chief Cook J. Leonard Osmundsen; Gunner Charles H. West.

EARLSTON: Lance-Bombardier Richard F. Crossley; Stoker A. J. Robinson; Cadet A. V. Watt, BEM, LM.

EMPIRE BYRON: Carpenter Frederick Cooper, DSM; A/B Walter B. Shepherd.

EMPIRE TIDE: Chief Officer George E. Leech, DSC; Boatswain C. L. Medhurst, DSM; Engineer Officer George Robinson; Fireman E. V. Williams.

HARTLEBURY: Gunner Arthur Carter.

OCEAN FREEDOM: Acting L/S Gunner Jimmy Gordon, DSM; Captain William Walker, DSO; Gunner Herbert Wharmby.

RIVER AFTON: A/B Adam J. O'Hagan; A/B W. N. Marsh.

DUTCH MERCHANTMAN

PAULUS POTTER: Gunner David J. Richards.

RESCUE SHIPS

RATHLIN: Junior Officer Ernest M. Bentley.

ZAAFARAN: P/O (Sick Bay) L. A. Bryant; Carpenter James Ramsay.

ZAMALEK: Chief Engineer A. S. Dawson, DSC; Surgeon-Lieutenant N. H. R. McCallum, RNVSR.

BRITISH TANKERS—R.F.A.

ALDERSDALE: Chief Engineer W. J. Brown, DSC; Captain Archibald Hobson, DSC; Third Officer Henry W. Phillips; Gunner Thomas W. Urwin.

GRAY RANGER: Chief Engineer D. L. S. Hood, DSC.

BRITISH CLOSE ESCORTS

AYRSHIRE: Sub-Lieutenant John F. Aylard, RNVR; Lieutenant Richard W. H. Elsden, RNVR.

DIANELLA: A/B Kenneth J. Richards.

HALCYON: Telegraphist J. A. Hart; Stoker S. Isam; Sub-Lieutenant James McDowall, RNVR; P/O J. T. C. Welch.

LA MALOUINE: Sub-Lieutenant F. H. Petter, RNVR.

LORD AUSTIN: T. O. Telegraphist Hugh Davey; Signalman Gordon Hooper; Leading Seaman Arthur W. Mallett; Signalman Jim Morris; Telegraphist Johnny Rose; Lieutenant E. Leslie Wathen, RNR, commanding.

LORD MIDDLETON: A/B (SDO) Arthur Jones; O/D Murdo MacGregor; Chief Engineer John P. Mair; Stoker Alex Milne.

NORTHERN GEM: Coxswain S. A. Kerslake; Skipper-Lieutenant W. J. O. Mullender, RNR.

PALOMARES: Signalman Douglas Blamey; Sub-Lieutenant (Sp) Leslie Clements, RNVR; Leading Telegraphist Maurice Davies; Signalman J. B. Taylor.

POPPY: Lieutenant John Beardmore, RNVR; Sub-Lieutenant Denis C. Brooke, RNVR; Leading Stoker Reginald Lantsberry; O/D H. V. Pittman.

POZARICA: A/B Walter Edgley; O/D Charles Gooch; A/B (ST) William S. Mayne; C.P.O. (Q.R.1) Peter Reid; A/B A. G. Webster.

SALAMANDER: Stoker Thomas McClements; Stoker G. Moore.

Also: Asdic Rating Alex Atmore (*Britomart*); John G. Galley (*Pozarica*); A/B Jim Harber (*Pozarica*); Radar Operator Glyn A. Hughes (*Pozarica*); Stoker E. Jeffries (*Britomart*); Coder R. C. Kimberley (*Palomares*); Arthur E. Lay-Flurrie (*Pozarica*); P/O Arthur H. Norton (*Britomart*); R. J. Smith (*Palomares*).

Destroyers

FURY: O/D (C.W.) Norman V. Smith.

KEPPEL: A/B A. E. Davies; P/O Frederick Wicks, RN; A/B Harold Williams.

LEAMINGTON: A/B Oswald Tranter.

LEDBURY: Stoker P/O G. H. Smith.

OFFA: Chief Bosun's Mate Danny A. R. Daniels; Signalman Richard Hodgett; First Lieutenant W. D. O'Brien, RN.

WILTON: Sub-Lieutenant Michael R. Collins, RN.

The authors acknowledge the kind permission of Captain Jack Broome, DSC, and A. M. Heath and Co., Ltd., to quote from his article 'I Am Ready And Willing To Go Back', featured in 'Freedom's Battle' (Vol. 1, The War At Sea 1939-45); Hutchinson.

They also express their deep appreciation of the valuable help and comments of Vice-Admiral W. D. O'Brien, CB, DSC, Commander Far East Fleet.

U.S./U.K. CRUISER FORCE

HMS LONDON: Telegraphist C. E. Blakeborough; C.P.O. Herbert G. Bull, RN; A/B D. Murray.

USS WAINWRIGHT: P/O John W. Crawford; Signalman First Class Merlin J. Ewing.

USS WICHITA: Lieutenant Douglas Fairbanks, USNR; Signalman G. Edward Young.

The authors thank Captain Douglas Fairbanks, USNR (Retd.) for his kind help and permission to use comments from 'Knight Errant' (Brian Connell; Hodder).

OTHER U.S/U.K. WARSHIPS

HMS AVENGER: A/B John A. Annand.
HMS SOMALI: Stoker First Class A. Bailey.
USS WASHINGTON: Lieutenant (jg) Daniel W. Jones, USNR.

The authors thank Vice-Admiral B. B. Schofield for his very helpful interest in this book and for permission to quote from 'The Russian Convoys' (Batsford).

They record the kind co-operation of more than 80 U.S. newspapers and 40 U.K. newspapers, together with maritime unions and organisations of both countries, all of whom played a part in the long search for ships and men, also the efforts of a host of helpful correspondents. Especially, in America: Howard Bethell (Brooklyn, New York); Frank H. Cressey (Portland, Maine); Marc Enright (New York); Charles Hollisian (Cambridge, Mass.); Robert Kissel (Cincinnati, Ohio): John F. Laird, Ex-Commander, USNR (Colorado); Robert L. Mahar (Randolph, Mass.); George Edward Stanley (Memphis, Texas).

And not least, for all her hard work, Mrs. Mary Vaughan (California).

The lines from the song "Jingle, Jangle, Jingle" (Composer Joseph J. Lilley; lyrics by Frank Loesser) are quoted by kind permission of Chappell and Co., Ltd.

Index

Trawlers Go To War

THE STORY OF 'HARRY TATE'S NAVY'

Trawlers Go
To War

THE STORY OF
'HARRY TATE'S NAVY'

by
PAUL LUND
and
HARRY LUDLAM

LONDON
W. FOULSHAM & CO. LTD
NEW YORK   TORONTO   SYDNEY

W. FOULSHAM & CO. LTD.
Yeovil Road, Slough, England

This book is dedicated
to every 'sparrow' who
passed through the Nest

CONTENTS

Introduction

'Harry Tate's Navy'

The Royal Naval Patrol Service was a very special service indeed. It was, in fact, a navy within the Royal Navy, down to the unique distinction of having its own exclusive silver badge, worn by sea-going officers and ratings. Its unlikely headquarters was a municipal pleasure gardens by the sea at Lowestoft with the odd name of Sparrow's Nest. Its fighting fleet consisted of hundreds of coal-burning trawlers, drifters and whalers brought in from the fishing grounds and dressed for war with ancient guns, most of which had been used to fight World War I—and some the war before that.

Fish holds became messdecks, and trawls were swapped for mine-sweeping gear; asdic sounding equipment was fitted for anti-submarine patrol. Then off went the fishermen to the bitter waters of the Northern Patrol, to the Channel and 'E-boat Alley', to the Atlantic and Arctic convoys, to the U-boat ridden U.S. east coast, Gibraltar and the Mediterranean, Africa, the Indian Ocean and the Far East. Vessels, many of them as old or older than their out-dated guns, made astonishing journeys of thousands of miles, fighting in strange waters and braving heavy odds. Other Patrol Service men helped to crew the small nucleus of Admiralty-built trawlers which existed at the beginning of the war, and others as they left the shipyards, besides a variety of requisitioned craft including armed yachts, boarding vessels, and paddle-steamers converted for minesweeping.

To start with, the ships of the Patrol Service were manned almost exclusively by skippers, mates and men of the Royal Naval Reserve, except for communications ratings, who came from a white-collar world. The crews were fishermen, tugmen and lightermen, and their officers were skippers from the fishing fleets, with a leavening of senior ranks from the Royal Navy and RNR to ensure that a modicum of naval discipline was observed. But as the war dragged on, the huge expansion in Patrol Service shipping had to be matched in its crews, and so there poured into Sparrow's Nest an ever-increasing flood of ordinary civilians from all walks of life, many of whom had not been to sea even on a seaside pier. As they went off to join their ships, their ignorance of nautical matters was a source of wonder to the fishermen, who also found it hard to understand what these men were doing in *their* navy, while the outlook, customs and language of the seamen produced no less wonder among the white-collar brigade. Yet somehow, with toler-ance and good humour on both sides, the mixing process worked.

However, in spite of all the efforts of the naval men in charge and the great influx of newcomers, including RNVR officers, the casual, haphazard atmosphere of the fishermen's navy persisted, as did its fiercely stubborn independence, if not downright cussed-ness. The fleet of rust-stained, weather-beaten fishing craft—'minor war vessels', in the official language of the Admiralty—earned the nickname of 'Harry Tate's Navy', after the famous comedian of the 1920s and 30s who was eternally confounded by modern gadgets and contraptions, the embodiment of the ordinary man struggling with irritations he could not control.

So the 'sparrows in the Nest', as Lord Haw-Haw called them, went forth from the efficient madhouse of their central depot to fight the war in many parts of the world, facing enemy planes and warships, U-boats, E-boats, mines and terrible weathers with a courage, skill, endurance and determination which won the admira-tion of their comrades in the big ships.

Grim statistics tell the measure of the contribution by the Patrol Service in World War II, for at the final count it had lost more vessels than any other branch of the Royal Navy.

Starting with 6,000 men and 600 vessels, 'Harry Tate's Navy' grew to 66,000 men and 6,000 vessels of all descriptions. One very green Ordinary Seaman who joined it was a bank clerk named Paul Lund, and it is from his experiences, together with those of more than a hundred officers and men who generously contributed their diaries, letters, papers and fresh personal testimony, that this book has been written.

It hopes to tell for the first time the eventful story of His Majesty's other navy, just how it was.

I

The Death of 'Cocker'

Anything less like a British warship it would have been hard to imagine. She lay in Tobruk harbour, H.M.S. *Cocker*, an unlikely ship in unnatural waters, far, far from home.

Even her saucy name was unreal. She had been launched in the 1930s, all 300 tons of her, as the more prosaic *Kos 19*; for she was a sturdy Antarctic whaler, and had served her peacetime masters well in the most relentless of oceans, doing one of the toughest and bloodiest of jobs, that of killing whales. Now here she was, on a June day in 1942, lolling in warm waters, renamed and fitted out with guns, asdic and depth-charges, all the paraphernalia of war.

Requisitioned only the year before, *Cocker*, like others of her kin had been brought up from the bottom of the world for service in the Mediterranean as an anti-submarine vessel; but call her what you will, try to hide her under Admiralty grey paint, dress her crew in the rig of the day, still at sea doing a punishing fourteen knots, with her midship deck awash, she was an ugly duckling.

In her brief year of war so far she had been a maid of all work, escorting, towing, 'arse-end Charlieing', and had earned several commendations escorting supply ships along the North African coast on the Tobruk run.

On this day, as on many previous occasions, *Cocker* slipped out of Tobruk harbour just before dusk to carry out the necessary asdic sweep of the harbour approaches prior to the arrival of her charge, a single-funnelled freighter. Once the freighter appeared, *Cocker* and her infinitely more imposing companion ship, the naval corvette H.M.S. *Gloxinia*—nearly three times her size—would take up escort stations, and as fast as *Cocker's* tired reciprocating engines would allow, they would steam down to Alexandria and the 'big eats' at the Fleet Club which all the naval crews dreamed about.

On this night, however, there were snags. The wayward freighter did not appear at the appointed time, so *Cocker* swept and re-swept, probing with her asdic for any sign of the underwater enemy, whose habit it was to sit quietly outside harbours for just such situations as this. Her crew, still at 'leaving harbour stations', began to get irritable when the skipper showed no sign of setting the watch, which would have allowed most of the men to have gone below.

By now it was quite dark, and tiring of the constant pressure, with the added danger of crossing courses with her sister escort in the blackness, *Cocker* hove-to and carried out a 360 deg. sweep. The air was like velvet, the ship blacked out, yet all men were aware of the intense urgency. Didn't the crazy, laggardly merchant-man realize that by dawn they ought to be well beyond the German dive-bomber range? Apparently not, so they cursed her, the slab-sided bastard, for the longer they waited for her to appear, the more certain they were to have Stukas with their breakfast.

Then, 'Captain, sir—vessel passing through the boom!' reported *Cocker's* sharp-eyed lookout. The whaler immediately stirred to life and, much to the surprise of her crew, took up station on the freighter's port quarter—her seaward side. *Cocker's* more usual, and safer, billet was on the shoreside of the ship she was escorting, a position which took her comfortably along under the coastal cliffs. Now this station had been pinched by *Gloxinia,* pushing *Cocker* out to the fully exposed seaward side of the miniature convoy.

But at least with the watch now set and the comforting vibration of *Cocker* at her best 'seven-o' revolutions they were thankfully on their way. Among those on watch was Petty Officer Coxswain Bertie Male.

'I was relieved at midnight, and savouring the now cool air I went aft, where, following instructions that all off-watch personnel must sleep on deck while in this danger area, I had brought my camp bed up from below. Having set up the bed I stood eating a door-step of a third-grade salmon sandwich before getting my head down to the pure bliss of, at the most, three hours' undisturbed sleep.

'The jangling alarm bells jerked us into life for action-stations. Then, as if driven by a monumental sledgehammer, an enemy torpedo rammed itself into the very vitals of *Cocker.* Instantly our ship and home was no longer either—she seemed to disintegrate, almost dissolve into the sea. A second explosion followed, probably a boiler going up. By the light of flickering flames it was obvious that the ship had been blown almost in two. This, and the effect of the engines being at full-ahead, had collapsed her at about midship point into a mass of rending metal.

'The stern half, still motivated by a revolving propeller, seemed now to be crushing forward and downward on to the rapidly sinking bow section. There was the noise of grinding metal, rushing water, steam gasping out of fractured pipes, bulkheads collapsing, the agonized cries of trapped shipmates. The stern began to rise clear of the water, the activating arm of the whistle on the funnel dropped forward and there began a long drawn-out wail that lasted until she died.

'I ran up the canting deck to the stern rail, climbing over the rail out on to what normally would have been the vertical plates of the stern. Now they were nearly horizontal, so steeply had she sunk by the head. There to my horror I saw the propeller still furiously turning at 'seven-o' revolutions. So *that's* what 70 revolutions looked like. My racing thoughts were now playing me tricks, and I recalled in absolute detail the day when, as a boy, wilfully playing with a chaff-cutting machine in a friend's farmyard, I accidentally cut off another boy's thumb. I thought, was I now to be chaff for these great revolving blades?

'Although I had seen similar disasters overtake a dozen other ships I still could not believe that it had actually happened to us. But the noise was real, and so was the flotsam now swirling past, and men in the water gasping with the shock and immersion in fuel oil. My brain cleared. I had only seconds to get clear, not only of the revolving scythe but also from the ship's depth-charges. We had forty charges in the racks and some of these were primed and at the ready, which meant that when the mangled ship had sunk to a certain depth they would go up.

'In a frenzy I stripped off all my top gear, but a navy blue roll-necked sweater recently arrived from home defied all my efforts to get it over my head. Coolly now I selected a space among the floating debris and jack-knifed into the hole, surfacing in thick oil, gasping and conscious of the sodden weight of the sweater. Try as I would while treading water, I still could not get the sweater over my head, nor could I swim a yard with it on. There was nothing else for it but to cut it off, which I did, blessing the fact that I had kept my knife on me and wondering oddly at the same time what my sister would have said at her knitted labour of love being cut to ribbons. Then I swam like the devil as far as I could get from the ship's suction and the slowly sinking depth-charges.

'It was hardly minutes since the torpedo had struck, though it seemed a lifetime. In the darkness I could hear men talking in the sea quite close to me. I eased my swimming pace and looked back at the remains of the ship now bolt upright in the water, with the propeller still slapping round. She began to slide, accompanied by the never-to-be-forgotten death noises of a ship broken and doomed. Bulkheads were crashing, great bubbles of air vomiting up to the surface—the nudity of those parts of a ship normally seen only when she was in dry dock was as starkly shocking as one's first view of female nudity. Above all this I heard a voice nearby call out in agony, "I can't swim! I can't swim! . . ." and a callously matter-of-fact voice from another direction answer "You've left it bloody late to learn, chum!"

'*Cocker* vanished in a welter of volcanic eruptions, leaving a sudden heavy silence, and those of us struggling in the sea began the soul-destroying task of finding out who was left. The fuel oil was warm and smooth to the touch, but tasted vile—choking coughs in the darkness began to indicate the presence of survivors. There seemed to be a fair number of us in the water, but sound at sea-level is deceptive. Calls of men to their mates, and the shouts of others telling what wreckage they were hanging on to confused the air; it seemed that half a Carley float was the best there was to offer. Then we were aware of the thud of approaching propellers, and pent-up feelings gave way to rousing cheers—it seemed as if half the ship's company had survived and were intent on making themselves heard.

'But then our shouts and cheers died away miserably as it slowly began to register on us that the approaching vessel, the *Gloxinia*, was not bent on rescue, but at full-ahead was, with regret carrying out the newest Admiralty Fleet Orders—that the enemy must be sought out *regardless of survivors*. We were now consumed by a slow build-up of hatred for the men in the fast-coming corvette, who in seconds would be hurling depth-charges among us; yet, bitter as we felt, we knew that this was a captain carrying out his instructions.

'*Gloxinia* came hounding on at a great pace, and as more men in the water realized what was about to happen great oaths were hurled at the ship which only half an hour before we had chatted with via the Aldis lamp. "Swim away—get out!" cried my brain, and being naked except for my khaki shorts I struck out in the water as fast as I was able. And here, for me, fate took a hand. From close by came the panic-stricken screams of a young seaman, all tangled up with what he thought was some undersea monster. I stopped swimming to help him; it turned out that his belt had broken and his trousers had slipped down around his legs, hindering his leg movements. By great good luck we came upon a dan buoy which had been spewed out by *Cocker* and I hoisted him up on to this, following quickly myself and getting the buoy under our stomachs with our legs still dangling in the water. We had only just made it when *Gloxinia* fired a pattern of depth-charges.

'I have never been kicked in the rudder by a mule, but that is the best way I can describe it. Three pairs of depth-charges, three mule-like kicks which, beginning at my tailbone, travelled up my spine and clamoured to get out of the top of my skull. It was sheer hell, but being halfway out of the water we were relieved of the full force of the explosions and so survived, while others around us died horribly.

'Afterwards it went strangely quiet, no chattering voices or calling to shipmates. It seemed that each of us still alive was now afraid to call in case he should find himself the lone survivor from the assault of the corvette, which had vanished into the darkness to continue her search and escort duties. . . .'

Gradually *Cocker's* survivors did come together. There were only a dozen of them, including the skipper (Lieutenant John Scott, R.N.V.R.) whose own escape had been one of the narrowest. He was in his cabin, dazed and going down with his mutilated ship, when he heard quick voices above saying 'The Old Man's dead!' This roused him and he rallied and managed to slither out through the porthole, which had only been enlarged three months before for just such an emergency. But the following blast from the depth-charges rammed the skipper hard in the stomach and paralysed him from the waist down.

The survivors now struggled on in the sea, some twelve miles from shore and twenty miles from Tobruk.

Coxswain Male: 'We had only the half of a Carley float, into which we packed the injured until it settled so low in the sea they were sitting up to their armpits in water. The remainder of us kept off the float, as in this condition the injured had just positive buoyancy. Here our messdeck comedian came into his own to equal even this situation, as with great deliberation he said: 'If Noel Coward were here I suppose he'd be singing "Roll Out The Barrel". Well, I bloody don't feel like singing—not even "Show Me the Way To Go Home"!' It was about four hours to dawn and we could only hope that *Gloxinia* had wirelessed our position and that daylight would bring a rescue ship before the Stukas found us.'

The initial shock and the effect of the depth-charges slowly wore off; men began to chatter a little, and some in answer to questions disclosed that they had injuries, the true extent of which would only be made apparent by daylight and death; one man's head was so torn open that the brains were showing.

The waiting hours to dawn, and the uncertainty of what might or might not arrive with it, proved too much for one man. From out of his utter all-night silence he suddenly went berserk, thus seriously endangering the precariously situated inhabitants of the damaged liferaft. It needed great courage for one of the other survivors to save the rest by hitting the crazed man with a piece of debris. The man slipped away and sank, to join those who had already died.

It was nearly noon before the remaining exhausted survivors were picked up by a British motor torpedo boat.

Cocker's skipper, Lieutenant Scott, recovered from his ordeal to return to sea in command of one of the bigger frigates. Awarded the DSC, he later added a bar to this when he destroyed a U-boat.

Coxswain Male, who had joined the Service as an ordinary seaman and progressed to leading seaman and then petty officer, went on to take a commission and reach the rank of Lieutenant, RNVR, with his own command—an unusually talented rise from rank to rank.

And *Cocker*? Her death added yet another hard statistic to the appalling losses of the trawlers, drifters, whalers and other craft that comprised the unlikely warships manned by the Royal Naval Patrol Service—'Harry Tate's Navy'. Nearly three hundred such ships had been lost to date; by far the largest losses of any section of the fighting Fleet.

It had all begun in the grounds of a seaside council's pleasure gardens, three years before. . . .

2

A Nest of Sailors

It was a sunny August day at Lowestoft in 1939. Though the storm clouds of war were about to break, the little Suffolk fishing port and holiday resort seemed as yet untouched. In the walled municipal pleasure gardens called Sparrow's Nest, overlooking a flat beach lapped by a lazy North Sea, all was peace. Green lawns, bowling greens, colourful flower beds and lily ponds, strolling holidaymakers and others lolling in deckchairs.

It was a brochure picture of the most easterly town in Britain, 'first in the land to greet the rising sun.'

Next day all was abruptly changed, as into the Nest strode the Navy.

Telegrams had gone off to retired officers standing by for the emergency. Now in they came to Lowestoft to take over Sparrow's Nest as a transit depot for the Royal Naval Patrol Service. Trawlermen already in port, members of the Royal Naval Reserve, hurried to report there. One of the first to arrive on that day—August 24th—was William Thorpe, mate of a Lowestoft trawler just docked.

'It was eleven o'clock on a brilliantly sunny morning when I got to the Nest. Sunning themselves in deckchairs on the main lawn were Elsie and Doris Waters—"Gert and Daisy"—and members of the cast of their seaside revue showing at the Nest's concert hall, but there was no show for them that night. By the afternoon there were several of us there, besides some naval Regulars from Chatham. We took the seats out of the concert hall, altered all the stage, and stowed beds and blankets where we could, working on till midnight. Next day more RNR men arrived and we all slept there. On the third day we were made up into crews, given £5 each to post to our wives and sent off by bus to Hull. There we

took over six trawlers and sailed them down to Dover to convert
them into minesweepers.'

At the Nest, the idle summer was ended. Gert and Daisy's revue
vanished overnight, the only reminder of it being a parcel of props
in the centre of the stage marked 'To be Forwarded.' So swift was
the takeover that the local newspaper went to press carrying an
advertisement for next week's shows at the concert hall, shows
which could never take place. But it did manage to get in a rushed
paragraph on another page which explained, rather mysteriously :
'Sparrow's Nest Closed—Owing to last-minute developments the
shows at Sparrow's Nest, advertised on another page of this issue,
have been cancelled. All the other entertainments will be as usual.'

That was the last notice about the Nest the newspaper carried,
and while the fishermen, as they arrived in port, streamed to its
gates, the other entertainments did go on as usual, notably at the
cinemas, showing such popular new films as Robert Donat in
Goodbye Mr. Chips, Ronald Colman in *Lost Horizon,* and Gracie
Fields in *Shipyard Sally.* Holidaymakers still abounded in the town
and the local regatta went on as planned, though a small item in
the *Lowestoft Journal* reported that sailings of steam trawlers for the
North Sea fishing grounds had been stopped, and that those at sea
were being recalled by radio.

By August 29, when the order went out for general mobilization
in Britain, Sparrow's Nest was already flying the White Ensign.
Many more men like William Thorpe had joined the Navy's
requisitioned fishing vessels and were busily stripping them for
conversion to war service. Into Lowestoft by every train came a
fresh influx of RNR men from other ports; seamen from the coal-
burning trawler and drifter fleets which fished around Britain's
coasts and out on the Dogger Bank, and others who went farther
afield in their deep water trawlers to the icy Barents Sea and
remote Bear Island. All well experienced men, they were passed
quickly through the Nest and on to ships hurriedly converted and
armed, and given a white, instead of a red, ensign to fly.

On September 3, officers and men at the Nest paraded on the
lawn before the naval officer commanding. To the younger RNR
men he seemed so old as he leaned, puffing, on his stick, and told
them the dramatic news of that morning : 'Gentlemen, I have . . .
(grunt) to tell you . . . (grunt) . . . that we are now at war with . . .
(grunt) our old friend . . . er—enemy, Germany. . . .'

Men from the main fishing ports of Milford Haven, Fleetwood,

Grimsby, Hull and Aberdeen now flocked to the Nest, arriving in a hundred different ways.

Some heard of the emergency at sea. Like Skipper John Harwood of Aberdeen, a veteran of the Patrol Service in World War I. 'I was fishing off the Minch, and was changing grounds to a position off the Butt of Lewis when I heard on my wireless that the liner *Athenia* had been torpedoed by a U-boat. The same day I saw a number of naval ships making for Cape Wrath. I knew then it was war, and made tracks for home. I didn't see any other ships all the way to Buchan Ness, so I decided to go on to harbour at Aberdeen. It was packed with ships, all awaiting mobilization. Within a week I was sent to the Nest to await an appointment.'

Some men were already in port when they answered the call. Like Douglas Finney, an engineman trawling out of Aberdeen, who the morning war was declared, was at home recovering from dermatitis. 'All my relatives in the RNR were getting their call-up papers and knew they were due to leave, but there was no word of my papers. My wife became convinced that the recruiting office hadn't heard of me, and she promptly marched me down there. The RNR commander told me not to worry, that I'd be called up in due course, and to get off home again. I *was* called up in due course : they were at the door with my papers the very next morning, and I left for the Nest the same evening, arms bandaged and all. My relations in the RNR didn't leave until about a month later. So much for a patriotic wife!'

The RNR men were fishermen of all ages who had each undergone three weeks' annual naval training. For other men now wanting to join up with their colleagues there would have been sore disappointment had it not been for the experience of Skipper Sidney White, of Hull. When the first trawlers were being requisitioned, Skipper White, who had been at sea since the age of sixteen, volunteered for the RNR but was told that the age limit was 35, and he was two weeks over age. The skipper went to his MP and questions were asked in the House of Commons, with the result that the rule was speedily altered to allow men over 35 to join up.

Throughout September the numbers of men arriving at Sparrow's Nest increased daily. The Nest's incongruous name, which came from its wealthy former owner, named Sparrow, was replaced by the temporary ship name of HMS *Pembroke X*. There were sentries with fixed bayonets at the gates now, but men could still walk in or out at any time, and inside there was no Service discipline, nor would it have worked had there been. To help kill the boredom of men waiting for ships—and to get them out of the hair of the overworked administrative staff—route marches were devised; but although these started out in orderly fashion, when the marchers got back a good many men would have disappeared. The one time everyone turned up in strength was on pay day.

These Patrol Service fishermen were tough men. Out trawling they thought nothing of working sixty to seventy hours on deck without sleep; they could carry on gutting and washing fish automatically, and fall asleep at meals eaten while on the job. Like the man who was given his breakfast of fish and fell asleep over it; his mates took it away and replaced it with a plate of fish-bones. When the fisherman woke up he carried on with his work immediately, thinking he had eaten his meal.

Skippers and mates of the fishing trawlers were all-powerful and had to be obeyed. The dictum was if the skipper could stick it, so could the rest; though there was the certain Norwegian skipper who, for a respite, would tie his scarf round the bridge voicepipe, put his woolly cap on top, and return to his cabin, hoodwinking the crew into believing he was still up on the bridge.

Most skippers were uncommonly stubborn, many were thoroughly harsh men. There was the trawler master on an Arctic trip who, after calling all hands on deck to shoot trawl, suspected one of his crew of feigning illness, and flushed him out of his bunk with jets of icy water from the ship's hose. But the man really was ill, with a high temperature, and died as a result of the brutal treatment. After a court of inquiry this same skipper was a changed man, and if any crewman was ill or hurt he couldn't do enough for him. Once, when a deckhand got a septic hand from a wire cut, the skipper took him on the bridge, dressed the wound and told him to stay there until he was better and to do no more work. The skipper then departed to his cabin and brought up a music-stand and a violin, which he played for the sick man between conning the ship; an experience worse, said the deckhand afterwards, than the pain from his throbbing hand.

Mates were required to command absolute authority over their crew, even to fighting them if necessary. There was the skipper who, when one of his bigger deckhands was polishing a ventilator, told the mate, a small man, to order the deckhand to do the job

over again . . . and again . . . and again, until the deckie lost his
temper and challenged the mate to a fight, in which the mate
received a terrific thrashing. While getting beaten up, the mate saw
the skipper roaring with laughter on the bridge. Afterwards the
skipper told him : 'Well, Mr Mate, you needed taking down a peg
or two. . . .' The mate discovered that the big deckhand was a
former champion boxer, and the skipper had put him up to the
whole thing.

Rough and tough, and little time for lyrical romancing about
the sea. These were the trawlermen. Skippers and men went fishing
for one purpose only, to earn themselves a livelihood. A £700
catch was a good trip, and the skipper took ten per cent of this,
but he had to pay all manner of expenses out of his money,
including use of radio and baskets, watchman's fee, electricity,
water, 'stage' expenses, and food for everyone aboard. Often, after
paying out all the bills, he would be left with only £10 for himself
after three weeks' Arctic trawling; sometimes he would actually owe
the company money, which would be deducted from the proceeds
of his next trip.

The mate got $7\frac{5}{8}$ per cent of the catch. He and the skipper were
the only shareholders of the ship's company, which gave them
certain powers of action. One hard-up skipper sold his anchor and
cable for a little ready cash, which was quite legal as skippers had
the right to sell gear if they wanted to.

The true measure of a skipper was his ability to 'smell' fish,
which he did without instruments and purely from his own intui-
tion, plus the contents of his little 'Black Book'. This was the book
which all skippers kept, in which they entered, and kept to themselves, the knowledge gained of fish movements from year to year.
The true North Sea skipper scorned the use of charts and was
reputed to be able to tell where he was at any time merely by
dipping his finger in the sea and tasting it, or by observing the
nature of the seaweed. If a crew ever saw the Old Man studying a
chart they would believe the worst—that they were really lost. For
a skipper's pursuit of a catch might take him long distances to
bitter waters in some of the fiercest weather to be found anywhere
in the world. It was not unusual for a weather-battered trawler to
run out of coal and finish up burning deckboards, cabin bunks,
pannelling, anything, in order to get home.

These, then, were the kind of skippers, mates and men who came to Sparrow's Nest dressed in their once-a-year RNR uniform, or with it stuffed in their seabags. The majority went off to join trawlers converted to shoot out minesweeping gear as they had formerly shot trawl, for the great need in these early days was for minesweepers. Other men joined trawlers fitted out with asdic apparatus for anti-submarine patrol, 'pinging' the depths to detect the presence of U-boats.

Men from the Nest were very quickly in action in the Channel, in the North Sea, and off the north coast of Scotland, guarding the waters between the Orkneys and Iceland. It was here in October, after the first few weeks of war, that the trawlers suffered their first casualty. The *Northern Rover*, patrolling from Kirkwall in the Orkneys, suddenly vanished without trace. Later the *Barbara Robertson* was sunk by gunfire from a U-boat off the Hebrides.

Other trawlers fell victim to enemy mines laid in the Channel and off the Thames estuary, where Hitler's 'secret weapon', the magnetic mine, had begun to wreak havoc among shipping. Even with the threat of mine and U-boat, however, the stubborn habits of the fishing skippers died hard.

The Fleetwood trawler *Gava* was given an old 12-pounder gun and took a naval lieutenant aboard when she went out with a sister trawler, similarly armed, to guard six other trawlers while they fished. But *Gava* and her companion ship began to fish too, and were taken unawares when an Aberdeen trawler steamed up to say she had sighted a U-boat. *Gava's* naval lieutenant gave orders for immediate action to protect his small convoy. 'Chop away your gear, skipper,' he commanded. But *Gava's* skipper, with little regard for the danger they were in, bluntly replied : 'Not so bloody likely—I'm not chopping a good set of gear away !' He coolly had his men haul it in. 'Now,' he said, 'we'll go and pick up the marker buoy, and after that we'll attend to the U-boat.' Fortunately the German was never sighted.

Nor could hoisting a White Ensign sweep away old super-stitions, as the non-fisherman telegraphist sent to another aged trawler soon found.

'We had a black cat, which all our fishermen crew thought was very lucky, and once when we were due to sail they all stepped on to the jetty at Harwich and refused to go to sea, because the cat was missing. After a thorough search of the ship we found the cat in the provision locker lying under a sack of potatoes, nearly flattened but otherwise unharmed. And off we went to sea.

'We always wore our lifebelts at sea and the cat was the only one aboard without one. So one of the seamen got a Durex, blew it up and tied it round the cat's neck. It looked so funny, but we got used to it, and the cat went around like that for months. It really seemed the ideal thing.'

This old trawler was early in action during the bleak period of fighting the magnetic mine. In the space of five days in mid-November, mines accounted for fifteen merchant ships as well as two minesweeping trawlers and a destroyer. One of the merchantmen to go down was the Japanese liner *Terukuni Maru,* sunk off Harwich. The old trawler steamed out with other ships to pick up survivors.

'It was a terrible sight seeing this big ship go down. The sea was littered. But most people were picked up, and among them was a woman from Cheshire. At Christmas she sent £20 to our trawler group of five ships to buy ourselves a Christmas dinner. This was a lot of money then, and it was divided £4 to each ship.

'We were going to sea on Christmas Eve, so some of us took our £4 to the NAAFI to buy a turkey, a leg of pork and some vegetables. We had a cook who couldn't cook, no rarity then, and on Christmas morning our purchases were still lying around. A slight collision in the fog forced us to anchor, so I tried to get the crew busy. They chopped the head and legs off the turkey and I told them it would need stuffing. One man broke a loaf up into filthy crumbs and was about to stuff the lot in when I told him to mix it with water first. The result turned out rather like black plaster on the galley bench. One man then held the turkey while another stuffed in the breadcrumbs, but as fast as he stuffed them in, they came out of its neck. So I told them about skewers. A seaman got his jack-knife and hacked bits off the coalbox, sharpened them, and skewered the bird.

'I put the leg of pork on the galley bench and chopped the trotter off. This caused an uproar—"Friday, and a pig on the bench!" They thought it by far the unluckiest thing that could happen, and every man of them rushed to heave the trotter over the side. Later that day a pigeon came from nowhere and settled on the gun platform. This, they thought, was great—a lucky omen —and were soon up there feeding the bird on bread and saucers of tinned milk. Apparently its arrival was considered enough to wash out our earlier bad luck.'

Not all the early trawler crews were exclusively fishermen, there

were already some cases where 'outsiders' had turned up in force.
One RNR fisherman from Hull, still only nineteen but with years
of hard experience of trawling behind him, went from the Nest
to a trawler in which most of the crew had never been to sea
before. Her skipper and coxswain were both RNR, as were her
chief engineer and second engineer, but the other officer was a raw
sub-lieutenant RNVR, fresh from officers' training at Skegness.

'We were at Milford Haven, with four of our flotilla out in the
Haven, and our ship in dock behind the lock gates. The skipper
and coxswain were in the nearest pub. When they finally rolled on
board the coxswain immediately collapsed and had to be carried
below, while the skipper, who was three sheets to the wind,
staggered up to the top bridge. I was in the wheelhouse as his
surprise order came down from the bridge—"Let go for'ard, let go
aft—full-ahead!"

'We were only a hundred feet from the dock entrance and
pointing directly at the lock gates, which were closed. I sang out
that the Chief wasn't ready to start engines yet, and managed to
delay us to give the harbourmaster time to get the gates open.

'Eventually I eased her out into the Haven. The other four
trawlers outside had got their "picks" up and were heading out to
sea at half speed to allow us to catch up—we were going to the
Clyde for a big refit, and home for Christmas. However, our
skipper's next order was to stand by to drop anchor! Our poor
sub-lieutenant, who had come into the wheelhouse to be out of the
skipper's way, said desperately: "What the hell are we going to
do?"

'I told him to go to the foc'sle head, and when the skipper
shouted "Drop anchor!", let it drop just to the waterline, but not
into the water, and leave the rest to me. I blew down the voicepipe
and warned the Chief of our predicament and told him that whatever I did with the telegraph he was to ignore the signals and keep
the engines going at slow-ahead.

'Down came the skipper's next order, "Stop engines!" which I
dutifully rang up, then the second order, "Drop anchor!" and the
Sub did as I had told him. After a short time the skipper shouted
to the Sub: "Where's she heading?" The Sub pointed straight
ahead, so the order came down "Ring off!" and I rang "Finished
with engines" on the telegraph. The skipper then staggered down
to tell me to keep a good lookout and to call him at breakfast—
though it was still only half-past four in the afternoon. He lurched

off to his berth just below the wheelhouse and I gave him a quarter of an hour to doze off, still moving the ship slow-ahead. When I judged him to be asleep I signalled to the Sub to get the anchor up again quietly and blew down to the Chief to ease her on to full-ahead, as I didn't want to wake our skipper with any bells ringing or sudden vibrations.

'In the meantime the leader of our flotilla had been flashing at us impatiently with his Aldis. We had no signalman—the skipper or coxswain did that job—and when I asked the Sub to reply he confessed miserably that he could neither send nor receive morse. I tried what little I knew but I was dead slow, and after a few attempts the man at the other end must have thought "There's a right idiot over there" and slowed down to my speed. He was sending "What's the trouble? Get into your appointed position." I asked the Sub, "For God's sake, what's our position?" But he said he didn't know that either. "Hell," I said, "you'd better get to the skipper's berth and find the orders—but don't wake him up!"

'After what seemed an eternity he came back empty-handed— "Can't find a thing—what are we going to do?" I'm sure he could see his newly-won braid going for a Burton. However, I finally hopped the ship along until I got her into position No. 2 in line, and as no one said anything I assumed I had found the right place.

'We arrived at the Clyde the next day and the skipper was duly called at breakfast. He didn't say a word, no more did we.'

On Christmas Day the Hull trawler *Loch Doon,* minesweeping off Blyth struck a mine and sank with the loss of fifteen men. She was the last of fourteen trawlers and drifters to die in 1939. Most were sunk by mines, along with them a little drifter by the name of *Ray of Hope*. She was part of a very strange and special Patrol Service flotilla.

During the first days at Sparrow's Nest, Skipper Sidney White and five other RNR skippers reported to the concert hall to be told they were going on secret work, and could pick their own crews of twelve from men willing to volunteer for a private mission. They were then to report to Commander Charles Hammond, DSC, RN, in his 'office', a tumbledown shack on the Lowestoft dockside.

The skippers found that the ships allotted to them were six small wooden herring drifters, all much less than 100 tons. Skipper White: 'We refitted and commissioned in about 14 days, with a lot of cajoling and swearing from "Bill" Hammond over the length of time it all took. Our ships were to comprise the Mine Recovery

Flotilla, formed to undertake special mine recovery duties for HMS *Vernon,* the Navy's shore-based research establishment at Portsmouth.'

Skipper White took command of *Silver Dawn,* and the other drifters in the flotilla were *Ray of Hope, Jacketa, Lord Cavan, Formidable* and *Fisher Boy.* The little boats, their only armament consisting of a few rifles, were fitted with a small trawl sweep to drag along the sea bottom to recover ground mines, though every rock threatened to carry the trawl away. It was hoped they might recover intact one of the magnetic mines which were hitting at shipping so mercilessly, and bring it back for examination. To this end, although their first base was at Margate, the drifters were sent anywhere that a suspected magnetic mine was reported to have been dropped, according to reports of enemy ships or parachutes seen off the south-east coast. No magnetic mine was actually swept up by them or anyone else, though at last, in late November, two were found on mudflats in the Thames estuary, where they had been dropped from aircraft. They were recovered intact for the experts at HMS *Vernon* to examine and find a counter measure.

Skipper White was among the selected few taken by closed truck to the secret naval research section near Havant, where a motley crew of boffins in beards and sandals were locked in for weeks to work on the magnetic mine problem and produce an answer to it. When, near Christmas, Winston Churchill announced that 'The magnetic mine is being mastered', it was in fact still taking heavy toll among shipping.

It was the engineer officer of Grimsby base who first thought up the idea of 'degaussing' the ships—having them set up their own magnetic field to foil the mine. Initially this meant running some three miles of copper wire round a ship's scuppers, but this wire was often knocked and damaged. Later the idea was improved to fitting a single wire, powered by the ship's dynamo, in a casing round the outside of the ship.

But all this took time to evolve, and in the meantime the drifters of the Mine Recovery Flotilla, or 'Vernon's Private Navy' as they were quickly called, carried on with their hazardous fishing for mines. In December they were working from Ramsgate when two vessels were called for to tackle a specially dangerous job. Skipper White of *Silver Dawn* and Skipper Walter Hayes of *Ray of Hope* volunteered, and went out to shoot their trawls some five miles east of the swept war channel used by the convoys. The two drifters took it in turns to sweep, the other standing by, in waters where parachute mines had been seen to drop.

All went well until *Ray of Hope* got her sweep fast on the bottom. Skipper Hayes heaved on the winch, drawing his ship back, but in reversing she passed over a magnetic mine, which was promptly triggered off by the metal of her engine and fittings. *Ray of Hope* went up immediately in a terrific explosion, blowing Skipper Hayes from his bridge. The skipper and his second hand, John Bird, were the only survivors, and were picked up by *Silver Dawn* along with two or three bodies of dead crew. Though a southbound convoy was passing at the time, no help was forthcoming from its escorts, who would not venture into the dangerous waters. The remainder of the flotilla steamed from Ramsgate to help search for the lost men, but their efforts were fruitless.

The disaster was not taken lightly by bluff, bearded Commander Hammond. He was a perceptive man who worked by a frank and simple code: 'You can't drive a fisherman, but a little leadership and understanding and they'll win the war for you.' Immediately following the loss of *Ray of Hope* he called a meeting of the crews above decks in Ramsgate harbour, in sight of the distant sea where the drifter had perished, and told them that in view of the loss, any man, repeat *any man,* could opt out if he chose and return to Lowestoft. They were to think of their families and domestic commitments; he preferred uncommitted men and would not blame anyone for quitting the flotilla.

The invitation was something unheard of before in the Navy. Only about half a dozen men did choose to leave, which pleased Hammond very much. This was the situation when a new party of volunteers from the Nest came to join the flotilla, among them two RNVR signalmen. One was Signalman Bev Smith.

'At the Nest we volunteered for "special dangerous service", having romantic ideas about blockships or some such thing. Romance went by the board when we arrived at Ramsgate in the dark, at low tide, to find five scruffy little steam drifters tied up to the wall. The majority of us found we were required for *Fisher Boy.* We clambered down to find the ship occupied by a stoker, a deep sea trawlerman, who told us that only he and the skipper remained of *Fisher Boy's* crew. The skipper himself left shortly afterwards and we were taken over by Skipper George Brown, a very able Yarmouth fishing skipper.

'My signalman companion joined *Silver Dawn.* In the whole of

the flotilla there were only us two signalmen, which made communications between ships difficult, as all we had were a pair of
hand flags and an Aldis lamp.

'The method of sweeping devised by Commander Hammond and
the skippers after the *Ray of Hope* disaster was that in future two
drifters would tow one trawl along the bottom of the sea bed. In
the event of something being picked up in the trawl, one ship
would pass her end of the trawl over to the other, which would
then steam in to a gently shelving beach until she virtually went
aground. She would then slip both ends of the trawl attached to a
wire with a buoy, and steam off to anchor safely offshore while a
dinghy party went out to haul the trawl up on the beach with the
aid of any suitable towing vehicle they could find. Then the trawl
was carefully opened and the contents examined.

'We trawled many a time in snowstorms, and on one occasion
when there was a big fall of snow and the decks were covered,
Commander Hammond was leaning out of the wheelhouse window
with watchful eye when, as our two ships came together, the crews
started snowballing each other. I couldn't help thinking how
tolerant the old Commander was, with his RN background, to
allow his two minesweeping crews to skylark in this manner. But
no doubt with the *Ray of Hope* affair still very fresh in his mind he
was disposed to be tolerant with us all at that time. We were an
easy-going, pretty rough-looking crowd, many of the fishermen
having brought with them their old fishing gear of oily jerseys,
fearnought trousers and seaboot stockings.

'We hadn't a cook on *Fisher Boy* and the galley stove was
cracked. Several people had a go at cooking and the whole thing
was a pretty miserable business. Commander Hammond eventually
arranged for us to buy a new cooker or coal burning range for the
galley from a local ship's chandler. This was duly installed, and
the next time we sailed from harbour the old stove was cere-
moniously slung overboard.

'We swept for six or seven days after this without catching
anything in the trawl. Then came a day when we found by the
way the ships were moving that something had been picked up,
and we went through the whole performance of beaching the trawl.
What with the tenseness that always went with this procedure and
the opening up of the trawl, everyone's feelings may be imagined
when we found we had recovered our old galley stove.

'Christmas Day came. It was bitterly cold and we hadn't been paid since we joined the ship. One of our crew had been ashore in the morning and found a pawnshop, where he'd been able to hock some odds and ends and raise a few shillings. We had secured from the base a joint of pork, which was bunged into the oven, and we were all sitting in the little after cabin feeling pretty miserable. At this time rum was not being issued to the ship, probably because the depot at Ramsgate was not properly organized.

'It was my first Christmas away from home and I was feeling pretty dejected, when a lad from one of the other drifters came down and said Commander Hammond had sent a message round for us to call up at his office. We went up there to find that the ladies of his village had got together and baked a cake for every crew, besides sending us pairs of knitted socks and other comforts. All of which helped to brighten our day, plus the fact that the Commander told us that if we went into the local pub there was a pint of beer waiting for everybody. It was typical of the way he always thought of and looked after his men. I must say it went a great way to livening up our Christmas Day, and somehow or other, having got into the pub, we all seemed to manage to get hold of more than one pint, and came back feeling that perhaps things weren't quite so bad after all.'

3

The Fighting Fishermen

It was January 9, 1940. Around dinnertime. The trawler *Calvi* was busy minesweeping off the North Foreland when a big convoy began to pass slowly by in the swept war channel. A routine scene. But suddenly there was a tremendous explosion as the second ship of the convoy, the 10,000-ton liner *Dunbar Castle* triggered off a magnetic mine and blew up right under her bridge. She sank within minutes close to the North Goodwin Lightship, where the tip of her mast was to mark her grave for the duration of the war.

Calvi was quickly to the rescue along with other ships and picked up two lifeboats of survivors. There were 73 of them, including women and children, two nuns, and some completely naked firemen. In one of the boats was the body of the liner's captain, who died in the boat even as rescue came. Every other occupant of this boat was quickly hauled out except one dazed man, severely shocked, who refused to budge. All aboard the trawler yelled to him to make a move and grab a willing hand, but even as they called, he sat there in his terrible stupor and died.

Calvi ran out of rum trying to comfort her big load of distressed passengers. Men and women were shocked and injured, children were sick all over the ship, and through it all the nuns remained calm.

After taking her survivors safely into Ramsgate harbour, *Calvi* kept the two lifeboats as salvage, and later towed them into Dover harbour and sold them for £14.

It was just another day's incident in the sea war, now five months old, in which the ships of the Patrol Service were ever prominent, patrolling and minesweeping, and adding their names to the spiralling casualties; blown up by the mines they were seeking to clear, or devastated by bombs from raiding enemy aircraft. Like the trawler *Valdora,* an aged survivor of World War I, which was sent to the bottom by German bombers off Dover; and three trawlers which met with a similar fate in the North Sea. The *Robert Bowen,* swooped on by Heinkels while minesweeping out of Aberdeen, broke in half and sank with all hands; her companion ship, *Fort Royal,* sank in minutes. *Fifeshire,* a big new trawler which had seen scarcely any fishing time before she was given a gun, died off Copinsay, in the Orkneys, under a pall of flame and smoke from Heinkel bombs. She sank rapidly under the feet of her captain, a naval sub-lieutenant only twenty years old, leaving only one survivor to tell the tale.

Other trawlers and drifters limped back to harbour heavily damaged by bombs or carrying the bodies of crew killed by the spraying machine-guns of raiding aircraft. But it was not all one-sided. In a spirited action off the north of Scotland, three patrolling trawlers, *Arab, Gaul* and *Stoke City,* determinedly attacked a U-boat which tried to escape by lying on the sea bottom; they banged away in turn with their depth-charges until they had completely broken up the U-boat and collected evidence of their 'kill'.

Just prior to this, in dirty weather early in January, two other trawlers, together with a small destroyer, had run a U-boat on to the South Goodwin Sands, a bold action which earned each of their skippers the DSC. The trawlers, *Cayton Wyke* and *Saon,* were working from the Dover Patrol. There was a break in the Goodwin Sands where a ship could get through on a good tide, and this gap was protected by an electric loop cable. On a dark night with a strong gale blowing, the trawlers received a coastguard alert that a crossing had been detected on the loop. The three vessels steamed up and down the break in the sands, dropping 82 depth-charges, and eventually drove the U-boat on to the west of the Goodwins. Commanding *Saon* was Chief-Skipper William Mullender.

'We went in and saw the U-boat stuck fast on the sands, but couldn't approach it because of the strong gales. A cable ship came out and joined us as we waited for the weather to ease before trying to save the U-boat, for it would have been a great prize if captured intact, the first of the war. But as we watched and waited, the sands slowly swallowed the U-boat up, and its crew.'

Little 'Billy' Mullender, five feet of pluck, was without a doubt the embodiment of all the finest qualities which the Royal Naval

Reserve skippers brought to the war at sea. His private battle had begun at a very early age, for he was born such a delicate child that he was not allowed to go to school. He was plagued by an illness which cost the lives of a brother and sister, and when he was nine years old the family doctor told his father, a Lowestoft fisherman, that there was only one thing he could do, and that was to take the boy to sea on a kill or cure basis. So the ailing young Mullender began his life at sea in a sailing smack, sleeping on the upper deck with only a canvas screen between him and all weathers. It cured him. By the age of 21 he had obtained his skipper's ticket and was running his own ship, after teaching himself to read and write along the way. The outbreak of war had found him, in his late thirties, the only skipper on the coast to be master of two ships at once, running a pair of colliers between Blyth and Lowestoft; the ships had separate crews and he captained one ship at a time as the other was being unloaded—and he'd been doing this for 12 years. Like whipcord was Billy Mullender.

Back at Sparrow's Nest in the early months of 1940 activity increased tremendously. Landladies of Lowestoft who were evacuated when the Navy declared the port depot a restricted area, had to be speedily brought back to their homes to provide billets for the sailors, who now thronged the town. As the trainees generally returned to their boarding houses for mid-day dinner, it meant that regularly, four times a day, hundreds upon hundreds of men were either converging on the Nest or passing out of its gates on their way home. To avoid congestion in the town's main street they were ordered to walk along the seafront. Enemy planes over the North Sea became aware of this practice and fighters on sneak raids would skim in from the sea or swoop over at rooftop height, machine-gunning as they went, causing the ratings to fling themselves under any cover available. There was many a man who lay with his face in the grass and numbly asked himself: 'Am I going to be killed before I even get to sea?' On the lighter side, down into unwritten history went such incidents as that of the man who emerged from the lavatory in his billet with his trousers round his ankles, quite dizzy from going round and round dodging a richocheting Jerry bullet that had sought to keep him company.

Basic training was going ahead now. 'Square bashing' was done at the Oval, the former sports ground only yards away from the Nest on the seafront. Here the stokers were marched across from

the Nest by a Scottish chief stoker who played the bagpipes as they
went. On the now dishevelled cricket ground the hardened stokers
derisively shovelled pebbles into dummy furnaces—square holes—to
simulate their future work at sea.

Already there had appeared some tough, gritty characters among
the Patrol Service instructors, and perhaps none more so than
Chief Petty Officer Edward Pugh—or 'Ted the Bastard' as he
became known to all and sundry. Ted, a trawler chief engineer from
Milford Haven, had been called up to the Patrol Service at the
war's outbreak. He was in his late forties, now an instructor at St
Luke's, the big hospital on the seafront where engines removed from
ships had been set up for training engine room personnel. Brought
up under the strong discipline of a military father, Ted had been a
young Royal Artillery sergeant in World War 1, winning the Croix
de Guerre for gallantry at the Battle of the Somme. At the Nest
he was a holy terror on parade and knew his nickname full well.
He sent home to his wife for his birth certificate, and on its arrival
had it framed and mounted on his office desk. He then fell in the
'Awkward Squad', his more charitable description for the latest
batch of recruits and made them line up to read it, after which he
bellowed: 'So I'm "Ted the Bastard" am I? But only on the
parade ground with a shower of mechanical crabs like you bloody
lot! . . .'

Among the recruits coming to Lowestoft now, besides the fishermen, tugmen and lightermen, were many men who had volunteered
for 'special service' with the Royal Navy and so were sent to the
Patrol Service. Frequently the reason for a man volunteering in
this way was from a desire to escape the tedium of life in the bigger
warships; sometimes it was as a matter of expedience when in high
desperation. For instance, many naval trainees at HMS *Royal
Arthur,* the Butlin's camp at Skegness, were so desperate to quit
the camp under practically any terms that they opted for the Patrol
Service as a quick and thankful means of exit. The trouble with
the Skegness camp was that it took the full brunt of the bitter
winter of 1939-40, when, although temperatures tumbled well
below freezing point for long periods, there was no heating in the
chalets, the walls of which became coated with ice from the breath
of their occupants. The only heating for the trainees was in the
lavatories, and this provided by coke braziers made of buckets
punched out with holes and stood on a couple of housebricks.
Several ratings died, either as a result of huddling over the braziers

to keep warm, or through taking the braziers into their freezing chalets. Men who chose to escape through the Patrol Service were highly relieved to bid the place earthy farewell and unroll their hammocks on the floor of the concert hall at Sparrow's Nest.

However, many an unknowing volunteer from Skegness was in for a surprise when finally drafted from the Nest to his 'warship'. Like Seaman Robert Muir.

'We were ordered to Dover to join the *Nautilus*. We thought she was a destroyer, but when we walked along the quay at Dover and asked a man where the *Nautilus* was, he replied: "You're standing right over her!" And sure enough, as we looked over the quay at low water, there she was, a little motor fishing drifter. Still, she was nice and comfortable after we got used to her.

'Her job at that time was going out with the paddlesweepers and laying the dan, or marker buoys, also shooting and exploding mines as they were swept up. Our armament consisted of one Lewis gun and two rifles. To combat the magnetic mine we were given a "skid", a small raft with coils of wire on it, which we towed behind us when sweeping. A "skid" could cope with about three mines, after which it sank.

'Following this we became a mark-ship for one of the mine-sweeping aircraft brought in to help in the fight against the magnetic mine, which was still doing a great deal of damage. The plane had a big hoop right round it from wing-tip to tail and nose, and had to fly at about 25 feet above the water for the contraption to be effective. We hove-to at one end of the sweep, flying an extra large black flag, while the plane swept in over us, making something like 50 runs until it had cleared the area. Of course, if we had happened to anchor over a magnetic mine it would have been our bad luck!'

Came the day *Nautilus* was selected for an important cloak-and-dagger operation. All very hush-hush.

'We took on extra stores and six extra jars of rum, and prepared a berth for a naval commander. When he came aboard we sailed from Dover under secret orders. These were opened three miles out and simply told us to proceed to Sheerness for further orders. When we arrived there, the commander went ashore for his secret instructions, and on his return we moved out into the harbour and anchored. The whole crew was invited to the wardroom, and all six of us went down to find a rum jar ready opened on the table. After we'd had a liberal tot, the commander broke it to us. We had been selected to put the blockships into Zeebrugge. Our job would be to lay the dans after the sweepers up to the mole, after which we were to carry on to the mole, go alongside and find out if the lock-keeper was a fifth columnist. If he was, we were to shoot him and give the blockships the go ahead. The commander added that anyone who wanted to cry off could do so there and then and he would be replaced. None of us stepped out. "Thank you, gentlemen", he said—"I am proud to sail with you".

'Well, we made three attempts to get over there, but on each occasion, after covering about twenty miles, we were recalled, as the time was not right. By this time we had knocked back three jars of the extra rum. After the third attempt the Admiralty decided that the poor old *Nautilus* was too slow with her seven knots and took us off the job. We were left wondering what eventually happened to the lock-keeper.'

When you came from civvy street as a clerk, underwent a crash course as a telegraphist and found yourself in an old trawler with a crew of ex-fishermen, you were also due for some surprises. Like Telegraphist Thomas Burn, who had never in his life seen such hard days.

'We had to coal the ship, all hands. 180 tons shovelled through the little deck coal-holes, and we worked all night. We had very little money but broke off about 9 p.m. and went to the dockside pub for a pint. The cook was a proper rogue and flogged the little carpet out of the skipper's cabin for his beer. He later flogged his hammock, which he didn't need as we slept in bunks. We went nine weeks without pay, through moving around; no cigarettes or anything. It was a real lean time.

'We couldn't get any proper signal pads. I had a sheaf of square lavatory papers in my kitbag and this was all I could use to write my signals on for the first few weeks. There was no ship's clock and my pocket watch had to keep me in touch with the world. I controlled the radio set from the wireless room below, and if anyone on the asdic bridge wanted to pass an R/T message he had to ask me to switch on. One day as an enemy plane flew over us the skipper, up on top, snatched up his handset and bawled: "Bloody German bomber flying south-east!" The message didn't go out as I hadn't switched on, just as well, considering we had been strongly warned against using plain language; there were code groups to cover such messages.

'The crew had no idea of naval discipline. In harbour we were supposed to keep deck watches in case of prowlers, but they never did—I think I was the only one to stick to the rules! Luckily I was deck watchman late one night when two of the crew fell over the side as they were coming aboard drunk; I called the rest of the lads and we fished them out, or they'd have been gonners.

'We were working with a convoy in the North Sea in horrible weather when the destroyer in charge of the escort called us up by lamp, but as the skipper couldn't read the signals he called me up top and I staggered from one well, to deck, to well, to get the message. The destroyer was ordering us: "Proceed with consort to search area—suspected U-boat in the vicinity." The skipper said to me: "What the hell does he mean—what's a consort?" I told him, and we went off with the other trawler escorts. It was a terrific sea but we got a good contact, attacked with depth-charges and saw some commotion, though whether it really was a U-boat no one ever knew.

'Depth-charging by some trawlers could be murderous. There was one skipper who foolishly stopped his ship to do depth-charge trials, and blew half the stern off! Some skippers just hadn't a clue when it came to naval drill, either. To position their ship alongside, many depended on the jetty stopping them, and at one time it was reported that they'd done £9,000 worth of damage at Harwich. After that they were ordered to tie up to buoys in mid-stream.

'For a time my trawler escorted convoys up the east coast and we were based on the Tyne. We were in harbour one wild night, pitch dark and stormy, all ready to escort a south-bound convoy formed up outside, when the NOIC came on to the jetty and called for our skipper. I went up with the skipper, and this RN commander called from the jetty: "You've got a change of destination, skipper, can you read morse?" The skipper, knowing I was beside him, bellowed "Yes!" The commander then said we were to proceed with a convoy going north, not south, and he spelt out its destination in dot-dash fashion, in morse: ".-. ./././-/...." I whispered to the skipper "Leith," and he shouted out to the commander "LEITH!" The commander choked with fury. "You silly bugger!" he yelled. "What the hell do you think I gave it to you in morse for?" Just to add to that poor commander's sorrow, as we moved from the jetty the skipper put our sharp bow into the bows of a Norwegian passenger ship lying close by. We could see light showing through the hole.

'At sea in this old trawler we got an awful lot of water down the hatch into the messdeck, the former fish hold. This had a sloping deck, and invariably, in spite of baling out, we had about six inches of water lying at the bottom end. It swished around night and day and when the ship rolled, the water was three feet deep at the "deep end."

'The pump in the crew's lavatory never worked, so all business was done over the side. This apparently was nothing to our hardy fishermen, who said it was normal practice with them. In peacetime they reckoned that when the weather was bad they just performed on the fish, and they solemnly advised me never to eat fish. I've seen us stop a minesweeping trawler on occasion and swap them some tobacco for a basket of fish, but none of our fishermen would eat it.'

The long fight against the magnetic mine continued, now with pairs of steel-built trawlers dragging thirty magnets between them on a sweep. And still engaged on its risky task of mine recovery was 'Vernon's Private Navy.' Two of the five wooden drifters, *Fisher Boy* and *Silver Dawn,* left Ramsgate to sail down the Channel and work off Falmouth, sweeping the war channel and outside it, towing their 'catches' into the mouth of the Helford river. Here they ran their ships ashore and warped the sweep wires round riverside trees, so as to bring the catch ashore between the ships in case it blew up.

In this way they caught some ordinary mines, but none of the magnetic type, and mostly, just shellfish.

One morning at Helford, after *Silver Dawn's* crew had enjoyed the respite of a day's shore leave, oysters appeared on the breakfast table; the hands, while ashore, having scooped them up with nets and buckets. During this splendid meal in walked Commander "Bill" Hammond.

"What the hell are you eating?" he demanded.

"Oysters, sir."

"I should think they're bloody oysters!" said the commander. "Don't you know this is the Duke of Devonshire's estate and these are the King's oyster beds? You'll all be for the high jump over this—fry me a bloody plateful!"

Far from the "high jump" however, Skipper White of *Silver Dawn* found himself awarded the DSC, along with Skipper Wally Hayes, for the operation in which *Ray of Hope* was lost.

Commander Hammond at the same time received the DSO.
Skipper White:

'The air raids made it a long wait at Buckingham Palace and
we were not allowed to smoke. We began fidgeting, and I asked
the Equerry for the lavatory. "Tch, tch!" he said irritably—
"Follow me." We followed him upstairs and he opened a door.
"This is the Queen's toilet—as the West Wing is being redecorated
I suppose you'll have to use it."

'We all got in, it was a large room, and lit our cigarettes and took
our turns, but then we couldn't find the chain to flush. The Equerry
returned to find the place full of smoke. "Tch, tch!" he said, "you
could all be shot according to the ancient laws of the land!" I told
him we couldn't find the chain, and with a sigh he went up to the
lavatory, which had two lionesses for arms, pressed the nose of one
and flushed the pan.

'We were then led through room after room to the Throne room,
where stood the King with a senior officer from each of the three
Services. For us, an Admiral had to hand each decoration on a
velvet cushion to the King, who then put it on a hook already sewn
in place on our tunics. A petty officer had rehearsed us for this
every time we were in harbour. The drill was to take three paces
forward, receive the medal, take three paces back and say "Thank
you, Your Majesty." Being a small man I found that after three
paces I was still not within the King's reach, so I had to shuffle up
to him. The King began: "I-I-I-....h-h-h-h-h...." He took
ages to get the words out and they were very embarrassing moments
for all of us. When he finished at last, I boobed and said: "Thank
you, sir—I mean, Your Majesty." As for Commander Hammond,
he fell over the cushion going backwards.'

Coxswains John Bird of *Ray of Hope* and Harry Bunce of *Silver
Dawn* were each awarded the DSM. The decoration of Coxswain
Bunce was memorable in that he was the only man in the war to
have two actual DSMs pinned to his chest. He was presented with
the first one by the Duke of Kent. Not long afterwards Bunce
marched out on to a parade ground again to be presented with a
second DSM, all because of a records department mix-up. Humour
never being far from bravery he treated it all as a huge joke, one
he told rather than the citation for his award—that, although a
poor swimmer, he had dived into the sea and saved two lives.

After the decorations there was an unkind relegation for another
vessel of the flotilla. It happened this way. One day when the

drifter *Formidable* got into port, her skipper, the ship not having had any mail for some time, sent his leading hand across to the mail office. After an hour or so had passed he began to get anxious, but eventually the leading hand reappeared, towing a GPO trolley piled high with letters and parcels. *Formidable's* skipper looked up incredulously from the bridge of his little drifter, which lay well below the level of the jetty. "Hell!" he exclaimed— "That's a lot of mail for eight men!"

Eagerly they pulled the mail on board and sorted it, only to find that not one letter bore the name of a member of the crew. Suddenly they realized that all the letters and parcels were addressed not to His Majesty's Drifter *Formidable*, but to His Majesty's Ship *Formidable*—a newly launched aircraft carrier. Despondently they had to tie the mail up again in neat bundles, rebag it and get it on its way to the proper vessel.

Shortly afterwards *Formidable's* skipper received instructions that, to avoid further confusion, his ship was being renamed . . . *Fidget*. It was a blow from which he never fully recovered.

4

Where's Namsos?

One day in April 1940 as signals, far too many of them for his inadequate staff to decipher, kept streaming in from the Fleet, the harassed Duty Commander at Combined Operations Headquarters at Donibristle, Fifeshire, suddenly spotted the name of "Namsos" mentioned in one of them. Puzzled, he checked the big operational map on the wall, but Namsos was not there. The map stopped halfway up Norway.

'Good God!' he exclaimed—'it's not even on the map. Anybody got a map of Norway?'

Someone produced a school atlas, and there they found it. Namsos, a small coastal town about 100 miles north of German-held Trondheim.

If the Combined Ops staff knew little about Namsos, the non-fishermen among the crews of the trawlers hurriedly despatched there knew even less. But they were soon to find out as a strong contingent of ships of Harry Tate's Navy took on their first major concerted action of the war. In all some thirty trawlers joined in with the Fleet warships to aid the British Expeditionary Force sent belatedly to assist the Norwegians against the fast advancing Germans. The British troops landed north of captured Trondheim at Namsos, Narvik and Harstad, and south at Aandalsnes. The trawlers were to provide anti-submarine protection for the troopships and also to help ferry the troops ashore. But as it transpired, in one of the swiftest turnabouts of the war, they were soon to revert to the more dismal role of assisting in the hasty evacuation of Norway.

Eight big trawlers of the 15th and 16th Anti-Submarine Striking Force sailed from Scotland to Namsos to find that it wasn't very much of a place at all. White wooden houses and a wooden pier, reached twenty miles up Namsen Fiord; a small fishing and timber town whose inhabitants were far fewer than the 5,000 Allied troops landed there. In the course of a week's bitter fighting, however, Namsos became an inferno, and three trawlers were so badly damaged by the fierce attacks of German bombers that they had to be abandoned and sunk.

During the hours of daylight the slow moving trawlers everywhere in the Norwegian operation were constant targets for the marauding enemy planes. At each alert the ships would make at full speed for the nearest cliffs under which they could shelter, thanks to the deep water even at the edge of the fiords. Wherever possible, crews went briefly ashore to chop down small firs and branches from the larger trees, and uproot evergreen shrubs; all the greenery was then draped over the decks and rigging as a camouflage against the searching bombers. Soon a number of trawlers were steaming about the fiords looking like mobile Christmas trees. But still their losses mounted under the relentless air attacks.

Here, there and everywhere in the thick of events at Namsos, was the Hull trawler *Arab*, commanded by Lieutenant Richard Stannard, RNR, an ex-merchant officer. *Arab* was always at hand to aid her sister ships in trouble and she also rescued the survivors of a bombed and burning sloop. Her outstanding moment came when Lieutenant Stannard put his trawler against the blazing pier at Namsos and resolutely fought the fire that threatened any moment to ignite an ammunition dump and send it sky high. For this action Stannard won the VC—the second naval VC of the war—together with awards for four of his crew.

After the week of desperate fighting Namsos was evacuated. On the last day at the battered town only three trawlers remained to nose alongside the shattered pier in the dark and ferry the remainder of the French troops aboard the waiting transports and a warship. Then a stop to bury the dead, including the commander of one of the trawlers, before moving off for operations elsewhere.

Meanwhile, more than 300 miles north of Namsos, *Northern Spray* and other trawlers had arrived at the naval and army operational headquarters at Harstad. They were under air attack within half an hour of their arrival, and saw half the jetty blown away. The advancing Germans, they were told, were already 'just over the hill,' while to the south, in bitterly contested Narvik, there were some two thousand of the enemy and more arriving hourly. *Northern Spray's* captain, Lieutenant-Commander D. J. B. Jewitt,

RN, was group commander of the five trawlers including *Spray*, which formed the 12th Anti-Submarine Striking Force. He stationed two trawlers in Vest Fiord, the main approach to Narvik, to observe movements and challenge any vessels moving in or out, the latter proving to be refugee craft carrying escaping Norwegians.

The trawlers generally remained stationary, sheltering under the high cliffs to escape attack from the enemy planes which swooped down in the pale light of the midnight sun.

Northern Spray took up patrol in calm and broad Ofot Fiord with her sister ship *Northern Gem*. Among *Gem's* crew was young ex-trawlerman Sid Kerslake, RNR.

'*Spray* took the port side of the fiord and *Gem* the starboard This became our regular beat, with an occasional run into Lödingen in the Lofoten Islands, for coaling and supplies. Once, while we were alongside at Lödingen, the alarm went and we tumbled on deck to see a Hurricane chasing a German plane. We were delighted to see the frantic enemy fly straight into a cliff face, and wildly cheered the Hurricane as it flew back performing a victory roll.

'Shortly after this, when patrolling Ofot Fiord in the early morning in thickly falling snow, we received a signal that destroyers and a heavy unit, believed to be hostile, were moving up the fiord. We were ordered to challenge them. Some time later we were horrified to see these ships emerge out of the snow. But challenge them we did, in true naval fashion, being greatly relieved to find that it was the *Warspite* with her covering force of destroyers on the way to stir things up in Narvik. This they proceeded to do almost every morning with clockwork regularity, and it made us feel safer to know they were around. It gave us all a great feeling of patriotism, for at this early stage of the war it was still a sort of game and we did not realize that people actually could be killed— you always thought it couldn't happen to you.'

Hearing the heavy gunfire and seeing all the naval vessels going about their deadly business set *Northern Spray's* Commander Jewitt stamping impatiently about the bridge. At last he could bear it no longer. He ordered: 'Hoist battle ensign and get all H.E. ammunition up at the ready,' and set course for Narvik. There was mist, smoke and snow all around. Soon a warship signalled *Spray*: 'What ship and what do you want?'

Jewitt answered: '*Northern Spray*—am coming to join in the bombardment.'

Back came the reply : 'Fuck off !'

And there was the passing sloop that took a good look at *Spray's* camouflage of fir trees and signalled : 'The decorations look pretty —when is the wedding?'

But *Spray* and *Gem* were soon involved in an action of their own. Seaman Kerslake : 'On the evening of May 8 we were having tea in *Gem* when the alarm went and a German plane shot over the mountains on *Spray's* side of the fiord. *Spray* fired a fierce burst at it, but by the time it was in sight of her it was also past her, as both ships lay within feet of the shore edge and were almost overhung by the sheer rock walls. From *Gem* we saw that one of the plane's engines was on fire and smoking badly. We gave the plane a full broadside from our two twin-Lewis guns, all we had time for before it passed over and disappeared beyond the steep rock wall, losing height rapidly.

'*Gem* signalled : "Have you seen our bird?" To which *Spray* replied : "You mean OUR bird !" The plane was obviously making for Narvik, so the trawler crews stood down and went back to their tea. An hour later a Norwegian "puffer"—a small motor fishing boat—entered the fiord and went alongside *Spray*. It was crewed by three Norwegians who, unable to speak English, got their message across with the greatest difficulty : they had seen the plane come down and would take men from the trawlers to the spot, which was just by Ae Fiord, not far away. Lieutenant-Commander Jewitt decided to put half a dozen men from each trawler aboard the puffer, with orders to capture any survivors and bring back confidential books and codes; the plane was assumed to have a crew of about three. The seamen concerned were not asked to volunteer, they just happened to be about on deck at the time and all were very keen to go. *Gem's* contingent included Seaman Kerslake.

'We were armed with .303 rifles and wore our tin hats, but on a lovely evening we had on only various old clothes, myself wearing a fisherman's jersey and a muffler and ordinary shoes. After all, it was always flat calm in the fiord, no need for seaboots, and we were only going after a crashed plane's crew—or so we thought.

'The puffer nosed down the fiord and we lost sight of our two trawlers on turning into Ae Fiord. After a few twists and turns we rounded a small headland and there was the aircraft. It had crash-landed on the island shore with part of its port wing under water. The ground from the shore rose up 2,000 feet and was covered with fir trees and bushes, rocks and snow. If there were any survivors from the plane they were somewhere in hiding.

'*Gem's* gunner, Fred Powell, a retired RN gunner called back to service, lay on deck on the puffer with his Lewis gun resting on the stem-post, covering the area. We nosed into the shore, but the boat touched bottom some six yards from dry land, so we had to jump in and wade ashore with the water up to our waists. Eight of us followed in line behind the officer-in-charge from *Spray*, a small, bespectacled skipper from Grimsby.

'We were laughing and joking about our unexpected "paddle" when Gunner Powell suddenly shouted: "They're up on the hill— I'll give them a burst over their heads!" I guess he thought they would then give themselves up, but he had only fired a few rounds before the Germans opened up with a Spandau firing explosive bullets and blew away half his head.

'Our shore party dived across the shingle for the sheltering rocks, the enemy bullets whistling over our heads. I levelled my rifle at a German up on the hill, but in the excitement I hadn't slipped the safety-catch. In the second or so before I could release it, Jack Sullivan, *Gem's* asdic operator, said urgently: "Don't look now, Sid, but there's a dirty big Jerry behind you!" I then felt a bayonet at my back, and that was it. We all surrendered, being overwhelmed by German troops. Too late it was realized that the plane was a troop carrier and their casualties on crashing had been small. But one of us did escape. This was our officer, who hid in the water behind some rocks and later crawled away unseen.'

All three Norwegians aboard the puffer were killed by the German's hail of fire, leaving the boat going round in circles. Every other man on board—all from *Spray*—was wounded, some very seriously, but despite being shot up in both ankles, and in great pain, Asdic Rating Sid Gledhill courageously struggled into the wheelhouse, pulled aside a dead Norwegian whose body was jammed in the wheel, and steered the boat away.

Seaman Kerslake: 'It was all over in minutes. We saw the puffer disappearing stern first out of the fiord, and the Germans gathered our rifles and threw them in the water. Then they searched us. They were a company of crack Alpine troops from a Jaeger battalion, thirty-five strong, plus the plane's crew. Taking us up to the top of the hill, where they had set up an emergency camp, they got a fire going and gave us some bread and a hot drink of ersatz coffee. After being questioned we were allowed to settle down on the ground on rocks that were free of snow. We were all bitterly cold and shivering as our wet clothes were beginning to freeze on us, but we would have felt far worse had we known that the survivors on the puffer, on their return, reported that we had all been killed.'

The plane had initially been damaged by a Skua aircraft from the *Ark Royal*. The German pilot, although with one leg completely shattered, had brought the plane down to a forced landing just short of the water's edge without a single extra casualty. They had then made their high camp commanding a clear view of the plane far below, and the entrance to the fiord.

Seaman Kerslake: 'We had been in the camp for about three hours when we saw a British destroyer come in and land a party of Marines. At this the Germans decided it was time to be off. The Unteroffizier gave us German greatcoats to warm us, and ordered us to carry their equipment, including guns, boxes and bandoliers of ammunition, and the machine-gun. We were warned that we would be shot if we tried to escape, after which we began a march inland across the hills. The Germans planned to strike directly across the island to a tiny village on its opposite coast, where they hoped to seize a boat to take them to the mainland. And so we set out, the wounded pilot being carried on a door from the plane rigged up as a makeshift stretcher.

'All the time we marched a brutal-looking little man in uniform took photographs. An officer of the plane's crew told me this was the Nazi of the group, and they all had to jump to his orders. He warned that if we tried to escape the Nazi would kill even those who made no attempt to do so. When we had walked a considerable distance waist-deep in snow, crossing streams of icy water, I was desperate for a "slash" and asked permission from this crewman. He told me not to be more than a minute or he would be obliged to shoot, as my move would be taken as an attempt to escape. I had my quickest "slash" ever! Afterwards we talked as we marched and he told me he had flown to London in civil aircraft pre-war and liked London very much.

'It was daylight when we reached the opposite coast, and to their dismay the Germans saw that *Northern Spray* had rounded the island and was steaming at sea off the village shore. She opened fire and shells began thudding into the hillside above us, far too close for the nerves of the Germans. They hurriedly put us in a shepherd's hut together with their wounded flyer, and cleared off.

We lay low during the shelling. At last it stopped and we heard rifle and machine-gun fire close by.

'Our signalman in *Gem*, Charlie Keen, opened the hut door cautiously, and there facing him was a hefty Marine with bayonet fixed, all ready to skewer him. "A bloody Jerry!" yelled the Marine, and only Charlie's dire mouthful in the most violent English caused him to stop the bayonet in mid-air. We all ran out waving madly and shouting that we were British matelots.'

Events had moved swiftly since the return of the puffer, which was a distressing scene. In the darkened hours of late evening, Telegraphist Eric Bardsley, of *Northern Spray*, had looked down on its arrival from the trawler's wheelhouse veranda.

'From the returning boat came a flashed SOS, repeated again and again. Commander Jewitt was suspicious and ordered the gun crews to cover the boat. When it arrived alongside, the scene on board was one of utter shambles and horror. *Gem's* gunner lay dead in the bows, and the three Norwegians, all dead, were jammed in the wheelhouse. There was blood everywhere, with every man aboard wounded and in pain. Our own gunlayer had a nasty wound in his back, and Sid Gledhill, who had been sending the SOSs, was suffering from the wounds in his ankles. Seaman Yardley was shot in the leg, while Seaman Wood had a huge hole in his back and was carried aboard spreadeagled with his shirt off, showing all the extent of the hole. He called out jokingly to his helpers, "They got me, pal!" Harry Peak, a Hull fisherman, was the worst injured, he had been raked by bullets and the whole side of him from thigh to ankle was laid open.

'We now had six badly wounded men aboard with only rudimentary medical supplies and medical knowledge, so we had to act quickly. We made for Lödingen, which was only a few miles away, towing the damaged puffer to hand over to the Norwegians there. We flashed the sloop *Stork* for a doctor, but her reply was that we should proceed to Skanland. We did so and found the *Resolution*, flagship of the FOIC Narvik. It took us two hours to reach her with our badly wounded laid out in the wardroom. Harry Peak was in a dreadful state, stretched out on a couch. Ramsden was kneeling beside him and saying: "Harry, can't we harmonize 'Somewhere In France With You'?" and in spite of his great pain Harry managed to sing it with his chum.

'All the wounded were taken aboard *Resolution* while 150 Marines came aboard *Spray* with the object of rounding up the

German force. The question was, where had they gone, and how? It was a desolate, untracked area. The major in charge of the Marines guessed that they would try to obtain a boat, so we went along Ae Fiord inquiring at each village, but without result. We almost gave up, but then decided to visit a small, uninhabited place called Skjellesvik, on the far side, and there we found the Germans up on the hillside. The Marines put ashore parties which made a pincer movement on the hut, another squad approaching from the rear in case of escape that way. From *Spray* we could see them crawling up the ground on either side of the hut while the gunners on board fired thousands of rounds from the Maxim at anything else ashore that moved. The Germans were seen leaving the hut and moving up the mountainside, and when the hut was stormed the Marines found only the prisoners from *Gem* and the wounded pilot.

'During this action we received a signal from *Resolution*, "Where are the Royal Marines?" so on our way back we signalled a brief report. We reached *Resolution* to find the Marine Band on deck playing "Life On The Ocean Wave" and all on deck gave three cheers for the Royal Marines and the RNR. At this moment an enemy plane flew over and was shot down by *Resolution's* ack-ack guns, at which there were three more cheers!

'Poor Harry Peak died after having his leg amputated, and he was buried in a civil ceremony at Skolund. We now had a very depleted ship's company of only 22 fit men.'

As for the Germans, the Marines captured nearly all of them and handed them over to a company of French Alpine troops. Seaman Kerslake: 'The French, we learned later, stood all thirty-four Germans up against the rocks and shot them, their explanation being that they did not take prisoners.'

Next day *Northern Gem* was ordered to shell the island village, in case any more Germans were in hiding. This she did with her ancient World War 1 four-inch, also spraying Lewis gun shot over the entire area. But there was no sign of a living thing until suddenly a Norwegian puffer appeared from the land side of the jetty and made off at speed along the coast. *Gem* hailed her to stop but she did not, so the trawler gave chase and fired a warning shot across her bow.

Seaman Kerslake: 'The puffer then came alongside us, throwing out a line for'ard and another aft, which we made fast. Our replacement gunner, together with a seaman and an officer—our leader on the plane party—dropped on board the vessel to investigate for Germans. But immediately they set foot on deck the man in the puffer's little bridge put his engines full ahead and simultaneously the two men at the ropes cut them through—and away she went.

'We dared not shoot for fear of hitting our own men, who were fiercely attacked with knives and axes by five Germans (so we thought) dressed as fishermen. Eventually our three men, after shooting two of the attackers, jumped overboard. As we picked up the gunner he laughed, said "Thanks", and died immediately. The seaman was severely cut, but our bespectacled officer was a terrible sight. He had been chopped with an axe right between the shoulder blades, and there it stuck. Our deck ran with blood, and it was a miracle he survived.

'We chased after the puffer, firing with machine-gun and Oerlikon until she stopped. She was riddled like a cullender when we drew alongside, there were four dead men on deck and another shot to bits in the wheelhouse, which had been blasted to a shambles. This time our men who boarded the boat did so with caution, and hearing a noise down in the foc'sle one man fired a round down the hatch and yelled: "Come up—out, out!" At this a very old man and a very old woman came up on deck, followed by a young woman carrying a baby in her arms.

'I can't describe the silence that followed. I thought all the crew were going to cry—I certainly felt like it myself. We brought the frightened trio and the child on to the *Gem* and sank the puffer. Only after questioning did we learn that the old people and the young mother and baby were the survivors of two families of Norwegians joined by marriage. When we had fired on the village their menfolk thought we were Germans and decided they should all make a dash for it in the boat. Why they had not recognized our White Ensign was a mystery.

'One of the men we had killed was the young woman's husband. We had a whip-round the crew for her, it was all we could do.'

On *Northern Spray* in the quiet hours of the night they began to pick up German wireless transmissions in morse. Regularly every night at 2 a.m. the same station broadcast a half-hour "programme" in the German language and in groups of cyphers, always signing off with "Heil Hitler." Telegraphist Ken Edwards, with his schoolboy knowledge of German, managed to understand one word in twelve and also recognized Norwegian place names from that area.

The first part of each message appeared to be in the form of a navigational report, the word *fyr*, Norwegian for lighthouse or lightbuoy, being repeated often, while the last part of the broadcast seemed to be a weather report. Commander Jewitt was informed, and at the next 2 a.m. "broadcast" *Spray's* wireless cabin was filled with people listening in with the loudspeaker switched on. At a guess, they placed the transmitting station as being about twenty miles away. Commander Jewitt alerted *Resolution*.

One night shortly afterwards, as *Spray* was alongside a small village, the German station came in as usual and "flooded the dial" —they were right on top of it. *Resolution* took a "fix" with direction-finding equipment, and confirmed that the mystery station was in the village. The next night an armed party went ashore and captured the enemy operator, a Norwegian fifth columnist. Jewitt was complimented on the vigilance of his wireless staff, which might well have saved the lives of many troops in the hard fighting which was still going on.

For both *Northern Spray* and *Northern Gem* there now followed a welcome break from weeks of almost ceaseless patrol, as each ship went for a week's boiler clean at Svolvaer, the chief town of the Lofoten Islands. Here the friendly and hospitable people could not do enough for the trawler crews, and there were parties galore during their stay. *Northern Gem's* arrival at Svolvaer was auspicious enough. All her ammunition spent, she was about a mile from the port when an enemy bomber zoomed to the attack. The trawler could only retaliate by firing starshells from her four-inch, but fortunately this was enough to drive away the German. *Gem* drew in to the dockside to be greeted by most of Svolvaer's inhabitants, who had watched the duel. They were led by the smiling mayor, who presented the trawler's skipper with the case of one of the starshells she had fired; it had landed in the local cemetery close to where the mayor and his friends had stood watching the fight at sea.

The hospitality of the people of Svolvaer made *Gem's* return to Svolvaer soon afterwards, during the evacuation from Norway, all the more bleak.

The trawler was ordered to escort to the UK a small Norwegian passenger ship, the *Ranen*. This coastal vessel had become a buccaneering auxiliary of the Royal Navy armed with Oerlikon and Bofors guns and crewed by an enthusiastic motley of naval ratings, Marines and soldiers. She was skippered by Commander Sir

Geoffrey Congreve, RN, who had promptly taken the ship over after losing his trawler, the *Aston Villa*, to enemy bombs.

Ranen and *Gem* left Lödingen together, steaming out of Vest Fiord with the object of doing as much damage as they could to what was now virtually enemy held territory.

As they approached Svolvaer *Gem* was challenged and fired on by a vessel which seemed to be an enemy trawler. *Gem* replied immediately with her starshells and started a fire on her attacker, at which the mystery ship went behind some rocks and vanished completely; neither *Gem* nor *Ranen* could discover any further sign of her, or any wreckage.

The two ships then steamed to Svolvaer and, with *Ranen's* piratical crew in their element, pumped lead and shell into the harbour installations, blowing up all the oil tanks and setting fire to the jetties. Then, the very last ships to leave the Narvik area, they started off for home.

Halfway across the North Sea a dozen enemy planes, evidently ignoring the *Ranen*, swooped down on *Gem* and for the next five hours gave her hell. Time after time the planes, in turn, roared over her, dropping a single bomb on each run—and missing. Finally one plane dropped low to the sea and made two vicious wave-top machine-gun attacks, spraying the decks, windows and waterpipes and wrecking both the trawler's smallboats, but incredibly in this hail of explosive bullets containing tiny steel darts, and with one twin-Lewis out of action, *Gem* did not suffer a single casualty.

Her luckiest escape of all came when the frustrated enemy plane flew low again and dropped what looked to be an aerial torpedo about twelve feet long; as *Gem* heaved over to starboard the menacing object literally slid down her port bow—if the ship had rolled to port instead, it would have dropped square on the foc'sle head and probably finished her. The plane flew off with smoke pouring from one engine—a good hit from *Gem's* Oerlikon, bolted to railway sleepers on the foredeck.

And so back to the UK. Both *Gem* and *Ranen* were supposed to steam for Scapa, but *Gem's* skipper quickly knocked that instruction on the head. As he acidly observed: 'Once you get to that damn place you never know when you'll get out!" So instead he headed for Aberdeen, where his war-weary crew secured an immediate two weeks leave.

Fourteen trawlers were lost in the Norwegian campaign, all

falling victim to enemy planes. Among those were some so badly damaged that they could not make the crossing home and had to be sunk by British forces. The Germans, however, were able later to salvage seven of the trawlers and sail them again under the enemy flag.

One of the earliest losses was the *Larwood*, sunk at Narvik, and one of her wounded survivors was none other than Ted the Bastard —Chief Petty Officer Edward Pugh, back at sea again as a relief from suffering the raw recruits at the Nest. He escaped the Germans and came back to Britain in the cruiser HMS *Glasgow*, which brought King Haakon and Crown Prince Olaf to safety.

On the lighter side was a cameo of Harry Tate's Navy retained by men of the warships. When all the destroyers were speeding out of Ramsdal Fiord, a trawler signalman with a small, battery-operated signal lamp stood on top of one of the cliffs asking the first destroyer for instructions for the asdic trawlers. Owing to the speed of the destroyers and slowness of his signalling, each destroyer down the line got a piece of the message . . . .

As a further instance of what the individual trawlers went through there was the *St Cathan*, which survived no fewer than twenty-nine attacks by enemy bombers while operating in Vest Fiord. *St Cathan* went to Norway armed with one Lewis gun, 350 rounds of ammunition, and her four-inch. Like several others she came away loaded with guns, her crew armed to the teeth; and with other "loot" besides. For with the Army retreating so fast, culminating in the complete evacuation of Norway, equipment of all kinds had to be abandoned—headquarters gear, the contents of officers' messes, radios, staff cars, and a whole assortment of supplies. Much of this abandoned gear was hustled on board by trawlers taking off Allied personnel and Norwegians wanting to escape to the UK. Towards the end the scramble of men and goods became chaotic.

Fitted carpets found their way on to trawlers' messdecks; even Austin motor cars of the wartime utility type were swung aboard and later used by the ship's officers—until reclaimed. Some other items came from shattered shops and buildings, for in Jack's fair reasoning nothing was stolen but merely saved from the advancing enemy.

When *Arab*, the VC trawler, steamed triumphantly back to her base at Belfast it was her multitude of scroungings that seized the eye. A seaman who saw her come in describes the fantastic sight.

'She came into Pollock Basin late one grey day, to the whistles and cheers of trawlers tied all around, a heroine ship, with the star performer on the bridge, the captain himself. But the really interesting thing was her appearance, for she looked like a Robinson's removal van. One forgot to look at the bullet holes, the dangling radio aerial and halyards and other marks of battle, because rivalling them in attention, and in the end completely overshadowing them, were the contents which this pantechnicon from Norway had brought back with her.

'She looked like a second-hand shop, with every conceivable item of movable equipment loaded all over her decks. On the well-deck some musical matelot strummed out "The Fleet's In Port Again" on a brand new grand piano. Leaning against it were numerous new motor cycles and next to them some prams. The remaining welldeck space was thickly covered with tables, chairs, mattresses, rolls of lino, deck chairs, and all the contents of an ironmonger's shop. More gear lined the port and starboard gangways and the after end, with the lighter, smaller bits stacked up all over the engineroom casing. But all this was extra to what was hidden below decks, where enough was stored to start up several shops.'

The humour, however, could not disguise the melancholy at the sudden withdrawal. As Telegraphist Bardsley of *Northern Spray* noted : 'We are amazed by the news that units of the Navy, the NWEF, and certain French and Norwegian army units are being completely withdrawn from Northern Norway. Narvik has been destroyed by the Allied forces so as to render it useless to the Germans for some time to come. A great proportion of Germany's light naval forces are at the bottom of the fiords and scores of her planes lie wrecked on the mountains, but the cost has been heavy for us, too. History may never know of many of the gallant deeds done on bleak mountainside or along the calm fiords, but from French Foreign Legionnaire to Grimsby trawlerman, all have put their whole heart and soul into the bitter struggle to save Norway.'

The trawlers' last loss of the campaign came with the tragic end in action of *Juniper*. On June 7 *Juniper*, commanded by Lieutenant-Commander Geoffrey Grenfell, RN, sailed from Tromso, far north of Narvik, escorting the tanker *Oil Pioneer*. At dawn next day she sighted heavy warships, and wirelessed an urgent signal reporting her discovery. Then, ordering the tanker to sail independently, she bravely turned and challenged the big ships. Back came the reply from one of them that she was the British cruiser *Southampton*. But she was not, she was the German *Hipper,* and her heavy guns proceeded to blast *Juniper* out of the water. Only four of her Patrol Service crew survived, and were rescued from the water along with a score of men from the tanker, to be taken to German prison camps.

Even before the tragedy of *Juniper*, however, other ships and men of Harry Tate's Navy were fighting and dying in a bigger and more dismal evacuation. Dunkirk.

5

'Gracie Fields is Making Water'

In May 1940 the five wooden herring drifters of 'Vernon's Private Navy' were all together again at Ramsgate, but working under the temporary command of Lieutenant-Commander A. J. Cubison, RN. He was a man with an orderly turn of mind and, unlike his predecessor, decided that his first duty was to organize the flotilla on proper RN lines. This included trying to improve the drifters' rather haphazard system of communicating with each other at sea.

Signalman Bev Smith of *Fisher Boy:* 'I was landed with the job of devising a simple code of signals that the skippers could easily understand. I managed to compile one and it was typed out by Commander Cubison's secretary. To give some idea of its extreme simplicity, the signal flag letter "A" meant "Form single line ahead," while flag "C" followed by a number gave the true course on which to steam; and so on.

'Having distributed the code to all the skippers, Commander Cubison importantly hoisted his first signal somewhere off Ramsgate harbour, and sure enough the drifters got into a line. He then hoisted a course signal. The response was that some of the ships altered course as soon as the signal was hoisted, while some decided to stay in line and change course in line ahead. The result was that in an astonishingly short time he had the five ships of the Mine Recovery Flotilla spread out from the North Foreland pretty well to Dover. But he wasn't deterred and tried two or three times to get these signals right, though really with little success. Shortly afterwards we had other things to think about when little coasters from Holland and Belgium started to arrive in Ramsgate harbour carrying a mixture of civilians and Dutch and Belgian seamen. We heard that things weren't going too well in France.

'One day Commander Cubison was observed standing on the

steps of his office with a handkerchief in each hand, waving like fury at our little fleet moored across the other side of the harbour. Someone alerted me to the fact that the Commander was "doing something a bit odd on the steps" and I realized he must be trying to send a semaphore message. It read: "All ships raise steam immediately and prepare for sea." He came down to us very soon afterwards, had a quick word with the skippers, then joined *Lord Cavan* and hoisted his now famous signal "A"—"Form single line ahead." We steamed out perfectly and took a short cut across the Channel, regardless of minefields, to Dunkirk harbour.

'We were to go in, bring off British troops and load them on to transports which would be lying off Dunkirk. When we got into the Dunkirk Roads there were some noisy bangs and flashes which had us all pretty frightened. With the sky lit up from the glare of burning fuel storage tanks, our flotilla milled about off the harbour, undecided. I was at the helm of *Fisher Boy* with little Skipper George Brown standing beside me. *Fidget* closed us and her anxious skipper hailed across to ours: "What are you going to do, George?" Promptly George Brown pushed his head out of the bridge window and bawled: "I'm a-going in, boy!" And with that he told me to bring *Fisher Boy* well over and we steamed for the harbour, the other drifters deciding to follow us in.

'I was smoking Craven A cigarettes and gave one to Skipper Brown, who, I noticed, was trembling violently. He popped the cigarette into his mouth the wrong way round and made three attempts to light the corked tip end before I saw what he was doing and told him to reverse the cigarette. He was an amazing man. I was just as frightened as him—we all were; none of us knew what had happened so far at Dunkirk and for all we knew the harbour was already occupied by German troops. But George Brown always visibly shook with fright in such cases, which made it even more courageous the way he would go into any danger. I never knew him to do anything other than carry out his instructions, regardless of how he felt at the time. He was a very brave man.

'It was something of an anti-climax getting into Dunkirk harbour. We managed to make fast to the mole, then looked around for soldiers but couldn't find any. However, we worked our way down into the general harbour installations, found some troops and encouraged them to come aboard. They were very weary and were glad to join us. Our cook was kept busy making tea for thirsty mouths. We finally left the harbour with about 250 troops crammed aboard and went out to find one of the transports supposed to be waiting outside. Seeing the silhouette of a ship in the distance we steered for her, and promptly went aground on a sandbank. Too late we found that the ship had been hit and abandoned, and was in fact sunk. Fortunately the tide was making, so we came off the sandbank without too much trouble.

'George Brown now searched around to see if any other ships were available, and finding none, decided we'd have to take the troops back to Ramsgate ourselves. We were all relieved to get back and see the troops safely ashore, but were none too happy when a naval officer ordered us to load up again with stores and get back to Dunkirk forthwith. This we did, in daylight, and though we had a few shocks we made the crossing without harm. This time we took scaling ladders made by Ramsgate carpenters to help the troops climb down from the mole on to our little drifters.

'By now Commander Cubison had established the *Lord Cavan* in Dunkirk harbour as a command vessel, and was terribly busy about the place. I was up on the mole with him and two or three others, trying to encourage more troops to come aboard down the scaling ladders, when we heard sudden great crashes and bangs as the German big guns shelled the harbour. The troops, being quite used to this by now, smartly dropped flat on their faces—and as we felt they knew what they were doing, we got down beside them pretty quickly. But Commander Cubison remained standing amid the shellfire and gave us one hell of a coating—told us to get up and get on with it. He seemed to have absolutely no fear at all, in fact one almost felt he revelled in things getting so lively. We loaded troops aboard *Fisher Boy* until it was impossible to move anywhere on deck or to remove the scaling ladders from the mole, so we just steamed away leaving them there.

'*Fisher Boy* was still in one piece when we got back to Ramsgate on this run, though the main steam valve was leaking badly and I doubt if we were making more than four knots. We were terribly low in the water with all the troops on board, but fortunately the weather was calm and somehow or other we stayed afloat. The troops sat on their haunches and as a destroyer raced by, her wash caused us to roll, the water seeped on to our deck and thoroughly soaked their backsides; but they were so packed that they were unable to stand up, and too tired to worry much about it anyway.

'All our drifters were by this time working independently. *Silver*

Dawn struck an obstacle in Dunkirk harbour which took a chip out of her propeller, and she vibrated and throbbed in the most hair-raising fashion all the way back to Ramsgate, but they got their troops back.'

It was *Silver Dawn's* only trip to Dunkirk because of this damage. 'Things were now getting too lively to continue going into Dunkirk in daylight so the rest of *Fisher Boy's* trips were timed so that we arrived after dusk. On each journey we took additional scaling ladders with us, as we were piling so many troops aboard that we could never recover the ladders. Night after night we steamed there stocked up with tea, cigarettes and full water tanks to recover our biggest possible quota of exhausted troops.'

The drifters had originally been instructed to limit their loads to a hundred men each, but this rule was forgotten from the start. The astonishing loads they did carry were made possible only by a generally calm sea.

At Dover the old minesweeping drifter *Nautilus* received orders to make for Dunkirk with her sister ship, the drifter *Comfort*. But they were only halfway across when they ran into trouble. Petty Officer Robert Muir, of *Nautilus*:

'It was a pitch black night and suddenly an E-boat loomed out of the darkness. We had the sauce to engage it with our full armament—one Lewis gun. I suppose it thought we weren't worth bothering with, for it pushed off at full speed. Our skipper was rather pleased with our performance, but shortly afterwards there was a terrific explosion and next moment there were men in the water screaming for help. We stopped and managed to pick up nine men as they were swept by us on the tide. *Comfort* picked up about sixteen. They were survivors from the destroyer HMS *Wakeful;* the same E-boat we had brushed with had put a couple of torpedoes into her. Her captain was among the survivors picked up by *Comfort*.'

Wakeful had been returning from Dunkirk with a load of troops below decks when she was struck amidships. She broke in half and sank immediately, taking most of her hundreds of soldiers down with her.

Comfort was ordered to take her survivors back to Dover, but in a night of chaos she was doomed to be the victim of a terrible confusion. Shortly after the sinking of *Wakeful* the destroyer *Grafton* was similarly torpedoed, and she and the Fleet minesweeper *Lydd* both opened fire on *Comfort,* thinking the drifter to be an

E-boat. Finally *Lydd* rammed *Comfort* and the drifter's men were
fired on in the sea. It was a cruel and ghastly mess. The captain of
Wakeful was picked up from the sea for the second time that
night; there were few other survivors from *Comfort*.

Nautilus escaped the horror because her orders were to carry
on to Dunkirk and put her survivors aboard the cruiser *Calcutta*.
Petty Officer Muir:

'We located the *Calcutta* and went alongside her to discharge
our survivors. We hadn't been alongside for many minutes when
she decided to fire an eight-inch broadside inland. I was down in
the mess having breakfast when she fired the first rounds. We were
lying right below her after turret, the messdeck hatch open, and
the flashback seemed to come right down the hatch. I was up on
deck in two seconds flat and after that went down again and
changed myself.

'We pushed off inshore—*Nautilus* had a very small draught—
and anchored off the beach. There were all sorts of craft around
and lines of soldiers on the beach, and we could see there wasn't
much organization at that time. Stukas were dive-bombing and
machine-gunning everything in sight. We were lying close to the
destroyer *Greyhound* and her captain decided to go ashore to try
to get things organized, so my mate and I were detailed to take our
smallboat and ferry him to the beach, bringing back a few soldiers
on the return journey. Away we went, nursing a jar of rum in the
bottom of the boat. We arrived at the beach, put the captain ashore
and never saw him again. We picked up four soldiers, all we could
manage in the boat, gave them a good tot, had a couple ourselves
and then made for *Nautilus*. But we arrived to find her ablaze from
stem to stern, with ammunition shooting off all over the place.
Apparently she was hit by a bomb in the engine room and had
begun to sink, so the skipper set fire to the ship's papers down in
the wardroom and the ship, being all wood, caught ablaze. The
crew were picked up by *Greyhound*.

'So my mate and I carried on and took our four troops to one
of the paddlesweepers, then headed back to the beach for more.
We got to within 200 yards of the beach when over came the
Stukas again and a bit of shrapnel from one of the bombs they
dropped went right through the boat's bottom and sank us. It was
quite a swim, but we made sure to take the jar of rum with us, it
was our saviour. We made the beach and found an abandoned
lifeboat fitted with Robinson's gear—its propeller worked by man-

power on the handles. We got this afloat, then had another good drink from the rum jar, which was getting pretty low by then. We picked up eight soldiers, set them to work on the handles turning the propeller, and got them across to the paddlesweeper with the others. We then turned the boat to go back for more, but were unlucky again, for as we neared the beach there was another raid and bang!—two holes in the boat and down she went. Once more we had to swim ashore—after rescuing the rum jar.

'We decided to empty the jar and look for something else that would float, but there was nothing. Then a small naval landing craft came in to the beach to pick up troops, and we asked its commander to take us as crew. We were lucky, he needed extra hands and we were detailed to drop the kedge-anchor aft so that the boat could pull itself off again after loading up. After about two or three trips I noticed that the commander kept taking a swig out of a bottle which I thought contained water, and being thirsty I asked if I could have a drop. He said certainly, and I had my first introduction to gin. He didn't get much more after that as my mate and I nearly cleared the lot.

'Conditions on the beach were getting worse; we saw soldiers go mad and threaten to stab their pals. Eventually our landing craft was almost out of fuel and had to cease operations. The commander had no room for us on the return crossing but offered to put us on board the paddlesweeper *Gracie Fields* to take us back to Dover. We said we'd rather go on another paddler, the *Sandown,* as she was due to sail about midnight, so he took us to her on his last trip. It was the best decision we ever made. We knew some of *Sandown's* crew and they bedded us down in their quarters with a bottle and a couple of sandwiches. I didn't remember anything else until we arrived in Ramsgate and they told us that the *Gracie Fields* had been sunk on the crossing.'

No one was likely to forget the grimly humorous signal that went out above the hell of Dunkirk: 'Gracie Fields is making water in Dunkirk harbour and requires immediate assistance.'

She was one of some thirty river and seaside paddlesteamers which had been taken over to help with minesweeping, painted battleship grey and showing only a number. *Gracie* came with the first paddlesweepers on the scene, from Dover; they arrived each day at dusk, spent the early night hours filling up with troops and tried to sail before midnight.

It was on her second trip that *Gracie* was bombed by enemy

planes and hit in her engine room. The old naval minesweeping sloop *Pangbourne*, returning to Dover jam-packed with troops, tried to tow her with the sweep wire but *Gracie's* rudder jammed and she sank slowly. *Pangbourne* was able to save all her crew and passengers.

The paddler *Sandown* had a charmed life. On one occasion thirty-seven dive-bombers made a mass attack on her and failed to score a hit—though just one bomb would have been enough to sink her. And there was the old *Emperor of India,* another from *Gracie's* flotilla, which made four trips to and from Dunkirk, once towing twenty small craft astern : lifeboats, yachts, motor boats, and a rowing boat with an outboard motor which had picked up two soldiers from the beach.

But other paddlers besides *Gracie* were lost. *Brighton Queen* went down under heavy gunfire, and *Devonia* was bombed and beached, while *Brighton Belle* struck a wreck on her first return passage. As she was sinking, another paddler from Dover, the *Medway Queen,* went alongside and took off survivors. The *Medway Queen* herself, in an unbroken week of nightly visits, brought a record 7,000 troops back to England.

A terrible disaster overtook *Waverley,* one of four paddle-sweepers from Harwich. On her first day, *Waverley* had embarked 600 troops and begun her return passage when twelve Heinkels swooped down on her in a concentrated attack. She fought back strongly, but a bomb struck her on the port quarter and crashed right through the bottom of the ship, leaving a gaping hole. The troops kept up rapid rifle fire and no more bombs hit the ship, but she would not answer to the wheel and began to sink rapidly by the stern. Within a minute of the order being given to abandon ship she had vanished, taking nearly 400 troops down with her. The survivors, including her captain, were picked up by a French destroyer and several drifters.

The three others of *Waverley's* flotilla, *Marmion, Duchess of Fife* and *Oriole,* their crews working for four days and nights without sleep and almost without food, between them brought nearly 5,000 troops safely home. But yet another paddler, the *Crested Eagle* was lost, and her story comes later.

At Dover, Second Hand William Thorpe took over the trawler *Calvi* and steamed her to Dunkirk. To help him, he had the ready assistance of Sub-Lieutenant Everett, a very popular young officer fresh from officer's training at King Alfred. Thorpe took *Calvi* in and moored alongside the jetty with two other trawlers. But the berth quickly became *Calvi's* grave, for in the heavy air raids which immediately followed she never really stood a chance.

The destroyer *Grenade*, berthed ahead of *Calvi*, was the first victim. In spite of all her guns she was soon severely hit and ablaze from stem to stern. *Calvi's* crew were among those who, in the confusion, helped to drag survivors from the oily water. Another of the trawlers managed to tow the blazing *Grenade* away from the jetty out into the harbour, where she continued to burn all night, erupting with frequent explosions until she finally sank. Before this, however, one of the trawlers with *Calvi*, the *Polly Johnson*, after being hit by bombs which killed her gun-crew, broke adrift and sank near the harbour entrance. And then *Calvi* herself began a fight for life. Second Hand Thorpe:

'I was firing the port Lewis gun, the steward loading the pans for me, when we saw a bunch of bombs coming down very close to us. We ran to take shelter in the wheelhouse, but as I opened the door to go in, the blast from the exploding bombs blew me inside, down the skipper's hatch, and before blacking out I saw everything in the cabin thrown up on to the deckhead. I don't know how long I was unconscious, the next thing I heard was the steward calling me. By this time *Calvi* was near to settling on the bottom and we staggered out of the wheelhouse to find ourselves down in the water on a level with the rail of the next ship, the trawler *John Cattling*.

'A bomb had gone through *Calvi's* counter-stern and exploded beneath her, and most of our crew had scattered. Our second engineer was in the water, and two men helped me to get him out. He was badly cut about and we stayed with him, giving him morphia tablets, till we got back to Dover in the *John Cattling*, which was well loaded up with soldiers. On muster we found we had lost only three of our company, including Sub-Lieutenant Everett. We had about forty troops aboard when we were hit, but what happened to them in the confusion we never knew.'

One of the three men missing from *Calvi* was Leading-Seaman Ernest 'Lofty' Yallop. He escaped from the sinking trawler to find himself near the *Crested Eagle*. The paddler, heavily laden with troops, was about to push off and he had just time to swing his legs over the side and get aboard before she was away. Morale was low on *Crested Eagle*, two captured Germans were shot out of hand and the gunners had panicked and left their pom-poms as screaming, diving Stukas came down so low that their tails almost touched the water.

Yallop had just gone below decks when one of the planes dropped a bomb between the funnel and the engine room.

'There was a huge explosion and she started to turn over on her side, making horrible noises. We were trapped as we stood, about thirty of us, for wreckage was strewn all over the funnel and the upper deck and we could not climb out. We all, sailors and survivors of other ships, put our arms round each other's shoulders and sang "Roll Out The Barrel." She continued to roll over to port, very slowly, with the sea creeping up to the closed portholes. Just when it seemed we were done for we managed to smash some portholes and let the air in. They worked like demons on deck to pull us up through the wreckage, the lucky ones of us. I got out to find a terrible mess. The troops had been packed tightly aboard so there was no escape from the bombing. When I came on deck it was like being in the fish hold of a trawler, except that it was humans squelching underfoot instead of fish. Blood ran everywhere and it was so slippery I could hardly keep my feet. I passed a soldier with a huge hole in his side, he was all screwed up and shaking his fist in the air at the Stukas. The ship was starting to go up in flames. Troops jumped for the water too quickly, putting their arms up in the air as they jumped, with the result that their lifejackets jerked up as they hit the water and broke their necks. A Dornier came down and machine-gunned those still alive, about thirty or forty of them, killing them as they struggled in the water.

'Sitting among the mess on deck I found Sub-Lieutenant Everett —he'd also managed to get to the paddler before she sailed. He was nursing a badly injured foot, but when I went to help him, waved me off, saying "I'm all right, Lofty—you look after yourself." The ship's bridge had gone. I scrambled to find the captain and asked him what I could do to help, but he said there was nothing that could be done and told me to get over the side immediately and try to swim across to a small troopship. As I jumped from *Crested Eagle* the flames were shooting high. After swimming for some distance I looked back and saw a man hanging on under the paddlers. It was my great pal, Johnny Stone, the ship's steward, and he couldn't swim. He was a man full of life and jokes, and now he clung on below the paddles, yelling for me to come back—I think he had hurt his spine. But I couldn't swim back to help him, it was impossible, with the ship already a blazing inferno.

He kept calling to the end and I was helpless and could do nothing.'

Crested Eagle sank only minutes after *Calvi,* taking down with her more than 300 troops.

The armed fishing trawler *Gava,* her crew not yet Patrol Service men but still civilians, had just landed her catch at Fleetwood, when she was told to steam for Ramsgate and there received naval orders to make for Dunkirk. Gunner Amos Sumner :

'It wasn't until we pulled nearer the bigger ships anchored outside that we felt the atmosphere of war. The noise of battle was loud and there was a lot of shouting. Our naval lieutenant ordered us into the harbour. There was a slight lull in the fighting as we went in, which was most uncanny. There were bodies floating all around among the debris.

'We tied up alongside the jetty and had begun to take on board the remnants of a French tank corps when suddenly there was a loud humming. We looked up and the sky seemed black with Stukas. While we were still loading the Frenchmen the planes began to dive-bomb us. It seemed a hopeless task but we kept blasting away with our old 12-pounder for all it was worth.

'I was only a lad and I was scared, and I certainly wasn't alone. Fortunately the Stukas didn't dive too low, and they took it in turns to run over us rather than coming down in force. Eventually they gave up, luckily for us, as we were getting flash-blind from the continual pounding of the gun. We were both surprised and delighted to learn afterwards that we had actually shot down three of the planes.

'We managed to rescue 376 French soldiers, but one French officer refused to sail with us. Nobody really knew why, it seemed he felt it more patriotic to remain on French soil. He stood to attention on the quayside and saluted his comrades as we sailed away.

'Outside Dunkirk we picked up the crew of a French destroyer which had been dive-bombed. Several troops aboard her fell into the water when the destroyer sank and three of our crew unhesitatingly dived in and saved them, a brave rescue for which each of them received the OBE. We finally steamed for Ramsgate well down in the water, carrying more than 500 troops and survivors—there was hardly any room to move in the old ship. One of the French sailors we'd pulled out of the sea appeared to be dead, so we covered him with a tarpaulin. On our arrival outside Ramsgate someone accidentally stood on him; he gave one big moan and sat up—what a shock!'

By dawn on what was to be the last day of the Dunkirk evacuation—June 2, 1940—a score of trawlers and drifters had added their beaten and sunken hulks to those of the paddlesweepers and other requisitioned craft operated by men of the Patrol Service. On this last day the asdic trawler *Arctic Pioneer* was patrolling the channel being used by the crowded ships crossing from France to England when through very thick fog she heard a distress signal. Powerless to help in these pre-radar days, having no idea of the stricken ship's whereabouts, she sadly fished from the sea later, a Kisbee lifebelt belonging to the trawler *Blackburn Rovers*.

The grim fate of this trawler was bound up with two others.

Blackburn Rovers was leading *Westella* and *Saon* on patrol of the waters crossed by the ships from Dunkirk when *Blackburn Rovers* made an asdic contact. Commander Rex English, RN, senior officer of the group, who was aboard her, felt sure she had contacted a U-boat, and took her in after it. But Chief-Skipper Billy Mullender in *Saon* was convinced that *Blackburn Rovers* was, in fact, 'pinging' on a wreck, and more importantly, in going in to investigate she was running right over a British minefield. He flashed urgently to *Westella* not to follow, but she did.

Blackburn Rovers erupted on a mine so suddenly and disastrously that her crew never knew what hit them. She blew up in the magazine, broke in half and sank at once. As she did, her depth-charges went off among the survivors struggling in the debris-strewn sea. *Westella* began rescue work, but then she also struck a mine. Her bows were blown off and she began to settle. Now the *Saon,* already battered from an earlier action, was forced to enter the minefield to rescue survivors from both vessels. Chief-Skipper Mullender:

'We saved thirty-six men in all from the two crews. Many of *Blackburn Rovers*'s survivors were suffering from internal haemorrhage as a result of being caught in the depth-charge explosions. The messdeck of *Saon* was like a slaughterhouse, with blood running everywhere.

'*Westella* was sinking gradually by the head, and I realized she could not be allowed to sink in her own time, as her asdic dome was still intact and this equipment was secret. I thought I heard a man cry out aboard her, and her skipper confirmed that one of his crew might still be in the ship. I called for two volunteers to go off in the smallboat to try to find this man, though I told them I couldn't wait for their return as I must go at once to Dover with the injured. My asdic-rating and steward, both Grimsby men, immediately stepped forward and were soon on their way over. I told them to put all depth-charges to safe as soon as they got aboard, in case the ship went down under them, then to make a thorough search for the missing man. They knew I had given instructions for *Westella* to be sunk by gunfire from another ship as soon as they had left her, which meant they would be left adrift in mid-Channel in a rowing-boat. But this did not deter them in any way. It was two months before I saw them again. Then I learned that they'd found the missing rating under the anchor chain for'ard, his leg broken. They got him into the smallboat and after being adrift for some time, at last hailed a tow which brought them to Margate.'

One survivor from *Blackburn Rovers,* after being rescued by *Westella,* was plunged back into the sea again when she was hit. 'I found myself with another man clinging to the large wooden nameplate which had previously been attached to *Westella's* bridge. That was just after 4.30 p.m. We clung to that nameplate and floated for two days and nights before being picked up, pretty well done in, and landed at Dover. There we lay for some hours in a quayside shelter before being taken off to hospital, where my injured legs were put in plaster.'

Commander Rex English was among the survivors picked up by *Saon.* He, like so many others, was suffering from internal bleeding after the depth-charge explosions. Chief-Skipper Mullender:

'Because of being such a mess, he wouldn't allow a steward to attend to him. So I bathed him myself, dressed him up in my own underwear and shirt, and eventually managed to get him to go to hospital.'

As this unhappy episode of the three patrol trawlers was being enacted out in the Channel, the drifters of 'Vernon's Private Navy,' which had been crossing to and fro from Ramsgate with their mercy loads of troops, each made their last journey. Signalman Smith of *Fisher Boy* :

'On the last day of the evacuation, things having got pretty desperate, *Fisher Boy* made her way to Dunkirk in daylight. But before we got to Dunkirk harbour, out in the Roads, we came upon a big troopship, the *Scotia,* which had been blasted by German bombers and lay on her side in the sea, burning fiercely.

'There must have been two thousand French soldiers struggling in the water, and there were hundreds more standing on the side of her hull, all being continually machine-gunned by enemy planes. We were the only other ship in sight, but Skipper Brown did not hesitate. We steamed in, never feeling so small with our crew of thirteen, and two or three lads went off in the dinghy to drag exhausted men out of the water while I and another of the crew slung heaving lines and hauled aboard those who could grab hold of them.

'There were hundreds of tin-hats floating on the water, and when you came up to them you saw that they were really French soldiers, who had donned small Board of Trade type lifebelts, kept on their helmets, greatcoats, bandoliers, field boots and other gear and jumped trustingly into the water in the belief that these little life-belts would keep them safe, the result being that they now floated dead in the water with just their helmets showing. It was a tragic sight which scarred us all mentally.

'When our crowded little ship got back to Ramsgate we heard that the evacuation was finished, and Dunkirk had fallen. In a way it was lucky we had come upon the *Scotia* and stopped to work among the survivors rather than going on, as George Brown would have done, into Dunkirk harbour, and probably falling victims to the Germans.'

Two other drifters *Fidget* and *Jacketa* also picked up some survivors from *Scotia*. The final casualty on that day was the 'command' drifter, *Lord Cavan,* from which almost until the last minute, the indefatigable Commander Cubison had continued organizing the beach rescue work.

An hour before *Lord Cavan* was due to sail a shell smashed through her wooden side and exploded against the harbour wall. She quickly sank. All hands got off safely and were brought back to Dover by a destroyer.

Signalman Smith: 'The crew were especially sad about the loss of *Lord Cavan* as she was well stocked up with cigarettes and other little items which they had "won" from NAAFI lorries and so on while working in and around Dunkirk.'

When the final count was taken, Cubison's little drifters had rescued no fewer than 4,085 troops from the beaches and waters of Dunkirk, and brought them safely home. *Fisher Boy*, in seven trips, had ferried one-third of these—more than 1,350 men. A truly remarkable achievement by a herring boat.

Two weeks after Dunkirk another evacuation was being attempted hundreds of miles to the south-west, at the port of St Nazaire on the Bay of Biscay. Here nearly 100,000 British and French troops and some civilians, including women and children, were awaiting ships to rescue them from the half-ruined town under bombardment from the Germans. In one convoy which arrived to help in the pick-up was the asdic trawler *Cambridgeshire*. She was a Grimsby trawler, and her commander, Skipper W. G. 'Billy' Euston, RNR, and chief engineer, George Beasley, were both Grimsby fishermen.

On the calm and sunny afternoon of June 17 1940 *Cambridgeshire* was anchored with other ships off St Nazaire. George Beasley had just come off watch and was in his bunk when the trawler was shaken by a terrific explosion from across the water. He rushed up on deck to see the 16,000-ton troopship *Lancastria* listing right over after being attacked by German bombers. The planes had scored at least four direct hits on the huge ship and she was sinking fast with more than 6,000 passengers aboard.

Skipper Billy Euston did not hesitate for a second, steaming *Cambridgeshire* at full speed for the *Lancastria*. 'Masses of men were climbing over the ship and jumping from her as she turned, and when we were still some distance away we could hear them defiantly singing "Roll Out The Barrel".'

The great liner sank in less than twenty minutes, and during the horrific scene of her dying and for long afterwards, in spite of repeated bombing attacks and the machine-gunning of survivors in the water, *Cambridgeshire's* small crew of sixteen men doggedly pursued their rescue work. George Beasley:

'As we closed up to the sinking liner the sea was black with men and we started pulling them aboard from all sides, some covered in thick, slimy oil, and others wounded and badly burnt. It was a terrible sight, a terrible mess, yet there was no panic at all. Some men sitting on the keel of *Lancastria* were still singing just before she went down, they certainly had plenty of pluck.'

Man after man was hauled aboard the trawler, which under their weight settled dangerously low in the water. They were packed in like sardines, crowding the hold, the stokeholds and engine room, until there was hardly any room to move.

Skipper Euston: 'We stayed until we had loaded far more men than we could reasonably carry, and to our regret could take no more. We left our lifeboat and threw over the side all our liferafts and lifebelts, everything that was floatable, to help those we could not take on board. When we had finished we were packed solid, every inch of space below was full and the decks were just a solid mass. We nearly capsized under the weight, but managed to steam alongside the *John Holt,* one of the transports, and transfer everyone safely to her.'

All 1,009 of them—nearly half the total survivors. For between 3,000 and 4,000 men died with the *Lancastria.* It was an appalling disaster, made all the more bitter by the mystifying neglect of other ships to come to her assistance. Had others acted as promptly as the trawler, the staggering death roll must have been much less. Instead, the casualty figures were so shocking that Churchill forbade publication of the news, on the grounds that the British public had already been fed more disaster than it could stomach.

But work was not yet over for *Cambridgeshire,* the heroine of that terrible day. The same night she steamed quietly into St Nazaire under the guns of the German bombardment, with orders to take on Army personnel for passage to the U.K. Skipper Euston :

'I was not able to leave the bridge until we were several hours out of St Nazaire, and it was then I discovered that our passengers were, in fact, the General Staff of the British Expeditionary Force, headed by the commander of the Second Army, General Sir Alan Brooke. I jokingly asked if he and his staff could all swim, and when he asked why, pointed out that we had no life-saving equipment on board, having thrown every last thing we had to the *Lancastria* survivors. He just smiled and said, "We shall not worry about that." '

Nor did they have to. Gallant *Cambridgeshire* sailed them all safely home to Plymouth.

6

The Silver Badge Fleet

Even before Dunkirk, Churchill's top secret instructions had gone out to various commands for a withdrawal to Canada if Britain should collapse. After the Dunkirk evacuation Patrol Service skippers received similar secret orders which they were not supposed to open, but which, of course, they did. The orders were that in the event of overwhelming invasion they were to steam as far away as their coal and food would allow, and if possible to make their way across the Atlantic to Canada or the U.S., and carry on the fight from there. There was many an emotional scene on ships of Harry Tate's Navy when they received their special recognition signals—six feet square, made of canvas and painted in red and white stripes—together with these depressing orders.

Men talked it over on the messdecks. Some, especially the married men, swore that in the event they would disobey orders and slip back home somehow rather than leave their wives and children to the mercies of the Germans. Others found themselves in two minds, not wanting to desert their parents and families, but recognizing what would be a desperate need to fight on. They were days of agonizing personal decisions.

Not that any ship yet was actually poised to run, all were far too active. Many trawlers and drifters, besides a host of other craft, were taken from minesweeping and anti-submarine duties to form an Auxiliary Patrol against invasion, steaming close off Britain's shores to give the alert should an enemy force sneak past the 'front line' of warships.

In early July 1940 Churchill was able to note with satisfaction that the Admiralty had 'over a thousand armed patrolling vessels, of which two or three hundred are always at sea,' and that a surprise crossing 'should be impossible.' Among this vigilant thousand were the redoubtable drifters of 'Vernon's Private Navy', still operating from Ramsgate. Signalman Smith of *Fisher Boy*:

'Ordered to take up anti-invasion patrol for the time being, we were equipped with a radio and transmitter, two Hotchkiss guns and two Lewis guns. We'd managed to get quite a few other odds and ends of armaments while at Dunkirk, so *Fisher Boy* was bristling by this time. We were also equipped with six small mines carried in two coffin-like boxes over the stern. Each mine was linked to the other by a length of grass line, and our instructions were that in the event of sighting an invasion fleet we were to steam across their course of approach and drop these mines into the water. They would float just under the water and the invaders would foul the grass line, so bringing the mines into contact with their hulls.

'The whole thing seemed to be a pretty dodgy operation and thank God we never had to put it into practice. We did, however, spend many hair-raising evenings not far off the coast of Calais listening and watching for an enemy assault. Working round Ramsgate and Dover during that summer meant that we saw a tremendous amount of the Battle of Britain and we also on many occasions engaged enemy aircraft with our Lewis or Hotchkiss guns, all 1914 vintage.'

In these dark days immediately following Dunkirk heartening news came from overseas of a triumphant sortie by one of His Majesty's trawlers—one of the few that had sailed early to the war in the Middle East. It happened only a few days after Mussolini's braggartly entry into the war following the debacle of Dunkirk; an encounter in which the little Hull trawler *Moonstone* brought swift humiliation for the Italian Navy out in the waters off Aden.

Moonstone had begun life as the fishing trawler *Lady Madeleine*. She was bought and put into commission by the Admiralty early in 1939, before war began. For this reason her crew were general service ratings, and her captain a warrant officer of the Royal Navy, Boatswain William Moorman.

In mid-June *Moonstone* was working from Aden on anti-submarine patrol when a submarine, believed to be one of several Italian boats operating from Massawa, in the Red Sea, became active. The trawler joined with other vessels in an extensive asdic sweep of the area.

During the night of June 18 one of the searching ships, the destroyer *Kandahar,* was surprised to detect the submarine surfaced and busily transmitting its daily report back to the Massawa base. *Kandahar* gave chase, but the submarine dived in the dark and escaped, nor could it be traced again by searching aircraft.

Next day, just before noon, *Moonstone's* asdic operator reported a strong submarine echo and the trawler immediately steamed to the attack, dropping depth-charges; but again the enemy escaped. Then, barely an hour later, the trawler regained contact and dropped more depth-charges. The explosions had scarcely subsided before the submarine, a big ocean-going boat, suddenly heaved itself to the surface a mile astern, streaming the Italian flag from a pole above its conning tower.

Moonstone wheeled hard round and steamed full-ahead with all guns firing, some of the crew even joining in with rifles as the distance between the two vessels narrowed. Though the submarine, which was fully three times the size of *Moonstone,* quickly returned fire, the hail of lead and shell from the trawler prevented the Italians from getting to their big gun, and finally *Moonstone's* four-inch crashed a shell into the conning tower, killing all inside it. Some of the Italians began to wave white clothes in surrender, while others scrambled into the wrecked tower to haul down the flag.

There were far too many Italians for the trawler's small crew to handle, so after warning the enemy commander not to scuttle or she would reopen fire, *Moonstone* stood off while *Kandahar* raced in to take the prisoners aboard and fix a tow to the big submarine, the *Galileo Galilei.* Much to the mortification of the submarine's crew the confidential papers which they had hurriedly thrown overboard failed to sink and were fished from the sea by the destroyer's boarding party. *Kandahar* then towed *Moonstone's* prize to Aden.

There was a grisly sequel. On arrival at Aden *Kandahar's* captain cleared lower deck and asked his crew to keep strict silence about the captured papers. Next day *Kandahar* and two other destroyers, acting on information from the papers, set sail and were scarcely an hour at sea before they took a surfaced Italian submarine completely by surprise. *Kandahar*, then no more than half a mile from the submarine, fired a warning shot over its conning tower to give the Italians a chance to surrender. But to the amazement of the British ships the submarine began to return fire. Aboard *Kandahar* was Seaman Edmund Carroll.

'The combined armament of our three destroyers was eighteen

4.7 in. guns and the Italian commander must have realized that
he hadn't a snowball's chance in hell with his single gun. We
manoeuvred in such a way that he couldn't bring his torpedoes to
bear, after which a couple of well-placed shots blew the Italian gun
and its crew into oblivion. The submarine slowly settled on an even
keel and the crew were already abandoning her when to our horror
we saw the dorsal fins of dozens of sharks weaving in and out of the
poor wretches. We heard screams and shrieks as they were eaten
alive.

'All our boats were lowered at speed. I was on the point-five
machine-guns and the captain ordered me to fire short bursts to
drive the Italians back on to the submarine, which was still afloat,
and so save them from the sharks, but this only made more men
jump from the submarine into the sea as they misinterpreted our
captain's intentions.

'As our boats picked up what survivors there were, only the
conning tower of the submarine was still visible; one boat went
alongside and our big, burly coxswain reached over and dragged
the Italian commander out of it. On our return to Aden the
Kandahar's wardroom was used as an operating theatre and our
surgeon did wonderful work to ease the pain of the Italians, some
of whom were horribly mutilated. He was later decorated.'

As for the *Galileo Galilei,* for whose splendid defeat Boatswain
Moorman won the DSC and accelerated promotion to lieutenant,
it became a permanent, active insult to the Italian Navy, being
promptly refitted, commissioned and sent back to sea as one of
HM submarines.

In Britain at this time, survivors of Patrol Service ships sunk at
Dunkirk and just after, returned to Sparrow's Nest to find it had
been given a new name—HMS *Europa.* There were new buildings
and extensions, and the old house of Sparrow's Nest had been
transformed into barrack-like administrative offices. Nissen huts for
training classes had sprung up around the Oval, and other classes
were under way in empty schools. A former secondary school was
converted into a fully-manned and equipped hospital. Inside the
Nest, air-raid shelters were dug on the lawn. The order was always
'Muster on the lawn,' though every blade of grass on it had long
vanished under the tramping of thousands of boots. With the threat
of invasion, holes were cut in the Nest's walls for rifles to shoot
through, and the adjacent ravines and scores were mined, to be set
off in an emergency by press-buttons in The Cottage, the Com-

modore's office. In this cottage, while alterations were being made, old copies of *The Times* were found under the wallpaper, including one of 1805 giving an account of the Battle of Trafalgar.

As HMS *Europa* the Royal Naval Patrol Service took on its full and complete independence as a separate navy within the Royal Navy. Promoted from transit depot to a full drafting and holding depot, *Europa* assumed absolute responsibility for training men for His Majesty's 'minor war vessels'—the Admiralty's description—and set up its own promotions roster. It made its own rules. It was still under the general regulations of the Navy, but with adaptations proposed by the Commodore, Lowestoft, and approved and published by the Admiralty.

The Patrol Service even acquired its own special badge, a unique distinction which gave the final endorsement to its separate identity.

The badge came into being in a roundabout way. It had originally been suggested for the many civilian seamen who, in the first emergency, crewed vital auxiliary minesweepers as temporary naval volunteers, wearing their usual sea rig. The badge was intended both as a special emblem for them, and as a protection should they be taken prisoner, thereby ensuring military prisoner-of-war treatment. But by the time the badge reached the design stage, a strong plea had been made for the men of the anti-submarine trawlers; that they, too, should be afforded recognition along with the minesweepers. And so the badge was designed to cover both these divisions of the Royal Naval Patrol Service and, in fact, became exclusive to it.

The silver badge, about the size of a shilling, was in the form of a shield which showed a sinking shark transfixed by a marline spike (representing the anti-submarine service), against a background of a fishing net containing two trapped enemy mines (the minesweepers), the whole surrounded by a rope with two fishermen's bend knots and topped by a naval crown. Below was a scroll bearing the letters 'M/S—A/S'.

The badge was awarded after a man had served a minimum of six months on anti-submarine or minesweeping service in the RNPS, or less in special cases. It became the most prized 'medal' of the war, as men felt that six months sea-time in a minesweeping or asdic trawler really *was* sea-time under the worst conditions of danger and discomfort. The fact that naval general service men could not wear it was one of its main attractions. It was exclusive to the RNPS—and only to the men who served at sea. No shore-based man could have it.

It was worn on the left sleeve, four inches from the cuff, and when a Patrol Service rating became an officer, he could still wear it in the same place on his officer's jacket. No matter how many other 'gongs' its wearer might earn, the silver badge remained his proudest possession.

Throughout the long, hot, grim summer of 1940 as Britain stood alone, losses among the 'minor war vessels' manned by the Patrol Service mounted with alarming regularity and out of all proportion to the losses of any other naval craft. From June 1940 to the end of the year, more than ninety vessels were lost, half of them blown up by enemy mines. Some twenty others sank under the attacks of bombing aircraft, the rest went down to torpedoes and gunfire, or were wrecked in collisions or foundered in punishing seas.

During the invasion scare, reinforcements for the little ships in the south came from all directions. Down from the Clyde, in spectacular formation, steamed the five paddle-steamers of the 11th Minesweeping Flotilla, or 'Churchill's Secret Weapon—the Fighting 11th' as they were called, mainly because they had seen no actual fighting but had hitherto spent their time daily sweeping the Clyde estuary. Now they took over the sweep from Dover, combined with anti-invasion patrol at night.

The five steamers, which in peacetime sailed the Clyde, had been commissioned early in the war; they were fast, with speeds of 14 to 17 knots, and had a shallow draft, which was good for minesweeping. Their crews were a mixture of Patrol Service men, RN and RNVR ratings, and RN pensioners. Among them were hardened deep-sea trawlermen and real tough stokers from Glasgow. Their canteen messing was designed to save as much money as possible to spend on beer, which left many a man always hungry.

For weeks the five paddlers swept in front of the Channel convoys by day and went out on patrol every night. Telegraphist Leslie Clements, RNVWR, was in HMS *Scawfell*.

'We were armed with a 12-pounder gun which had the date 1898 stamped on the breech—it was said to have been made as a field-gun for the Boer War. We also had a Lewis gun with two mountings, one on each paddle-box.

'After a few weeks at Dover we went to Portland, and were in harbour there during the first heavy air-raids. We were on the spot when the *Foylebank,* a merchant ship converted to A/A cruiser, was sunk by enemy bombers. After this the paddlers earned a great reputation with the people ashore for our terrific A/A defence of the town! In *Scawfell* we shot down a Junkers 52 with our old 12-pounder, at which our crew leaped about the deck for joy. In another raid our sister ship HMS *Goatfell* was hit by a bomb. It landed on her 12-pounder mounting, killing several men.

'It was a period of considerable strain and one of our own seamen died of heart failure. Several men hardly ever went below decks, and we fired our gun so much that the supports under the deck were buckled.'

After a few weeks of this the 'Fighting 11th', real fighters now, were ordered back to resume their minesweeping on the Clyde.

The trawler *Marconi* steamed up from Torquay, where she had been under repair, to join the minesweepers operating from Harwich in 'E-boat Alley', the dangerous stretch of sea running from the Thames estuary north to Flamborough Head. Her first, ominous sight as she drew in to Parkeston Quay was that of the ancient, 1914 built trawler *St Olive,* so badly damaged that she looked like a pepper-pot. She had been attacked by planes the previous night, had seven hands killed and others wounded.

Marconi herself was no newcomer to danger, her recent repairs being the result of a fierce encounter with three dive-bombers. She was now put in a flotilla with three other trawlers and began her duties at once. This consisted of sweeping the war channel by day, both ways, before the convoy came through, and then patrolling the convoy route each night, keeping a sharp lookout for mine-laying planes and marauding E-boats. She was the new ship of Petty Officer Robert Muir.

'We followed this double drill for four days and nights at a time, having a break of two days and nights in harbour after each spell. During the four days it was hell on earth. We were continually at action-stations, being bombed and machine-gunned. After four months it was decided the strain was too much for us, as a lot of men were going round the bend and had to be sent off to hospital. So to give us some protection against the enemy planes we switched to doing our sweeping at night. We would leave the inside anchorage at about 8 p.m. and anchor about eight miles offshore till midnight, then make our way to the Orfordness lightfloat and patrol off there till 4 a.m., after which we swept the convoy route and steamed back to the inside anchorage off Felixstowe at about

8 a.m. The Ipswich patrol trawlers used to come out at midnight just as we were weighing anchor and patrol the outside line till dawn, then return to Ipswich.

'Night sweeping was still a hazardous job. We had to cope with E-boats in the dark, and having our sweeps down we weren't very manoeuvrable in an emergency, in fact we were sitting ducks. But for a time the switch to night sweeping foxed the enemy and we were not attacked quite as often.'

Not that any trawler was ever backward in showing her teeth. When *Red Gauntlet,* sweeping off Harwich, sighted an enemy bomber flying low with its deadly load for London, she manfully let go with her 12-pounder. She was the new ship of Second Hand Thorpe: 'We just missed him, and he got so annoyed that he turned round and came in to attack us. Our young gunner on the aft gun brought down the mizzen-boom in keeping him off and was worried to death about what the skipper would say, but I told him he could bring down the mizzen mast just as long as he could keep that plane off. The bomber pilot seemed to lose patience, for he finally dropped all his bombs at us at once—about 12. They fell to one side, shook us up a good deal but did no real damage. At least it meant twelve fewer bombs fell on London that day.'

What some trawlers managed to achieve with their meagre armament was nothing short of a marvel. Had they possessed the sharp teeth of some of the refugee vessels from the Continent which joined Harry Tate's Navy they might have done so much more.

Three French trawlers which escaped across the Channel at the time of Dunkirk each boasted the somewhat fantastic armament for those days of three 100mm. guns, one on the foc'sle and one each on the port and starboard sides; plus two 10mm. A/A guns in the port and starboard wastes, and two twin-Hotchkiss on the bridge.

These trawlers, *L'Atlantique, L'Istrac* and *Ambrose Pare,* were fitted with asdics and depth-charge throwers in Devonport dockyard and sent on anti-submarine patrol in the Channel with a mixed British and French crew under an RNR skipper and mate. They were big boats, but slow, and to those who sailed in them it seemed that after a few depth-charge attacks they might drop to bits. But two of the vessels clung on to life. The third, *L'Istrac,* met a quick and tragic end while on patrol when she ran into the guns of a German destroyer, which picked her off at leisure. Her commander was shot while on a liferaft.

L'Istrac had been working from Portsmouth along with other trawlers including the flotilla leader *Lord Wakefield,* commanded by Chief-Skipper John Harwood.

'We had many escapes during the heavy bombing at Portsmouth. One near-miss for us was when the Navy tugboat got a direct hit and just disappeared. We were berthed across from her, and in the explosion we went up into the air and dropped down to the bottom of the harbour. None of the crew was hurt, but the ship—what a mess. It landed us in dock for quite a spell, during which time the bombing was fairly continuous. One day I counted about 80 bombers over Pompey, and two squadrons of Hurricanes and Spitfires chased them right out of the sky. Several times we were attacked while at anchor, but thank God we suffered little damage except for our balloon being shot down and a few holes in our funnel.

'Another of our group, the *Warwick Deeping,* was not so lucky, meeting with a similar fate to that of *L'Istrac.* She was about 25 miles south-west from St Catherine's Point when she was gunned down and sunk by enemy destroyers.

'In *Lord Wakefield* we saw the tragic end of the destroyer *Acheron.* She was heavily bombed while in dry-dock at Portsmouth, and I think most of her officers were killed when the stern was blown to pieces. She was repaired and re-commissioned, and set sail to some west port. She passed us westward of Nab Tower, but only got as far as the Isle of Wight when she was blown to bits on a mine. We picked up two of her Carley floats, but I did not get any bodies, only pieces of sailors' clothing. Oil was everywhere and bodies were not easy to see in the mess.'

It was at Portsmouth that a memorable clash occurred between an exasperated RNR skipper and an RNVR lieutenant. The skipper, a gentle giant of a man, brought his minesweeping trawler, which had an edge of speed, into harbour ahead of the lieutenant, who was senior officer. The lieutenant reported him. By way of reply the big fisherman took hold of the startled officer by the underarms, hoisted him in the air like a baby and threatened: 'I'll hang you from the bloody cross!' The skipper was afterwards court-martialled. An unfortunate episode, but Harry Tate's men were contemptuous of 'bull' and only asked to be allowed to get on with the job in hand.

So many ships were engaged on anti-invasion patrol at this time that shipping losses in the depleted area of the Western Approaches mounted. The situation so worsened that numbers of trawlers had to be released from patrol to take up service as convoy escorts. One of these escorts was the *Cape Argona,* whose lot it was to be involved in a rescue operation following the greatest single merchant shipping disaster of the war. Aboard *Cape Argona* was Sub-Lieutenant Geoffrey Dormer, RNVR, who describes the events of October 26.

'We were on our way home with a couple of other trawlers from a convoy dispersal point about 300 miles west of Ireland, when a plane signalled that a ship was on fire about fifty miles away. We turned and made for her at full belt, pouring oil and water on our plummer blocks (the bearings through which the main propeller shaft runs), for we had a bent propeller shaft, the result of near misses at Norway and Dunkirk, and of a mishap with a depth-charge.

'We saw a great column of smoke from about 40 miles away, and it took us four hours to get there with our machinery literally red hot. Eventually a mast appeared and then another, so far apart that we thought it must be two ships, but on steaming closer we saw that it was indeed one, the liner *Empress of Britain,* the third largest ship in the world. She was burning well with a slight list, and had seven or eight lifeboats near her.'

The magnificent luxury liner, pride of the Canadian Pacific Fleet, was in service as a troopship, carrying 643 people including troops and their families. That morning as she steamed for Britain, enemy bombers had swept down on her out of the sun. The liner's gunners fought back until all were killed or disabled by the machine-gun fire which raked her decks. Then the planes swooped in to drop high explosive and incendiary bombs. Soon the liner was ablaze midships, some of her boats burning fiercely as they swung on the davits. Her master, Captain Charles Sapworth, stayed on the bridge until it burned away beneath him, manoeuvring the ship to minimize the effect of the flames.

Sub-Lieutenant Dormer : 'We made for one lifeboat and picked up 66 people, including women, children and wounded. The coxswain of the lifeboat was the brother of one of our seamen—they hadn't met for a couple of years—and they had two other brothers also in the *Empress,* who were picked up by other ships. As we came up to the boat the survivors were singing "Roll Out The Barrel."

'I learned long afterwards that a U-boat was watching the *Empress* but was deterred from attacking by our arrival. There was a Jacob's ladder hanging from the liner's foc'sle which seemed clear of the fire. Some of us wanted to board her and try to take her 42,000 tons in tow—enormous salvage! But the C.O. vetoed this idea and later two destroyers arrived.

'One of our survivors had both legs broken and a bullet through his foot. He sat in the scuppers, smoking, surrounded by children who were much amused by the funny shape of his legs. A boy of eleven and his sister of eight were specially fascinated by one or two bodies floating in the water, they seemed in their innocence to be thoroughly enjoying the whole thing. We had an eleven months old baby too, but the saddest case was a young girl whose fiance had been killed before her eyes.

'Luckily the weather was calm for once and the casualties were soon under morphia. Some of our tough young men were violently sick over moving them, but the children never turned a hair. The crew gave up most of their spare clothes to the survivors, who also helped themselves to a few things along the way, but we in return acquired all the lifeboat's equipment.

'We eventually transferred 61 of our survivors to one of the destroyers, which already had a number of dead laid out aft. We kept aboard only two women who were too ill to be moved, and an RAMC colonel, together with two nurses to look after them. One of the women, a Maltese Service wife, was soon to have a baby. She had both arms broken, both legs badly cut and burned and a couple of bullets in her from the Focke-Wulf that had bombed the ship and then machine-gunned the survivors. Yet she both survived and produced her baby successfully.'

The severely damaged *Empress of Britain* was taken in tow by the Polish destroyer *Burz,* but was torpedoed and sunk by a shadowing U-boat, the largest Allied merchant ship to go down in the war.

As for *Cape Argona's* final memory of the disaster—'There was a horrible smell and mess in the Subs' cabin afterwards, blood and dressings all over the place, and it took time to get used to sleeping there again.'

The following month of November 1940, saw 26 trawlers and drifters go to the bottom—very nearly one a day. Some sank under enemy bombs, the majority were torn apart by enemy mines. Like *Amethyst,* an asdic trawler operating from Parkeston Quay on patrol for the East Coast convoys. Steaming in the Barrow Deep on a beautifully fine and quiet November day she hit one of the very early acoustic mines—Hitler's latest 'secret weapon.' When the ship blew up at the stern, wounding seven men, all thought they had been bombed. *Amethyst* took ten minutes to sink, which allowed everyone to get off safely. They were picked up by the trawler *Le Tiger* and taken to Southend pier, where, adding insult to injury, they were promptly taken in charge by suspicious police, who had earlier arrested the survivors of a little Dutch schoot which had also hit a mine and sunk. It took *Amethyst's* crew half an hour to convince the police of their identity before they were released, and attention turned once more to checking the bona fide nature of the Dutchmen.

The acoustic mine was a new menace which gave shipping a thoroughly bad time. Minesweeping trawlers would sweep the convoy route for the usual mines, including the magnetic type, and then the convoy would come through. A number of ships might steam by unharmed, then, bafflingly, the fourth or fifth ship in the column would be blown sky-high. When it was realized exactly what was going on, the sweepers were fitted with "A" Frames and The Bucket, an electrical hammer device calculated to set off an acoustic mine about a mile away.

One of the test ships to go out with the first Bucket was the small trawler *Refundo,* an old veteran of World War 1. She got well outside the harbour, lowered her Bucket into the water, started the hammer and began to sweep. In less than half an hour she got a mine, but not where expected: it blew up under the bow, killing two men on the foc'sle head. The severely damaged ship was towed inshore, where she sank. This was on December 18.

From such mishaps were the lessons of the acoustic mine learned, until eventually all sweepers were fitted with reliable gear, an innovation which meant that they were now equal to dealing with three different sorts of mine.

The year 1940 ended with Harry Tate's Navy having lost well over 140 vessels since the outbreak of war. Among those which added a last sad statistic to the total was the aged trawler *Pelton,* torpedoed and sunk by an E-boat as she was sweeping off Great Yarmouth on Christmas Eve.

Christmas Day found the Clyde paddlers of the 'Fighting 11th' returned south to clear a minefield near Tuskar Rock, off the southern Irish coast. This was a tough, dangerous job in winter, especially for ships which, in peacetime, were only allowed in the upper Clyde and not in the open seas.

By Christmas Day *Scawfell* had swept up 25 mines and her crew ate their Christmas dinner of corned beef between runs over the minefield. *Scawfell* was working close to *Mercury,* whose crew had cheerily issued their own Christmas card. It showed Popeye the Sailor sweeping up a mine with a broom, and bore the message:

'HMS *Mercury*—we make a clean sweep of everything except our friends.'

Before the day was out *Mercury* got a mine tangled in her sweep, and as the wire came in the mine blew up astern. The explosion buckled *Mercury's* stern and she began to sink. Efforts were made to shore up the bulkheads and pump her out; if she stayed afloat, *Scawfell* was to escort her into Wexford. This led to much speculation as to whether they would be interned by the Irish for the duration.

But the water could not be pumped, and at 9 p.m. *Mercury* was abandoned and quickly sank.

Merry Christmas.

7

The Northern Patrol

The Northern Patrol. There was a certain bleakness about the name and a bleak life it could be, as the many men drafted to it quickly discovered.

The Northern Patrol was a special force of ships steaming up and down lines of patrol between the Faroes and Iceland, their main purpose being to prevent German raiders slipping out unseen into the Atlantic to attack the homing convoys. They also challenged all vessels using the northern waters, and kept a lookout for U-boats.

During the first months of the war, armed merchant cruisers had made the patrol, with small trawlers acting as armed boarding vessels. But they met with heavy losses. An early disaster was the sinking off Iceland of the merchant cruiser *Rawalpindi,* gunned down by the German battlecruisers *Gneisenau* and *Scharnhorst.* This was followed by the loss of nine more merchant cruisers, the majority torpedoed by U-boats while patrolling off Iceland and Ireland.

So naval cruisers took over the watch on northern waters, but they could not be spared for long, and in any event they suffered a great deal of damage from the appalling weather conditions. Destroyers, also in short supply, did not have the endurance, but the coal-burning trawlers were found to be ideal for the job. Their duty was to report enemy sightings before being blown to Kingdom Come, unless they could slip away before being detected. They were painted in anything but pusser warship grey, generally a valiant black and tan, for it was not intended that they should hide behind camouflage. The reasoning appeared to be that they were eminently more expendable than big, expensive warships.

And so the trawlers, all based on Kirkwall, ancient capital of the Orkney Islands, steamed to and fro on their lines of patrol between

the Faroes and Iceland for eight to ten days at a time; six knots
back and forth, in some of the roughest seas imaginable.

On the Northern Patrol a novice seaman soon found that trawlers
did not 'plough' seas, they rode them. As one rating describes it:

'Imagine the traditional Wild West bucking bronco enlarged to
some 400 tons and fashioned like a ship and you have a good idea
of a deep-sea trawler in a northern gale. She does everything in her
power to throw you off your feet, hurl you against bulkheads and
ship's fittings, stop you working, eating, sleeping, washing, shaving,
dressing, even carrying out calls of nature. She seeks to stun you,
maim you, hurl you overboard, destroy you utterly. She strikes at
you when you are least prepared and off your guard. In everything
you do, you battle against her relentless will to break you.

'She has two main weapons, the pitch and the roll; sometimes
she uses both at the same time. Let's take them in turn. First the
roll. On deck you reel drunkenly along, hanging grimly on to the
lifelines or any solid structure. If you let go, she'll fling you off
your feet to roll into the scuppers while icy water pours over you;
and a nicely timed big sea may wash you over the rails into
oblivion. Below decks you must struggle for everything. Getting
yourself clothed to go on watch is a feat in itself. You are hurled
from side to side of the messdeck as you let go for a moment to put
on a garment. It takes two hands to put on a seaboot stocking, so
you wait your chance. As you pull it on while sitting on your bunk,
a sudden lurch flings you to the deck, cursing roundly, so that you
have to pick yourself up and start all over again. The operation of
getting dressed for watch, which in calm weather you could
complete in three minutes, may take ten minutes in a gale.

'Eating is just as difficult. The messdeck table down aft runs
thwartships and the eaters sit on two benches on either side. The
fiddles are on the table to wedge the plates, but soup or any other
fluids have to be taken with a certain technique. The bowl must be
held in the hand, kept level, and spoonfuls taken when the roll levels
out. You need both hands to hold it on the roll, then you let go
one hand and spoon up rapid mouthfuls between rolls. As the ship
rolls, all the eaters slide heavily, one on top of the other, first to
one side and then the other, each man hanging on to his plate with
both hands. Much cursing follows, the favourite remark being:
"Roll right over, you fucking old bastard, and come up the other
side!" The messman struggles to reach down the heavy pans from
the galley above without scalding himself to death, while up in the

galley the cook fights a desperate battle with his steaming pots and pans, which threaten to run amok if left for a second. Ship's cooks are notoriously temperamental, and in heavy weather are driven almost to the limits of endurance and patience. At times they may drive out all the galley hangers-on with a carving knife. The greasy galley deck can start a slide for the unwary which will send him skating three or four times from end to end with a fanny of hot tea in his hand before he can get a handhold.

'When at last you reach your bunk, you find that this rolling demon will not easily permit you to sleep. The bunks are fixed but your body is not, so you roll steadily from side to side and it's not easy to sleep in this state of constant motion. In a hammock the body sways with the bed and this is much more comfortable, but hammocks are used only when bunks are too few, and hammocks are awkward beasts to lash up and stow in heavy weather.

'The pitch is more violent than the roll, but it is easier on the eaters and sleepers. The mass-sliding game is gone from meal times, the sleeper's body is stationary in the bunk, though the sensation of being on a roller coaster in reverse takes some adjustment at first. You sleep head-to-bow, so that as the ship climbs steadily up each huge wave, your body comes towards the upright position. Then, as she tops the crest and plunges down the other side into the trough, you have the sensation of standing on your head. But this does not disturb sleep like the body-roll; in fact it can, in time, actually induce sleep, with a gigantic rock-a-bye-baby effect.

'However, the pitch is harder on the lookouts and the men working on deck, because in addition to the bucking and crashing of the bow into the troughs, there comes the lashing of faces and hands by icy spray; you are drenched, stung and blinded by it. Normally simple jobs become nightmares of frozen, fumbling hands and sliding feet. You can anticipate the roll much better than the pitch, with its sudden, violent intensity.

'In heavy weather jobs about the deck can be dangerous as well as frustrating. A seaboat breaking adrift from its lashings can endanger the lives of those who have to secure it again. In really bad weather it is foolhardy to attempt to cross the open deck, lifelines or no. Only in cases of emergency, such as enemy action or damage, is it attempted. When darkness falls in a full gale those aft stay aft, and those for'ard stay for'ard, till daylight.'

Typical of the smaller trawlers which first steamed on the Northern Patrol was *Aquamarine,* a thirteen-year-old fishing vessel of some 350 tons. She began as an armed boarding vessel attached to Contraband Control at Kirkwall, her job being to intercept neutral ships.

Her crew were mostly RNR. The engine room staff were 'T.124' engagements—civilian seamen in uniform who did not consider themselves under naval discipline, not having undergone any service training. They were characters all, like the chief engineer, who once went off to visit his opposite number in a trawler shortly leaving for Aberdeen, had a glorious bender and woke up well on the way to that city.

Others of *Aquamarine's* crew came from the Western Isles and used Gaelic as much as English. Some of the younger seamen were local, from the Kirkwall district and were great hands at 'the dancing.'

The quiet nature of the older seamen from the Islands and remoter parts of Scotland, who were to be found in most of the trawlers, was a feature that never failed to impress their messmates. Most were deeply religious men and kept a Bible under their pillow, reading from it before going to sleep, and saying their prayers regularly. Aboard one trawler there was an Islander who each night before turning in used to kneel in the middle of the messdeck and say his prayers, while the rest of the crew hurled not only abuse at him, but seaboots and any other heavy articles they could lay hands on. The Scot never wavered, but continued to say his prayers, and as time wore on the attacks grew less and less, until at last he was left entirely in peace to say his nightly prayers. He had won the respect of every man.

Another characteristic of the Stornowegians particularly was their gift of extraordinarily keen eyesight. Unsophisticated and uncomplicated, almost childlike men, they had pale blue, rather dreamy eyes, with which they could detect an object at great distances long before other eyes could discern them. Many was the trawler steaming in bad visibility in dangerous waters whose Stornowegian was called to help save her from harm. It was uncanny the way those dreamy eyes could spot a floating mine or a small object like a buoy minutes before anyone else could catch a glimpse of it. Up on the bridge an officer might train his glasses in the direction indicated and take a full minute or more to spot the object which the Stornowegian's hawklike eyes had detected unaided.

Many Stornowegians could not bear to be cooped up aboard a ship of war. Like big Jim Reid, a whaler in peacetime, who would never go below decks in his trawler; he ate all his meals standing up in the galley and slept in a Carley float alongside the funnel. In a rare moment of confidence he told a shipmate: 'I'm no afeared o' dying, but when I do, I want to feel the fresh sea breeze on my face, not be caught like a rat in that hellhole of a messdeck.'

There were many other men who, like big Jim, pondered on their doubtful chances should the ship go down suddenly. But one with singular confidence was *Northern Duke's* wireless operator. At 'Up spirits' time, when the trawler was in harbour, he rashly bet that in an emergency he could escape through the messdeck porthole. He had plenty of takers, and got down to the job; but he finished up stark naked half in and half out of the porthole, stuck fast. As there were two other trawlers tied up alongside he had quite an audience when, after a good greasing, pushing and pulling, he was freed. Thereafter, that particular Sparks was always missing at rum time.

Among *Aquamarine's* representative crew were such fearsome Scots as 'Lofty' McDonald, a giant of a ghillie, who could lift a two hundredweight sack with ease, and who spat violently at the very mention of the name of 'Campbell.' There was also a professional yachtsman, a yachtmaster and the usual sprinkling of larger-than-life personalities. Signalman Gordon Hooper:

'There was a Manxman, Bob Holmes, a real "old un" who was said to have been round the world with a tug-master's ticket, but had fallen on hard times—he had no kit at all. He would go ashore on the booze then flop into his bunk with the excuse that he was suffering from malaria. His great pal was a little bald-headed Scot called McGregor, and it was Bob's great delight to wait until McGregor was asleep and then draw all over his bald head with an indelible pencil. At night Bob would wait until McGregor was on the wheel and then crawl through a scuttle at the back of the wheelhouse and quietly grab the bottom spokes of the wheel so that poor old Mac couldn't tell whether the wheel had jammed or what. Bob led Mac an awful life, but they were the greatest of friends.

'We also had a rather boisterous Irish Sparks—or "That bloody mad Irishman!" as the captain used to call him. *Aquamarine* had been at sea for a fortnight and we hadn't received a single W/T message, Sparks maintaining that "nothing had come through." But the captain got suspicious and contacted the next ship. They handed over a fistful of signals, and Sparks got the bullet. We discovered he hadn't done any proper radio work for years and couldn't even read the ship's call-sign, but he was quite cheerful about it all.

'And there was the sub-lieutenant who was a bit of a ladies' man. The first time *Aquamarine* went into Lerwick, in the Shetlands, he arranged a party ashore and decided to smuggle off a bottle of gin by holding it inside his trouser-leg. All went well until we got into the crowded main street, when he lost his grip on the bottle and it went down his leg and smashed in the street. Strong men wept, that's all I know.'

In due course it was decided that *Aquamarine* was to turn over to anti-submarine work, and she went to West Hartlepool for an extensive refit, during which the decks were reinforced, the A/S gear was installed and a new A/S bridge built on.

'After the refit some of the older hands had grave doubts about her stability, and they were proved right in a tragic way. We were off the Faroes, in a gale of hurricane force, the ship yawing and rolling all over the place, when suddenly there was a great crash and she lay right over on her side. The wireless room was partitioned off the messdeck and the water rushed through the vents and flooded it. There was a shout from the deck of "Man overboard!" One of the Kirkwall dancing lads, on lookout on the lower bridge, had gone over the side. He was one of the most popular lads in the ship and a strong swimmer. The ship was put about, but we never had sight or sound of him again. For a long time afterwards there was silence on the messdeck, men just looking at each other and not speaking.

'We could not get the ship upright again and it turned out that our ballast of pig-iron had not been properly secured in the dockyard, and had shifted. So we made for the Faroes, still half on our side. We arrived at Thorshaven and were met by a snipe of a naval officer who hailed us in a loud voice and told us to carry out our repairs and be off as soon as possible, as he had no room for us. He drew some choice remarks from the lads, and I think he'd have gone in the "drink" if they'd got their hands on him.

'*Aquamarine's* sister ship, the *Kingston Onyx*, had the same conversion and underwent a very similar experience. It was rumoured that her captain went out of his mind and was a mental case for the rest of the war.

'As for our own use as an anti-submarine vessel, early on we got a perfect asdic contact and dropped a pattern of depth-charges, but all we did was nearly to kill the cook. His galley door slammed to and shut him in, the hot water geyser flew off the bulkhead, the galley stove flew to pieces, the galley funnel broke off and filled the place with smoke and steam, and the cook was nearly smothered.

'Eventually all our little Kingston ships were deemed unfit for Northern Patrol and were replaced by bigger trawlers.'

The trawler which replaced *Aquamarine* was the former Hull fishing vessel *Lord Austin*—ten years younger and 200 tons bigger, with a crew of around thirty men. As *Lord Austin* steamed from Kirkwall on her first patrol it was the prelude to long months of wearisome work in a sea beaten by severe storms for most of the year, and bitingly cold in the winter.

The monotonous pattern of the Northern Patrol was the worst thing to bear. From the time the copper spire of Kirkwall's ancient cathedral faded from sight, it was two days at full speed out to the patrol line, then more than a week steaming back and forth at slow speed, until the magic moment when, to everyone's joy, the order was heard 'Full ahead!'—signalling the end of the patrol and a fast two day run back to Kirkwall. The lines of patrol were varied a little for each trip, the most northerly line being near to Iceland and the most southerly only miles from the Orkneys. Each patrol was followed by four days in harbour for coaling from the collier, storing up and repairing defects. After coaling up, *Austin* would go to a buoy where she 'drew fires' so that the boiler tubes could be cleaned, engineers descending on the ship like industrious flies, and there was the ring of hammers and raucous cries. There was also a spot of shore leave to sample the delights of Kirkwall, the gaunt Gaelic city of grey houses and narrow streets; then out again to the next patrol line.

By the book, each trawler should have steamed down to Grimsby for a refit every six months, but in practice this period was often extended to seven or eight months. After the six months was up, every return from patrol became a time of eager anticipation, often to be dashed by the signal to take on 200 tons of coal for another patrol. But if the long-awaited signal was received—'Proceed to collier and take on 60 tons'—it meant that the destination was 'GY' (Grimsby) and leave, and jubilation would break out all over the ship. A refit meant two weeks leave for each watch, and this was the only home leave available to men of the Northern Patrol.

Most of *Lord Austin's* crew were Patrol Service men. In addition to the hard core of experienced Scots and English fishermen, and ex-

Merchant Navy seamen, there were other strong personalities like Peter, the flame-haired son of a tug-master, who had lived all his life among the Thames barges and had all the Cockney aggressiveness, small, tough and afraid of no one, and 'Guns', who invariably brought the house down with his vivid rendering of 'The little dirty drawers that Maggie wore,' sung with great pathos and feeling. Guns had a most curious Yorkshire accent. 'Doo goes and does dis,' he would say, explaining the intricacies of his old four-inch, 'and den doo comes back and does dat.' He provided endless amusement for Sparks, a round-faced and rather balding salesman from Cumberland, who never tired of imitating him. Sparks, like Guns, was a specialist. In fact, as the only wireless operator carried on board he was a key man and a law unto himself. He was never heard to address an officer as 'sir'—'mister' was as much as he would allow himself in recognition of authority. He was in constant wordy warfare with the signals officer, whom he treated with scant ceremony.

The chief engineman, in his mid-fifties and now fighting his second war in trawlers, hailed from Grimsby; he had a suspicious eye and lived by his grumbles. He was engaged in continual warfare with the wardroom, and some of his replies up the engine room voice-pipe made stirring history. Down in his realm lived men like Paddy, the Irish stoker without parents, relations or friends, who spent his leaves living in Service hostels at one and sixpence a night, the rest of his money going on drink. And a fellow stoker, Bill, an ex-heavyweight boxer who had been round the world in the Merchant Navy and claimed to have possessed women of every nation.

On *Lord Austin* as with all the Northern Patrol trawlers, the rigs worn varied from the weird to the wonderful—seamen's jerseys and bell-bottoms, overalls, windcheaters, oilskins, duffle coats and kapok suits, topped by balaclavas, pom-pom and tea-cosy caps and even trilbies. But still among these, Ordinary Seaman Patrick Bryant was a 'loner' in his awful wreck of a leather coat, tattered and stiffened from salt water, and his battered cap.

Patrick had come over from Rhodesia to join up at the age of twenty-one, and he was both a mystery and a source of continual amusement to the rest of the crew. His pleasant, intelligent face usually sported several days' growth of beard, but in contrast to the variety of dialects on the messdeck he had a public school accent. His manner of speech left the crew flabbergasted, for instead of swearing he would abuse his mockers in long words foreign to their ears. He was, as they summed him up, a 'posh bugger—a broken down toff.' He had dramatic and literary ambitions, too, and these peculiar leanings were enough to earn him the label of 'crackers.'

In spite of—or maybe because of—the jibes that were continuously levelled at him, Patrick was popular on the lower deck. Legends of him persisted long after he had left the ship. His 'mourning' underclothes; his hammock, which he sometimes slung as a change from a bunk, and which he rigged so loosely that, when he was in it, it assumed the shape of a 'V' with his backside swinging about two inches off the deck; Patrick singing lustily, doing a ballet dance round the messdeck after a night ashore, or suddenly bursting into Shakespeare with dramatic intensity. Patrick playing tramcars while on watch on the veranda round the wheelhouse : 'Ting, ting, move along please, room for two more up here, standing room only downstairs, hurry along now, hold tight,' and he would work handles and ring bells vigorously. A man like Patrick was always an asset to the morale on the lower deck. His chief virtue was that he could 'take it'; an enviable gift. He also kept a diary, excerpts from which capture vividly the life of *Lord Austin* on patrol. First, the ever changing, rigorous weathers.

'Today has been rough. The messdeck is pure havoc; coal, tables, benches, gramophone records, boots, kitbags, all in together in anything but fine weather. It would seem that the following sea, from which we flee, is a horde of hearty sea-sprites, bluff creatures of blue-green glass and soda-water bubbles which speed us on our way, not gently, but in good heart, and if the sea should slap us and send spray bridge-high, it is only doing it in a non-malicious, sturdy way. The ship seems to take it all in the spirit of a rough game, and she is a good sport.'

And again : 'The weather is heavy. The bows seem to gouge the waters and shoot monstrous plumes of ice-green spray on either side, spray which gusts against the bridge windows like rain and makes crossing the open deck from the shelter of the bridge to the foc'sle companionway a hazard of skill and daring, if one is to avoid a wetting. Some dash the distance and chance that speed will outwit the weather. Sometimes it does . . . sometimes. Others move Apache-wise from cover to cover, with ever an eye for that momentary lull.'

Below, on the messdeck, there are matters of importance.

'A topic of absorbing interest for the major portion of this week has been Peter Piper's constipation. In these days, trifles become matters of much moment. Day in, day out, all minds have revolved about this singular stoppage of the bowels. So universal has this topic been that echoes of it must have reached the wardroom. In vain were administered the most potent pills and draughts, but today the blockade is broken, amid general and sincere relief.'

Then back to the demon weather. 'It has snowed today, soft, slushy stuff which clings for an instant then melts, and the view from the wheelhouse window was that of an old, scratched and flickering film, with the snow streaming before the wind.' 'A freak hailstorm. It came out of a clear sunlit day; over a black-blue sea it advanced like a light mist and rattled down on to the deck, stinging the face and tickling the ears and filling the pockets. It was over as swiftly as it had begun. The sun is warming again and we can see distant rainfall all about us like crude daubs of purple and off-white.'

The diary begins to record the work of *Lord Austin* on her long patrols.

'A convoy was dispersed last night, whether by the enemy or the weather we did not know, but the merchant stragglers beating it for the place of new rendezvous served as admirable targets for our gun crew while each in her turn was challenged and made satisfactory reply. The scene presented rather the one in which the small boy pursues an elderly gentleman with catapult fully tensed; the old man maintains an unhurried dignity while the boy, for apprehension, will not fire but thinks he frightens. Stragglers passed during most of the day, heavily laden—one bore planes on her decks, perhaps from the States—and all had a bearing of dogged persistence, no, placidity, as they hitched their way home. There is about these cargo vessels an almost ox-like, unhurried gait. A couple of them had an ox-herd, a destroyer, for guidance.'

And on another day: 'Smoke was seen during the "Dogs" and, as is our duty, we set full speed towards it. It proved to be from another patrolling trawler, but as we drew nearer a greater shape loomed up, three-funnelled and very large. We must have seemed very impertinent as we made towards her with gun crew at their station, but she resigned her dignity and hove-to, to be duly challenged and to give satisfaction. She was the *Empress of Russia*.

'Later, horizon-smoke was seen to port and away we went again at speed, gun crew to station and Aldis flashing. This second ship, however, did not answer our flashing nor our pennants, but continued across our beam. George, our valiant gun-layer, was eager, as he always is, to plug first and ask questions afterwards, but he was forced to restrain his blood-lust. This flouting of authoritative questioning brought the inevitable result, the firing of a blank. For a half charge the noise was highly satisfactory, the suspect ship altered course. Far from our expectations the ship did not stop, so again the detonation; still she didn't stop. Instead she sent out an alarm that she was being pursued by a suspicious-looking vessel— us. This is, I think, the only time upon which one of HM ships about her lawful occasion has been announced over the air as "a suspicious-looking vessel." On reflection we must have presented an oddly piebald effect, since we are wildly daubed with red lead, being in the throes of painting (intermittently, in these severe weathers). Small wonder that our warpaint, combined with detonations, struck fear.'

There could, on occasion, be more to the day than the simple challenging of every passing vessel.

'The day began on a note of excitement. During the night we received instructions to rendezvous with another trawler and her suspect, a Finnish merchantman, and it was thought that each patrol vessel would put aboard an armed party. So it was that some of us quickly won George Crosses in imagination. In minutes (in our daydream) we were designated for the armed party; fifteen minutes later we were defending the bridge against hordes of fiendish Finns . . . But the cancelling of orders made us just seamen again.

'An armed party goes aboard well prepared. It takes its own food—parties have been poisoned before now; and one is warned against seduction by cigarettes or French postcards. One uses the eyes to convey what ignorance of language cannot get across. So it was, until the cancellation of orders, that we practised withering glances lest the Finns should try to fraternize with the dignity of RN personnel.'

'Night watch : Yesterday we had three calls to the gun. One was an Icelandic trawler, the *Eldborg,* of very modern lines. The horizon silhouette was very much like that of a surfaced submarine, and her actual identity disappointed. We got out of our tin-hats and it was Watch-Ho.

'We later made use of our searchlight for the first time, and a dazzling white pen wrought blots of ultramarine on the surface of the sea. Then peace reigned for a little while, but soon the beam was probing the dark waters again, fine on the starboard and along our length. There was not an exploration for some time, then the captain came down and asked had we heard anything scrape alongside, as the sound had been reported by the engine room. He said calmly: "Oh, it was probably a mine." This as simply as he might have said "It's ten to six." '

It took a great deal more than a loose mine to disturb *Lord Austin's* captain. He was Lieutenant N. P. McLeod, RNR, a ruddy-faced Scot who had been *Aquamarine's* last captain, and had taken command of *Lord Austin* when she replaced the smaller vessel. McLeod was a master mariner, formerly a first officer in the biggish ships of the Bank Line. He was very pusser navy—very much resented being addressed as 'skipper'—and kept a captain's remoteness from his crew, leaving the ship's routine entirely to his officers.

Stocky and bluff, he was a man of variable moods, gay at times and drily humorous, but often bitingly sarcastic. He liked to hum hymn tunes on the bridge, and 'Deutchland Uber Alles'; hated Lord Haw-Haw and forbade anyone to listen to his broadcasts. He was always in command of his ship and men and stood no nonsense, roaring his orders in powerful voice when needed. One of his favourite sayings was: 'A sailor without a knife is like a woman without a fanny,' and he looked with quizzical eyes on his mixed crew. Once, coming from cabin to bridge, he stopped to stare at Patrick Bryant, leaning in elegant attitude on the wheel, and said: 'And I'll bet he's wearing a wristwatch!" To a crewman who, on pay day, refused to join the Savings Stamps scheme, he declared: 'Och, lad, ye'll wish ye had when ye're swimming about in the water one day!'

The crew, in return, had their own measure of McLeod, including a memory of him brought from *Aquamarine*. The most popular rig with Northern Patrol officers was a white polo-neck pullover worn with uniform trousers, and the fashion was not lost on the Scot. He was sent a beautiful white sweater by his wife, with instructions that when necessary it was to be sent home for washing. One evening McLeod wore it for drinks aboard another ship, and returning to *Aquamarine* late but very happy, decided to climb aboard up the ship's side. That day the crew had been painting the hull—black. Every man wondered what story the captain told his wife.

Pusser navy as he was, McLeod retained a strong belief in the old seamen's superstition that it was unlucky to pack in anticipation of leave. He never would pack, with the inevitable result that the steward and signalman would be summoned half an hour before his train was due to leave, to help him wildly open drawers and wardrobes and tumble everything into his suitcases.

Often, as *Lord Austin* steamed her dreary patrols, McLeod's first words when arriving on the bridge would be: 'They also serve who only stand and wait. . . .' For there was no disguising the sense of futility felt by most officers and men of the Northern Patrol, having to follow, day after day, what seemed to be the most unnecessary operation of the war. While they sailed the northern sea virtually untroubled by the enemy, many of their families at home were being subjected to German bombing. Far out in the ocean, crews would crowd round their radios and listen anxiously to the BBC's announcement that 'a certain Midlands town' had been heavily bombed the night before.

The unreality of the patrol was gently probed by a newcomer to *Lord Austin's* crew, who asked the officer of the watch just what they would do if they encountered the *Tirpitz*.

'He replied, without hesitation: "Go in and attack her, of course."

'The idea of our trawler, with her single worth-while gun, going in to engage the pride of the German Navy struck me as so ludicrous that I ventured the suggestion that it might be better for all concerned if we sheered off, hoping that we'd not been spotted, and radioed the position of the battleship to headquarters. Number Two drew himself up and withered me.

' "It is not in the tradition of the British Navy to run away."

'But a strategic withdrawal, sir?'

' "Certainly not. What is one trawler and thirty odd men to the chance of getting one hit on the enemy!" '

Some slight relief on patrol was afforded by exploding or sinking floating mines, usually those which had broken adrift from the British minefield laid to the north-east. Bryant's diary:

'In a heavy sea, the day's highlight—a floating mine. She was sighted after tea. The ship slewed round and made circuit about it, while all with the inclination made to sink or explode it by rifle fire. Number One was at the Hotchkiss and I must admit his aim was good. The horned emblem of menace reeled and mounted on the swelling sea. About and about we steamed, and the air fast became bitter with cordite vapours, and ears sang with the detonations of the rifles. The Hotchkiss splashed the waters and an occasional tracer ricocheted off the water and danced high in the air. As the firing progressed and the mine, though hit often and sinking, showed no sign of sinking rapidly, McLeod grew impatient and shouted down to the miniature Bisley on deck : "If you don't get her this time round we'll lower the smallboat, fix bayonets and charge !" '

There were sights at sea very strange to the non-fishermen.

'The night was heavily uncomfortable and eerie with Northern Lights. To see this strange ivory fire in the heavens, raying, peaking and fitfully flickering, is to sense loneliness and desolation; such loneliness and desolation as the ice-deserts of the far north, whose reflection, some say, gives this light.

'We passed a Swedish ship and they heartened our fishing hopes by demonstrating great beating silver cod, freshly drawn from the sea. Barter swiftly followed. We got £5 worth of fish in exchange for half a pound of not-to-be-disposed-of-contrary-to-regulations tobacco. The fishers drew alongside and threw fish, not to us but at us, for some ten minutes. The heavens rained fish, and all we could do was to take cover. When the downpour ceased, the after deck was heavy with haddock and whiting.'

Constant reminders of the true occupation of men in the stormy waters crossed by the patrol were the fishing boats sighted red-sailed in the fitful northern sunlight. They came from the Faroes.

'Unlike the Orkneys, these Danish islands are golden like hay, and the cold air has the sweetness of crisp clipped grass. These are precipitous bays, and their waters Prussian blue. The Faroes spring prominent from the surrounding mist like dragon-teeth soldiers. All other land looms slowly; these islands, one just comes upon.'

The Faroes were defended by British coastal batteries which became rather bored and trigger-happy. One day *Lord Austin* was steaming up a fiord when there was a 'wham' from the shore and a heavy shell ricocheted off the water in front of her bow. She hoisted her recognition signals and steamed on. On her next call at the Faroes there was a parcel from the Army awaiting her. Inside was a four-inch shell, beautifully polished and mounted on an oak base, together with a card which read : 'Yours—we believe.' The shell had landed on the opposite side of the fiord, been found, polished and presented to the ship. It was displayed in the wardroom ever afterwards.

The story went that these impetuous shore gunners tried the same stunt on a passing British destroyer. But she promptly retaliated by training all her gun-turrets on the Army camp, which was swiftly evacuated.

But *Lord Austin's* most memorable visit to the Faroes was when, while on patrol, she experienced serious trouble in the exterior fittings of her asdic dome. It was decided she would have to enter Thorshaven and obtain the services of a diver. Signalman Hooper:

'It was a fine summer's evening and we were secured alongside the wall. Ahead of us was a Tribal destroyer, HMS *Bedouin,* about to leave. It was soon apparent that something was in the air, loads of activity among the locals ashore and the racy-looking Faroese longboats assembling. And then the shindig started. A shoal of whales had been sighted just offshore, and apparently this was one of the great events in the Faroese calendar. All the longboats set off down the fiord and formed a wide circle round the whales. Each boat carried a large stone on a length of rope, which its occupants kept hurling over the side into the water and then drawing it out again. In this way they drove the whales like a flock of sheep up into the shallow water, and then the local lads, armed with knives and harpoons, threw themselves into the water and on to the backs of the whales and started doing battle.

'It was an astonishing sight, with the old *Lord Austin* tied up in the middle of it and the *Bedouin* trying to get under way.

'When all the whales had been despatched and hauled up, most of the locals went off on an almighty bender lasting all night in the village hall. Our lads who could scrounge shore leave were not slow to take advantage of the celebrations, which resulted in some fat heads the next morning. In the midst of all this we awaited the arrival of the base engineer officer and a civilian diver. Eventually they arrived, the RN officer in a towering rage and the Faroese diver so tight he could hardly stand on his feet.

' "Drunk or not, he's damn well going down to do the job!" said the officer, so the old diver was literally levered into his diving suit and down he went. He did a first-class job and then trotted off back to his drinking.

'We discovered that these annual whale hunts were one of the main sources of food for the Faroese. They hung the whale meat up in strips outside their homes to let it be cured by the weather.'

There was another, less happy occasion when *Lord Austin* again had trouble with her asdic. Big trouble. She was on passage from Iceland to Kirkwall and running before one of the worst 'blows' anyone could remember. Finally she sighted the lighthouse on North Ronaldsay, Orkney, and was fast going ashore. Lieutenant McLeod said there was only one thing he could do—turn and steam against the wind, and he told his crew to 'hang on' as the helm was put over. *Lord Austin* shot into the air and came down across a heaving sea. All her asdic gear snapped off and was lost, but she made it to Kirkwall. The 'blow' was a hurricane which had swept across Iceland and demolished most of the army camps.

There followed more repairs and then back on patrol, once more challenging everything in sight. Bryant's diary:

'Mist persisted through the night and into the early morning, at which time we ran upon a convoy silhouetted in the mist, sharp bows and many stacks. A Tribal challenged us and an American destroyer steamed round us. We allowed her to proceed—so says the logbook for each and every occasion on which we contact a ship, be it an Empress liner or the lowly bellying sails of a Faroese fisher. Such is the conceit of the Patrol Service!'

And later: 'A pursuit in the dark. She did not answer our signals at first, a lax watch no doubt, but after an hour the captain was satisfied and we resumed our job. No sooner had we settled down to the heavy roll of head-on winds than we were away again with all speed. Over the air had come an SOS. A torpedoed vessel, one of two which have appealed tonight. The first one had a vessel to aid her almost as soon as she called, it was to the assistance of the second ship that we now sped. And as we steamed before the wind with engines pulsating with urgency, what were the thoughts and words which passed on the messdeck? Not all so humanitarian, I think, as the occasion might have merited. We were anticipating towage—the saving of the ship and the resultant salvage money—and high were the tales told of similar incidents and the sums of money collected, money which would make us comfortable sailors in a matter of days. With the slowing down of the engine beats, our dreams of opulence died. Once again our good intentions had been done to death by another and nearer ship. Thank God that someone was near.'

A rescue attempt on another occasion merited only brief mention in *Lord Austin's* logbook. But Bryant documented the haunting scene.

'We received orders to go to the assistance of a ship on fire, and set off full belt northwards. It was thought there was a crew of 80, so blankets and food were prepared for that number. We sighted first a thin stream of grey smoke on the horizon, then the mast and funnel became visible. Calamity had given a fine purple cloud-curtain for the drama, against which the flames shone fiercely. All hands were on voluntary lookout as we approached our objective.

'It is a popular conception that a fire at sea is dramatic. Not so, for a burning ship is an abject object of resignation, rather like a woman in great pain; she bears it bravely without show. We steamed past to the windward looking for signs of boat or survivor, but there was none. The fire, which had taken a strong hold aft, "morsed" at us as it moved swiftly forward. More than once we mistook the flame-flickers for distress signalling and turned to look hopefully, but were confounded. So we steamed east in hope of survivors, turning only when the ship had receded to a mere cigarette-glow in the dark depths of the night. Our searchlight probed the darkness but found nothing. The howl of the gathering gale fanned the flames maliciously, seeming to laugh mockingly at our earnestness and our straining eyes. As we returned to steam about the ship her sampson-posts were silhouetted against the light, and an underglow illuminated the sea, the driving cloud and the drooling smoke. We stood by her all night, and at dawn were relieved by an Admiralty tug and an escort vessel, who took over the watch from us.'

Then a rescue attempt that did come off, in part.

'At four o'clock this afternoon we contacted *Northern Chief* and took aboard two British airmen she had rescued from the sea when their Lockheed-Hudson developed engine trouble. The plane blew up as it hit the water. Of the four who had baled out only two survived. The others died, one by drowning, the other by being strangled by his shirt collar and tie, which shrank in the water and choked him. An ugly incident and an odd one.'

So life on patrol continued, relieved only by such melancholy incidents and by shooting at mines, and grappling odd bits of wreckage from the sea.

'The ocean is a voracious creature which tires quickly of its hastily snatched prizes. Witness the small collection we have accumulated during the job—a destroyer's lifebuoy, a raft, lifebelts, a body, spars, planks, logs, drums.' More items were added as the days passed. 'Two rafts were picked up with a man's suspender as evidence of late human tenancy. They were Swedish out of Bergen, by name *Rimfrashe*. The biscuit and water barrels having been investigated, matches, flares and a battery were found. . . . We are rapidly making a name for ourselves as a picker-up of junk, much of which is useless, but it gives the grappling party practice. Planks, a jib-boom and an AA kite fell to our vigilance today. Four destroyers crossed our bows and stood off to the south, throwing spray over themselves as an elephant throws sand.'

If the monotony of life in *Lord Austin* differed little from that in the other patrol vessels, she was different at least in one comforting respect. As one of her crew discovered when, at Kirkwall, he went over to the *Kingston Agate* to see how a friend of his was faring.

'His trawler was very similar to ours—except that the messdeck was alive with small red beetles of the cockroach strain. There were tens of thousands of them; they were everywhere, on the deck, the bulkheads, the deckhead, the tables, the bunks and even on the occupants of the messdeck, who seemed supremely indifferent to their presence. The whole place seemed alive with crawling, scurrying insects. They ran over the food on the plates and had to be brushed off before a mouthful was eaten; they dropped on to your hair and shoulders as you sat at the table.

'Good God!' I said. 'How the hell do you put up with this lot?'

'He laughed and replied: "Oh, we're so used to them, we hardly notice them."

'I thanked my stars that *Lord Austin* was free from such infestation and for once was thoroughly glad to get back aboard her!'

Though it was part of the duty of the asdic trawlers to watch for and listen out for U-boats, few U-boats were ever contacted or seen. They must have crossed the British patrol lines on their way to and from the Atlantic, yet if they saw the trawlers they did not waste either shot or torpedo on them. It was said the U-boats fixed their positions on the slowly plodding Northern Patrol trawlers when going out and coming back; certainly it was felt among the trawler crews that there was some sort of gentlemen's agreement that if they did not attack the U-boats, the U-boats would not attack them.

This theory of a strange truce existing between the trawlers and the U-boats was given added strength by the affair of the trawler *Visenda*. While on patrol she contacted a U-boat and depth charged it, bringing back evidence of having at least damaged the German, if not actually sinking it. One Sunday afternoon a few weeks later *Visenda's* aft lookout went into the galley for a warm, and at that precise moment a U-boat surfaced astern. *Visenda's* officer of the watch called the captain, at the same time giving the order 'Hard-a-port!' to bring the forward four-inch to bear. But *Visenda's* captain, on coming up, unknowingly counter-ordered 'Hard-a-starboard!' (single-screw trawlers turned more easily and quickly to starboard because of the clockwise thrust of the screw). This unfortunate muddle gave the U-boat's crew time to man their gun, loose off about nine rounds at the helpless trawler, and crash dive before she could reply. The shells thudded into *Visenda*, shrapnel filling the galley and entering the bread which was just being baked; they struck the bridge, and the captain was killed by flying glass from the shattered bridge window.

Was it revenge by the U-boat she had attacked? Or, if this had been lost, by one of its fellows? There were many who held strongly to this belief.

There were two direct results of the *Visenda* incident. One was that all the patrol trawlers were eventually fitted with protective triplex-glass bridge windows. The other was that they were sent in turn to the newly opened sea training establishment at Tobermory, on the Island of Mull, for an intensive work-up under the gimlet eye of Commodore Sir Gilbert Stephenson. The already legendary old 'Monkey Brand' himself.

8

The Terror of Tobermory

Tobermory! The order to proceed there for work-up was received with apprehension by all crews and positively dreaded by the officers. Not because of the rigours of the battle school, but because of its fiery Commodore, a heavily bewhiskered vice-admiral brought back from retirement to lick the convoy escorts into shape.

Commodore Gilbert Stephenson was known in more polite terms as 'Monkey Brand' or 'Electric Whiskers,' or simply 'the terror of Tobermory.' Even his wife admitted : 'My husband is a very fierce man.' Very fierce, very efficient and, despite his years, very energetic and full of drive, for he was in his middle-sixties. At this age he had broken out of retirement to fly his flag at Tobermory in an old Dutch horse boat, once used to run live horse flesh to Rotterdam. This, his base ship, was renamed HMS *Western Isles*. His battle school commenced in mid-1940 and the tremors of its lively coming reverberated throughout the Fleet.

Soon 'Monkey Brand' had secured the aid of Fleet Air Arm aircraft, submarines, motor launches and speedboats to help reproduce battle conditions for the benefit of new corvettes, frigates and sloops sent to Tobermory fresh from the shipyards; and for the veteran ships sent there for refresher courses, like the Patrol Service trawlers.

'Monkey Brand' achieved splendid results by methods which owed nothing to the naval drill book. He worked by fear, surprise and shock tactics. Thorough to the last degree, he would remove on the spot any officer he considered inefficient, once signalling a trawler's C.O.: 'Suggest I remove all your officers and have replacements sent forthwith.' To his credit this C.O. declined. The Commodore really had no power to remove an officer from his ship, only the Admiralty could do so, except when an officer was guilty

of misbehaviour—drunkenness, madness or assault. But the
Commodore would whip off an officer he considered not up to
scratch, then signal the Admiralty that he had taken Lieutenant X
ashore 'for training,' and would their Lordships please send a
replacement for the ship. . . .

The trawler crews on their work-ups, which lasted from two to
three weeks, found themselves on day and night gunnery exercises,
mock U-boat hunts with a real live submarine, boat-pulling
instruction and even field training on the hillsides. A piratically
black-bearded chief petty officer with waxen ends to his moustache
would give lurid and bawdy lectures on the duties of lookouts,
warning them in spectacular language that the Germans knew
exactly when the watches on British ships were changed, and often
attacked just after a new, sleepy-eyed watch had taken over.

The trawler men had not undergone such vigorous exercises since
their early training, and some not even then. They were not
enthusiastic about it.

'Gestapo' parties in smallboats sneaked up on the trawlers to
catch out unwary quartermasters. 'Monkey Brand' himself, in a fast
motorboat which he used to make sorties round the harbour,
delighted in getting aboard ships unobserved by day and night,
and if possible removing valuable gear from the wardroom. The
morning after one of his night raids some unfortunate ship would
receive the dismaying signal: 'I have your sextant in my cabin—
come and retrieve it forthwith.'

He had other ploys. He would slip aboard a ship, creep up to a
rating and suddenly growl in his ear: 'There's a U-boat on the
port bow—do something about it, man, do something!'
Occasionally, just occasionally, he met his match. Coming thus
aboard *Lord Austin* one day he crept up to two ratings and hissed:
'There's a fire on the messdeck!' To which one of the men calmly
replied: 'Oh yes, sir—we always keep a good fire going down there.'

They deserved their small victory, for *Lord Austin's* arrival on
'Monkey Brand's' territory had been unsettling enough. She had
sailed into Tobermory Bay, all four of her officers on the bridge
wearing clean collars and ties and a worried look. She picked up
her buoy perfectly, a model demonstration, and the officers relaxed
—at least they had made a good start. But then came the
thunderous signal: 'Why have you gone to the wrong buoy?
Proceed to number four buoy forthwith!' They need not have
despaired, for 'Monkey Brand,' who watched every ship come in

and timed them with a stopwatch as they made their buoy, often used to order them to another buoy just to see them go through the whole performance again.

But for *Austin* there was worse to follow. It was 'Monkey Brand's' rule that all men aboard should be able to switch roles and do the jobs of others, which created chaos on exercises with everyone frantically changing posts and seamen going to the stokehold while stokers launched the whalers and manned the guns. On one dreadful occasion when all this was going on during a night shoot, some stokers were on *Austin's* four-inch preparing to fire starshells, when at the critical moment a shell stuck in the barrel. The starshells, being delicate, had a grommet or rope ring round the base to prevent damage, and in the dark the stokers had thrust a shell into the breech without noticing the grommet still on it. The gunner's mate fussed and jittered around trying to dig the shell out with his ramrod. 'Oh dear, oh dear,' he wailed in most un-mate-like language—'My goodness, what a terrible thing to happen at a time like this—what would the Commodore say?'

Austin was exercising with two other trawlers at the time and the most successful feature of the affair was that nobody hit anybody else. They were luckier than some. Like the trawler *Quadrille*, which achieved notoriety by firing both depth-charge throwers while secured to a buoy with another trawler alongside. The depth-charges were set to 150 feet, and the ensuing explosions, besides causing interior damage to both ships, were felt in the church ashore where the Commodore happened to be reading the lesson. His comments are not recorded.

'Monkey Brand' had a wonderful and unnerving memory for faces. He would suddenly roar to a petrified officer : 'You've been here before, haven't you?' To which there was scarcely any answer. Another characteristic was his rigid distinction between lunch and dinner. Every so often, two or three officers from ships working-up would be invited to eat with him aboard *Western Isles*. As the duty-boat brought them aboard, 'Monkey Brand's' chief steward would be waiting alongside the officer of the watch and the boatswain's mate. If it was dinner, the guests would get drinks and plenty of interesting talk until the early hours of the morning. But if it was lunch—nothing but water. It was eat up and away, with 'Monkey Brand's' parting shot ringing in their ears : 'Well, you'll be anxious to get back to the job!' Fortunately the wine steward always knew who had been asked to lunch, and those guests, when they went to their cabin to wash, always found a couple of drinks with which to fortify themselves before facing up to the Commodore.

One of 'Monkey Brand's' favourite tricks was to speed over to a ship in his motorboat, hustle up the ladder on to the assembled quarter-deck, grab off his gold-braided cap and throw it to the deck, shouting: 'That's a bomb—what are you going to do about it?' The ruse never failed to create momentary panic. Until one day, when he tried it out on a trawler. As he flung his cap down in front of the startled company and made his challenge, a rating stepped smartly forward and kicked the cap overboard. The surprised Commodore gazed unbelievingly at his cap floating away on the water. But he was not beaten. 'Good work,' he said approvingly— 'splendid.' Then pointing to the cap, he roared: 'Quick, that's a survivor who can't swim—save him!'

Among the honoured few who actually did get the better of 'Monkey Brand' was the C.O. of a midget submarine exercising at Tobermory. After suffering the lash of the Commodore's tongue he took his tiny craft alongside the old *Western Isles* and left a dummy limpet bomb with a rude message on it directly below 'Monkey Brand's' porthole. It was said that when the 'bomb' was discovered the voice of the Commodore addressing his unlucky officer of the watch stampeded sheep on a hillside four miles away.

But it was the trawler *Rumba* that won perhaps the most satisfying victory of all. Her number one was Sub-Lieutenant Jim Fowler, RNVR.

'We had been accused by "Monkey" Stephenson of having been boarded during the night and found to have no gangwayman or anybody on watch. I personally was rather incensed about this, so was the coxswain and others; we were quite sure this hadn't happened. So that evening, when our captain was having dinner with the Commodore, four of us took the boat away and went up to cable length from *Western Isles*. Leaving one man in the boat, we boarded the depot ship without being seen. Two of us then got on to the bridge, leaving the other man keeping lookout on the foc'sle head in readiness for a quick getaway. It was pitch dark up on the bridge, and we were just getting the magnetic compass out of the binnacle to take away with us when there was a movement in the corner. It was an armed guard.

'He said, "Can I help you?" We replied: "Yes please, can you give us a hand getting the compass out? We'll hold your rifle for you." Trustingly he gave us his rifle and then we were all set; we took the compass and with the guard in tow, went down to the officer of the watch's cabin, nobody questioning us on the way. We entered the cabin and got the O.O.W. to sign a form—we had the rifle—saying that we'd boarded his ship at such a time and taken away his compass. Then we left hurriedly.

'Next morning we got a signal saying, would we please return the compass? And that was all. We had no more trouble after that.

'Next time I went to Tobermory for working-up I was in command of a trawler, and I wasn't looking forward to it very much. But I had a very easy time indeed, as I was "killed" in the first two minutes of the main exercise and it was left to everybody else to carry on.'

Away from the mock battles of Tobermory the war continued hard for Harry Tate's Navy, more than thirty vessels being lost in the first three months of 1941 and the losses piling up with each succeeding month. During January nearly all the losses were from mines. Many other trawlers were damaged, and some, like the former Hull fisher *Bernard Shaw,* had the narrowest of escapes. Her newly promoted commander was Skipper William Thorpe. 'One night while sweeping the Barrow Deep we nearly met our end. It was raining hard and a nice breeze, so I told the gun crew to get under the whaleback for shelter as we were approaching number four Barrow buoy. I heard a plane fly overhead, and trying to spot him with the binoculars saw a parachute mine being dropped. I caught sight of it just under our starboard crosstree, ordered "Hard-a-port!" and the parachute slid over the foredeck into the water. Three more feet to port and that would have been the finish of us.'

Another minesweeper, the old *Stella Rigel,* had swept all day long off the Essex coast without getting a single mine. She went on working through the moonless night. Skipper T. Spall, RNR, kept a wary lookout as he passed each buoy, knowing that an E-boat might be hiding in its shadow. He continued sweeping till the end of the middle-watch, then told the tired hands to pipe down for a few hours rest.

He left the bridge for the first time since *Stella Rigel* had put to sea, but did not go down below to his cabin, remaining on deck near the ready-loaded Oerlikon mounted aft. Suddenly hearing aircraft engines he ran to the gun, and as a searching plane zoomed over low he fired. He did not order action-stations, which would have brought the crew from their bunks, for to do that, as he explained afterwards: 'I would have had to run to the bridge to sound the bell, and by the time the hands had closed up, the Heinkel might have been back in Germany.' So he tipped the Oerlikon skywards and kept up rapid fire. The Heinkel lost height and moments later blew up in the sea half a mile ahead. The action had lasted a matter of seconds, but now the hands were astir. Skipper Spall went for'ard and shouted down the companion-way leading to the foc'sle. 'Just come up and have a look at this, lads!' They tumbled up on deck to watch the Heinkel blazing in the sea.

That's how Skipper Spall won his DSC.

In the Channel the trawler *Syringa,* commanded by Skipper W. Ritchie, RNR, was sweeping in company with another trawler when they sighted a Junkers 87 flying in at about 300 feet. *Syringa's* sister ship challenged and was answered by a burst of machine-gun fire. She opened with her 12-pounder and Lewis gun as the plane crossed her quarter and dropped a salvo of bombs on either side.

Then it was the turn of *Syringa.* The plane sprayed her bridge and deck with machine-gun bullets, and dropped two more salvoes, one narrowly missing to starboard, the other to port. The plane then went back to attack the other trawler, injuring her skipper, after which it returned again to *Syringa.* Seaman-Gunner Colyer, at *Syringa's* Lewis gun, was killed by a burst from the German rear-gunner as the plane passed over, and a bomb pierced the engine room casing. It crashed down on to the platform on the fore side of the engine but failed to explode.

The Junkers circled and returned for a third attack on *Syringa,* but it seemed to be losing height and dropped down within range of the trawler's 12-pounder. Two well placed shots sent the German crashing into the sea a mile away.

Skipper Ritchie, a braw Scot, went down to the engine room, where, despite the presence of the unexploded bomb, Stoker Petty Officer G. Wood had remained at his post. With the help of Chief Engineman E. Clinton the skipper carried the heavy bomb on deck and threw it derisively over the side. That was how Skipper Ritchie earned his DSC and the other two men the DSM.

Skipper Ritchie was indeed a man to be reckoned with. 'It was on *Syringa,*' a member of her crew recalls, 'that we had a skate of a Welshman, an AB, who was always dodging work, usually by pretending to be sick. One morning he asked to see the skipper, and being at sea he did so on the bridge. I was at the wheel, and down the voice-pipe I got this end to the conversation by the skipper—"Now you go away to your hammock, sonny, and turn in. It takes a man just fifteen minutes to die—if ye aren't dead in fifteen minutes, get back on this bloody deck!" '

As ever, the drifter *Fisher Boy* was in the thick of it. Early January 1941 found her helping in the rescue work off Clacton when the motorship *Strathearn* went down to a mine. Sixteen men were picked up alive out of *Strathearn's* crew of thirty-four.

Later the same month *Fisher Boy* was on patrol out of Brightlingsea when she anchored in thick weather. All hands turned in with the exception of Signalman Bev Smith and Seaman Cyril Paine. Signalman Smith :

'We heard quite a noise going on out at sea and assumed that a passing convoy was being attacked. I left Cyril in the wheelhouse to go down to the galley to make a pot of tea, when there was an almighty roaring sound and a Junkers 88 came in very low, machine-gunned us and dropped several bombs. We both dashed to the Lewis guns and managed to get them going, but after half a dozen shots both our guns jammed. I got my gun released and trained on the aircraft again just in time to see what I thought was a mine floating down on a parachute. I aimed at the mine, hoping to explode it while in the air, but to my surprise it swung its legs apart—it was one of the crew, the pilot. The plane crashed and the pilot landed in the water. By now, with all the noise going on, our crew had turned out in a bit of a hurry and we found we had barely enough steam to get the anchor up. The wind had caught the German pilot's parachute and he was skimming across the water on his way back across the North Sea—it took us some time to catch up with him. Eventually a neatly thrown lead line fouled his parachute rigging and we hauled the frightened fellow aboard. We dried him down, dressed him up in a sailor's suit, and I called ashore on our radio for someone to come and take him off the ship. An Air Sea Rescue launch came out and we put our prisoner aboard dressed as an English matelot. He had got over his fright now and was a bit cocky. But not half as cocky as we felt, having brought the plane down with a few Lewis shots. We celebrated, highly illegally, with neat rum which we kept bottled, and were highly pleased later to hear it announced over the BBC that the drifter *Fisher Boy* had shot down an enemy plane.'

Success of a different kind came to the trawler *Tourmaline* while on convoy escort. Unlike most other trawlers she had never gone fishing in her life, having been bought by the Admiralty as she was built. In late January she had just been refitted and looked more like a yacht, her decks as white as snow and even her brass polished, though this was an error in wartime.

One night *Tourmaline* was at her station on the port side of a convoy when her officer of the watch, Midshipman Allan Waller, was alerted by starshells fired by the destroyers ahead. Looking towards the land he saw a tell-tale splash of foam and rang the alarm bell. The crew ran to action-stations. Suddenly an E-boat was seen approaching on the port bow at high speed and *Tourmaline* let fly with everything she had—her port Lewis gun, the twin point-fives aft, the Savage guns on the welldeck, and her 12-pounder. As the E-boat shot across her bow only 100 yards away *Tourmaline's* guns kept up a hail of fire from her starboard side. Answering machine-gun bullets from the E-boat peppered her funnel, and one of her own Lewis guns, which had no stop, slewed right round and drilled holes in the break of the foc'sle just below the 12-pounder platform, narrowly missing the gun's crew. During this encounter a second E-boat sped up astern and began firing. *Tourmaline's* aft point-five gunners emptied their guns at it, scoring repeatedly with their tracer shots. The damaged boat sheered off and attention was focused again on the first one, which after a crippling shell from the trawler's 12-pounder, had swerved hard to port. Now its engine had stopped, and it was awash and covered in foam. *Tourmaline,* still firing, turned to ram it, but had to hold back when a ship of the convoy came into line. The E-boat sank without survivors, a definite 'kill'.

But it had been a very near thing. In his official report *Tourmaline's* captain commented: 'The success of this short action was entirely due to the fact that the ship was at full action-stations as a result of seeing the starshells fired by the destroyers. If the warning had not been received, the only armaments ready to engage the enemy in the short time available would have been the point-fives. The ship's complement is inadequate to keep continuous watch on the other guns in the severe weather conditions prevailing at this time of year.'

Unhappily *Tourmaline's* taste of victory was short-lived. Just thirteen days afterwards, on February 5th, she was again on escort duty, almost at the rear of a convoy as it passed Dover. This convoy was enjoying the welcome air cover of four Spitfires. When a Junkers 87B attacked one of the merchant ships *Tourmaline* fired and took the top of its tail off, and away it limped, hotly pursued by all four Spitfires, who finally shot it down. Unwittingly, however, by all chasing after the German, the Spitfires left *Tourmaline* to her fate. Directly above her was high cloud. As the Spitfires vanished, down through a hole in the cloud zoomed a second Junkers 87B, straight for the hapless trawler. After half a dozen rounds *Tourmaline's* point-fives jammed and she was helpless; down came three bombs, one of which crashed through the engine room casing and exploded, throwing everyone to the deck and blasting the ship's point-fives off their mounting.

Two of her gunners were injured, one being blown over the side of the sinking ship. Three men were killed and others burnt and scalded. One boat was got away, the other men jumped over the side.

Quick revenge for *Tourmaline* came when the low-flying plane continued over another part of the convoy. The Hull trawler *Lady Philomena* wheeled to the fight and Leading-Seaman Alec Dodd let blast with his four-inch, sending the German crashing into the sea. It was an action for which he won the DSM, and his wiry commander, Skipper Albert Robinson, RNR, the DSC.

Philomena picked up some of *Tourmaline's* survivors, the others being rescued by a tug acting as a balloon ship. One stoker was so badly scalded that he only lived for a few days afterwards. Among the badly injured was Midshipman Waller. When the ship was struck he was hurled to the deck from the point-five zareba and blacked out. On coming dazedly to his senses he staggered for'ard through steam and smoke, his face and hands scarred by steam, and passed out again on the well-deck. He recovered consciousness to find himself in a boat with five of the crew, and suffering badly from facial wounds and scalded wrists. Taken ashore at Sheerness, he went on to Chatham naval hospital and was there for some weeks, being treated by a surgeon who had been a member of Sir Alexander Macindoe's team of plastic surgeons at East Grinstead. Waller was given only morphia and his face felt as if it was being scrubbed with sandpaper—a very painful process. But the treatment was highly successful, and weeks later he was back at Harwich looking for another ship. However, his reputation as a survivor from two sunken trawlers, *Amethyst* and now *Tourmaline,* in little more than two months, besides being in the corvette *Primula* when she was rammed and badly damaged, had preceded him, and he was almost thrown off two trawlers he visited, being dubbed as 'The Jonah of Parkeston Quay.'

Waller's unfortunate record was not unique. With more than 160 Patrol Service vessels now sent to the bottom there were many other survivors like him. And the ship casualties continued to rise steeply in the early months of 1941, reaching a peak in May of one vessel lost every two days, this chiefly as a result of enemy bombing. There were, in the midst of it, some memorable escapes and none so weird as that of the small and very old Lowestoft drifter *Young Mun*. Her engineman was Walter Walker.

'We were detailed to accompany a group of trawlers steaming out to clear some mines which had been laid near Folkestone, and were only two miles out of Dover when two German bombers swooped down on our small fleet of ten ships. All the vessels opened fire, the trawlers with their anti-aircraft guns, the drifters with their double-barrelled machine-guns. I was at my post at *Young Mun's* engines when suddenly there was a terrific crash and water poured down through the engine room skylight. I stopped engines and ran up on deck to take a look. It was a fantastic mess. A Junkers 88 had crashed down on our deck, bringing down the mast and covering the ship with wreckage. Two of its crew had been flung out and one hung on a small derrick, the other on the ship's quarter, both bodies with their legs missing. We were ordered to return to Dover, which we did after dropping all the gruesome parts in the water. As we were about to enter harbour we were stopped by the suspicious officer on the mole—because our mast was down we were unable to run up any identification signals. It was only after taking a good look at the evidence piled up on the deck that he allowed us in, much to the amusement of the crew.'

The losses from enemy bombing continued, among them three vessels which went down off Lowestoft, almost within sight of the Patrol Service depot, in as many weeks. These were the trawlers *Ben Gairn* and *King Henry*, and the drifter *Uberty*, which was blown to pieces just outside the harbour. They were joined by the drifter *Thistle*, wrecked by a mine.

June was a shattering month, every lost vessel but one falling a victim to the attacks of enemy planes. But it did not stop the convoys. On the Channel convoys, Portsmouth to Southend, usually five trawlers swept abreast, followed by a destroyer and then the merchant ships, mostly coastal colliers bringing coal from South

Wales to the power stations on the Thames; for the railways could not cope with the coal traffic and it had to come by sea, even through the Straits of Dover. When the convoy reached the Straits the trawlers broke formation and two continued to sweep with shortened depths. The three others became additional escorts on the flanks of the convoy, and eventually all five were purely escorts as they approached Southend.

The trawlers spent a night in the Medway and began their return voyage the following night, again passing through the Straits in the dark. Invariably they were shelled from the French coast on the westbound trip, while passing through at about 10 p.m., but on coming east, between 2 a.m. and 3 a.m., they were allowed a peaceful passage by the enemy gunners. It appeared that even the Germans liked their sleep.

Time and again the phlegmatic quality of the trawler skippers showed itself in the most heated moments. There was the occasion when a trawler patrolling five miles out of Grimsby, watching for minelaying aircraft, was attacked by a Heinkel. The ship disappeared in bomb splashes but reappeared seemingly unharmed. However, she made no response to signals from the shore station, so a boat was sent out to investigate. They could see no sign of life on board and the quiet scene had all the eeriness of a *Marie Celeste* mystery; until on the vessel's other side were discovered smallboats with almost the entire ship's company in them busily picking up dead fish.

The trawlers continued to play a large part in rescue work in E-boat Alley and many merchant sailors had cause to bless them. Like Fireman Joseph Willis of the SS *Westbourne,* which was dive-bombed in a convoy passing north of Flamborough Head.

'I had just come off watch at midnight and everyone was in the galley, thinking they were safe at last, when it happened. I was on the poop deck aft with two shipmates, holding a mug of coffee in my hand. The blast of the bombs blew us all overboard. Next thing I remembered was coming to my senses in the cold sea. I swam about in the dark till I got hold of some old hatch-board, which I clung on to and managed to stay afloat, A destroyer raced past, a voice shouting through a megaphone that he would send help.

'Everyone amidships in the *Westbourne* had been blown to pieces. As I hung on to my float in the dark I could see her burning and hear the ammunition exploding. I must have been in the water for six or seven hours, for it had turned daylight, when out of the blue came a Patrol Service trawler and her sailors fished me out of the sea. "God blow me, Geordie," said one, "couldn't you find a better time than this to take a bloody bath!" They plied me with Craven A cigarettes and plenty of rum.

'We could see the *Westbourne* miles away, still on fire and her ammunition going off. Next day at Hartlepool, where I went into hospital, I saw her after she'd been brought in by tugs. Her bridge, funnel, boats, everything was completely gone; she was just like a flat-iron. They found a charred body which they thought was the skipper's, and another body, that of the wireless operator. Others had gone down to Davy Jones, and if it hadn't been for Harry Tate's men he'd have got me too.'

Many Patrol Service men were sent straight from Lowestoft to the trawler base at Belfast. Here, trawlers were employed both on Atlantic convoys and on minesweeping. Within weeks of joining the old Dutch trawler *Friesland*, Seaman Robert Thomas was involved in the tragedy of a sister ship.

'It was a Sunday, and we were duty ship. At about 2 p.m. the quayside telephone started ringing. The sentry who should have been on the quay was on the messdeck, and the rest of the seamen were in their bunks. An argument started between them and the sentry as to who should answer the phone, which kept on ringing. Eventually a young Scotsman with more imagination that the rest said it might be important and dashed up on deck to answer it. He returned with a message that there had been an explosion down Belfast Lough. As duty ship we steamed out to investigate, but when we reached the scene all that remained on the surface was some floating wreckage and a lifebelt bearing the name of the drifter *Jewel*, an inshore minesweeper. She had gone up on a mine. In among the wreckage was the body of her young sub-lieutenant; we found no survivors. Ironically, one of *Jewel's* Patrol Service crew had only just joined her; he'd been sent to recuperate at a quiet base after a harassing time minesweeping at Dover.

'Soon after we returned to harbour the quayside phone rang again and this time I answered. A woman's voice asked if she could speak to Sub-Lieutenant ——, of one of our minesweepers. I told her that his ship was at sea, which was true enough. The *Jewel* would never return, and Sub-Lieutenant —— was lying on our deck, his broken body covered with a blanket.'

In the North Sea, typical of the small trawler minesweepers was the *Contender*. She operated with three others in a group of four, carrying out regular Oropesa (moored mine) sweeping duties from Lowestoft to Sheringham Shoal. Her signalman was Colin Brown.

'Though we were never actually involved in any skirmishes with the enemy on the water we frequently heard their engines and witnessed the night engagements with the convoys, which were always just astern of us, doing a little better than our sweeping speed of about six knots. With our World War 1 vintage 12-pounder and two single Lewis guns on their bridge mountings, I, for one, was always relieved when we left the swept channel at either end of our stint.

'There was always the floating mine, particularly after a spell of easterly gales, and rifles were handed out with armour-piercing ball ammunition for our "marksmen" to have a bash. Most of these floating mines were ours, washed away from the East Coast minefield, and most were set safe and had to be punctured a number of times before they would consent to sink.

'Our main bugbear at this time were the Junkers 88s which sneaked across the North Sea in periods of poor visibility. Often their real targets were on the East Coast, but they could make our lives miserable, shooting us up with their cannon and machine guns. Lots of our little ships had small steel boxes with peepholes set up behind the bridge, in which the skipper could shelter during an attack and continue to con his ship.'

Nogi, the senior vessel of *Contender's* group, fell victim of a near miss by a bomb one evening as they were nearing the end of the sweep off Cromer. She started to founder by the head. *Contender* and *Solon* went alongside and with bow and stern ropes secured, steamed all out for the shoreline to drag the wreck off the swept channel. They just managed to do this before the respective skippers had to give the order to chop the hawsers.

Contender's own brush with the enemy had a happier result. It occurred when a Heinkel attacked the group as they were sweeping. 'He made a dummy run, circled and pointed towards the last in line—us. Swooping down he dropped two big bombs at masthead height, and both were travelling almost horizontally when one crashed on to the 12-pounder gun platform and shot off into the sea beyond, where it exploded. The tail of the bomb was sheered off and wedged under the gun mounting, effectively putting the gun out of commission. The bomb must have been a 1,000-pounder, for it so damaged the gun mounting and platform that we were in dock for a fortnight while the plates were straightened out. Had it gone off on impact instead of in the sea, I would not have been able to tell the tale. I was standing on the wing of the bridge at the crucial time with a jammed and useless Lewis gun in my hand, when a fire bucket dislodged by the impact sent sand shooting across the foredeck and over the bridge. I very nearly collapsed with fright, but was able to put on a brave face with the rest when we were congratulated on our return to harbour. We'd had a miraculous escape, and for some reason which I am not able to explain we were treated like heroes, which we were very far from being.'

Another member of the foursome, the *Force,* was not as fortunate. 'We were anchored off the mouth of the river at Great Yarmouth when she caught a packet. Visibility was extremely poor and we had a couple of shackles out waiting for the mist to clear. Unfortunately *Force* did not have a shackle on deck ready to slip in an emergency, and when a Jerry plane loomed up and dropped a stick of bombs across her bows the steampipe to her windlass was fractured and she was unable to pick up her anchor and beach herself. Despite frantic attempts to run out more cable and knock out the next shackle pin she slid to the bottom in about twenty minutes. It was Harry Tate's Navy after all, wasn't it?'

Higher up the East Coast, at North Shields, the 8th Mine-sweeping Flotilla was based. It consisted of eight paddle steamers with names nostalgic of an idle peacetime : *Laguna Belle, Thames Queen, Glengower, Glen Avon, Glen Usk, Southsea, Snaefell* and *Medway Queen.* Gunnery officer of *Thames Queen* was Lieutenant James Reeve, RNVR.

'The paddlers were especially well suited for conversion to Oropesa minesweepers because of their shallow draught, which was up to about seven feet, and their extensive decks, which allowed them to be fitted with powerful steam winches from which sweeps could be streamed on either quarter, and with protective armament —if available ! This same extensive deck, however, offered an unpleasantly large target to hostile aircraft, and if the deck was wooden and well scrubbed to please a zealous first lieutenant, it made the ship a conspicuous target on a moonlit night.

'The usual armament of these old paddlers was a 12-pounder on the foredeck, two or more Lewis guns on or near the bridge, a couple of Brens if they had been able to "win" them from the grateful soldiery at Dunkirk or elsewhere, half a dozen rifles for sinking mines, and half a dozen depth-charges. Towards the end of 1941 we carried balloons when sweeping, and there was one other piece of defensive equipment that was unique, the Holman projector, used also by the trawlers. This was the most frightening thing I ever had to handle during the war. It fired a Mills bomb into the air to deter and destroy aircraft engaged on a low-level attack. It consisted of a length of steel piping forming a six-foot barrel which could be swung about freely. The firing power was either compressed air from a steel bottle, or a steam supply from the boilers. Experience was to show that the compressed air was some-times only powerful enough to spit out the bomb so close to the ship that it broke the lavatory basins, and that the engine room staff objected to their steam being continually leaked away when the projector was in a state of readiness. After one night air attack I was approached by the old "Stripey" who had charge of this infernal machine, with the confession that he had put in a bomb upside down and it was still there after the projector had been simmering away all night. The junior engineer and I got it out and back in its tin, and away into the deep without delay; and when I came to leave *Thames Queen* the Holman projector had ceased to be regarded as an effective weapon.

'*Southsea* had the distinction of shooting down an attacking aircraft, but alas, was blown up just outside Tyne harbour after completing a search-sweep, the victim of an acoustic mine.'

A few months later *Snaefell* met her end, bombed by enemy planes off the Tyne, while down at Harwich the paddlers *Marmion* and *Lorna Doone* were constant targets for enemy cannon shells and machine-guns, suffering damage almost every time they poked their noses out of harbour. *Marmion* finished up a total wreck from enemy bombs. Later, and sensibly, all the surviving paddlers were to be stripped of much of their sweeping gear, fitted with extra guns and converted to anti-aircraft vessels.

In the heat of action collisions were inevitable, and the terse official description of 'Lost by collision' formed an unfair epitaph for some unlucky trawlers which had fought bravely through other hazards. Like the bomb-scarred *Marconi*. Petty Officer Robert Muir:

'Our flotilla sailed from Harwich in the evening as usual for the night's sweeping. At midnight, when we had anchored to a buoy, out came the Ipswich patrol ships at full speed. It was a pitch black night, you could hardly see a hand in front of you. Suddenly the Ipswich vessels were attacked by enemy planes and the noise of battle was terrific. There was a resounding crash and *Marconi* heeled over. We dashed on deck just in time to see one of the Ipswich patrol ships drawing her bows out of our boiler room. The skipper, giving orders to get the lifeboat and raft ready, hurried down to see the damage but was met by the chief engineer coming out of the engine room. "It's no good, skipper," he said, " she's sinking—the engine room's half full already." Out went the order to abandon ship and the boat and raft were launched. The enemy planes must have seen our lights flashing—we were using torches to see and get everything away—and one dropped a stick of three bombs just alongside us. The ship shuddered—it was the finishing touch. The skipper told me to see if there was anyone left down on the messdeck. I shot down and sure enough there was Horace, one of the stokers, fast asleep! I pulled him out of his bunk, dragged him up on deck and pushed him into the raft—poor devil, he didn't know what was going on and was petrified. I then scrambled into the boat with the rest of the crew and the skipper told the rating standing by the bow painter to let go and climb in. He did so, but let the painter trail along the deck and it caught up on one of the dan buoy anchors. *Marconi* was going down fast. The skipper quickly seized an axe and chopped us free, or she would have dragged us down with her—as we tried to row away, the suction of her was so great that I broke an oar in half with the strain. But we got clear at last, and after rowing for over an hour were picked up by a small tug.'

Such was the dismal end of *Marconi,* veteran of two wars; launched 1916, lost 1941.

One of the most bitter collision disasters struck on a North Sea convoy in July.

On the night of the 19th, the brand-new submarine HMS *Umpire* was making her first sea voyage northwards from Chatham, bound for trials on the Clyde. She sailed on the surface in a convoy of merchant ships escorted by trawlers and motor launches. About nightfall *Umpire* developed engine trouble which caused her to drop astern of the convoy, and a motor launch dropped back to act as her escort until she was able to catch up again.

The convoy was due to pass a southbound convoy at midnight somewhere off the Wash. It was a calm night, very dark, but no lights could be shown because of the ever roaming E-boats. *Umpire* and her guardian motor launch lost touch, and when the two convoys met up, the submarine was some miles astern, alone and almost invisible to other ships even at close range.

By international rule ships in a channel-way should keep to the starboard side and pass port-to-port, but on this night the two convoys passed each other on the wrong side : that is, starboard-to-starboard. Consequently *Umpire's* surprised captain found the oncoming convoy approaching him head on. He altered course a few degrees to port and the first six ships of the convoy passed safely down his starboard side. But one of the trawler escorts, the *Peter Hendriks,* keeping station on the flank of the convoy, suddenly loomed up almost dead ahead. *Umpire's* captain took the only action possible to him and ordered hard-a-port. Unfortunately just as the submarine began to turn, the trawler saw her low, dark shape ahead and naturally swung to starboard, making a collision inevitable.

Peter Hendriks struck *Umpire* heavily near the starboard bow. For seconds the two vessels stayed locked together, then the trawler fell away and within 30 seconds *Umpire* sank, taking down all but two officers and two lookouts with her. Thanks to good use of the Davis escape apparatus, many of her company were saved, but two officers and twenty men were lost.

No blame could attach to the *Peter Hendriks*, but that was small consolation to her horrified crew.

In the following month of August a handful of Northern Patrol trawlers played a major part in one of the most remarkable incidents yet in the war at sea, when a U-boat surrendered in the Atlantic to an aircraft of Coastal Command.

On the furiously blowing morning of August 27th the surprised pilot of a Lockheed-Hudson flying on anti-submarine patrol from Iceland saw a big U-boat surface almost directly beneath him. Diving immediately almost to wavetop height the Hudson dropped four depth-charges, which rocked and damaged the U-boat before it could crash-dive, then quickly returned to spray it with gunfire, so preventing its crew from getting to their deck guns. The officers and crew packed the conning tower, and as the Hudson came down on its fourth pass the U-boat's commander held aloft a large white-painted board in token of surrender.

The victorious Hudson wirelessed Western Approaches, and soon British sea and air forces were converging upon the tossing speck in the ocean. The trawler *Northern Chief* was on patrol only a hundred miles away when her commander, Lieutenant N. L. Knight,

RNR, picked up the Admiralty's instructions that the U-boat was to be prevented from scuttling by any means. While he pushed his ship hard through a westerly gale a Catalina aircraft, together with a reinforcement of Hudsons, kept watch on the U-boat, ready to attack again should it attempt to escape.

Northern Chief arrived just before midnight, picking out in the darkness the faint yellow distinguishing light which the planes had ordered the U-boat to show all night. In the rough seas it was impossible for the trawler to launch a boat, so Lieutenant Knight ordered his signalman to warn the German commander not to scuttle; that if he did, his crew would not be picked up. Knight was really bluffing as the trawler would not have left her enemies to drown, but back came the plaintive reply from the U-boat: 'I cannot scuttle or abandon. Save us tomorrow, please.' However, it was not going to be as easy as all that.

Knight switched on a searchlight, playing the beam along the length of the heaving U-boat. It was one of the enemy's new ocean-going boats, more than 100 tons bigger than his own ship. Shortly after midnight the trawler *Kingston Agate* arrived to help in the rescue operation, but then undersea tapping was heard from the German, and the trawlers were instantly on the alert for the presence of another, rescuing U-boat. The tapping then stopped.

Dawn brought another two trawlers, *Wastwater* and *Windermere*, to the scene, also two destroyers. The six ships now ranged close to the U-boat, their asdics still probing for any warning of an enemy rescue attempt. But when danger did come it was not from the enemy but from an Allied aircraft from Iceland; the Norwegian pilot of a Northrop, suddenly breaking from the clouds and seeing the U-boat, thought it was poised to attack a convoy and immediately dived low on it, scoring very near misses with two bombs. The pilot gave no reply to recognition signals made by the trawlers so *Northern Chief* opened fire—until they saw the plane's marking as it vanished again into the clouds. Meanwhile, in the heavy seas with half a gale blowing, the U-boat was dipping her bows deeper and deeper. The senior destroyer ordered the German commander to blow ballast and pump oil, and when there was no reply to this repeated order, fired a burst over the conning tower until the Germans obeyed and the trim of the sluggishly riding U-boat improved.

Skipper-Lieutenant Mawer of the *Windermere* now tried to drift a Carley float down to the enemy, but the waves overturned the float and tossed it back. Another attempt made with a fog buoy was similarly unsuccessful and oil poured on the water also had no effect, while a line fired by rocket simply vanished into the sea.

So the six ships withdrew beyond collision distance to await a lull in the gale. When it came, *Kingston Agate,* skippered by Lieutenant H. L'Estrange—his first command—took a hand. Jock Campbell, *Agate's* first lieutenant, was convinced he could now get across to the U-boat in a Carley float and asked for two volunteers from the messdeck to go with him. A line was shot from the *Agate* to the U-boat and Campbell and the two ratings got aboard the float. In no time they were making the crossing—one minute in sight of *Agate's* crew, tensely lining the deck, the next hidden by the towering sea. They completed their hair-raising journey without mishap and hauled over a heavy tow rope from *Agate.*

For nearly five hours Campbell and his men were busy aboard the U-boat. When Campbell forced its crew to come on deck and lend a hand they seemed reluctant to do so, but eventually the tow was secured, though twice Campbell was nearly swept overboard by the heavy seas when crawling along the vessel's narrow deck.

The Germans were then ferried over to *Agate,* but when it came to the turn of the U-boat commander and his two officers, he refused to step into the float—perhaps with some desperate idea of being able to effect a last-minute scuttling. Campbell signalled this refusal to *Agate,* at which L'Estrange bluntly instructed his signalman : 'Tell them there's a four-inch gun here that says he gets into that boat pretty damned quick!' The commander and his officers took the hint and got into the float, Lieutenant Campbell being the last to leave the U-boat. This was at 6 p.m., just thirty hours after U-570's surrender to the Hudson.

When the sea had calmed *Northern Chief,* being the bigger and senior trawler, took over the tow, while *Kingston Agate* made off at full speed with her prisoners. Throughout that night and the next day *Northern Chief* and her escorts struggled northwards against the boisterous weather, finally reaching the shores of Iceland. There the big U-boat was towed in and beached to cheers from the other watching ships. The greatest naval prize of the war had been successfully brought in by one of His Majesty's 'minor war vessels.'

U-570 was soon declared seaworthy again; the Germans appeared to have panicked unnecessarily, for the interior damage was comparatively slight. The boat returned to the sea war, though this time on the side of the Allies and renamed HMS *Graph*—the only U-boat in naval history to sail under the White Ensign.

Meanwhile an even more astonishing encounter took place in the seas off Gibraltar when a U-boat was humbled by a lone trawler, the redoubtable *Lady Shirley*.

9

The Triumph of 'Lady Shirley'

There was nothing to single out *Lady Shirley* from the other converted fishing vessels based at Gibraltar. Nothing whatever. A Hull trawler built in the mid-1930s and taken over by the Admiralty as war loomed, her 470 tons was typical of other ships of Harry Tate's Navy. She berthed quietly with her sister trawlers at the northern end of the Rock.

Lady Shirley's earlier war service had been sound if unspectacular, though she had once come through a fierce attack by enemy aircraft while on patrol, and her name was on the honours board at Sparrow's Nest.

Then had come her orders to proceed to Gibraltar. After a work-up at Tobermory she had reached the Rock in the early months of 1941 and settled to a routine of convoy escort and anti-submarine patrol duties.

Lady Shirley was constantly at sea, which was no real hardship for her crew. Several were from the pre-war fishing grounds and all except one of the twenty-six were Patrol Service men from the Nest.

Their captain was a thirty-six-year-old Australian, Lieutenant-Commander Arthur Callaway, RANVR; quiet, thoughtful and full-bearded. At the outbreak of war Callaway had been managing-director of a bedding factory in Sydney, and an active member of the local RANVR unit. The young number one was Sub-Lieutenant Frederick French, RNR, with neat pointed beard. Just 24, he was an alert and determined officer from Kent, whose war had begun early with service in an armed merchant cruiser.

Another Australian, Lieutenant Ian Boucaut, RANVR, a Sydney solicitor, was second officer; and the third and junior officer, now a Patrol Service veteran but still looking considerably younger than his twenty years, was Acting Sub-Lieutenant Allan Waller, the 'Jonah of Parkeston Quay.'

Shirley's capabilities—and handicaps—were much the same as the majority of her sisters, including a full speed of only ten knots. The crew used to keep their own 'rattle schedule' which graphically informed them of their ship's passage. As one crew member describes:

'We always knew when we were at our full speed of ten knots because the bridge windows began to rattle. Nine knots was when the bridge flag locker shook; eight knots down to five produced minor shakes in the bridge ladder. An extra burst of speed needed in an emergency shook the whole bridge works in harmony.'

But for all her limitations *Shirley* was a highly efficient ship. She carried out a full set of drills every day, wherever she was, and practised her gunnery. A .303 rifle was fixed on the four-inch gun to provide firing practice at barrels and other floating objects in the sea. Many of her crew were highly competent at other jobs besides their own; 'doubling' on the asdic, for instance.

It was this extra 'edge' that was to win the trawler a proud place in naval history.

Lady Shirley did a lot of her work from Gibraltar in company with the trawlers *Erin* and *Lady Hogarth*. Poor *Hogarth* at this time had become popularly known as *Mrs* Hogarth, having been 'demoted' by the senior officer, Gibraltar Escort Force, for the cardinal sin of making too much smoke in a convoy. Frequently *Erin* and *Shirley* were sent out to escort tankers coming in; they brought in the tanker *Denbydale,* later mined by Italian frogmen in Gibraltar harbour.

In early September 1941 the two ladies, *Hogarth* and *Shirley*, went out to find another tanker—and *Shirley* broke down with engine trouble. *Hogarth* was obliged to tow her into neutral Madeira for repairs. Aboard *Shirley* then was Signalman Neville Wilson.

'In the harbour we were at once surrounded by local natives in small boats offering us all the products of Paradise. "Anything for buy?" they chanted, and if not for buy, then for flog. So over the side began to go at first items of personal equipment, and then certain pieces of ship's gear. Before long there were few messdeck blankets left and pillows were a scarcity, as were old suits, trousers, leather boots, rope and hawser. The captain, of course, knew nothing of this; he was to learn of it safely afterwards, when some suitable punishments were meted out.

'It seemed it would only be a matter of time before the four-inch gun went over the side, along with the point-fives and two Hotchkiss guns. One wag pinned a placard on the four-inch : "Useful fowling piece for flog or buy. Needs some attention but could be put in working order. Apply Stoker I/C Govt. Surplus Disposal, aft." Fortunately there were no takers, though at one time it seemed that if things were allowed to continue, a price for the whole ship as a going concern might be worked out.

'On the credit side, *Shirley* was bedecked with flower garlands and bowers of fruit such as might have put the hanging gardens of Babylon to shame. No lady ever looked more ladylike, and all at Government expense. You had to duck along the decks to avoid the net bags of swinging onions, whole vine branches of grapes and tastefully arranged swags of pineapple, figs and oranges. Naturally we very quickly had to get back to naval trim, and after the first rush most of the native boats were kept off by the Portuguese Navy.

'On our second day in harbour a funeral procession filed slowly past the ship on the far side of the quay. Little did we know we were being thoroughly scrutinized, for we learned afterwards that it was a fake ceremony organized by the local Nazi gauleiter. Really, the exercise was pretty pointless as we were moored inside the mole and not far from the road which ran round Funchal Bay.'

Shirley's captain was told by the resident British naval liaison officer that a U-boat was suspected to be operating to the north, off the little island of Porto Santo, and arrangements were made for a system of warning flares between ship and shore in case of trouble. *Shirley* then sailed away at dusk on the third day, anxious fingers on the triggers and butterflies in the stomachs of her crew until she cleared the Porto Santo area. But she saw no sign of the U-boat she was deliberately seeking, and so steamed uneventfully back to Gibraltar.

Shirley and *Erin* were next ordered to escort the 6,000-ton ocean-boarding vessel *Maron* to the Canary Isles. *Shirley* took along with her on this trip two Royal Engineers corporals, to give them a welcome change from tunnelling in the rock. They were not deadweight passengers, for in action they could serve as additional lookouts and gun-loaders.

It was a pleasant job for the two trawlers, steaming along with the plum-coloured *Maron* with her six-inch guns—and in the comforting knowledge that she was the bigger target. They left *Maron* south of the Canaries to look for the Allied tanker *La Carriere* coming from Barbados, which they were to escort to Gibraltar. But then *Shirley* was detached to patrol in the vicinity of Teneriffe, because of an anticipated breakout by three enemy tankers harboured there.

For two days *Shirley* conducted a lone patrol south of the Canaries. Signalman Wilson had now left the ship but he recalls those waters.

'It could blow hard and bring up a heavy swell, but more usual was a boundless placidity of ocean, the sort of weather met with in the holiday brochures. When a convoy or a patrol was ended and you were released from worries about mass U-boat attacks and could contemplate the pleasant run back home, you were tempted to idealize about life and became a brochure advertisement yourself, lolling about the sunbaked decks, the engine room casing, the gun decks, and even the bridge top, in holidays-abroad atmosphere and without a care in the world. Providing of course you were not on watch, when naturally you did jump to it a little more. There did, however, always lurk at the back of one's mind the nagging reflection that this same calm weather was a U-boat's high delight. In it, a torpedo ran magnificently straight and untroubled towards your hull, and the end could be sudden. quick and total, and thus the end of your holiday.'

While *Shirley* continued her lone patrol a holiday atmosphere could not be indulged, so the early morning of October 4 1941 found her keenly alert. The weather was fine and calm, and the visibility very good, as her great drama began.

The lookout in the crow's nest spotted something that looked like a ship's funnel and reported it to Sub-Lieutenant French, who was officer of the watch. French went up to see for himself, and as he was studying the object it disappeared. It could have been either the funnel of a ship or the conning tower of a U-boat refracted over the horizon. *Shirley's* captain immediately altered course towards the position.

Sub-Lieutenant Waller, the young signals and navigation officer, had taken middle-watch, and was just about to turn out again.

'At four minutes past ten the alarm bells went. I grabbed my lifebelt and tin-hat and went off to my U-boat action station aft at the depth-charges. I then went up to the bridge to see what was happening and was told we had made a firm contact at about 1800 yards. We were going for it at top speed.

'We had been having trouble with the asdic and had managed to mend it so that we could "ping", but the recorder part of it on the bridge was useless, which meant that distances of echoes had to be measured by a stopwatch, and it was by this means that we went into the attack.

'I ran back aft and waited for the signal to fire the depth-charges, and when it came we dropped a pattern of five. While we were preparing to reload I made my way round to the port side to see how the loading was going on there—and got the most tremendous shock of my life. About four hundred yards astern, amid the disturbed explosions slightly off the port quarter, there appeared first the grey bow of a U-boat, then the periscope, and then, very slowly, up came the conning tower. It was a huge ocean-going U-boat, fully twice the size of our little ship. It was a nightmarish experience—I felt like a small boy caught robbing an orchard.

'Our drill quickly switched from undersea to surface action stations, and being action officer of the watch I had to be on the bridge. When I scrambled up there the captain hadn't got over the shock either, he was just ordering hard-a-port, to give us a chance of bringing our four-inch to bear and also to ram the U-boat if we could get there. Before leaving the twin point-fives aft I had told the gun's crew to open fire on the conning tower in short bursts as soon as they could get a range on it, and this they did as *Shirley* came round hard, steaming flat out.

'We saw that the U-boat had a large gun up for'ard, about the size of a four-inch, and a gun like a Bofors abaft the conning tower, also a cannon-like Oerlikon on the conning tower itself. When our point-fives opened fire this cannon answered with a stream of shells.

'Our only other guns besides the point-fives and the four-inch were a Hotchkiss .303 each side of the bridge. When our four-inch could bear it opened fire, but the first round was a near miss. The U-boat opened up at the same time and there was a flash of tracers all over the place. This burst mortally wounded our gun layer, Seaman Leslie Pizzey, who was hit by a cannon shell. Calling out "They've got me!" he staggered back, collapsed and died at the back of the gun platform. The gun's crew quickly changed round and another seaman ducked under the gun and took over as layer.

They opened up again at the U-boat, firing shells in quick succession, a mixture of semi-armour piercing and shrapnel. Our Hotchkiss gunners also kept up a constant fire.

'We could not understand why the U-boat hadn't opened fire at us with its big gun. We could see several members of this gun's crew scattered around it and we had soon killed or wounded most of them without suffering a single shell in reply. It was mystifying. But we took a real hammering from their conning tower cannon. Our bridge was riddled and a steampipe up for'ard was punctured, sending clouds of steam flying about the deck. I had been quickly working out *Shirley's* position and the captain told me to take the signal down to the wireless cabin, also to yell down to the engine-room to get the steam turned off smartly so that we could see what we were doing.

'The wireless cabin was behind the wheelhouse, but when I tried to leave the bridge by the back door I found it obstructed by one of our two signalmen, who had been hit in the thigh by a cannon shell—one of the Army corporals was trying to patch him up. I dashed back into the bridge, got out through the front window and slid down the ladder at the front. There was a fresh stream of fire from the U-boat as I went down and I felt a shell narrowly miss me. I reached the wireless cabin to find Sparks there all ready to send, but coolly leaning out of the scuttle taking photographs. I gave him the signal and he whipped it off straight away. Just as I was leaving the cabin I heard our helmsman, Leading-Seaman Blowers, give a loud cheer and shout: "The bastards have finished, I think."

'I flew back to the bridge and found that both our Hotchkiss gunners, Billy Windsor and Sydney Halcrow, had been hit in the legs by cannon shells. Halcrow, in spite of his pain, asked me, " Will you reload the gun, sir?" I grabbed hold of the gun and—so they told me afterwards—yelled, "Get off that bloody gun and let me have a go!" I had just reloaded when we were treated to the extra-ordinary sight of the U-boat's crew all abandoning ship. They jumped into the sea, groups of them, all keeping together in perfect drill, until there seemed to be hundreds of them in the water waving their arms and shouting. We had seen two wounded men still lying forward of the U-boat's big gun, which although we were now only about 100 yards off had surprisingly been trained away from us. All very puzzling—I thought something must have gone wrong with its firing mechanism.

'The end for the U-boat came very quickly, her bow rose up and she just slipped away—at which all her crew in the water gave three cheers! But I was sure we had sunk her, rather than some of her crew opening seacocks. Our depth-charges had forced her to the surface—they must have split her aft, as she never got her stern out of the water. Besides, she had taken at least nine direct hits from our four-inch; she was finished all right.'

And so U-111 took her 740 tons to the depths. The time now was 10.27. The action had lasted just twenty-three minutes from start to finish.

'Everybody lined the ship's side with whatever arms they'd got—rifles, revolvers—as we hauled the Germans aboard one at a time. It was the first time we realized they *were* Germans; we'd thought them to be Italians as they were all so dark, but instead they were just deeply sunburned. We kept pulling them in, dozens of them, until at last there were only two men left in the water. One of these was very badly wounded with a leg shot away at the knee, the other was his comrade.

'Some of the Germans wore Davis escape apparatus, others simply lifebelts, and all were clad in shorts or drill trousers. On counting them up we found we had forty-five prisoners as against less than thirty of us—and four of these wounded and out of action. Eight of the U-boat's company had been lost, either killed or drowned, including the captain, whom we never saw.

'There were two officers among the prisoners. One turned out to be a commander who was learning the job. He was a nasty bit of work and had an injury to his forehead. The other, the U-boat's engineer officer, seemed more amenable. Some other prisoners were injured but the only very serious casualty besides the man who had lost a leg was another with a bad leg wound. We put them down in the wardroom, all except the legless man. There wasn't much room there but it was the safest place for us to lock them up, heavily outnumbering us as they did.

'That afternoon we held a funeral service for Seaman Pizzey, who had been a very popular member of the crew. Tragically, by rights he should never have been with us. He'd hurt his leg playing football and ended up in hospital, but had been so keen to get back to *Shirley* that when our cook fell ill he came back, his ankle in plaster, to take the cook's place. It was an example of the comradely spirit of everyone who served in *Shirley*. The captain read the service and we then stopped engines to put poor Pizzey over the side.

'We had kept the legless German on deck and tried to make him comfortable, but he never really recovered consciousness and died that evening. As we didn't like to stop the ship at night the captain held a second burial service the next morning. We allowed six prisoners on deck for this, and they were very impressed and pleased that their colleague should be given a proper burial. We put him over under a black flag, the captain apologizing for the fact that we hadn't a German ensign to drape him in.

'We were four days out of Gibraltar at our ten knots and didn't know if anybody had heard our signals. We naturally didn't like to make too much fuss about the action for fear of drawing enemy attention. It was only afterwards that we discovered that another U-boat had in fact seen everything and sent frantic signals back to the U-boat base at Lorient, not daring to sink us because of the many prisoners we carried.

'So we steamed on, the blood mopped up from the bridge, and several small fires started by the U-boat's incendiaries safely put out, but with the ship full of holes. Our smallboat was holed and there was an ominous hole in a depth-charge which had been struck by a cannon shell; we carefully dumped the charge overboard first chance we had. Fortunately we had no trouble with our prisoners, though we were all ready for it. We discovered afterwards that one or two Nazis among them had tried to dig through the floor of the wardroom, which was over some of the ship's tanks, but it wouldn't have got them far as we'd already thought of that one and stationed a man down there with a Hotchkiss gun unshipped from the bridge. In addition the officer of watch always carried a couple of Mills bombs, and we kept two or three men on deck similarly armed.

'The Germans were dumbfounded and bamboozled by our victory over them and wanted to know "where all the guns had come from." However, it was not the number of our guns which had beaten them, it was the speed and efficiency of our drill. It was at this point we discovered why we had not been shelled by their own four-inch : the German gunners had acted so hastily that they forgot to take the tompion out of the gun; they fired their first shot with it still in and blew up the barrel.

'Their engineer officer, Gunther Wolf, was most co-operative. He noted down in meticulous fashion a list of the U-boat's company—names, numbers, addresses, the lot. He had been to Birmingham University and his English was perfect. We got on very well with him. One of our enginemen who could speak German also managed to get a lot of information out of the prisoners.

'Lieutenant Boucaut, though actually a solicitor, had had three years' medical training, and he and the Royal Engineers corporal who was skilled in first-aid looked after the casualties supremely well, so we did not have anyone else die on us.

'About two days out of Gibraltar, when it grew dark, we sent off another signal; the Vichy French were none too friendly and we had to steam past Casablanca. But we finally got a reply saying we would be met by the destroyer *Lance*. She duly came along, put her doctor aboard us and escorted us the rest of the way.'

Here was *Shirley's* big moment. Instead of sailing unnoticed to her usual berth at the trawler base end of the Rock, she went straight alongside the nearest mole to be boarded by Vice-Admiral Sir George Edward-Collins, Vice-Admiral Commanding North Atlantic. Everyone knew she was coming. Every ship in harbour loudly tooted a victorious welcome.

'We had half the Gibraltar army on the quay to take the prisoners off. The Admiral came aboard with the base surgeon commander. The surgeon, who spoke good German, told the wounded prisoners where they were going, but they refused to believe him—they'd heard that Gibraltar had fallen long ago to the Germans and so were absolutely lost.

'We said our goodbyes to Gunther Wolf, all *Shirley's* officers shaking hands with him, a gesture which appeared to upset the waiting soldiers. Once clear of prisoners we went up to the trawler base, cheered by all the trawlers in the pens. Later we had to take *Shirley* down to the other end of the dockyard for a refit and much needed repairs. As we went past, Force H was in harbour and we were cheered by all the ships, including the *Ark Royal*. We were forgivably pleased about that.'

Winston Churchill cabled his personal congratulations to *Shirley*. Lieutenant-Commander Callaway was awarded an immediate DSO —'For daring and skill in a brilliant action against a U-boat in which the Enemy was sunk and surrendered to HM trawler *Lady Shirley*. . . .' In fact his award came just short of being a VC. Other awards followed. Sub-Lieutenant French and Lieutenant Boucaut each received the DSC; only the junior officer went un-decorated, and this for the simple reason that *Shirley* ran out of her quota of medals. No fewer than six of the crew were awarded the DSM, while for Seaman-Gunner Halcrow there was a special award of the Conspicuous Gallantry Medal. In the words of the citation : 'Although so badly wounded that he was ordered to go below, he stood to his gun until the action was over.' Five Mentions in Despatches completed *Shirley's* honours and one of these was for the Army corporal who had helped so ably with the wounded—a most unusual honour for a soldier, for it entitled him to wear the Atlantic Star.

But after all this, red tape still won the day. Sub-Lieutenant Waller :

'We had to account for all the depth-charges we'd used, and to produce the keys used for setting the depths at which they were to explode. We were one key short. This had been in the depth-charge holed by a German cannon shell, and which we had hurriedly dumped over the side. We had to put in a full report as to why we hadn't first removed the key. . . .'

After her great glory *Lady Shirley* settled once more to the humdrum routine work of one of His Majesty's trawlers. But sadly her final drama was only weeks away.

Early December found her with largely the same victorious crew, except for the wounded and one or two other crew replacements. There had been one change among her officers. Sub-Lieutenant Waller had entered hospital for further treatment of an injury received when one of his earlier trawlers sank, and on coming out found himself swiftly drafted on to Admiral Edward-Collins' shore staff. 'The Admiral was very short-staffed, so they grabbed me. My first duty was to look after the harbour defence asdics; then I became responsible for the U-boat plot.'

And so Allan Waller, his place in *Shirley* taken by a Polish officer, escaped the fate that now awaited his former colleagues, yet by reason of his position at headquarters was to be made grimly aware of it as it occurred.

'There had been some U-boat activity in the Straits, so four trawlers were detailed off to do an asdic sweep. *Shirley* was one of them and another was the *St Nectan,* whose Lieutenant Osborne, an Australian, was a friend of Lieutenant-Commander Callaway.

'The trawlers were carrying out this sweep on the night of December 11 1941. At 3.45 a.m. Lieutenant Osborne came on watch in *St Nectan* and looked across at *Lady Shirley.* She was about a mile off, perfectly in station. Then a sudden rain squall descended on the ships. When it cleared away at about 4.10 a.m.

Lieutenant Osborne looked across again at *Lady Shirley*. But she was not there. At some time during those twenty-five minutes she had vanished.'

Nothing more was heard from *Shirley*, but at 5.10 a.m. there came news of a casualty in the area when the armed yacht *Sayonara* wirelessed Gibraltar: '*Cable Enterprise* blown up, have eleven survivors on board.' *Cable Enterprise* was a mercantile cable ship taken over by the navy. Not long after this signal came another one, somewhat obscure, saying that the armed yacht *Rosabelle,* patrolling in the same area, had been blown up and sunk. Both these signals were intercepted by the trawler *Arctic Ranger*. Intercepted, in fact, by *Shirley's* former signalman, Signalman Neville Wilson.

'I had heard some dull explosions and then came these two signals about *Cable Enterprise* and *Rosabelle*. Not until 9 a.m. were we informed that *Lady Shirley* had vanished. It was a very confused situation. *Arctic Ranger* had been helping another trawler to shadow a French convoy; at 10.30 a.m. we completed this support duty and went off to join in the hunt for the missing *Shirley*. We carried out an extensive search east of Gibraltar but there was no trace of her.

'We could hardly conclude that she had been torpedoed, since there was not even the smallest trace of wreckage, or of the many loose items scattered about her decks which I knew from experience would have floated off had she been tin-fished. There was nothing at all to explain her mysterious disappearance.'

Some wreckage was found by other searching ships, but not *Shirley's*. It was Sub-Lieutenant Waller's unhappy task to verify this when the wreckage was brought in.

'*Rosabelle's* captain and I went to identify the bits and pieces retrieved from the sea. *Rosabelle* was a poor little yacht about 40 or 50 years old. I knew her captain well. He had complained bitterly about the condition of his ship and been temporarily relieved of his command as a result; and so she had sailed without him.

'He easily identified some bits of *Rosabelle* among the wreckage, but I couldn't recognize anything from *Shirley*. This was very strange. In particular, on top of *Shirley's* bridge we had kept two small rafts which rested loosely on a splinter mat and were held in place by vertical brackets; if she had been torpedoed and sunk, these rafts would have floated right off; yet there was no sign of them or of anything else.

'We knew that at least two U-boats had gone through the Straits at the time and the old *Rosabelle's* end was perhaps inevitable, but the double mystery about *Shirley* was why, if the victim of a U-boat, she should have been so instantly overwhelmed; and secondly, if she had been torpedoed, why—in those waters—there was not a single item of wreckage to tell the tale.

'Another thing. If, as was suggested, the Germans had smarted under little *Shirley's* defeat of a U-boat and sought revenge upon her, why hadn't they jumped to announce the glad news of her sinking? In my position on the U-boat plot, information came to hand from all kinds of quarters and it was part of my job to read up all the U-boat reports; but the Germans made no claims about *Shirley*—none whatsoever.'

A possible pointer to what could have happened to *Lady Shirley* came at Gibraltar only a few weeks later, in January 1942. Sub-Lieutenant Waller:

'I was then living in a mess just outside the dockyard and working in the tower, the flag officer's headquarters. I was getting ready to go on watch when at 6 p.m., there was a terrific explosion in the dockyard and a huge smoke ring drifted right up over the Rock, a remarkable sight. I dashed out to see that a big fire had broken out in a corner of the dockyard just astern of the aircraft carrier *Argus*—her officer of watch was killed in the explosion. It was a shocking sight in the dockyard, where three trawlers had been tied up. The middle trawler, the *Erin,* had blown up and sunk instantly, while the one on the outside, the little *Honjo,* was fiercely ablaze from stern to stem, another total loss. The inside trawler of the three, the *Imperialist,* was on fire aft and her first lieutenant called to me to help him with the magazine stopcocks—I knew their whereabouts as I had served in *Imperialist* for a few days at Harwich. We managed to do this job although she was really going up fast, and luckily they were able to save her, though badly damaged.

'The explosion was believed to have been caused by a time bomb placed in one of *Erin's* depth-charges by a Spannish agent for the Germans. And this, to my mind, is the most likely explanation for what happened to *Lady Shirley*. A bomb was placed in one of her depth-charges and she blew up at sea and sank immediately. This would explain everything, including the absence of any wreckage.'

Captured enemy documents at the end of the war ascribed the

sinking of *Lady Shirley* to a torpedo from U-374. But as this U-boat was itself sunk by a British submarine only a month later there are no details to support this claim; and as has been seen, two other ships were torpedoed in the area at around the same time. U-boats generally had little opportunity to check their victims; all the British anti-submarine trawlers looked more or less alike, and in the near darkness no one would have known which ship was sunk.

The mysteriously sudden fate of the fighting *Lady Shirley* and her four officers and twenty-nine men, remains unsatisfactorily explained.

10

'Don't Hang Your Bloody Heads'

By late 1941 the 'efficient madhouse' of Sparrow's Nest had changed considerably from its early days. It was busier, more efficient, and in some respects even more mad.

The rapid expansion of the Patrol Service had seen its ranks thrown open almost entirely to a new type of recruit. Gone to war were most of the fishermen, tugmen and bargemen, and the week-end sailors with a smattering of what it was all about. Now in came civilians from all walks of life, many of whom had not the slightest idea what the Royal Naval Patrol Service stood for. A popular belief was that it was a force of naval police; other ideas varied from flotillas of motor torpedo boats and gunboats to a special fleet of patrolling destroyers.

When the type of ship they were to serve in was unceremoniously revealed to the trainees it was in many cases a severe shock. They would be led past the sleek, rakish motor torpedo boats in one dock to the rusty, battered, ponderous fishing trawlers tied up in another, and be told by a brisk, no-nonsense instructor: 'Them's *your* ships, lads. Not much to look at but fine sea boats. Not speedy but sturdy.' And, ignoring the obvious dismay of his audience, he would continue: 'I know you're all eager to go to sea —I wish I could go with you, but they won't let me now.' His tone belied his words.

New entries were streaming into Lowestoft at the rate of hundreds a week. Naval lorries met the trains as they arrived and ran the newcomers to the Nest. There they were mustered in batches on the stage and names and details taken by the Regulating Chief Petty Officer. Much harassed, but always commanding, this majestic personage did much to allay the doubts caused on arrival by the curious sight at the gates of the two sentries lounging with cigarettes in their mouths, or sparring playfully at one another with their bayonets. A strange introduction to a naval training establishment.

Signed in and told to report back at 0800 hours next morning ('And do not, repeat NOT, be adrift first morning!'), the new entries were marshalled outside the concert hall to join a big queue awaiting transport to billets. Returning lorries were filled to capacity and roared off to town, weaving in and out of roads branching off the main street and stopping at different houses.

A rating would leap down, knock on each door and call out: 'How many, Ma?'

'I'll take two, son,' would come the reply, and the two men nearest the back of the truck would be ordered down and into the billet.

So it went on until the lorry was emptied and went speeding back to the Nest for more. Billets were entirely a matter of chance and on the luck of the draw would depend either misery or comfort for the newly-joined men. Some billets were little better than doss-houses, others were homes-from-home. All depended on the character of the 'Ma's,' as the landladies were universally known. Some greedy, avaricious women saw the war as an opportunity to make as much money as possible and give as little as possible in return. They would squeeze the maximum number of men into their small boarding houses, cram together beds, tables and chairs, give as meagre rations as they dared, and make handsome profits out of the plight of the poor ratings. Some would bunk two, or even three, men in a bed together, though this was against strict naval regulations; they banked on the new entries being too green to complain.

Again, some billets might be filthy, with one lavatory to eighteen men, and infested with fleas which waxed fat on human blood. Rooms were unswept, meals had to be staggered for want of space, and the second sitting might not even have time to finish. Some landladies and their families lived and cooked below ground in the basement, and plates of food came up at the end of an apparently disembodied hand. By these means, unscrupulous land-ladies ended up with fur coats and their own cars.

Many were the men's complaints about fleas, but they had to learn to live with them or find their own remedies, which was hard on those particularly susceptible to the insects, like Ordinary Seaman Paul Lund. By bitter experience he found that the only way to catch fleas successfully was to dab them with a piece of wet soap; they stuck to the soap and you'd got them. For many nights it was a common sight to see Lund standing over his bed, a candle in one hand and a piece of soap poised in the other. To the amusement of his room mates, who seemed to escape the attentions of the fleas entirely.

And there were more vivid experiences, like that which befell Rupert Garratt, bundled into a billet in Nelson Street. 'On our side of the street there were few houses standing and my billet hadn't a whole window—there was oilcloth or something similar for glass, and a cracked and broken front door. All the "livestock" from the bombed houses sought the human warmth of those that were occupied, so my first night was a nightmare. The next night I used a packet of Keatings which I shook liberally over the sheet on which I lay, and although later in the night I applied a more liberal covering, they still got me. The last impression I wished to give was that I was "soft," but after some days my wrists were so swollen that I could not button my cuffs and my bootlaces were well stretched to go round my swollen ankles, so I reported to the Sick Bay with a request that I be moved to another billet. The MO was young, supercilious and probably unsure of himself, or he would not have asked "How do you know they are not gnats?" "Sir," I replied, "gnats do not bite at that time of day, at this time of year, late September, under bedclothes." I got my move and the old billets were closed.'

The majority of men, however, were stuck with the billet in which they had landed. Billets of awful meals and gross over-crowding, where in the morning miracles had to be performed by twenty men in the use of one bathroom and lavatory at more or less the same time—a nightmarish version of the small boarding house in Blackpool at the height of the season. Billets like that of the coalman's terrace house, where every evening the carthorse was led through the hall from the front to the back of the house for stabling. And like the one where the poor, long-suffering trainees pushed a piece of gristle masquerading as liver into the parrot's cage. Whether it was this tasty morsel which choked the bird or the whisky which the frantic landlady poured down its throat to revive it they didn't know, but they did take the precaution of burying the creature to prevent, as one man suggested, having it served up as chicken at dinner the next day.

At first, in all billets, there was no dinner at all on one day a week, for on that day the landladies had to go to the Nest and queue up for their pay. Later they were paid by postal orders sent through the post.

In theory all the billets provided by nearly a thousand landladies were supposed to be inspected regularly by billeting officers from the Nest, but at this period of intensive call-up of civilian personnel there was little time for such niceties; and the newly-joined rating, expecting to endure all kind of hardships, was not likely to make an official complaint at the start of his naval career. The bad landladies banked on this and generally won.

Those landladies of goodwill and real patriotic spirit were fortunately in the majority and they made the utmost sacrifices for their billetees. By limiting their numbers, providing clean, comfortable quarters and as much good food as their naval allowances would provide, they made real homes for their sailors without profit for themselves.

Many, after all, had sons of their own. Like one 'Ma,' who had lost her husband at sea in World War 1 and now had a son in the Army in India. She looked after every one of her lodgers like her own. She fed them like fighting cocks and was not above slipping any hard-up Jack the price of a night at the pictures. She even did their washing; no light task considering she took in seven or eight men at a time.

Other good 'Ma's' saw hope in the young men they cared for in their own private grief. Like one whose youngest son was killed with others in a depth-charge explosion on his trawler. The pieces of his body were sent to Lowestoft, where he was buried, but as she knew, they may well not have been him, or only partly him. Then his kit was sent back to her, and turned out to be another man's. Such bereaved women cared for the hundreds of men who passed through their homes as their own sons.

The names of the good landladies would be passed from mouth to mouth so that on their next return to the Nest the unfortunates could change their luck. The drill was to go to the landlady before reporting at the Nest, and if she was willing to take them, to tell the RPO on the stage that they had already fixed up a billet. Fait accompli.

It must be said that it was not all honey for the landladies, who had to put up with many varying types of men. Here again there were unfortunates, as instanced by the curious but necessary institution of the Wet-Bed Book, kept by the Pay Office at the Nest. The combination of East Coast air and the amount of beer drunk had a potent effect on the ratings' bladders. Beds were wetted every night, rising to a grand climax on pay nights, when many more pints of beer were drunk. The landladies naturally complained, hence the Wet-Bed Book. Landladies reported men who had wet their beds and 2s 6d was deducted from their pay. There was quite a harvest in these 'fines.'

With the trainees and other men waiting for ships, together with a procession of survivors from vessels that had been lost, there were as many as six thousand men attending the Nest at one time. As the town billets could not cope, many had to spend a fortnight or so sleeping on the floor of the concert hall with a gas mask for a pillow, nowhere to wash, and eating their meals at the NAAFI set up in the Nest's confines. Some, no doubt, would have welcomed the use of any billet, fleas and all.

Each new intake of trainees attended the first morning's Divisions, a motley crowd in rig ranging from smart lounge suits to open shirts and patched trousers. The Chief Petty Officer barked his welcome.

'After Divisions the Commodore will inspect you. He'll ask you a few questions. And remember this, he likes a man to look him straight in the face, so don't hang your bloody heads as if you've done something to be ashamed of. Even if you have, the police won't get you here !'

And so the new men had their first meeting with Commodore Daniel de Pass. There would be nearly two hundred of them, but he would exchange a few words with every man. De Pass was short and broad, with a pair of brown eyes in which lurked much good humour. He left a rating with the feeling that he knew exactly what sort of a man he was—his strengths and weaknesses, his virtues and faults. Even the biggest 'skates' liked and respected the Commodore. He had the pleasantest and yet the most telling way of delivering a 'bottle' to a man, and he had an amazing memory for faces.

De Pass took over HMS *Europa* in April 1941. Till then he had captained the *Cossack* as Divisional leader in a flotilla of the famous Tribal-class destroyers. His life was the Navy. He had joined it as staggeringly long ago as 1905 and served in Admiral Beatty's Battle Cruiser Fleet throughout World War 1. Between the wars he had devoted himself to training cadets and young ratings. He took over the Nest at a time when the fishermen's navy had to be brought

into line with the Royal Navy, though still retaining its strong
independence. A lesser man might have fallen down on the task.
By being too lenient he could have let the ever-present slackness and
un-pusser-like conduct continue; by being too harsh he could have
had half the inhabitants of the Nest doing punishment. But De Pass
had a deep understanding of men and of the peculiar composition
of the Patrol Service, and he steered a wise middle course to make
a grand success of the job.

After the initial words with the Commodore there followed days
of getting kitted out. Then the start to six weeks' training: square-
bashing and rifle-drill at the Oval; classes in seamanship, gunnery,
depth-charges, signals and semaphore, minesweeping and asdics.
The instructor at the Oval might be a very young-looking
Newfoundlander.

'If you play the game with me, lads (some of the trainees were
old enough to have been his father) then I'll play the game with
you. But if any of you think you can get the better of me, then
you'd better think again. You'll never do ut! No, you'll never do
ut! When I tell you to do a thing, I just want you to do ut,
that's all.'

This was not easy, as the Newfoundland fishermen, though first-
class seamen, were not usually good at explaining things to others.
They were essentially doers, not teachers. There were a great many
of them passing through the Nest at this time and a number could
not, or would not, read and write, though they were no worse
sailors for that. They could steer a ship perfectly, but could not
box a compass. They were the most happy-go-lucky crowd one
could imagine, and on pay nights went on a glorious bust which
left them broke for the rest of the fortnight. On that night they
would treat anyone within range, for they were recklessly generous.
One seaman went on leave to Edinburgh and spent forty pounds; in
those days a small fortune.

The Newfoundlanders' speech, like a mixture of Manx and Irish,
was equally fascinating. They invariably began a sentence with
'Jeez' or 'Jeez hell,' and seemed to have difficulty in pronouncing
'th.' 'Jeez hell, we've got to do ut at tree-tirty!'

Earlier, when a large contingent of these Newfoundlanders
arrived in England to join the Patrol Service there was no
immediate room for them at the Nest and they were put on forestry
work in Scotland. After some months had passed they organized a
lie-in strike and refused to leave their beds. They had come over

to join the Navy, they said, not to cut down trees. The strike had the desired effect for they very quickly found themselves at Lowestoft.

Gunnery was taught by instructors who were a race apart and had a staccato language all their own.

'When the bullet leaves the barrel—or-right?—the gasses escape through here—or-right?—and take up against the piston—or-right? —forcing it to the rear—or-right?—thus bringing the breech-block and moving parts to the rear—or-right?—and then the sear—or-right?—takes up against the cutaway portion—or right?'

Gun drill was an endless repetition of numbering, doubling, falling over each other, clangs, thumps and yelling. Men confused the four-inch with the 12-pounder, and the 12-pounder with the point-five. According to the instructors they were 'solid.'

Semaphore was taught by a three-badge AB nicknamed Donald Duck. He spent ten minutes of each period teaching semaphore and the remainder telling the trainees of his past experience and warning them of the fate in store for them. Pointing dramatically out to sea as in the painting 'Boyhood of Raleigh' he would thunder ominously: 'I've been out there—I know what it's like. I was out there last war, but I'm finished with it now. But you lot are going out there to get bombed, mined and torpedoed—and you won't enjoy it. And if you don't *pay attention* to what I tells you, you'll like it a bloody sight less!'

Less dramatic but more to the point was the instructor who used to tell his class: "When the action bells ring you don't walk and you don't run, you just fly—your feet never seem to touch the deck.' Thousands of men who wondered at his words later found themselves doing just that.

There had to be some practical training in seamanship, so to be taught helm orders and steering, recruits went to sea in a vessel called the *Umbriel*. She had been intended as an upriver steamer somewhere in Africa, and was rather slow in the tides of Lowestoft. Later, because of the constant enemy raids, it was decided that helm training should be done in the harbour, and sea trips were confined to going out in smallboats and trying, mostly unsuccessfully, not to be seasick.

Those who were to become ship's cooks were taken to a school of domestic science in Lowestoft which, up to the outbreak of war, had been used to teach little girls cookery. There they patiently took tuition from young women teachers. Some men had not even boiled an egg in their lives before, but there were also former employees of large hotels and restaurants; chefs, head waiters, hotel managers. They stood it very well, starting right from the bottom by learning how to wash up, wipe the galley deck and peel potatoes. They were also taught how to cook some very dainty dishes and four-course lunches, though these for four persons, not for a whole ship's company. And they were not told that the galley would, in some cases, be no larger than the average bathroom, and that they would be lucky if they had sufficient cooking utensils to do a decent job. Nor were they told of the agonies of getting meals in a full gale, with pots and pans breaking loose and the cook sliding about and hanging on like grim death to galley supports; or that the crew would demand as good a dinner when a trawler was bucking like a broncho as when she was alongside the harbour wall.

All instructors struggled with and heaped curses on the trainees, each intake according to them being more hopeless than the one before. 'If you don't bloody well pass out, you'll bloody well stay at the bleeding Oval and do another bleeding six weeks!' This threat hung over them constantly like a thunder cloud. In the event they found that 'passing out' was a myth and a mirage. There was a slight formality of some squad and rifle drill under the eyes of the training commander, and a written test on depth-charges, the answers to which were told them beforehand by a kindly petty officer. And that was all. It was impossible *not* to pass out.

For relief for all, there were stage shows of outstanding quality at the Nest, which was not surprising considering that Petty Officer (later Sub-Lieutenant) Eric Barker, supported by his wife, produced and starred in them. And there was also Trevor Little and the Blue Mariners dance band, which included in its players a number of ex-members of famous dance bands, and gave regular BBC broadcasts. They gave the same show on several nights so that all would have a chance to see it. There was Russ Conway, who also occasionally entertained on the piano of The First And Last pub, and there were concert parties and Ensa shows. Tickets for these entertainments were limited, and at the Oval they had their own way of making 'fair distribution' of them.

'Married men with more than five children—prove it. Right, here's your tickets. Single men with more than five children? You don't get 'em for being careless! Single men who should have had more than five children but haven't? Right, you get 'em for putting the latch to safe in the proper manner! Men who've been to jail—

prove it! Right, you've done your time—come and take 'em. Men who ought to have been in jail? OK that's being honest. Men with two wives—and I mean real wives—come on, don't be shy, this isn't the Law! But you don't get tickets—you've had enough entertainment already!'

And so on. It was original and it caused a laugh; and more to the point, it wasted a lot of training time and was a buckshee stand-easy.

Novel local 'entertainment,' especially for the Wrens on staff at the Nest, was provided by a boatman who delighted in rowing parties along the coast to neighbouring Pakefield, where cliff erosion was causing the whole of a row of cottages to topple one by one into the sea. Falling over the cliff, too, was part of Pakefield Churchyard. The old boatman landed there and went round picking up old bones and skulls expelled from burst coffins and showing them to his horrified passengers. The Wrens themselves were popular for even more than the usual reasons; sailors could only visit the Church Army canteen if escorted by one, which led to the not uncommon sight of a Wren doing her patriotic duty by taking six or more Jacks in tow for a cuppa and a sandwich.

When men had finished their training and passed out they were incorporated in the guard at the Nest until drafted to sea. The guard, when not on watch, slept 'booted and spurred' on the concert hall floor. They spent many weary hours praying for a ship while standing with a bayonet at the gates of the Nest, or at the mail office or the fishnet store. At one time there was a craze for trying to catch the sentries out. This culminated in a certain Chief receiving a bayonet thrust through his forearm while crawling in the bushes, which caused the sport to become less popular. On another occasion, having ordered the sentry to open the gate and receiving no reply, a lieutenant-commander going his rounds called out: 'If you don't open this gate I'm going to throw a grenade over at you.' Back came a sleepy voice: 'If you're going to fuck about like that, I'm going home!'

The guards did have their small triumphs. There was the day Commodore De Pass approached the gate in plain clothes. The petty officer in charge challenged him. 'You know me,' said De Pass, 'I'm the Commodore.' But the petty officer, not to be out-witted, threatened him with his bayonet and said: 'I don't care if you're the King of England, you're not coming in here till you *prove* who you are !' Seven days later, on 'the lawn,' the approving Commodore presented the petty officer with his long serving medal.

Men discovered that a simple way to escape from the general misery of the guard, and the duties of sweeping up leaves and scrubbing floors, was to go to the Regulating Office and say they had been an office worker in civilian life. As the Nest was always chronically short of staff they were quickly snapped up as extra clerks. Within ten minutes of asking, Ordinary Seaman Lund found himself installed as an office boy in the Pay Office under a benevolent old Chief who seemed to have a specially soft spot for bank clerks turned seamen. From there, Lund, still waiting for a ship, was switched to more exacting work in the Divisional Office, which gave a green newcomer an insight into the wiles and dodges and cunning of the 'skates,' as well as the problems of the honest matelot.

Daily a long procession of request-men, defaulters, men who had lost their kit, and prospective CW candidates (ratings recommended for a commission course) passed by the windows of the small hut. The two lieutenant-commanders who ran the office, named Wheeler and Jordan, had a window each and shared the work. They were complete opposites in temperament. Jordan was gruff, brusque, ruddy-complexioned and short-tempered, and could be frightening to the timid request-man; Wheeler was quiet, calm, soft-voiced, judicial, and possessed of a dry humour.

They did not always see eye to eye, these two dispensers of justice. Wheeler's calm would irritate the choleric Jordan and they would dispute freely. But then, the people they had to deal with were often enough to try the patience of a saint.

The perpetual request-man used a carefully planned technique. Having had enough of the oceans and wanting to spend the rest of his naval career in a shore billet, his method was to put in a request from, say, seaman to stoker. All requests had to receive due consideration, and by the time a request had been round the interested departments and been finally rejected, some considerable time had elapsed—and while a man had a request in being he would not be available for draft. After each rejection the request-man would immediately put in a new request, and when all possible variations had been used up and he actually found himself on draft, his masterpiece of strategy would appear in the shape of Loss of Kit. A man could not be sent on draft without his kit, so while the routine inquiries were being made to railway departments and the like, another man would have to take his place in the draft. And so it went on.

There was 'Lord Haw-Haw,' whose accent equalled that of his infamous name-sake. It was said that when he joined the Patrol Service he arrived with a Bentley, a blonde, two spaniels, a check suit of plus-fours and a silver-topped stick. He had become a CW candidate, done his sea-time, gone the way of all flesh to King Alfred, the officers' training college, and there 'dipped.' He entered the hut one morning, very hurt about it all. There had been a mistake. King Alfred were getting in touch with the Commodore, and the Commodore was seeing him about it. The error would soon be put right. In the meantime he simply desired a good billet and a decent job.

Next day he was listed on the drafting board, and appeared at the Divisional Office more hurt than before. It was ridiculous! Monstrous! Impossible! There had been a mistake. It was....

'You will have to take that draft,' said the voice of authority.

Lord Haw-Haw drew himself up with supreme dignity.

'Ai shall not take it. Ai could not pawsibly go back to sea on the lower deck.'

'You realize the consquences of refusing to obey a lawful command?'

'Ai do, sir.'

'Very well, you will be given three hours in which to reconsider your decision.'

At the end of three hours he was unchanged. He refused to go. He was taken up on the stage, a warrant was read, and he spent the next week in the cells. What happened to him after that no one quite knew.

One day a man was brought in who boasted that he had done 362 days of cells or detention since joining the Service. He had no kit, was heavily in debt, and said that if drafted he would simply steal another man's kit.

Lieutenant-Commander Wheeler threw out his arms. 'What can you do with a man like that? You can't send him back to civvy street, but he's no damn good at all in the Navy.' The real bad-hats were a problem to the authorities.

Requests, defaulters, advancements, compassionate drafts, CWs, losses of kit; the queue was unending.

'I'll tell you this,' the Regulating Chief PO would emphatically declare, 'we've forgotten what we're here for—we've forgotten what it's all about!'

Amid the tangle of administration it seemed he was right. The pantomime went on at all levels. Two pay sub-lieutenants joined the Pay Office and were there for at least a year before it was discovered they were not in the Navy at all; they had obtained uniforms and faked draft-chits to join.

For a long time the simple business of drafting men had produced its own muddle. The early stages at the Nest were the worst, both through misunderstanding and deliberate switching by ratings. Men awaiting a train at Lowestoft to join a certain ship would find a friend going to a different ship, and swap with another man in order to accompany him, the result being that the wrong men were on the right ships, with wrong pay and allotments, and their letters wrongly directed. The most serious aspect of this was in the event of casualties occurring; a true relative might know nothing, while someone else would mourn a loved one who months afterwards would walk through the front door on leave. It took time before every ship could make a correct return of her crew and their next-of-kin.

Another aspect was the wait for a draft. Men were given their station cards on joining and had to report every day until ships were found for them. There was no other record of them inside the Nest, so some men found that if they went home for a long weekend leave no one would miss them. The weekends stretched to weeks and even fortnights at a time, till the numbers at the Nest each day were so noticeably diminished that the racket was exposed and a new card system installed. Even then, many were the tales of men getting drafted to the ship or trawler base they preferred by slipping a bribe to one of the drafting clerks. Some cases, undoubtedly, were true. In the quick expansion of the Patrol Service almost anything was bound to happen, and did. Starting with 6,000 men and 600 vessels, the RNPS grew to 66,000 men and 6,000 vessels of one sort and another. Besides trawlers, drifters and whalers, it also took in other craft ranging from fuel carriers, motor launches and seaplane tenders to dinghies on reservoirs, these being employed to row about the reservoirs and break up the smooth surface of the water to reduce its effectiveness as a guide to enemy aircraft.

But the drafting system settled down eventually with Wrens sharing the work. And a firm step was taken to prevent liaison between drafting staff and men awaiting ships. This was the opening in Lowestoft of the Drafting Office Club, membership of which was exclusive to the drafting staff, giving them somewhere to gather for music and dancing without mixing with the rest of the depot. It was highly successful in its purpose, though when moved to new quarters above a store it was very nearly a disaster. The Commodore and his wife attended to open the club on its first night, but so did the enemy. In a fierce air raid on the town it appeared possible that at any moment the entire drafting staff of more than a hundred might be missing, which would have caused chaos in the depot. However, the danger passed, though Lord Haw-Haw, in one of his 'Jairmany calling' broadcasts, gave dire warning that 'We haven't forgotten the sparrows in the Nest at Lowestoft. . . .'

Air raids remained a part of the Nest's daily life as Lowestoft went on to earn the unenviable record of the town to receive the third highest number of alerts. In addition to the normal air raid warning Lowestoft operated a 'crash' signal, 'the cuckoo,' to warn of the straffing planes which continually ran in low to pepper the coast. The town suffered much damage, but in spite of Haw-Haw's threat no bomb fell on the Nest, nor was the old lighthouse adjacent to it, set in its unusual position high on the town's main street, damaged beyond having two of its windows blown out. The wags said that the lighthouse, which signalled the Lowestoft channel, was a good landmark for the German raiders so they probably wanted to keep it intact.

A man awaiting draft expected at worst to be sent up on the Northern Patrol, if not to one of the home trawler bases at Belfast, Scapa, Swansea, Brightlingsea, Plymouth, Milford Haven, Portland or Hvalfiord (Iceland). He rarely expected to be put on foreign draft, and many of those who were, complained bitterly, on the grounds that the Patrol Service didn't go abroad but was responsible only for coastal patrol and minesweeping.

However, abroad they went. Some, like a particular batch at the end of 1941, to Tobruk.

11

From Tobruk to the USA

The first stage of the journey to Tobruk was by train from Lowestoft to Glasgow, a slow, endless crawl most of the way. There were a few desertions en route, especially at Glasgow station, where it was easy to slip away unseen. Then on to the troopship *Cameronia,* with more desertions when the ship was held up for a week, anchored at Tail of the Bank, off Greenock. Some Army, Navy and RAF personnel who went ashore with working parties were not seen again.

This was not surprising, for conditions for the luckless 5,000 aboard the *Cameronia* were appalling. With fresh water available for fifteen minutes night and morning, and twelve wash basins to serve 350 men, the only way many could wash was by using the sea water in the urinals. Food was dished out quite haphazardly, the doler-out himself often not knowing what was in the food containers till they were opened for the meal queues, so that anything might turn up. Every man was issued with a hammock but there was no space to sling them, so they had to try to sleep in them laid flat on the deck. Sleeping out on the upper deck was forbidden, but because of the gross overcrowding below many men were driven to do so.

Smoking on deck was strictly forbidden too, but one Patrol Service man at least found a modicum of comfort. 'I had several Hurricane pipes with me, which showed no glow at all, so I was able to enjoy my smokes, though they caused much mystification and annoyance to the naval police, who could smell the smoke but couldn't find the culprit.'

The *Cameronia's* voyage to Durban took four weeks, and as she reached the heat of the tropics the overcrowding became unbearable; three men committed suicide, there was a near mutiny and a riot below decks had to be quelled by force. The only temporary relief for her miserable passengers was when the *Cameronia,* or the 'Altmark' as they nicknamed her, after the German hellship, put in calls at Freetown and Capetown.

Possibly the only man actually to enjoy the voyage was the soldier barber who cut men's hair at sixpence a time all day and every day, and landed at Durban with a small fortune to carry happily to the bank.

After a few days' respite at Durban all were re-embarked in the *Mauretania* for a further grim voyage up the east coast of Africa to Suez, which took another week. From Suez the naval men went by train through the cold night desert air in old, spartan carriages to Sidi-Bish transit camp, just a tram ride out of Alexandria. Here it was the now usual business of 'Fall in, RN ratings on the left, RNPS on the right.' This was an unfortunate arrangement which never failed to cause friction and animosity among the seamen; it was as if they were fighting two different wars. Separation of the divisions was inevitable for the purposes of pay, records and drafting, but such open segregation, the apparent weeding out from the RN ranks of lesser men, the Harry Tates, only served to magnify the differences between them. It was still remembered at Sidi-Bish how, earlier in the war, the *Ajax* had put in at Suez after the Battle of the River Plate, her captain needing fifty men to make up for those killed and wounded in action. He had picked his replacements from an RNPS contingent in transit, but on discovering they were Patrol Service men had turned them down.

So at Sidi-Bish in February 1942 the Patrol Service men who had come out with the *Cameronia* kicked their heels until sent off to various small ships. The ship chosen for one group of men was the old naval trawler *Moy,* a veteran of World War 1. She was an Oropesa sweeper with a maximum speed of only seven knots, and had been run by the RN in peacetime, and in the opening years of the war, in a variety of jobs including boom defence and store carrying.

Moy steamed off to Tobruk to sweep the harbour approaches. Tobruk had been under siege by German-Italian forces for eight solid months of the previous year, and during this time many Patrol Service manned ships, in addition to minesweeping and patrolling, had also ferried thousands of prisoners and carried stores and armaments. Under constant enemy attacks the ships' own casualty list had grown. Those lost included the whaler *Southern Floe* and trawler *Ouse,* both mined, and four other vessels sunk by enemy bombers: the whalers *Thorbryn* and *Skudd,* the drifter *Aurora II* and trawler *Sindonis.*

Moy arrived at Tobruk to find the whole place, not surprisingly, 'bomb-happy.' She berthed alongside an abandoned merchant ship, the *Urania,* which had been put out of action by the enemy months ago; she had been hit for'ard by bombs, and *Moy's* crew had to go through the hole in her side to get ashore, each time stepping gingerly over an unexploded 500-pound bomb.

The frequent Stuka raids made the crane on the jetty spin round with each explosion like the dummy on a swivel at bayonet practice. Ships were regularly shelled by a German big gun known as 'Bardia Bill,' driving them all to another part of the harbour, whereupon the Stukas came over and strafed them there. When a hospital ship came into harbour one day the Stukas concentrated all their attacks on her. Seething with anger, every ship fired everything she had at the planes. One loader, instead of dropping clips of ammunition into his gun, pushed them in as hard as he could and kept pushing, so that his gun got a terrific rate of fire. Even so the hospital ship was straddled again and again, but escaped a direct hit. One damaged Stuka flew off so near to the cliffs that soldiers jumped cursing out of their slit trenches to throw helmets, boots and shell-cases at it.

There was a Bofors gun on a hillock manned by the Army. In return for rum from *Moy's* crew, they agreed to fire at any Stukas coming for the trawler—a new kind of 'protection racket'. The Stukas came over regularly every day at 2 p.m. and 5 p.m. except Wednesday, which was the British naval men's 'make-and-mend', and presumably the enemy's.

One of *Moy's* crew: 'Food was very short so we pinched what we could from stores left on the jetty. We would take the whaler in below the jetty level and pull the sacks of food down into it. One day we were nearly caught. The guards noticed the sacks disappearing and came to investigate, but we all hid under the jetty and they saw only an unmanned boat. We also acquired some extra guns to augment our meagre armament. Our cook brought aboard a Lewis gun which he said he'd found in a gunpit and which "nobody seemed to want." This made our armament up to five Lewis guns, on one of which was a plate which said "Made in Belgium, 1914." '

But *Moy's* greatest capture was a Breda gun—the Italian equivalent of the Oerlikon. Some of *Moy's* crew 'won' this prize from an Italian outpost in the desert near Tobruk, after the outpost had been abandoned. Having installed the gun they nonchalantly went back and retrieved the ammunition for it.

'If troops on patrol came across Italians in the desert the Italians generally fled, so salvage was easily obtained. By this time the Italian soldiers' morale was very low and the Germans had taken over the war. The Italian prisoners at Tobruk were allowed to work or go about practically unattended, as there was nowhere for them to escape to except the desert.

'The Breda gun was an excellent gun, better than the Oerlikon, having twice the range, and it placed its empties back into the tray instead of all over the deck. We set it up nicely on *Moy's* deck over the galley, the only snag being that every time it was fired, the cook and the cooking got covered in soot.'

Moy spent nearly forty weeks at bomb-happy Tobruk, which had its certain effects. 'One of our crew went to visit a pal on a trawler just arrived from Alex., got filled up with rum and started to walk back to *Moy* on the sea. He said that as Jesus Christ had done it, he didn't see why he couldn't. Naturally he didn't get far.'

Moy finally went off for a refit in Alexandria, and remained there to sweep the approaches to Port Said. At this time Alexandria was expected to fall imminently, and to guard against frogman attack, standing orders instructed all trawlers and other small craft to lay alongside the valuable RN warships at dusk each night to provide some sort of buffer against one-man torpedoes. One night a dirty old trawler dutifully lay up against a destroyer, but the sight of the warship's beautiful new fenders was too much for Harry Tate's men, who could get no sea stores at all. In the quiet of night it was no trouble for the trawler's middle-watch quartermaster to swap over adjacent knots on the rails and exchange the trawler's filthy fenders for the destroyer's magnificent white ones. When the destroyer left at dawn, eyes popped and men stood aghast. A short, sharp signal from her RN commander caused the position to be righted forthwith.

Then there was the case of the trawler with the Crumpled Funnel. Funnel stay-wires were always left slack when the funnel was cold, for when it heated up the wires went tight. A zealous ordinary seaman, seeing the slack wires, decided it was his duty to tighten them, with the result that when the funnel got hot either wires or funnel had to give—and it was the funnel which gave and crumpled.

At Port Said ships flew small barrage balloons during the day to give them added protection against diving Stukas, the balloons having an explosive charge fixed to the wire. Each evening the balloons were taken back to an RAF compound, to be brought aboard again the following morning. The drill was to harness a balloon to an aircraftman, who then made his way with it to the harbour in a series of hops. One man was bringing a balloon back to *Moy* when, as he hopped round the harbour corner, a gust of wind blew him into the water to be towed at high speed across the harbour all the way to Port Fuad on the other side; he had to pay his own ferry fare back to Port Said. It was the first known example of water-skiing.

Also into *Moy's* unwritten log went the episode of the oil drums. She was alongside the jetty and had to take aboard some oil drums from another ship, but some buoys obstructed the passage between the two vessels. A wire was rigged to heave the drums across and over the buoys on to *Moy's* deck, but unfortunately the winchman took up the slack of the wire too suddenly. It went taut and sprung a coil round the door-handle of the captain's lavatory, pulled the door clean off and revealed the captain sitting on his throne to the gaze of a bevy of Maltese Wrens in the office alongside.

That was a trawler's life at Port Said; bombs and shells, madness and monotony, as they went out on sweep carrying an assortment of pets from dogs and cats to ducks, and even trusting doves that made their nests in the mast. And each man with his ready-money kept in a blown-up Durex, so that if the ship went down and he with it, someone at least might benefit.

Among other Harry Tate craft working in the Mediterranean, few were so defiantly debonair as the minesweeping yacht *Calamara*, which was furnished with a grand piano. As she sailed along, the first lieutenant played the piano while the skipper accompanied him on the violin. This skipper was very single-minded about his fresh cup of cocoa, which he would refuse unless it had the requisite circle of bubbles spinning round in the middle. His steward grew so tired of having to carry the rejected cup back to the galley that thereafter, just before delivering the cocoa, he would spit lightly into it to achieve the desired effect.

In pure comedy vein was the performance aboard a whaler bringing a very high-ranking, self-important Italian officer prisoner-of-war from Tobruk. He was confined to the captain's day cabin for most of the day, but allowed exercise under guard. He came aboard the whaler with a mass of trunks and other luggage which astonished both officers and crew. The voyage to Alexandria took longer than usual, owing to the whaler being detached for a time to hunt a U-boat. One day the Italian demanded to see the captain, protesting volubly and quoting the Geneva Convention, complaining that he had been robbed of all his decorations and orders. He got little change from the captain and was finally put ashore at Alexandria, in charge of the Redcaps, still protesting loudly as he flounced down the gangway. Three weeks later, with the watch on deck scrubbing down at 5 a.m., a petty officer was roused by gales of laughter. 'Dashing up to see what was going on, and to stop it before it woke the captain, I found our tiniest AB and biggest comedian scrubbing down decks with his overalls turned up to his knees, bare-footed, but with a full dress plumed cocked hat sideways on his head, a marvellous blue silk sash carrying a dagger across his chest, and half a dozen orders and decorations pinned to his overalls. I don't think I ever laughed so much in my life.'

The trawler *Cumbrae* also acquired a singular passenger. She was escorting a convoy from Cyprus to Port Said when, near midnight, the Commodore ship signalled that she had heard 'voices in the water.' *Cumbrae* was leading escort at the time, but she reversed course and eventually traced the 'voices.' It turned out there was only one voice, that of the captain survivor of a sunken Greek coaster. Seaman John Paterson:

'As well as having a Kisbee lifebelt round himself he had lashed himself to a lot of wooden deck-housing. We got him alongside, hacked him clear of the deck-housing and heaved him aboard. He told us in broken English that an enemy submarine had surfaced and shelled his ship until she sank and he was the only survivor. This would have been his third night in the water, and "No save tonight, tomorrow we fineesh!" He had lost the use of his legs so we carried him for'ard and took him down to the messdeck. While we were easing him down the ladder his arm hit the rail and he called out, very upset, "Mind arm—smash watch!" A chance in a million of being picked up, and that was his chief worry! He had some banknotes packed in his oilskins, and the first lieutenant told me to take them into the galley and dry them out. I spread the money round the galley, it came to fifty Egyptian pound notes. The first lieutenant came and asked me how much there was and I told him, "Fifty pounds, sir." "That's right," he said, "the captain told me." I thought, that captain is a very long way from being "fineesh!" '

When the Fleet evacuated Alexandria and most ships went to Haifa, *Cumbrae* and a sister ship, *Islay*, went on patrol out of Haifa nightly, returning at daybreak. But one day at noon they received the unusual order to sail immediately. *Cumbrae* had trouble at her buoy, so *Islay* was through the boom before her. It seemed she was hardly through before she was dropping depth-charges, and in no time at all she had brought up an Italian submarine, close enough to encourage the shore batteries to join in the fight. When *Cumbrae* caught up *Islay* was doing nicely. Two destroyers came and finished off the badly damaged Italian, but it was *Islay's* 'kill'; she had used up all her depth-charges in the battle. Three days later the Palestine police brought in three bodies from the sunken submarine, which had been carrying one-man submarines on its deck.

Another trawler to put paid to an Italian submarine was the *Lord Nuffield*. This was off Algiers, shortly after the Allied landings in North Africa. *Lord Nuffield* made an underwater contact and was preparing to lay a pattern of depth-charges when the submarine, the *Emo*, came up to periscope depth almost underneath her. *Emo* crash-dived but took a hammering from *Lord Nuffield's* depth-charges as it did so. The trawler ran in for a second attack, lost contact but dropped a single depth-charge, and the submarine panicked and came to the surface again. Unable to start his diesels and pull fast away from the trawler, the Italian commander ordered his men to the guns, but *Lord Nuffield*, captained by Lieutenant D. S. Mair, RN, was far too quick for him. Her four-inch, Oerlikon and machine-guns raked the submarine and smashed the conning-tower, effectively stopping all enemy resistance, and with most of his crew already in the water *Emo's* commander gave orders to scuttle and abandon ship. Eleven Italians died in the battle, the remainder being rescued and taken to Algiers.

Over at Malta in the meantime, the trawler *Beryl* had become the Navy's lone bulwark in the long and bitter siege of the island. *Beryl* was an old hand at work in the Mediterranean. She had been bought by the Admiralty in the mid-1930s and sent out on the Abyssinian Patrol. The outbreak of war found her at Malta under the command of a warrant officer of the Royal Navy, Boatswain Victor Rhind. As the island came under siege both of *Beryl's* sister ships, *Jade* and *Coral*, were wrecked early in 1942 by the enemy bombers which raked the island, but *Beryl* went on to weather the siege and win the same sort of reputation and undying admiration of the islanders as the three aircraft which were all the local defence available at one time. The islanders called her 'the flagship of Malta,' for she flew the flag of the Flag Officer, Malta, when there was no other naval ship afloat.

Beryl's first big exploit involved a merchant ship which she found bombed and on fire. Despite continued attacks by enemy planes, *Beryl* rescued the crew and stood by, trying to put out the flames, but the blaze had taken too big a hold. Nevertheless she fought the fire until it was too dangerous to stay near.

She next took part with minesweepers in bringing the heavily damaged and blazing tanker *Ohio* into harbour. Though attacked by aircraft for four days, the crippled *Ohio,* making hardly any speed and looking all the time as though she would crack in half, was finally brought into harbour. The *Ohio,* after her epic run, was a total loss.

One of *Beryl's* trickiest jobs at the height of the siege was as mark-ship for a minelaying cruiser which used to dash for Malta to run in supplies; the trawler would wait for the cruiser at a buoy to lead her in. One night while *Beryl* waited, five E-boats spurted out of the dark to attack her. Cannon shells splintered her bridge and wheelhouse, but she evaded all the enemy torpedoes and came back strongly with her limited armament—her strongest gun was a three-inch for'ard. She sank one of the enemy boats and damaged at least one other, and the rest turned tail. Because of this enemy activity Boatswain Rhind decided to lead the cruiser into harbour by the inshore route, even though there was a danger of mines. It was remarkable foresight and good luck on his part, for in the morning they found that enemy mines had been strewn down the other, 'swept' channel and the cruiser would have been a certain victim. *Beryl* also met and guided in British submarines which sneaked into Malta to land vital supplies of oil and food, patrolling watchfully for U-boats and E-boats while they were discharging.

When an ammunition ship was bombed and set ablaze in the harbour *Beryl* attempted to save her. Braving repeated attacks by enemy planes she went alongside and tried to fight the fire, but the decks of the stricken ship were red-hot and burned through all the hoses that were put aboard her. Finally a lieutenant went aboard her and carried out scuttling work to ensure that she sank without blowing up, an exceedingly dangerous task for which he earned the George Cross.

As the only warship to serve day and night throughout the siege of Malta, *Beryl* had many narrow escapes. Just one instance of her charmed life was when an aircraft carrier was in harbour and the naval authorities foxed the enemy by moving the carrier to a new anchorage. Unluckily for *Beryl* her berth for the night was near that previously occupied by the carrier, and when the enemy swooped over to the attack she found herself the centre of a hailstorm of bombs; but miraculously she escaped with her stern riddled with bomb splinters.

When Malta was relieved *Beryl's* work was still not ended. She laid the buoy which guided the small landing craft to shore on their invasion of Sicily. Later this buoy, at the end of the Malta swept channel, was used for the rendezvous with the Italian Fleet which surrendered and was laid up in St Paul's Bay, Malta; *Beryl* met the ships and led them to the anchorage.

She also helped on experimental work with two-man submarines in a bay at Malta, 'pinging' the bay with her asdic while the miniature subs tried to get in and stick a mine on her. Exercises completed, she would hoist the two-man craft on to her deck and ferry it home to base. Yet another duty found her as a survey ship when the various harbour and approach hazards were plotted by the hydrographical officers of Malta. Towards the quieter days in the Mediterranean she took on convoy work up to Italy.

Though she had many changes of first lieutenant, Boatswain Rhind remained her captain. He was dedicated to his ship and must have spent more hours on the bridge than any other commanding officer in the Navy, for on *Beryl,* with only two officers, it was always, at best, watch-and-watch; and in action, watch-on and stay-on. Rhind, who was awarded the DSO, was a quiet man who seldom mixed much when ashore, although he had friends in the dockyard whom he visited. He was very proud of his position, and of his ship and her record, but he never spoke of his exploits, which accounts for *Beryl* never having received her due, though her log-book showed her to have been in everything, and sometimes as the leading light. She was in commission in the Mediterranean longer than any other ship in the Navy.

Early in 1942 twenty-four anti-submarine trawlers each equipped for the first time with an early type of radar, steamed from Britain across the Atlantic to America, on loan to the U.S. Navy. In charge of Commander Rex English, RN, they went to help the Americans, who, having recently entered the war, were sorely in need of anti-submarine vessels to help them in their struggle against the U-boats now rampaging among shipping off the U.S. east coast. Among the half a dozen Northern trawlers, fine, sturdy sea-boats all, which formed part of the fleet to make the journey was the *Northern Princess,* commanded by Lieutenant Dryden Phillipson, RNR. Like the other commanders, Phillipson did not know his destination until his ship put out to sea from Londonderry and he opened his sealed orders, yet he had been particularly anxious to see his wife before he sailed, which unhappily could not be managed. It was almost as if he had some premonition of his ship's fate.

Among *Northern Princess's* crew was an eighteen-year-old seaman fresh from Sparrow's Nest, young Alec Macleod. Alec, a very likeable lad, had come over from Shanghai to join up, and was expecting his parents to follow him over. He was a member of the raw bunch from Lowestoft, including Ordinary Seaman Paul Lund, who to their dismay had been sent up to Kirkwall to join trawlers of the Northern Patrol. 'Well, never mind,' young Alec had grinned, 'it's only for three months, and then we'll be back in Brighton to get our gold stripes.'

Poor Alec, to be drafted to *Northern Princess,* for he never received the call to do his commission course—never survived the three months.

On March 6 1942 *Northern Princess* was steaming across the Atlantic to St. John's, Newfoundland, in company with her sister trawlers including *Northern Chief, Northern Isles, Northern Dawn* and *St Cathan.* On the Grand Banks, the fishing ground a few hundred miles from Newfoundland, they ran into patches of fog. Next morning at dawn, *Northern Princess* had disappeared. The other trawlers immediately searched the area but not a trace of her could be found; no wreckage, nothing. It was a complete mystery. The sea was oily calm, there had been no explosion, no radio call-up; *Northern Princess* had simply vanished in the night. The only possible explanation was that she had been torpedoed and blown apart or sent to the bottom within seconds, yet no U-boat ever claimed her. So she joined seven other ships of Harry Tate's Navy which had already vanished without trace, their ghosts now ranging over waters from the Barents Sea to the far Atlantic.

All the other twenty-three trawlers made the crossing safely.

They were fitted out American fashion with such sophisticated equipment as air-conditioning, iced water fountains, coding machines and typewriters, and based at New York, Boston and Charleston, South Carolina. From Charleston *Northern Dawn* went twenty miles up the Cape Fear River to Wilmington, North Carolina, where she was given an enthusiastic reception as the first vessel within living memory to visit the place flying the White Ensign.

The Britishers escorted convoys from Boston down the eastern seaboard to Key West in Florida, making calls at New York, Norfolk (Virginia), Wilmington and Charleston. For a long time the only assistance given them by the US Navy was provided by four old American destroyers and some assorted motor patrol boats. There were no blackout restrictions on land and at night the coastal lights silhouetted all the ships to the further advantage of the enemy. In the first mass slaughter by the U-boats many oil tankers were torpedoed and frequently it was impossible for the trawlers to rescue survivors because of the blazing oil on the surface of the water from the dying ships. But the knowhow of the British vessels was invaluable to the hard-pressed US Navy, and one trawler, *Le Tiger*, achieved a triumphant victory in sinking a U-boat. Against this, Harry Tate's men lost five vessels. The *Bedfordshire* was sunk by a U-boat south of Cape Lookout, North Carolina, two months after her arrival; *Kingston Ceylonite* was sunk by a mine off Chesapeake Bay. The others were lost through collisions: *St Cathan* after being hit by a merchant vessel off New York, the *Pentland Firth* also off New York, and the *Senateur Duhamel*, a huge 900-ton French vessel acquired after Dunkirk, plunged to the bottom after a collision off Wilmington.

During their stay in America the trawler men were treated exceptionally well, enjoying all the facilities of the USO with free tickets for Broadway shows, concerts and operas. As an instance of the generosity of some American citizens, while *Cape Warwick* was in Charleston three members of her crew on shore leave were treated to a six-day holiday in Greenville, North Carolina, at the expense of one of the residents, with first-class hotel accommodation and spending money. Even the shops in Greenville refused to accept payment for anything they wanted to buy.

The shades of Harry Tate, however, followed the trawlers even to the U.S. Followed, at least, *Northern Dawn*, when Leading-Coder David Willing, together with the signals officer, Lieutenant R. B.

Belas, RNVR, was summoned to a Court of Enquiry convened aboard a British destroyer in the Charleston Navy Yard, there to answer for a priceless incident that happened aboard *Northern Dawn* just before she left Londonderry. Leading Coder Willing:

'At the time we thought we were going to North Russia, not the States, so there was gloom in the bunkhouse. We had instructions from NOIC Londonderry that certain of our secret signal books were to be handed in at the naval base. These included most of our code books and some special codes used in conjunction with RAF aircraft. Lieutenant Belas and myself were ordered by the captain (Lieutenant J. O. Williams, RNR) to get all the books ready and mustered in his day-cabin. We worked most of one afternoon and evening getting this done.

'The captain was ashore so we had the run of his quarters, putting all the books into the usual heavy canvas bags full of eyeleted holes for quick sinking in an emergency. We decided to leave the bags in the cabin overnight and take them ashore first thing next morning. Belas would go ashore to get transport, and when he reappeared on the quay he would wave—and I, with the help of one or two of the hands, would start lugging the bags ashore.

'The next morning happened to be Friday the 13th, a date we were both to remember. At 7.15 a.m. Lieutenant Belas appeared and waved. I nipped down to the bunkhouse and shook Sparks, Bunts and one or two others to come and give me a hand, but was told fiercely to "get bloody lost." I dashed on deck again to see Belas getting very agitated at the delay, so decided to try to heave the first two bags ashore unaided. Some of the books were quite big, with leaden covers, so the bags were pretty heavy, but I managed to get them down to the main deck then heave them up on to the ship's side. A USN minesweeper lay between us and the quay, and we were linked to her by a hefty plank, on to which I now dragged the bags. Needless to say, on that cold winter's morning there wasn't a quartermaster to be seen.

'Suddenly I lost my balance on the plank and dropped the two bags between *Northern Dawn* and the sweeper. Down they went in a mighty splash, almost taking me with them. When Lieutenant Belas realized what had happened there was great excitement. I was slapped under close arrest in the hands of the coxswain while Belas rushed off ashore to summon the captain. The captain appeared, closely followed by none other than the NOIC himself. Things really began to happen. I was called to the wardroom and in the presence of the coxswain, first lieutenant, sub-lieutenant and captain, I was questioned by the NOIC.

'*Northern Dawn* was then shifted and other ships around us moved, and a diving operation begun. This went on throughout Saturday and Sunday, our crew having to take it in turns on the pump taking air down to the diver—I wasn't at all popular. To the best of my knowledge the bags were never found, and because of their loss new codes and cyphers were brought into force for the whole of the RN and RAF operating in Western Approaches.'

In America, *Northern Dawn* and her sister trawlers remained with the US Navy for several months until the autumn of 1942, when they had to be withdrawn and sent over to South African waters, where a fresh burst of U-boat activity was worrying the South Atlantic convoys. But other Patrol Service men crossed to America at this time to crew the new British Yard Minesweepers, or BYMS, being built over there for the Royal Navy under the Lease-Lend agreement. The BYMS were sturdy wooden ships— the wood to protect them against magnetic mines—with a top speed of about 15 knots, and their main armament a three-inch gun. Many of these little ships steamed thousands of miles to their stations, crossing the Atlantic quite alone. Petty Officer Robert Muir was among a squad sent out to bring the brand new BYMS 51 over to the UK.

'We went by train from Halifax, Nova Scotia, to the U.S., finally landing up in a little holiday resort in New Jersey called Asbury Park, where we were billeted in two lovely hotels. Here we were split into two watches and given various duties. At first I was put in charge of a working party to help clean and alter another big hotel being converted into a White Ensign Club for the boys, and in charge of this place was the famous tennis player Miss Betty Nuttall; of course, she loved us all and gave us a very good time. We also used to go up to New York at weekends.

'I got collared two or three times for the town patrol and had to take four men down to the local police station, where we did an hourly routine patrol then waited in the station in case of trouble in any of the bars. When an alarm came, the cops rushed us to the spot in the "Hurry Up" wagon and we'd go in with pick handles flying and bring out our own boys—they took care of their own men. One noted joint was Fox's Bar, which was guaranteed to produce a couple of calls a night.

'After three months we were sent down to Portsmouth, Virginia, and billeted in the U.S. naval base. The food was marvellous and there was a beautiful canteen in which we spent our evenings, but twice our matelots got fed up with the American "bull" and had a sort-out, smashing the place to pieces. You couldn't really blame them as some of the Americans plainly hated us.

'We were finally sent on to the U.S. Navy camp at Charleston. Here we were treated very well, but in Charleston some of us came up against the racial thing. After having a few drinks, a pal and I got on a bus to return to the docks, and of course the buses were divided into two sections, one for whites and one for coloureds. The white section was full so we went into the black section. Up came the conductress to tell us "You're not allowed to sit here." We said we didn't mind where we sat and that we weren't going to stand, so she immediately stopped the bus and said : "All right, bud, you can walk." And the driver chucked us off two miles from the docks.

'We eventually took over BYMS 51. She was a little motor mine-sweeper about 135 feet long, but nicely accommodated and fitted with every type of sweep. After doing two months' trials out of Charleston we at last received our orders for home. We came right up the east coast to Staten Island, spent a night in New York, then on through Long Island Sound and the Cape Cod Canal, on to Boston and finally to St John's, Newfoundland, where we waited three weeks for good weather. We took a full load of diesel oil and also fifty 50-gallon drums on deck to get our little ship across the Atlantic. As we used the drums we lashed them round the ship's side to act as buoyancy tanks. We made the crossing in six and a half days with a gale of wind up our stern, and berthed at Londonderry. A stop of one day here, then across the Irish Sea, through the Caledonian Canal and down the east coast to Great Yarmouth, where we arrived nearly a year after leaving Britain. We were given ten days' leave and on returning received orders to sail to Milford Haven, take on a full load of oil at Milford and join a convoy to the Azores, which was to be our operational base. We arrived at Milford, and just as we were coming into the fuelling wharf the skipper rang full-astern, but instead of going astern she went full-ahead and hit the quay at 16 knots. She smashed all her bow and was starting to sink alongside the quay, but they managed to tow us into Milford Haven and put us on the slip before she went. And that, after thousands of miles, was that. Back to the Nest we all went.'

The flow of British Yard Minesweepers continued by the hundreds. Chief Petty Officer William Davies, RNR, went out to commission BYMS 2188 at Brooklyn Navy Yard.

'We were at Staten Island, Coney Beach and Iona Island for about five months, during which we experienced the usual epidemic of brawls. In "Pop's Bar" on Staten Island the old 'un who ran the place would climb on the bar and wield a baseball bat at whoever came within range. Once, as we were going along the main "drag," the sounds of catchy music attracted our attention and we all piled into this hall for the local hop. There were some red faces when we were stopped in the foyer by a coloured man who told us: "I'm sure sorry, boys, but you can't go in dere—it's de house of de Lord, and I don't reckon as how you're looking for him right now." Well, Negro spirituals always did sound gay and lively.

'From New York we called at Boston, where we were involved in what became known as "The Battle of the Silver Dollar." That's where it started, over a girl of course, at the Silver Dollar in Scully Square. From there into the street and down the subway the fight raged with US Marines. The police and the USN Patrol rushed along, but an officer yelled: "Let the stupid bastards fight it out down there—we'll clean up later!" Which they did, and a sorry looking lot were bailed out of the "cungee hole" in order to sail BYMS 2188 out of Boston—all under stoppage of leave and pay.

'En route for the UK we were held up by the Royal Canadian Navy at Halifax, Nova Scotia. U-boats had laid a minefield outside the harbour, blocking the entrance to Bedford Basin; the Canadians didn't know how to deal with the situation so our flotilla, the 170th, was attached to the RCN to do the job for them. We cleared eighteen mines. No sooner had we done this than the Germans laid another minefield outside St John's, Newfoundland, so away we had to go and sweep up that little lot. We blew up sixteen mines, and were iced in, but finally returned to Canada.

'Eventually we sailed home via the Azores. On calling in there for three days we were honestly shocked to find a chap bringing his "good lady" down to the jetty wearing only a Burberry, his price for her services being just one woollen sweater, of which we had plenty. None of our crew availed himself of this service. We still had some pride.'

12

'Tally-Ho, Drive on!'

In home waters early in 1942 *Fisher Boy* was helping the old 'Smokey Joes' of the 14th Minesweeping Flotilla, led by the elderly naval minesweeping sloop *Fitzroy*.

Mines laid between the Thames estuary and Great Yarmouth were causing the sweepers a great deal of trouble, their wire cutters were getting caught and not managing to cut through the mooring wires.

To try to overcome this, boffins at HMS *Vernon* invented an explosive wire cutter—a small charge snapped its cutting edges together—and *Fisher Boy's* job was to steam up and down behind the Smokey Joes, retrieve mines that were cut loose and tow them to the beach intact. It was hoped the explosive cutter would also clamp on to the lower part of the mooring wire, so that the wire could be hauled in together with the all-important mine sinker; but unfortunately the charge not only blasted the wire apart, it also blasted the sweep cutter and everything else.

This operation saw the death of the old *Fitzroy*, when she struck a mine just off Yarmouth. *Fisher Boy* hurriedly steamed out to find the sloop rolled over on her side and men struggling to keep afloat in the water. She was successful in saving most of the crew. Signalman Smith :

'One old Stripey we picked up caused us great amusement. He was in his mid-fifties and seemed quite elderly to me, but after we had given him hot rum and a mug of tea he was quite lively. He told us that when *Fitroy* rolled over he got on to the hull, quietly looked round and assessed the situation. He decided *Fitzroy* was going to sink and that the best thing to do was to get the hell away from her. So he dived into the water and swam like fury for half an hour, after which something hit him in the back of the neck.

He looked round and saw it was the keel of *Fitzroy*. He'd been swimming in the wind, and it had brought the capsized ship hard up behind him. But he was a brave old boy and could see the funny side of it.'

In a further effort to recover one of these same troublesome mines, *Fisher Boy* moved to Harwich and picked up a diving crew from HMS *Vernon*.

'The diver was "Pincher" Martin, a little fellow who, in his diving kit, was virtually lost and quite helpless until we lifted him over the side. Working with the yacht *Bystander* we swept with a single wire off Orfordness for a couple of days and finally did come fast with the wire. *Bystander* passed her end to us and we hauled on it till it was taut, then hove-to beside what we hoped was a mine. We had to wait some hours for Pincher to go down and investigate, and this waiting period was heavy with suspense. We'd been given a little fox terrier in London which we had christened Blitz, and during the time we were moored to the mine two of the crew cut up an old sailor's suit and made a smart little rig for the dog; it was one of the odd ways people found to ease their minds in times of tension.

'When slack water came we were able to send Pincher down the wire. Divers had to wait for slack water because the tide in the North Sea ripped along fairly smartly, stirring up the sandy bottom, and according to Pincher it was like a thick fog down there at any other state of the tide than slack water. He got down and we passed a wire down to him which he secured to the mine sinker. We hauled this up, released the mine from the sinker and towed it behind us, rejoicing, to Harwich. Here all this gear was put ashore and specially dealt with, then sent down to *Vernon* for them to devise ways and means of sweeping it. We got our usual reward for a dangerous piece of work : five days' boiler-clean leave—whether or not the boiler needed cleaning.'

Shortly afterwards the minesweepers operating from Grimsby had trouble with a protective device which the enemy began mooring outside their minefields. This was an explosive cutter which blew up the sweeps as the trawlers went in.

'At Grimsby one day Lieutenant Armitage came to *Fisher Boy* and asked me to go up to an office where he'd been allowed some accommodation. One of the sweepers had brought in or towed in a pear-shaped metal canister standing some 3ft. 6in. high. Somehow or other Armitage had got it up into the office and he told me he'd been on the phone to Lieutenant Glenny, RN, down in Portsmouth, and Glenny thought he knew how the thing should be taken apart. We had some tools in the office, so Armitage now took instructions over the phone which he passed on to me while I got busy with a screwdriver and spanner. Just then the RN captain of the base came into the office and asked what we were doing. When he heard, he almost exploded, telling Armitage where to go and how to get there. I suppose it must have been somewhat upsetting for the old boy as his office could quite easily have gone up in smoke.

'After this, Armitage sent me home for a couple of days. On getting out of the train at Peterborough I saw a porter helping Armitage with his luggage. The porter was carrying a wooden box on his shoulder, something like a 3 ft. 6 in. coffin, which contained the works of this small mine, together with a potato sack containing the casing. I doubt very much whether he had any idea what he was lugging across Peterborough station.'

A little later, with her mine recovery officer away at *Vernon*, *Fisher Boy* was quietly lying up in her favourite corner in the Royal Dock, Grimsby, when a damaged fishing trawler was towed into the fish dock.

'She had been skim-bombed by an aircraft coming in low over the water. The bomb had smashed through the hull into the living accommodation aft and the crew had promptly abandoned ship, though the bomb hadn't gone off. Someone had heroically towed the trawler in, and she was moored on her own away from the other ships. The base maintenance commander, faced with the problem of what to do with the trawler and the bomb, sent for an Army bomb disposal lorry. This came and parked alongside the trawler, but the bomb being on the ship it was argued that naval personnel must remove it. The maintenance commander, remembering that the mine recovery vessel *Fisher Boy* was in harbour, decided we were just the people to handle it. We really knew nothing about the technicalities of handling mines and bombs, all this work being done by our officers. However, together with the skipper, about six of us went over to the trawler and found this 500 lb bomb down in the after cabin. Trying to get it up the ladder out of the cabin was quite a task; we were all scared to death and hadn't a clue what to do.

'At last we got it up the ladder and on to the concrete quay, and gingerly carried it to the tailboard of the lorry. As we lowered it on to the tailboard someone pulled his hands away quickly because his fingers were being trapped. The bomb started to fall and we all ran like hell and got down flat. The bomb, fortunately, just lay there, a lump of useless metal on the quay. After a while, the thing not having gone off, we got up, hoisted it back on to the lorry, wedged it so that it couldn't roll about, and wished the Army driver a fond farewell.'

Down at Portland the small and very old Lowestoft trawler *Thrifty* was working with her port sister ship, *Kindred Star*. They had as consorts two French diesels, *Cap Ferrat* and *Pierre Gustave*, together with an ancient wooden tub of a drifter, B.T.B., which had been pulled off the beach inside Lowestoft harbour to go sea-faring again. Commanding *Thrifty* after his long spell with the paddlesweepers was Lieutenant James Reeve.

'Our motley group would sail at dawn from Portland harbour searching the approach channels southwards of the Bill and eastwards to St Alban's Head, for enemy mines. Of the five ships *Pierre Gustave* was always the smartest—and the least used. B.T.B. leaked and was likely to sink from sheer old age, while *Thrifty* and *Kindred Star* had old boilers which, conveniently for us, had to be cleaned every three months if we were to reach our ten knots.

'*Thrifty* and her flotilla each carried at the bow an enormous bracket and bucket containing the noisy automatic hammer designed to trigger off acoustic mines. Astern, to counter the magnetics, we streamed almost a mile of two heavy rubber-covered copper cables which pulsed electricity into the sea. This unwieldy tow wrapped itself round the propeller when I put the ship slow-astern to help the crew manhandle it inboard after my first trip in command. *Kindred Star* towed us home, and there a diver cut us free. Experts found that the cable had been pierced in many places by some reluctant, seasick conscript, who would commit sabotage rather than sail in HMT *Thrifty*.

'Navigating with our cumbersome gear between the Shambles and Portland Bill, where the race at spring tides ran faster than our own speed, caused more anxiety than the hazards of war. Sometimes these anxieties came from an unexpected quarter. In the middle of Weymouth Bay, *Thrifty* and *Kindred Star* were surprised and straddled by a double fall of shot coming from a shore battery doing a practice shoot. Then there was the torpedo, again a blank practice shot, which sped straight for a motor torpedo boat but stopped when it got alongside *Thrifty's* well-worn plates.

'Returning to harbour in line ahead, *Thrifty* could put up quite a bow wave, but sweeping against a head sea made her old engines squeak and splutter. Her venerable engineer, Chief Petty Officer Brown, who knew her from her fishing days, nursed her jealously and well. Anxiously sounding the siren in thick fog, I received via the voice-pipe the message : 'If the Old Man doesn't stop blowing that bloody whistle we shan't have enough steam to get home tonight !'

At Dover, eight former fishing trawlers from Hull, Grimsby and Fleetwood, together with a dozen assorted drifters, comprised the Dover Patrol. In the Channel front line, under constant attack from raiding aircraft and shellfire from the big guns of Calais, theirs was an eventful life of minesweeping, escorting convoys, rescuing ship survivors and ditched airmen, besides undertaking peculiar duties like releasing pigeons in mid-Channel at fixed times; where the birds went to they never discovered.

Easter Sunday 1942 found the men of the Dover Patrol marching through the town on church parade to Dover Priory, whose old pile, though damaged by bombs, was still usable. After the hymns came the sermon. The parson mounted the pulpit and silence reigned except for the cooing of pigeons in the eaves. The parson announced : 'My sermon today is "Who Moved the Stone?" ' At that moment a small stone, no doubt dislodged by the pigeons, fell into the church. In the hush that followed a voice from the back said : " 'Itler !"

It needed a strong sense of humour to survive the daily pressures. One drifter, the *Ut Prosim* was sunk by shellfire even as she moored in Dover harbour. There were other losses, but the saddest of all was that of the trawler *Waterfly*. A short time before she went down under the bombs of German aircraft off Dungeness, Leading Seaman J. P. Rampling went to *Waterfly* as a relief gunner from his own trawler, *Yashima*.

'We in *Yashima*, *Adam*, *Wigan* and the other trawlers had our own routine at sea. Leaving harbour for sweeps or escort duties we would load all guns and keep the gun crews closed up ready for action. Only on "out-sweep" and "in-sweep" did they leave the guns to help, and then there was always someone standing by. These precautions were very necessary as it was Jerry's habit to pay us a sudden visit. Pairs of ME 109s would sweep in low over the water, give us a stick of bombs and zoom off again. They seldom came back for a second go, so it was the sudden first attack that mattered. We were always ready to let go with everything we had; it accounted for our scraping through with minor damage. However, not *Waterfly*.

'She was the smartest looking trawler in the Dover Patrol, commanded by a lieutenant-commander who was a real Navy man. His ship was not as the other Harry Tates, she was always spick and span.

'When I was loaned to her as gunner for one trip, as we left harbour I carried out the routine job of loading the guns and closing up the gun crews. After we had been steaming for about ten minutes the Chief Petty Officer came on to the 12-pounder platform and asked why I had the gun crew closed up. I said it was the usual practice in *Yashima*, but he replied: "In this ship everybody is working party—out-sweep, in-sweep, and then part of ship. Action-stations will be sounded on the enemy being sighted." Well, on that day's sweep nothing happened, but I told some of the crew that I didn't like it, and that if she continued in this fashion some day she was bound to "get the works." It seemed she did—that action-stations was sounded, but Jerry was first.

'We heard that *Waterfly* took a direct hit in the magazine and there was only one survivor, the Bunts, who went insane.'

Up in northern waters the fight was more often with the weather. Sub-Lieutenant Dormer graphically logged *Cape Argona's* experience on Bill Bailey's Bank, between Scotland and Ireland.

'Hove-to at midday, the first of the convoy escort to give up. The next forty hours were memorable. The vicious shriek of the wind, the great ridges of water appearing level with the hounds (the point at which the rigging is attached to the mast), their last ten feet or so as steep as a wall. . . . The lovely green of the crests just as they curl over to break, and the ship climbing, climbing, and the sea piling up, leaping up, like two rugger players jumping for the same ball. Every so often she didn't quite make it and tons of water crashed on board, springing the wooden deck till it leaked like a sieve, carrying away wardroom ventilator and stovepipe, smashing the bridge ladder, buckling the Carley float frame, and throwing a depth-charge clean out of the port thrower, over the galley to the starboard quarter, sending most of the others rolling about the deck, washing away the log and line streamed from the stern, and the collision mat, and a dozen other things. We waded around trying to lash things up. I crawled round the gun platform in my pyjamas to throw away the fused H.E. shells after their rack had gone; the coxswain declared it was too dangerous to send a man, so I left my last dry clothes in the wheelhouse.'

And again in *Hornpipe,* when Dormer was first lieutenant. This naval-built Dance-class trawler left South Shields bound for work-up at Port Edgar.

'Sailed in a terrific gale. My fault . . . . NOIC phoned for the CO who was not available, so I took the call. If we liked, our sailing could be postponed in view of the weather. I had never heard of such a thing . . . we were tough. I said : "Oh, we'll sail—doesn't worry us." Just outside the piers both seaboats started wandering. We had to heave-to and all hands got soaked and were nearly blown overboard while securing them. The ship leaked like a sieve and rolled very badly, often to 40 deg. Everything was flooded out and almost everyone seasick, even the CO. In the afternoon the ship "fell over" on her beam ends. I was on watch. Down in the seamen's mess Johnnie Bentham was thrown against a stanchion and fractured his knee-cap. Simultaneously the paint locker door at the top of the companionway burst open and several hundredweight drums of paint spilt, largely into the seamen's mess, as well as over the deck above.

'Ready-use ammunition lockers, welded on to the superstructure, broke adrift, and great concrete dan-sinkers, weighing two hundred-weight if not five, were wandering about, while the whole ship was swept by a continuous storm of cutting spray as cold and painful as powdered ice. There was indescribable chaos below, two or three inches of paint on the deck and everything in the seamen's mess smothered with it. The place was ankle-deep in water, broken crockery, clothes and furnishings. The watch below were being sick over everything while more water poured through the leaky deck, and because of the violent motion and the paint it was impossible to stand up. Poor Johnnie yelled with pain every time his leg moved. We had quite a job to fix it.'

Fog, too, was a great menace. It resulted in another Dance-class trawler, *Sword Dance,* coming to a miserable end off the north-east coast of Scotland. In her life of less than two years *Sword Dance,* employed almost entirely on escort work with coastal convoys, had taken a severe shaking from a bombing Heinkel and been caught up in air raids on Hull, when she lost two ratings. In the early morning of July 5 1942, while senior escort of an eastbound convoy, she was rammed in dense fog by one of the merchant ships. She was holed in the starboard coalbunker and the boiler and engine rooms immediately flooded, taking her down in less than an hour. Another escort rescued her company.

Over at Belfast the trawler *Friesland* led a dull but reasonably safe existence sweeping off Northern Ireland. Until she became a plague ship. One of the crew contracted typhoid, at which she was quarantined in a far corner of the dock. Seaman Robert Thomas:

'We were all innoculated, the ship scrubbed down with disinfectant and a watch kept to see that no one came near us. The skipper blamed the cook, which was unfair, though allegedly he had on one occasion been mistaken for a stoker coming off watch. The crew knew the source of the trouble, however. It was the rats. They were everywhere, infesting the galley and messdeck and nesting in the provision store. The bins containing rice and lentils were obviously contaminated by them, and lentil soup and rice pudding disappeared from my menu. A loaf of bread left on the messdeck table was torn to pieces by the brutes. One night coming off watch I saw two running up and down a man's bedclothes. We tried trapping them, and inside a quarter of an hour there were half a dozen in the cage. A heaving line was attached to it and it was lowered into the sea. Half an hour later the cage was hauled up with one rat still running round. Much as I loathed them I felt there must be a better way of despatching them than this. Finally, fumigation was tried, the crew being turned adrift for twenty-four hours while the operation was on. This seemed to be successful. But the rats had the last laugh, for when the cold weather came and we dug out our overcoats, there wasn't a button to be found on them.'

The *Friesland* captain's suspicions of his cook were probably not entirely without foundation, for a legion of stories grew up around the trawler cooks, perpetually harassed men as they all were. Cooks were notorious and cooks were fiercely individual.

There was the excellent one aboard a motor minesweeper who put on a lunch for the Paymaster Commander at Harwich in order to qualify as leading cook. He was helped by a friendly petty officer who washed up his pots, and fortified by the coxswain's rum bottle. The lunch was perfect, the sweet out of this world; then came the cheese and biscuits and coffee. By now the cook was dangerously well fortified. He pushed up the wardroom hatch and passed the cheese and biscuits to the steward, commenting boldly: 'I dinna make these, and if he doesn't like 'em, he can stick 'em up his fat arse. Never wanted to be a bloody leading cook anyway. . . .'

But of all the ratings aboard the Patrol Service ships the 'asdics' were perhaps the most remarkable. It was generally agreed that they were without exception quite mad. This because of the hours spent with a continuous 'ping' in the ears while on watch, and the special training that they all had to undertake for the job. A prime case was Andy, of the naval trawler *Fir*. For justice Leading-Cook F. J. Scadeng tells Andy's story.

'He was from the North and never went ashore without coming into contact with the police. He was once removed by his ship-mates from the middle of a fountain, from whence he was determined to annexe a statue nearly as big as himself. On another occasion he had to appear in court to answer a charge of damage to a weighing machine. Found guilty, he was given time to pay the fine. He always forgot it, and at regular intervals would be seen strolling along the deck saying with great dignity: "I've just had a letter from my solicitors. . . ."

'His great day came when, as we were entering Plymouth, he reported "Something, sir!" and gave the estimated direction and distance. Great excitement was felt when he convinced the skipper that it could be a U-boat. In the galley I had no warning of what was about to happen until a terrific explosion, much heavier than any mine I had experienced, shook the ship and lifted her stern well out of the water. The galley clock started to race, the minute hand whizzing around at the rate of knots. The coal shot out of the bunker and joined pots and pans on the galley deck. I found afterwards that they'd failed to calculate the depth for the depth-charge to go off as against the speed of the ship.

'Undaunted, Andy insisted that he could still hear "echoes," so the skipper ordered a turn round and another run. This time they got it right and the depth-charge waited until we were clear before exploding. After three or four runs and some wonderful depth-charge practice somebody spotted oil on the water and we started to congratulate ourselves. Highly pleased, we turned to continue our way back to Plymouth. The skipper stepped down from the bridge to make his way aft, probably to commend the depth-charge crew on a fine piece of work. He was making his way along the port waist when he saw a stoker lolling against the stokehold hatch. The skipper stopped dead in his tracks. "Have you thrown any oily waste over the side lately?" he demanded suspiciously. "Oh, yes, sir," the stoker replied—"I thought we'd better get rid of it before we entered harbour." The skipper did not finish his journey aft and the depth-charge brigade did not receive their commendation. He went sadly but thoughtfully down to his cabin.'

Further sadness for *Fir's* skipper came in Plymouth harbour. 'We had to allow another trawler to move out from an inside berth and go to sea. We got out of her way all right, then made to get back again. The sea wall at this point was built at right angles to another, forming a corner, and there were some steps down to the water. Against the steps was tied an old steam picket boat used to take mail and stores to ships in the stream.

'We had to get back against our wall with the stern about thirty feet from the picket boat. The engine room telegraph worked overtime and we went backwards and forwards in a whirl of water that stirred up more muck than a messdeck "buzz." Eventually the skipper forgot to telegraph full-ahead in time to stop his "way" before we went in and sat on that poor little picket boat. Fortunately the boat's crew had foreseen what might happen and scrambled up the steps in time. It was quite a peaceful end. The little boat just folded up with a long "Weeeeeeee . . ." from its boiler and went down without a splash.'

On the small ships the rum was always 'neaters,' but once on the trawler *Hazelmere* they started to issue grog (two parts water, one part rum). The only way the men had of voicing their protest was to empty the grog into a bucket, which was then taken by the leading seaman to the first lieutenant. 'The grog, sir,' he reported, and emptied it over the side. After a few days of this the astute coxswain sorted things out. He made the men drink their rum neat, then follow it down with two tots of water. And gradually the water was forgotten.

On the bridge of *Hazelmere*, Lieutenant-Commander Nichols had his regular saying for the day. 'Do you like Hitler?' he would ask. 'No, sir,' his crew would reply. 'Good! Tally-ho, drive on!'

At the other end of the scale to the sometimes stiff-upper-lip command of some trawlers was the jolly lot of the motor minesweepers or 'Mickey Mouses,' small ships with a crew of fifteen. Like on one MMS when the skipper and his first lieutenant both got plastered while out sweeping and were beyond bringing their ship back to Parkeston Quay. The leading seaman, a fisherman from Aberdeen, donned the skipper's cap and went on the bridge, while the coxswain, a fisherman first mate from Hull, went on the wheel; and with Bunts making all the correct signals to Shotley Tower they brought the ship into harbour, and no one was any the wiser. But the climax came when the skipper, on sobering up, played merry hell with the leading seaman for getting his cap dirty. You couldn't win with the wardroom!

Unfortunately some officers carried their drinking bouts too far, which resulted in such farcical situations as at Grimsby, when Chief-Skipper Sidney White had to take an officer under arrest for being drunk on duty. 'I was driving him through town when he asked to go to a public lavatory. I agreed and he went down the steps while I and my Wren driver waited outside. After ten minutes I got suspicious and went down to find that he'd ducked out by another entrance. I was in dead trouble for losing him. However, three days later he was brought in. He'd left his false teeth on a ledge in the lavatory, gone back later for them and been caught by waiting police.'

But the most remarkable escapade of all, even including that of the cook who deserted *Foxtrot* and was picked up in Liverpool passing as an admiral's son, concerned the strange disappearance of Sub-Lieutenant 'X' of the trawler *Turquoise*.

In very rough weather, *Turquoise* was bound for her base at Harwich with a southbound convoy. One of two lookouts standing the morning watch on the point-five guns aft was William Davies.

'I called the forenoon watchkeepers at one bell, and as I returned to my post Sub-Lieutenant 'X' came from the bridge and told us to tighten up the gripes on the lifeboat, saying, " I'm just going to check the log." The lifeboat gripes seemed all right so we returned to the guns, were relieved and went below for breakfast. At 0900 hours word was passed round that Sub-Lieutenant 'X' hadn't returned to the bridge, and that his scarf had been found wrapped around the log. A thorough search of the ship was made, even to the chain-locker, while the officers checked their quarters, but there was no sign of him. We got permission from the convoy escort leader, the destroyer *Richmond,* to leave convoy and search the sea. In such rough weather this was difficult and proved fruitless, so we entered harbour with our flag at half-mast, Sub-Lieutenant 'X' being presumed lost at sea.

'It was a great puzzle to us all how he had gone overboard, though of course such things could happen. He was a pleasant enough young officer, well liked by the lower deck; he suffered from seasickness but so did thousands more. He was the grandson of the founder of a well-known shipping line, so his family were among the gentry and he himself was the perfect gentleman. His mother came down to the ship and collected his things, spending a little time with the captain, and we all felt sad at her distress.'

Sub-Lieutenant 'X' was officially reported missing, his name appearing under 'Fallen Officers' in *The Times*, which also published, by a correspondent, a full and wistful appreciation of the young man, whose mind, the writer said, 'was always alive with some fresh enterprise.' A memorial service was held at St Paul's, London, with many VIPs attending, besides another held at his parish church.

A month afterwards *Turquoise*, returning from convoy duty, was putting into Parkeston Quay when her crew saw an astonishing sight.

'There on the jetty under close arrest was our Sub-Lieutenant "X." He was court-martialled on the base ship, and I believe as he left the quay and stepped on to the station he was taken by MPs as being eligible for military service. The grapevine said that he had somehow retained his OD's paybook and drafted himself into Devonport Barracks, where he was awaiting draft. How was he discovered? How did he hide? How did he get ashore past the quartermaster? Was he helped by someone? And the biggest question of all—why did he do it and cause so much distress? We never knew. Authority, his family and the newspapers were all silent.'

Turquoise's finer claim to fame came when she sank an E-boat during a big sea-air attack on a convoy off Sheringham, in E-boat Alley. Seaman Davies:

'Each of our convoy trips had its moments of excitement with the usual attacks by aircraft, but this one was really special. Our charge numbered 72 ships, including tankers, the largest convoy to date. It had been a balmy sunny day and the second dog-watch came round with one of those glorious sunsets travel agents speak of, on a calm, oily sea. It all seemed rather unreal, until shortly after my arrival on duty at the twin point-five aft the alarm went, and over on the far side of the convoy the firework display of tracers etched their wonderful pattern in the evening dusk. The time was 6.10 p.m. It wasn't long before we were engaging enemy aircraft, Heinkel 113s, and the sky now seemed full of these roaring, bat-like messengers of death. Our entire ship was shrouded in gun-smoke and the pungent smell of burnt cordite hung in the still air. One lost all sense of time and between the frantic bursts of firing, of near misses, it seemed that an unearthly, ghost-like silence descended over the area of the sea with *Turquoise* appearing motionless. The moon was now shining and suddenly the four-inch crew shouted "E-boat—Green 10, sir!"

'At this time the angle was too acute for us to see the German, but our forward guns were letting fly. In the starboard wing, manning the Lewis gun, was the steward, a Cockney veteran of World War 1. He was a four-foot-nothing man and had a beer crate to stand on, and we could see him up on his crate blazing away. Now the E-boat was in sight at 80 yards, the whine of bullets was loud in the air and the thud of them finding a home in the padding round the bridge sounded clear above the turmoil. Our little steward raked the German gunners at their guns and, doll-like, they fell over and firing ceased from her. She was now running broadside on to us and our guns methodically raked her, then as she sheered away from us one had the impression that she was finished. But before we had time to collect scattered thoughts a cool voice ordered "Shift target—aircraft bearing Green 90, angle of sight 20 degrees."

'The rest of the night wore on—"Load, open fire, shift target"— until the sun came up over the horizon, bathing the sea with its shimmering yellow light. "Stand down—tea up!" Blessed relief. Now was the time to feel scared. Later the *Richmond* came over and congratulated us on defeating the E-boat, which had sunk some hours after the action. Some of the Germans had been rescued.

'On our return to Harwich we were given twenty-four hours excused duty and a bottle of beer each. Later our CO (Lieutenant C. M. Newns, RNVR) received the DSC, and there were four Mentions in Despatches. One of these was for the steward, who had been more instrumental than anyone in saving casualties among our ship's company. My wife sent me a telegram : " Heard news on wireless—write—worried." The news item she had heard stated that a large-scale air and sea attack on a big East Coast convoy had been repulsed with the loss of only seven ships . . . HMT *Turquoise* pursued and sank an E-boat. "Pursued" be damned with a 7-knot trawler!"

The E-boats had a lean time of it during 1942 as the Patrol Service ships found their measure; only three trawlers went down to their torpedoes. The U-boats were stiffer opponents, destroying twelve trawlers for certain and possibly more among other ships lost by 'cause unknown.' Less than a dozen of the minesweeping trawlers, now more adequately equipped, were sunk by mines, but more than twice that number were overwhelmed by the attacks of enemy bombers. The year's total of more than seventy vessels lost was considerably lower than the previous year, but it still raised the losses of the Patrol Service since war began to well over three hundred vessels.

The last entry on the casualty list for 1942 was dated December 5th. It was a curious one recording the loss of three trawlers at once 'by accidental explosion and fire' at Lagos. Brief accounts of the incredible disaster filtered their way through Harry Tate's Navy, but the full story was never told. Now it can be.

Early on the morning of that fateful December day the trawler *Kelt* tied up to the Nigerian Marine wharf at Apapa after bringing in the motor tanker *Athelvictor,* which she had escorted four hundred miles from Takoradi, in the Gold Coast (Ghana). The *Athelvictor* berthed port side to the jetty at the Shell Company's wharf upstream to discharge her cargo of high octane petrol. Aft of her lay three trawlers in port for refitting, with native workmen busy on each of them. The vessels were the *Canna,* a naval trawler only two years old, and two requisitioned fishers, the *Bengali* and the *Spaniard. Kelt* lay astern of these three. A handful of her crew had gone ashore on store duties and her captain had also left the ship, leaving her chief officer, 23-year-old Sub-Lieutenant Jim Fowler, in charge.

'During the forenoon a report came round that the tanker had accidentally discharged about 20,000 gallons of petrol into the harbour, and we doused our galley fire and told everybody to stop smoking. We were well aware that there was petrol on the water as the fumes made our eyes sting.

'There were four of us down in the wardroom, myself, two other officers and the steward. We were having coffee. Suddenly there was a rumble as if an oil drum was being rolled down the deck above us, followed by shouting and the noise of running feet. Next thing we knew there were flames coming down into the wardroom. It was immediately clear what was happening—that somehow the petrol had caught alight. In seconds we decided we had better get ashore quickly because of the danger of the ammunition exploding if the ship got properly ablaze.

'It was at the bottom of low tide and the petrol was surrounding the four trawlers. *Kelt,* as did the others, lay with her gunwhale below the level of the hollow quay, and the fierce flames were acting like a giant blowtorch, blowing straight across the ship. The heat was tremendous. Our only gangway and means of escape, having so recently arrived, was a wide plank going up rather steeply from the foredeck on to the quay.

'The other two officers and the steward took it in turns to go up the companionway from the wardroom and out on to the burning deck. Two got ashore but none survived. As they were disappearing into the flames I had a little extra time to think things out and decided it would be wiser to get thoroughly wrapped up in anything I could find. I realized I wouldn't be able to have my eyes open in the flames, so I kept a visual picture in my mind of where the gangway plank would be, and went out on deck quite slowly. The heat was intense, but I found the front end of the plank with my foot, lined myself up by running my foot over the width of it, and then ran up the plank, luckily without falling off. When about twenty yards from the edge of the quay I stopped—it was as close to the ships as one could bear in the fierce heat. Several men, all badly burned, came by me and I shouted to them to run on to the main entrance gate of the dockyard, 400 yards away. My own injuries were slight, just burns along the side of my face and on one hand, and I was standing there waiting to see if anyone else was coming off when the three trawlers ahead of *Kelt* went up into the air. There wasn't a sound, they went up absolutely silently, bits and pieces shooting up into the air in front of me. I think I probably then did the silliest thing of the lot, which was to lie down, because by the time I was flat on the quay everything had gone up and was coming down; stretched out flat I was a bigger target than if I had remained standing. A lot of things bounced around for quite a considerable time, and then, when it was all over, I stood up again, turned round to go to the entrance and see what was happening, and found that the whole of the very big sheds behind me had gone. I still had no injury, I was not blown over or anything, and the only thing I had lost was my hat. What had happened was that I was at the apex of a great piece of the quay which had been carved out by the explosion and all the blast had gone over my head. I had heard no sound because I was in the dead spot of the explosion.

'There was a tremendous amount of damage to the dockyard, the main building 400 yards away being severely damaged at the entrance, and as for the three trawlers, when I looked back they had vanished completely—they just weren't there. All their depth-charges had blown up, which was astonishing in itself, as depth-charges were never known to explode, only to burn. The explosion had put out the fires on *Kelt* except on the boat deck, but her bow was blown off and the front of the bridge pushed in, while the foredeck had collapsed. Her steam whistle was blowing furiously, an eerie sound in the sudden stillness.'

An RN captain arrived at the main gate and Sub-Lieutenant Fowler told him the three ships had blown up. They went back to *Kelt* and he and Fowler removed the primers from the ship's depth-charges, which were hot. They found one of the native stewards on board who had been blown out of the foc'sle head and was sitting on the remains of the foredeck unhurt. The boy died of fright three days later—he was sure he had died in the explosion and refused to speak to anyone. He was another casualty in a huge death roll.

'About twenty-six of our crew were caught in the fire, and hardly any survived. They had been caught on deck, most of them not even wearing a shirt, and although the majority got to hospital they were so badly burned that despite living in some cases for several days, they eventually died. One or two men never got ashore and their bodies were recovered from the water.'

And so Sub-Lieutenant Fowler had the traumatic experience of being almost the only survivor of the men aboard *Kelt*. A later official account gave the total number of dead in the disaster as sixty-eight, but these figures represented only those people who could be reliably checked.

'The authorities were never really able to take a complete account of the natives who were lost, many of whom jumped into the water. Very few bodies were recovered from the water, so I should think the dead numbered many more. We were told at the time that an estimated 200 people had lost their lives. *Kelt's* losses were the heaviest among the naval men. The casualties among crews on the other three trawlers were small, as the ratings were living ashore and few were on board at the time, the ships having been taken over by large numbers of West African workers.'

The badly damaged *Kelt* herself survived to steam on to the end of the war and be sold back for use in her rightful occupation of trawling. Also at war's end, in a case which dragged itself through the law courts to determine the liability for damage arising out of the disaster, the cause of the *Athelvictor's* lethal leakage of sixty tons of petrol into the harbour was established. Three sea valves used to admit water ballast, and to flush the pipeline when cleaning it, had negligently been left open after use, so allowing the petrol to escape when the tanker discharged her cargo.

13

The Grim Run to Russia

Of all the jobs given to the trawlers the most dreaded was the Russian run, helping to escort Allied supply convoys to North Russia.

There was a special horror about working up there on the icy roof of the world which struck at a man's heart. It was an emotion compounded of the sick fear of those dark, desolate waters, which froze a man as he fell into them; fear of the treacherous weathers; fear of the enemy sea and air raiders; and last but not least, a nagging distrust of the almost unknown Russians themselves.

The Russian run undoubtedly was one of the toughest jobs afloat. The slow moving convoys had to fight, besides the enemy, ice-strewn seas and black fogs, and sub-zero weathers unequalled for their gale-torn ferocity. If anything showed the superb seaworthiness of the converted fishing boats it was the Arctic convoys, when ships cleaving their way through the grim Barents Sea in mid-winter threatened to capsize under the weight of quick-frozen ice, listing at 30 degrees and more with their signal halyards thickened like stove-pipes.

The trawlers' exposed steampipes on deck constantly froze up and had to be thawed out with burning paraffin rags. Their guns, winches, and all exposed deck gear also became sheeted with ice and had to be thawed in the same way, or by blow-lamp, or by having boiling water poured over them. Their bows had not been strengthened to resist the constant heavy blows from the floating ice, and they were still in the black-and-tan garb of the Northern Patrol, while all other escorts wore Arctic camouflage. They lacked effective anti-aircraft armament, and their slow speed was a bar to U-boat chasing. Even in their additional role of rescue ships they were greatly handicapped, having limited accommodation, no doctor nor sick bay attendants, and no spare crew to look after injured survivors.

Yet in spite of it all, the trawlers earned considerable honours in this, one of the strangest theatres of war.

The convoys to Russia sailed from Hvalfiord, near Reykjavik, and steamed north up the west coast of Iceland, turning eastwards into the Barents Sea, travelling as close as possible to the polar ice-field in order to keep the greatest distance between them and the enemy planes which flew out in droves from the North Cape of Norway. The majority of convoys steamed supplies to Murmansk, the only North Russian port which remained ice-free all the year round; other convoys, or sections of them, sailed 400 miles farther on to Archangel, which was clear of ice during the summer.

The famous 'PQ' series of convoys began in late 1941 and carried on all through the black hell of the Arctic winter, when every day was darkness except for a brief period of 'twilight' at noon. Despite increased resistance by the Germans, more than half the battle was fought with the shocking weathers, and by the time PQ 12 sailed, only six merchantmen had been lost through enemy action, though there had been losses among the escorts.

Where possible, four trawlers were employed on a convoy, helping both as anti-submarine vessels and rescue ships. Among the first trawlers to join the Russian run was the *Lord Middleton*. She saw her first enemy action off the North Cape on PQ 14, which sailed at the tail-end of the Arctic winter in April, 1942. *Lord Middleton* was steaming close to the *Empire Howard*, the Commodore ship (leader of the merchantmen), when *Empire Howard* was struck by two torpedoes from a U-boat. Engineman Douglas Finney:

'As I looked across I heard three explosions, saw her shudder, and in three minutes she had gone, taking the Commodore and many others down with her. We managed to pick up fourteen survivors. Among these was a young lad no more than fourteen years old and in a state of shock. He had probably lied about his age to make the voyage. He recovered, but four others died. The night before entering Murmansk we stopped ship in a howling gale to hold a burial service and put them overboard. During the service we heard enemy aircraft overhead, but luckily the storm screened us, and we steamed into Murmansk safely next day.'

In Murmansk *Lord Middleton* was used to ferry some badly frost-bitten British airmen to the cruiser *Edinburgh*, which was to take them back to the U.K. To the *Edinburgh*, too, went the survivors of *Empire Howard*, relieved at the thought of safety in a big ship. The transfer was not made without incident. An enemy plane dived on the *Edinburgh* and let loose its bombs, narrowly missing both the cruiser and *Lord Middleton* as she lay alongside.

'We left in convoy again to return to Iceland, and were six days out when a Russian ship lying 13th in line was suddenly torpedoed by a U-boat. We started to pick up survivors immediately. It was intensely cold, I had never encountered anything like it—our hands were so numb that it took four of us to lift one man out of the water. Hearing shouts from starboard I ran across to see a young Russian girl, probably a stewardess, desperately hanging on to a rope in waters that could stop your heart in a minute. I called to our wireless operator to help me drag her in, but our hands were so numb that try as we would, we couldn't do it quickly enough. I'll never forget how she gave one last cry and lost her hold, and we could do nothing as she slipped away. Just then I realized that shells were exploding around us. Three German destroyers were steaming on the convoy. The *Edinburgh* stopped one of these, but was then hit by torpedoes, and the order came to us to get to hell after the rest of the convoy.'

Edinburgh struggled on in tow but was hit again by a torpedo which almost cut her in half, so all aboard her were taken off and a British destroyer sank her with a final torpedo. The *Empire Howard* men saved by *Lord Middleton* were among those taken off *Edinburgh* by minsweepers; shocked men who, aboard the cruiser, had felt themselves to be safe.

Lord Austin, also making her first Russian run, should have gone through to Murmansk with *Lord Middleton* on PQ 14. But hers was a woeful tale. Through frequent snowstorms she steamed with the convoy steadily north around the snowbound Icelandic coast, fog and icy winds making it difficult for her crew even to keep their eyes open, and frozen snow having to be scraped regularly from the bridge windows. Iceland behind her she forged on, but on the third morning, daylight broke after a night of particularly vile visibility to reveal herself and six large merchantmen alone in a waste of grey sea. The rest of the convoy had vanished.

The convoy's Vice-Commodore was aboard one of the merchantmen and he signalled all ships to turn about and and return to Iceland. So *Lord Austin* took them back, out of stormy seas into a placid fiord in the north of Iceland, at the naval base of Akureyri.

She quickly received a 'rocket' from the NOIC Reykjavik. He demanded: 'Why have you become detached? Sail forthwith and rendezvous convoy at position X.'

Austin's captain, Lieutenant E. Leslie Wathen, RNR, saw that this would entail him taking a more northerly route than the rest of the convoy, in an effort to catch up. Two of the merchant ships conveniently developed 'engine trouble', but the other four sailed out with the trawler, and out into drifting ice, with grey masses of snowstorms bearing down on them across the water and blanketing them in a swirling whiteness.

Two more merchantmen returning from the convoy were sighted, one with a gaping hole in her bows where she had run into ice. The undamaged ship turned round and tagged on to *Austin*, flashing the warning signal 'Bad ice ahead.' Later another straggler passed, homeward bound and so disgruntled that she refused even to answer *Austin's* signals.

It was a filthy night. *Austin* made a violent entry into some ice-floes and in the process her asdic dome was sheered clean off. Rough repairs were made and she pushed on, through intense cold and fog, into a huge field of ice-floes stretching as far as the eye could see. The merchant ships had vanished and she found herself alone in a weird and desolate sea of ice where the only sign of life was the occasional seal scrambling on to an iceblock or bobbing in the water, but she struggled on.

The chief engineer gave the captain high warning not to run the engines in thick ice or they would lose the propeller, so *Austin* took to drifting through the ice-floes, only using her engines in clear patches. Iceblocks banged against the hull day and night, and if a swell had sprung up the trawler would have been crushed like a matchbox, but fortunately the sea remained calm. Lieutenant Wathen was on the bridge for almost every minute of five days, his hair visibly greying under the strain.

At last they reached position X, only to find no trace of the convoy. They steamed on in thin fog in the hopes of finding it, but still no ships were seen, even though a lookout was sent up the crow's nest, a move which added to the tension for it was the first time the nest had been used, and there were fears the ratlines would break. The fog thickened, and suddenly from the hollow depths of it was heard the siren of one of the corvette escorts, giving her pennant numbers. *Lord Austin* urgently replied on her steam whistle, but because of the dense fog the two ships were unable to make firm contact. The sound of the corvette's siren grew weaker, and was lost.

As a consequence of her battering in the ice, and of being so far north, *Austin's* magnetic compass was now nearly 40 degrees out. She was eventually forced to turn in the dangerous ice and make for home, frozen up even in the engine room, having a near miss with the cliffs of Iceland on her return.

Lord Austin was defeated, but not disgraced. The Admiralty had placed the edge of the polar icefield, in which she had spent six frustrating days, a hundred miles farther north than it actually was. When Lieutenant Wathen made his report they were 'most surprised' and said they had based their calculations on information received from the weather men. In fact they were calculations that not only led *Lord Austin* astray, but which resulted in no fewer than sixteen of PQ 14's twenty-four merchantmen, and two of the escort ships, having to turn back because of the ice. With the loss of the *Empire Howard* only seven merchantmen had reached Murmansk.

Such Admiralty errors, and the old, outdated and inadequate charts with which they had to work, were by no means the only sufferances of the trawler commanders on the Russian run. For the remoter outposts of war like the Arctic were unfortunately riddled with gin-soaked recalled naval officers who appeared to care nothing for the trawlers' welfare but only for their own comfort and pleasures. When *Lord Austin* called at Seydisfiord to make reports and carry out various duties, her first lieutenant went ashore to see the senior naval officer and ask for shore leave for the crew. He found a doddering old man, recalled from retirement, pacing up and down his 'quarter-deck'—a space on a wooden jetty marked out by two white lines.

'What the hell do you want?' barked the SNO.

'Permission for shore leave for the crew, sir,' replied *Austin's* number one.

'Certainly not. I'm not letting any more trawler crews ashore here after the way the last lot behaved. They can stay aboard!'

But *Austin's* captain and his lieutenant resorted to playing by the book and put in a request for the crew to go ashore for 'necessary exercise and recreation.' This time the request went through.

A high-ranking officer afloat at Reykjavik was a classic example of the worst type of senior officer to be found in such circumstances —hard drinking, womanising, bullying his inferiors. He gave *Aus*-

tin's first lieutenant a severe reprimand in front of a bevy of Icelandic girls in his cabin, and bullied a rating into confessing to a crime he had not committed. He was constantly under the influence of alcohol, but his watchful first lieutenant kept him out of trouble. At last some of the disgusted trawler officers caught him drunk without the protection of his watchdog, put him under arrest and took him ashore, where he was finally court-martialled. All this and Russia too.

PQ 15, which sailed early in May, saw *Cape Palliser* join the Arctic run, still in her black-and-tan of the Atlantic patrol, which made her stick out like a sore thumb in the white wilderness. During the night hours the convoy was steaming along in hazy half-light when six enemy torpedo-bombers streaked in low and dropped their 'tinfish'. Three planes were shot down, but three merchantmen received fatal direct hits. Young Leading-Seaman Raymond Smith was aboard *Cape Palliser*.

'Horrified, we saw one of the merchant ships go straight up and disappear in a purple flash. All that was left of her afterwards was a mass of floating debris of deck cargo, all else had gone to the bottom.

'Our four-inch was practically useless as the low-flying planes were on us before we knew it, and it was impossible to bring the gun to bear. As I was strongly built my action-station was on the stripped Lewis gun, a contraption which could be fired from the shoulder, like a rifle, instead of from the usual tripod. Only someone with a bit of weight could fire the monstrosity—if you didn't hold on tight you spun round with it.

'I was on the starboard side of the bridge near the wheelhouse when a low-level bomber swept over us from the port beam. Its rear-gunner was 'hosepipe firing' and I could see him as clear as day working the gun in a figure of eight—and not too bad with his gunnery, either. I was told later that his shot fell just short of the starboard waterline—I don't think I'd time to look. I managed to get off somewhere near a pan-full, gradually spinning round and trying to keep the Lewis somewhere near the target; it was a hell of a thing to use. Our point-fives also got close to the target, but the two twin-Hotchkiss, one each side of the bridge, proved useless.

'The survivors we picked up were mostly lascars, but among them was one Nigerian, whom they seemed to resent and wouldn't have in their presence, until after much trouble we told them they were all in the same boat—and lucky to be in it, too!'

At Murmansk all hands set to and painted the black and brown *Cape Palliser* in Arctic camouflage in double quick time. On her return journey she also brought back some of the crew of the luckless cruiser *Edinburgh*.

The next convoy, PQ16, sailed in the round-the-clock daylight of the Arctic summer. With nothing but intermittent fog to hide it from the enemy, it suffered the heavy losses of seven merchantmen; and the trawlers *St Elstan* and *Lady Madeleine* were loaded to the gunwhales with survivors, some of whom later died from their injuries and were buried at sea. It was on this trip that a third trawler, *Northern Spray*, was given the task of towing back to Reykjavik a damaged American merchantman, the *Carlton*, crippled when an enemy bomber shot down by the escorts crashed in the sea and blew up right beside her. *Northern Spray* hitched herself to the 5,000-ton vessel and successfully brought her home, fighting off another plane which attacked them both. A shell from *Spray's* four-inch exploded under the German's tail and sent him packing.

Ironically the *Carlton* was saved only to be torpedoed on the next convoy, the disastrous PQ17. She was the first ship to die when the Admiralty ordered the convoy to 'Scatter' because of a believed threat from the immensely powerful battleship *Tirpitz*. *Lord Middleton, Lord Austin, Northern Gem* and *Ayrshire* were the four escort trawlers and narrowly escaped in that dreadful holocaust which sent twenty-four ships to the bottom.

Again, on PQ18, four trawlers were with the escorts, and prominent among them was the Hull trawler *St Kenan*, and the German-built *Daneman*, a reparation ship. After the bitter lesson of PQ17, this convoy of forty merchant ships had a formidable escort of eighteen destroyers, a cruiser, an aircraft carrier, two anti-aircraft ships and the four trawlers, but still in devastating attacks by the Germans, thirteen vessels were lost. On September 13 two ships were sunk by U-boats, the Russian *Stalingrad* and the American *Oliver Ellsworth*. *St Kenan* rescued the master and three other survivors of the *Oliver Ellsworth* from a raft. Later that same day there was a mass attack on the convoy by ninety torpedo-bombers, which produced the fantastic sight of more than one hundred torpedoes racing for the convoy. Eight ships were hit. *Daneman*, steaming at the rear of the convoy, picked up four survivors from one of the stricken ships, the British *Empire Stevenson*. Seaman-Gunner G. R. Lunn:

'One of these four seamen couldn't swim and we put it down to his threshing madly about in the sea which kept him afloat and warm enough to survive. Another older man was about to be rescued when the planes attacked again and we had to get under way and leave him to drown. I can still see him, cold in the water, trying to reach one of our sailor's hands to get a grip so that he could be pulled aboard to safety, but we were being attacked by a torpedo-bomber and the skipper rang full-ahead. We had to leave him and watch his bald head and red football jersey vanish behind us; as we were the last ship in the convoy he would never be picked up.'

St Kenan rescued 64 survivors during and after the mass torpedo-bomber attack. These included the entire ship's company of the Panamanian ss *Macbeth*, all picked up from boats and rafts, and survivors from the American ss *Oregonian*. Ten of these were grabbed from the sea in a shocking state from their icy exposure and the oil and water they had swallowed. When rejoining the convoy with her mercy load *St Kenan* was attacked by a twin-engined bomber which hurtled in on a shallow dive, but the trawler's pumping Oerlikon forced the German to release his bombs prematurely and harmlessly, and smoke was seen to break from the plane as it made off. *St Kenan*'s crew then set to caring for their passengers, and in the words of her captain, Lieutenant J. Mackay, RNR : 'Though exhausted by prolonged action-stations many gave up their bunks and hammocks to survivors, and the hardships of feeding and sleeping so many men in cramped quarters was cheerfully accepted. The behaviour of the ship's company as a whole was excellent.'

Still the attack on the convoy by planes and U-boats went on. The American *Mary Luchenbach* went up in a flash and a bang— she was said to be carrying H.E. ammunition and gelignite fuses. Gunner Lunn : 'There was a tremendous explosion and debris showered down on us on *Daneman* like hail. Nothing and no one was left when the smoke cleared.'

For four more days convoy PQ18 fought off its attackers, and then the weather took a hand. As the ships neared the River Dvina leading to Archangel they ran into a fierce gale. Several merchant-men ran aground. *St Kenan* was dangerously unstable and had to heave-to. When caught in the trough of the sea she took an exceptionally heavy roll which carried away her lifeboat and badly bent the davits, but she righted herself and rode out the storm. For *Daneman*, however, the luck ran out. Gunner Lunn :

'When the big gale blew up in the Dvina we were entirely without coal and having to chop up all the woodwork to get some steam on. The skipper ordered a rum for everyone, but it was found that the rum jar had already been broken open and many of the crew were quite drunk. We had a terrible night; tossing about like a cork, no fuel for the engines, and just burning anything that would burn to try to keep the engines going, but we still finished up by running aground on a sandbank. Next morning we abandoned ship, but then went back as she lay on her side. And there we were marooned for days. We made rafts and pulled wood from the shore to get a bit of power up so that we could charge the batteries to listen to the six o'clock news; and that's just about all the listening time we did get, for all our day's toil.'

It was hoped the Russians would pull *Daneman* off the sandbank, but they could not be prevailed upon to do so until two weeks later, by which time *Daneman* had completely run out of food. She then limped home to Belfast with a return convoy, for her damaged plates to be repaired.

PQ18 was the last of the 'PQ' convoys, for the code letters were then changed. It was on the first of the new convoys, which pushed on now in the pitch blackness of the Arctic winter, that the veteran *Northern Gem* played a strong mercy role in the fateful last voyage of the destroyer *Achates*.

In December 1942 convoy JW51 sailed for Russia in two sections. The first, sailing in mid-December, successfully reached the Kola Inlet, leading to Murmansk, on Christmas Day. But the second section, JW51B, which sailed on December 22 was destined to have a more eventful passage.

JW51B consisted of fourteen merchant ships escorted by seven destroyers, two corvettes, a minesweeper and the trawlers *Northern Gem* and *Vizalma*. Other cover was to be provided later by the two cruisers returning from Russia after escorting the first section.

The troubles of convoy JW51B began six days out, when a destroyer had a compass failure and lost the convoy. The same night a severe gale overtook the ships and the *Vizalma* and five merchantmen lost contact. Three of these ships found the convoy again next day, but *Vizalma* and two others never returned, making their own way to Russia miraculously unscathed.

The dark morning of New Year's Eve saw the storm abated and the ice-covered ships of the now depleted convoy pressing on under constant snow squalls. Elsewhere in the darkness, unknown to them, the enemy cruiser *Hipper* and pocket battleship *Lutzow*, together with six destroyers, had sailed out from Norway to the attack. Aboard *Northern Gem*, rear escort on the convoy's starboard quarter, they saw the first gun-flashes in the blackness astern as the enemy destroyers moved in; it was 9.30 am. At fast speed the destroyer *Achates* steamed across the convoy laying a protective black smoke screen, but within minutes she was hit, partially flooded and ablaze with several fires. The fires were quickly brought under control and she carried on laying smoke as the escort's senior officer, Captain R. St. V. Sherbrooke, in *Onslow*, took the remainder of his destroyer flotilla to meet the enemy.

From *Northern Gem* they could see the faint outlines of the British destroyers and the repeated gun-flashes as they harried the *Hipper*. But the German cruiser scored several hits on *Onslow*, causing considerable damage and casualties and severely wounding Captain Sherbrooke, blinding him in one eye (for this action he was awarded the VC).

The blizzard came down again, but the one-sided battle went on. The minesweeper *Bramble* was sunk, then it was again the turn of *Achates*. *Hipper's* guns blasted and damaged her severely, a direct hit on the bridge killing her captain. The coxswain and signalman, the only survivors on the bridge, carried on until the ship's second in command, Lieutenant Loftus E. P. Jones, DSC, who had been controlling work against the floodings, returned and took over. He steered the crippled *Achates* on a zig-zag course, still valiantly making smoke to protect the merchantmen. For four hours the battle went on, until the returning British cruisers finally drove off the raiders, sinking one German destroyer.

Achates was now nearing her end. Hit again on the port side, which was like a pepper pot from shrapnel holes, and with more men killed and the boiler room flooded, still she tried to protect the convoy, reducing speed to keep afloat. But her engineers reported that they could not keep speed on her one remaining boiler, so she stopped engines and her wounded signalman flashed to *Northern Gem* to stand by.

But when *Gem* closed the *Achates* it was already too late for many of the destroyer's crew, including some thirty-five badly wounded men gathered in the captain's day-cabin, and cared for by two volunteers who elected to stay to help them when the order was given to abandon ship. Acting-Coxswain Sid Kerslake of *Gem*:

'Suddenly *Achates* rolled over on to her port side. In the darkness we could see the red lights on the lifebelts of the men and the red-tipped cigarettes of some ratings who were even smoking as they clambered over the rail and on to the ship's starboard side, which in a few seconds had become the "deck". Seconds later the ship's bottom started to rise out of the water as the superstructure vanished from view on the side away from us.

'The men began to slide into the water off the ship's bottom, laughing and joking as they did, then to our astonishment someone started singing "Roll Out The Barrel" and soon, even above the noise of the wind and the sea, we heard them all singing as they fought their way over to us. Some men still smoked, or tried to, as they swam in the icy water, others held up wounded shipmates or dragged them along. *Gem* acted as a kind of lee for them in the heavy sea and our skipper (Skipper-Lieutenant H. C. Aisthorpe, RNR), taking over the wheel, kept giving a touch ahead or astern if he spotted anyone in danger of floating past. In spite of this a few men did drift past, but they must have been dead, either from wounds or from the killing cold of the water; our main concern was for those who were now struggling for their lives.'

Achates sank in three minutes, taking all the wounded in the captain's cabin down with her. Coxswain Kerslake:

'We had dropped our rescue nets over the side. We had no boats to lower, our port boat had been washed away in the gales, while as for our starboard boat, none of its running gear would work—we hadn't been able to get to it to clear it of ice, and everything was frozen solid. In the waist of the ship some of us dropped over the side and hung on to the rescue nets with one hand, pulling and pushing the frozen survivors up to where other willing hands could lift them on deck. As we clung on to the nets we would first be lifted right out of the water as the trawler rolled to starboard, then when she came back we would be plunged up to the neck in the freezing sea, but we managed to come up again each time clinging to a man and pushing him up the ship's side to those above.

'Every member of the crew was at *Gem's* side. Those not busy in the waist or on the rescue nets stood throwing out heaving lines to men still struggling in the sea. I left the nets and ran to the port quarter to help throw out these lines and tow in the men who caught hold of them. One very young sailor, scarcely more than a boy, began drifting past the stern. We threw him a line which he caught, but as we pulled at the rope it slid through his frozen hands. Again we threw the line, but as he grasped it he panicked and started to cry "Mother, mother!" It was heartrending. We yelled to him to hold his hand up so that we could get a turn or two of the line round his wrist, but he slid out of sight for ever with the rope still slipping through his fingers and still crying for his mother.

'Our rescue work reached a point where we seemed to have saved all but a number of bodies floating by with no sign of life. At this moment there was a huge underwater explosion as the *Achates'* depth-charges went off, certainly killing anyone still left alive and lifting *Gem* almost out of the water. So great was the blast that we thought at first that we had caught an enemy torpedo on our starboard side; pots were smashed to pieces, cupboards blown open, clocks stopped; but she didn't take any water and luckily escaped damage to the hull, so we turned again to helping our survivors. Except for a few who had got over to us in liferafts they were so frozen they could not stand or help themselves in any way; we had to carry them below, strip them and rub them down as dry as possible to help get their blood circulating again. We had to do this very quickly, and possibly did not spend as much time with each man as we should have done, but there were eighty of them, nearly twice as many as us, and some of us had to carry on with the duties of the ship as well as doing battle with the ice rapidly freezing all over the superstructure and threatening *Gem's* stability. About half an hour after being rubbed down the circulation would come back again to the survivors' shocked and maimed bodies, it was agonizing for them and their screams had to be heard to be believed.

'The wounded sat or lay down as they could, shocked and staring into nothing, or groaning with pain; others were seasick, some vomiting fuel oil, which covered them from head to foot. Being only an escort trawler we were not rigged out for dealing with severe casualties. Our crew gave up their bunks and spare clothing and did all they could, but we had no doctor on board and our medical resources were practically nil.

'One lad I helped to strip kept looking over his shoulder, though due possibly to shock or cold he never said a word. Yet as we pulled his jersey over his head almost the whole of his right shoulder came away with the jersey, and we had to separate the wool from the flesh. All we could do for him was to put antiseptic lotion over the wound and bandage the loose flesh back in place. Fortunately one of our crew, Seaman Edward Mayer, a former bank cashier from Rotherham, was able to give some treatment to the wounded; he had learned quite a bit from his wife, who was a nurse.

'I went the rounds with the rum jar both for the survivors and our own men, for we all badly needed a tot, and in the galley I came upon a lad of about twenty sitting on the cook's seat locker. He was shivering with cold even though the galley stove was glowing red and someone had given him their duffelcoat to wear. I gave him a tot and asked if he was okay, and he said his ear hurt. I examined it and saw that sticking out of the bone behind the ear was a piece of shrapnel an inch long. When the surgeon who eventually got aboard us saw it he could do nothing, but when the shrapnel was removed in hospital at Murmansk it was the length of a cigarette packet; it was remarkable that the lad recovered.

'One very young sub-lieutenant who had swum over to us with the strength of an ox rapidly showed signs of weakening. We couldn't make out what was wrong, for there was no sign of a wound, so we put his quietness and pallor down to shock, and tried to make him comfortable in a bunk on the messdeck. When the surgeon examined him later he, too, could do nothing, the unfortunate man had taken the full blast of a shell explosion in the stomach and was smashed up internally. We gave him everything he asked for, but he died soon afterwards and was buried at sea.

'With the *Gem* crowded with the sick and wounded it was a ghastly night. Everything was blacked out, no lights at all allowed on deck. It was like living, or rather existing, in a howling, raging and totally black hell on some other planet; black, that is, except for the snow blizzards and the ice. Not until late morning did the wind and sea drop slightly, and it was then, despite a heavy swell, we managed to get the surgeon aboard from one of the destroyers. During the brief lull in the weather and the slight greying of the darkness at noon, the destroyer went head-on into the wind and sea at a speed just fast enough to give her steerage way and slow enough for us to come up astern of her and place our starboard well-deck alongside her port quarter. With a heavy sea running this was no mean feat by our skipper. As the two vessels closed, our starboard rail was bent inwards when the destroyer's quarter dropped on to us, and as she lifted up again her depth-charges came up smack under our remaining lifeboat. But the eyes of everyone were fixed on the surgeon, who stood poised, waiting his chance, and when the destroyer reared up again and looked dangerously like coming aboard the *Gem*, which was now in the trough of the sea, he jumped feet first and bag in hand, landing safely by the grace of God on to our heaving, pitching, roller-coaster deck and being caught in the waiting arms of some of our crew. It was a fantastic leap under any conditions.

'As the weather rose again there began the grim business of performing what operations we could on the badly wounded. All the time the surgeon was busy *Gem* was blown by gale force winds and tossed by mountainous seas that swept over the entire ship. Everything was frozen, the rigging swollen to four times its normal size and our lifeboat, boatfalls and boatdeck just solid blocks of ice. It was treacherous to move about the deck anywhere. Below, meantime, no fewer than twelve emergency operations were performed on the messdeck table, one after the other. Each time, so that he wouldn't be flung off by the pitching ship, the patient had to be held down on the table by two or three of the crew or the fittest survivors, anaesthetic being administered by Lieutenant Jones of the *Achates*.

'No words of mine can describe the courage and skill of that surgeon. We all thought he deserved a medal. Whether he received one or not I don't know, but I do know that he lost his life a year later on another Russian convoy. On that occasion he was passed to a merchant ship to look after a sick member of the crew, and in the early hours of the next morning the merchantman was torpedoed. His first thought was to get his patient into a lifeboat, and he only just succeeded in doing this before the ship sank with him still on board. A very gallant man.

'For the rest of *Gem's* voyage through the dark to Murmansk everyone helped each other, sharing sleeping quarters, clothing and cigarettes, and the only moan to be heard was: "When's this bloody wind going to drop!" '

Gem's Skipper-Lieutenant Aisthorpe received the DSC for his trawler's heroic rescue work.

And so the work of the trawlers in the Arctic went on. *Northern Spray*, towing home a second, and bigger crippled ship, the 12,000-ton *Empire Unity*, after she was torpedoed. This mammoth tow was being made at a painfully slow two knots when a U-boat was sighted on the surface. It dived to the attack, but *Spray*, having quickly slipped her tow, steamed hard for the U-boat and rammed it, smashing up her asdic dome as evidence of her bold assault. With the U-boat claimed as a "possible" she re-engaged the tow and pulled her huge charge home.

And on the trawler *Paynter*, there was a poignant rescue involving none other than that terror of the Nest, Ted the Bastard—Chief Petty Officer Edward Pugh. When a merchantman carrying passengers was torpedoed he dived overboard to save women and children struggling in the icy water. Among those he saved was a child who later died without anyone ever knowing her name; he gave her the same name as his own daughter, and stood by her grave as she was buried at Seydisfiord.

He received the DSM. And lost his nickname for good.

14

One of Our Ships is Missing

In the Capetown Officers' Club, the skipper-lieutenant of a trawler took a long, cool look at a monocled RAF squadron-leader, and told him in blunt terms that he only needed a monocle in another part of his anatomy and he'd make a 'bloody fine telescope'.

The Harry Tates had arrived. In December 1942 the trawlers loaned to the U.S. Navy were withdrawn to South African waters, to combat growing U-boat activity there. From the American east coast the trawlers steamed down through the Caribbean Sea to Trinidad, then on to the Brazilian port of Pernambuco, where they coaled up for the passage across the South Atlantic. En route to Pernambuco they engaged in a fruitless reconnaissance off the French penal settlement of Devil's Island, French Guiana, where the presence of U-boats had been suspected. Then across from Pernambuco to Freetown, Sierra Leone, and on down the African west coast.

Some interesting, if uncalled for, advice was given to *Lady Elsa's* first lieutenant by a Belgian pilot taken aboard at Pointe Noire, in the Congo. 'He gave me the "useful" hint that when flogging natives, always string them up in wet canvas, as it left no marks. The advice did not pass unheeded by our asdic operator and signalman, and for some time afterwards my movements were closely watched to see if I intended getting in a little practice on the ship's company.'

And so on to Walvis Bay, German West Africa, down to Capetown and up the east coast to Durban. The trawlers were to remain in South Africa until the war's end, the crews being relieved after a long spell. Joined by a handful of other trawlers to make up for their losses in the U.S. they were employed on asdic patrol and as escorts for convoys from Walvis Bay round the Cape of Good

Hope and up to Durban and Mombasa. It was generally wearisome work, though occasionally highly eventful. Like the adventure of *Cape Warwick*.

Captain of this trawler was Lieutenant W. E. 'Paddy' Goggin, an Irishman of great renown among the Harry Tate commanders. There was the time when *Cape Warwick*, working in Icelandic waters, took in tow a merchantman which had grounded on the coast. After losing most of her cables, *Cape Warwick* managed to get the cargo vessel into Reykjavik. On the way into harbour a tug attempted to take over the tow, only desisting when Paddy Goggin vigorously promised to use his four-inch. Paddy lodged a salvage claim and a year later the princely payout was made by the Admiralty. Paddy, as captain, received £10, his other officers £4 each, and the ratings £1.

A jaunty and a strong-hearted ship was *Cape Warwick*—even if it was aboard her that an officer was about to tuck into his lunch when the steward shot into the wardroom and suggested that he skip the soup, as they had just got to the bottom of the pot and found a black sock resting in the remains.

At 4 p.m. on April 2 1943 *Cape Warwick* and *Northern Dawn* set out from Walvis Bay, a known hot-bed of German spies, as escorts to a small convoy of three ships bound for Capetown. Two of these were cargo vessels, one carrying a large quantity of ammunition. The third ship was the 7,000-ton *City of Baroda*, with more than 300 passengers and crew aboard, including ninety European passengers and a hundred lascar seamen in transit. As darkness came a thick fog descended, and the speed of the convoy was reduced. Coder Jack Clegg, of *Cape Warwick*:

'About 9 p.m. a dull thud was heard from what appeared to be a considerable distance. The ships in convoy were not visible owing to the fog. Shortly afterwards a mysterious SOS was received from a ship whose identity was unknown, and whose position given was on dry land! At the first light of dawn, when it was discovered that *City of Baroda* was not in line with the convoy, *Cape Warwick* was ordered to make a search.'

What happened between the time of the 'dull thud' of the night before and 9 a.m. the following morning was told by survivors when *Cape Warwick* found a lifeboat from the liner.

Without warning a torpedo from a U-boat had struck *City of Baroda* on the starboard side, destroying one of her lifeboats. Almost immediately a second torpedo exploded, again on the starboard side. The captain gave the order to abandon ship and six lifeboats were quickly filled and lowered. A seventh boat upended, throwing the occupants into the sea and five people were drowned, including a mother and child. The attacking U-boat was never seen. All night the survivors kept afloat in the fog and dark, until five hours after beginning her search, *Cape Warwick* came upon the first lifeboat. Within a few hectic hours she had found other boats and picked up a total of 260 people. Among them were score upon score of lascar seamen, together with European crew and passengers, among them three children and a dozen women, including some Quaker nurses on their way to Burma. Gallantly Paddy Goggin handed over his cabin to the womenfolk.

Paddy and his officers, with fresh visions of salvage in mind, wanted to take the stricken *City of Baroda* in tow, as she appeared to be floating fairly well, but orders came for him to abandon the hulk and proceed to Capetown with the survivors. This was a four-day journey which no one aboard was ever likely to forget. Coder Clegg:

'Conditions on board with 300 souls were terrible, and everything that could possibly be jettisoned went over the side. Every inch of deckspace, chartroom, wireless cabin, officers' quarters, was occupied during waking and sleeping hours. The crew gave up their bunks to survivors and slept on deck, but even here people had to sleep sitting up because there was insufficient room to lie down. The lascars were accommodated in an unused fish hold and the for'ard messdeck, and the scenes here were unbelievable.'

The trawler men distributed all the clothing they could rake up among the survivors, but food was a different problem. It was perilously short and the only way they could give everyone a meagre two meals a day was by using up all the concentrated rations kept in the lifeboats for emergency use. For some of *City of Baroda's* crew who had been torpedoed before—one man had been sunk nine times since war began—every discomfort was small; even so, there was hearty relief when the grossly overladen *Cape Warwick* reached Capetown. And a pleasant surprise. Coder Clegg:

'While there were supposed to be security restrictions in force, every ship in the harbour sounded their welcoming hooters as we sailed alongside. Even more remarkable was the sight of trestle tables laid out on the quayside laden with food, and more than 300 chairs. The food had been provided by the WVS of South Africa. All 260 survivors, together with our forty crew members, sat down unshaven, unwashed, and in many cases only partly clothed, to enjoy their first real meal for four days. Before leaving, all the survivors expressed their thanks to us by singing "Auld Lang Syne".'

Captain Paddy Goggin afterwards received a letter of gratitude from the High Commissioner's office in Capetown. It was sent on behalf of the survivors and thanked him for the manner of their rescue and the 'overwhelming kindness and hospitality displayed by his officers and crew'.

Sub-Lieutenant 'Mick' Hargraves: 'A month afterwards we were in Durban and came across a paymaster lieutenant-commander, RNVR, who had been one of the survivors. He was looking a little down in the mouth and quite naturally so, as he told us he had just been landed at Durban after being torpedoed again and losing all his belongings for the second time in a month.'

A final sadness was when the Quaker nurses rescued by *Cape Warwick* joined another ship, only to lose their lives when she also fell victim to a U-boat.

In home waters in 1943 the long struggle against the E-boats continued. In February, after a heavy E-boat attack on a convoy of ten ships off Start Point, Devon, there were jubilant claims by the Germans. A cargo ship hit by a torpedo broke into pieces, a tanker was sent to the bottom, and another freighter was left sinking, the escorts faring just as badly. When a big 900-ton tank landing vessel was hit but did not sink, German sailors boarded her, killed some of the crew with revolvers, took a dozen prisoners and then sank the ship with a torpedo. Another E-boat torpedo sank the minesweeping whaler *Harstad*, leaving only one survivor; another sank the escort trawler *Lord Hailsham* along with eighteen of her crew.

Weeks later another E-boat victim, this time off Lowestoft, was the RDF or radar equipped trawler *Adonis*, based at Ipswich. Among the few survivors who lived to tell her story was young RDF rating T. Roy Sparkes.

'Running out of Ipswich at that time were two flotillas of patrol vessels, each with an RDF-equipped master ship, one of which was *Adonis* and the other the *Norland*. The RDF (early radar) had a range of only six miles, and was a diabolical and misleading thing of false comfort. Both our ships were converted French trawlers, possibly the ugliest and without doubt the roughest boats to put out from Ipswich. Many was the time in heaving *Adonis* that I prayed for death as I stared at the green grass in the miniature cathode, trying to distinguish echoes from ground-base waves, writing my log and vomiting profusely into that vital piece of equipment, the bucket.

'Towards the end of March 1943 we entered Immingham Docks for a refit and leave, and sailed again on the ominous date of Friday, April 13 1943. I had a premonition that something was about to happen, the feeling being so strong that I sewed a pocket into my old Mae West lifejacket, bought from a crewmate for a dollar of beer money, and into it stowed my wallet and a few personal photographs.

'On the night of the 14th, after manoeuvring my way across the pitching deck to take over the middle-watch, I had been settled down in the radar caboose astern for about an hour when I became aware of a movement on the screen. There was a blip or two at about 6,000 or 7,000 yards. With the general conditions and the hand-turned radar "aerial" to contend with, the blip was at about 2,000 yards before I could make any really definite report. At 1.15 a.m. I whistled up the old voice-pipe to the bridge to report my suspicions, but they could see nothing. The range then closed to 1,700 yards. From the bridge I heard the muffled order given to fire starshells, a task for our foc'sle gun crew with their pride of weaponry, an old Japanese 14-pounder.

'Then all hell was let loose. Faintly I heard the gun's report, followed almost immediately by a huge explosion—the whole ship appeared to heave her guts and shudder. Up in my radar caboose, on its four spindly angle-iron legs, I was flung violently forward, crashing my nose into the radar tube. All the lights had gone out and I felt the floor beneath me begin to tilt.

'Not having the full picture of what was going on I sat there calmly awaiting instructions, but none were forthcoming. I whistled up and called the bridge again, but my voice was obviously lost on the night—I was cut off. Even then the full truth didn't strike home. Other than blurping, muffled gun reports I had no feeling of life outside, no sound of a voice. I stood up, grasping the voice-pipe, and tried again to get some information, though inwardly I knew it was hopeless. Turning and slithering on the now frighteningly sloping iron floor, I tried the cleats on the watertight door; one moved, but the rest seemed to be solid and would not budge. I was trapped in an expensively attired steel coffin. For a brief second I visualized the whole thing at the bottom of the sea and myself waiting for the water to slowly seep in, then nothing. I stood there unemotional, coldly resigned.

'There was a further lurch, the whole cabin tilting even more alarmingly towards the bows. At that moment a quiet voice spoke to me, seemingly out of the air. It insisted that I try the door again. With one mighty sweep of the palm of my hand I clouted each cleat in what seemed one movement. Destiny or luck was with me, the sinking movement carried the heavy door the right way and it swung away, the open space now rising above me. The night sky was lit by tracer flares. With an effort I clambered through the door on to the small cat-platform, but a sudden lurch flung me down. I grabbed a rung of the narrow steel ladder which led to the deck and found myself twisting until I was hanging by one hand underneath the slope of the ladder. I remembered stories of men clinging to guardrails and going down with their ships, absolutely terrified to let go, clinging on as if the cold iron was a life-saving straw, and even though I was considered a strong swimmer I just couldn't let go of that ladder and drop clear into the lapping sea which I had glimpsed beneath me.

'Then a rumbling noise arrested my thoughts and anchored my mounting panic; the depth-charges astern were loose and threatening to roll in my direction. I let go and dropped into the icy North Sea, kicking and threshing, catching my legs and shins on floating wood and wreckage as I tried to make clear of the stricken ship. A large wave caused me to all but give up the ghost there and then, for in spite of the lifejacket in which I had lived, eaten and slept, I was almost a gonner. Then I kicked out strongly and began to make headway through the seething black water, while around me I was aware of lads and men shouting, throwing up their arms and sinking from sight, and large timbers suddenly shooting up from out of the depths like huge rockets. One poor lad was impaled on one such murderous length before being carried down and out of sight.

'I continued swimming. I then heard my first coherent conversation out of the chaos, voices crying out for guidance on freeing rafts or cutting a boat adrift from the fast sinking debris, though icy water, rusty cleats, and rope that had not been disturbed for months, resisted all their attempts. I swam on in no particular direction, not caring so long as I cleared the two halves of *Adonis* which I saw standing starkly, bow and stern to the night sky. The rising moon helped to illuminate the ghastly picture. Away to the stern I was aware of small pockets of stabbing lights and tracers as the E-boats, for that is what the echoes had turned out to be, continued to pump death-dealing lead into the fast disappearing trawler.

'I saw a group of heads bobbing about and recognized one voice as that of a leading seaman. I struck out in that direction, but then again that "voice" I had heard in the radar cabin spoke to me clearly : "No, no—this way". As if to confirm it someone shouted : "Over this way—the skipper's here !" I changed direction, swam towards the sound and came upon a well-laden Carley float with the second-in-command, Skipper Cyril White, there among the survivors (our commanding officer, Skipper Draper, had been lost in the first few seconds of the action). But there was no more room on the liferaft and I could do no more than grab a loop of rope and continue to dangle in the freezing water.

'After some time it became obvious that I couldn't hold on to the thin line much longer, so with struggling effort and rocking change of position, everyone sitting straddle fashion, a small space was made on the raft and I was lugged aboard, or rather placed in a position of semi-submerged floating, for with eleven souls aboard the raft was well below the surface, in fact we were up to our waists.

'A biting wind seared across the sea and only by grabbing pieces of scrap wood and attempting to keep up a form of useless paddling did we prompt blood to circulate. The moon had fully risen and by its light we did at one stage glimpse a launch silhouetted against the horizon, but despite our shouting and waving it churned away. Singing half-heartedly to try to keep up morale, and encouraged all the time by Skipper White to keep paddling we drifted for the better part of the night. In the early dawn, just as two or three men were beginning to give way to the effects of exposure, we heard again the throb of engines, and into view loomed the craft we had seen before, now about half a mile away. We shouted and waved, at the same time holding aloft a rather dim Carley light on a lanyard. The boat carried on, and for a moment our hearts sank as we felt that our last chance before our energy and will faded had deserted us; then to the amazement of us all she heeled and turned. This time there was no doubt—she was making for us straight as a homing pigeon.

'As she drew near we managed a feeble cheer. She was an RAF rescue launch and we were soon being dragged aboard. The RAF crew were the Samaritans that night, giving us their last smokes and brandy, even their personal and precious stored caches were brought out of hiding. They said they had been almost to Rotterdam seeking a ditched bomber and failed to locate it, but none the less their journey had been necessary—sentiments we were quick to echo.

'We reached Harwich about 6 a.m., and fixed up with some temporary gear we eventually returned to the base at Ipswich which some of us had given up hope of ever seeing again.

'The loss of *Adonis* was summed up in a communique which my mother heard the next day over the BBC: "One of our ships is missing . . . the Admiralty regret . . ." What was not given was the fact that only eleven of us out of a total crew of 32 had escaped. Some six of those lost were barely eighteen, having joined the Navy about eight weeks before; it was their first trip to sea, and their last.

'Next day, destroyers from the Harwich flotilla took part in a revenge raid on the E-boat pens at Rotterdam, putting the base and craft out of action for many months. Surveying the area of the action, many bodies from *Adonis* were picked up, including the luckless leading seaman and his group of men to which I had originally been swimming.' Such were the victims of the E-boats.

The trawler *Red Gauntlet* was sweeping out of Harwich early one morning when an E-boat attacked her. With her sweeping gear out and so unable to make a quick counter, the fight was short and *Red Gauntlet* went down with heavy casualties. Weeks later the *Franc Tireur*, also sweeping from Harwich, was torpedoed and sunk with half her crew. In this desperate action with the E-boats two trawlers collided, with the result that one of them, the *Donna Nook*, foundered. Yet further losses were the *William Stephen*, torpedoed by an E-boat off Cromer, and the *Avanturine*, sent to the bottom off Beachy Head.

The old minesweeping trawler *General Botha* found herself abruptly removed from these realities of war to take on the surprising role of an enemy ship—unsettling for a veteran trawler which had served through half of World War 1. It was all to do with the documentary film 'For Those In Peril', a story of the Air Sea Rescue units being made by Ealing Studios. *Botha*, based at North Shields, happened to be the first ship of Seaman-Gunner Lionel Gray.

'When I joined her she was already at work in her film role and I was given a German naval suit and hat with the name *Königin Louise* on the hatband; *Botha's* name had been changed to this for the film. It was a bit embarrassing filming out in the North Sea with a damned great swastika flying from the ship. The film took three months to make and we seemed to be the laughing stock of all the other sweepers and drifters as we sailed from the fish quay in North Shields in our German gear and with this big German flag flying. Once at sea we began to film, firing round after round from the old 12-pounder, running and shouting around the deck. It was a worrying moment one day when we heard a plane overhead, but it went off all right, and for our efforts at film acting each member of the crew received a whole pound note.

'It was not until much later, when I was home on leave and went to the pictures with my future wife, that I found out what the film was all about. It appeared that we were a German armed trawler steaming through thick fog to reach a British bomber crew which had ditched in the Channel, while racing out from the British coast was an RAF rescue boat with the same intentions. They sank us in the film, and there we all were on the *Königin Louise*—"Germans" panicking as we went down. It was an especially comical sight to see one of my pals, Jimmy Bentley, doing his acting bit, running around in his German uniform with the seat of his pants out and his shirt-tail blowing.'

Another unusual role, though a real life one, came the way of the small but fast Aberdeen trawler *Star of Freedom*, working as a store carrier from Longhope, in the Orkneys. She was given the job of taking small mines and arms to Lerwick, in the Shetlands, where members of the Norwegian Resistance, in fast motorboats, ran out from Norway at night to pick them up. The mines were the size of a football, with a grass rope for securing to the seabed; the Resistance fighters laid them in the fiords.

Perhaps the most unexpected duty was that which befell *Cape Portland*. She was an escort trawler with good service in northern waters, and her ship's company consisted of Yorkies from Hull and Geordies from the Tyne, together with a few Scots, East Anglians and Cockneys. Her chief engineman, John Brown, had been with the ship fishing in peacetime and continued to nurse her engines with supreme care. Once, when she refitted at Hull, the owners came aboard for a look at their requisitioned vessel. On seeing the spotless condition of the engine room they presented John Brown with a handsome cheque.

In the summer of 1943 *Cape Portland* was at Liverpool. Her number one was Lieutenant Arthur Miles, RNVR.

'There was great speculation when we were first fitted out with de-freezing equipment, as though to cope with iced-up conditions in the Arctic. Then came a full issue of tropical uniforms and kit. After one or two false starts we at last set off, and our sealed orders informed us we were bound for the Azores. Before leaving, Burton's of Liverpool had measured every man aboard for a civvy suit, so we had suspected it would be a neutral country—the "buzz" was Turkey. We officers had trilby hats and the ratings cloth caps, but I never saw any of these worn ashore!

'In fact, the true purpose of our voyage was to hand over the *Cape Portland* to the Portuguese Navy.

'The first few days at the Azores port of Ponta Delgada were alarming. A nucleus of Portuguese officers and ratings came aboard and we were required to circle the islands keeping an asdic watch and burning full navigation lights. My opposite number informed me that he had taken the German hydrophone course at Bremerhaven as well as an asdic course with our people, so he had the best from both sides.

'At last we went ashore, leaving only an anti-submarine officer and six key ratings with the ship. They did well, drawing Portuguese pay as well as their own, I believe. The rest of us had three delightful weeks ashore before passage home.'

Cape Portland was one of several escort trawlers handed over to the Portuguese Navy on lease-lend for patrol duties off the Azores, when the Allies were granted the use of bases for air protection of Atlantic convoys.

At this time, in 1943, the trawlers still on Atlantic convoy work began to take on more the roles of additional escorts and rescue ships, as proper naval escorts became more plentiful. Many trawlers were engaged on 'buttoning' and 'unbuttoning' convoys; that is, leading sections of incoming convoys to ports, or taking out groups of merchantmen to the convoy assembly points. These duties were not without incident, but it was in their mercy work with the actual convoys that the trawlers earned eternal gratitude.

In May 1943 *Northern Spray* was involved in a fantastic battle by a U.S.-bound convoy against wolf-packs of some thirty U-boats. In four days of attacks ten ships of the convoy were sunk, the escorts in reply destroying five U-boats, two by ramming, and claiming a further four 'possibles'. As the incredible battle went on, *Northern Spray* steamed among the chaos and carnage saving exhausted and wounded men from the sea, picking them up from boats and rafts, rescuing them as they clung to wreckage or struggled in the oil and debris-strewn sea. As one British merchantman was sunk, *Northern Spray* got a U-boat contact on her asdic and had to steam through the screaming, cursing survivors in the water to drop depth-charges; afterwards she turned back to rescue the men, many of whom had suffered badly from the explosions. One man was unhinged by his ordeal and had to be put in a strait-jacket; a lascar fireman who had floated up through the ship's vents as she went down clung to a floating wooden box, unable to grasp lifelines, so he was hooked aboard with a boathook. In one day *Northern Spray* packed 145 survivors aboard, the officers and crew giving up their cabins and bunks and sleeping where they could. The American seamen rescued all volunteered to help clean up the ship and assist in the galley, but the lascars sat around on tables and would not move, drawing knives and threatening to use them. *Spray's* commander formed an armed party to round them up and lock them in the chain-locker. The trawler then detached from the convoy with her survivors and steamed on to St John's, Newfoundland. Here, in thick weather, an American destroyer challenged and was ready to fire on *Spray*, until her angry captain ordered a huge battle ensign to be flown at the starboard yardarm and the four-inch to be uncovered and manned, at which forceful display the deflated destroyer signalled 'Sorry, buddies' and offered penitent escort to harbour.

Another battle-weary trawler to enter St John's after a long, hard fight against the U-boats was *Northern Foam*, commanded by Lieutenant 'Bryn' Harris, RNVR. *Foam* had set out across the Atlantic as additional escort and rescue ship to one of two convoys sailing separately from the U.K. Gales slowed the convoys on the first part of their voyage, and on the evening of their fifth day at sea the battle commenced. An escort destroyer, sighting a U-boat well astern, made several attacks on the enemy vessel but had to retire from the fray after a serious explosion aboard. Next morning it was decided to merge the two convoys and so increase the escort power considerably. By nightfall the convoys were almost together when a U-boat closed in again and torpedoed the destroyer *St Croix*, which instantly blew up. Shortly afterwards the corvette *Polyanthus* was torpedoed and sunk. Then fog closed down and shrouded the harassed ships.

In thick fog next day *Northern Foam* sighted a U-boat running awash only 300 yards off her port beam. She turned immediately to ram, but the U-boat just managed to get across her bow. Quickly opening fire with her four-inch, *Foam* hit the U-boat abaft the conning tower, and was manoeuvring to ram again when the U-boat dived, so close that the trawler passed over the 'flurry' of its diving. Getting a firm asdic contact *Foam* next fired a 10-charge pattern of depth-charges. Hardly had the explosions subsided when the U-boat was heard blowing tanks in order to surface, and shortly afterwards was heard and seen surfaced, making off fast to southward. *Foam* valiantly gave chase, but the U-boat was doing at least 15 knots and was soon lost in the fog. Nevertheless, it had been heavily damaged by gunfire and shaken up badly by the depth-charges, which had forced it to the surface.

Hours later the fog lifted and the convoy tried to form up into some semblance of order, but the result of an alteration in course was an unwieldly formation which exposed a long flank to attack. Sighting another U-boat about 1500 yards off her port quarter, *Northern Foam* again turned to ram, firing a starshell as she did so, but by the time the starshell burst, the U-boat was nearly submerged. *Foam* tenaciously went in and attacked with patterns of depth-charges . . . once, twice, until her charges caught the zigzagging U-boat on the point of its course. A very loud and prolonged bubbling noise was then heard coming from undersea, and *Foam* stopped engines and turned ship to listen. The bubbling was heard for some time, gradually growing fainter, until at last it faded. A large patch of oil had welled up to the surface and a sample of this was taken, the strong smell of oil hanging over the dark sea. As the convoy was by then several miles ahead *Foam's* commander decided to leave the scene and regain his station, as the convoy was seriously threatened and he considered the U-boat destroyed.

Foam had only just reached her station when the main enemy attack started and three merchant ships were torpedoed. Immediately the trawler switched to her role of rescue ship, steaming to pick up survivors in the darkness, though she was now totally exposed to the enemy, the heavy depth-charging having put her asdic out of action. First to a raft to rescue the solitary seaman aboard it, then to a large lifeboat carrying 30 survivors of the ss *Fort Jamseg*. This merchantman was still afloat but settling down, and as *Foam* approached, the calls of an injured man still aboard were heard. In the heavy swell running it was too dangerous to go alongside, so *Foam* lowered a boat, and away went Sub-Lieutenant

Morgan to board *Fort Jamseg* and rescue the injured man. Then on to pick up 40 more survivors, mostly Norwegians, from another sunken ship. When *Foam* had finished her part in the mercy work she carried 75 survivors; but the injured man from *Fort Jamseg* died and had to be buried at sea. The rest of that long day consisted of a hard chase to regain the convoy before darkness fell again, and with Chief Engineman Crosland and his men cursing and coaxing the badly shaken engines, she just made it. There followed a night of alarms, the fog closing in again thicker than ever. As *Foam's* commander commented in his official report : 'I look back on the remainder of the voyage as a nightmare. The convoy was very scattered and all the escort vessels in a state of nerves. I think it doubtful whether the U-boats were still around, but many depth-charges were dropped, including three more by us, probably on unsuspecting whales, of which there were many, and which added to our discomfiture. It was with considerable relief that at last the time came for us to leave the convoy, the thick fog following us right up the entrance to St John's harbour.' Lieutenant Harris had then been five and a half days on the bridge of *Northern Foam* and was thankful for some rest.

Unhappily, in their rescue work the Atlantic trawlers frequently had the task of burying at sea numbers of survivors so badly wounded or affected by exposure that they died after rescue. Holding the solemn burial ceremony was one thing, preparing for it was another. Coxswain Sid Kerslake of *Northern Gem* :

'Our asdic operator and myself often found ourselves being the ones who had to stitch up the dead in their canvas shrouds after putting fire-bars at their feet. We used to get a good tot of rum before and afterwards, and it was always badly needed; you never got used to the job and it was worse if it was one of your own crew, as was the case with us on three occasions. Once, when an American we picked up died, we had to use thick sackcloth and found we hadn't a needle strong enough to go through it, so we had to bind the cover round him with twine. I couldn't get it done fast enough, as I had the eerie feeling he would get out of the cracks or vents I'd left in the cloth. This fear was with me for weeks afterwards, and if I had to go on deck during the night, when all was dark, I had the overpowering feeling that he was after me for not giving him a proper shroud.'

The final chapter in the story of the unfortunate Arctic trawler *Daneman,* after her rough grounding in the River Dvina, began at this time when, her repairs at Belfast barely completed, she was ordered to a North Atlantic convoy. Her new commander was Lieutenant Stanley Lock, RNVR.

'The ship was recommissioned and we were ordered off to Tobermory for a "crash" work-up. Several civilian shipyard workers were still on board when the time came for sailing and they had to be turned off whether they'd finished their work or not. After work-up we were appointed to a convoy, and I then realized that our bunker capacity would be insufficient to see us across the Atlantic except under the most ideal conditions and by the shortest route, neither of which was likely. We accordingly had to take tons and tons of coal on deck, to be shovelled down as the bunkers emptied. I was also advised by Captain (D), Belfast, to ask one of the merchantmen to give me a tow if I ran short of fuel!

'When the convoy sailed from Londonderry we were given station astern in view of our rescue duties. All went well until about the third or fourth day out, when the chief engineer reported flooding in the engine room. The pumps were kept going but were unable to prevent the water rising. I reported this to the senior officer escort in destroyer *Keppel*, as we were beginning to lose speed and consequently were unable to maintain station.

'As darkness approached it became obvious that the engines would soon be put out of action. We organized a bucket chain of all hands except those on essential duties. Every bucket and can available was passed along a chain of about forty hands from the depths of the engine room along an iron cat-walk and up a steep iron ladder to the deck, and emptied over the side. It was not very effective, but at least it gave our crew something positive to do.

'We had now dropped miles astern of the convoy and with our last flicker of auxiliary power I reported our plight to *Keppel*. It must have been very difficult for him to decide what to do. The convoy had already lost one escort in ourselves, should he weaken the screen still more by detaching another to stand by us? He would probably have been correct had he decided the safe arrival of the convoy to be of more importance, and left us to our fate. However, he detached not one but two escorts to come to our aid. One was the ocean rescue tug *Bulldog*, and the other a Free French corvette.

'We were now in the middle of the ice zone, at the time of year when the ice breaks away from the polar icecap and drifts southwards either as icebergs or small "growlers" which are very difficult to spot if there is any sea running. I counted no fewer than thirty icebergs on the surrounding horizon. Not that there was any fear of collision; I reckoned we would all drift together at the same speed.

'We were listing heavily to starboard when *Bulldog* arrived. She said she would try to lie alongside our port side and pass one of her enormous six-inch pipes down through our skylights into the engine room and get her powerful pumps to work. It was very difficult keeping our two ships alongside, for although there was not a very big sea running it was enough to cause the ships to separate and crash together intermittently. All the fend-offs we could find were ground to pulp. Still, after the heavy silence that had pervaded our ship for the past ten hours it was good to hear the rhythmic throb of *Bulldog's* pump. We couldn't see where the water was going and the level did not seem to be going down. We soon saw the reason why: after one particularly bad lurch a bight of the pipe was crushed between the ships' sides—and the inside of the pipe was bone dry.

'*Bulldog's* captain and I then held a megaphone conference, and it was decided they would ship one of their donkey engine pumps aboard *Daneman*, with an operator, and then take us in tow. I also suggested he should take half my crew on board, in case the situation got really difficult for us, but he was unwilling to do this.

'The pump they passed to us was a pretty hefty affair about the size of a lorry engine. *Bulldog* rigged up a derrick to get this over to us, but there were some perilous moments as the thing swung around in the air and a few feet above our heads. Meanwhile we were preparing for tow, and soon had the tug's enormous steel wire hawser led through the fairlead on the stem, twice round the base of the gun platform and aft on to some very stout "bits" amidships, all well padded with chunks of timber at any likely chafing points. Having no power for the windlass we could not follow the correct method of attaching our own cable to the towline as a "spring". All this time the corvette had been lying off, giving us a protective screen, though it was doubtful if a U-boat would have thought it worthwhile to waste a perfectly good torpedo on us.

'The wind increased and the sea got rougher. *Daneman* by this time was half full of water and had a list of 40 degrees; it was really like trying to tow a covered swimming bath through a fairly heavy sea. *Bulldog* cracked on the knots and I was concerned that she was going too fast, for *Daneman* was travelling through the water faster than she had ever done under her own steam.

'After some anxious hours the inevitable happened and the tow parted. It was night, there was a heavy sea running, our list had increased to 45 degrees and the level of water was rising more rapidly as a lot of the sea breaking over the ship was finding its way below. Our whaler, carried on deck amidships, had been stove in by the heavy seas. I seriously considered whether it was worthwhile renewing the tow under these conditions, even if it were practical to do so. How long would she stay afloat? Certainly not long enough to make harbour, even under a reasonable tow. I decided we would have to abandon ship as soon as daylight broke.

'We had one Carley float, and the idea was that this would take its full complement of fifteen men and drift down to the corvette, which would take them aboard. The rest of us would have to jump for it on to *Bulldog*, which would do her best to lie alongside our starboard, windward and "low" side—the starboard rail was well under water by this time. Our confidential books and documents were sunk in their weighted bags, the Carley float party was selected and all the ship's company instructed on the drill for abandoning ship.

'At dawn the Carley float was launched and manned with a junior officer in charge. There was a very big sea running. Although the first lieutenant supervised this operation he could not prevent one of the ratings left on board from suddenly scrambling over the side on to the raft, followed by two or three others. Consequently the raft was seriously overloaded and three men were lost from it, slipping away in the freezing water. Of the others, taken aboard the corvette, one subsequently died from cold and exhaustion.

'*Bulldog* did her best to lie alongside us and tried to keep her bridge-deck aligned with our foc'sle and four-inch gun platform, which were roughly on a level when *Bulldog* was on an even keel. But now she was rolling madly in the heavy seas and both the level and the space between the ships were varying all the time. At times there would be 15 to 20 feet between the hulls, then they would crash together. One had to choose the right moment to jump decisively. If you chose the right *second* you could step over the rail on to *Bulldog*. Some men did this, some hesitated a few seconds then jumped and clung on to the rails of *Bulldog's* bridge-deck, where they were clawed inboard by her crew before the ships crashed together again. Two men jumped at the wrong moment and went down between the ships.

'*Bulldog* had meanwhile been preparing a large net on her towing deck aft. This was held out by about ten of her crew, fire-brigade fashion, and the remainder of our crew jumped into this. This also needed correct timing, but it was easier and safer than before. When my turn came the only other man left aboard *Daneman* was *Bulldog's* pump operator, who had been trying to make up his mind to jump ever since the operation started. I mounted the gun platform, got on to the outside of the rail beside him and told him to jump when I gave the word. As the ships rolled together and the net was about 15 feet immediately below us I bellowed " Jump!" and descended fairly comfortably into the net. I looked back—he was still there! However, he did make it a few minutes later.

'*Bulldog* then sped on while the corvette gave *Daneman* the coup de grace with a few rounds of shell from her four-inch. Rather surprisingly *Daneman* caught fire and finally settled in the water belching smoke and flames. So ended this depressing episode.

'The loss of six lives in this way was particularly tragic. Fortunately the convoy was not attacked, but it seemed incongruous that the rescue ship herself had to be rescued, and that the rescue tug had to desert the convoy to do so. An inquiry was held at St John's on our arrival and the finding was that *Daneman* had sustained damage by floating ice which caused flooding and subsequent loss. I wonder. It was my belief that the repair job down below, following her misadventure in the Arctic, was never really completed. In normal circumstances I would have insisted on a proper survey, but in this most critical period of the Atlantic war you just had to get on with the job and hope for the best.'

Tragedy upon tragedy among the trawlers. And yet, as was the way with men in constant danger, it was often the humorous incidents that registered most. *Quadrille*, returning to the trawler base at Liverpool in thick fog on the Mersey; she took on about ten pilots and they were all on the bridge when she touched bottom and lost her asdic dome. *Lady Madeleine*, complimented by King George VI on her smart appearance when he visited her base; he was not to know that she was painted on one side only—one side of the ship, one side of the funnel, one side of the whaler; simply because there wasn't the manpower to get the full job done in time. And on *Northern Gift*, escorting one of the HX convoys from Newfoundland to Belfast, the priceless moment when her captain was caught with his pants down. Lieutenant Fred Bentley:

'We were, of course, always fully clothed all the time on convoy, and on a beautiful day with a calm Atlantic swell I thought it would be a safe time to take a bath. My number one offered to look after the ship, and I fell to temptation. Halfway through my bath the alarm klaxons went, so hastily putting a towel round my middle and my uniform cap on, I belted up the steel ladders to the bridge. On the last ladder the towel came off and I arrived before the startled signalman in my uniform cap and my birthday suit. It was a false alarm as many were, and it was the laugh of the ship that the Old Man had been caught with his trousers down. However, mine was the last laugh, for when we got to Liverpool I had all their trousers down by ordering an F.F.I. (free from infection).'

The weather, as ever, produced its constant punishments, and one of the most bizarre experiences was that of *Cotillion*, when she rode into the dead centre of a storm. She sailed from Londonderry in December 1943, attached to a Gibraltar-bound convoy and commanded by Lieutenant Jim Fowler, survivor of the Lagos disaster the year before.

'We were routed to about 25 West before turning south and the weather was extremely hard. In the first week, steaming through a series of storms, we got exactly 800 miles, which was very slow going. On the morning of the eighth day the wind was gusting to a hundred miles an hour, quite the worst I ever experienced in the Atlantic. The waves were very far apart but completely flattened out, and we could see little because of the flying spray. It was more or less darkness at that time, eleven in the morning, and the convoy had scattered long before.

'We suddenly came out into brilliant sunshine with a very, very confused sea running, a frightening sea. Visibility was about three miles all round and spiralling helplessly were millions of seabirds, all in a very exhausted state; they had been trapped inside the centre of the storm and couldn't get out—they poured on board the ship in their thousands. After ten minutes, however, we were almost from a flat calm straight back into the full force of the wind, hove-to in a completely different direction, having cut across into another sector of the storm. The contrast from no wind to force 12 again was really remarkable and frightening, and it was during the course of this afternoon that we failed to rise to one of the big seas.

'By this time I had been alone on the bridge for a long time, for the simple reason that anyone who had gone below to the wheelhouse had not been able to come up again, so my only communications were with the people in the wheelhouse, round which all the weatherboards were up. I was standing behind the binnacle, as I had to watch the compass fairly carefully. Visibility again was very bad. We were being blown off as much as 90 degrees and putting our stern right under when we went over the crest of the waves, having to bring her round again in the troughs; so we were going as slowly as possible. Then came this giant wave and we went right underneath it.

'I was just able with all my strength to hold on to the compass platform under the weight of water which came over the top of the bridge. For a second or two the whole bridge was completely filled with water, until it began to drain out down the two companionways. We lost both our boats and the boatdecks with them, the windlass shifted for'ard, part of the four-inch gun platform was bent right back, and all the small ventilators and suchlike simply vanished. For a time it felt that the ship was never going to come up again, she was quite dead under my feet. But at length she did come up. . . . From that point onwards the storm seemed to ease off fairly rapidly. I went down to my cabin to find it under two feet of water, but turned in and just slept.'

In the Mediterranean, 1943 saw increased activity by Patrol Service vessels as patrol and supply ships, especially with the Allied landings and the capitulation of Italy in September. But at the start of the year the picture did not look as favourable. In February, when a group of asdic trawlers including *King Sol* left Milford Haven for Gibraltar they did an anti-U-boat sweep in the Atlantic en route. It was the height of the U-boat war, as was vividly brought home to *King Sol's* telegraphist, Fred Howson.

'One night a coder passed me a situation report after he had decoded it, and it really showed us for the first time just how serious the position was. The details read something like this : "15 U-boats shadowing X convoy, 20 U-boats shadowing Y convoy, 12 U-boats inward bound Bay of Biscay, 25 outward bound". Yet somehow we got through without seeing a thing.

'*King Sol's* first trip out of Gibraltar was quite something. We coaled and watered, and steamed out with other escorts to rendezvous a convoy from the U.S. about 250 miles west of the Rock. There was a long, slow swell and one or two of us remarked how little movement there was, especially considering the extra top-weight on either side of the bridge. After twelve hours the asdic packed up and the leading asdic operator had to take a look at the works. These were situated under the messdeck, and as soon as he lifted the trapdoor it became apparent why we were riding through the swell so smoothly—we were flooded to within a few inches of the messdeck.

'Immediately the pumps were started up, but within minutes they too had packed up. The reason was that our entire stock of Naafi cigarettes and chocolate was stored down there and it blocked the pumps. The C.O. decided there was no alternative but to bale out the ship by bucket and hand. For two days and nights it was a case of coming off watch, grabbing a meal, then joining the human bucket-chain from the trap to the deck. The cause of the flooding was discovered: a seacock was found turned to "open", and it was suspected that this had been done by one of the Spaniards aboard while we were coaling. Ever after that there was always a deck guard and a quay guard when we were tied up at Gibraltar.

'But this was not the end of our troubles. The coal we had loaded was of very poor quality, more like black sand, and the convoy was quite fast, about 10 knots. Our daytime station was ahead of the convoy, and our night station at the rear. Everything went well the first night, but next morning, when we had to take up station ahead, it proved almost impossible. We eventually made it, but only after hours of work and sweat by the stokers; it was so hard on them that we were given an extra stoker when we arrived back at the Rock.

'Ships kept leaving the convoy at intervals for various Algerian ports and eventually we sailed into Bone, the Allied base. Here we cleaned out properly below the messdeck and stacked up all our sea-spoiled Naafi stores on deck so that they could be declared unfit by someone from the base, and reimbursed free of charge. This done, we were told to throw them over the side. I could scarcely believe my eyes at what happened next. None of the harbours out there was tidal, the result being they were full of filth and oil scum; but as we threw the stuff overboard the Arabs scooped it out of the water, ate the sweets and chocolate and put the cigarettes on one side to dry out. For the first time in my life I saw the results of extreme hunger and poverty.'

Another trawler which reached the Mediterranean at the same time as *King Sol* was *Foxtrot*. From patrol off Algiers she went as additional escort to a convoy which took a bitter hammering. Her commander was Lieutenant John Bald, RNVR.

'It was a lovely misty morning. We had just secured dawn action-stations and I was arranging myself on the deck of the bridge for a nap, when there were three very loud bangs. A U-boat had slung a handful of torpedoes into the convoy and hit three ships. One, a tanker carrying high-octane, just disappeared in a white flash, and by the time I had leapt to my feet all that was left of her were pieces coming down out of a grey mushroom-shaped cloud. Another of the torpedoed ships was the *Siddi Bel Abbes*, a Frenchman, carrying 1,500 Senegalese troops; she turned on her side and sank in three minutes. The third ship, the American *City of Michigan*, slowly settled by the stern and remained hanging like an unkempt lighthouse before sliding to the bottom fifteen minutes later. The senior officer escort, as he dashed past me on the hunt in his destroyer, signalled me to pick up survivors. With the aid of another ship we managed to rescue 400 men in many stages of mutilation, and these we took to Oran.'

Just two or three weeks before Italy's surrender the trawler *Hornpipe* was on patrol off Bougie, near Algiers. Her number one was Lieutenant Dormer.

'There was an eclipse of the moon, very beautiful and weird, and portending strange events. It was midnight and I was asleep when there was a roar of aircraft, followed by the alarm. I tumbled up on the bridge in bright moonlight to see the sea ablaze. What the hell? My first thought was that a tanker had been hit, but no, it was a Heinkel 111 which, after having a good look at us, had dropped a torpedo fine on the starboard bow about 600 yards away; it splashed twice and ran down the starboard side as the ship went hard-a-starboard. The plane, turning away, somehow crashed into the sea and became a mass of flames from which there was one man shouting as we passed.

'We could not stop and did not think of throwing him anything as there was a second plane about, which shortly came at us. We let fly at him with everything . . . four-inch shrapnel, Oerlikon, twin-Vickers, twin-Brownings, and certainly gave him a damn good fright as he practically looped the loop to get away. He, or another, returned a few minutes later in a rather half-hearted manner, but a burst from all guns quickly drove him away and, after circling out of range, he disappeared for good.

'The authorities ashore jumped to the conclusion that we had shot the plane down and were full of congratulations. It was rather embarrassing for the C.O. to have to explain that it had flown into the sea by itself, without us firing a shot. The officer of the watch rather prided himself as an aircraft recognition expert and had "recognized" the plane, which was in fact Italian, as one of ours, and had allowed it to take a good look and then attack before realizing anything was wrong. Luckily he woke up in time to comb the track of the torpedo. The Italian communique announced the loss of two aircraft, so perhaps we did the second one no good.

'The body of one of the Italians was recovered and we inspected it with mixed emotions. A dark little chap, somewhat burned and battered—I wondered who he was. So unnecessary, the Italian surrender was already being arranged.'

The following month found *Hornpipe* at Phillipville, some 120 miles along the coast from Bougie. Lieutenant Dormer's diary:

'Liberty men came back aboard . . . an inoffensive little chap is talking quietly on the deck outside my cabin. Suddenly he says in an offhand way: "Excuse me a minute, I'm just going to strangle the C.O." He trots to our door with someone in pursuit warning him: "Now don't do anything you'll regret in the morning". He insists: "But it won't take a minute . . . I'm just going to strangle him". He is dragged away, disappointed.'

Later, at Malta. 'Stored up with everything we could get, using our own two pulling-boats which had to row miles and miles. The Sub. was so late that I got worried and borrowed a motorboat from a fleet sweeper, *Clacton*, to look for him. *Clacton's* officer-of-the-day was very snooty and would hardly speak to me although of the same rank. His ship is not all that much bigger than ours but, because it is a different shape, there is an unbridgeable social gulf.'

Fate knew no such distinctions. Only weeks later *Clacton* was sunk off Corsica, after hitting a mine.

And so late October found *Hornpipe* at Naples. 'Broken down . . . no lights, no radio, no hot water. A five o'clock curfew makes the evening gloomy, but we are having mild air-raids which happen just after supper and conveniently fill the time till bed. Everyone blazes away at random, balloons come down in flames, we shoot each others' masts, and there is a terrific din and fireworks display. Any bombs are lost in the uproar. Great fun. There is nothing to do ashore except for the very foolish . . . one can get anything for tobacco.'

In November an unusual event took place back at Algiers, where

Admiral Sir John Cunningham, the C-in-C Mediterranean, had his headquarters ashore. The Admiral would fly his flag on a warship in harbour, generally a destroyer or cruiser, or something larger, but in an unexpected departure from routine he asked the trawler *Staffa* to fly his flag—a rare distinction. So there followed the unlikely spectacle of the beflagged trawler returning the salutes of warships large and small moving in and out of harbour at all hours of the day. It imposed quite a strain on her company, but the four days of glory was well worth it, and afterwards her commander asked the C-in-C's permission for *Staffa* to keep the flag as a memento, a request which was speedily approved. The Admiral added : 'I would not hesitate to order you to hoist it again should the occasion arise.'

Well, that was the trawlers, always equal to the occasion, big or small. Like the captain at Gibraltar, who, having an appointment with the Admiral, and his trawler being involved in the filthy business of coaling up, donned impeccable white uniform and had himself wrapped up in sheets and carried off the ship down the quay to a safe distance from the flying black dust.

Of the trawler losses in the Mediterranean in 1943 two, the *Jura* and the *Bredon* were sunk by U-boat torpedoes and two more, *Horatio* and *Tervani*, were torpedoed by Italian submarines. Three others were destroyed by mines.

At the year's end the total casualty list of Harry Tate's Navy now stood at more than 350 vessels lost. The last entry was a stark Christmas Day tragedy in home waters. *Kingston Beryl*, on convoy duty off Skerryvore, ran on to some floating mines which had broken loose from a British minefield.

She sank with all hands. British mines were supposed to go 'safe' when they broke loose, but these were not.

15

'Sir, the Wheel's Come Off'

January 1944 and a renewed burst of E-boat activity. The trawler *Wallasea* was escorting a convoy section from the Bristol Channel round to Plymouth when E-boats struck off Mounts Bay, sending *Wallasea* to the bottom along with two of her charges. In a similar attack off Beachy Head the trawler *Pine* also lost two of her flock and had her own bows blown off by a torpedo. She carried on fighting the E-boats until help arrived, only to sink when taken in tow.

In the North Sea the E-boat pack found easier prey in the mine-sweeping *Cap D'Antifer*, which they despatched within minutes.

However, the trawlers' overall losses at the beginning of the year were light, and for most Harry Tate vessels in home waters it was a case of plodding on with their usual unspectacular duties during the massive build-up for the Second Front. Like the old drifter *King's Grey*, based at Devonport; her routine consisted of Channel sweeping by day and putting into a different port each night, Brixham, Falmouth, Dartmouth, and then back to Devonport. It was a humdrum existence repeated hundreds of times on similar ships, but that a Second Front was coming at last was made evident by such scenes as the handing over of the old *Monique Andre*, a converted French trawler operating from Plymouth, to the Free French. Cook Scadeng:

'The *Monique Andre* was as dirty as they come, we'd lie in our bunks at night and hear the rats scurrying along the steampipes within six to eight inches of our faces. So there were no regrets when we were told she was to be returned to the Free French Navy.

'Never was there a greater ceremony. We spent days getting all the stores listed and ready to be returned to the depot. The turn-over was ordered to take place at Ardrossan, not far from

Glasgow, so we steamed our way there up the west coast.

'The great day came and everything movable was transferred to the jetty, every pot, pan and item of stores, to be carefully stacked in a large covered van. Off went the van, and the skipper asked us all to get into a decent suit and get our personal gear on the jetty, ready for transport. "Now," he said, "when these froggies come along we have to line up along the jetty, facing the ship so as to witness the hauling down of the Ensign and the raising of the Free French flag!"

'What a performance. The French arrived in another covered van and piled out of the back. First, an armed guard of two French sailors who stood rigidly to attention while the standard bearer placed himself between them, then the French relief crew. Their officers arrived by car.

'We lined up facing the forward part of the ship while the French faced the after end. Simultaneously, and to commands of "Present Arms!" in French, and a modest request from our skipper to stand to attention, accompanied by some blasts from a French bugle, our Bunts hauled down our Ensign and the French hauled up theirs. A few handshakes and goodbyes were exchanged, the new crew climbed aboard, and we got into their wagon. Off we went, to a chorus of groans when, a few yards along the jetty, we passed the van with our ship's gear and stores still aboard and untouched going back to the *Monique Andre*, where the French were to take it all back again.'

In the spring of 1944 the Royal Naval Patrol Service reached a working strength of 57,000 officers and men. Overwhelmingly now its ranks were filled with hostilities-only ratings, but Harry Tate's Navy retained its spiky, pugnacious, defiant identity.

The old trawler *Clythness* had been a minesweeper at Dover, was at Dunkirk, and all in all had gone through a rather eventful time. Recommissioned as a water-carrier she had spent the winter of 1943-44 watering the landing craft assembled in Cromarty Firth. When she left Aberdeen on this task there was the moving scene of her skipper bellowing at his seasick sailors as they struggled to get the smallboat swung out. He had asked for seamen, he said, and been sent bloody farmers. A few days later he presented the messdeck with a brown paper parcel in which was a book from the comforts, entitled 'How to be a Successful Farmer'.

This skipper was a wiry ex-fisherman, a small man in his middle-thirties but with a powerful voice that could be heard all over the harbour. A thoroughly tough man, he nevertheless had a sentimental and generous side to his nature and his bark was generally worse than his bite. But there was fierce rivalry between him and the chief engineman.

There was the day *Clythness*, which had been steaming in the centre of a convoy, discovered at daybreak she was alone on the sea with the convoy a far-off smudge of smoke on the horizon. A destroyer flashed urgently from a discreet distance that *Clythness* was steaming through a minefield, or so the more pessimistic of the crew judged the signal to read. This was too much for the chief engineman, who afterwards drew up a 'round robin' petitioning for a new C.O. However, the skipper got wind of it and cleverly prevented his arch-enemy from going ashore; much to the secret relief of the chief, whose enthusiasm had waned.

When the 'bond'—the monthly supply of whisky and gin—came aboard, a skipper would throw a party for brother skippers from other trawlers, and they would get down to steady drinking for the next twenty-four hours until the liquor was finished. As one seaman describes:

'During these parties anything could happen. First they became mellow and sent a bottle down to the messdeck, whereupon someone would open a bottle of illicitly stored rum and another party would start there. Then the skippers became a nuisance, ordering the steward, or if he had conveniently disappeared, the member of the crew who was on watch, to dish up a meal for them, anything from a plate of sandwiches to a fry-up of bacon and eggs. After this they might get sporty and hold a shooting competition with the revolvers kept in the wardroom, when it was as well to keep below under cover. It generally ended up with a fight between a couple of the skippers and the cook chasing a seaman out of the galley with his carving knife; or, as on one occasion, the chief engineman trying to put a troublesome stoker over the side. Next day, after a twelve-hour lie-in, everything would be back to normal.'

Very occasionally a determined attempt would be made to shake some sterner discipline into the Harry Tates, as at Granton, on the Firth of Forth, when an RN commander assumed command and looked with jaundiced eye on the motley collection of Patrol Service craft which included a fair complement of little motor minesweepers or 'Mickey Mouses'. Taking a leaf out of the book of old 'Monkey Brand' Stephenson at Tobermory, the commander, along with a working party, raided unguarded ships and dismantled parts of their

guns—a bit off an Oerlikon here, a little off a 12-pounder there—
had them all labelled and dispatched to his office, and sat back to
await the inevitable result, a steady stream of furious skippers to
retrieve their losses.

One sight to cap all others was that of the skipper of a whaler
going ashore three sheets to the wind, coat slung over his shoulder,
cap at an angle of 45 degrees, his pet Alsatian bounding along
beside him, giving loud voice to blistering remarks about the RN
which were exciting in their inventiveness and a revelation to the
ears of the Wrens.

But perhaps no better illustration of the root spirit of Harry
Tate's Navy, undiminished by four years of war, could be the
experience of a party of senior naval brass who set forth from Scapa
Flow one fine afternoon, bent on a fishing expedition to Hoy.
Admiral Burnett, in HMS *Belfast*, flagship of Cruiser Squadron 10,
had organized the party and a drifter arrived to transport them.
The crew were no doubt impressed by HMS *Belfast* but hardly by
the relaxed group of men in old jackets and flannels, led by an
elderly, red-faced man in a cap and dirty raincoat.

To the flag lieutenant's inquiry, 'Who is the captain of this
driftah?' there was no reply, so Admiral Burnett reverted to the
Buchan dialect and asked, 'Fa's skipper o' this boatie?'

A youth eventually looked up from the drifter's wheelhouse and
said slowly and very deliberately: 'This iss a Stornoway ship, and
we're aall captainss here. . . .'

In the Mediterranean, minesweeping had been stepped up in all
areas. Ships were constantly busy, like the whaler *Satsa*, working
on the Italian minefields at Pantelleria, Sicily, Sardinia, and along
the coast of Italy. *Satsa* did the sweeping at night for the landing
on Elba, and when dawn broke, found herself surrounded by
twenty-seven floating mines, a sight that froze the blood of her
crew at the thought of their hairbreadth escape.

The trawler *Hornpipe* was in at the Anzio landing. Extracts
from Lieutenant Dormer's diary describe the build-up at Naples,
and afterwards.

'The typhus has spread, and we are not allowed ashore at all.
Nor can laundry be sent. We have all been issued with anti-louse
powder. Some "enterprise of great pith and moment" is in the
offing. The port is crowded, heavy air-attacks are expected, and
we close up at dawn and dusk. The burning question is, are *we*

going? Will the steering be repaired in time? We coaled today, a hopeful sign, since there had even been talk of digging our coal out. They brought a coal barge to *us* . . . never before. Confinement on board is no joke. Some of the sailors have even taken to writing letters to each other for the benefit of the censor . . . me. They tell each other what they think of "Jimmy-the-Bastard" . . . me.

'*Tuesday*. We are very likely to go on the party now, so there is a crescendo of excitement, and grim jokes. The whole area is in a fever of preparation. German reconnaissance planes have been over, so they'll probably be waiting on the beaches. The only question is, where? Funny to think that some unsuspecting little town or village will, in a few days, be world famous.

'*Wednesday*. The steering is mended, and excitement increased so much that people worked overtime without even remembering to grumble. At last, extricating ourselves with great difficulty from the mass of ships and landing craft, we sailed to Castellamare for the night, with best wishes from the stay-at-homes. There, as soon as dusk fell, every sort of flap arose . . . human torpedoes, E-boats. . . . But nothing happened, though we spent the evening at action-stations with a boat full of bombs patrolling round the ship.

'*Thursday*. Checked up on everyone's lifebelts and tin-hats. Issued field dressings and checked every detail of organization and equipment. The C.O. went to a most secret conference, of which no details are to be released until actually under way. Let's get cracking, waiting is a strain. Only four trawlers are concerned, we are lucky this time . . . I wonder if we shall say "lucky" later?

'*Friday*. "Never sail on a Friday", but we did, about noon, behind a big convoy of landing craft. The officers were only told of the plan in the evening, though Sparks, a leading telegraphist, has known all along. So far, at 2000 hours, all is well. We can see gunflashes, as usual, from the Minturno area, and various aircraft are about.

'*Saturday*. 1100. The night passed quietly, but the landing craft were hard to see, and by 0300 the convoys were in a fair state of confusion. At 0500 the course seemed wrong, and the speed too slow. I asked the nearest LCI . . . we were with the wrong convoy. Cracking on we found our flotilla of fleet sweepers at daybreak, and spent a hectic day picking up dan buoys. We had hardly ever done this before, and found it difficult. I spent much of the day in the sea, swimming to shackle on wires.

'*D-Day*. A lovely, calm, sunny day, almost cloudless blue skies. The multitude of ships off the beaches look more like a review than an invasion. The sweepers cut several mines, one of which damaged the A/A cruiser *Palomares*. We are now about to escort her back to Naples, in tow of tugs. There are a few columns of smoke rising from the shore, and every now and then a dull thud. Sometimes a cruiser does a bit of bombarding or a few enemy planes approach. There are constant red warnings, but no attacks yet.

'*D-Day plus 2*. Escorted the tug *Evenshaw*, towing two lighters to Anzio, but had to sink one of them by gunfire as it broke adrift and the sea was too rough to recover it, in spite of using oil. Arrived off the American beaches at 1500. The town was being heavily shelled, and shells were bursting on the beaches and in the sea. Return fire from U.S. warships was landing quite close inland. At 1600 three dive-bombers attacked the HQ ship, without result, but one American vessel was sunk, with its bows sticking out of the water. At dusk, just as we were setting off with a Naples-bound convoy, the Luftwaffe arrived in force, and the next two hours were a terrific muddle of flares and tracer and bombs in all directions. We hardly fired at all ourselves, but I saw four aircraft go down in flames and the destroyer *Janus* badly hit and burning. We had a nasty half hour later, well out on our own, having lost the convoy in the confusion. Enemy planes dropped dozens of flares in a circle round us, but we made smoke and were not attacked.'

On the fourth day after the landing *Hornpipe* arrived at Anzio again—'just at dusk, the worst possible time, with the convoy of LSTs disorganized by a gale. There was a heavy air attack which lasted three hours. A Heinkel attacked us with a torpedo, which I saw drop. We had a go at him but missed, as the ship was rolling in a heavy sea. There were attacks about every half hour all next day as we hung about in the anchorage. I attempted to have a wash, but a stick of bombs came down just ahead as soon as I got my shirt off. At 1500 the BBC boasted about "our complete mastery of the air over the beach-head". There were two formations, each of 12 aircraft, cruising overhead, all silvery in the sunshine. We felt nice and safe, until they peeled off and attacked, one after the other. One of them dived straight into the sea, it all looked too like the films to be real. We were very worried about the evening, but the sun went down in a glory of crimson and gold, and it got dark without anything happening. No one dared to be the first to say "I don't think they're coming". And so it went on.'

The trawlers were switched from escorting convoys to Anzio to make anti-submarine patrols between the Pontine Islands. The aim of this was to seal off the inshore shipping route, but it was not a success, the cruiser *Penelope* being sunk by a U-boat inside the 'sealed off' area. The trawlers resumed their journeys to the beach-head.

'One could see for miles, all the beach-head, and the Alban hills, the poplars of the Pontine marshes, and the great snow-capped mountains beyond. All around the perimeter little white puffs appeared, grew into tall columns, and faded away. Against the dark of a leafless wood, we could see the flashes of our own artillery.'

The Germans had perfect observation from the Alban hills; Dormer later saw enemy photographs in which one could easily pick out an individual trawler. The Germans also had one or more very long range guns known as 'Anzio Charlie', which made life hotter all around.

'The afternoon was quiet until the Jerries noticed an LST that had anchored away from the rest. They started shelling it with a most enormous great gun whose shell sent waterspouts up some 150 feet. After the fifth shell, at exactly three-minute intervals, the LST was seen to be moving. The sixth shell was close astern of her, but after the seventh they gave up. We, and the merchant shipping, remained several miles off shore, the latter unloading into DUKWs.'

Later on, the beach-head was kept perpetually shrouded in smoke, and mines were the main problem. *Hornpipe* went on to dan-laying.

'One day we were looking forward to provisions from a fleet sweeper, but they unfortunately hauled up a mine in their sweep which killed their first lieutenant. "Oh dear," said my C.O., "we can hardly ask them for 40 pounds of fresh meat now".

'Near the end we arrived in the smoke screen one morning, simultaneously with several German midget submarines. They hadn't a chance, being clearly visible in a glassy calm.

'Finally, just before the breakout from the beach-head, we had to get our own sweeps out, to sweep a convoy into Anzio. All the sweeping gear was stowed away, and we had forgotten how to use it. Surprisingly we got it running, but most of the sweep was done in a thick smoke screen, where none of us could see each other, and the convoy did not follow in the "swept" water anyway, so the whole thing was a bit of a farce.'

Work went on off West Africa, and it was these waters which saw the end of one of the most notable ships sailed by Harry Tate's Navy.

Southern Pride was a big whaler of nearly 600 tons. Under construction at Blyth at the beginning of the war, she was taken over on the stocks for Admiralty service, and when completed in 1940 she and *Southern Gem*, of the same tonnage, were the largest whale-catchers in the world.

Southern Pride arrived at the Belfast trawler base late in 1940. With a very low well-deck constantly under water—she had a nine-inch freeboard when fully loaded—she was the prototype of the Flower-class corvettes, and did twenty knots on trials with a bronze propeller. She had been designed to reach South Africa on her way to the whaling grounds without refuelling, travelling rather like a submarine, and the effect of the addition of a four-inch gun, ammunition, depth-charges and the rest was very nearly disastrous on her first convoy trip into the Atlantic. After losing the convoy a few days out in heavy weather, *Pride* was forced to heave-to for forty-eight hours, during which time her boats were damaged and the charthouse structure on the upper bridge wrecked. She subsequently never took on her full capacity of oil fuel; except once, in the South Atlantic, and then she was nearly driven under.

The middle of 1943 saw *Pride* operating from Freetown, she and *Southern Gem* working as a pair, taking merchantmen round to various surf ports on the West African coast, where the ships were unloaded by surf boats, and escorting cable ships. On one such tour of duty *Pride* crossed the Atlantic to Pernambuco, Brazil, with a cable ship, patrolling round and round her charge while the vessel hauled up and repaired undersea cables. Then *Pride* had the task of escorting across to Dakar, via Freetown, about twenty little motor fishing vessels built in the U.S. The MFVs mostly seemed to be manned by retired Army officers, including three full colonels. One of the boats broke down on the equator, crossing the line dizzily back and forth all night, and *Southern Pride* with it. Finally *Pride* towed the boat back to Pernambuco.

At this stage the whaler's number one, Lieutenant Allan Waller, had a recurrence of ear trouble and had to go into hospital. On recovering, and with *Southern Pride* gone, he attached himself to the U.S. Navy, along with an engineman from *Pride* now fit again after breaking a leg while playing football, and the first lieutenant of *Southern Gem*, who had been to hospital to have his tonsils out.

The USN tried to arrange passage to the States for the trio. However, the whaler *Buttermere* turned up bound for Freetown, and so the three men joined her. She was only a year older than *Pride*, but she put the fear of God into the passengers. She had been in Rio for a couple of months refitting, and the ship's company of thirty-six was highly demoralized; some thirty of them had got VD, or were just getting over it.

Buttermere was loaded up with quartz for asdics and was also escort for eight MFVs. She had not been long out at sea when the helmsman reported to the officer of the watch: 'Please, sir, the wheel's come off'. The O.O.W's reply was, 'Well, put it back on again!' which they did, fixing it in position with the marline spike of a pusser's dirk. After a few days the ship stopped completely, the chief engineer mournfully telling the captain 'The whole job's fucked, sir.' A pump had broken down in the engine room. Help came from a totally unexpected quarter when an engineer of one of the MFVs, Lieutenant (E.) Lance Harrison, RNVR, brought his boat alongside the stranded whaler in the flat calm. He climbed aboard *Buttermere* and made repairs using two galley stove lids, one from the whaler and one from his own boat. And so they made it to port—and never were the three passengers more grateful to get back to their own ships. Unfortunately, for the two men of *Pride*, it was not for long, though Allan Waller, the 'Jonah of Parkeston Quay', had no idea that he was soon to have a third ship go down beneath him.

In June 1944 *Southern Pride*, in company with a trawler, was escorting a merchant ship to a Liberian port, but never reached there. Off Marshall Port, about thirty miles from Monrovia, she ran on to a shoal. The time was four minutes past 7 p.m. Lieutenant Waller:

'I was sitting with the chief engineer outside the wardroom on the starboard waist when the ship struck. It felt as if she had been mined by an acoustic ground mine. I seized my lifebelt and hurried to my action-station on the bridge, while the chief ran aft. There were more shocks as I arrived on the bridge, like exploding depth-charges this time.

' "We're hit," said the captain—"Unprime depth-charges!" While we were doing this the ship rocked heavily but was not sinking, and seemed to have stopped. There were more shocks, and it now seemed we were striking either rock or hard sand. In four minutes the depth-charges had been made safe and I was back on the bridge. A signal was sent to the trawler *Pict* and I tried to fix our exact position—we were about three miles from shore in shark infested waters—but this was impossible in the failing light.

'The cox'n took over the wheel and the captain tried to move the ship at slow-ahead, without success. The engines were then tried at slow-astern. The wheel would not answer, but the ship appeared to move very slowly. Soundings were taken and two fathoms reported; the bangings and grindings ceased. The captain decided to anchor, as the ship seemed to have cleared the rocks and was riding well, but the chief engineer reported that the pumps were unable to cope with the water and it would soon be necessary to draw the fires. The captain then decided to try to beach the ship, and we began to heave in the anchor, but before this could be done the chief said that the engine room would have to be abandoned. More cable was let out and the anchor secured. The ship was still rising buoyantly and was well out of the water, though she had in fact been holed right under the Scotch boiler. The asdic well had been made watertight.

'It was now two hours since we had struck the shoal and there was not much more we could do. I helped the captain to decide on the ship's position and compose a signal to senior officer West Africa which we tried to send off over our own set, an attempt which was abandoned when the lights failed and power was low.

'Rum was issued, all hands gathered on the well-deck to hear a reassuring talk by the captain, and a sing-song was organized to help keep up morale. Some men broke into the wardroom spirit locker, and one troublesome seaman had to be shut up in the heads.

'Watches were organized, those off watch trying to rest. Still the ship showed no signs of sinking, though water was rising slowly in the engine room. Shortly after midnight several shocks were felt and the ship suddenly began to settle port side aft. We had already lost one boat, so a few of us now tried to build rafts by lashing together empty oil drums. There were four of us, Sub-Lieutenant Dunn, Lieutenant (E) Johansen, the chief engineer, Telegraphist Roberts and myself. But there was a heavy swell running, and just as we had completed one raft the ship lurched heavily to port and lay over at an angle, a huge sea came over and carried away our raft and all other floatable gear on the boatdeck. We ourselves escaped by each selecting a funnel guy and, when the sea came over, swarming up it, though I suffered a badly lacerated leg. A Carley float with three native stokers on it was also swept away, but kept afloat.

'I went down to the main deck to see if everyone there was all right. The ship was now listing to an angle of about 30 degrees; most of the hands were sitting on the starboard rail, which was well clear of the water. I remembered the seaman we had shut up, and making my way forward with difficulty because of the angle of the ship, found him lying completely unconscious outside the heads, the tapes of his lifebelt wound round his neck. Shaking him did no good, so in desperation I kicked and punched him. At last he came round a little and started raving. With the help of two men I sat him up with his lifebelt well inflated and securely fastened round his chest, then got him to the rail, where he seemed to realize to some extent his danger. I left him hanging over a rail with a rating on either side, satisfied that if he kept only slight control he would easily save himself, for at that end the ship was only about four feet under water.

'Scrambling back along the ship I then tried with Signalman Stone to get a message to a boat from *Pict*, which seemed to be having difficulty in finding us, and in the process was nearly washed over the side. *Pride* was righting herself quickly and the rising waters forced us to climb upwards to the lower bridge veranda and the Oerlikon and four-inch platforms. *Pict's* boat finally took off the first load, and as the lower bridge was crowded I climbed to the upper bridge, and from there on to the searchlight platform on top. There was nothing to do now but wait to be taken off. *Pict's* boat came over four or five times for new loads, during which time the swell moderated and it grew lighter.'

On the top bridge were Paddy Swanson, the assistant cook, and Seaman Field, an asdic rating. Paddy could not swim and had anxiously equipped himself with three lifebelts. Field promised faithfully to jump into the water with him when the boat arrived, which he did, but in swimming to the boat Paddy reached a speed which astonished everyone and was hauled aboard well ahead of his shipmate.

Finally the boat made its last journey to pick up the remaining six people aboard: the captain, chief engineer, engineman, telegraphist, Sub-Lieutenant Dunn and Lieutenant Waller. 'We abandoned ship from the port side and I looked at my watch before I jumped; it was 5.17 a.m., ten hours since we had struck the shoal. The captain followed me into the water and after a short swim we reached the boat and were pulled aboard.'

Only one man was lost, and this a seaman who was swept away despite the best efforts of his comrades to save him; the three stokers washed over earlier with the Carley float drifted safely ashore. Even the ship's dog managed to swim the three miles to the beach, though the ship's cat and three kittens were never seen again.

Adding to the melancholy of the disaster was the loss of the cash in the wardroom safe, for *Southern Pride* had been due to make another crossing to Pernambuco, and so they had bought all the cruzeiros available in Freetown and put them in the safe—which now lay abandoned under water. However, there was a bright sequel when, on returning to the wreck with a salvage party from a tug, Lieutenant Waller managed, with help, to get down and rescue the cash, and spent most of one day drying it out.

In the same week that saw the ignominious death of *Southern Pride*, the trawler *Birdlip* also met her end off the West African coast. *Birdlip* was one of three trawlers escorting a merchantman from Takoradi to Freetown when she was torpedoed by a U-boat. Half of her company, including the captain, were lost, the remainder managing to reach the shore on two rafts.

Birdlip's swift fate was very much on the minds of the crew of another escort trawler, the *Duncton*, as she approached those same waters less than a month later. *Duncton*, based at Freetown, was returning north from Capetown after a three-month refit when she broke down. Her number one was Lieutenant Arthur Miles.

'A few days out of Walvis Bay, where we called for repairs to our W/T transmitter, the engines were stopped owing to leaking boiler tubes. Spare tubes were fitted, but more leaks developed. Our transmitter remained out of order so we couldn't wireless for help, and it was a case of improvising as best we could to stop the leaks, which now affected a great number of the tubes. Several times the boilers were refilled by hand pump, all hands from the captain to the cook taking a spell, but steam was raised only to produce further leaks, and repairs had to be started all over again.

'Fortunately the weather was perfect, whales and sharks playing around our silent ship. One evening a sing-song on deck came to an abrupt end when the lookout sighted mysterious green flares, and action-stations was sounded. Nothing happened, but we felt like sitting ducks, remembering the fate of *Birdlip*.

'Food and water were now rationed, no fresh water at all for washing, and everyone grew beards. Somebody joked "Why don't

we sail her?" and very soon the idea was being taken seriously. The
big foredeck awning made a good mainsail, and every bit of canvas
aboard, together with some pretty odd bits of bunting, was hoisted
until the ship was festooned with "sails". As one of the crew described it, we looked like the washing on the Siegfried Line. There
was a steady wind on the beam and the quartermaster steered from
the auxiliary wheel aft. By Dutchman's log *Duncton's* speed under
sail was a good one knot! The wind blew steadily off the coast so
that we could not, with our unwieldy rig, even tack towards it,
and the best we could manage was to continue heading north.

'Every day our dinghy put off on a practice cruise in preparation
for sending a volunteer crew hundreds of miles north to the
Portuguese island of Sao Tome, to fetch help. This would have
been very much a last resort, and luckily the most they did was
take snapshots of us—the last sailing man-o'-war. For at last steam
was raised and our engineers' makeshift repairs enabled us to limp
slowly into Lagos after about a fortnight without engines. We
learned that aircraft had made several fruitless searches for us and
our next-of-kin cards had already been taken out at the base. We
were back from the dead.'

16

The Last of 'Lord Austin'

Flotilla upon flotilla of Patrol Service minesweepers, together with scores of anti-submarine trawlers, were among the thousand warships that led and supported the great invasion of Normandy on D-Day—June 6 1944.

For some it was a dangerous front seat, given the hair-raising task of sweeping ahead of the mammoth invasion fleet. Like the old trawler *Ijuin*, whose tottery engines mustered a full nine knots with her safety valves screwed tightly down. She was dan-layer to a flotilla of fleet sweepers ordered to sweep and light a channel from St Catherine's Point, Isle of Wight, to Normandy, then to clear an anchorage close inshore for the invasion force to Juno beach-head.

Signalman Leonard Stent:

'We left anchorage at St Helen's Bay at dusk on June 5 and carried on with our job until the change of tide, when during the hours of slack water we lay quietly waiting to stream opposite-hand sweeps for the remainder of the journey. As we rested for this brief spell a motor launch came close by to greet us with "Hey there, don't look now but you're being followed!" We all strained our eyes through the gloom until a frantic yell from Leading-Seaman George Swallow froze us all with fear, for right under our counter lay a mine, and as we pitched, so the thing rolled back and forth, the horns at times only two or three feet from contact with our hull. George tore along the deck, grabbing a long-handled deck-scrubber as he went, and hung over the stern to fend off almost certain destruction, until the chief engineman, with coolness and presence of mind, strolled down to his control position and gave the engine a kick ahead, the turbulence causing the mine to drift clear but with agonizing slowness. Of all the stories of minesweeping

I'm confident that our George was the only man who used a broom successfully.'

In the great offensive some trawlers earned their battle honours early, like *Grenadier* on D-Day. She was off Arromanches when she fired at an enemy plane, causing it to drop its bombs in a hurry. One bomb hit *Grenadier*, making a great hole in her side, but they coaxed her back to Portsmouth, where her wound was fixed up with a concrete patch.

Other Harry Tates pressed on with humbler tasks. The trawler *Clythness*, carrying fuel oil and petrol, left Poole harbour on the night of June 5 for the Normandy beaches. All next day, D-Day, she was at sea, having become separated from the convoys of the night before. Seaman Thomas:

'By nightfall we anchored in a small cove under the cliffs somewhere on the French coast. We were alone except for a barge which we had found broken down and taken in tow. The young sub-lieutenant RNVR commanding the barge had gratefully accepted the skipper's offer of the tow in spite of the dire warning he received from our chief engineman, who spent more time on deck than in the engine room, that our Old Man had lost the convoy and would get us all blown up. Next day we found the invasion beaches proper at Arromanches, and the Sub., overjoyed at his safe arrival, invited us all across to splice the mainbrace, a rather peculiar little "party" on the edge of battle. But not for long, for very soon we received orders to proceed to Omaha beach, where the fighting had been fiercest.'

The trawler *Cevic* had returned from the Mediterranean, where she had been water-carrying, to have her tanks refitted for carrying oil to the Normandy beaches. Skipper Thorpe:

'We arrived in Portsmouth Harbour on D-Day plus one to see notices stuck up all round the harbour saying "This is D-Day". We had to pick up 120 drums of oil as deck cargo, distributing them evenly each side of the ship. When loaded, however, I found we had sixty drums on the port side but only fifty-six on the starboard side, and demanded to know where the other four had gone. It turned out that the lorry driver had been trying to keep them for himself. It stuck in my mind for days, how he could come to do such a thing when so many men were being killed on the beaches.'

Incredibly, though the trawlers took a thrustful part in these early stages of the Normandy invasion and many had their scars to show for it, only one was sunk. Hers became a lone statistic among the losses of hundreds of landing craft and several small warships. The date was June 24, and the trawler the veteran *Lord Austin*.

Austin had returned, very thankfully, from her last Russian convoy six months before, in December 1943; by sweeping coal dust from every nook and cranny she made enough steam to get up the Mersey and dock at Birkenhead at midnight. She paid off, the crew departed on leave, and for the Hull trawler it was the end of her rigorous life in the northern seas. When recommissioned she was a greatly altered ship and had a new captain, though he was no newcomer to the vessel. Lieutenant E. S. Terence Robinson, RNVR, had joined *Austin* as a 'new boy' on Northern Patrol, and his promotion to command followed service as her number one.

'We now had an open bridge. We had radar, and had lost our trawler mast; we had large sponsons on the wheelhouse deck with Oerlikons, and stripped Lewis guns on the bridge. We also had radar operators and coders, and were nearly a large enough crew to have a Naafi manager. But we still made only ten knots flat out except when going downhill, and we still made lots of smoke except when burning good Welsh coal.

'After several training work-ups we were ordered to the Clyde to pick up some dumb-barges—barges without means of propulsion —in company with two other trawlers. We found ourselves towing a barge filled with water-tanks for the invasion; it was fully as big as *Lord Austin* and we had to take it down to Falmouth. On the journey we got mixed up in a bit of a battle in the Bristol Channel when some E-boats got rough with our motor gunboats, but I decided we were non-belligerent. I named our barge "Fanny" and for the most part she behaved herself well.

'We arrived in Falmouth with Fanny, but nobody wanted us. Instead we were ordered on to Southampton, where we arrived eventually after a number of adventures. Here again, nobody seemed very enthusiastic about Fanny, but by this time I'd had enough of her and gave her to the Sea Transport people, receiving, almost in exchange, my sealed bag of orders for Operation Neptune —though no one thought to tell me that I was entitled to open it. Eventually I did so, weighed anchor from close in to Seaview, Isle of Wight, and picked up the right convoy of tank landing ships bound for Juno beach. The sea was much smoother than on the day originally planned for the invasion, nevertheless at dawn the next day I could see the unfortunate troops hanging over the sides of their ships being thoroughly seasick. We closed the coast and the LSTs went ashore in turns to land their follow-up troops.

'It was certainly a wonderful sight. Heavy ships carrying out bombardments, ships everywhere and the sky dominated by the RAF. What a change from our convoy PQ17 to Russia, and my own earlier memories of the French coast in 1940 at Dunkirk and after.

'Towards the end of a long day I was ordered to take a tank landing craft in tow. She had struck a sea-defence mine on the way in to the beach, and although badly damaged had somehow managed to get her tanks ashore. We took her in tow and beached her near Portsmouth. Back we went again, and soon we were spending our days patrolling on anti-submarine and E-boat work.

'Then came the great gale. I hadn't liked the look of the weather when we anchored for the night, and had put down both anchors. I went up on the bridge at midnight to have a last look round before turning in, and found we were dragging. We got under way, found we were an anchor short when we weighed, and man-oeuvred somehow all night without hitting anything. There were plenty of casualties among the landing craft but we were lucky, except for one of the stewards who hurt his back so badly I had to get a doctor over from a destroyer.

'On most nights the enemy planes came over dropping mines and the odd bomb but the battleships and cruisers kept very quiet to avoid giving away their positions. We tried to mark the position of some of the mines with dan-buoys, and often this was a help to the sweepers in the morning.

'One night while we were anchored a plane came over low. One of the gunners asked permission to open fire with the Oerlikon, but as we were anchored near a big ship I ordered him not to fire. The plane dropped a bomb which we heard coming down, and it went off alongside, so disposing of a theory I had held that you never heard the bomb that hit you. It made a great mess, putting our radar out of action and making a hole in the ship's side near the engine room, but we were able to plug this successfully and were lucky to escape without casualties. My cabin was a shambles. The radiator had been torn off the bulkhead and lay flat on the deck; in the bathroom my shaving brush had been lifted off the shelf, blown out of the door, and the door then shut after it. Blast did some extraordinary things.

'Each morning at dawn we weighed anchor and set off to patrol the lines. As the minesweepers started their work the battleships took up positions for long-range bombardment, and it was an incredible sight to be able to pick out 15-inch shells at the height of their trajectory and see them quite clearly.'

The big ships were the *Rodney* and *Nelson*, which bombarded the shore batteries at Le Havre and drew the enemy's fire in reply. During all this spectacular shooting match a Marine band played encouragement on the deck of one of the battleships. Shells landed so near to *Lord Austin* that her crew had to duck to dodge the water-splashes. German spotter-planes flew over very high, but before dark *Rodney* and *Nelson* moved anchorages—leaving *Austin* to endure a rain of bombs intended for them both.

'One day we saw our first flying bomb. No one knew what to make of it and all ships were ordered not to fire. It seemed to circle the anchorage and then turn inland, probably coming down on the Germans themselves.'

And then it was Saturday, June 24. A warm day that broke with blue skies and a fairly calm sea. *Lord Austin* weighed anchor at 5.30 a.m. She had ten miles to go to take over patrol round the anchorage, and the watch-below was asleep.

Parachute mines had been dropped in the night, and soon after getting under way *Austin's* asdic operator, George Edwards, reported he was "pinging" mines. When they neared the trawler *Northern Reward*, Lieutenant Robinson called over to her: "My asdic operator reports this place is lousy with mines".

' "Yes," replied *Northern Reward*—"don't touch 'em".

Only minutes afterwards a mine went off right below *Lord Austin*. The time was 5.55 a.m. Lieutenant Robinson:

'Because of the distance we had to go to take up our patrol I had been hurrying; had we been making seven knots or less we might not have triggered off the acoustic mine. When the explosion came we were thrown about heavily on the bridge, the ship's siren was jammed wide open and making a terrible din, and the engines stopped dead. I rushed to the voice-pipe but there was only a roaring sound of steam from the engine room.'

The mine had struck in the engine room, where some of the men must have been killed instantly. *Austin* heeled over to port. She had barely ten more minutes to live.

When those on the bridge had scrambled to their feet Lieutenant Robinson ordered a boat away, but in the explosion both boats had been smashed and the davits and tackle bent and twisted. Liferafts were got away and scrambling nets dropped over the side, some men leaving before the order to abandon ship was given. Others followed orders and ran to remove the primers from as many depth-charges as they could. Among these men was George Edwards.

'I ran down and looked into the messdeck, but it was half full of water with no sign of life. With another of the crew I ran to the engine room, but we could see nothing except steam. Then we heard cries of "Help!" coming from the "fiddley"—the engine room grating. We opened it and hauled up a stoker so badly scalded that as we pulled him up by his hands all the skin came off his fingers, but we managed to get him into a raft.'

The ship's confidential papers were dropped overboard and now the rest of her company hurried to leave the quickly dying *Lord Austin*. Just before she struck the mine, George Edwards had gone below to make an adjustment to the asdic gear, and on passing through the messdeck had noticed his lifebelt hanging over his bunk. Normally he did not bother to wear it on the bridge, but this time without thinking he took it and put it on. This action undoubtedly saved his life later, as he could not swim. After jumping into the sea he struggled on until an officer thrust him a piece of board, on to which he and another man clung as the ship started to go down.

Lieutenant Robinson was the last to leave the ship. 'I carefully took off my shoes, they were nearly new and I hated losing them. I then went down to the sponson and did a swallow-dive. The group of us swimming together were anxious to get farther away as the ship was going down fast by the stern and we didn't want to be sucked down with her.'

After heeling to port, *Lord Austin* righted herself and heeled to starboard, then straightened up again and sank quickly stern first, bows up. There were two more explosions as she went down, possibly the boilers going up.

One seaman who could not swim, and was without his life-jacket, clung to a liferaft which was secured to the ship by a lanyard, and was dragged down with the ship to drown because he had no knife to cut the raft free.

As the ship sank, smooth and ladylike to the end, with scarcely a ripple, Edwards thought a mast would hit him and his companion on the plank, but it just missed them.

'Other men in the water were shouting to me to get away from the suction of the ship, but I *was* sucked down and could only see foam and bubbles as I fought to get to the surface. Suddenly I saw a clear picture before me of my wife and baby standing over my own grave. Then I got clear of the water, breathless.'

Seven of *Lord Austin's* company were lost. Her portly old chief engineman, the engineman and a stoker were either killed or trapped by the explosion; the other losses were two seamen, the assistant steward and the leading steward, who, still recovering from the back injury received in the gale, had been caught lying helplessly in his bunk. All the survivors were rescued within minutes by an American coastguard cutter, which later transferred them to *Northern Reward*. A number of injured were then passed to a destroyer, which in turn transferred the more seriously hurt to *Rodney*. Lieutenant Robinson:

'*Reward* was very good to us, fitted us up with survivors' clothing, dried our clothes, fed and consoled us, and had to carry on with her normal patrol in addition. *Rodney* sent across eighty loaves of bread in a whaler. During the morning we saw a "Mickey Mouse" motor minesweeper also blow up on a mine; when the smoke cleared there was nothing left, just pieces of wood. Later we passed the cruiser *Scylla* under tow. She, too, had struck a mine early in the morning, and although they got her home, her back was broken and that was the end of her.

'Eventually *Reward* transferred us to a Blue Funnel liner being used as an accommodation ship. Here I had a stand-up row with the naval lieutenant-commander who wanted to keep all our company aboard his ship as crew replacements. I told him I wanted us landed on the beaches and we'd find our own way home. In the end, after we had spent a night in the ship, he reluctantly had us put ashore.

'I walked along the beach until I saw an American tank landing ship with her ramp down, and asked the captain if he could give us a lift home. "Sure, skipper", he said—"hitch a ride with us". They were a very hospitable lot.

'We had one or two scares on the way back, and one in particular I wasn't likely to forget. Among my survivor's clothes I had been given a pair of combinations. These had a "trapdoor" in the stern which was very difficult to operate. At quite the wrong moment a mine went off rather close, and my nerves not being very steady I leapt out of the heads and arrived on deck in a considerable state of disarray. It was a long time before I was able to get back to a state of decency.

'On a more serious note, the ship was carrying some German

prisoners from the First Panzer Division, and during the night one of my petty officers came to me and suggested, quite soberly, that we should dispose of the prisoners—"Let's put the bastards over the side". He was not alone in his bitter feelings, which took some calming down. When your ship is sunk, and your shipmates with her, it can prove too much.'

They were landed near Southampton, Germans and all. The crew were then sent off to Lowestoft while the officers went to Portsmouth to report the sinking.

'Lord Austin was a fine, stout vessel, a wonderful seaboat. I had been in her for three years, we had experienced many adventures together and had got through safely. It was a terribly sad thing when she went below, because I loved her. Some fine men went down with her, too.'

All through the early landings and in the months afterwards, Patrol Service ships were involved in every describable operation and service at sea.

It fell to the old trawler *Ijuin* to help sweep in the combined British and American fleet to bombard Cherbourg. Signalman Stent: 'Our task completed, we prepared to lay off and watch the "real navy" do their stuff, but try as they might, the Germans refused to play. Every enticement was offered to the enemy shore gunners to open fire and so disclose their positions, but all to no avail. So the Admiral ordered our flotilla of sweepers to offer ourselves as bait, which we did, almost to the point of thumbing our noses. The poor German gunners, their patience exhausted, let fly at us at last, the cruisers and battleships replied, and there we were, caught in the middle of a king-sized duel. Our flotilla leader hoisted "Retire independently" and retire we did; the *Ijuin*, her ancient engines leaking steam from every pore, lifted her skirts and rapidly fled the scene with a bow-wave like a destroyer, closely followed and sometimes overtaken by very large H.E. shells, which happily all missed. We were told afterwards that we'd clocked nearly 12 knots!

'We then had a grandstand view as our naval gunners proceeded to show our American cousins how to reduce shore defences to rubble.'

BYMS 2188 arrived at Cherbourg to suffer a surprise blast of shells from the one remaining fort, which the U.S. army had said was cleared. Chief Petty Officer Davies: 'Next day the fort was in rubble, thanks to the work of RAF Tempests, and the job of clearing Cherbourg harbour began. Every night the Germans would mine the entrance, and next day our flotilla would go out and clear it. For three days the body of an American soldier face down in the water, floated back and forth on the tide inside the breakwater; as it floated past us yet again, an ironic voice would call out "Hi, Joe!" The body was eventually recovered and I trust laid in peace somewhere in the Cherbourg Peninsula.'

The little *Fisher Boy* earned further honours at Cherbourg. When a bargeload of mines was sunk at the entrance to the harbour she anchored over it and recovered the mines, so re-opening up the harbour. Later she went up one of the German rivers, where various forms of obstacles had been sunk or moored, and cleared the lot.

In late July the Harry Tates suffered a heavy loss when the trawler *Lord Wakefield* was bombed and sunk by German aircraft while working off Normandy. Twenty-six of her company were lost, including her commander, a skipper-lieutenant, and two skippers.

Then came the battle for the River Scheldt, with small motor minesweepers doing excellent work as part of a large force which sailed for Walcheren Island, the key to the Scheldt. It was vital to clear the river to Antwerp to allow the supply ships to get right in behind the advancing armies. Chief Petty Officer Davies:

'In the early dawn our fleet of sweepers under the guidance of the base ship, *St Tudno*, hove-to and waited for the *Warspite* and *Black Prince* to finish their pounding of the town of Flushing. When they had spent their deadly cargo and came speeding out, their massive black shapes made us feel rather proud and patriotic, and at the same time made our small wooden ships seem very insignificant, until word was spread that *Warspite* had made the signal: "My part was easy, yours is vital, good luck and God speed."

'Our objective was to get to Terneuzen and Breskens, which were in British hands, on the other side of the estuary from Walcheren, but we only managed to stream sweeps and get a couple of mines before it was realized the Germans were far from finished at Flushing—they let us know of their presence in no uncertain manner. Word was sent to Army headquarters to bring fire to bear on the town to enable our fleet to make a dash for the harbour, such as it was, of Terneuzen. We made it, though not without casualties on some of the ships. Then came a waiting period while the Marine commandos went across and stormed the fortress-like wall of Flushing, and the RAF, with Dutch approval, blasted the dyke and flooded the island. After this our work began without interference and we cleared the Scheldt from Flushing right into Antwerp with the loss of only three ships, a small price to pay when reckoned against the sight of the big merchantmen immediately sailing up with urgent supplies.'

On November 29 1944 a special signal from General Eisenhower congratulated the minesweepers on the successful conclusion of the operation to open up the Scheldt and the arrival of the first convoy at Antwerp. . . . 'The work has been completed in the face of adverse weather conditions in almost a week less than the estimated time, which reflects great credit on all concerned.'

Chief Davies: 'For us, it was a case of well, the job's finished, how about a run ashore to see what the girls are like? We did not mean to be unsympathetic or uncaring for the casualties; we weren't tough, we were scared and alive, and so our relief took this form.

'There was an amusing experience involving our petty officer engineman. During the brief visit ashore in Terneuzen he found himself a lady friend who was married, and was caught by the husband's unexpected return. On being chased out of the house he was told in broken English to the effect: "I don't mind you sleeping with my wife, but leave your shoes on the doorstep like any good Dutchman." '

One of the Mickey Mouse sweepers which helped in the Scheldt operation was MMS 44. Afterwards she went on to Ijmuiden, where the Germans were still around. Cook Scadeng: 'The watch ashore found an abandoned German officers' canteen with its well stocked wine and spirit cellar, and came back very, very drunk.

'In a few days Captain Hopper arrived in St Tudno, the base vessel, to demonstrate that he, too, could take a leading part in the mopping-up activities. Together with the commander of the Canadians he arranged a drumhead service and the troops of a Scottish regiment beat a retreat on the jetty. All this was to impress the Germans, who were being marched off in their thousands, disarmed and disillusioned.

'After Ijmuiden we were based in Amsterdam. Captain Hopper promised us leave for Christmas, and just before we sailed, our number one, Sub-Lieutenant "Lucky" French, came to me to discuss Christmas dinner. He had some inside information which resulted in he and I going ashore to bargain with a local small-holder for a couple of geese in exchange for a carton of duty free cigarettes. Our Sparks and a seaman volunteered to pluck the geese on the way over and stowed themselves away in the ship's small air-raid shelter to do the job.

'It was a lovely sight as we made for home, the *St Tudno* steam-ing ahead with her two minesweeping flotillas following in two single lines astern, reminding us of a big swan with her cygnets trailing behind. Halfway across the Channel Captain Hopper made the signal "Leave to one watch from the day before Christmas", and everyone cheered up immensely. It was a bright day but with a stiff breeze blowing. I peeped into the air-raid shelter to see how the two lads were getting on with their plucking and was astonished at the pile of white feathers they'd made, they were standing in them up to their waists. They wouldn't be long, they said. The fleet sailed on for another half an hour, when suddenly the pluckers opened the shelter door. The breeze caught the feathers and soon the whole fleet of sweepers was steaming through what looked like a snowstorm, a beautiful sight. Our skipper nearly blew his top.'

Christmas for others was spent at the rear of the big push into Europe. *Clythness* arrived at a small village about twenty miles upriver from Brest, where she worked completely on her own for the next three months. After carrying oil for the invasion her tanks had been cleaned out and now she resumed her earlier role of water-carrier, taking fresh water to the American ships in Brest harbour. Seaman Thomas: 'Brest was a shambles, all the water-mains broken and the town in ruins, the nearest quay with fresh water being the small village of St Nicholas, where we used to load up. During this period we were isolated from all contact with the Navy and hadn't been paid for weeks.'

All the ship's company enjoyed some very lively nights ashore—especially the skipper.

'One night he returned aboard and found no quartermaster on duty to welcome him. From the messdeck he sent a search party to find the erring seaman. A blank being drawn in the galley and stokehold, the favourite places for a quartermaster on a cold night, he left a message that if the miscreant hadn't fallen overboard he would deal with him in morning. A new quartermaster was appointed and he helped the skipper to his quarters, switched on the light and disclosed the missing man sound asleep in the skipper's armchair, an empty bottle of the skipper's whisky by his side.' Next day the skipper had forgotten the whole incident.

Bartering occupied the attention of many of the Harry Tate crews at this time, as indeed it did the rest of the Forces. Like on one old minesweeping trawler from Dover, as told by her gunner.

'We had to go across to sweep off Dunkirk and the French coast, operating from Calais and Boulogne, returning every fortnight to Dover for stores. In Dover we spent all our fortnight's pay on cocoa or anything that would sell in the black market and in this way earned thousands of francs, which enabled us to live it up well over there. Then we were offered English pound notes for English tea, and as I was friendly with the steward we were able to pull off this deal, only to discover on our way back that the notes were all counterfeit. However, on going ashore in Dover we took a trip on several buses and to quite a number of pubs, and changed the lot.

'Another time we were not so lucky. We spent our fortnight's pay on cocoa, ready to go back to France. Then the ship broke down on her way across and had to be towed back. After repairs we were told we were going to Plymouth, so there we were with all that cocoa and no ready money. It was mid-evening. We collected all our kitbags containing the cocoa, knocked up all the shopkeepers and asked them to buy it back. They did so—after all, we had been good customers. We then had a good drink and went off back to the ship, only to be told that our orders had changed again and we were leaving for France after all. . . .'

In the Mediterranean in 1944 it was the same story of trawlers, drifters and motor minesweepers assisting in almost every operation as the tide of war turned heavily in favour of the Allies.

One 'invasion' with a difference was that of a trawler group which swept the channel into Heraklion, Crete, and were the first ships to enter harbour there. This was in late November. The group, led by the trawler *Staffa*, was a mixed force of six trawlers and whalers, two motor minesweepers, two motor launches and a dan-layer. Crete was still largely in the hands of the Germans and when the sweepers' senior officer, Lieutenant-Commander Geoffrey Syrett, RNVR, went ashore with two other officers he entered a cafe which, the proprietor told him, was frequented by the local German commander, who was very fond of a game of chess. However, Commander Syrett decided that such a meeting might not be quite the most suitable way of ending the war in that locality, and he did not stop to meet the German.

In mid-December there followed off Northern Italy a unique action in which a group of trawlers, so accustomed to taking the defensive role, were actually used as an attacking force against an enemy convoy. The action took place north-west of Spezia, and became known as the Battle of Mesco Point. One of the five trawlers involved was *Hornpipe*, whose number one was Lieutenant Dormer.

'Earlier in 1944 our trawler group had moved up to Leghorn, south of Pisa, as soon as it was taken, and spent a very dull period doing patrols off the harbour and to seaward of the front, which became static a few miles north. There was little or no enemy activity at sea, though the Germans were running coastal convoys from Genoa to Spezia. British and American coastal forces attacked these regularly, but had trouble with the very heavily armed German flak-lighters.

'One night Lieutenant-Commander W. B. T. Bate, RNVR, our senior officer, in *Minuet*, was on the northernmost patrol when he intercepted a signal from an aircraft that an enemy convoy of four barges was approaching Spezia. Being always a very enthusiastic warrior he requested permission to leave his patrol and attack, but was, of course, refused. Strangely enough, that same night I dreamed of *Hornpipe* attacking an enemy convoy. As, up till then, no one had ever thought of trawlers doing such a thing, this seemed an odd coincidence, but months later, in December, the operation was at last laid on.

'After a preliminary sweep to clear and mark a passage through the enemy's offshore minefield our five trawlers—*Hornpipe, Minuet, Twostep, Ailsa Craig* and *Gulland*—plus a number of motor torpedo boats were to waylay an enemy convoy. The trawlers were to engage with gunfire at long range, to distract attention, while the MTBs attacked. The RAF wanted to join in too, by firing the coastal forest and silhouetting the enemy against the flames. But the Navy had little enthusiasm for this idea, as I'm afraid we thought they'd be just as likely to bomb us too.

'In the event the MTBs didn't carry out their torpedo attack, though Commander Allen, senior officer of the Inshore Squadron, controlled the whole affair with his high-class radar.

'Before the operation we had an intensive work-up in which we learned to keep station in line ahead at 50-yard intervals, which was not easy. I, as first lieutenant, handled *Hornpipe* throughout, leaving the C.O. (Lieutenant-Commander H. D. Legh, RNR) free to look at the wider picture. The effort of station-keeping was so intense that I hardly had time to be frightened, and rarely to look round.'

Lieutenant Dormer wrote the following account of the battle on *Hornpipe's* way home afterwards.

'Just after dark we arrived off the enemy coast, met our coastal forces and stooged slowly in. Suddenly starshell burst just short of us, and we had a nervous half-hour while the German shore batteries searched and searched. It was eerie, shells whistling over us, gun-flashes along the coast, and starshell all over the place. I don't think they saw us . . . at least, nothing solid came near. We heard asdic transmissions, and thought an enemy force had come out to intercept, but they kept away. We closed the coast to about two miles and stooged around until 0200 hours. Several times there were false alarms, as our scouting MLs and MTBs made contacts.

'We had just about given up hope—I had long ago taken the cotton wool out of my ears and let the air out of my lifebelt. We were simply manoeuvring around at 50-yard intervals, everyone rather tired, bad tempered, and longing to go home. Then . . . ALARM GREEN 100. . . . "Oh, just another false one." But no. the range is given over the R/T . . . OPEN FIRE.

'The first salvoes of starshell, from the 12-pounders of *Ailsa Craig* and *Gulland*, stationed at each end of the line, burst short; nothing to be seen. Then . . . there they are . . . several low, beetle-like objects in the glare, with splashes rising among them as the four-inch guns of *Minuet, Twostep* and ourselves open fire. But stuff is coming back, bunches of gentle-looking tracer shells come sailing over to accelerate and pass with a whoosh, or splash in the sea alongside. The fire becomes heavy. One flak-lighter is pouring out so much muck that it looks like a bloody catherine wheel. Shells of all sizes, 88mm., 40mm., 20mm., even down to .303 or somesuch are whistling and splashing all around as shore batteries and land ack-ack sites join in.

'FULL-AHEAD . . . We had been going dead-slow, even astern . . . then "turn in succession straight towards the enemy." I thought it was a mistake—we are third in line and I am praying hard: "Our Father, which art" . . . steer two degrees to port. . . . "Hail Mary" . . . 45 revs . . . "God Almighty" . . . Whoosh, bang, crackle,

splash . . . the Bofors come in groups of five. One can tell pretty
well where they will land. Of one group three went over, two fell
short. *Ailsa Craig*, leading, pours a long burst of 20mm. into the
nearest small craft. The craft, actually an R-boat (German motor
launch) burst into flames, whereupon the Germans started pouring
tracer into it also. . . .

'We were steaming now at full speed straight for the shore.
Ailsa Craig yelped something over the R/T about being 800 yards
off. . . . RED 18. . . . Turn about together. . . . Maximum speed. . . .
Make smoke . . . off we go. Never have trawlers gone so fast, under
a blaze of enemy starshell, with heavy stuff from the shore batteries
splashing all around. A storm of red-hot splinters passes my face
from a near-miss to starboard.

'The C.O. had scarcely needed to say a word throughout. Now
he ordered me to steer for the shell splashes, to put the enemy
gunners off, but I was more worried about finding the gap in the
minefield and mutinously clung to the course provided by our DR
plot. Commander Allen was checking up. . . . "Report state, pup-
pies." "Titus O.K." "Harry O.K." "Jack injured, No. 1 in command." "Andy on fire aft, no casualties." And so on.

'At last we were out of range and by a miracle not hit. It only
remained to get the force into some sort of order and go home. We
thought the affair had been a complete failure, the gunners said
they had hardly been able to see their targets for the smoke and
glare, and we were tremendously surprised when Commander Allen
announced success—"A gallant and determined fight against heavy
odds" he called it in a signal. Apparently there were eight enemy
ships in all. Three of our trawlers had fired about 100 four-inch
rounds between them, the other two only providing illumination.
Our only casualty was the C.O. of *Twostep* (Lieutenant J. Nye,
RNR) who had his right arm broken by one of eight rounds which
hit their bridge. On *Hornpipe* we merely collected one hunk of
metal, just where I'd been standing.'

Away to the east at this time the trawler *Moonstone* was patrolling the Greek island of Corfu. On Christmas Eve in harbour
Moonstone wore a festive air, with home-made trimmings in place
and the galley stove working overtime; but what promised to be a
quiet Christmas was rudely interrupted. At 9 p.m., with her shore
party recalled, *Moonstone* steamed off in answer to an emergency
call from the Greek mainland, where civil war now raged, and in
the early hours of Christmas Day met up with two Greek ships

crowded with refugees. A pitiful avalanche of wounded, sick, cold, starved and malaria-ridden people clambered aboard the trawler. Seaman Albert Owen:

'Every inch of space in the old lady was taken up and, women and children sick down below, we set off on the return journey to Corfu. Our passengers' stomachs, through lack of food, must have felt like gaping wounds, but they still suffered from seasickness and everything was a mess and a shambles. As they began to recover, our Christmas fare became a story of forty loaves and fishes; all the food was given out and chocolate rations became the refugee children's presents as we played real Father Christmases in the most pathetic circumstances. We reached the island of Paxos at early light, and what a welcome we received; the inhabitants had a diet of what appeared to be dark bread dipped in the local ouzo, very potent. There was some wonderful singing that night in the local tavern.'

While on patrol in this area *Moonstone* was also successful in capturing a Greek vessel employed on smuggling guns and ammunition to the rebels. Her commander was a much-wanted man with a few murders behind him, and a grateful government official later visited *Moonstone*, shook hands with all, and presented medals to three members of the crew.

For another trawler, *Sheppey*, acting as dan-layer to a group of fleet sweepers working off Piraeus, life was neither so eventful nor so adventurous. In a largely monotonous routine, 'flogging' was the main occupation of the day. One of her crew: 'We flogged all sorts of gear to the Greeks—stores, ship's equipment, clothing, comforts. Someone got the equivalent of £7 for a pullover with a large burn hole in it; I got £14 for an old overcoat. When we went to sea afterwards we couldn't swing the smallboats out as all the ropes had been sold.'

No medals in this case; but that's how it was.

Meanwhile, away across in the Far East, a far flung group of little BYMS sweepers worked as industriously as their sisters in Europe. One of these craft was BYMS 2006, engaged on special duties with the Army during the campaign in Burma; in naval slang she was 'chaung hopping', doing any job along the Arakan, working the river and salt water inlets. Tough as her crew were, one special incident made them feel just a little queasy, as Petty Officer Coxswain Charles Ridsdale describes.

'After the landings at Myebon we were ordered to ferry troops

of the 25th Indian Division to Akyab. These were mainly men of
the Yorks-and-Lancs, Gurkhas, and some Punjabis, and by a
strange coincidence I found that one of the soldiers in the Yorks-
and-Lancs belonged to Hartlepool, as I did, and I knew him well.
He was a sergeant in Army intelligence.

'During the trip we nattered together for hours, and he introduced me to his "oppo", a corporal in the same regiment. This lad
looked a kind and gentle youth, something like my idea of a young
Mr Pickwick, but was actually a real tough nut. One evening, while
we were having a quiet smoke, my friend asked the corporal to show
me what was bulging his pocket out, and quite casually the corporal
withdrew a fairly big bundle wrapped in a filthy bloodstained rag.
When undone it proved to be full of gold teeth, which puzzled me
until my friend gave the grisly explanation. It appeared the corporal
always managed to have himself included in burial parties, especially
those of dead Japanese, and by some means arranged to leave a
marker where the body was buried—a hand or a foot protruding
from the soil. When the chance came he went back to the grave,
scraped the soil away, knocked the gold teeth out of the corpse's
jaw and added them to the store in his pocket.

'Months later, while in Singapore, I learned from a friend that
the corporal had made a considerable sum by selling the teeth to
Chinese dentists.'

17

Take My U-Boat

Northern Isles, a big and sturdy Grimsby trawler, had been among the first vessels of the Patrol Service to put to sea on the outbreak of war. The start of 1945 found her with a splendid, unblemished record of long years on the Northern Patrol, followed by escort and patrol work off the U.S. coast, and now, in South African waters, with two years' good work round those tropical coasts to her credit.

Good work, but monotonous work, such as steaming out of Durban on loop patrol, on which duty she was engaged on the morning of January 19 1945, working under the direction of the South African Navy. Because of the humdrum, largely unhurried nature of her job, *Northern Isles* would often fish. Telegraphist James Brown: 'We did this to help with our rations. We were on canteen messing; any money not spent at the end of the month was disbursed among the crew to augment our wages. Therefore the more fish we caught, the less food we had to buy, and the more beer money for the lads at the end of the month.'

So on the morning of the 19th, because the fish were close inshore, *Northern Isles* went in after them. She had three spinners and fishing tackle over the stern; the spinners belonged to the captain, which was not unusual as many trawler captains did their own share of fishing, it was a common practice. Unfortunately for *Northern Isles*, in her preoccupation with following the fish she ran on to the rocks at the Bluff. Telegraphist Brown: 'She struck the rocks at 9.45 a.m. As soon as it became obvious she was stuck fast, I wirelessed for tugs, but they could not budge her. The constant swell hindered matters and the tugs were scared to get too close to us in case they should suffer a similar fate and pile up alongside.

'When the tugs retired, the captain ordered all non-essential ratings to leave in the ship's two lifeboats, which left about a dozen of us remaining on board. I asked if we were likely to get any of our personal gear off, to which the captain replied, "You'll be bloody lucky to get off yourself!' For the ship was well and truly stuck, and heeled over at a steep angle.

'At 2 p.m. the signal station on the Bluff started flashing. I was now the only one on board who could read the light, my good friend the Bunts having conveniently decided he was non-essential and gone with the boats, so I had to make the difficult climb to the bridge and take the message. It was from the South African Navy, telling us to place ourselves under the orders of the Royal Navy forthwith. In other words, they wanted nothing further to do with us.

'When it was clear nothing could be done for the old *Northern Isles* the captain asked me to send for the lifeboats to come and take us off. This I did, and got the alarming reply that the sea was now too rough for them to risk coming alongside. Ever since we'd stuck, a party on the beach had been trying to fire rocket lines out to us, but the wind always blew the lines off course. We hadn't been paying much attention to their efforts, but with this development we started to take them much more seriously. Seaman Sandy Reid, one of the smattering of peacetime sailors found on most RNPS ships, tied all our heaving lines together, secured a lifebelt to one end and threw it over the side, letting it drift ashore successfully on the flowing tide. Under Sandy's expert guidance a breeches buoy was then made fast. Determined to save the best of my personal gear, I dressed in my number ones and took my seat in the breeches buoy looking more as if I was going on a long weekend from Sparrow's Nest rather than a dip in the Indian Ocean. Our wise Chief, Jock Cowie, put his watch in a Durex and tied a knot in the neck before taking to the breeches buoy. I had a waterproof watch and so I didn't bother. But when we got ashore my watch had stopped, while Jock's cheap ten-bob effort was still going strong.

'After we'd dried ourselves out we were taken to a camp along the front at Durban. About 4 a.m., the unearthly hour when the continuous Durban swell was at its quietest, I was awakened with some other men and we set out in the ship's whaler under the command of the captain, in an attempt to get back on board. But the sea was still too rough and the attempt had to be abandoned.

'Our confidential code books had been put in weighted bags and cast over the side as per pusser's procedure, but to our mortification one of the bags was cast up on Durban beach. The swell got the blame, but our crew was promptly organized to mount a 24-hour watch along the beach. We didn't find anything more and the watch was only just called off in time before some of the wilder sparks planned to get back on board via the breeches buoy to recover the contents of the ship's spirit locker.'

At separate courts-martial the captain of *Northern Isles* and the officer of the watch were found guilty of negligence and received sentences which included each to be 'dismissed his ship'. As *Northern Isles* had, in the meantime, died miserably in sight of shore, the formal naval language seemed ironic.

As for Telegraphist Brown, he managed to wangle himself aboard the trawler of his choice, *Le Tiger*, famous for her killing of a U-boat off the U.S. coast, but at this time more noted for a special survivor she had snatched from the sea. A bitch called Pruddie.

'*Le Tiger* picked her up from a piece of wreckage in mid-Atlantic. A survivor from some torpedoed ship, she adopted *Le Tiger* and some wit christened her Pruddie. I say wit because she was anything but prudent, being almost constantly in whelp. When the South African newspapers got to hear about Pruddie's adventure, they pestered us all for the details. This was at rum time, and some of the accounts given the reporters were pretty lurid. One had the rescue taking place in the midst of a howling gale, with the captain calling for volunteers and the crew stepping forward to a man! There must have been some red faces in the Durban newspaper offices next day when the highly-coloured and conflicting reports appeared.

'When Pruddie had pups she would allow no one on board who was not crew. One day our group commander came down to inspect us. We were lined up on deck and the old boy was stepping down on deck with his hand up at the salute, when Pruddie dashed out of the foc'sle and sunk her fangs into his well-fed calf. For a second or two we didn't know what to do, and simply stood to attention as the commander hopped about the deck with Pruddie hanging on like a limpet. Then a seaman, who was Pruddie's special favourite, broke ranks and persuaded her to relinquish her grip.'

The loss of *Northern Isles* coincided with other melancholy losses among trawlers and drifters early in 1945. *Golden West*, foundered off Aberdeen, *Computator*, lost by collision off Normandy, and *High Tide*, foundered off the Welsh coast. Mines too, continued to claim their toll, from the *Arley*, mined in the North Sea, to the *Treern*, which went down thousands of miles away off Greece. And four vessels were torpedoed by U-boats. *Haybourne Wyke* and *Ellesmere* both fell victims in the Channel, while *Nordhav 11* was torpedoed off Dundee, and the whaler *Southern Flower* plunged to the bottom off Iceland.

On March 3 1945, the day *Southern Flower* died, the patrolling *Northern Sun* was detached and ordered to an area south of Reykjavik to hunt the whaler's killer, though without success. Lieutenant Geoffrey Howarth:

'*Southern Flower's* Skipper Brown was a great friend and frequent visitor to our wardroom. He was a quiet, inoffensive little man, completely opposite to the usual run of skippers, and out of uniform could easily have passed as a country parson. Our information was that *Flower* had gone down in seconds and there was only one survivor. We learned on returning to port that it was Brown. Sitting up in bed in hospital he was a very sad man and extremely lucky to be alive. He told us he was leaning out of the bridge window when the ship was hit, and as she went down beneath him, miraculously he was sucked to the surface and saved.'

Northern Sun had recently come through a very rough round of 'met' reporting trips in the middle of the winter-bound Atlantic. Trawlers given this duty spent three weeks on station, which in the rigorous weather conditions was a daily nightmare. Only when two Wallasey-based trawlers limped back to base having burned their mess furniture to keep up steam was the stint shortened. Lieutenant Howarth:

'On one occasion we knew that two U-boats were engaged on similar work in the same area. I was on watch when the wireless operator handed me an immediate priority message from the Admiralty, which said they had intercepted a U-boat transmission to Bremerhaven in which our sighting had been reported. Weighing up our chances we thought it likely that the Germans' own met reporting would be considered more important than risking a brush with us, and so it turned out, for we saw nothing of them.'

Another winter adventure of *Northern Sun* happened when she was ordered to take over the escort of an auxiliary floating dock, off the south coast of Iceland. The dock, built in the U.S., was intended for the war in the Far East, and *Northern Sun's* job was to escort it to Gibraltar, on the second stage of its trip across the world. An earlier attempt to get one of these huge docks across the South Atlantic had ended in disaster when the well escorted convoy, which included an armed merchant cruiser, was attacked by U-boats. The

dock broke its back and was lost. And so, because of the desperate
need for a floating dock in the Far East, the Admiralty had decided
to risk the next one in the North Atlantic in wintertime. AFD 17
reached Iceland safely but then hit bad weather, and the tow broke.
The dock wallowed around for days but amazingly stayed afloat.
Lieutenant Howarth :

'We met it off the south of Iceland and relieved the escorts,
which were low on fuel. The two ocean-going tugs also needed to
refuel, so they detached in turn to go to Falmouth for oil. While only
one tug had the tow, no progress was made and the most that could
be done was to keep the dock head to sea. It was the best part of a
week before the double-tow was resumed and seventeen days later
we reached Gibraltar, having taken well over a week to get through
the Bay of Biscay. The most serious mistake we made was in joining
the T. 124-crewed tugs at a celebration party on the Rock; it was
surprising the length of time it took the bloodstream to absorb a
mixture of Export Guinness and port."

After the casualties among Patrol Service vessels in the early
months of 1945, April was a quiet period. Though there was no let-
up in duties at sea, the war in Europe was coming to a close. When,
on the last day of April, Hitler committed suicide, Germany's unconditional surrender was only days away.

Berlin surrendered to the Russians on May 2nd. That day also
saw the last loss in action among the Patrol Service ships operating
in home waters. The minesweeping trawler *Ebor Wyke* was working off the east coast of Iceland when she was attacked by an E-
boat, torpedoed and sunk. Only one man survived; a particularly
grim loss considering that it was all over less than a week later.

In these last days of hostilities trawlers were still showing their
teeth against the U-boats. *Arab*, the VC veteran of the Norwegian
campaign so long ago, made a U-boat contact off the Minch and
steamed in to attack, but a depth-charge went off on the surface,
breaking just about every pipe in her engine room. She was towed
into Tobermory by one of the destroyers on work-up there, arriving
in the early hours of the night to be greeted typically by the fiery
'Monkey Brand' Stephenson firing dozens of snowflakes to light up
the harbour while a tug took her to a buoy. By the time *Arab* was
repaired the war in Europe was over.

What must have been virtually the last attack on a U-boat was
that made by *Northern Spray*. It happened off Garosskagi, a

promontory in the approaches to Reykjavik, and the awful place on which ships would try to make a landfall on the way in, if the compass did not spin off by up to 25 degrees because of magnetic variation. Commanding *Northern Spray* was Lieutenant Geoffrey Thorpe.

'I was senior officer of the escort force based on Reykjavik, escorting in a small homebound convoy including a tanker, the *Empire Unity*, when we were attacked just off Garosskagi. The tanker was hit and the crew abandoned ship.

'*Spray* was astern of the convoy when we sighted the U-boat's periscope only a cable away. We went hard over and full-ahead and dropped a shallow-set pattern of depth-charges. We must have been close, as we subsequently found we were without our asdic dome—it had presumably been knocked off by the U-boat's conning tower or wire cutter. We never heard what finally happened to that U-boat, as the end of the war in Europe was declared the next day.

'We picked up a boat containing *Empire Unity's* chief engineer. He told us that the tanker's engines were all right as he had actually stopped them, so we decided to re-board the derelict; her captain and deck officers had been picked up by another trawler and were already on their way to the U.K. I put our coxswain and a small boarding party aboard the tanker, plus her chief engineer and some of her engine crew. In minutes she was under way and we successfully took her in and anchored her at Hvalfiord.

'Full of hope we slapped in a salvage claim, assessing the ship and cargo at £2 million! Unfortunately, due to some technicality the ship was said to be owned by the Ministry of War Transport, and all we got was fourteen days' pay. My coxswain got the BEM and I got a Mention in Despatches, but I often thought of the £2 million that got away. I didn't understand at the time why *Empire Unity's* crew had abandoned so quickly, but I learned later she either carried aviation gas, or had carried it immediately before, and they obviously expected the ship to go up. We, in our youthful ignorance, knew no better.'

Up on the north coast of Scotland, off Loch Erriboll, Skipper-Commander Billy Mullender, DSC, was finishing the war as he had begun it, on the bridge of an asdic trawler. He was steaming *Stella Canopus* on patrol when suddenly a U-boat surfaced not far off. Mullender boldly turned to the attack. The trawler's guns were swiftly manned and they had a shell in the breech when, to their skipper's surprise, the U-boat hoisted a black flag of surrender. Mullender steamed alongside and ordered the U-boat commander to hand over his sextant and chronometer. 'But captain,' protested the German commander, 'I am giving you the whole ship!'

It was the day of Germany's surrender and Mullender didn't know it. *Stella Canopus*, however, was cheated of her final glory. Before Mullender could take the U-boat in, an armed yacht with a senior officer on board raced up and took possession of the prize.

Now followed the mass surrenders at sea, and to the trawler *Guardsman*, which had been on west coast convoy duty, came a signal honour: she was ordered to the Kyle of Lochalsh to represent Western Approaches trawlers in an escort of the first surrendered U-boats to arrive. On reaching Lochalsh, *Guardsman* found representative destroyers, sloops, frigates and corvettes already gathered round four U-boats, and next morning the convoy sailed for Londonderry. But, shades of Harry Tate to the last, because of her slower speed, slower even than the U-boats, *Guardsman* was soon left miserably behind and, losing the convoy altogether, turned despondently for Greenock. A little later she did actually escort a big U-boat on a short voyage, and her best moment, representing the asdic trawlers, came when in Wallasey Dock she stood alongside a U-boat placed on view to the people of Liverpool and Birkenhead. The sight of the German, and the kind of vessel that had helped to hunt such killers for nearly six years, was an eye-opener. Then away went *Guardsman* to Devonport, to join trawlers coming in from all parts of the world to tie up at buoys below Saltash bridge.

Just what they had been up against in their counterparts in the enemy fleet came home to the Harry Tate crews who assisted in rounding up the German armed trawlers. For the trawler *Skomer* it was a proud moment when she took possession of the surrendered German minesweeping flotilla based at Jersey. The German crews brought their ships to within ten miles of Plymouth under Royal Marine escort, then a British officer and signalman took over each ship to bring her into Plymouth harbour. The resplendent trawler which *Skomer's* captain and her signalman K. N. Williams took over was a stunner. Signalman Williams:

'When *Skomer*, being a coal-burner, was at full-ahead we could rely on 12 knots with a fair sea. So when my C.O. gave the order for full-ahead on the German trawler you can imagine his feelings and mine when the stern went down and the bow came up like a motor launch. As for armament, she had some kind of rocket-firing equipment right on the bow, a four-inch quick-firing gun on the foredeck and numerous machine-guns all over her. On her funnel were the silhouettes of various RAF aircraft.

'To negotiate the boom defence at Plymouth we had to stop the trawler's powerful diesel engines and proceed by trial and error. Meanwhile the people of Plymouth and Devonport had learned of our approach and collected all along the cliff walks and quays to cheer us in—a very proud moment indeed.

'For a time, *Skomer* helped to escort German prisoners-of-war from Jersey via LCTs, and we spent some time ashore viewing their defences and the huge camouflaged naval guns sited on top of the highest hill. These guns were at least 16-inchers, but I don't think they were ever fired. On Jersey we were able to buy creme-de-menthe by the glassful for sixpence, for there was nothing else available in the way of food or drink. The inhabitants were living on rats, cats, or anything that moved in the animal world, and we were offered carrots as sweets! There was a woman on the island whose husband, the authorities discovered, had been an inmate of the notorious Belsen concentration camp. We had the glad task of bringing her to the U.K. to be with her husband again.'

In September came the Japanese surrender, but even yet it was not all over. The Patrol Service's last three trawlers were lost in October 1945, ending an eventful summer of further casualties from mines, collisions and bad weather in the minesweeping operations that had to be continued in the wake of victory.

When the last entry was made, Harry Tate's Navy had lost well over 400 trawlers, drifters and whalers, while the casualties among other RNPS-manned craft including motor minesweepers, motor fishing vessels, BYMS sweepers, armed yachts and small auxiliary vessels took the total to almost 500.

They were losses far in excess of those of any other branch of the Royal Navy, and were actually more than the combined losses of destroyers, sloops, corvettes, frigates, fleet sweepers, motor torpedo boats and motor gunboats

No Grave But The Sea

On a June day in 1946 Lieutenant Roger Geary-Hill, RNVR, commander of the trawler *Staffa* at war's end, put on his wartime uniform again and caught a train for Leiston, Suffolk. He took with him the flag of Admiral Cunningham, Commander-in-Chief Mediterranean, which *Staffa* had flown for four days at Algiers in 1943. *Staffa* had now been sold to the depleted Italian Navy; Geary-Hill had taken the flag which hung in her wardroom and decided the best home for it would be Leiston, in appreciation of the town's generosity in adopting *Staffa*, whose three-inch gun had been made in a local factory. So, with permission from the Admiral and the Admiralty, he presented the flag, and copies of signals, to the assembled town council.

Some other Admiralty-built trawlers like *Staffa* went into service with the Italian and other foreign navies; many more were sold for mercantile use. As for the requisitioned fishing vessels, most were stripped of their guns, asdic and sweeping gear, refitted, given back their trawls and returned to their peacetime owners. And Harry Tate's Navy was no more.

At Sparrow's Nest the White Ensign was lowered. The sentries vanished from the gates, the wartime buildings were removed or altered, and grass began to grow on the lawn again. The seats went back into the concert hall and the first seaside show returned. Across at the Oval, the training huts were dismantled, and they began to think again of cricket.

When all the naval trappings had gone from the town the Royal Naval Patrol Service might never have existed, except for the new addition to the landscape made in 1953. This was a memorial, a tall, fluted column, topped by a bronze ship, erected high above Sparrow's Nest with a clear view out to the grey North Sea. It was unveiled by the First Sea Lord, revealing seventeen bronze panels set in its broad circular base, bearing the names of 2,385 officers and men of the Royal Naval Patrol Service aged from sixteen to the late sixties, fathers, sons, brothers, cousins, who died in the service of their country and found 'no grave but the sea.'

So it stands today, in the busy little fishing port where traffic still stops in the main street while trawlers sail across it, through a retracting bridge. This memorial, and some wooden panels listing men and ships, set in the interior walls of the concert hall, are all that remain to show that 'Harry Tate's Navy was here.'

Holidaymakers loll in their deckchairs in the summers at Sparrow's Nest, the flower-beds a mass of colour and the turf evergreen. But to many men who revisit it with their families, men in possession of a somewhat worn silver badge about the size of a shilling, the scene reverts in fresh memory to one of bare earth flattened by the marching and trampling of a million feet, while once again the air is punctuated by the raucous voice of the loudspeakers issuing a constant stream of commands. . . . 'Attention—D'ye hear there? —The following ratings report to the Drafting Master-at-Arms— Men under punishment to muster on the stage—All ratings who have rejoined the depot and not passed the doctor, fall in on the roadway outside the concert hall at once—By the right, men of the Royal Naval Patrol Service quick march!'

For such visitors, to stand at the base of the memorial in Belle Vue Park and read the long register of names, is to think of those men, as with kit-bags over their shoulders, they piled into the lorries for Lowestoft station, bound for destinations all over Britain to join the small ships in home waters, or take passage for the Patrol Service bases in the Mediterranean, Africa and the Far East, never to return.

Harry Tate's Navy had its shortcomings and its frustrations, and was bloody-minded to the end. It also had a special brand of determination and sheer guts.

It is remembered with pride.

Acknowledgments

The authors gratefully acknowledge the generous help given to this book by officers and men of the Royal Naval Patrol Service, the Royal Naval Reserve, the Royal Naval Volunteer Reserve, and the Royal Navy. In particular they thank the following for their valuable contributions :

Seaman George A. Adams.
Lieutenant G. James Allen, RNR.
Lieutenant-Commander Stanley F. Archer, RNR.

Telegraphist Eric H. Bardsley.
Chief Engineman George R. Beasley.
Lieutenant-Commander F. N. Bentley, RNVR.
Leading-Telegraphist A. Blakeburn.
Lieutenant Ralph Boddis, RNVR.
Lieutenant Colin F. Brown, RNVR.
Telegraphist James Brown.
Seaman Patrick Bryant.
Seaman Norman Burgoyne.
P.O. Telegraphist Thomas E. Burn.

P.O. Edmund Carroll.
Captain R. V. E. Case, DSO, DSC, RD, RNR.
Leading-Seaman T. A. Charge, RN.
Lieutenant Peter H. Clarke, RNVR.
Coder Jack S. Clegg.
Lieutenant Leslie Clements, RNVR.

Chief P.O. William J. Davies, RNR.
Lieutenant-Commander Geoffrey Dormer, RNR.
Surgeon-Lieutenant Allan Douglas, RNVR.

T.O. Telegraphist E. F. J. Edards.
P.O. George Edwards.
Skipper-Lieutenant W. G. 'Billy' Euston, RNR.

Engineman Douglas Finney.
Seaman (SD) Leslie Forster.
Lieutenant-Commander S. G. 'Jim' Fowler, RNVR.

Lieutenant Rupert L. Garratt, RNVR.
Lieutenant Commander Roger M. Geary-Hill, RNR.
Seaman-Gunner Lionel Gordon Gray.

Lieutenant A. L. Hargraves, RANVR.
Lieutenant-Commander Bryan W. Harris, RNVR.
Commander Guy Harris, OBE, RN.
Hon. Lieutenant-Commander John E. Harwood (QC), RD, RNR.
Acting Leading-Signalman Frederick Hazell.
Leading-Signalman Gordon Hooper.
Lieutenant J. B. Hornby, RNVR.
Lieutenant Geoffrey R. Howarth, RNVR.
Telegraphist Fred H. Howson.

P.O. Coxswain Sid A. Kerslake, RNR.

Lieutenant-Commander Stanley W. Lock, RNVR.
Seaman-Gunner G. R. Lunn.

Leading-Seaman Harold McCall.
Chief Engineman John P. Mair, RNR.
Lieutenant H. G. F. Male, RNVR.
Leading-Seaman Arthur W. Mallett.
Lieutenant Arthur H. G. Miles, RNVR.
T.O. Telegraphist J. A. Mitchell.
P.O. Robert H. Muir.
Commander William J. O. Mullender, MBE, DSC, RD, RNR.
Lieutenant T* John Oakey, RNVR.
Seaman Albert Owen.

P.O. John S. Paterson.

Leading-Seaman J. P. Rampling, PSGL.
Lieutenant-Commander James G. Reeve, RNVR.
P.O. Coxswain Charles Ridsdale.
Cook William Riley.
Lieutenant E. S. Terence Robinson, RNVR.

Leading-Cook F. J. Scadeng.
Signalman L. B. Smith
Leading-Seaman Coxswain Raymond Smith.
RDF Rating T. Roy Sparkes.
Signalman Leonard Stent.
Chief P.O. Amos W. Sumner.

Seaman Robert Thomas.
Lieutenant-Commander Geoffrey Thorpe, RNVR.
Skipper-Lieutenant William H. Thorpe, RNR.

Leading-Seaman S. D. Varley.

P.O. Engineman Walter Walker.
Lieutenant-Commander Allan Lansley Waller, VRD, RNR.
Seaman James Waterson.
Lieutenant-Commander E. Leslie Wathen, DSC, RNR.
Lieutenant-Commander Richard F. Wattam-Bell, RNVR.
Chief-Skipper Sidney A. White, DSC, RNR.
Signalman K. N. Williams.
Leading-Coder David Willing.
Signalman E. Neville Wilson.

Leading-Seaman Coxswain Ernest Claude 'Lofty' Yallop.

The authors thank Mrs Jean de Pass, wife of the late Captain Daniel de Pass, CBE, RN (Commodore of the RNPS, Lowestoft, 1940–44) for kind assistance with information; Mrs Frieda Shillan, wife of the late Lieutenant-Commander A. A. Shillan, RNVR; Lieutenant T* John Oakey, RNVR, Secretary of the Irwell Association, and Lieutenant-Commander E. B. West, RNVR, VRD (and Bar), for providing the official Scrapbook of the Association; Mrs Hilda Mothershaw (Wren Hilda Ralph); Fireman Joseph Willis, Merchant Navy; Mr David A. J. Pugh; Northern Trawlers Ltd., Grimsby; together with the *Grimsby Evening Telegraph*, *Eastern Daily Press*, *Hull Daily Mail*, and many newspapers which kindly helped in the search for 'Sparrows' from the Nest.

Index

NIGHT OF THE U-BOATS

NIGHT
OF THE
U-BOATS

by

PAUL LUND
and
HARRY LUDLAM

LONDON
W. FOULSHAM & CO. LTD
NEW YORK   TORONTO   SYDNEY

W. FOULSHAM & CO. LTD.
Yeovil Road, Slough, England

SC7 was one of many convoys to sail the North Atlantic. This book is written to the memory of them all, and the men who sailed and escorted them.

Of the events that have taken place during the last few hours of this 'Black Friday' I will write again if we are spared to get through this next day and night. Suffice to say at present that I was never so glad and thankful that during these months I have been back at sea I have each day said my prayers as I have been in the habit of at home. I am sure that during the last twenty-four hours only something higher than any good fortune has enabled us to be still sailing on this Saturday morning. For which fact I shall always return thanks.

— From the shipboard diary
of Radio Officer Kenneth
Howell, ss. *Corinthic*;
dawn, October 19th, 1940.

CONTENTS

Introduction

The Darkest Days

OCTOBER, 1940. In this fourteenth month of the war with Germany, Britain stood alone with her back to the wall. After a winter of 'phoney war' the year had seen disaster after disaster. The withdrawal from Norway. The fall of Denmark, Holland, and Belgium. The evacuation from Dunkirk and the capitulation of France, followed by Mussolini's entry into the war on the side of Hitler. Day by day, the rolling tide of Nazism had spread over the newspaper maps of Europe like some great black evil blot.

Young men had gone fresh to Norway and France and returned disillusioned, though not beaten, veterans. The carefree notes of the popular song 'We're Going To Hang Out The Washing On The Siegfried Line' had gone sour.

Now, invasion of England by the Germans seemed inevitable.

The first enemy onslaught in the skies had been beaten off gloriously by the RAF in the Battle of Britain, but now hordes of German bombers were coming nightly, as many as a thousand planes at a time. In London, where on some nights bombs fell every few minutes, the sky raged red from the glare of burning buildings. Stabbing fingers of criss-crossing searchlights sought the deep droning high flying bombers; there was the thump-thump-thump of anti-aircraft guns and the whistle of bombs; explosions, alarms and cries, and shrapnel hissing down in the streets.

At this time of crisis people anxiously scanned the newspapers and listened for the news on the BBC, sturdy reliable voice in a tumbling world. The communiques, coming between such reassuring programmes as 'Hi Gang', 'Thanking Yew!' and Sandy Macpherson at the organ, were grim. They were days of 'Music While You Work' and nights of misery, death and stubborn heroism. By the end of September, the month in which the great bombing Blitz began, seventeen thousand men, women and children had been killed or seriously injured in the savage air-raids. In bleak October the casualties continued to rise.

Above it all, despite the constant hammering of enemy Channel ports by the RAF, hung the dark cloud of imminent invasion. Churchill frankly admitted to the nation that Germany had ships and barges ready to transport an army of half a million men to the beaches of Britain—if they could make the crossing. 'We are waiting,' he said pugnaciously. 'So are the fishes.'

Also waiting were a thousand British fighting ships of all descriptions, some three hundred of which were always at sea on anti-invasion patrol. Many of these ships had been withdrawn from duties in the Atlantic and the Western Approaches for the emergency, with the consequence that convoys crossing to Britain from Canada were desperately short of escorts for the ocean voyage. And the warships that sailed out to meet the convoys and bring them safely home were also severely depleted in numbers.

Losses of merchant ships had risen alarmingly as the rampaging U-boats grew in numbers and daring. Since June, 1940, the losses had multiplied, until in September, U-boats sank fifty-nine ships of 295,335 tons, most of these off the northern coast of Ireland, well named the Bloody Foreland.

It was now the blackest period of the sea war, the zenith of four months' slaughter which the U-boat commanders were to look back on as 'the happy time.'

At first only fast convoys had sailed homeward across the Atlantic from Halifax, Nova Scotia. These 'HX' convoys were made up of ships capable of maintaining a steady eight or nine knots. But to increase the flow of supplies across the ocean lifeline and to make use of slower ships, a second type of convoy was begun. These were the 'SC' convoys, which sailed from Sydney, Cape Breton Island, Nova Scotia. The plan was to sail these convoys of old, slow cargo vessels during the good summer weather, taking sixteen days to complete the passage at a laborious six or seven knots. But the urgency of the situation demanded that they should continue to sail throughout the winter. And so ships that had never before risked the hard and turbulent waters of the North Atlantic in winter had the special light loading line drawn at the base of the loading marks on their sides; the mark for WNA—'Winter North Atlantic'. And into the teeth of winter they sailed.

SC7, the seventh of the slow convoys, sailed from Sydney, Cape Breton, at twelve noon on October 5, 1940. It was a convoy of thirty-five ancient ships carrying mundane, if vital, cargoes of timber, grain, steel, scrap and iron ore. It was nothing special. It might have lost one ship or a few, then won through to home waters and been quickly forgotten, just another convoy among hundreds.

But it did not happen that way. SC7 sailed into history as the victim of one of the biggest and most painful surprises sprung by the Germans in the war at sea.

This is the story of convoy SC7, and the men who were there.

I

The Admiral's Daughter

Within hours of the long awaited telegram arriving in Cleveland, Ohio, two attractive young mothers were in the air, their gay little red and blue aeroplane firmly on course for Halifax, Nova Scotia, a thousand miles away. They had only one parachute between them, and for Fynvola James it was only her second time in a plane, but Mary King was an experienced pilot and this was all set to be one of the happiest flights she had ever made.

It was October 2, 1940. The telegram had told Mrs James the glad news that her father, a retired Admiral now back in service as a Commodore of convoys, would be able to see her at Halifax before leaving for Britain with his next convoy. Mrs James had sailed out to Cleveland with her three young children in the grim, uncertain days following Dunkirk. Now, with her father and her husband, a naval commander in the Admiralty, both far away in the war, this brief chance to see her father was not to be missed. Mrs King, who owned the plane, had seen to that.

The Stinson light aeroplane flew due east at its one hundred-plus miles an hour, following the shore of Lake Erie, then on to Schenectady to land and fill up with thirty gallons of fuel to take them on to Portland, Maine, by nightfall. On they flew, over tree-covered hills in the full glory of autumn scarlets, yellows and oranges, and bright blue lakes that reflected the white clouds above. After an overnight stop at Portland, the Stinson took off at dawn for Bangor, the last airport inside the United States. There it landed on a bumpy runway and filled up with fuel to the brim for the non-stop flight to Halifax, for with Canada at war the two women had been warned not to land anywhere else than their permitted destination.

There were no maps of Canada available in wartime, nor were there any radioed weather reports or flight instructions; the plane's radio now remained stubbornly silent to their every call. After the busy, friendly airwaves of neutral America, it was very disconcerting. It also made the flight much more difficult. All Mary King had to navigate by was an ancient road map of very small scale, and as they flew on across wild, wooded country they hugged the one and only road for most of the time, it being their only hope of making a forced landing should the plane's single engine fail them.

But it did not, and they successfully reached the port of Saint John, New Brunswick. Here again, though, there was still no reply from the radio, and after circling round fruitlessly they headed east across the Bay of Fundy to Nova Scotia. It was the shortest and quickest route, instead of going north and swinging round to Halifax overland, and they were in a hurry, for it was only a matter of hours before the Commodore was due to leave to join his convoy. But crossing the bay meant flying over twenty miles of open sea in their small one-engined landplane. They held their breaths, murmured a prayer, crossed their fingers . . . and reached the far shore. From then on it was an easier journey, flying overland, and at noon they sighted Halifax harbour, but still with the radio eerily silent in spite of their repeated calls.

They were now at the end of their thousand-mile trip, looking down on the port where the ships gathered for the big convoys to Britain—they counted no fewer than sixty vessels waiting at anchor. But where was the airport? As the radio gave no help they looked again at the old road map. It indicated an airport on the north side of the harbour, and sure enough, on searching around they sighted it—a fine big one, it appeared. They circled it once, then Mary King brought the Stinson gently down to land.

Unbelieving eyes watched the little red plane taxi to a halt in the middle of the airfield, where great camouflaged bombers stood ready with their deadly loads. For this was the airfield of Eastern Air Command, Royal Canadian Air Force. Scarcely had the plane's wheels stopped before a plain clothes detective jumped in, shut the doors and windows and started to question the two women, while a Mountie stood guard outside. Crowds of curious airmen gathered round to see the plane and catch a glimpse of its two most unlikely occupants.

The plane had been silently tracked through the skies from the moment it had come wandering over the border—it had come very, very close to being shot down. Who were they? asked the detective, and where were their papers? The two spirited young women obediently handed over their documents. Everything had been planned for the flight and the necessary papers obtained from Washington as soon as Mrs James had first heard by letter that her father would be coming to Halifax. Everything, they said, was in order.

But it was not. Some vital landing permits were missing, and Mrs King realized, too late, that Washington had neglected to send them to her.

Now the questions came thick and fast. They were going to meet father? Who was father? Vice-Admiral Lachlan Donald Ian MacKinnon, CB, CVO. Where was he? Oh . . . er . . . he must be waiting at the civil airport. After a flurry of telephone calls the little plane was taken away and locked up, and the two 'suspects' driven from the airport under police escort.

So Mrs James was eventually reunited with her father under circumstances which neither they nor the Royal Canadian Air Force were ever likely to forget. Fortunately the admiral's departure had been postponed by one day, so that he was able to accompany the two women as they went from one office to the next, swearing in triplicate who they were and answering a battery of official questions, while the authorities checked with Washington and delighted newspaper reporters jostled for the story of the saucy flight. What a lark and a laugh and a gift for the front page to relieve the gloomy news from the old country.

Even after the admiral had gone it still took his daughter and her friend another twenty-four hours to get things sorted out to every official's satisfaction. Then, with smiles all round, the Stinson aeroplane, considerably polished until it shone, was released from its locked hangar, filled up with fuel, and Fynvola James and Mary King climbed back into it for their thousand mile journey back to Cleveland, armed with navigation papers kindly provided. The airmen stood around and waved, and waved . . . but the plane did not move. Mary King had carefully put the main switch in a safe place and now couldn't find it. There followed a minute or two of deep embarrassment while everyone took a turn at searching the plane, then the switch was found—put tidily where it should have been. The Stinson took off, circled and vanished into the sky, and the Royal Canadian Air Force shook its head in wonderment and went back to war.

Admiral MacKinnon, meanwhile, having seen the funny side of the affair in spite of all the fuss and bother, had left by train for Sydney, Cape Breton, to take up his next convoy. He was last seen by his daughter walking off with a light suitcase containing all his personal belongings. In itself an unusual sight, for it was so at odds with the important naval life which he had led before Hitler's war began.

Lachlan MacKinnon, the son of a parson, had joined the Royal Navy as a thirteen-year-old cadet in the days of Queen Victoria. Now, a grey-haired fifty-seven, he looked back on an eventful career. The first World War had seen him as gunnery officer of HMS *Indomitable* at the Battle of Jutland, service which gained him special promotion, and he went on to become the first commander of the proud new battle cruiser HMS *Hood*.

MacKinnon was always a man of the big ships, and always zealously on top of his job, whether as captain of a cruiser in the China Seas or, in later years, as Rear-Admiral commanding the 2nd Battle Squadron, Home Fleet. His multitude of honours included the award of the CVO for organizing the King George V Jubilee review of the Fleet in 1935, though a lesser known but especially pleasing honour was the result of his service as an instructor to the Turkish Navy when a young lieutenant. The Turks dubbed him 'Mac Kinnon Bey.'

MacKinnon was not a tall man, but he bore himself very erect and was a stickler for deportment. He could not abide to see a man with his hands in his pockets. He was a disciplinarian, and liked to see things done just right. But he also had a zest for living coupled with a deep sense of humour. He enjoyed gay company, and as a senior officer in the big ships was able to indulge in, and organize, the social round. Although used to having officers and men jump to his every need and command, and quietly enjoying the fact, he was extremely popular with both. He was Navy through and through, but possessed of a vivid personality that was not bound by the gold braid.

Had war broken out earlier, as threatened at the time of the Munich crisis in 1938, when he commanded the 2nd Battle Squadron, Admiral Lachlan MacKinnon would have jumped straight into an important active service command. Instead, the immediate threat of hostilities receded, and the following January, after forty-two years in the navy, he retired. When, only months later, war came after all, he was quickly back to volunteer his services. But his situation had changed. He was offered a post as Commodore of Convoys.

There could hardly have been a greater contrast with his past career. The Commodore of a convoy sailed in one of the merchant ships and was responsible for keeping the merchantmen in formation, passing them signals for altering course, zig-zagging and other evasive manoeuvres, and generally keeping some order among the flock, working in liaison with the senior escorting warship. The Commodore's 'flagship' could vary from a substantial cargo-liner to a dirty old tramp, and his staff was never more than a handful of naval signalmen. A far, far cry from other days. But Lachlan MacKinnon, like many another retired senior naval officer or merchant officer of the Royal Naval Reserve who took on the onerous job of Commodore, put into it all he knew. Though the standard of signalling among the merchant ships, to say nothing of their station-keeping, was enough to try the patience of a saint, he had adapted himself to the job with a keenness and level temper that brought good results.

Only once in several convoys had he been known to air a mild complaint; about the master of his 'flagship' whose billious delight it had been to stuff himself with steak and cabbage for breakfast every day.

Long before Commodore MacKinnon caught the train for Sydney, the ships that were to form convoy SC7 had been loading their cargoes in readiness for the homeward passage.

Some went to ports of the United States for their loads. To New Orleans, in the south, for grain and aluminium ore; and to Baltimore, in the north, for strip-steel, pig-iron and scrap. Some of these vessels then continued on to New York to top up their cargoes with more loads of food, pitprops, railway lines and scrap. It was hardly a wildly exciting cargo, a load of junk iron and steel dumped aboard by a giant magnetic grab, but it was precious enough. As some United States Army ordnance officers had worked out very precisely, from every ton of American scrap iron, Britain could manufacture either one 75-millimetre field gun, twelve machine-guns, one 16-inch battleship piercing shell, or nine 500 pound bombs.

All they had to do, of course, was to get those precious tons across the U-boat infested Atlantic.

But the great majority of ships destined for SC7 went to load up at Canadian ports, some of these so small and outlandish that ships' captains had never heard of them and had to call in at other ports first to ask the way. However, soon all these vessels were busy taking aboard their cargoes at various points in an area of activity stretching high up the eastern coast of Canada.

For some ships the loading port was the familiar one of Saint John, chief port of New Brunswick, on the Bay of Fundy. Here they took on timber, copper ore, steel, grain and trucks. Others went up to Campbellton, the hunting, fishing and lumber centre, to take on a full cargo of timber—rough-sawn planks of varying lengths.

Other ships journeyed still farther north to Gaspe, on the Gulf of St. Lawrence. Here the local men and girls came down to watch as great bundles of pitprops were swung aboard. The winches worked in pairs, one doing the lifting and the other the swinging of the cargo. Once the holds were filled, additional logs were stacked on top of the steel decks of the steamers, like thousands of giant matchsticks.

Some vessels had to make the journey into the St. Lawrence River itself, up past Anticosti Island, where great schools of whales played, blowing their steaming breath a stone's throw from the ships, leaping spectacularly and then plunging deep from gaping gazes. Two busy river loading ports were Quebec, city of a million lights on both sides of the river, and Rimouski, the pilot station of the St. Lawrence, where the pitprops could be seen rushing down the hillside in long troughs or flumes, into which local streams were diverted high up the slopes. After their spectacular wet glissades, sawmills in the valley cut the long logs into short lengths with far-ringing noises and puffs of white steam.

Farther up the St. Lawrence at Three Rivers, ships loading grain anchored alongside a gigantic grain elevator with many cylindrical storage buildings more than two hundred feet high. A discharge tunnel ran down to the quayside and from it came four large pipes which swung out over the holds of the ship to be loaded. With a hiss a torrent of grain would start pouring in a dusty golden cascade into four holds at once, the dust soon settling over the ship like pale fawn snow.

At Three Rivers, too, ships came to load steel and timber. Two such vessels were the *Beatus* and the *Fiscus*, big steamships of nearly 5,000 gross tons. Both were built in the 1920s and hailed from Cardiff, where they were among the best kept ships in and out of that port, each a fine floating advertisement for her owners, the Tempus Shipping Company.

Captain Wilfred Brett took the *Beatus* into Three Rivers for a load of oblong steel ingots weighing five tons each. Once these were safely stored down in the lower holds *Beatus* took on a load of timber laid on top of the steel and also piled twelve feet high on deck. The cargo for *Fiscus*, on the other hand, was composed almost entirely of the steel ingots, together with a number of large crates containing aircraft repaired in Canada for return to the U.K. *Fiscus*'s master, Captain Ebenezer Williams, looked on with sad eyes as the two ships were loading and observed with much feeling, 'I wish I had your cargo instead of mine . . .'

Captain Williams did not seem his usual self. At forty-eight, he was nine years older than Captain Brett of *Beatus* and had done his turn at sea during World War I. Never a talkative man at the best of times, he now seemed full of the gloomiest forebodings. He was due for leave on his return to the U.K., but seemed convinced that he would never see his home in Anglesey again. He confided these fears to other masters, too, and would not be consoled. In truth there was not much they could say. When it was common knowledge that a ship loaded with steel, like *Fiscus*, could sink like a stone when torpedoed, there was little one could reply to his firm presentiment of disaster, except to encourage him to have faith in God and the convoy.

Far to the north, round the eastern hump of Canada, on the coast of Labrador, other ships steamed in to collect their cargoes of timber. Two which found their way to the little-known port of Francis Harbour, at the mouth of the Alexis River, were the *Scoresby* and the *Clintonia*. Smaller ships these, and older, the *Clintonia* having braved the assaults of U-boats in the last war. Francis Harbour was not much of a place, there was hardly anything there but the church of St. Francis after which it was named. For *Scoresby* the load was 1,586 fathoms of pitprops slung and heaved up straight from the river; many had been spilled out by a ship which came to grief on rocks near the coast. The props had been rounded up into rafts secured by chains, and were brought alongside *Scoresby* and winched aboard in slings. The props were stowed below and on the decks, and over all the hatches including the cross-bunker hatch. This meant that one had to climb a makeshift ladder outside the crew quarters aft, the apprentices' quarters for'ard or the saloon entrance, and get to the top of the cargo before being able to see around the horizon. But although so well loaded *Scoresby*, and other timber-carrying ships like her, were not laden to danger point and all had to take in water ballast to counter top weight for seaworthiness for a normal sea journey.

Clintonia's load was pulpwood, also fished straight out of the water. The pulpwood floated at an anchorage in the sea near the beach, enclosed by big booms; it was towed out to the ship and winched into her holds.

And so it went on, the ships that were to join SC7 taking on their loads at a dozen different ports. Not only British ships but many of other nationalities, vessels which had either been taken over by the Ministry of War Transport after the collapse of their countries, or which were still neutral but chose to sail in British convoy rather than cross the Atlantic alone. Neutrals were always offered this choice, and the majority wisely decided that there was more safety in numbers. Hitler had yet to make his stormy declaration that 'every ship with, or without convoy, which appears before our torpedo tubes is going to be torpedoed,' but for months the U-boats, in complete disregard of international law, had been doing exactly that, regularly sinking neutral as well as Allied merchant shipping round the coasts of Britain. Huge national flags painted on the sides of a neutral vessel never stayed the passage of a death dealing torpedo.

One of three Swedish ships destined for SC7, the small 1,500-ton *Gunborg*, was outside the enemy blockade when the Germans swarmed across Norway, and so like many vessels had been chartered by the British authorities. Her arrival now at St. John's, Newfoundland, to pick up a cargo of pulpwood was of fateful importance to one young Swedish seaman.

Sture Mattsson, just sixteen years old, was hardly yet recovered from the shock of having his ship go down beneath him on the voyage across to Canada. He had come out in convoy in a Swedish ship which was torpedoed and sank in two and a half minutes, taking down with her many of his shipmates. Young Mattsson was among the survivors picked up by a British ship called the *Empire Soldier* and brought to St. John's, where he had been for six weeks when the *Gunborg* called. He had lost all his possessions, but had been kitted out and told he could go home to Sweden by a Swedish ship sailing from New York to Petsamo, in Finland. This was fine offer, and yet the lad could not bring himself to accept it. It had a lot to do with something he had heard the master of the *Empire Soldier* say. The master, Captain H. A. Lego, was an old man in his seventies, drawing a well earned pension. One day Mattsson heard someone ask him why, at his time of life, he should still be at sea, to which Captain Lego quietly replied, 'If there is something I can do for old England, this I want to do before I die.'

It was a modest remark that made a profound impression on the young Swede, as did another incident involving the old captain. When *Empire Soldier* picked up Mattsson and the other survivors her crew threw a wooden-runged rope ladder over the side for them to climb up. Unfortunately the ladder struck the wife of the Swedish ship's engineer on the head and split it open. Calmly, Captain Lego set to and expertly sewed up the wound. It was a fine piece of work that earned the congratulations of doctors at St. John's.

So Sture Mattsson chewed it all over and went to the anchored *Gunborg*, which was bound for the Clyde, and found they needed an able-seaman. His friends all advised him to take passage home to Sweden, but he firmly did not heed them. He shouldered his seabag, collected his pet dog and stepped aboard the ship due to sail with SC7.

The previous SC convoy, SC6, had left Sydney, Cape Breton, on September 27. Soon after its departure the first of the motley ships of SC7 began to arrive.

Unlike in blacked-out Britain, Sydney wore its lights at night, and an intermittent heavy glare came from a point on shore near the steelworks, where white-hot slag was tipped at the water's edge. Some ships of the SC convoys took on their loads of steel at Sydney and went on to top up with timber elsewhere, then return. It was no hardship to leave Sydney for there was nothing prepossessing about the place for seamen to remember. Those who went ashore found a ramshackle main street of wooden houses where they waited for a bus into town. The town itself seemed very much a shanty affair, though there were also some substantial brick buildings. But anyway, who was here for the sights? The one appeal of Sydney was that it was the last stop on the way home.

On a warmish day at Sydney it was tempting to go over the side for a swim, though those who attempted it soon clambered out again fighting off an attack of the shivers. The water was always far colder than the sun made it look. In deep winter the harbour became covered with pack-ice and often froze over altogether, so firmly that the local inhabitants could drive their cars over the ice.

A swim would have been welcome after the business of coaling up. Ships bunkered at the coaling station of St. Pierre across the bay, where from great wooden erections trucks ran out to supply the shutes. Coaling-up shot coal all over the decks, while fine coal dust invaded all rooms and cabins and got up everyone's nose. It was a mercy if it rained. In the evening after the day's toil, crews might go ashore to a dancehall where strong men in lumber jackets swung girls around in the air in true lumber-camp style while the band played nothing but variations of the tune 'Blueberry Hill' all night.

As the ships earmarked for SC7 were entered in the official lists, so the structure of the convoy began to take shape. There would be about thirty-five ships in all, half of these British. The foreigners would include the three Swedes, six Norwegians, four Greeks, a French tanker, two Dutch ships and one Danish.

'Old wrecks and barnacled tramps' was the laconic description unofficially applied to the greater part of the convoy. It was not far from the truth. For what the convoy papers did not show was that half the ships of SC7 were old vessels dating back to World War I and some even to the turn of the century. The four venerable Greek ships, for instance, had sailed the oceans under a total of ten different names, the oldest vessel among them having carried her first cargoes way back in 1906. But the Norwegians had the oldest ship of all. She was the small and ancient steam tanker *Thoroy*, built as long ago as 1893! *Thoroy* was a credit to her British builders, Armstrong Mitchell of Newcastle, who had constructed her in those pioneer years of tanker building. Launched as the petroleum tanker *Snowflake,* she had become a veteran of the high seas long before the Boer War began, and had sailed for forty-seven years under four different names and nationalities. She excusably drew the admiration of other SC7 masters, mainly for the fact that she was still cheekily afloat.

Several of the other foreigners were also British-built and formerly British owned.

At least two ships in the convoy should have sailed with the previous SC convoy, but to their shame had missed it, while two others had been directed to one of the fast HX convoys from Halifax, but had to drop out when found woefully incapable of keeping up the required speed. They were then shuttled off to join 'the slow buggers' at Sydney. There were no illusions about the vessels sailing in the SC convoys, least of all among naval control; as one senior officer admitted, ships were sailed from Sydney that would never have been given a seaworthy ticket in peacetime.

Among the British ships of SC7 was one which had actually lain under water for some time. Several vessels had been resurrected from rusting graves pegged out for them during the great shipping depression of the 1930s. This was especially true of the tramp steamers, vessels which in normal times had no fixed routes but touted their way around the seas, available to any merchant who could provide a cargo, working from one port to the next, lifting cheap and handy bulk loads such as they were now carrying for war. The depression had laid up hundreds of tramps and other cargo vessels to idle away their days at desolate moorings until, in December 1939, the Ministry of War Transport began requisitioning them; when overnight, almost any vessel that could still ride the water became at once precious and vital to the country's needs.

Such a ship saved from a rusting eternity was the *Corinthic*, from Hull. She had been laid up for years in the River Fal in Cornwall, the tourists' river which, during the depression, had held as many as eighty unwanted ships, a never-ending line of silent, ghostly vessels inhabited only by nightwatchmen. *Corinthic*, on her earlier voyage out to the United States, had arrived twelve days overdue, having spent many hours on many days quite motionless at sea, while her engineers sweated to repair various peculiar breakdowns. A hair-raising experience, knowing that at any moment she could be the target for a scavenging U-boat. Now here she was, reporting for SC7 laden with another eight thousand tons of scrap and steel, though this time with her crew feeling quite swanky, for the heavy junk cargo was topped by a somewhat more respectable load of railway lines, plus a pile of strip-steel for plating aeroplanes. *Corinthic*'s fiery little master was Captain George Nesbitt from Hull, who had reason enough for not being very fond of Germans. When World War I broke out he was in a British ship lying in a German port, and was promptly interned for the duration of that war. Captain Nesbitt was resolved that Hitler's war would not find him so easily removed from the fight.

Another British ship rescued from the scrapheap was the *Botusk*, from London. This strange, jungle-sounding name was not the one with which she had started out in life. In common with some other vessels her name had been changed to give her the prefix 'BOT', standing for Board of Trade. Meanwhile, the dubious honour of being the oldest British ship in the convoy was shared by two hard-worked vessels dating back to 1912. One was the *Creekirk*, now loaded with iron ore for Cardiff, and sailing under her third name since leaving the Glasgow shipyards so long ago. The other was the *Empire Brigade*, which after an eventful career had been sold to Italian owners, but was now back in the fold after being taken in prize by the Royal Navy on Italy's entry into the war and given her third, resoundingly English, name.

Among all this odd assortment of ships, however, the strangest by far were three British vessels from the Great Lakes of North America. All the other ships of SC7, even the smallest and rustiest old tramp, pitied the Lakers—'Too bloody slow to get out of their own way!'

The Lake boats—never 'ships'—were weird looking vessels with a high bridge-house set almost on the bow, and a funnel placed well aft, above the engines. With their long, flat midships in between, it was as if the people at each end of the vessel would never meet. Nor did they, except at mealtimes in the messrooms aft, for in the bow section lived the captain, his deck officers and crew, while back in the stern section lived the engineering staff and stewards. But it was all to a purpose in the Lakers' natural habitat; the curious forward bridge-house was to give the captain maximum visibility when negotiating the narrow channels connecting the Great Lakes.

Even if the Germans did not pounce on these 'sweet water' vessels the winter storms of the Atlantic must surely break their slender backs, thought the ocean seamen. But in fact all three boats, two of them less than 2,000 tons, had been built in Britain and sailed across the Atlantic to begin their life on the Lakes. Admittedly this ocean voyage had been made in the best of weather conditions, in high summer, and they had not tasted salt water since, nor ever been intended to. Yet now, after long years spent carrying cargoes round the inland ports of the Great Lakes, here they were, facing the uncompromising Atlantic at the stormy time of year. And this with puny engines of around a hundred horse-power or less, compared with the 300-plus horse-power of the most elderly ocean freighter.

Masters and crews had been sent out from Britain to bring over the Lakers. It was to be a once-and-for-all crossing for the vessels, carrying timber cargo to help keep them afloat, for on reaching Britain they would be put to work round the coast mainly as coal-carriers. But whether they could make the journey was another matter. The unexpected antics of the first Lakers to attempt the passage, sailing in the calmer days of August with SC1, left the Commodore of that convoy totally bemused. 'I

had five Lake boats,' he said, 'which appeared to yaw 60
degrees each side of their course, but later I discovered that
this is their method of advance if they think they are closing
ahead.' One of the five was so helpless she had to return to
Sydney only hours after SC1 sailed, while another had to turn
back the next day. The harassed Commodore thought he would
also have to write off the remaining three, but to his surprise
they were still in sight next day and gradually took up their
correct stations, though their steaming eccentricities continued
throughout the voyage. Two other Lakers which set out with
SC4 in September found it difficult to keep pace with the
convoy even in a smooth sea, and in rough seas later could
hardly move. Yet to everyone's astonishment and delight they
still won through.

But it was now October, and how SC7's three Lakers would
fare in this month's wild seas was anybody's guess.

This, then, was the motley collection of ships which Commodore Lachlan MacKinnon was to lead across the Atlantic.
These, and one other, the British steamer that was to be his
'flagship'. Her name was *Assyrian*.

As the Commodore took the train for Sydney, *Assyrian*'s
captain was ploughing his ship there along the east coast of
Nova Scotia. Neither of them knew of their forthcoming meeting,
nor could they have had any idea of the arduous course on which
Fate had, even now, launched them both.

2

A Ship Called Fritz

The *Assyrian* was actually a vessel from the other side. The Germans had built her at Hamburg in 1914 as the *Fritz*, but at the end of the Kaiser's war she was handed over to Britain as a reparations ship. When the Ellerman and Papayanni Lines acquired her they rechristened her *Assyrian*, and at their hands she changed much more than her name.

The Germans had built *Assyrian* as a diesel engined motor-ship, one of the first of her kind ever to put to sea. But on joining the Ellerman fleet she was very soon converted to a more conventional steamship. In the hard costing of a British cargo vessel, pared down to the smallest fractions of a penny, there was no room for new-fangled diesels. For one thing it was difficult to get spares for the engines, and for another, they needed to be operated by twelve engineers! So out came the Sulzer diesels, and in went the steam engines.

To save expense, it was decided to keep *Assyrian*'s original propeller shafting and propellers. This complicated matters as it limited the choice of suitable engines, but she was eventually fitted with two trawler-type steam reciprocating triple-expansion engines. Old-fashioned and slower they might be, but infinitely more reliable.

So *Assyrian* became a coal fired twin-screw steamship, though keeping at least one tangible reminder of her revolutionary origin. Her mainmast was still fitted with the running gear which had enabled her former German crew to hoist a trawler-like sail whenever her experimental diesels became troublesome.

For the next twenty years, from her new home port of Liverpool, *Assyrian* voyaged about the oceans of the world on different trades, striving to achieve a ten-knot average for at least one voyage but never quite managing it. In calm seas and light winds she might maintain nine knots steaming flat out, but in heavy weather her progress was likely to be no more than four or five knots.

On being requisitioned for war service she first worked in the Mediterranean, carrying general cargoes, until Italy came into the war. Then she was transferred to the Atlantic. As she had no such refinements as a refrigerator, only an ice-box, carrying perishable foods for lengthy periods made things difficult as far as the crew's feeding arrangements went, as the ice dwindled; but still, with all her limitations *Assyrian* was a well loved 'old tub.'

Early in August 1940 she loaded up at Liverpool with a cargo for the West Indies. She carried a gun now. It was fitted in the Barry Roads, an old four-pounder of 1914-18 vintage, set up on the after deck. Some of her crew went ashore for brief instruction on how to use it. The first time they fired the gun it shook everything up both above and below her wooden decks, and broke the bottom of the ice-box. Ah well, maybe it would cause bigger discomfort to the Germans. All hands eventually had some rudimentary training on it so that they could double as members of the gun-crew in an emergency.

Although she was a Liverpool based ship and so had many men from Cheshire and North Wales in her crew of thirty-nine, *Assyrian* also had men from Bristol, Hull and Devon, and some Irishmen.

Her master was Irish. Captain Reginald Kearon, a youthful thirty-five years old, came from a large seafaring family in Arklow. Stocky and well built, with black wavy hair and a healthily ruddy clean-shaven face, he was both a crisp professional mariner and a very likeable personality. Reg Kearon was not stand-offish, nor did he pull rank, and was greatly respected by all hands, with whom he enjoyed mixing freely as 'one of the lads.' His chief officer was Irish, too. John King came from Rush, in County Dublin. He was touching sixty and had served the shipping line for many years. But although to the younger elements in the ship's company he seemed a ripe old age, he lacked nothing in vigour and enthusiasm, and like his captain was popular with everyone. The other two deck officers, the second and third mates, were also well experienced men in their thirties and forties, while at the other end of the age scale the youngest crewman aboard was a cadet of sixteen.

It was to Captain Kearon's credit that he kept a happy ship in which almost every member of the crew got along well together. They all knew their job, although one or two among them were men who had been forced by the great shipping slump to quit the sea and find a job ashore . . . until war called them back. Like Robert Stracy, the ship's quiet-spoken radio officer. After being laid off during the slump which rendered one in every four British seamen unemployed, Stracy took a shore post, but remained in the Merchant Navy Officers' War Reserve, and so was hurriedly recalled for service at the outbreak of war. How ironically the pendulum had swung back for previously unwanted men and ships.

Assyrian's fateful passage to SC7 began when she left Liverpool in August. Five days out she lost her convoy and had to steam on alone south to Barbados, which she reached without incident. Her next call was at Georgetown, British Guiana, and here occurred a warmly sentimental interlude which, in the light of later events, was to become a poignant memory. Chief Officer John King had not seen his sister for some twenty years. She was a nun in a convent far out in the wilds of Brazil. The ship's agent, asked to pull a few strings for a faithful employee, had arranged that King should at last meet his sister, and from Georgetown he was flown several hours away to a midway point where she also had been flown to meet him. The chief officer was a very happy man when he returned to the ship two days later.

From Georgetown *Assyrian* steamed north through the Caribbean to New Orleans, there to load up for her return voyage across the Atlantic. In the light of the grave news from home, with hundreds dying nightly under the rain of enemy bombs and Britain facing an invasion by the might of the German armies it seemed a strange situation for them to be in, sailing through the sunny Caribbean playing deck quoits to while away the hours, Captain Kearon joining in with everyone, cook, firemen and all. To some, in fact, it seemed altogether wrong to be idling their time away in this manner when the old country was in such desperate straits and urgently in need of supplies. But *Assyrian* was forging on to do her bit in the best way she could.

After loading up with grain and other cargo at New Orleans she made ready for the long voyage home. She was ordered to join a convoy going north from Bermuda to New York, there to top up her cargo, but in spite of the willing work of her twin screws she was quite unable to keep up with the convoy's fast speed of eight or nine knots and had to drop out and plod on to New York alone. Tumbling weather made this long journey an eventful one in which so much crockery was smashed that they were left with barely enough cups to go round. As a final disappointment she arrived at New York too late to catch another convoy sailing to Halifax, Nova Scotia, on the next stage of the journey home.

However, she made it to Halifax, and her arrival there brought particular joy to three French naval men. They were billeted in the *Champlain*, a French ship which had lain for a long time in the Bedford Basin, her crew undecided which side to be on after the fall of France. The three men had finally opted to throw in their lot with the Free French, and were accepted for passage to the U.K. aboard the first available ship. So Lieutenant Gabriele Andre Sauvaget of Bordeaux, and ratings Oliver Paupon and Marcel le Meur, an exuberant trio, happily joined the ship for the last leg of her voyage to join SC7. This was a journey some 230 miles north-east along the coast of Nova Scotia to Sydney.

She only just made it, arriving the day before the convoy was due to sail. But this was one convoy she would not—could not—lose, for to everyone's surprise they learned on arrival that they were to lead it. The old *Assyrian*, Commodore ship! Never in her twenty-six years had she known such an honour.

Down below, bespectacled William Venables looked over the engines on which he had lavished so much care during seven contented years as her Second Engineer.

Assyrian, at only 2,962 tons, was one of the smallest British ships in the convoy, besides being one of the oldest. But she could do it. Of course she could!

Commodore Lachlan MacKinnon boarded *Assyrian* late that evening, together with his staff of five naval petty officers and ratings: a yeoman of signals, two telegraphists and two signalmen. He was to share the captain's cabin, while his staff were found accommodation in the ship's four passenger cabins, where the Frenchmen, too, were berthed.

Chief Steward James Daley went ashore by naval launch to order the essential provisions needed to make good the ship's depleted stores. Plus a crate of crockery, for there was hardly enough left for the use of the ship's company, never mind the extra nine people now aboard. He was promised that the stores would be alongside by 10 a.m. the following morning, two hours before sailing time.

Just before midnight the big dark shape of the last of the British ships destined for the convoy nosed its way into Sydney harbour. She was the 5,000-ton *Somersby*, a West Hartlepool vessel carrying a cargo of grain.

Next day was Saturday, October 5, 1940. Dawn broke clear and bright over the groups of anchored ships and brought a warm morning sun. But with everyone due to move out on the stroke of noon there was little time to enjoy the weather. Breakfasts were cut short as launches picked up the merchant masters, together with an accompanying officer, and took them ashore for the official convoy conference.

It was not a very long conference. The masters were given the by now usual pep talk about keeping good station according to their allotted numbers in the convoy, which would take the general formation of six columns of five or six ships each. They were urged to act smartly on the Commodore's signalled instructions, and warned against lagging behind and becoming a 'straggler', with the probable dire consequences of collecting a torpedo from a prowling U-boat.

As the Navy strove to ram home its advice, the masters digested it all impassively in that deceptively casual manner which had caused an earlier Commodore to complain testily 'little notice was taken of points made by the officers speaking . . .' But there was another side to it. The SC briefings were by no means as well organized as the conferences at Halifax for the HX sailings, and it was still sorrowfully remembered how one SC Commodore had missed the conference altogether through being given the wrong orders.

The masters of SC7 learned that they were to have just one naval escort across the Atlantic, a little sloop smaller than the smallest tramp steamer among them. There would also be an armed yacht and an 'aerial escort'—a seaplane—for the first two days, but these would then turn back and the convoy would be on its way with only the sloop for protection until they reached the Western Approaches. No amount of pep-talking could make the one small warship seem any bigger, especially when considered against the limited, and in some cases ludicrous, armament of the merchant ships. Perhaps a dozen among them had an old four-inch or four-pounder mounted aft, two or three of these vessels having the added advantage of a Naval Reservist gunner to lead the merchant gun-crew. But other ships had only a machine-gun, or perhaps two, mounted on the bridge, while yet others had merely the odd rifle; like the British *Carsbreck*, whose sole defensive weapon was a rifle in charge of the chief officer. The more fortunate *Beatus*, which boasted an old four-inch on the poop, had also possessed two rifles . . . until these were taken away for anti-invasion use.

So SC7 would have to sail on for ten days until it reached the point of rendezvous where warships of the Western Approaches would come out to meet it and escort it in. With Hitler's big new ocean-going U-boats already reported to be ranging farther and farther west across the Atlantic, this seemed to be cutting it rather fine. But that's how it was.

A more optimistic note was struck when Commodore Mac-Kinnon, drawing calmly on his pipe, was introduced as one who had never lost a ship in convoy—and who had no intention of blotting that record. The masters liked what they saw, a fit, precise and clear-thinking man, obviously well on top of his job. Even if he was a retired admiral.

And that was that. 'Best wishes for a safe passage, gentlemen . . .'

After the conference most of the masters had a drink and a chat before returning to their ships. Still full of gloom was Captain Ebenezer Williams of the steel laden *Fiscus*. He had heard nothing in conference to alter his conviction that this was to be his last voyage, that doom was staring him in the face. Could it be the Welshman's aptitude for second sight that had given him this persistent, nagging premonition of disaster? It was going to need great effort for him to hide his feelings from his crew.

Meanwhile aboard *Assyrian* Chief Steward Daley was a very worried man. Ten o'clock had come and gone, and there was still no sign of the promised stores. At 11 a.m., with the captain and Commodore now returned to the ship, he was called to the lower bridge. Where in heaven were the stores? asked Commodore MacKinnon. Daley told him of the assurance he had been given, but still the minutes ticked by and nothing arrived. At 12 noon the naval escort sloop slipped out of harbour and *Assyrian* was due to start leading the ships of the convoy. Daley was again summoned to the bridge. This time Commodore Mac-

Kinnon was pacing to and fro in exasperation. He was very
displeased.

'Mr. Daley, can we proceed without the extra supplies?'

Daley quickly ran his mind's eye over the ship's reduced
stores, now required to feed an extra nine mouths. Yes, he said,
they could just about get through if they used, in rotation, fresh,
canned and salted meats, for luckily the ship had stored to
capacity on canned meats at New Orleans. But bread was the
big problem. The stock of flour would never last the journey.
However, if they used part-bread and biscuits . . .

Ships around *Assyrian* had now begun to move off. A naval
launch hove into sight and the Commodore took up a loud-
hailer and cracked an order to its officer in charge. 'Take an
urgent message ashore,' said the Commodore grimly, 'that if this
ship's stores are not alongside in fifteen minutes, someone's head
will roll!' The launch shot off at speed.

To the consternation of the chief steward, *Assyrian* then
started to get under way, the Commodore determined to make
up for precious minutes lost and sail the ship to schedule. But
after an anxious interval there came a gladdening shout from
one of the crew—'Chief, the stores have come.'

In response to the Commodore's fierce warning a hurried
flotilla of motorboats chugged alongside the slowly moving ship
and Daley and his staff quickly gathered aboard in welcoming
arms sides of meat, bags of potatoes and flour, and a precious
crate of crockery, managing to complete the loading just in
time before *Assyrian* increased speed and steamed importantly
out of harbour to head the convoy.

The good weather continued throughout the afternoon as the
thirty-five ships ponderously took up their positions in the convoy
formation, *Assyrian* at the head of the centre column and the
escort sloop out in front, together with the armed yacht. And
then, in the early evening, they were off. Unlike an earlier SC
convoy, which had taken no less than twenty-nine frustrating
hours to form up.

Meanwhile, back in Sydney harbour a latecomer for the
convoy had arrived in the shape of the little Norwegian tramp

Sneland 1. Her passage to Sydney had been a laborious one. After loading aluminium ore at New Orleans she had gone north to the Hampton Roads, Virginia, to get concrete protection for her wheelhouse. She was delayed there for a long time and when about to leave was so heavily encrusted with barnacles that she was unable to keep up with a convoy. So she steamed on alone to Halifax, where shore workers armed with long scrapers got to work and the ship was made to list with the aid of her ballast tanks so that some of the offending barnacles could be removed. Then on she ploughed to Sydney to join SC7.

As *Sneland 1* dropped anchor her master and chief officer went hurriedly ashore to the convoy office for instructions. Sorry, they were told, the office was short of convoy documents, but they could get a set from a naval launch in the harbour. Captain Laegland and his chief scoured the water for the launch but could not find it. They decided the best thing they could do was to carry on and try to catch up with the convoy—and just hang on to it.

So *Sneland 1* steamed out determinedly after SC7 and, like some tardy Disney cartoon character, managed to catch up with the dark ranks of the convoy during the night. She crept in on the starboard wing as the last ship of that column, and steamed on in comfortable station for all the world as if that had been her rightful position all along. She had no knowledge of the convoy and no papers, and would not be able to understand a single signal from the Commodore, whoever that might be. But she had caught her convoy!

3

The Steaming Herd

Sunday, October 6, and already SC7 had suffered its first casualty. It was a fine morning on this second day at sea, and in the excellent visibility ships gradually became aware that one vessel was missing. She was the *Winona*, the oldest and biggest of the three Lakers, and therefore the most conspicuous. What had happened to her?

Aboard *Assyrian*, Commodore MacKinnon put a cross beside the name of *Winona* on his official convoy list. The Laker had turned back in the early hours of darkness of the previous night. Despite the efforts of her chief engineer and his staff, her dynamo had failed to operate, and much to his disappointment Captain John Stevenson of Newcastle had had to turn his ship and head back to Sydney for repairs.

So now there were two. Eyes went to the other Lakers, doggedly struggling along in their erratic fashion.

In a clement sea the convoy steamed steadily along at its planned speed of seven knots, sometimes in good order and sometimes in rather haphazard fashion after a change of course had been ordered by the Commodore, for already he was busy making signals and reflectively watching their effect. The seaplane droned through a clear sky overhead, and close at hand was the armed yacht, HMCS *Elk*, a converted mercantile vessel known in more tranquil days as the *Arcadia*. Out ahead, the escort sloop HMS *Scarborough* led the smokily steaming herd, which now covered a sizeable piece of ocean. The length of each column of ships was some three miles, and the six columns sailing abreast presented a broad front three or four miles across.

It was a workmanlike formation, and yet the scene did not at all resemble an illustration from a textbook of war. Far from hiding their identities in drab anonymity, most of the ships, British and foreign alike, sported the colours of their respective shipping lines on their funnels. At the start of their war service the British ships had been painted an anonymous grey with buff superstructure, in accordance with Ministry of War Transport regulations, but on next painting ship they had promptly put their peacetime colours back on the funnels, and many had reverted to their more familiar black hulls. Now it seemed to add that extra touch of defiance.

HMS *Scarborough* herself was hardly a textbook warship. She had been launched in 1930 as a naval survey vessel, and had spent practically all her life pre-war in the China Seas. She still had a large charthouse built out over the quarter-deck as a continuation of the foc'sle deck, so that although the after gun mounting remained, there was no after gun. Her only big gun, mounted for'ard, was an old low angle four-inch of Japanese make which she had picked up off the jetty at Hong Kong. Stamped with the date 1920, it was, in plain language, a 'bloody awful old thing', yet it worked and had been put to good use on more than one occasion.

Scarborough just topped a thousand tons, rather more than half the size of the smallest freighter in the convoy. She was a good seaboat, though with a bit of a list to starboard and a tendency to buck and roll alarmingly in heavy seas. At such times a rope was stretched across the wheelhouse and the helmsman put his arms over the rope to steady himself and keep an even course. It was painful on the arms, but effective. The sloop's top heaviness was partly due to another legacy of her peacetime occupation, an extra large motorboat used for surveying, which she still carried on big davits on the port side. The cumbersome boat was a great nuisance, and as offensive to her good lines as the unsightly charthouse.

She had wooden decks, which a former commanding officer had demanded should be kept scrubbed and burnished bright. As at that time she had no deck hydrants, no means of pumping up water for scrubbing the decks, her crew had to lower heavy wooden buckets over the side and haul them up filled with sea water, a long and arduous process which was agony on the muscles of the scrubbers, none of whom would forget the weight of those buckets as long as they lived. War or no war, they were kept hard at it holystoning the decks until one day the tell-tale shine from the sloop's decks was reported by an aircraft, and to everyone's immense relief the practice was ordered to be stopped forthwith.

Since being recalled for war *Scarborough* had managed to scrounge two stripped Lewis guns, which were mounted each side of the bridge—a token defence, at least, against aircraft. Her only other artillery was a saluting gun, a ceremonial piece which fired at a fixed angle from one side of the ship only.

She had also kept the sensitive hydrophones used for surveying, not for her the newer asdic equipment for detecting the underwater enemy, but she did carry a good quota of depth-charges. And she had seen one major change. Gone, along with the burnished decks, was the commanding officer who had believed in the little sloop observing big ship 'bull', with the blowing of bugles and all the rest. Her commander now was a tall, athletic Dartmouth trained man who, as the lower deck soon concluded to their satisfaction, 'really knew his stuff.' As almost all *Scarborough*'s crew were naval regulars, this was no mean accolade.

Commander Norman Vincent Dickinson, at forty, had already fought one war. He entered the Royal Navy as a cadet in 1915,

and during World War I served in the Grand Fleet as a midshipman in the battleship *Royal Sovereign*, gaining the DSC.
After the war he specialized in physical training, putting cadets
in the *Erebus* and at the Royal Naval College, Dartmouth,
through their paces, also seaman boys at Shotley. Later, back
at sea, he was squadron P.T. officer with the 1st Cruiser
Squadron, and with destroyer flotillas in the Mediterranean,
before becoming assistant superintendent of the Physical and
Recreational Training School at Portsmouth.

Quick, firm and decisive in manner, Commander Dickinson
was a popular commander not only because it was plain he knew
how to handle a ship, but because he had a good sense of humour
and was eminently more approachable than his predecessor.
Immediately he took command there was a new and better spirit
among *Scarborough*'s company.

Before taking up duties in the North Atlantic the sloop had
acted as the lone escort for several convoys from the U.K. to
Gibraltar. In the early months of the war this had been a
comparatively trouble-free passage, with the U-boats concentrating nearer Britain's shores, but lately *Scarborough* had seen
a good deal more action, and there had been a very hot time
on the outward bound convoy she had helped to bring out of
the Western Approaches before continuing independently to
Sydney, several ships of the convoy falling victim to U-boats.

Scarborough's duty now was to get SC7 safely to the rendezvous in the Western Approaches where other escorts would meet
them. There were no special plans of action arranged between
the sloop and the Commodore ship other than the general tactics
laid down for the convoy. Commander Dickinson and Commodore MacKinnon had met only briefly at the Sydney
conference, and their sole communication now would be by
means of flag and lamp, for wireless telegraphy—morse transmission—was to be avoided, and no ships yet were equipped with
radio telephony.

Sunday continued fine, and late afternoon found the convoy
sailing eastwards below Newfoundland in position 45 deg. 17
min. N, 55 deg. 43 min. W. Next day they could expect to sweep

round the far eastern corner of Newfoundland and begin the slow, steady passage north and east across the North Atlantic in a great curve.

In the underground Operations Room in London the position of SC7 was plotted on the huge map covering the whole of one wall : another slow convoy had begun the long voyage home. In the meantime the previous convoy, SC6, was nearing the Western Approaches. From an Admiralty point of view the record of these slow convoys so far was satisfactory. Though a U-boat on weather-station had sunk one hapless ship of SC1 so easily that the German commander was able to cruise around and take striking photographs of his slowly sinking kill, the losses had on the whole been relatively few. Only SC3 had encountered any great U-boat activity, when at least two U-boats had been seen cruising on the surface at night, in and out of the convoy. But even then, only four vessels were lost, two of these on becoming stragglers, and official opinion was that these sinkings might never have occurred had not the convoy arrived at rendezvous a day too early. In fact, the losses of the SC convoys so far had been much more damaging on the naval side, two escort sloops having been sunk by U-boats. The main troubles of the convoys, as successively reported by their harassed Commodores, had been those of very bad station-keeping and signalling, particularly by the foreign merchantmen, painful weather conditions, persistent straggling and near collisions, especially when some SC convoys had cut dangerously across the course of outward-bound convoys. There was no reason to suppose that SC7 would experience anything more than these now common hazards.

As the convoy steamed quietly on during the second day, the lookouts took stock of their companion ships, some familiar, others not.

Smallest of all the merchant vessels was an old Norwegian tramp, the *Havorn*. She had been sailing the seas since 1902 under three different names, and was now bound for the Mersey stacked high with pitprops. She was little more than 1,500 tons, but in the eyes of her crew it was better to be small, they were far happier than the crew of the convoy's biggest vessel and its most tempting target. This was the French tanker *Languedoc*, a splendid new motorship of nearly 10,000 tons which had been taken under the British flag in tropical waters after the capitulation of France. Now *Languedoc* was on her way to the Clyde, having been ordered to join SC7 after missing a fast HX convoy. She was a most beautiful ship, very neat and clean and painted a smooth light grey. Cruising easily on the port wing of the convoy she stood out from the other vessels like a swan among geese, though her seeming pride did not extend to her cosmopolitan crew, headed by a British master. Being such a size meant being twice as vulnerable. In many another ship, too, they looked across at the big, sleek *Languedoc* and decided among themselves that if any ship was to be torpedoed, she would be the first to go.

The biggest British ship in the convoy, the 6,000-ton *Empire Miniver*, was not really British at all. In fact she was an American vessel of the 'three-island' type from Texas, and as old as the last war. Formerly the *West Cobalt*, she had been bought by Britain for war service—a sort of early lease-lend deal—and now carried a full load of steel and pig-iron on this, her second voyage to Britain under her new name, and with an all-British crew. Although like *Languedoc* she was oil-fired, and therefore a cut above the coal burners, *Empire Miniver*'s advantages beyond that were few. She had been used to carrying cotton, and her steel cargo made her very heavy and sluggish in her movements. Nor was her armament any more splendid than the rest. Her very old 4.7 in. gun, in charge of a Royal Marine Reservist gunlayer, had no protective shield, and its ammunition was in separate pieces consisting of shell, cordite bag and firing cartridge.

Less than half the ships in convoy had been 'degaussed.' That is, fitted with an electric cable run round the scuppers, which set up the ship's own magnetic field to counter magnetic mines. The 'degaussed' ships were easy to identify, a buff cross being painted on either side of the ship just under or just forward of the bridge structure. This was an official marking, and one criticized in blistering terms by the crews of the marked ships, for a better lining-up target for the crossed hairs of an enemy periscope could hardly be imagined.

Another uncomfortable target was provided by one of the Swedish ships, stubbornly intent on proclaiming her neutrality. The Swedish flag was painted large on her sides fore and aft, and the crosses were in luminous paint, which could be seen at night more than half a mile away. They were the cause of much anger aboard other ships, especially those nearest to her. Since when had any neutral flag deterred a U-boat?

There were many vessels which had already seen a fair bit of action.

The old *Trident*, a tramp from Newcastle upon Tyne, had even arrived at Cape Breton on her outward voyage carrying survivors whom she had rescued in mid-Atlantic. It happened that the *Trident* was steaming along one morning when there was a U-boat alarm from the bridge—they had sighted a lifeboat ahead with sails set. Captain Lancelot Balls thought the boat might be a decoy, but as it was dead ahead he kept on course with the gun-crew standing grimly by for action. However, it turned out that the lifeboat held seven survivors from the Norwegian ship *Karet*, which had been torpedoed at midnight. On their safe arrival at Sydney the grateful Norwegians presented *Trident* with a silver cocktail set, and the mates with fountain pens.

A brave ship was the old *Trident*, even if in bad weather she was always more under the Atlantic than on top of it, being constantly awash. Among her earlier adventures she had escaped from Narvik with 10,000 tons of iron ore only hours before the Germans went in. A very cool master, Captain Balls. Once, when a periscope was sighted, he turned his ship full on to it so as to present a smaller target, clapped on all steam and prepared to ram the U-boat. Luckily for all, perhaps, the 'periscope' turned out to be nothing more than the mast of an empty water-logged lifeboat from a sunken British liner.

Her crew loved the dirty old *Trident*, for she worked hard and always got through in her slow, ponderous way. They liked to joke that any U-boat commander who torpedoed her would get the sack for wasting a torpedo, for they reckoned she could fall to pieces at any time without any assistance from the Germans.

Empire Brigade, the ship snatched back from the Italians, had had a nerve-racking encounter with a U-boat on the way out, after losing her convoy. In heavy weather she suddenly came upon the U-boat on the surface and, each as surprised as the other, ship and submarine both fired one shell before the bad weather took over completely. The German's shell missed *Empire Brigade*, but the roaring gale that followed gave her a real hammering and shifted her centre castle back five inches; she had needed substantial repairs before she could join SC7. Her huge cargo now was 7,000 tons of copper ore, 3,000 tons of grain, great quantities of tinned foods, and eighteen Army lorries secured on the after deck.

At least one of the foreigners, too, had had an eventful outward journey from the U.K. This was the Dutch tramp *Soesterberg*. Her first fortunate escape had been when the east coast convoy with which she started out from Tyneside was attacked at night by enemy dive-bombers. Three ships immediately in company with *Soesterberg* were all struck by bombs, the convoy scattered and *Soesterberg* cracked on full steam to round the northern coast of Scotland and reach the waters of the Pentland Firth, south of the Orkneys. From here that same night she slipped out in the darkness and set course for Canada alone.

In the meantime the surviving ships of her convoy had reformed and she was reported missing, believed lost. It was a tense lone voyage for *Soesterberg*. Three days out they thought their number was up when a plane swooped out of the clouds towards them, for no one aboard could tell one plane from another, friend or enemy, but resolutely they ran up the Dutch flag. The plane circled round, asking the name of the ship, and when they signalled this, it asked for a repeat. It then gave the recognition signal and disappeared in the direction of the English coast. The crew sighed with relief as the plane flew off . . . fortunately it was a British plane, which duly reported them to be still in the land of the living. And so *Soesterberg* had successfully made it to Canada to load up her vital cargo. Pitprops.

Sunday evening, and SC7 continued on course, sympathetic eyes again watching the two remaining Lakers steaming along in their peculiar manner, each looking like two metal islands with a stretch of white water in between. Crazy, just crazy, that vessels like these should have to make such a voyage.

Night came, a glorious night with the new moon shining as a new moon should, and the stars amazingly brilliant. Silent and dark, completely blacked out, the thirty-four ships progressed across the unusually calm and quiet ocean.

But the air waves were busy. Ships' radio officers picked up a message giving warning of a U-boat plotted at 51 deg. N, 27 deg. W. *Twenty-seven degrees West!* With the convoy scheduled to meet its Western Approaches escorts much farther in, at twenty-one degrees West, this really was too close for comfort.

Monday, October 7. Dawn broke, bringing more remarkably settled weather. The sun shone brightly, the sea was very slight, and although the wind was not exactly warm, still it was far from cold.

An ideal day for putting the masters on their mettle. Commodore MacKinnon was active very early, exercising his charges in emergency alterations of course. As the radio officer in one steamer noted in his diary: 'Apparently this Commodore does the job properly!'

Aboard *Assyrian* it made them feel very important as the Commodore's signallers hoisted the bunting giving the orders, which were relayed throughout the convoy, ship to ship. This flag signalling would continue day by day, for complete radio silence had to be observed and the radio officers in the various ships kept a listening watch only. By night, the Commodore's signals were made by a system of red and green lights, a few selected ships being designated as light-repeating ships, so that the whole convoy did not hoist its lights and become lit up like the Blackpool illuminations. When each and every ship had digested the instructions, the executive signal actually to make the required manoeuvre came when the lights were switched off on the Commodore ship.

For the second day running the officers of *Sneland 1*, the barnacled latecomer, looked on in puzzlement at all the busy flag signalling without understanding any of it, not having any convoy papers; but this time the Commodore detected that something was wrong, and the ship ahead of *Sneland* was detailed to fall out of the column, drop back and take up position behind her, so as to be better placed to give assistance. But no sooner had this situation been sorted out than a ship appeared unexpectedly over the horizon ahead of the convoy, with the seeming intention of joining the flock.

The big British steamer *Shekatika*, only four years old but her steel decks already rusting, had set out from Halifax with a fast HX convoy, but found herself completely unable to stay the course. She was loaded with steel below, and pitprops piled high on her decks. In fact, so stacked with timber was she that the well-decks were full, and poles standing ten feet above the bulwarks prevented wholesale log cascades into the sea. Plank walks with wood handrails were nailed in place on top of the last of the mighty stack; by this means the crew walked from aft to duties amidships, and to the galley.

Shekatika had failed to keep up with the fast convoy mainly because of the poor quality Canadian coal in her bunkers. The firemen had done their best, coming up only to get great pickle jars of slightly salted drinking water at the galley pump. But no matter how hard they sweated and drank water to restore their body fluid, they could not keep the ship in station, especially at the end of each watch, when they 'ashed out' from the furnaces great lumps of clinker six feet long. So Captain Robert Paterson had been ordered to turn back and join the slower convoy coming up in the rear. *Shekatika* was less than a day on her own before the ships of SC7 crept masts first round the curve of the world into her circle of sea, and at two o'clock in the afternoon she took up station as the last ship of the port column. Her armament? Just a single rifle used for anti-sabotage watch on the gangway when she was docked.

So, one ship gone, another gained. SC7 sailed on at seven knots. At 6 p.m., ships' clocks were advanced one hour. Clocks would be advanced regularly now throughout the voyage, as they progressed the five hours from Eastern Time to Greenwich Time. At 9 p.m. the yacht HMCS *Elk* left the convoy for other duties, and the seaplane, too, was seen no more. The convoy was left alone with its single escort, the *Scarborough*, and would remain so for another ten days at least.

Just before midnight, course was altered for the night. And still the weather continued fine.

Tuesday, October 8. More settled weather, the morning sun shining brightly on the trim lines of ships. It took some believing . . . was this really the tempestuous Atlantic? There was a much bigger swell, however, causing ships to roll.

Commodore MacKinnon was very persistent in his exercises this morning. Besides zigzagging, the ships were put through a long sound-signals exercise, and hooters were blowing all over the convoy from 10 a.m. to 11.30 a.m. It offered some passing entertainment, picking out which ship was blowing by the sound of her hooter. *Corinthic* had a good strong one which acted straight away and was quite definite . . . *Beatus*, next door to her, would do a 'sisssss' of varied length before she started to 'hooooo', while *Blairspey*, on the other side, made heavy weather of it with someone pulling the lanyard who took a long time over the dots and dashes. *Assyrian*'s hooter had a double note. Above them all sounded the posh modern hooter of the big French tanker.

Besides the hooter-blowing, flag signals went up at frequent intervals, and there were many men who derived great interest from trying to learn the various flags.

Whether by good luck or good schooling, it was all a sight more orderly than on previous SC convoys, whose Commodores had wept in fury at the lackadaisical standard of the simplest flag signalling and roundly cursed the foreigners who could not—or would not—read semaphore. When, as on one well remembered occasion, two hoists from the International Code Book had taken three hours ten minutes to pass through a convoy, such anger was well justified. The Germans could have sunk them all in less than half the time.

But if he had achieved tolerable order among his flock, one failing that Commodore MacKinnon could not correct was the prolific smoke they made. It wafted upwards in a clear sky, a treat for enemy eyes. Steamers were made to steam, and testy signals of 'Make less smoke' brought little result from ships doing their best on poor quality coal. The *Assyrian* herself, denied her good Welsh coal, was just as guilty as the rest.

At noon the convoy, still maintaining a good seven knots, reached position 46 deg. 35 min. N, 49 deg. 13 min. W. They were beginning to rise sharply northwards now.

In the quiet of the afternoon crews prepared their 'sub bags' once again. These were the small canvas bags, like miniature kitbags, into which each man packed his most valued personal possessions, all ready for the lifeboat. The lifeboats themselves were checked over and things generally got ready for entering the danger zone. Those ships which had guns made sure they were in working order. In convoy there could be no more practice, no more popping off at a barrel dropped overboard. The next shots, when fired, would be at the enemy.

Apart from these activities crews settled to the business of overcoming the feeling of tenseness coupled with sheer boredom which was the merchant seaman's lot for long, monotonous periods in convoy.

For most men that meant cards. Cards, whether played for money or matchsticks, was more than a relaxation, it was a kind of religion. And a special part of that religion was the game of cribbage. Once, not so long ago, aboard the newcomer, *Shekatika*, when a great shout went up and the din and cheering was immense, people rushed into the saloon thinking wildly that perhaps the Germans had given in. Not so. It was just that twenty-nine, the greatest score mathematically possible in the game of cribbage, and one almost impossible to achieve statisti-

cally speaking, had just turned up in the 'box' in a game of
five card, four-handed crib.

There were other forms of recreation, too. Aboard *Assyrian*
the three French sailors sat on a hatch singing happily along
with 'Chippy', the young ship's carpenter from Anglesey. The
Frenchmen and he had found to their delight that the songs
of Brittany and Wales both had a Celtic origin and could be
sung by either. Below, Second Engineer Bill Venables, when
off watch, studied his notes on the Flying Flea he was making
to the design of its inventor, Henri Mignet. Venables had been
building the little aeroplane in his spare time for two years now.
On other voyages he had completed the fuselage, rudder and
framework of the wings, working in the space for'ard where the
twin-screw *Assyrian*'s two shaft tunnels converged. It made an
ideal workshop, though he had had to make the fuselage half an
inch narrower than specification in order to get it through
the tunnel door into the engine room. Back home in Liverpool
he had a brand new 34 horse-power Anzani engine, and now
he was saving money for the linen and dope for the wings . . .
quite an item when as second engineer his wages came to only
£17 10s a month. When war broke out he had transferred his
dissembled Flea from the ship to his home, but he was still
reluctant to relinquish his dream of building and flying his own
plane, which he hoped to do when the war was ended. So he
had spent a voyage designing and making a propeller of
laminated beech and mahogany, which now hung over his
bunk.

Yes, one day he would fly. Bill Venables was determined
about that.

Wednesday, October 9. It was still gloriously fine and sunny,
and everyone was astonished at the continued good weather. A
little uneasy, too. Seas like this favoured a searching enemy, and
there were a few quiet prayers offered that the weather would
eventually revert to its normal stormy self, when the rough
conditions would make it more difficult for a U-boat to find
them.

The flag-painted Swedish ship had inexcusably shown a light during the night and was severely reprimanded by the Commodore. Blackout was very strict and most ships exercised their own discipline on this. Like on the *Corinthic*, where any light shown after blackout time was liable to cost a man a fine of five shillings. The long and lonely night hours were always a time of extra tension. Tell-tale sparks might suddenly come from the funnel . . . someone on deck might forgetfully light a match . . .

There were more manoeuvres this morning for over an hour as Commodore MacKinnon ran up his various flag commands. Everyone seemed to be performing pretty satisfactorily.

They were moving more sharply to the east now in their northerly climb. For the listening ships' radio officers this meant farther and farther away from the New World's cacophony of commercial radio and back into the bleak ocean area of monotonous morse navigation warning signals and the occasional faint yelp of hurried distress signals, which sometimes at night could be heard from thousands of miles away. Good-bye to all the cowboy songs . . . 'Ya gotta rope and throw, leave Oklahoma when the sun is low, if ya wanna be a cowboy . . .'

It was always a novel experience for merchant radio officers making their first trip out to Canada, accustomed only to the wartime diet of the BBC's Home and Forces programmes. On nearing Canada the background chatter of the radio networks would begin to break through on the ship's primitive two-valve set, pouring straight down the hundreds of feet of aerial wire and making raucous interference. Now, for SC7, the situation was in reverse, the aerials beginning to clear except for the last sounds of station VONF, Newfoundland, which often held the whip-hand in the interference. Lone announcers on VONF held the fort for hours at a time, playing records, giving news of the twins just born up in the backwoods, and relaying sweetheart messages to men out fishing on the foggy Newfoundland Banks. A tune, a chat, and a bit of fun. Like the girl disc jockey who recited, apropos of nothing, between records:

'If a cargo ship, ten thousand tons,
Had sailed ten thousand miles,
With a cargo large of overshoes, and carving knives and files,
If all the mates were six feet tall,
The engineers the same,
Would you subtract or multiply to find the Captain's
name . . .?'

Generally only the radio officers on their listening watch were treated to these delights, for the use of personal radios aboard ship by anyone was forbidden, such sets being either confiscated or dismantled for the duration of the voyage, though there were always some seamen who managed to hold on to their sets and have a listen in occasionally. It was questionable whether any U-boat ever did home in on a ship or convoy through tracking a seaman's radio, but there was no doubt of the disturbing oscillations produced in the 160 metre trawler-band by the cheap super-heterodyne radio sets.

The ships' own receivers were often just as guilty of oscillation, which was a far more serious problem. Commodores of earlier SC convoys had vigorously complained of W/T oscillation from ships, especially the foreigners, and urged that wireless cabins and sets should be sealed before sailing. On some earlier convoys many ships had had only one radio officer, which meant that sets could not be manned round the clock but only during the hours these officers were on watch. The result was that at certain watch commencement times, all sets were switched on at roughly the same moment. The discordant chorus of oscillating whistles and howls, grunts and groans on the air waves that followed could have alerted any listening U-boat and informed him of the coming-on-watch times. At least on SC7, with most ships having two radio officers, the watch was continuous and much of this row was avoided.

6 p.m. Clocks were advanced 30 minutes. The barometer was falling rapidly, and the wind had increased to Force 7 southerly, blowing a near gale. The longed for change in the weather had not been slow in coming.

And what was the radioed news from home, as against the sarcastic prattling of the traitorous Lord Haw-Haw?

The Germans were sweeping into Rumania . . . London had suffered its biggest night bombing raid yet, with very heavy casualties . . . the German invasion fleet was poised to strike . . .

Thursday, October 10. The strong wind continued, and it began to rain. It pelted down all morning. The wind gathered force and ships were taking seas. As the going got more difficult they started to roll a good deal. One or two vessels, labouring heavily under the strain, began to lag behind, earning swiftly signalled rebukes from the Commodore.

The noon position was 51 deg. 47 min. N, 43 deg. 43 min. W. It had been a steep journey north, and now the convoy's path would taper into a more north-easterly curve, though as the voyage continued they would go still higher north to a point below Iceland, where, if a ruler were laid across the chart, they would be on a level with the Orkneys. But this would not be for another six days yet.

On they sailed, taking heavy seas consistently throughout a wild, uncomfortable night.

Friday, October 11. This morning the sun shone, but the heavy seas continued unabated. Decks ran with water as ships pitched and rolled, and breakfast was an adventure. The balancing of a cup of tea in one hand while manoeuvring curry on to a fork with the other, at the same time swaying sideways in rapidly alternating directions, was a very complicated operation.

The storm was in for the day, no doubt about it. The once calm, unruffled convoy presented a far different spectacle now. One minute ships rode right on the heights of the waves, and the next they had practically disappeared below them. It was impossible for the lookouts on any one ship to count more than about twenty other vessels in company. Several ships thrown out of formation by the rough seas of the night were struggling to regain their positions, but it seemed clear that others, noticeably the two Lakers, were no longer in sight.

After a flurry of signalling through the tossing ranks, Commodore MacKinnon and Commander Dickinson, in the attentive *Scarborough*, reached a final count of the ships in convoy, or at least in sight of it. Four vessels were missing : two big old Greek tramps, each well over three thousand tons, and the two Lakers.

The Greeks were the *Niritos*, loaded with sulphur, and the *Aenos*, carrying grain. The Lakers were the *Trevisa* and the *Eaglescliffe Hall*.

All masters had been advised of the daily 'rendezvous' positions of SC7, so that they might hurry their way back to the convoy should they become detached from it in darkness or bad weather. Would these four storm-tossed absentees manage to fight their way back?

The two Greeks, perhaps. But the slow, erratic Lakers? At most it now seemed a faint hope.

4

The Luck of the Lakers

In the growing seas, the Laker *Trevisa* had fought a steadily losing battle. For most of the twenty-five years of her life she had been employed on the unadventurous routine duty of carrying coal between Lake Erie and Montreal, and her 1,800 tons were not designed to withstand the punishing Atlantic rollers.

While the weather was calm to moderate she had been able to keep up with the convoy, but she had no reserves in power or speed, and as the seas and weather worsened she dropped astern, the convoy drawing well ahead of her and finally vanishing over the horizon.

Left to struggle on alone in the heavy seas, *Trevisa*'s situation was not a pleasant one. She was a straggler, and everyone knew what happened to stragglers. Also, there was an additional factor which gave her crew cause for alarm.

Like all the Lakers the *Trevisa*, from Montreal, was being sailed to the U.K. by a British crew sent out specially to Canada to collect her. The officers in these crews stayed as a rule at the same hotel in Montreal while the boats were got ready and their engines adapted for salt water, and it was here that *Trevisa*'s officers had first become aware of their master's excessive liking for his liquor. The captain was in his fifties, and seemed to have acquired a lifetime's thirst. Nor did his drinking slacken off at all when they steamed down to the Bay of Fundy to collect their load of prepared spruce, intended for the construction of fighter aircraft. And once SC7 put to sea he went on the grog in earnest, being patently under the influence of liquor for more than half his waking hours.

Now, with the convoy out of sight, the master of the *Trevisa* ordered a change of course, and although his officers and most of the crew knew him to be still well in his cups, they expected him at least to be following the official instructions for stragglers which had been given to all the masters. And so the old Laker pushed her way onward at the best speed that her limited engine-power would allow.

As time went by, however, the *Trevisa*'s new course took her strangely farther south, and her officers grew worried. It was then discovered that instead of steering a course to pass between certain secret map reference positions set up across the North Atlantic, the captain was in fact steering a course to pass *through* the first of these reference points, and then presumably through all the others, one by one. It was a huge and totally unnecessary detour to make, if not an extremely foolish and dangerous one; but it was the master's decision, and as such could not be questioned.

On October 15, five days after losing the convoy, *Trevisa*, travelling far south of SC7's curving northerly route, neared 21 degrees West. This was the meridian that marked the outer limit of the Western Approaches—the farthest point in the Atlantic to which British warships came to shepherd in the homeward-bound convoys. But no escorts came this far south, more than 120 miles below the route of SC7.

As the old Laker plodded on over mile after mile of dangerous ocean Radio Officer Charles Littleboy was seized by a feeling of impending disaster and determined to do something about it.

He made every possible preparation in the radio room to keep going in the case of a total power failure, and also rigged up an emergency light. At 9 p.m. on October 15 he went into the chartroom and, with the second mate's permission, estimated and drew up a list of *Trevisa*'s positions by latitude and longitude for every half hour during the coming night. He took the list down to the radio room and fastened it down beside the morse key. He then went to his cabin, which formed part of the radio room, and lay on his bed, fully dressed and wearing a partly inflated life-jacket. . . .

It was after two o'clock in the morning when, in the moonlight, U-124 came upon its prey. Kapitanleutnant Wilhelm Georg Schulz could hardly believe his good fortune. A seasoned Atlantic commander, he was out on the twelfth day of his patrol from the U-boat base at Lorient. U-124, with Schulz's edelweiss emblem painted on its conning-tower, was one of the big new ocean-going U-boats with a surface speed of well over sixteen knots, and it was faster than *Trevisa*'s six or seven knots even when submerged. It carried twenty-two torpedoes, though for the curious looking ship which now laboured surprisingly across its path only one would be necessary.

However, Kapitanleutnant Schulz took no chances. He submerged and made a textbook attack. The torpedo sped to its target and struck with a great flash in the night. *Trevisa* seemed to disappear. Schulz marked 'Sunk' in his logbook, and U-124 continued on patrol.

The torpedo ripped into *Trevisa* and blew off the whole of her stern in a thousand flying fragments. The explosion disembowelled the engine-room, killing all the engine staff . . . the chief, second and third engineers, a donkeyman and a fireman. The ship's lifeboats were blown to bits and the vessel plunged into total darkness.

For Radio Officer Littleboy, who was lying on his bed when the torpedo struck, pressure seemed to predominate over noise. His body appeared to be held against the ceiling, but in the darkness it was impossible to identify walls, ceiling or floor, until gravity caused him to fall back to the sloping deck. He then saw faint moonlight coming through the open doorway and reasoned that the radio room was still right side up. Scrambling up and with the doorway to guide him, he quickly found and switched on the emergency light which he had prepared. It undoubtedly saved many lives, including his own.

Using the emergency power he started up the transmitter, suddenly remembered the radio antenna and dashed out on deck to find it still luckily in place with both masts nearly vertical, then ran back to the radio room, and without waiting for the captain's authority tapped out the distress signal '. . . SSSS . . .' together with his own estimate of the ship's position as shown by the list he had put ready. It was a good feeling to get an immediate answer from both sides of the Atlantic. He repeated the distress call several times, stressing the fact that *Trevisa* was turning over and sinking, firstly to give any nearby ship a chance to take radio bearings, and secondly to assure the U-boat that its job was completed—they didn't want a second torpedo. It was reassuring to hear a British coastal station speedily repeat his message on the distress frequency.

He then hurried back on deck. *Trevisa* was sinking slowly by her shattered stern and listing ominously as she made to turn over. There were just over a dozen survivors and only two rafts between them, primitive affairs consisting of four 40-gallon oildrums in a wooden lattice framework. Some men in their panic wanted to sit on the rafts and let the dying Laker sink beneath them, but Littleboy suggested they should carry the rafts to the water's edge and launch them properly. It would be safer and would keep them busy. All agreed to do this, and it was only when they tried to move the rafts that it was discovered they were both chained firmly to the deck. The horrible thought of what would have happened had they simply sat on them as the ship sank below the surface came as a cold douche upon fuddled minds.

Littleboy and the second mate now became aware of the curious absence of the captain and hurried to investigate. The mate led the way for'ard to the master's cabin, and there they

found him in a drunken stupor, totally unaware that anything
was wrong. They had to throw respect for authority to the winds
and use considerable physical force to bring him round and get
him on his feet. When the situation finally dawned on him he
sobered up fast.

On returning to the deck Littleboy and the mate helped to
release the first raft from its chain and launch it over the side.
The first man to jump aboard was a frightened young seaman
who immediately pushed it away from the ship and started to drift
off to sea alone. It took much cajoling by the elderly chief officer
to persuade him to paddle the raft back to the side of the
listing ship, after which another seven men clambered on and
the raft moved away fully loaded.

In the meantime the second mate had disappeared, so those
remaining prepared to launch the second raft without his help.
They had got the raft on to the sloping deck, ready to slip down
into the water, when the mate reappeared. He had rushed to his
cabin to pack his personal effects, and now arrived on deck
humping two large suitcases, together with a typewriter tucked
under one arm and the ship's chronometer under the other, and
his pockets and clothing bulging with every possible domestic
commodity other than food and water. In the midst of grave
emergency he cut a tragically ludicrous figure, for there was no
possible stowage space for any of his luggage aboard the raft.
But his foolishness did not justify the action that followed.

The bleary-eyed captain, taking the opportunity to perform
his one and only authoritative act of the night, angrily snatched
the baggage away from the second mate and hurled it piece by
piece into the sea. It would have been easier for him to leave
the pathetic load on deck and show a little consideration towards
the man who had just helped to rouse him and save his life,
but only now was the captain beginning to show any signs of
command. He had taken no part in the abandon-ship routine
nor given any orders about sending a distress message or disposing of the ship's secret code books. The radio officer had
locked these books in the steel lockers of the radio room so
that they would go down with the ship. The flimsy code 'key'

sheet he kept in his pocket to hand to his captain later—if they survived.

By this time the ship's starboard rails were well under water and they had no difficulty in launching the second raft. The remaining six survivors who scrambled aboard it were the captain, chief officer, second mate, radio officer and two young seamen. They paddled the raft to a safe distance away from the overturning ship and waited. It was a strangely calm, moonlit night as they huddled there, gently riding the slight swell, only the radio officer in uniform, the others wearing whatever clothes they had been able to grab in the emergency. At frequent intervals came the question, 'Did you get the distress message away, Sparks?' and repeatedly he assured them that the message had been sent and acknowledged. But what were their chances of being picked up? This question was not one to be debated, every man chewing it over to himself in agonised silence.

Then, just as dawn was breaking on the eastern horizon, there came the threat of high danger when the chief officer saw a vague shape in the distance. Everyone was convinced that it was the lurking U-boat, now moving in to spray the rafts with machine-gun fire, and they crouched down in fear. In a little while, however, what they had thought to be a conning-tower turned into a topmast and bridge—it was a British destroyer. Jubilantly the chief officer and second mate set off signal flares, and as the ship closed, the radio officer flashed a warning message with his torch . . . 'Sub near.' Within minutes the two rafts were being circled by three destroyers, one of which dropped speed and closed in alongside. It was HMS *Keppel*. 'Hurry, there! Hurry!' came the shouts from her bridge, and they lost no time in climbing up the scrambling nets lowered over the destroyer's side.

With all fourteen of them safely aboard, *Keppel* drew away from the scene, as did HMS *Sabre*, leaving the third of the trio, the Canadian destroyer *Ottawa*, to stand by the now completely overturned and half sunken *Trevisa*. At 8.21 a.m. she wirelessed the Commander-in-Chief, Western Approaches: '*Trevisa* bottom up, 25 feet of her showing, five feet above water, propose to sink . . .' It did not take much effort from *Ottawa*'s gunners to send the Laker's remains sliding below the surface of the compassionate sea. She died in position 57.28N, 20.30W. For a quarter of a century she had hauled her cargoes round the sweet waters of the Great Lakes, now her distant grave was the deep mid-Atlantic. She took down with her six men.

Aboard *Keppel* the survivors were given a quick examination by the destroyer's doctor, who found no bones broken. The prescription was a hot bath and bed, *Keppel*'s officers and crew willingly doubling up to provide accommodation for them.

Saved, and comfortable . . . the idle unemployed. For as *Trevisa* sank, so did the jobs of her crew. Their term of engagement ended on October 16, 1940 at the hour the waves closed above her. In most ships perhaps one or two officers would remain on salary, but for the rest, and the seamen, the loss of their vessel rendered them unemployed and so unpaid.

Such were the unreasonable conditions under which Britain's merchant seamen at this time loyally fought the war.

On this same day, October 16, hundreds of miles away to the north-east, the other Laker which had lost the convoy was still pressing on determinedly for the U.K.

The *Eaglescliffe Hall* was only half the age of *Trevisa* and at 1,900 tons was a hundred tons bigger, but her handicaps were much the same, if not greater. Her three-cylinder steam reciprocating engines were of a mere 81 horse-power. They had been designed to ease her over smooth inland waters, and the strain of keeping up with a seven-knot ocean convoy had finally proved too much. She gradually lost ground due to steering, engine and steaming difficulties, and in the end had just had to stop. By the time the trouble was cleared sufficiently for her to continue, the convoy had long disappeared.

On finding himself alone in mid-ocean without the remotest hope of catching up with SC7, Captain Charles Madsen followed his own counsel. Although only in his early forties, he was a well-experienced master who had sailed all kinds of general cargo ships all over the world, and what was more he knew the North Atlantic like the back of his hand. In spite of all the dangers that ocean might now hold, he knew that with *Eaglescliffe Hall's* severe limitations there was only one course of action for him to take, and that was to make his way home by the shortest route. Accordingly he laid course direct for the Butt of Lewis.

And so for five days now, since losing the convoy, *Eaglescliffe Hall* had pressed ahead, her dogged performance being something of a tribute to the Middlesbrough shipyard that built her back in 1928, and to her crew, mainly Tynesiders like their captain, who almost willed her through the waves.

Like *Trevisa*, the *Eaglescliffe Hall,* also a Montreal boat, was stacked to capacity with timber. Her sole armament consisted of a Thompson gun which had been delivered aboard in pieces at Sydney, together with a book of instructions on how to assemble the weapon, and a small amount of ammunition. By trial and error they had put the gun together, but a positive gnat's sting it seemed as they steamed on through dangerous seas.

Captain Madsen had not left the wheelhouse by day or night since leaving Sydney, nearly two weeks ago now. The dark early hours of October 17 found him there, keeping alert watch on the night sea, when suddenly he saw a mysterious craft low in the water and travelling at considerable speed pass by on *Eaglescliffe Hall's* port side. It was a heart-stopping moment, for it could only have been a surfaced U-boat, racing along on its fast diesel engines. Yet the next anxious minutes brought no further sign of the marauder. To their immense relief either they had not been seen or the German had bigger fish to fry.

Shortly afterwards another traveller emerged out of the night, this time the solid dark shape of a large steamer, which overtook and passed the Laker on the starboard side. She was so close that in the moonlight Captain Madsen immediately recognized her as the *Aenos*, one of the two Greek vessels which, unknown to him, had also lost the convoy. He identified *Aenos* from her clipper stem, for the thirty-year-old ship was originally the *Cedar*

Branch, built in Sunderland, and Captain Madsen had known her well before she was sold off to the Greeks.

Nearly twice the tonnage of the Laker, the more powerful *Aenos*, loaded with grain, steamed ahead into the night and was gone, leaving *Eaglescliffe Hall* to continue her lone passage.

The rest of the night passed quietly and dawn broke on an empty sea, but the mid-morning brought more company, this time in the sky. It was a patrolling plane from Coastal Command. Circling low, it began to blink out a message on its Aldis lamp . . . 'Lifeboats, rafts and men in distress 25 miles ahead . . .'

It was 10.20 a.m. Captain Madsen asked his chief engineer for every ounce of power, stretching *Eaglescliffe Hall*'s engines to their utmost speed of seven knots, and after three hours' hard steaming the Laker sighted two lifeboats, two rafts, and some miserable pieces of floating wreckage, all that remained of a big steamship of 3,500 tons. At 1.45 p.m. in position 58.56 N, 13.03 W she took aboard twenty-five shocked survivors of the ss. *Aenos*.

Captain Laskarides, very distressed, described as well as he could in broken English how his ship had been torpedoed, the explosion killing three men in the engine-room. After they had abandoned ship and the crippled *Aenos* showed no immediate signs of sinking, the U-boat had finished her off by gunfire. His ship went down at 8.30 a.m., and he and his men had been adrift for some five hours in the waterlogged lifeboats and on the rafts.

It seemed clear that *Aenos*'s killer was the U-boat which had sped past *Eaglescliffe Hall* during the night. The unfortunate *Aenos* had steamed on close behind it, right into the German's patrol area and into his waiting jaws. The U-boat, its job done, had obviously cleared away from the scene fast on sighting the patrolling aircraft. Had it not been for the timely presence of the plane, the Laker would without doubt have been the U-boat's next victim.

Fortune had smiled on them. After taking aboard the exhausted Greeks, Captain Madsen set course to pass outside the Hebrides for Barra Head, hoping to avoid the route of further trouble and in addition to make landfall nearer in case of accidents.

Held as they were in the gunsights of the Germans there had been no time for the Greeks to abandon ship with any ceremony, and they had only what they stood up in, together with a few valuables such as watches and money which they had carried on them at the time the ship was struck. They were in a state of acute shock and bewilderment that it could have happened to them, not seeming to have any notion what war conditions were. Their sole desire was to get as far away as possible from the scene of their encounter with the enemy.

As the Laker slowly ate up the miles they continued very jittery, peering anxiously ahead for the first sight of land. When at last it came, the faint outline of the rugged islands of St. Kilda, they nearly wept for joy. But on learning to their dismay that *Eaglescliffe Hall* did not intend to call there, their emotion knew no bounds. All they desperately wanted was to feel firm earth under their feet, far away from the waters which any minute might release another killer torpedo. A deputation begged Captain Madsen to put them ashore at St. Kilda. They did not seem to know or care that the austere islands were now totally unoccupied, the remaining few dozen inhabitants having been evacuated to the Scottish mainland, more than a hundred miles away, years earlier. The Laker's captain tried to explain to them that if he landed them there they would be in for a very long wait, quite apart from the serious problems of trying to keep themselves alive. His ship, he repeated, was bound for the Clyde.

At this many of the Greeks broke down and some openly sobbed. Through tears they pleaded with him that they could go no further—that they were terrified that even now a U-boat might be shadowing them to send them to the watery grave from which they had only recently escaped. But Captain Madsen was adamant. It was to be the Clyde or the enemy, he told them. The ship would take her chance, and so must they. Sorrowfully they resigned themselves to this fact.

The master now grimly faced the last lap of his dangerous

journey. *Eaglescliffe Hall*, he was determined, would bring herself, her crew and her load of survivors into Rothesay Bay intact.

Incredibly, her weird and wonderful engines responding gamely to the last calls made on them, the Laker did just that. At 10 p.m. on Saturday, October 19, 1940 she steamed safely in, alone and unheralded in the pitch dark blackout.

But next morning it was different. As she moved up from Rothesay Bay to Gourock pier she was greeted by rousing cheers and an exuberant fanfare of ships' hooters.

Too slow to get out of her own way? Slow, yes, but bloody sure!

5

The First of the Hunters

Saturday, October 12. Two days after the disappearance of the
Lakers and the two Greeks, convoy SC7 forged on through heavy
seas. Ships had tossed and rolled throughout the night, and
so it continued for most of the morning, seamen holding on to
any and everything as their vessels rode the boisterous Atlantic.
In spite of the awkward conditions the Commodore still sent
up many flag hoists, a number of vessels being ordered to change
their positions and group up with others bound for the same final
destinations.

During the afternoon the buffeting wind began to die down
and progress became fairly comfortable again. Only a thousand-
odd miles to go as the crow flies!

Sunday, October 13. It poured with rain, and the glass went
down once more. But there was a cheering sun and they were
managing a consistent seven knots now, after the previous day's
struggle to keep at six knots. The noon position was 55.59
N, 32.48 W, and the convoy commenced zigzag No. 17. From

tomorrow night they would be entering the high danger zone.

There was much speculation as to when ships would arrive at their various ports. The lucky ones were those that would end or break their journey at Rothesay, as against those bound for the east coast. The Rothesay ships should arrive late on Friday night or early Saturday morning. It depended on the weather, U-boats, enemy aircraft, and a few other minor details . . .

The convoy continued zigzagging throughout the night.

Monday, October 14. They were now less than 30 degrees West and into the straight for home. Metaphorically 'straight', for they were still furiously zigzagging, to the regular ten-minutely discomfort of everyone as each vessel rolled over on to her new course.

The wind was kinder, and a weak sun shone; only an occasional sea now flopped on to the deck.

Several of the timber ships had noticeably increased lists, but all vessels kept good station. The daily manoeuvres were carried out with an easy familiarity, flag signals going up with promptitude, and altogether *Assyrian*'s admiral had got them running in real Navy fashion.

They were farther north than ever now, having passed beyond 57. N, and were still climbing. Yet it was not too cold.

Tuesday, October 15. The convoy continued rising north towards Iceland, the weather beginning to feel like it. Both sky and sea were grey, and the wind had turned decidedly wintry. They were above 58 degrees North, and passing 25 degrees West.

The day brought a piece of good cheer. One of the four missing vessels had managed to rejoin. She was the Greek *Niritos,* carrying a cargo of sulphur. A typical sturdy, ageing old tramp was the *Niritos.* Greek she might be now, but she had started out as a British ship from West Hartlepool, three names and thirty-three years ago, back in 1907.

There was still no sign of the other missing Greek, *Aenos,* and the two Lakers. There was little hope felt of ever seeing them again now.

The convoy moved on steadily throughout the day, *Scarborough* retaining her pathfinding position ahead as though fastened by an invisible tie to the leader of each column of ships.

During the afternoon the Commodore made the warning signal: 'Keep sharp lookout for submarine astern.' They must be on their guard now for any shadowing U-boat.

In the evening zigzagging began again in complicated style. Shortly after midnight an outward-bound convoy passed by, faintly visible in the distance, steaming safely out of the danger zone SC7 was now entering. Ships that pass in the night . . .

Wednesday, October 16. It was a pleasantly sunny morning, though with the wind very cold, but aboard the *Assyrian* and other ships which had picked up the distress message, they knew that the crew of the *Trevisa* would not be thinking much about the weather or anything else, for she had been torpedoed far to the south. Sadly, some radio officers did not even recognize the name or call sign as being that of one of the lost Lakers, it remained just one more distress call among several heard during the night. But in *Assyrian* they knew it only too well. With mixed feelings Commodore MacKinnon took up his list of ships and struck off *Trevisa*'s name. She was the first convoy vessel he had lost through enemy action. There had to be a first victim, and he had been prepared for it each time he sailed, but now that it had happened it was none the easier to accept. Each ship, even the dirtiest and most troublesome tramp, was a living thing, besides being of great need to Britain's war effort, and *Trevisa*'s crew were not just another cold statistic but a company of human individuals. What had been their fate?

At noon the convoy reached its highest point on the chart, 59. 31 N, 21. 39 W. From now on its path would follow a steady curve to the south-east, advancing east much more rapidly than on the climb to the north.

Late in the afternoon a lone ship hove into sight, travelling far over on the port side of the convoy. As she steamed abeam of them the end of a rainbow showed immediately behind her. A strange, enchanting spectacle, it probably would have been regarded as an omen of something or other by superstitious seamen of bygone days.

And then suddenly there was a signal lamp flashing to the north, and as the dying rays of the sun moved slowly across the horizon, crews were relieved and pleased to see the silhouettes of two small warships coming to meet them. Were they guardian ships of the Northern Patrol, or the convoy's long awaited escort?

They were not left in doubt for very long.

The sloop HMS *Fowey* and corvette HMS *Bluebell* had anticipated meeting up with SC7 soon after 9 p.m., but instead both sighted the convoy at 6 p.m. They therefore decided to leave the outward-bound convoy they had been helping to escort, and join SC7 immediately.

Under the orders of Commander Dickinson in *Scarborough* each now took up their escort positions. *Scarborough* herself moved to the port wing of the convoy. *Fowey* took the starboard wing, and *Bluebell* went astern.

It was a cheering sight for the merchantmen, now at least the convoy could show a few teeth. But they might not have been quite so pleased had they known that *Fowey* already carried a large quota of survivors. They were the entire crew of the New Zealand Shipping Company's big 9,000-ton steamer *Hurunui*, which had been torpedoed and sunk two days earlier on the outward convoy. Some of these men now stood on *Fowey*'s deck and looked on apprehensively as she joined SC7. They had just escaped a watery tomb and now here they were, having to sail back again over each dangerous mile.

Fowey was about the same size as *Scarborough*. She had been launched the same year, too, in 1930, but unlike *Scarborough* she had not been adapted for surveying but was designed to serve the multi-purpose role of escort sloop, minesweeper and admiral's yacht. Her pleasurable peacetime occupation had been that of generally showing the flag as a gunboat in the Persian Gulf. War had brought her to the Atlantic.

Camouflaged, and with four-inch guns fore and aft, *Fowey* looked a very purposeful ship. But it was always a surprise for

others to see the pennant on her side, painted large and clear—
'U-15'. More than that, a first sight of it often made hearts
jump for a painful second or two. It was easy to understand
how already one merchant ship had rammed the sloop in error
for a U-boat. Those responsible for the 'U' marking of some
warships seemed to have little idea of the instant suspicion if
not terror it could create in the minds of seamen, especially
among harassed ships in darkness or bad weather.

The *Bluebell* was quite a different vessel. She was a corvette,
only five months old, one of the new and strange breed of
warship now beginning to make their mark in Atlantic escort
work. The corvettes were in fact a development of the trawler,
and had been intended for use as coastal escorts, but because
of the desperate shortage of ocean escorts they were pitched
almost at once into work for which they had never been designed
—'Cut off by the yard like a string of sausages', as one naval
critic wryly observed. It made one dizzy to watch the corvettes
in heavy seas. Like the trawlers they did not cut through the
waves but rode over them. They bobbed and weaved, sat on the
tops of waves, spun round like corks and generally bounced
about in an alarming manner. But, overgrown trawlers as they
might be, the corvettes could withstand exceptionally bad seas.
Rather smaller than the sloops, they were very manoeuvrable
and could reach a speed of fifteen knots. *Bluebell* had a four-inch
gun, Lewis guns and, importantly, the latest type of asdic set,
as against the earlier type fitted in *Fowey*.

There was another great difference between *Fowey* and *Bluebell*. While the sloop was commanded by a naval lieutenant-
commander, with a largely naval crew, *Bluebell*'s commander
was a Merchant Navy officer of the Royal Naval Reserve, and
her crew mostly inexperienced hostilities-only ratings. The fact
that Lieutenant-Commander Robert Aubrey, RN, of *Fowey*
and Lieutenant-Commander Robert Evan Sherwood, RNR, of
Bluebell had never even met, meant little. The commanders of
Western Approaches escorts at this time more often than not
were complete strangers to each other. There had been no special
training in working together against U-boats and there were no

common plans of action. All escorts worked independently. They would accompany an outgoing convoy, then receive wirelessed instructions from Western Approaches Command, in Liverpool, to detach and rendezvous with an incoming convoy at a certain position, and escort it in. Off they went, and if they were lucky they found the convoy—if by the time they arrived it had not moved to another position. They never knew which other warships, or how many, they would meet on the same mission. As they arrived singly at the convoy the escort senior to the others would assume authority and position them, and the command could be always changing with the arrival of a more senior ship.

So in the late hours of October 16 the two newcomers settled in with SC7 for the homeward run. To them it was just one more convoy among many, they had brought one out and now they were bringing one in, and the cycle would be repeated again and again, until they were deemed to have earned a break. Their duties with SC7 would last a bare four days and nights, during which time they would hardly get to know the name of a single ship. That is how it was, and there was no reason to suppose that this convoy of slow and aged ships would be any different.

Each of the new arrivals was a reflection of the character of her commander, both of whom had, in their respective ways, chosen the sea as a career at a very early age.

Fowey's Lieutenant-Commander Aubrey was a skilled naval officer of thirty-one, well-built and broad-shouldered, with plenty of drive and determination. He had entered the Royal Naval College at Dartmouth and first gone to sea in 1926. He had come to *Fowey* from commanding a destroyer flotilla leader, and had already seen plenty of action, including the Norwegian campaign. He was the type of man, a dedicated naval officer, who drew an easy respect from his juniors, even when they disagreed with some of his personal views. They counted their time with him as valuable experience.

Aubrey was a 'salt-horse' and disdainful of specialists, especially as to their ability in ship-handling. He was a prodder, a fighter, a man of swift, decisive action. Every forenoon his officers would be summoned to the boatdeck which he was pacing to 'tell the story of their lives,' which meant telling him what they had been doing so that he could find out those things they had not done. His terse comments would remain with them always . . . 'Procrastination is the thief of time' . . . 'Never volunteer any information' . . . 'I wouldn't know—I haven't taken a course' . . . 'How *right* are you?' . . . 'I don't give a fish's tit' . . . Blunt and pugnacious, but always fair was Aubrey, and as jolly as he could be assertive. He delighted in singing Frances Day songs such as 'Blue Champagne' and 'I'm just a little girl lost in a fog . . . Me and my dog, lost in a fog . . . Won't some kind gentleman see me home' . . . when his jowelly face would wreath in smiles as he beat time on his thighs.

Bluebell's Lieutenant-Commander Sherwood, RNR, stocky, bearded and bright-eyed, was the son of a merchant captain. Aged thirty-three, he began his apprenticeship at sea at the age of fifteen, and went on to become mate and then master in various East Coast vessels. Then, from 1935 onwards, he progressed from junior officer to master on the Holyhead-Dublin steamers.

On the outbreak of war Sherwood commanded trawlers on the Dover Patrol. He left Dover in May, 1940 to stand by *Bluebell* as she was being built, one of the very first of the new corvettes. He was then called to Dunkirk, as so many were, to join in the rescue work, and captained a tug which saved hundreds of exhausted soldiers from the beaches and brought them safely to Ramsgate. He returned to the Clyde to find *Bluebell* launched, and commissioned her in late August. Though the corvette had since been active for only two months she had seen plenty of sea time. After a week's 'work-up' at the battle school at Tobermory she had begun escorting convoys from Methil up round the north of Scotland into the Atlantic, and was then switched to Liverpool to escort outward-bound convoys and bring in the homecoming ones.

Sherwood never left *Bluebell's* bridge, sleeping there in a hammock in the asdic house. He was a quick and confident commander, as well as displaying a keen sense of humour. He certainly needed to keep tight hold of the reins, for unlike the sloop, whose company was composed mostly of Naval Regulars, *Bluebell*'s crew were pretty raw. For three-quarters of them, conscript seamen ratings fresh from training school, *Bluebell* was their first ship—the first time they had ever been to sea. A handful of experienced A.B.s and petty officers, among them the coxswain, a recalled naval pensioner, served to inspire the rest. As for the officers, *Bluebell*'s number one was an RNVR lieutenant whose pre-war experience had consisted chiefly of yachting round the East Coast, while the two juniors, both Canadians, were young RCNVR sub-lieutenants only just out of training college.

Fowey and *Bluebell*. Apart from the Commodore ship and *Scarborough*, no other vessels in the convoy were yet aware of their names. But they would be, soon enough.

Thursday, October 17. In the old *Corinthic*, Second Radio Officer Henry Simpson, a nineteen-year-old from Aberdeen, was on listening watch in the dead hours after midnight. He had considerable misgivings about this date. His previous trip to sea had been for a few days only, when his ship was torpedoed— on the 17th. Indeed, the figure seemed to haunt him. He had joined the shipping company on April 17, been torpedoed on July 17, and signed on with the *Corinthic* on August 17. Now, in the early hours of another 17th, he was full of forebodings. He had been nervy all the previous evening, and hesitated a long time before turning in, even with all his clothes on, the practice they had been following for the past few days.

Just before Henry came on watch at midnight, First Radio Officer Kenneth Howell had picked up a distant message warning of a U-boat far ahead, and he half-jokingly told the mournful Henry to have a special listen-out at about 3 a.m., for he had worked out speeds and distances and thought perhaps the German might come their way.

As the convoy steamed silently on through the occasionally moonlit night, Henry Simpson sat glued to the radio, like his counterparts in the other merchant vessels, while men off-watch dozed fitfully on their bunks. From every bridge, eyes searched the fluctuating darkness. The weather remained clear with very good visibility, and the night clouds gradually dispersed to bathe the convoy in the light of a bright full moon.

It was a silent, almost mesmeric scene for the ships' lookouts, the convoy moving alone through the still night sea. But they were not alone. Unknown to them the first of the hunters had arrived. On its conning-tower, the emblem of an arched cat with glowing eyes. Waiting to pounce . . .

In the early hours of darkness before midnight U-48, a big new ocean-going boat commanded by Kapitanleutnant Heinrich Bleichrodt, had cruised easily over the surface of the fairly gentle sea, enjoying the welcome break in the weather after a stormy north-wester. The watch on the bridge could move around freely without lifebelts, looking poetically on the white horses of the sea shimmering in the silvery moonlight; the mood was rather that of an unhurried night-ride on peacetime manoeuvres rather than a wartime patrol searching for the enemy convoy lanes. But in a fraction of time all that was changed.

'Shadow in front!' went the message to the U-boat's commander. After only a few seconds on the bridge Kapitanleutnant Bleichrodt saw that there were indeed several small shadows ahead to starboard. He brought the U-boat full speed ahead closer to the shadows, and ordered the crew to battle stations. The first officer of the watch and the battle watch on the bridge took their positions. All could now see that they were in the presence of a considerable convoy. They counted more than thirty ships. The columns of smoke from the convoy formed avenues of poplars in the night sky.

Bleichrodt manoeuvred the U-boat still nearer to the convoy, and the Germans could then make out the shapes of the escort vessels. Bleichrodt turned the U-boat on to a parallel course, so as not to be seen and driven away. He then made U-48 follow all the movements of the convoy; its zigzag course was logged, and they were very soon able to establish its general eastward course and speed.

The glad tidings were wirelessed to the U-boat base at Lorient:
U-48 had sighted a large convoy at map reference AL3388,
heading East at seven knots.

Meanwhile they had been noting the movements of the three
escorts. One (*Scarborough*) steamed on the port wing and ahead
of the convoy, another (*Fowey*) patrolled the starboard wing,
and the third vessel (*Bluebell*) was on station astern, as 'sweeper'.
U-48 was in a favourable position, having the convoy and its
protecting vessels between itself and the moon. The silhouettes
of the ships were clearly visible, while the small shape of the
U-boat would be hard to make out against the dark horizon.

Bleichrodt now had the task of bringing his U-boat into a
surface aiming position without being seen. He could only
manage this when *Scarborough* was at her farthest point to
starboard on her sweep ahead, and *Bluebell*, similarly, was sweeping to starboard astern, thus leaving the port wing temporarily
unguarded; but every time U-48 tried to steer in towards its
goal one of these two escorts would change course and come
steaming back, causing the U-boat to turn quickly in order to
avoid detection.

Bleichrodt could not wait much longer; once dawn came he
would have to withdraw, as he could only continue to shadow the
convoy during daylight by remaining outside the range of
visibility. He was quietly cursing his luck when suddenly, with
both escorts steaming to starboard, the opportune moment came.
He passed a message to his crew: 'Attacking enemy convoy.
Firing three-pronged blast.'

U-48 now moved in on the convoy's port bow, heading for
the first column of ships. They went in slowly, for Bleichrodt
did not want to betray his presence by the strong phosphoresence
of the water churned up by the screw. The first officer of the
watch was ordered to aim three torpedoes at three different
vessels, which overlapped one another in their staggered course
so that they appeared like one huge vessel.

The convoy loomed up in the moonlight until they were about
three-quarters of a mile away from the target ships. Bleichrodt
ordered the first officer to fire, and swung the boat over to star-

board. All three torpedoes left their tubes smoothly and headed silently for their targets. U-48 then retreated in a north-westerly direction, first at low speed then at full speed ahead. The stop-watches of the first officer and first mate would tell them when the 'eels' should have reached their destinations.

Scarborough and *Bluebell* had by now changed course and were steaming back to the exposed port side of the convoy. Tense moments followed for the U-boat's crew. Would the torpedoes hit their mark? And would U-48 be far enough out of danger when they did?

Then they saw flames shoot up from the convoy and shortly afterwards heard in quick succession two dull detonations roll across the sea.

Kapitanleutnant Bleichrodt gave the order for emergency speed, it was imperative that he should get clear of the scene and back into the protective night shadow. The U-boat's radio operator was picking up strong distress signals on the 600-metre waveband, but because of the suddenly busy air waves it was not possible to make out from which ship or ships the signals were coming. Standing on the bridge of the U-boat, Bleichrodt had to keep warning his men to pull their eyes away from the flare-lit convoy and search the dark areas of the sea for a possible pursuer . . .

It was exactly 4 a.m. when the first of U-48's torpedoes struck home. There was a loud explosion astern of *Corinthic* . . . and then, almost before anyone could scramble up on deck, another explosion as fierce as the first. Immediately the unsleeping Commodore made the light signal from *Assyrian* for an emergency turn to starboard, and all ships wheeled away from the direction of the attack.

Two of U-48's torpedoes had found their targets. The first struck the great tanker *Languedoc* and sent her reeling.

In the Vice-Commodore ship *Scoresby*, forward and to starboard, they saw the brilliant orange flash of the explosion on *Languedoc* and the second mate called Captain Lawrence Zebedee Weatherill to the bridge. Below, Chief Officer Ronald

Coultas sprang from his bunk the second he heard the explosion. He had just put one foot outside the saloon entrance preparatory to climbing the makeshift ladder which would allow him to see over the top of the great stack of pitprops on deck, and the captain had only that moment reached the bridge, when the second torpedo struck—blasting full into *Scoresby*'s side. It exploded in No. 3 hold aft of the engine-room, starting to flood it immediately, and rocked the teetering stacks of pitprops, which started to move dangerously, threatening the safety of the men aft. The ship's after end was sinking into the sea and after a speedy check of the damage there was no doubt that she had received a fatal hit.

Scoresby's captain and the entire ship's company made their way to the boats and all four lifeboats, still thankfully intact, were launched successfully in the light wind and moderate swell. Shortly before the master got into the last of the boats *Scoresby* began to sink by the stern.

Less than five minutes after the boats had drawn away the dying steamer reared her suffering bulk up to an almost vertical position and slid back until only her forecastle head was above water. For another three or four minutes she hung there, then suddenly she was gone, leaving only a mass of swirling pitprops and wreckage to mark her grave.

Languedoc's crew, too, had managed to get their boats away without mishap after first sending up a distress rocket. But their stricken ship still remained afloat.

Fowey, stationed two and a half miles from the convoy on its starboard side, heard the two explosions over the asdic, saw the distress rocket shoot up into the sky and the convoy make its emergency turn to starboard. It was clear the enemy attack had come from the port side, where *Scarborough* would be in need of assistance. Commander Aubrey increased his sloop's speed to her full fourteen knots, steamed round the rear of the convoy and took up station one mile on the starboard beam of the searching *Scarborough*. Together the two sloops, in company with *Bluebell*, which had steamed up from astern, now began an exhaustive moonlight hunt up the port side of the convoy, but it was entirely fruitless. Where the attacking U-boat had vanished to was a complete mystery, for none of the ships could gain an underwater contact.

Scarborough signalled *Bluebell* by dimmed morse lamp to return and pick up survivors while she and *Fowey* continued the search. None of the merchant ships had stopped to help the men from the torpedoed ships. Such action was considered too dangerous and was strictly forbidden by Defence of Merchant Shipping orders.

An hour after the attack the green light showed at *Assyrian's* masthead and the convoy swung back on course, ships which had dispersed now rejoining, until once again the body of ships were proceeding in near perfect formation.

Bluebell, meanwhile, had gone off to hunt in the dark for the survivors, keeping a wary lookout for signs of the enemy. While the corvette was searching in the vicinity of the still floating *Languedoc* some shells whistled alarmingly over her. There was no evidence as to who it was who fired, it could have been any frightened merchantman, but whoever was the culprit the shots were too damned close. Eventually *Bluebell* found the French tanker's crew in their boats, scrambling nets were thrown down over the side and they were helped aboard. The corvette then continued her search for the survivors of *Scoresby*.

It was just before daylight when she located them, and it was an astonishing sight that met the eyes when the corvette drew near to the lifeboats, for all around the four boats there appeared to be a great black mass on the surface of the sea. As *Bluebell* drew closer still they were aware of a strange squelching noise rising from the black mass, an eerie sound quite unlike anything they had ever heard before. Commander Sherwood decided to keep clear of the spot till daylight, so that he could see what he was up against. It was a wise decision, for as dawn broke he discovered that the black mass was a huge cluster of pitprops disgorged by the torpedoed ship; they were moving up and down in the water, creating an odd squeaking noise as wood rubbed on wood. Wires which had been used to secure the pitprops on deck were now streaming among them in the sea and could have put *Bluebell* out of action had they fouled her propellers.

Sherwood manoeuvred the corvette carefully in and took the survivors aboard, all being safe and well. Never would he forget the eye-opening sight of *Scoresby*'s master coming aboard from his lifeboat, a very tall and handsome man, imposing in stature, and dressed in quite the most beautiful new uniform *Bluebell*'s commander had ever seen in his life! The explanation was that after giving the orders to take to the boats Captain Weatherill went into his quarters, put on his new uniform jacket, gathered an attache case containing the ship's papers and discharge books, also some loose clothing, and threw them down to the port side bridge lifeboat before going over to the starboard boat.

Bluebell now closed the crippled *Languedoc*. Although the tanker was very low in the water there still seemed to be half a chance of saving her, so her master, Captain Thompson, rowed over to the ship with his chief officer, second engineer, and some of the crew. But it did not take them long to discover that the engines could not be restarted, and that her hull was so damaged and open to the sea that it was only a matter of time before she sank. Until she did so she was a hazard to shipping, so *Bluebell* fired a few rounds from her four-inch into her, and as she was then obviously sinking, left her.

Bluebell now set out to catch up with the convoy, which had pulled away in the darkness hours ago. The seventy survivors she now carried well outnumbered her own ship's company of fifty-six and it was becoming more than a little crowded. . . .

While *Bluebell* was busy at her rescue work the two sloops had continued the hunt for the U-boat, but still without success. *Scarborough* then rejoined the convoy, leaving *Fowey* to carry on with the search for a time, but *Scarborough* had hardly regained her station when a Sunderland flying boat loomed out of the morning sky and flashed a message that it had sighted and attacked a U-boat a few miles to the north-west of the convoy. The time was 7.30 a.m.

It *had* to be SC7's attacker, and now that the aircraft had forced it to submerge there was every chance of moving in to the kill. Commander Dickinson made a rapid decision. *Bluebell* and *Fowey* would both be rejoining the convoy within a few hours and other escorts were expected, also there had been no wireless signals warning of U-boats anywhere near the convoy's route. So Dickinson turned his sloop, intent on putting paid to SC7's shadower.

After U-48's safe withdrawal to westwards from the convoy Kapitanleutnant Bleichrodt ordered his men to stand down from battle stations and the cook to give everybody a good breakfast. Bleichrodt decided that his best plan now was to shadow the convoy from a distance and keep reporting on it, as U-48 had only three torpedoes left, with only two of these usable. The U-boat's course of action during the daylight hours therefore seemed assured, when suddenly their plans were shattered.

Bleichrodt was standing on the bridge when it happened.

'Aircraft ahead!' shouted the second officer.

Bleichrodt gave the order to dive, and the men of the bridge watch sprang into the turret hatch. He was the last to go in, and as he did so he saw the Sunderland flying low towards them, already very close, winging in out of the early morning sky like a prehistoric monster after its prey.

'Depth regulator hard down!'

After some fifteen to eighteen seconds they had reached a depth of ten fathoms, and Bleichrodt was turning the handle of the turret hatch still tighter when the Sunderland hit them. Two bombs exploded so close to U-48 that it seemed as though a giant was shaking them in his mighty fist; the lights went out and water rushed through the hatches into the boat. The dials of the pressure gauge burst. The steep angle of dive caused everything that was not fixed to the bulkheads or deck to come crashing down and roll about. The crew had to cling on at their battle stations to prevent themselves being tossed forward. Bleichrodt took such a knock on his hands that he could not feel them, nor his arms, for some time; they hung lifeless at his sides. Wrapped in darkness, U-48 continued its headlong dive.

'Keep your heads,' Bleichrodt calmly told his men, and

ordered the first engineer to continue diving still faster to 450 feet. 'Standby lighting.' It took a little time before the dim light from the emergency system was switched on.

Then came the Sunderland's second attack. First, the U-boat's operator on listening-post duty reported bombs hitting the surface of the water, then the boat was rocked by two waves of detonations. This time, however, they had reached a good depth and suffered no damage.

The boat's descent was arrested at 550 feet and it was then righted. The flooding flaps were closed. Bleichrodt gave the order to start the bilge pumps and clear up the mess in the boat as soon as U-48 was on even keel. The crew were well experienced and it did not take long for them to repair the damage, though it was impossible to right the gyro-compass. The leakage of water in the conning-tower sprang from the periscope gaskets, which had been holed by the pressure waves and were letting in water.

The Sunderland's crew had done their job well. The first bombs must have been planted just where U-48 had dived, and detonated just in front of the conning-tower. Had they landed on the bridge it would have been all up with them.

Bleichrodt could now feel his hands and arms coming back to life. He gave the order to proceed at half-speed submerged, steering westwards to get further away from the scene of the aircraft's attack. He intended to stay underwater for another hour and then surface to approach the convoy again.

The cook had just received orders to distribute the breakfast interrupted by the bombing, when a report came through from the radio room : 'Direction sounding aft. Propeller noise, turning fast, coming close at speed.'

Bleichrodt rushed into the radio room and jammed the headphones on his ears. The propeller noise could be clearly heard, and there was no mistaking that it came from a warship and not a merchantman. He realized at once what it meant. The Sunderland had reported to the escort vessels that it had driven U-48 below the surface. Now he would have to reckon with a depth-charge attack—and by how many vessels? He ordered the U-boat's engines to be set at crawling speed and called for strict silence in the boat. The hydrophones then told them that the searching vessel had slackened speed and finally stopped altogether, listening. Warning the crew to expect a depth-charge assault he sank the boat to 600 feet. The bilge pumps had to be started up again, for it was necessary at such a depth to ensure that the boat was not over-heavy. But in spite of the need to get rid of the water, after a time he ordered the pumps to be switched off again as they were making too much noise.

All remained quiet, and they could only sit and wait. At times like these, when being pursued by surface vessels, Bleichrodt's station was always by the dished bulkhead dividing the control room from the radio room. He sat there, with one foot in the radio room and one foot in the control room, able to watch both the radio operator and the depth regulator. All orders and reports were now passed in whispers or signs. The crew sat or squatted at their posts. The officers and petty officers were all positioned so that they could see their commander and watch for his signals.

For a time it semed that U-48 might not be detected. Then, 'Surface vessel approaching to port.' Now everyone could hear the noise of the propellers even without headphones. All waited for the signal of a hand being dropped . . . and it was, six times. *Scarborough* had fired a pattern of depth-charges.

Aboard U-48 a stop-watch timed the depth-charges to work out the depth at which they were set to explode. From the time *Scarborough* went over to top speed ahead, Bleichrodt did the same with U-48, turning away from his pursuer at 90 degrees. The essential thing was to get the U-boat out of the line of fire, even if it was only a few yards. One after another, as they had been discharged, the depth-charges went off with a great rumbling explosion which shook the U-boat but without causing any damage. All the charges were over their heads; the stop-watch indicated that they had been set to go off at depths between 250 and 450 feet.

When the explosions had died away Bleichrodt brought U-48's revs down again to crawling speed. There then followed another long wait as *Scarborough* began listening and sounding once more. Then again, another pattern of depth-charges, with the U-boat following the same tactics as before.

All through the morning and into the afternoon *Scarborough* harried U-48, losing contact, regaining it, attacking, and then losing contact once more. Meanwhile the convoy had sailed on far ahead. *Fowey* hurried to rejoin it and caught up with the columns of ships at 3.15 p.m. When *Bluebell* also rejoined a few hours later Commander Aubrey, now the senior escort, stationed the corvette on the port side of the convoy and steamed *Fowey* across to the starboard side. Both escorts kept a constant listening watch on the asdic, but throughout the afternoon and evening and into the first night hours, all remained quiet and uneventful. Mile by mile, SC7 drew nearer home. They passed 15 degrees West, following a course that would take them north of Rockall, the bare upthrust of rock 200 miles from the Hebrides.

For *Scarborough*, left far to the rear, it had been a frustrating day as she kept after the U-boat, playing a long game of cat and mouse and refusing to give best to her quarry. For more than eight hours U-48 was unable to get properly clear of the tirelessly searching sloop; the most Kapitanleutnant Bleichrodt could do was to manoeuvre the U-boat yard by yard outside of *Scarborough*'s area of search, hoping that she would at last give up and return to the convoy. Their good luck lay in the fact that none of the sloop's depth-charges came lower than about 400 feet; had they done so it could have been a very different story.

Finally their pursuer seemed to lose contact entirely; there were no more detonations, no more propeller noises. But Bleichrodt did not yet dare to surface. How often had it happened that searching warships had just stopped engines and waited, after their depth-charges were exhausted, until a U-boat was forced by shortage of oxygen or weak batteries to surface, when they moved in to the kill with their guns, or rammed the boat. He decided he would have to remain submerged until dusk at the very earliest; he must err on the side of safety.

When still no more depth-charges came the tension eased a little. Someone started to grumble that he was hungry, and everyone relieved their feelings in laughter. Bleichrodt had to warn his crew to silence again, although he did not find this easy. Eventually the ventilators were switched on and the foul air whipped into motion. Now at last the cook was able to serve up fresh coffee, and life came back into wan faces. Bleichrodt let the boat rise to 200 feet and every arrangement was made to surface; he felt it was high time that everyone should be freed from the long day's tension, not to mention certain human needs. While the U-boat was submerged the lavatory was out of use, and they had to resort to a couple of buckets placed in a corner of the control room near the periscope shaft, where they could do their business undisturbed. No one had had a warm meal since the midnight soup of the previous night, before the attack on the convoy; events since then had interrupted their meals. Now the crew's favourite dinner was ordered: rice soup with beef.

As night fell, U-48 went up to periscope depth. The gun-crew stood ready in the control room, the munition store was opened, the escape apparatus checked, and the security arrange-ments for destruction of the boat in an emergency were gone over. All waited as Bleichrodt scanned the horizon. He trained the periscope all round and saw nothing. Extending the periscope further, he searched again, but still saw nothing but the shadows over the sea. He gave the order to surface. The boat gave a slight shudder and pushed its way yard by yard out of the water until it broke surface. Bleichrodt opened the hatch and entered the conning-tower alone, drawing air greedily into his starved lungs. When he had made quite sure that U-48 was alone, he ordered the diving cells to be blown out with the diesel engines until the boat was right out of the water.

The bridge watch was set up and U-48 began its surface voyage again. The batteries were recharged. One by one, men were allowed on to the bridge to fill their lungs with good air. . . .

Elsewhere in the night steamed *Scarborough*, still searching for her elusive foe. Grimly through the night hours she con-tinued to search, her reward coming next morning, October 18, when U-48 was sighted on the surface far away. *Scarborough* immediately gave chase and fired her old four-inch gun, but the German was well out of range. And this time, U-48 had no need to submerge. As the sloop crammed on all speed in an all-out effort to overtake it, or at least come within firing range, the U-boat struck westward, showing a derisory clean pair of heels. It was a good three or four knots faster than its aged adversary and the distance between them increased to a hopeless expanse of ocean.

Despondently, Commander Dickinson abandoned the chase, and in the early afternoon set off after the convoy at *Scarborough*'s maximum speed of 14 knots. His efforts seemed to have been entirely wasted, and worse still, at this speed he had little hope of ever catching up with the convoy again.

In fact he would not, but neither would U-48, much to the disappointment of the German U-boat command. When Bleichrodt had signalled his discovery of the convoy to the U-boat base at Lorient, instructions had speedily gone out to five other U-boats operating to the east and north of Rockall to converge upon the convoy. It was confidently expected that U-48 would continue to shadow SC7 and report its course, so leading the other U-boats straight to it. But *Scarborough*'s relentless pursuit of U-48 had ruined everything, preventing Bleichrodt from ever finding the convoy again.

The German command had no knowledge of SC7's actual route, so at U-boat headquarters now the vexed question was: how can we re-establish contact with the lost convoy? The man who came up with the simple but effective answer was the Commander-in-Chief U-boats, Admiral Doenitz.

6

The Wolves Gather

Admiral Karl Doenitz, master-mind of the German U-boat Arm, had now reached the position in the sea war towards which he had been working since hostilities began. He commanded sufficient U-boats in the North Atlantic to deploy them in attacking groups—or 'wolf-packs' as they were soon to become known.

At the start of the war Germany possessed only fifty-seven U-boats, many of these of a small type, and during the first nine months there had been many calls on them for service in different areas of operation, including the Norwegian campaign. Even now, because of losses cancelling out the increasing numbers being built, the total number of U-boats had scarcely changed. But the summer of 1940 had seen more of the new big ocean-going boats coming into commission, fast, modern craft with a deadly torpedo load, and commanded by men whom Doenitz had been training from the mid-1930s for this eventuality. Now, greater efforts were being made in the North Atlantic, with damaging results for Britain.

It was Doenitz's firm, unswerving belief that the surest and quickest way for Germany to win the war was by cutting Britain's Atlantic lifeline. And this job, he was convinced, could best be done by U-boats, rather than by marauding warships.

As Captain Karl Doenitz he had been a U-boat 'ace' of World War I. Now, in supreme command of U-boat operations, he brought to the sea battle all his wealth of experience, plus carefully evolved plans which had been well tested over the past five years.

Doenitz, born of an old Prussian family, had entered the Imperial German Navy in 1910. He was twenty-three years old when the Kaiser's war began, and at the end of it was a seasoned campaigner of twenty-seven. Now, fighting Hitler's war, he was still only forty-eight, in the prime of active comand, and the lessons he had learned from the last war were to be exploited to the full by his protégé commanders.

In particular, Doenitz had long reached the conclusion that success for the U-boats lay in attacking convoys not singly, but in strength. In 1914-18 this was impossible, a situation dictated by the primitive wireless equipment available. Communications then had been by long-wave transmissions only, and a U-boat had to surface and erect an aerial before being able to send or receive messages. This was a time consuming procedure even in the best of conditions, and in many circumstances it was just not practical, especially when under enemy threat, or when everything depended on a boat remaining unseen. For these reasons among others, attempts to plan transmissions at pre-arranged times failed. They could not take into account the changing events at sea; and denied a reliable wireless link, there was a limit to the opportunities which boats had of remaining within sight of each other and keeping contact by means of visual signalling.

Even in spite of these handicaps Doenitz, as a U-boat commander, had on occasion tried to act in company with another U-boat, setting off together and with a common plan. But he was not successful.

Now, in 1940, all that was changed. There was short-wave

radio; U-boats could keep in touch with one another, and with the U-boat base, at most times. Doenitz at last had the means of organizing group attacks, and enough boats to carry them out.

At first he had visualized a surface warship or senior U-boat acting as 'command ship' to direct the U-boats into action. But he soon resolved that by far the best method was for all boats to keep closely in touch with base, and for himself to direct operations, leaving the business of the final assault to the individual commanders on the spot. This became a supremely practical solution after the fall of France, when the U-boat base was set up at Lorient.

The plan of attack by the 'wolf-pack' was simple. As a U-boat discovered a convoy it would report to base and continue to shadow the convoy while other boats in the area were directed to converge on the convoy and make the kill.

The second lesson which Doenitz had carried from the 1914-18 war was the value of a U-boat attacking at fast speed on the surface at night, when its small silhouette was extremely difficult to detect by lookouts. This surprise tactic had been carried out very successfully by some U-boat commanders, himself included, towards the end of that war.

So here was the double-edged master plan : U-boats attacking in groups, on the surface at night, and creating havoc.

There was, however, no question of Doenitz having kept these revolutionary tactics a deep, dark secret. As long ago as 1937, the German Navy had carried out its first large-scale manoeuvres in which U-boats tried out their group assaults, and this and subsequent exercises could hardly have escaped the notice of foreign naval intelligence. As for attacking by night, Doenitz had gone so far as to give warning to the world of his intentions. Just as Adolf Hitler had laid down his doctrine in 'Mein Kampf', so Doenitz also laid bare his thinking in a book. It was called 'Die U-bootwaffe' (The U-boat Force) and was published in Berlin in January, 1939—just after the Munich crisis, and eight months before war began. In his book Doenitz stressed very strongly, by means of words *and* illustrations, the great advantages to be gained by U-boats attacking on the surface at night.

Yet apparently no one in Britain took the slightest bit of notice.

In the years up to 1939, while the German Navy had concentrated on perfecting its hydrophones, the Royal Navy had felt itself secure in the possession of the much superior asdic underwater detector. This, basically, emitted a high-frequency sound beam which 'pinged' on an undersea object and gave a highly accurate bearing. So although British naval training between the wars did include exercises with surfaced submarines, these were purely incidental, and the whole accent had been on submerged attack, and methods of defence against it. The plain truth was that the submarine was still regarded as an undersea craft and not, as Doenitz now saw it, a surface attacker taking on the role of a fast torpedo boat. As far as the Royal Navy was concerned, enemy submarines were expected to attack by day, submerged, and the asdic was the finest weapon British warships could wish for. As for U-boat action at night, they would be all right as the enemy would not be able to see them.

As it transpired, the efficiency of the asdic did take the Germans by surprise, but it was soon discovered that it only worked underwater and was virtually useless against a surfaced U-boat. And radar was not yet used at sea, being still, in its infancy, used mainly as a warning system to detect enemy aircraft over British skies.

The position, then, in October 1940 was that reports of surfaced U-boats, and of attacks by night, had been made by some British warships during the past month or two, but these had not been seen to indicate that any special new tactics were being employed by the enemy. Similarly, where definitely more than one U-boat had been spotted during an attack on a convoy, still no particular construction was placed on this. But in fact Doenitz's new style of U-boat warfare had already begun. During the early part of September he had organized, from Lorient, the first successful attack by a group of U-boats, which sank five ships of a convoy, while in late September a second group attack had achieved the staggering result of eleven ships sunk in a fifteen-ship convoy. Yet in spite of this calamitous loss the idea of deliberately organized attacks by groups of U-boats just did not percolate through to the Admiralty. Or at least if it did, certainly no warning of it was passed on to the escort commanders.

This was the situation when Admiral Doenitz planned his 'wolf-pack' strike against SC7. Now that Heinrich Bleichrodt's shadowing U-48 had been chased away from the convoy, all they knew at Lorient was the convoy's last position as Bleichrodt had reported it. What course would SC7 now take? It was impossible to judge with any certainty, for there was no way of knowing what evasive action the convoy might have taken. But there *was* another way of re-locating it. Doenitz now sent out new instructions to the five patrolling U-boats he had contacted earlier. This time they were ordered to withdraw to a point far ahead of the convoy's last known position and form up in line abreast, miles apart, in a vertical north-to-south line, or 'stripe'. Into this line, with a morsel of luck, SC7 would unwittingly sail. It was planned that the line of boats should be in position by daylight on October 18.

The five U-boats ordered to lay this ambush were commanded by some of the élite among Doenitz's carefully bred U-boat officers. Four of the commanders had been in the navy since 1930, and all were members of the pioneer nucleus with which he had begun to build the new U-boat arm in 1935, after Germany won the right to expand her navy under the Anglo-German Naval Agreement. Doenitz had taught them all he knew, and gone out with them in their boats during training. They were now mature young men whose ages ranged from twenty-eight to thirty, and their experience and capabilities were of a very high order. All had graduated from smaller boats to their new big craft, which they had been sailing with success since early summer; and all had developed their talents in their individual ways, for Doenitz allowed his officers to evolve their own tactics in the light of practical experience. In this way, although the principle of night surface assault had not yet been written into the training textbooks, the 'aces' among them had already begun independently to use this method of attack.

So now the five commanders were to move their boats into action like a small fleet, hovering poised across the expected path of their prey. They were Fritz Frauenheim, in U-101; Karl-Heinz Moehle, in U-123; Engelbert Endrass, in U-46; Joachim Schepke, in U-100; and Otto Kretschmer, in U-99. Of them all, the two latter were perhaps among the best known U-boat commanders outside the service. Schepke, the tall and handsome twenty-eight year old with the ready smile, and Kretschmer, of the same age but with a serious look and demeanour.

Otto Kretschmer, the son of a teacher, was already well on his way to becoming Germany's greatest U-boat ace of World War II. 'Otto the Silent' was a disciplinarian, a cool, self-confident professional. He, more than any other, had been quick to see the advantages of surfaced attack by night, and in fact he had already abandoned completely the old practice of sub-merged attack on an escorted convoy by daylight, except when it was impossible for him to wait for darkness. His tactics now were to shadow by day and attack by night, moving into the convoy lanes and making every torpedo count, one to a ship, instead of standing off at a distance and firing what he con-sidered to be wasteful 'fans' of three or four torpedoes across the path of the convoy, the method still employed in the classic submerged attack by daylight. These and other tactics Kretsch-mer had set out in his new Standing Orders for U-99, the craft with the familiar golden horseshoe emblem on its conning-tower, and they were the result of hard and highly successful practical experience.

He had already sunk the remarkable total of twenty ships by going in at them on the surface.

As the five U-boats travelled from various directions to take up their positions in the line of ambush east of Rockall, one other boat was busy patrolling in the reverse direction, heading west-wards. This was U-38, commanded by Kapitanleutnant Heinrich Liebe. It was late in the evening of October 17, and Liebe could feel fairly satisfied with his day's work, for early that morning he had torpedoed and sunk by gunfire the Greek *Aenos*. Now he was searching for other game, and unexpectedly found it. Convoy SC7, sailing by right under his nose.

Near to midnight on the 17th, as the moon shone brightly, silhouetting the ships of the convoy to make them a dream of a target, he crept in close on the dark side to select his victims.

7

Don't Launch the Boats!

Friday, October 18. It was fifteen minutes past midnight, 0015 hours, when two more escorts sent to help bring in the convoy sighted SC7 ahead. The moon was behind cloud, but visibility was good, and the sea calm. All seemed quiet as the convoy forged on through the night. It had now reached position 58. 50 N, 14. 12 W, and would reach a point north of Rockall in less than six hours' steaming.

The two new arrivals, the sloop HMS *Leith* and corvette HMS *Heartsease*, were the last escorts allocated to the convoy. As they neared the columns of ships *Leith*, being the senior vessel, signalled the corvette to take up a flanking position while she herself took station astern. But just as they were positioning themselves the peaceful night scene changed.

U-38 had crept up unseen on the port side of the convoy, where only *Bluebell* was in station, the corvette's asdic being unable to detect the surfaced U-boat. *Fowey* was far away on the convoy's starboard side. As the masking clouds shifted from the face of the moon, Kapitanleutnant Liebe fired a salvo of torpedoes across the path of the convoy's silhouetted port column of ships. He was not very successful, scoring only one hit—on ship number thirteen of the convoy.

The Glasgow steamer *Carsbreck*, stacked high with timber, shuddered under the explosion and listed violently to port. As all hands rushed on deck the ship started to go down by the head. *Carsbreck* looked done for, some of her timber already on fire. Captain John Muir gave the order to launch the boats and abandon ship.

At the radios in other ships of the convoy they heard *Carsbreck*'s rapid distress call . . . 'SSSS' . . . repeated twice, followed by four or five attempts to tap out her call sign GYXB. The operator seemed unable to get it right, and his last attempt died off in the middle. They feared the worst.

On *Carsbreck* as the crew stood at their lifeboat stations a hurried roll call revealed that two young deck-boys were missing. The bosun and an A.B., together with the ship's cook, Hilton Brodie, ran down to the boys' accommodation, which was on the port side amidships, not more than forty feet from where the torpedo had struck. With difficulty they managed to open the door and found the two boys lying sound asleep, completely unaware of what was happening. The three men quickly roused the lads from their dreams and hurried them on deck.

The boats were being launched when Captain Muir, a Glasgow master in his sixties, suddenly reappeared on the boatdeck, very agitated.

'Don't launch them!' he cried. 'Don't launch the boats! It's all right, we are not sinking—come back, men—come back!'

As the captain's words were passed along from man to man they brought real confusion, for a change of order by the usually dour and very determined master was entirely unexpected and no one seemed to know how to cancel an order to abandon ship. But eventually the majority of the crew did come back, except for the men in one lifeboat which had pulled away from the ship.

The *Carsbreck* had taken a severe knock. The force of the explosion had swung her right round until she was now facing in

the opposite direction to the fast disappearing convoy; she still
listed badly to port and the foc'sle was almost under water, but,
said her master and the chief engineer, she was not sinking and
they were convinced she could still make passage. Once this was
made clear the returned crew accepted the situation with relief.
After all, they had withstood an attack without suffering a single
casualty, which in itself was very heartening, and the ship was
refusing to be beaten. Even the usually excitable Arab firemen
had shown a praiseworthy coolness, and strangely no one seemed
to fear the possibility of another torpedo.

Nor did it come. U-38 had used its superior surface speed to
race ahead and position itself for another strike at the convoy.
Half an hour after *Carsbreck* was hit, Kapitanleutnant Liebe
fired another salvo of torpedoes. This time, however, he was
completely out of luck, none of them striking home. Commodore
MacKinnon, looking out from the bridge of *Assyrian*, saw the
track of one torpedo as it sped across the path of his ship and
immediately signalled the convoy to make an emergency turn to
starboard.

Fowey, miles away to starboard, made all speed to get round
to the port side of the convoy and help *Bluebell* in her search
for the U-boat, but the sloop's fourteen knots was far too inadequate and she did not meet up with *Bluebell* until thirty-five
minutes after U-38's second salvo had been fired. The German,
however, made no further attack during this time, and now
the two escorts searched up the port side of the convoy, but
without result. They were joined soon afterwards by the newcomers, *Leith* and *Heartsease*, and the search was repeated up
and down the convoy's port side. But the U-boat had gone. Had
it submerged they would have had a fair chance of detecting it,
but the German had remained on the surface, using his fast
diesel engines to elude his pursuers.

In fact, although they could not know it, U-38 would not
renew its attack on SC7. After wirelessing the convoy's position
to Lorient, Kapitanleutnant Liebe returned to his patrol.

In these eventful early hours of the morning of the 18th, *Leith,*
being the senior of the escorts present, now assumed command.

She took *Bluebell* in company, sent *Fowey* back to the convoy, and detached *Heartsease* to look for the torpedoed *Carsbreck*. But it was *Leith* herself who, after having abandoned her search for the attacker and turned to catch up with the convoy, first sighted *Carsbreck* and the lone lifeboat which had pulled away from the steamer. The time was 6.10 a.m.

In the early morning light the full extent of the damage to *Carsbreck* could now be seen. The torpedo had struck her just forward of amidships on the port side at No. 2 hatch; they were lucky to be loaded with timber, which gave the ship extra buoyancy, for there was a gaping hole in her side about thirty feet across, out of which planks of timber were escaping and littering the sea.

Leith drew close and her commander spoke to *Carsbreck*'s master by loudhailer. Was she in distress? How badly damaged was she?

Captain Muir replied that his crippled ship had a good chance of staying afloat and he should be able to keep her steaming at a steady six knots.

This was good news, but it also presented a problem. In the state she was in, *Carsbreck* could not be left to limp along alone. *Leith* therefore signalled *Heartsease* to remain behind and escort the damaged steamer after first picking up the men in the lifeboat and returning them to their ship. *Leith* then, in company with *Bluebell*, set course for the convoy at fourteen knots, reaching it shortly after 9.30 a.m.

Leith now briefly exchanged signals with Commodore Mac-Kinnon in *Assyrian*. The sloop was commanded by Commander Roland Charlton Allen, RN, a Dartmouth man and a very efficient officer, as well as a popular captain in the eyes of his largely Regular naval crew. After his rudely interrupted arrival on the scene—Allen had only just reached astern of the convoy when *Carsbreck* was struck—he was now to take a major role in the events to follow.

Leith, which he had commanded for about five months, was somewhat smaller than *Fowey*, being less than a thousand tons. She was also newer and a little faster, but her other refinements were few. She was fitted with the early type of asdic set where the operator sat on an open bridge, training the oscillator by means of a handwheel mounted on the binnacle. And she had only a magnetic compass, subject to all kinds of fluctuations, unlike the newer gyro kind. Her armament was similar to *Fowey*'s, a 4.7 in. gun on the foc'sle and a 3 in. gun on 'B' deck.

Like *Fowey*, the *Leith* had spent most of her time pre-war in warmer waters. Shortly before the war began she was on loan to the Royal New Zealand Navy, and paid an official visit to the Tonga Islands, embarking Queen Salote for a tour round her domain. Memories of the jolly queen's voyage were still vivid. Naturally she had been given the best accommodation the ship could provide, namely the captain's cabin. Salote being a very substantial lady, over six feet tall and about 18 stone in weight, the captain's bunk suffered as a result; her majesty broke its springs, and it was never the same again. After this diverting interlude *Leith* was all set to begin a pleasant six months tour of the South Sea Islands when she was abruptly recalled for war.

Her forty-year-old commander was an orderly, meticulous man known as 'Maudie' Allen to his intimates, after the noted dancer, but, good-humouredly, 'Auntie' Allen to others, because of his apparent zeal for working by the book. However, Commander Allen, straightforward and courteous, was possessed of a know-how that was often an inspiration to brother officers. For example, when able to leave the bridge at night he slept on his bunk with a faint blue light over it. When the officer of the watch saw anything he pressed a bell, and in two seconds Commander Allen was up, through the bathroom—also with a blue light and ever-open doors—and thence to the bridge. He could reckon on reaching the bridge in five seconds flat *and* with his eyes accustomed to the darkness. There were no flies on 'Auntie' Allen.

To the other SC7 escort commanders, however, he was a completely unknown quantity. He had not met any of them before, not Aubrey of *Fowey* nor Sherwood of *Bluebell*, nor even Lieutenant-Commander Edward John North, RNR, of *Heartsease*, the ship with which he had arrived. So the situation remained that all four escort commanders and their ships were complete strangers to each other, and they had no common plan against attack. It was now up to Allen, as the senior escort, to deploy them as he saw fit.

The late hours of the morning saw SC7 curving steadily to the south-east, north of Rockall. The gap in the port column had been closed, ship number fourteen, *Shekatika*, moving up to take the place of *Carsbreck* at number thirteen. Superstition apart, it was not a very comfortable move for her crew, after having seen the *Carsbreck* hit directly ahead of them and watched her reel back in the haze of moonlight and mist. But they were not alone in their thoughts. None of the merchant crews felt that trouble was past, especially with the sharp reminder given by the occasional glimpse of survivors moving about the decks of *Bluebell* and *Fowey*. At such times a man would get to wondering quietly which part of his ship would be hit if she did stop a torpedo . . . whether it would strike for'ard or aft or amidships. Would there be a gigantic flash, roar or blast? Or would he be transported from this life to the next without knowing how it had happened? It was a numbing kind of thought born of a peculiar mixture of fear, fatalism, and an almost detached curiosity.

They were now entering the zone of greatest danger, and with the convoy spread out over such a big area—there were still twenty-nine ships—it seemed that their few escorts faced an impossible task in trying to give protection to them all. Shortly after midday some ominous bits of wreckage were spotted floating in the sea, and there gradually came into view the pathetically waving occupants of two rafts, a sudden huddle of forlorn life tossing on the expanse of ocean. The survivors had roped their rafts together so they would not drift apart, and each was crowded, many of its occupants having to stand up, for the simple reason that there was not enough space for them all to sit or lie down at once.

Always wary of a trap, of a U-boat perhaps lying in wait

near the scene for someone to take the 'bait', *Leith* and *Bluebell* searched the area around the rafts before the sloop finally closed in and took the survivors aboard. They were the master and eighteen members of the crew of the Estonian steamer *Nora*. They had been adrift for five days and nights, hanging grimly on to the rafts and praying for some ship to pass, since their vessel was torpedoed some fifty miles west of Rockall. They climbed aboard *Leith* weak and exhausted, but with their master still clutching two precious pieces of 'luggage': his sextant, and a briefcase containing the ship's papers.

It was a sombre rescue scene that caused nerves to be drawn a little tighter all round.

During the late afternoon Commodore MacKinnon began to run up signal flags. These gave early warning to all ships of his intention to alter the convoy's course by 40 degrees to starboard at 8 p.m., and then at 11.30 p.m., to swing the convoy back 40 degrees to port.

Commander Allen now formulated his plans for the escorts in the case of attack, and signalled them to *Fowey* and *Bluebell*. By day, he instructed them, *Leith* would pass through the convoy on a reciprocal course. The escort on the engaged side was to take station ahead, the escort on the other side to go astern, and then look out for the signal to turn 90 degrees. By night, the ship on the side not attacked was to take up station as directed and remain with the convoy. If the side of attack was unknown, both wing ships were to turn outward.

This understood, Allen now ordered *Fowey* to search five miles astern of the convoy at dusk, to shake off any shadowing U-boat, and then steam back to take up her position on the convoy's port side. Meanwhile *Bluebell* was to remain at her station on the starboard side.

Having delivered herself of these orders *Leith* steamed out in front of the convoy as *Scarborough* had done earlier in the voyage. *Heartsease* did not come into the scheme of things now, as she was far behind escorting the damaged *Carsbreck*.

The Glasgow ship, as good as her master's promise, was limping along at five or six knots, although every now and then there was a scare for her crew as she gave an extra heavy roll to port, when planks of timber would slip out through the huge hole in her side, leaving a plaintive trail across the ocean like in some weird paperchase.

It was an unusual role for *Heartsease*, playing nursemaid to a single damaged ship. The corvette was more used to being in the centre of any action, as on a recent convoy when she had run up her blue and yellow attack signal and depth-charged a U-boat. 'Heart Disease' her crew called her, for although a splendid seaboat she rolled frightfully and fairly rapidly. She was identical to *Bluebell*, having been launched during the same week, and like *Bluebell*'s commander, Lieutenant-Commander North had stood by his vessel as she was completed.

He was thirty-eight, and a man used to far bigger ships, having spent twenty years with the P. and O. Line; when war broke out he was chief officer of the liner *Strathaird*. But he had taken smaller ships in his stride and commanded anti-submarine trawlers before taking over *Heartsease*. A modest and unassuming Oxfordshire countryman with a big, hearty laugh, North was well liked by his officers and crew. He still managed to find humour in the fact that his stomach could never acclimatize itself to the small ships and that he was prone to seasickness when *Heartsease* left harbour, often sharing the same bucket on the bridge with his signalman. However, he bore the ship no malice, in fact he was well pleased with her. Pride of place in the wardroom was given to a little picture of wild heartsease growing on the fells above Tynemouth, which a friend had painted while on holiday.

In her short life *Heartsease* had already experienced some of the worst the Atlantic could offer. For half the time on her last trip out she had ridden a fierce gale during which she had lost her charges for nearly two days. The calmer weather now was altogether incongruous; was this really late October in one of the wildest of oceans?

The same thought was uppermost in the minds of many crews of the merchant ships in the convoy now drawn far ahead and out of sight. After a few days of turbulence the weather was once again proving far too kind; rough seas were infinitely preferable, for rough seas handicapped the enemy.

The daylight faded into darkness and at 8 p.m. as arranged, Commodore MacKinnon turned the convoy 40 degrees to starboard. The manoeuvre was carried out perfectly under the night sky and in a calm sea with a slight swell. The full moonlight had shone on them all as night descended, but now dark clouds veiled the face of the moon from time to time, and a fresh wind blew drifting patches of light mist.

The convoy settled down for the night. They could not know that in a matter of minutes it would begin to explode hellishly around them.

The five U-boats had formed their line of ambush well, helped by U-38's last reported position of SC7. The convoy had been sighted during the afternoon and the 'wolves' had waited for nightfall to pounce. They were uncertain about the strength of the escorts; the convoy had seemed from a distance to be guarded by at least three destroyers and several smaller warships, though this was certainly no deterrent. Each U-boat commander had his own plan of action. Some would fire 'fans' of torpedoes from outside the escort screen, or closer in as the action developed. The advantages of close-in surface attack would also be pressed. The boldest method was to be used by Otto Kretschmer in U-99, who intended to speed right inside the convoy lanes just as soon as he could dodge past the escorts.

This was the opportunity all had been waiting for. The big night.

At 8.15 p.m. Kapitanleutnant Engelbert Endrass in U-46 fired a first salvo of three torpedoes at the port bow of the convoy, which with *Fowey* still searching five miles astern was left completely unguarded. One torpedo found a target.

The destruction of convoy SC7 had begun.

8

The Night Explodes

The torpedo from U-46 ripped into the port side of the Swedish *Convallaria*, causing a huge explosion which shook the ship from stem to stern and shot parts of her deck cargo high into the air. She began to sink by the stern immediately. The order was quickly given to launch the two lifeboats, and in three minutes both boats were in the water with all hands, pulling hard away from the doomed vessel. Only five minutes later the 2,000-ton ship reared up vertically with her bow pointing to the sky, then slid back until only her foc'sle was above the surface of the water. She remained suspended like this for a full quarter of an hour, held uncannily afloat by her crammed cargo of pulpwood, then, with a sigh, she disappeared down into a thousand fathoms of the night black Atlantic.

Leith, steaming ahead of the convoy, had just reached the extreme starboard limit of her station when *Convallaria* was hit. She turned sharply and raced at full speed across to the port side, firing starshell to illuminate the scene as she went. She scoured the dark ocean for ten miles, but found no signs of the attacker and had to give up and turn back to the convoy.

Fowey, still making her asdic sweep astern of the convoy, saw the starshell fired by *Leith* and, in an attempt to find out what was happening, tried to call up *Leith* on the convoy manoeuvring wave—a special W/T wavelength on which suitably equipped escorts could communicate with each other by morse transmission. There was no response, so *Fowey* hurried to regain her position up the port side, but she was an hour's steaming from the rear of the convoy and at her limited speed it was a long, frustrating haul back. On the way she sighted two lifeboats ahead. Although Admiralty orders were against escorts stopping to pick up survivors, Commander Aubrey now justified his decision to pick up the men in the boats on the grounds that they might be able to give him some useful information regarding the attack, as well as the fact that they were completely alone with no other ship standing by them—officialdom required more than simple humane reasons. The boats were found to contain the crew of the *Convallaria*, whose ship had long vanished. There was little delay in getting them aboard the sloop, but from an information point of view the Swedes were a complete write-off. All one officer could tell Aubrey when he was questioned on the bridge was 'There was a big bang, and I yumped for the yollyboat . . .'

Once more Aubrey tried to call up *Leith* on the convoy manoeuvring wave, but again there was no answer; either *Leith* did not possess the necessary equipment or it was not tuned in accurately. This was highly frustrating. After an eternity, as it seemed to *Fowey*'s commander, more used to the quick response of a fast destroyer than to the limited engines of his sloop, *Fowey* met up with *Leith* and joined her in a new search up the wake of the convoy, but there was still no trace of the enemy. In the meantime, as the convoy sailed on ahead with only *Bluebell* in station on its starboard bow, the wolves closed in.

The Cardiff steamer *Beatus*, laden with steel ingots and timber piled high, sighted a shadowy U-boat skimming the moonlit surface of the sea off her port bow. The radio officer tapped out the alarm, but moments later she rocked as a torpedo struck her between Nos. 2 and 4 holds. The sea rushed in and the big vessel, more than twice the size of *Convallaria,* shuddered to a stop and began to settle. After a quick inspection of the damage it was clear it would be only a matter of time before she sank. Captain Wilfred Brett gave the order to abandon ship.

There was confusion as one of the two lifeboats was being prepared for lowering by the native stokers; when told to knock out the toggle to release the griping brackets, they chopped through the hauling part of the falls, with the result that the boat crashed down into the sea and was so badly damaged as to make it unseaworthy. But *Beatus* carried a jollyboat and this was launched along with the other lifeboat. Eventually everyone had got away to the boats except Captain Brett and the ship's naval Reservist gunlayer, together with an Indian fireman. The fireman was a fatalist and refused to leave the ship. His time had come, he said, and he was content to stay and go down with the vessel. He was stubborn and unyielding, and the only way the captain and gunner could finally persuade him to go was by telling him that they had to be the last people to leave the ship and he *must* go before them. Grudgingly the fireman then consented to join one of the boats, though still voicing his protests. No sooner had he gone than the gunner, with rather excessive devotion to duty, insisted that *he* should be the last to leave, after first seeing the captain safely off. It was hardly the time for further argument, so to settle the matter they jumped together into the waiting boat.

The broken *Beatus* took forty minutes to die. While she was still inching below the surface the Dutch ship *Boekolo* came upon her two lifeboats of survivors and, surprisingly, slowed down and stopped engines with the evident intention of picking them up. This comradely gesture was against all instructions and unfortunately brought disastrous consequences. Only one seaman from *Beatus* had managed to climb up the Dutch ship's side before she, too, was hit by a torpedo and lurched crazily in the water, never to start her engines again.

They saw the whole thing happen from the bridge of *Bluebell* miles away, and could scarcely believe their eyes when the tramp from Amsterdam, the Dutch colours bold on her funnel, suddenly hove-to.

'Good God, what's that fellow stopped for?' exclaimed Commander Sherwood to one of his officers.

Next minute, the torpedo, and the third victim. Fire broke out among the timber cargo as *Boekolo*'s crew got away in their boats.

Aboard the big *Shekatika*, which was astern of *Beatus* when that ship reeled and fell away, Second Radio Officer Raymond Baldwin had picked up the urgent distress signals of all three ships. Now he was trying to keep up with events between rushing out through the double blackout curtains up to the bridge to give information to the captain in the gloom, the captain reading the messages over the binnacle light.

Baldwin had just returned to the radio cabin after his third or fourth run up to the bridge when there was a thunderous boom and an almost instant lurch of the ship as *Shekatika* became the wolf-pack's fourth victim.

His chair canted, but he managed to avoid being flung on to the floor. He stood up, thinking 'Surely that couldn't have been?' Although wearing earphones he could hear crashing noises of descending wood, and what sounded like torrents of rain. The radio cabin began to tilt over at an angle . . . ten, twenty degrees . . . There was a scurry of feet from the outer deck and First Radio Officer Harris appeared—'This is it, we've been torpedoed!' Harris was carrying his life-jacket and now began to pull it on. Baldwin took his life-jacket down from the cabin bulkhead, put the blue kapok waistcoat on and tied its black tapes. . . .

The torpedo had struck *Shekatika* on the port side in the way of No. 4 hold, the explosion flinging up a mountain of pitprops aft by the mast where Nos. 3 and 4 holds joined. The noise of these pitprops hurtling back on to the deck and into the sea accompanied the torpedo explosion 'rain' which had been heard in the radio cabin—the ship's third mate narrowly missed being struck by one of the lethal lengths of flying wood.

The explosion, close to the men's quarters aft, had blown brass scuttles across cabins with terrific force, though fortunately hitting no one. The lights aft went out immediately. The descending waterspout roared down, making them think the stern was already awash, and men fled without pausing to snatch up belongings, scrambling in the dark over the great black pile of pitprops to amidships and the boats, bumping and bruising themselves and registering their curses as they went. By this time the ship's stern was already very well down.

Back in the radio room the heavy running of the captain was heard. 'Send th' SSSS, Sparrks!' Captain Robert Paterson's red face above the gold bands on his greatcoat shoulders vanished into the alleyway and the door of the safe in his day cabin clanged open as he seized the ship's accounts and stock of money. Harris began to send the SSSS message. Captain Paterson looked in again for a second, grasping a thick briefcase, then raced heavy footed back to the bridge.

Suddenly the listing ship seemed to right herself again. It came as a surprise, but the simple reason was that after bursting in on one side, the seawater had quickly run over the central propeller tunnel and flooded both halves of Nos. 3 and 4 holds, so that the water was evenly distributed. *Shekatika* was now kept afloat by her wood cargo.

In the moonlight the crew assembled on the boatdeck. The safety valve steampipe beside the funnel was fanning out steam in a steady earpaining hissing roar, for *Shekatika* had been thumping along at full speed when hit and great fires were fully stoked down below; the reciprocating engine was still, and steam roared skywards since the engine was not consuming it. On deck, conversation could only be carried on by shouting in each other's ears.

The captain again hurried to the radio room and it was decided to inform the shore that *Shekatika* had been hit. An international SOS message was now sent out and comfortingly answered by the coastal radio station at Valentia, in south-west Ireland.

Chief Officer Leask and Second Mate Alexander Smith went aft on deck to inspect the damage. The explosion had broken the tail-shaft and buckled the bulkhead between No. 3 hold and the engine-room, making it impossible to close the watertight door to the shaft-tunnel, with the result that the sea was sluicing into the engine-room pretty fast.

The dynamo, with excess steam and now untended, was running high voltage, and the radio room was so brightly lit that the lamp threatened to burn out. It was time to quit. 'What about the log?' There was a considerable litter of papers and hours of writing up. 'Leave it, we'll just take the code books.' Baldwin drew out the emergency carborundum crystal that Board of Trade regulations insisted all ships must carry. Such a crystal allowed messages to be received without any electricity supply whatever. It went into his pocket as a souvenir as they pushed out into the dark with the weighted code bag.

Hunched on the boatdeck stood the Scottish chief engineer. Into his hand Baldwin slipped a borrowed pack of patience cards which he had grabbed from his cabin along with his coat. 'Don't say I lost them, Chief!' he bellowed. The chief looked at him as if he were mad, but thrust the cards silently into his pocket.

Far below, the second engineer was at that moment studying the seawater pouring into the flooded engine-room through the buckled watertight door to the tunnel. When he admitted a little steam to the triple expansion engine it thundered round and the whole ship shook, for its great crankshaft had no load to carry. The main propeller shaft was broken and the ship helpless, but the captain had insisted that this should be made doubly sure of before they abandoned ship. The engineer on watch had previously shut down the flailing engine before fleeing aloft.

Looking aft, the once orderly stacks of pitprops were now a tangled mountain, while hundreds more props dipped and bobbed black on the surface of the sea under the cold light of the moon. The ship swayed with a new dead motion, her decks treacherously wet from the cascade of water that had followed the torpedo blast. Captain Paterson, an Edinburgh master in his late thirties, now had to make his decision. . . .

At this moment the searching *Fowey* sighted the dark, drifting shape of *Shekatika* from half a mile away. Her signal lamp blinked.

The sloop's morse message was read by half a dozen pairs of eyes on *Shekatika* and acknowledged by the chief officer with a brief flash of his hand torch at the end of every word.

'Are you in distress?' asked *Fowey*.

They grimaced their wry amusement. The fierce roar of steam made several rich comments inaudible.

'Yes,' flashed the torch.

' Are you abandoning ship?'

Captain Paterson looked around at the dark clusters of men, more than two dozen of them, awaiting his next word. Sadly, reluctantly, he nodded to the chief officer—'Aye.'

'Yes,' flashed the torch again.

They clambered into the boats in an orderly manner, and in the general air of politeness there was almost strong competition to remain on board to pay out the ropes. The boats jerked down the big ship's steel sides into the shadow, and when the sea slapped them, their occupants found themselves swirling up and down about eight feet on the agitated water. The falls were unhooked at the ends of each boat and the men who had paid out the ropes came sliding down. Shouts of 'Mind the blocks!' could be faintly heard above the still searing noise of the steam. Oars were unshipped and they crabbed away from the great moonlit hulk, pulling their way gingerly through menacing pit-props that continually bumped the boats. Once round the bow of the ship they could see for the last time the name *Shekatika*, grey painted over though it was. The men, some clad only in thin singlets, hunched together.

Captain Paterson was in charge of one boat, Chief Officer Leask taking the other, as they hauled across to *Fowey* in the moderate swell. Only when boarding the sloop did the company suffer their first casualties. It was a tricky business having to jump from boat to ship on the crest of the waves. The captain fractured his right foot when it was caught between the lifeboat and *Fowey*'s side, and a seaman fell and injured his ribs.

Fowey's engine-room telegraph clanged, and the empty lifeboats drifted quickly astern into the night. On the messdecks the men from *Shekatika* began to loosen their life-jackets and fling them down at their feet.

'Hey—don't do that!' exclaimed some of the survivors already on board. 'They say this tin can would only last about ten seconds if she got a torpedo.'

When *Fowey* drew away from *Shekatika* the big Scots steamer was still well afloat on her packing of wood. Steaming hard after the convoy now, *Fowey* had not gone far before she sighted two more lifeboats, and once again the desperate question of whether to stop and take on survivors or continue on to try to regain the convoy confronted Commander Aubrey. But he did not hesitate. *Fowey* closed the boats and took aboard the crew of *Boekolo*, together with the one seaman from *Beatus* who had managed to board the Dutch ship before she was hit. Then on again after the convoy, by now drawn many miles ahead.

But the wolves were striking again, and with terrible result. The old British steamer *Creekirk*, which had won safely through one war, now stood no chance at all when a torpedo tore a gaping hole in her side. The 4,000-ton vessel was loaded with iron ore and she started to sink at once. What drama was played out in the last quick minutes of her long life no one survived to tell. From Guernsey-born Captain Elie Robilliard to the sixteen-year-old cabin boy, all thirty-four of her crew were killed or drowned along with her as she plunged to the bottom without trace except for a few pitiful bits of wreckage.

Aboard the big ex-American *Empire Miniver*, leading ship of a column on the starboard side of *Assyrian*, they had watched explosion follow explosion and the sky light up with gunflashes, starshell and parachute flares. The protecting darkness when the moon clouded over had gone, and all felt very naked and exposed.

In the midst of it all the bosun, a big burly man with a woollen comfort on his head, climbed the bridge ladder to see the master. Captain Robert Smith, a North Shields master who was no stranger to action at sea, had ordered the crew to keep awake and fully dressed, every man wearing his life-jacket, and now the bosun asked if some of the men could stand-easy, as those due to take the middle-watch, midnight to 4 a.m., wanted to turn in and get some sleep. But Captain Smith told him that in the present dangerous situation it was more important than ever that every man should stay fully dressed and out of his bunk, and the master promptly gave a further shrewd order to ensure it. He instructed the chief steward that every man off-watch was to be given a large tot of rum, but that he must come amidships to drink it. The order worked.

Now, after having seen several ships torpedoed, two of them very close to *Empire Miniver,* Captain Smith was turning over the idea of trying to make a run for it, away from what appeared to be certain destruction. *Empire Miniver* being an oil-burner and turbine driven, her speed had been kept down a little to conform to that of the convoy. The master knew that if he left the convoy he would be breaking regulations, but that was really a secondary consideration now; if he could get away from the area at full speed he might have a chance of saving his ship and his men. He finally reached a decision and ordered Third Mate Gilbert Hing to ask the chief engineer to let him have all the speed of which the vessel was capable.

Hing made his way down to the deck, hurried along the port alleyway to the chief's cabin and passed on the captain's request, at which Chief Engineer Paul, from Glasgow, a quiet and likeable man, disappeared into the engine-room to begin the great race.

Farther on down the passageway Hing came upon Third Engineer Sneddon, wearing only a towel round his waist and nothing else but his slippers. Calmly, Sneddon said he was going to have a bath. Hing reminded him of the captain's 'all fully dressed' order, but it didn't make a scrap of difference, the engineer was determined to take his plunge.

Up on the bridge they saw *Assyrian*'s gun firing, and other ships seemed to be firing too. Some of the shells were coming dangerously close. After that everything seemed to happen very quickly.

The torpedo that found *Empire Miniver* should by rights never have reached her. It was heading straight for the old steamer *Clintonia*, less than half the size of the ex-American, but *Clintonia*'s Captain Thomas Irvin skilfully swung his ship away from its path and the torpedo ran across to the bigger vessel. Even in the tension of that moment Captain Irvin hoped that Captain Smith would forgive him for dodging the torpedo; they had both begun their careers with the Stag Line and knew each other well.

Chief Officer John Green had just come up on to *Empire Miniver*'s bridge and was standing in the port wing looking over the ship's side when he saw the track of the torpedo speeding towards them. 'Mind your hat!' he yelled. Seconds later the torpedo struck. It tore into *Empire Miniver* amidships on the port side between the engine-room and the tank where the fuel oil was carried, blowing part of the port side away and shattering the port lifeboats above, even though they were American boats made of steel. Pigs of iron in the No. 3 'tweendecks shot up into the air over the funnel and rained down on the poop, where the frightened gun-crew jumped overboard after releasing a raft into a sea already afire with burning oil. The ship's engines stopped dead, plunging everything into pitch darkness, steam hissing up from below where Chief Engineer Paul lay dead, killed instantly in the explosion along with the fourth engineer and a fireman.

The ship, heavily laden with iron and steel, rapidly lost way and began to settle. Her welldecks were quickly awash and all hatchboards on the hatch abaft the bridge had been blown away, leaving a gaping hatchway. She could break her back and sink very quickly. Captain Smith gave instructions to abandon, shouting his order from the bridge to hands on deck below.

Chief Officer Green rang down 'Stop' on the engine-room telegraph, an unnecessary action with all contact with the engine-room destroyed, but one that came automatically. Third Mate Hing, as officer of the watch, lit and hoisted the red lights which told other ships they had been torpedoed. Hurrying down to the lower bridge Hing then saw Captain Smith trying to open the door leading to his quarters, and lent him a hand. But despite their combined efforts the door remained jammed fast.

On deck, Hing and Second Mate Reginald Leach tried to release the starboard liferaft from its securing pins, but it would not run, so they made their way aft and climbed the ladder to the boatdeck. An engine-room grating had been blown away and they had to be careful moving round the exposed opening in the half light of the moon. Then Chief Officer Green suddenly spotted Captain Smith crossing the boatdeck. 'Leap, Cap!' he yelled. The master reacted instantly, only realising afterwards that had he not done so he would have fallen down the entire depth of the ship.

While all were busy launching the starboard lifeboats an apparition appeared flying across the boatdeck in the shape of Third Engineer Sneddon, clad only in his jockey underpants. In the explosion he had been spreadeagled on the floor of the engineers' bathroom, half covered with small octagonal tiles, looking dazedly up through the torn ship at the clouds and stars above. Another latecomer was a greaser, the only survivor of the explosion in the engine-room. When the torpedo struck he had been at his duties in the after end of the propeller tunnel and, escaping unhurt, had managed to feel his way through the ship in total darkness and climb up the Jacob's ladder to the deck.

Steam was escaping from pipes on the boatdeck and the glands of the ship's siren as the two lifeboats got away, the captain in charge of one and the second officer taking the other. It was only ten minutes since the torpedo had struck, and yet it seemed a lifetime. One boat picked up all but one of the gun-crew from their raft. The missing man, the young ship's carpenter, was believed lost. But an hour later much shouting was heard from a floating light in the water and they found the carpenter, who had jumped overboard, still swimming for all he was worth and pushing the light in front of him.

The two boats kept within hailing distance as their occupants gazed out at the dismal night scene around them. Small lights from other lifeboats and liferafts could be seen twinkling on the surface of the sea. They could also see a few ships, stragglers possibly, at the tail end of the convoy. Even from their own 'dead stop' position these vessels seemed to be moving painfully slowly. . . .

The Cardiff steamer *Fiscus* had pushed on at a punishing ten knots, laden as she was with her cargo of steel. For Captain Ebenezer Williams, who had lived with the morbid presentiment of disaster long before the convoy sailed, this night's pattern of destruction had already exceeded even his worst fears. More than anyone he must have watched in horror the slaughter around him. But what it felt like to see a premonition unfold in reality before one's eyes he would never be able to tell, for the torpedo that now struck *Fiscus* caused one of the most violent explosions of the night, the ship almost disintegrating under the master's feet. She plunged like a stone, taking every one of her crew with her. Twenty-eight souls, from the forty-eight-year-old master to the two youngest members of his crew, brothers aged fourteen and fifteen, the sons of a widowed mother back in Cardiff.

The almost unbelievable tragedy was witnessed by those aboard the steamer *Somersby*. One minute *Fiscus* was steaming hard, the next she had erupted and vanished from the surface of the sea as if sucked down by some evil whirlpool.

Far away to the rear of the convoy another explosion followed, but this time the torpedo rocked an empty, derelict ship . . . the *Shekatika*. A different U-boat from the one that had first attacked her had now found the silently drifting vessel and given her the *coup de grace*. The German withdrew, marking a 'kill', but when he had gone, still the battered *Shekatika* remained astonishingly afloat. . . .

Aboard the *Gunborg* earlier they had seen their fellow Swede, *Convallaria*, torpedoed and felt helpless when they could not stop to pick up survivors. But now they, too, fell a victim of the pack.

A torpedo struck *Gunborg* on the port side, causing such a wild explosion that an enormous sea was thrown up over the vessel and her master was twice knocked down by a wall of hurtling water. The ship began to list heavily to port. Everyone ran for the lifeboats, including the youngest able seaman, Sture

Mattsson, now torpedoed for the second time in weeks—he had lost his ship coming out, and here was his return ship shuddering and dying beneath him. On reaching the boatdeck Mattsson was suddenly aware of the strangeness of the moonlit scene, which was being enacted in complete silence, not a word coming from anyone as they got the lifeboats away as coolly and efficiently as if it was the kind of thing they did every day.

When the lifeboats had pulled away from *Gunborg* Mattsson remembered with a pang that in the rush he had left his dog on board. It was a fine dog, his German Shepherd, and, left shut up in his cabin, the animal was doomed to a horrible death as it went down with the ship. Mattsson told the master, Captain Jiewert, about the unfortunate animal. The captain studied the sinking ship. *Gunborg* was settling very slowly, kept afloat by her pulpwood cargo; he decided there was time to go back. As the lifeboat pulled close to the vessel's side, Mattsson jumped on board and ran to his small cabin, opened the door and let the dog out, raced back on deck with it and threw it into the lifeboat, though the animal was frightened and he thought it might bite him. Minutes later they had pulled away from *Gunborg* again and were watching her slowly settle into the black sea, the grim-faced men and the boy, now happy at having saved his dog.

When the sea closed above *Gunborg* they began to row, seeing ships burning around them. Then a big vessel loomed ι ρ out of the darkness, silhouetted by the moon. She was the old Greek *Niritos*.

'Stand by to come aboard!' came an unexpected shout from the Greek as she slowed down to help them.

The surprised Swedes quickly talked it over among themselves and decided to refuse the offer. The truth was they all felt much safer in the lifeboats while the attack on the convoy continued. They shouted their thanks across to the Greeks and told them of their decision.

'We wish you the best of luck!' came the reply from *Niritos,* and the big steamer made speed and passed on into the night. Hardly ten minutes later the lifeboats from *Gunborg* shuddered under the shock wave as the Greek vessel was hit by a torpedo. They could see the old sulphur-laden tramp across the sea in the moonlight, reeling from the explosion in a great cloud of dust and smoke. She sank very quickly, burning fiercely as she went. In Mattsson's boat no one spoke; silently their eyes followed the luckless Greek until she had gone, leaving only a wreath of smoking wreckage. They started to row again and, seeing a light on the water, pulled towards it to investigate. It was a lifeboat with a small lamp at the bow, its only occupant a dead seaman. They rowed on . . .

Across the sea strewn with shadowy wreckage, tossing and swirling, a single boatload of survivors from *Niritos* also pulled on their oars, though it seemed useless for them to head in any direction at all except away from drifting dangers. There were only fourteen of them, including the captain. More than half the crew had been killed in the explosion or drowned, or perhaps even now were struggling in the water somewhere in the dark. They would not survive.

It was now just after 10.30 p.m. In two explosive hours nine ships had been lost, though in the mass of distress signals received and half received by *Assyrian's* radio officer there was no clear count. Commodore MacKinnon had seen his convoy all but shattered. The remaining twenty ships were now steaming as fast ahead as they could go, the majority of them still clinging to a desperate formation.

It had all been like a nightmarishly unreal picture of events played out against a theatre screen. Everything in darkness except for the light of the moon as it broke through mist and cloud, and against this backdrop the sudden flashes and explosions, the fires aboard stricken ships, the bobbing lights of lifeboats and rafts, strange flares streaking the sky, and eerily bursting starshell. Through all this the unharmed ships had moved darkly over the water, fleeing from the revealing moonlight and the unseen enemy, sometimes the frenzied note of a ship's siren sounding as vessels narrowly escaped collision in the scramble to avoid torpedoes seen streaking across the sea. As they steamed on, every cloud that momentarily obscured the face of the moon seemed to spell the difference between life and death.

For the ever searching escorts, never able to rejoin the convoy, the prolonged slaughter was both appalling and mystifying. How could one U-boat, or even two, manoeuvre to make these persistent attacks? Why could the enemy not be detected? The effect on the asdic hydrophones from the engines of the scattered merchant ships, the noises of torpedoes exploding, the echoes from debris and half sunken wrecks, made conditions extremely difficult, but why was not one contact made with an enemy boat? The unexplained flares, ships on fire, explosions first from one direction and then another, gave them a feeling of impotence. Like a blind man in a boxing ring they were being hit but did not know from which direction.

Then at last something tangible and real offered itself in the confusion of the night. At 10.40 p.m. the searching *Leith* sighted a U-boat on the surface dead ahead, racing fast on the same course as the sloop at a distance of about two miles. *Leith* fired more ten-second bursts of starshell as she gave chase. The U-boat and its wake were clearly visible, but not sufficiently for the sloop's 4.7 in. gun to get its sights on the German before he submerged minutes later. Continuing hot in pursuit *Leith* gained an asdic contact at less than two miles and held it on a run-in up to 800 yards—but then lost it.

It was a bitter disappointment. Either the U-boat had changed course at a speed far greater than that believed possible, or else the contact had been made on the boat's wake and not on the boat itself.

Aboard *Fowey* there had been some sharp criticism of *Leith's* constant firing of starshell. It seemed totally unnecessary on such a night, showing nothing more in the moonlight than they could already see, and it was a giveaway to the enemy, quite apart from its natural handicap of the brilliant flash of the discharge temporarily blinding the ship's own lookouts. But perhaps *Leith* had orders which they did not have to take this course of action?

Bluebell, which had dropped back to help *Leith*, was now

ordered to join in the hunt for the U-boat, which went on for another hour. But it was no use, the German had got clean away. Ordering *Bluebell* to stand by and pick up survivors of a number of torpedoed ships *Leith* swept off after the convoy, which had pulled far ahead and out of sight.

For *Bluebell*, moving into the scene of incredible devastation, a sea covered with wreckage, there began the long task of rounding up everyone alive in the water. It was near to midnight when the corvette started her mercy work. After tracking down survivors in their boats she searched the vicinity thoroughly for a lurking enemy before closing in and bringing the men aboard, a laborious operation in the rising wind and swell. The rescued men were the Swedes from the *Gunborg*, their captain very irate at being torpedoed although a neutral, the two boatloads from *Empire Miniver*, and the lucky ones from *Niritos*. The Greeks, some of them injured but none seriously, took an interminable time getting aboard. For Commander Sherwood, who had looked on wonderingly at the dog brought aboard by the Swedes, it was too much.

'Someone,' he said, 'must be looking for his bloody parrot!'

Bluebell, already carrying seventy survivors before beginning this latest rescue work, was feeling the strain on her limited resources.

'Bring aboard any blankets or food,' the men in the lifeboats were ordered. 'Any clothes—anything useful you've got. And hurry!' Every minute the corvette was stopped increased the danger.

Empire Miniver's Third Mate Hing, having been responsible for his ship's boats, knew where everything was stowed in them and it took only a few moments to pass over blankets, tinned meat, and a bottle of brandy from his boat; unfortunately the captain's boat drifted away with its brandy. In normal practice the plugs would have been taken out of the lifeboats so that they would sink and not litter the sea, but on this occasion the boats were left intact . . . they might yet save the lives of any man swimming in the water.

It was 3.15 a.m. before *Bluebell* could wireless Western

Approaches Command: 'Have on board captain and crew of British ship *Empire Miniver* . . . Captain and 22 crew Swedish steamer *Gunborg* . . . Captain and 13 crew Greek steamer *Niritos* . . . Standing by for further survivors at daylight.'

Bluebell, the ship whose raw company had never in their lives even seen a U-boat, now carried more than 140 survivors, but her job was by no means finished yet.

On leaving *Bluebell* at midnight, *Leith* had hurried off at her best speed to catch the convoy. After ten minutes she sighted *Fowey* and they talked by signal lamp. *Fowey* was now crammed with more than 150 survivors—the crews of *Convallaria, Shekatika* and *Boekolo*, besides the men rescued from the ship lost on the outward-bound convoy.

Leith stationed *Fowey* a mile on her port beam and together they raced after the convoy at *Fowey*'s top speed of 14 knots. At half-past midnight, great flashes lit up the sky on the starboard horizon and the two sloops altered course towards them. But they were hopelessly too late. The unguarded convoy had already been set upon by the wolf-pack in a staggering new wave of destruction.

9

And Still the Slaughter

At almost the same time as *Leith*, searching miles from the convoy, sighted a surfaced U-boat, so did *Assyrian*, still leading the depleted convoy as the first ship of the centre column.

'Look, there goes Jerry!'

Captain Reg Kearon sent down from the bridge for Second Engineer William Venables, who hurried up to find the captain and Commodore pointing excitedly over the ship's bows.

'There's a U-boat ahead,' said the captain. 'Give us all the speed you've got, Sec, we're going to try and ram him!'

Venables shot a glance for'ard before making a run for the engine-room. On the moonlit sea barely a hundred yards ahead he could see the dark conning-tower of a U-boat.

Down in the stokehold the duty firemen, two young Liverpool lads and a first-trip trimmer, had been working steadily to keep the ship going at a good seven knots. Their faces lit up when Venables told them of the captain's plan, and that he was going to open the expansions to suck up every pound of steam they could produce. Grinning at the thought of the old ship ramming a

U-boat they set to work like the very devil and fired her boilers as they had never been fired before; even with both engines full out her steam was on the feather.

From the bridge, Commodore MacKinnon signalled other ships of his intention to engage the U-boat on the surface and ordered every vessel to fire at the enemy on sight. Then *Assyrian* began to pull ahead of the convoy.

In the engine-room as the steam pressure rose, Venables opened up the expansions of the ship's twin steam-reciprocating engines to increase the revs. *Assyrian*'s normal speed was 104 r.p.m., but now the revs were 110, the fastest those engines had ever turned. Never before had the old vessel vibrated with such power. For the first time in her life she actually made ten knots.

For forty minutes she remained so hot on the U-boat's tail that it dared not try to turn away from her, so exposing itself to her after gun. But *Assyrian*'s best was not enough. As dark clouds momentarily obscured the moon, the U-boat seized the opportunity to veer away to starboard.

For a fraction of time *Assyrian*'s gun-crew on the four-inch were given a clear sight of the German. They fired twice, but missed. In the poor light the U-boat either submerged or disappeared at a fast speed into the night.

Second Mate Frank Bellas, the ship's gunnery officer, cursed the fact that they had no for'ard gun, when they might have got in a perfect shot while on the German's tail. But guns in the forepart of merchant ships were banned by International Regulations.

Engineer Venables, who had raced back on deck to see the action, now went below to reduce speed to normal to save overheating the ship's engines. The Commodore ordered the gunners to set off some smoke-floats. At first these flamed, making the ship an ideal target, then a dense pall of smoke trailed from her stern. It was just as if an old hen had spread her wings to protect her chicks.

Gradually *Assyrian* dropped back to resume her position at the head of the convoy.

Two other ships close to her had glimpsed the U-boat. The

Dutch *Soesterberg* fired once, but then lost the German before the gun could be loaded with a new shell. The *Empire Brigade* also saw the surfaced U-boat only 200 yards ahead, surging along incongruously almost as if it were part of the convoy. But no action could be taken other than to alert the other ships: 'U-boat ahead on surface DE 53 . . .'

On the *Soesterberg* now all hands on deck except those on-watch stood by the lifeboats wearing their life-jackets. The chief officer paced the lower bridge, having made sure everything on the boatdeck was in order to lower the boats, while the gun-crew stood ready at their stations. The constant sharp lookout played tricks. Several times the bridge telephone rang as the gun-crew, thinking they could see a U-boat, asked permission to shoot. But Captain de Jong and his officers had good binoculars and could see nothing in the fluctuating darkness. He told the gunners not to shoot before he gave the order, as he was worried they might fire mistakenly at another merchant ship.

Assyrian's gunners were just as tense. After the nervous excitement of chasing the U-boat there had come the sobering thought that the Commodore ship, by her audacious attack, had probably singled herself out as a special target for the enemy. Tension mounted as she narrowly missed being hit by two torpedoes which skimmed past her stern. Two more barely missed her bow.

On the bridge, Chief Steward James Daley asked the captain if he should send up some tea. Captain Kearon told him to ask the Commodore, who was on the starboard side peering hard out into the night. Daley went across to him.

'Would you like me to send up some tea, sir?'

Commodore MacKinnon did not turn, or raise his voice. 'An excellent idea,' he said quietly, 'so long as it is for everybody.'

It was a reply Daley would think about many times afterwards, always with admiration, that in spite of the danger of the moment the Commodore could still remember his staff.

Daley left the bridge and went below to the pantry. He was completely unaided now, as the assistant stewards formed part of the gun-crew. But on the way down he met Engineer Venables, who was off-watch and quickly volunteered his help. Between them they made the tea, and Venables went aft to the gun-crew carrying a large well-filled jug and a pint mug.

But they never got their tea on the bridge.

The time was twenty minutes past midnight, although down in the engine-room, clocks and watches gave the time as almost midnight, for in the stress of convoy battle the usual practice of advancing the engine-room clock to compensate for west to east progression had been neglected. This discrepancy in time grimly affected the fate of the three firemen in the stokehold, who should have been relieved and on deck, and of their three mates now about to descend the 'fiddley' ladders to take over the watch.

Just before midnight by the engine-room's unaltered clock, Bill Venables, after taking up the tea to the gun-crew, looked into the stokehold to congratulate the two young firemen and the trimmer on their efforts in speeding the ship after the U-boat. He then went on deck to warn the oncoming midnight to 4 a.m. watch against making too much smoke. The watch, two firemen and a trimmer, had already gone to the fiddley, just forward of the funnel, and begun to descend the series of iron-runged ladders and gratings taking them down to the stokehold forty feet below, a hazardous job under blackout conditions. Venables ran along the port side of the ship to catch them up. As he did so there was a violent crash and explosion as a torpedo tore into *Assyrian's* starboard side just forward of the engine-room, flinging Venables heavily to the deck and knocking him unconscious.

One minute after the torpedo hit Assyrian *another torpedo ripped into the* Empire Brigade. Soesterberg *was close by both ships. Captain de Jong immediately gave the order 'Hard-a-port!', trying to turn* Soesterberg *180 degrees and steam away from the U-boat. But barely was the Dutch ship turned four degrees when she, too, was hit.*

Five men died in the shattering explosion in *Assyrian's* stokehold. On deck, three luckless off-watch firemen also caught the blast. They were standing in their life-jackets on the boatdeck beside the starboard lifeboat when the sudden fierce eruption

hurled them overboard into the sea. The bow of the starboard
lifeboat was smashed and the boat hung over the side swinging
uselessly from a single bent davit. A long steel hatch-beam burst
up through the hatchboards and tarpaulins of No. 3 hold and
stood poised like a finger of warning. The engines stopped on
impact, all lights went out and everywhere there was a loud hissing of steam.

Not realizing that he must have lain unconscious in the
scuppers for several minutes, Bill Venables scrambled to his feet
and ran along the deck to the engine-room entrance. A vestige of
moonlight crept through a shattered skylight and found evil
gleams in the black and oily water which surged sluggishly over
the submerged engines. The smell of steam was overpowering,
though by some strange quirk of the explosion not a steampipe
was fractured.

With little hope for the safety of the fourth engineer, who had
been on watch, Venables started down the engine-room ladder
calling his name. There was no answer. With a louder shout
he took another step down the ladder, slipped and plunged into
the black water. In a panic he threshed about in the darkness
until he regained the sanctuary of the ladder, to which he clung
gasping for breath. It was only as he wiped the oily water from
his eyes that he realised that his glasses had been lost and his
forehead was bleeding from the fall on deck.

He staggered to his cabin for spare glasses and a torch, and
again searched the water in the flooded engine-room. But there
was no sign of the fourth engineer or any survivor. Heartsick,
he hurried to the boatdeck.

But in fact Fourth Engineer William Dean had had a remarkable escape. The tremendous explosion had thrown him hard on
to the stopped port engine, yet shocked and bruised as he was,
he managed to climb up the ladder topside in the darkness and
make his way to the ship's port side. Here, in the moonlight,
under the supervision of the captain, men had been swarming
down ropes and ladders into the port lifeboat. Dean climbed
down after them and the boat began to drift away almost
immediately.

Steward Jim Daley, caught in the crash and the dark as he was about to take the tea up to the bridge, felt his way out of the pitch darkness of the pantry and up the ladder to the boatdeck. By now the well-laden port boat was away from the side of the ship but already in difficulties. It had been holed, and quickly let in the sea until it was floating below the waterline on its tanks. There being no part of the boat visible, it seemed to those on the ship gazing after it that its passengers were all standing in the sea, when in fact they were sitting on the submerged gunwales. Among them was Engineer Dean, still badly shaken from his ordeal in the engine-room. A greaser beside him sat on Dean's left leg to prevent it from dithering, not with cold, although all he had on was his boiler-suit and socks, but with shock.

Captain Kearon called from the boatdeck to Third Mate Robinson, who had charge of the precariously floating boat, to row or paddle it farther away from the ship in case *Assyrian* suddenly plunged. Meanwhile the ship's young third engineer had swung out Tarzan-like across the water on a derrick line in an attempt to reach the lifeboat. He succeeded in getting there, but on seeing that the boat was almost sinking held tight to the rope and had to be pulled back to safety aboard the ship.

Everyone left on board now hurried to launch the small rafts which the ship carried in her rigging . . .

Across the water in the mist, moonlight and dark, *Soesterberg* reeled drunkenly. The torpedo had struck her at the rear of the engine-room, the explosion sending a huge column of water cascading over the vessel. The engine-room watertight doors, kept closed as much as possible against emergencies, burst open with the enormous air pressure, the starboard lifeboat disappeared with its davits and all into the sea, and four of the crew were sucked up by the enormous waterspout and hurled overboard.

On the bridge, as all the ship's lights went out, the engine-room telegraph was rung to 'Stop', though the engine had already stopped itself. Everything in sight of the bridge was a dark mess of twisted and burst metal and scattered pitprops.

Captain de Jong ordered 'All men abandon ship in the port lifeboat.'

The ship was listing over, but the boat, like the one that had been blown away, was already swung out over the water and only needed to be lowered. The captain now wanted to give orders to his third and fourth mates, but in the general scramble both officers had already run off to the boatdeck with the seamen, while the gun-crew aft had taken a small raft, thrown it over the side and jumped after it; they were now clinging to it in the sea.

The master hurried to his cabin, grabbed the bag with the ship's secret papers and ran to the boatdeck. Everyone was sitting ready in the lifeboat, the chief officer at the rudder. The master grabbed an axe and started to cut the boat's lashings free. He called for help, and eventually the third mate scrambled back from the boat to lend him a hand. Together they freed the boat and paid it down to the water.

Second Mate Ort, who had been on radio duty, now appeared and tried with the help of a seaman to get the ship's remaining small boat into the water, but there was a knot in the tackle and the boat stuck fast halfway down the ship's side. The seaman gave up, jumped out of the boat into the sea and swam to the lifeboat.

The boat was anxious to go, but the master checked and found that the duty engineers were missing. He ordered the boat to wait while he and the second mate, armed with a torch, went to the black bowels of the ship in search of them. The steps in the engine-room had disappeared and the inrushing water was already some seven feet high, covered with a swirling mass of pitprops. There was no answer to their repeated shouts, and as they could not get down any lower they abandoned the search; all on duty must have died in the explosion. They returned to the lifeboat.

Soesterberg had now settled deeper in the water and the lifeboat was bucking and tossing just off her side. 'You jump first, Ort,' ordered the master, a small man but large in courage. The second mate refused, insisting that he would see his captain safely off first. In the end they jumped together, the master falling into the pitching lifeboat with nothing more than a bruise, but the mate, afraid of being trapped between the ship and the boat, jumping into the sea beyond the boat. The boat's line was cut and Ort was pulled aboard in seconds. To the captain's astonishment the boat was half full of water, and the level was rising. It must have been pierced by a lump of iron flung out in the engine-room explosion, yet no one was doing a thing about it.

'Bale!' ordered the captain. 'Bale as hard as you can, or we'll all drown!'

But those men who were not rowing simply sat there dull-eyed with shock. No one moved. 'I'm wounded,' one seaman weakly excused himself.

Angrily Captain de Jong grabbed a bucket and started quickly baling out, at the same time keeping an eye on the oarsmen to see that they pulled in the right direction to pick up the four gunners from the raft. Second Mate Ort, his only staunch helper, groped in the dark water in the boat searching for the leak. He found it, a big hole in the bottom.

'Take off your boots and shoes and bale out!' the captain ordered everyone. ' And give me your socks—quickly!'

This time they did as they were told. The master collected the socks and stuffed them together to make a huge makeshift plug. The second mate rammed the plug into the leak and sat with his feet on it to hold it in. They were just in time, for the boat was now very low in the sea. With boots, shoes and the bucket they scooped out the water until the boat was fairly dry.

Now they came upon the raft. The gunners were burning a Holmes light, but even if the lifeboat had not seen it they would have found the gunners from the noise they were making. Once the gunners were aboard, the empty raft was taken in tow behind the boat, for it might yet be needed in an emergency . . .

Aboard *Assyrian* they were busy launching the small liferafts, all they had left now that the half-submerged lifeboat had floated off, when suddenly the lifeless grey hulk of *Soesterberg* loomed out of the darkness. Though a smaller vessel, she seemed higher out of the water than *Assyrian*.

'Couldn't we board her?' Engineer Venables suggested to the captain.

Captain Kearon studied the drifting Dutchman.

'No,' he said, 'she's sinking—could go any time.'

On came the eerily floating Dutch ship to kiss very gently stern upon stern with the doomed *Assyrian*, as if in sympathy, before swinging away.

What followed shortly afterwards came as a cruel stroke of fate. *Soesterberg,* still quite close, rose up by the bow a little and then slowly, like some stricken elephantine creature, reared up on end. Her bow thrust up almost vertically above the sea and she whined as she slid below the water. As she sank, thousands of pitprops burst from her holds and leapt high into the air, hurtling down again to skid across the surface of the sea and crash into the side of *Assyrian*. All the rafts were smothered, if not shattered, by the onslaught.

Venables and one of the Commodore's naval telegraphists had just got away on one of the rafts when the cannonade of pitprops came smashing over the sea. Their raft was hit and began to break up. The telegraphist scrambled back on board *Assyrian*, now settled low in the water. Venables also tried to make a jump for the ship's side, but his hands were numb with cold and he missed, falling into the sea beneath the jostling pitprops. He struggled his way back to what remained of the smashed raft and made another attempt to reach the ship. This time a strong hand came over the ship's rail to help him aboard. It was the Commodore.

'All right, Second?'

Those now left on board were in a terrible plight. They had neither boats nor rafts. The ship's bow was submerged and she had an ominous list to port. The water made a mournful sound as it soughed up and down the alleyways.

Venables ran off and shone his torch down into the engine-room. Surprisingly, the water did not seem to have gained, and he began to have faint hopes that the ship might even yet remain afloat. He went on to look in the fiddley space and found a fireman dazedly sitting there, his jaw and arm broken. Venables called Steward Daley and together they gave the injured man rudimentary first-aid. They then secured him to a Board of Trade gangway, cut the lashings and let him float off, reasonably safe on his own personal raft.

There were about a dozen of them left on board now, including Captain Kearon, Commodore MacKinnon and two of his staff, the three Frenchmen, Daley, Venables, Radio Officer Stracy and the ship's carpenter. Captain Kearon called everyone together.

'Come on,' he said resolutely, 'we'll build our own raft . . .'

Under his prompt direction most of them now gathered under the poop and set to constructing a big raft out of painting planks and hatchboards. They were all soaking wet and their hands so cold they could hardly tie the knots to bind the raft together, but they started to joke and sing as they worked while the carpenter sawed the wood, even if at the back of their minds some were wondering what it would be like to die.

Commodore MacKinnon joined in, the soul of encouragement. His example, from a man nearing sixty, fired the younger ones among them with a cautious optimism. The main thing was to keep busy and not dwell on the horrible prospect of the drowning ship suddenly falling below the surface and dragging them all down with her.

Engineer Venables was hurrying off again to check the water level in the engine-room when he heard a voice calling his name from the sea. Looking across the moonlit mass of pitprops he could see Chief Officer King waving to him. King was hemmed in by pitprops some yards from the ship's side, and Venables ran for a rope to help him. But as he was doing so the wind and sea suddenly shifted the props and King was able to swim to the ship's side and clamber on board. For a moment the two men looked at each other, then as the absurdity of the situation mutually dawned on them they both laughed aloud . . . at the crazy notion that to them the deck of a sinking ship should appear as a place of safety.

Looking over the side now Venables saw the third engineer silently hanging on to a rope in the water. He lowered himself down to help the man, but could not unclasp the dead hands from the rope, for the man had expired even as he clung on.

Pulling himself back on board, Venables suddenly heard a voice calling for help. It came from the direction of the fiddley. He ran to it and his torch revealed the soot-smeared face of a young trimmer trapped beneath the top grating, his hands clenched on the rungs, his body below the shoulders immersed in dark, dusty water, a gash on his forehead bleeding into his eyes as he gazed pitiably up at the torchlight. Venables was doubly shocked to find the trapped man, as he had previously checked that no one was in the fiddley and nearly an hour had gone by since the ship was torpedoed. He called to Steward Daley, Radio Officer Robert Stracy, and a greaser named Bishop, to help him release the trimmer. Tenderly they laid him on the deck. He was terribly injured, his stomach torn open, his legs nearly off at the thighs. Stracy, a quiet man who normally could not bear to look at a cut finger, pushed back the man's spilling stomach and helped to apply a rough bandage. Daley placed a morphia tablet on the man's tongue and gave him some water. There was little else they could do except wrap him up warmly in blankets.

He was a Catholic youth from Liverpool's Scotland Road. As he lay suffering on the moonlit deck he kept moaning 'Holy Mary, Mother of God . . . Holy Mary . . .' He was to have been married when *Assyrian* docked. By rights he should never have been caught by the torpedo blast, for he was off-watch at the time and had only gone down to the stokehold for a chat with his mates.

A gangway lying on the deck nearby seemed a likely raft to carry both the injured man and his rescuers. They hauled it to the side of the ship and hoisted it over, preparatory to boarding it, but to their utter dismay it quickly sank.

Now two lifeboats could be seen rowing in the dark distance. They hailed them lustily, but a disappointing response came back across the water. 'We're full up mates,' and 'Sorry, we're sinking ourselves. . . .'

Unknown to them, one boat was from the *Soesterberg*, crammed full of men and towing the empty raft. Captain de Jong was faced with a dreadful dilemma. His leaking boat was fully loaded and he dared not pull too near *Assyrian* in case any men from her jumped overboard and tried to get into the boat, whereupon it would surely sink. All he could do was to row about wind, away from the ship, and release the raft so that it would float towards them. If some men could pick it up they would save themselves.

The other lifeboat, also unable to risk taking aboard a single extra man, was one from the *Empire Brigade*. . . .

The torpedo that tore into the starboard side of the *Empire Brigade*, a 6,000-ton vessel twice the size of *Assyrian*, blew a great hole in No. 2 hold at the side of the bridge.

Down in the radio cabin First Radio Officer Leonard Dewar, after picking up distress messages all night, had just remarked thankfully about their own ship 'Well, so far so good . . .' and was about to raise a hot drink to his lips when the torpedo struck.

'They've spilt my bloody cocoa!' he exclaimed indignantly. He tapped out 'No 53 torpedoed starboard side' and raced up to the bridge to report. Tall, balding Captain Parks was trying to assess the damage. There seemed no doubt that *Empire Brigade* had been fatally hit.

The captain and his officers now hurried down to the boat-deck to find that, incredibly, no lifeboats were left. The crew had gone without waiting for the order to abandon. One boat's painter had been chopped away and the boat launched with the way still on the ship.

A few men had not waited for the boats but dived straight over the side. One fireman-trimmer scrambled up the ladder from the engine-room and jumped into the sea to his death. Another casualty was the third engineer. Many times he had vowed 'If we're hit I won't trust you bastards to get me out—I'll trust to God to help me!' He did succeed in getting out of the engine-room after the explosion, but after having appeared on the boat-deck he was never seen again.

For the people scrambling down from the bridge there was no time to lose, as the ship's bow was already well down and her stern had risen high out of the water. Captain and everyone jumped overboard in the dark into the black sea. Radio Officer Dewar jumped from one of the Army lorries secured on the after deck, but no sooner had he jumped than he tried to get back, with the result that he slid heavily down the side of the ship, glimpsing the propeller still revolving in the air as he fell. He drifted away in the sea and was hit and knocked unconscious by an oar from one of the lifeboats, but they saw him and dragged him senseless into the boat.

All those from the bridge were eventually picked up by the lifeboats, though the captain himself was nearly lost. He was only spotted as he swam by his bald head shining in the moonlight.

Six men of the *Empire Brigade* lost their lives, either killed in the explosion or drowned, the big vessel sliding below the surface twenty minutes after being hit. . . .

On *Assyrian*, after unsuccessfully hailing the passing lifeboats, they were hurrying to get the makeshift raft ready for launching, but it looked doubtful whether it would carry everyone, even if it floated successfully. As time pressed, everything floatable on deck was flung overboard into the water in the hope that it might help to save a life. Engineer Venables and greaser Bishop even cut down the battered starboard lifeboat, still hanging by its one solitary fall. The boat fell into the water upside down. Bishop, together with a seaman and a fireman, sat on the cap-sized boat and made it fast to the ship's deck railing while Venables went back to the badly injured trimmer lying moaning on deck. He was now faced with the impossible task of getting the poor man across to the overturned boat. He searched around for some means of transporting him.

Meanwhile Chief Steward Daley, on going to the ship's rail, was surprised to see one of the small rafts put overboard earlier now floating intact only some twelve feet away from the ship's side. It was the kind of raft that carried a box containing biscuits and brandy. It was easy for Daley to reach, with lots of floating pitprops to help him and his Mae West life-jacket supporting him in the water. Manoeuvring the raft alongside the ship he called to the second steward, who came down and sat on the raft with his back to Daley's. They found it more difficult to get the raft away from the ship's side because the same helpful pitprops now hemmed them in, but they were joined by one of the Commodore's ratings and now the three of them, with the aid of a small piece of timber and by kicking out in the water, at last got clear. *Assyrian* now had almost no freeboard and was settling deeper every minute. They floated past the stern, where Captain Kearon, Commodore MacKinnon, Chief Officer King and at least three others were under the poop, still fighting against time to launch the raft.

Suddenly a tremor ran through the ship and it was clear she was going. 'Abandon ship!' cried the captain, and they began to push the makeshift raft over the stern. But even as they did so it began to break up. Hands had been too cold when tying the rope knots. Already the ship's stern was rising quickly out of the water. Men jumped from from the rail after the raft, one climbing down to the great propeller boss before jumping.

Away from the raft party Engineer Venables, in an agony of mind at having to leave the injured trimmer, had jumped hastily for the capsized boat. He and his three companions then shouted to let anyone who missed the raft know there was plenty of room for them on the keel of the boat. When no one answered they tried to push the boat away from the ship's side but could not, the suction of the sinking ship was holding it fast. Suddenly the ship's side seemed to jump up at them, the starboard davit swooped down through the air and sliced through the overturned boat between Bishop and Venables, who found themselves struggling underwater, fighting to free themselves from the pull of the ship.

Venables surfaced with difficulty, his skin scored by wires, his clothes torn and one leg of his trousers ripped to the thigh. He clutched his glasses to his eyes as he bobbed up, and saw the after part of *Assyrian* rear up above the sea. She stood on her bow, her twin screws high above, photographically etched against a moonlit cloud. He could see every plate of her, the sea grass vivid on her side. In front of him was the gaping black hole where the torpedo blast had ripped open her side, a frightening sight. He swam on his back away from it, deeply afraid of being sucked inside; he would have swum faster had he turned and used the breast-stroke, but he could not, for he was completely unable to drag his fascinated eyes away from the ship.

Assyrian hung poised for a moment above the water, and there was a tremendous crashing noise inside her, as if everything in the engine-room had broken loose. Then she slid beneath the dark surface of the sea, the displaced air from her holds droning through her ventilators like a mighty organ. And afterwards nothing, just a huge patch of frothing water, wreckage, and bales of cargo bobbing in the white foam as she sank to her grave more than a mile below.

The Germans had built *Assyrian*, and the Germans had sunk her.

There were voices now calling out from many directions, seeking comrades in the debris and dark. The raft, or what was left of it, had got away, but for several men a floating pitprop was their life-saver.

Commodore Lachlan MacKinnon never got on to the raft. As he struggled in the sea, his feet were grasped by Second Mate Frank Bellas and his head was held out of the water by Radio Officer Stracy, who hooked his arms through the Commodore's braces to tow him along until he had recovered sufficiently to strike out for himself. Stracy's own departure from the sinking vessel had had a touch of nonchalance about it. He simply walked off the vessel into the water, went down and down, and came up again with his uniform cap still firmly on his head.

Captain Kearon had floated off the ship and been sucked under as she plunged. A strong swimmer, he fought his way to the surface and came up beside a large spar to which Chief Officer King, nearly twice his age, was clinging for dear life. There was some rope trailing in the water and the captain used it to lash his elderly chief officer safely to the spar, after which he himself breasted the floating timber.

Now someone, somewhere in the dark, had burst bravely into song. It was the messroom steward, floating in the sea and singing in a discordant voice 'Roll Out The Barrel.' Elsewhere a seaman hanging on to a pitprop kept pulling something out of his jersey, waving it over his head and jubilantly shouting 'I've got my nylons!' Precious stockings for a girl friend, bought while in harbour at New York.

There was someone else half sitting up in the sea, holding on to a lifebuoy. It was Carrot, the Commodore's naval signaller. 'Are you okay?' someone called.

Cheerily Carrot replied, 'If it wasn't so bleeding cold it would be like being on the Serpentine!'

Soon men fell quiet as they floated aimlessly, and as the fitful moon came and went behind dark clouds they lost touch with one another and were left alone with their thoughts.

Steward Daley and his two companions on their small raft suddenly heard voices out of the silence, and looking in that direction saw a dark shape larger than themselves. They paddled and splashed their way across to it. The voices grew stronger, and the shape clearer. It was the port lifeboat, unbelievably still afloat on its tanks with only its occupants visible above the surface of the sea. Raft and boat drifted apart again and lost each other in the sea of pitprops. Everyone now was praying for daylight, and the chance of rescue. Could they stay afloat till then, and ward off the deadly effects of shock and exposure?

After the lifeboat had drifted on for some time there was great excitement when someone shouted 'Look—a destroyer!' Sure enough, about half a mile away there was something like a destroyer making straight towards them. But hearts dropped when, on coming closer, they found it was just another stricken merchant ship slowly sinking stern first.

Away across the sea of misery the occupants of Daley's raft now heard a lone voice calling out in a foreign tongue. They paddled towards it and found a seaman whom they judged to be a Greek. He grabbed Daley's side of the raft and hung on. Daley held on to him with one hand, and in doing so lost a briefcase containing the ship's articles and other papers which he had saved from his cabin and clung on to for so long; it spun away into the sea. It was impossible to pull the Greek up on to the raft, so Daley gave him some brandy and the man kept talking and talking, all quite unintelligible to them. He held on to Daley until the steward's arm was stiff and numb. With his free arm, Daley kept feeding the man brandy . . .

Engineer Bill Venables soon found himself swimming alone. He was fully dressed, complete with Merchant Navy muffler, rigged for a night in a boat or on a raft, not for swimming the Atlantic. He tried to take his shoes off to give himself more freedom, but the water had tightened the laces and his hands were too cold to undo them. His life-jacket was nearly in shreds after his struggle to escape when the *Assyrian* rolled over on top of him. For more than an hour now he swam alone with a pit-prop under each arm. He came upon dead men floating face-down in their life-jackets and turned them over to see if he recognized them. But there was no companionship even from the dead for they were all strange faces from other ships.

The water did not seem as cold as he thought it would be, but his hands soon lost all feeling and his stomach felt as if it was full of ice. He began to fear that even if he was eventually picked up he would be a physical wreck for the rest of his life.

Coming upon some packing cases floating in the sea he tried to climb up on to them, but as he did so the cases simply rolled over on top of him and pushed him under the water. He went back to the support of his pitprops.

Suddenly a new fear shot through him as he saw a periscope skimming along through the moonlight. The U-boat's conning-tower was almost awash and he thought it was going to surface. He hid behind a floating bale, greatly afraid of being taken prisoner, and to his intense relief the grim shape of the U-boat passed on.

As the time dragged on, the icy feeling in his stomach crept higher, and he felt that when it reached his heart he would die. The moon was lowering behind the scudding clouds and he was afraid it would vanish altogether, leaving him in darkness. He seemed to be the only thing that lived on the face of the sea.

Lived? He was as good as dead already, for they could none of them reasonably hope to be rescued at all. The surviving merchant ships had all gone on, and no doubt the escorts with them, for warships could not stop to search for men in the sea while the enemy still threatened. This they all knew.

Suddenly the awfulness of his situation was too much. Very deliberately, Bill Venables put his head under water and tried to drown himself, but found he could not do it . . .

In another part of the sea another lonely survivor clung forlornly to a supporting piece of timber. It was Commodore MacKinnon. After recovering from the first shock of immersion he had lost touch with his rescuers and swam alone for some distance before finding a small raft with six men sitting or lying on it. It was loaded to danger point, clearly unable to support another body, so he found a plank of wood for support and held on to the raft, adamantly refusing to board it in spite of the entreaties of its occupants, in case he should sink them all.

He clung on to the raft as long as he could, but as the numbness crept through his limbs he had to let go of it and drift away on his plank. Now he floated as the waters took him, feeling for the first time the full weight of his fifty-seven years. But it was not his growing physical distress and horror at being alone in the dark that finally drove through to his heart, it was the hopeless situation of everyone who might still be bobbing precariously on the littered surface of the sea.

His convoy had been massacred. His own ship had gone, and the Vice-Commodore ship, *Scoresby*, had been sunk long before. Any merchant ships that survived now had no merchant leader, nor, as far as he knew, any escorts.

As he floated on his life-saving piece of timber with all hopes of rescue fading, he mercifully could not know that the slaughter of SC7 was far from done.

When *Leith* and *Fowey*, racing hard for the convoy shortly after midnight, saw flashes on the starboard horizon and set course towards them, they came upon the big Glasgow ship *Blairspey*, loaded high with timber, stopped and drifting after being rocked by a torpedo blast.

Aboard *Blairspey*, her crew all either Scotsmen or Northerners, the night had seen a certain change among the engine-room staff. Beforehand when the convoy was quiet, her stokers had gone down to the stokehold to pitch, slice and rake the boiler fires, then returned to sit in the galley, deeming it to be safer there. But as the events of the night plunged them into the thick of danger the same men had stayed working like fury in the stokehold, not only those on duty but others off-watch, stoking up the fires to give *Blairspey* the steam she needed in her efforts to speed away from the enemy. She had thumped and dodged through the night at a rate she was not originally designed for, doing a good twelve knots with all safety valves closed down. But it was not enough. With her wheel hard over to port, she was torpedoed in No. I hold, port side, and quickly came to a stop, blowing off steam very hard.

In a moment of panic the starboard lifeboat was let down into the water, but Captain J. C. ('Jesus Christ') Walker, a Glasgow man like all the ship's officers, firmly ordered the boat to be re-hoisted. There was no question of abandoning ship, he declared, until the ship abandoned them.

It was then that *Leith*'s signal lamp winked across the water. 'Are you in trouble?'

Captain Walker signalled back that he was confident *Blairspey* could keep afloat and that he could steam her at six knots independently.

Leith replied that she was sorry she could not stand by but would try to send an escort shortly. Then off she vanished after *Fowey*, still trying to catch up with the convoy.

Only twenty minutes after the sloop's departure *Blairspey* shuddered and reeled in the water again as a second torpedo struck her, this time on her starboard side in No. 2 hold. It was the end. Captain Walker ordered abandon ship.

The captain took one lifeboat with nineteen members of the crew, and they got clean away in the darkness. Chief Officer

John Glasgow took the other boat with the remaining thirteen men, including Second Radio Officer John Crawford. They were not so lucky. Being on the port side, the windward side, they had difficulty pulling away from the stricken ship. They were still trying to get clear when a third torpedo hit *Blairspey* port side under the bridge. The fierce explosion blew timber high into the air and it came raining down into the sea, bouncing up again from the surface in all directions. The lifeboat fortunately escaped the flying timber but was thrown back on its beam by the surging water, hurling several men into the sea. Yet by some miracle no one was injured, and the men thrown into the sea were pulled back to safety.

The two lifeboats never joined each other. Far across the water, in the captain's boat, there was panic when a U-boat was spotted on the surface making directly for them. It came close and almost stopped, and there was a cold fear of spraying machine-guns.

'What ship?' asked the German commander.

'*Blairspey*,' replied Captain Walker.

Satisfied, the U-boat sped on into the night.

Twenty-five miles due south of the now silently drifting *Blairspey*, in an area of ocean covering some thirty square miles, the relentless destruction of SC7's scattered ships continued.

The small Norwegian steamer *Snefjeld* sank quickly when a torpedo tore a hole in her side. The thirty-nine year old vessel just seemed to fall apart, even her timber cargo could not keep her afloat.

The British *Sedgepool* was three times as big as the old *Snefjeld*, but again one torpedo was enough. The explosion blew away a wing of the bridge, killing the captain and his second officer—they simply vanished. Death also struck down in the engine-room, where the third engineer died instantly. The main wireless aerial broke adrift and part of it hung over the ship's funnel, while the emergency aerial was blown clean away.

Chief Engineer James Aves shut down the ship's engines and came on deck to find that he was left absolutely alone on a derelict vessel—the lifeboats had gone, except for one which had jammed at the side of the ship and been abandoned. Desperately he tried to free the boat, but in doing so he badly crushed his hand. He gave up and jumped overboard, having to swim around for some time before being picked up by a few of the crew who had got away on a raft. Later they were all taken aboard one of the ship's lifeboats. As they pulled away in the dark they could see the ship, loaded with grain, settling in the water but still well afloat.

Fifteen miles to the south the Greeks of the old *Thalia*, carrying a full load of steel to Liverpool, were not so fortunate. The big steamer, nearly 6,000-tons, sank almost as soon as she was hit. There were no survivors.

At this time the still floating *Shekatika*, drifting far to the rear, shook with the impact of a third torpedo delivered by a third U-boat. This third explosion was too much, even with her great packing of timber. Wood spewing from the big holes in her sides, *Shekatika* settled rapidly in the water.

And now, headlong into the most southerly area of attack by the wolf-pack, steamed the *Clintonia*, the Stag Line ship carrying pulpwood for Manchester. Captain Thomas Irvin had seen all five vessels leading their columns on his port side receive direct hits. One of them was the *Assyrian*, which had left *Clintonia* a 'sitting duck' and the convoy without a leader. After the loss of the Commodore ship a speaker for the officers and crew told Captain Irvin they were prepared to go it alone; that is, to sail independently, which *Clintonia* had been doing all the time up to joining SC7. Having had a brief gun battle with a U-boat on the outward voyage and got the better of the exchange, the crew believed they could now stand up to anything they could see. With these reassurances Captain Irvin set course away from the convoy's planned route in the hope of clearing well out of the area by daybreak.

But it was not to be. At 3 a.m., having run the gauntlet for the past two hours without sight or sound of the enemy, the master was remarking to his second officer on the bridge how lucky he felt, when they sighted a U-boat close to port. So close, in fact, that had there been a hand grenade on the bridge he could have lobbed it down the German's conning-tower. *Clintonia*'s gun-crew scrambled to their station as the klaxon horn gave the alarm.

Captain Irvin skilfully brought the German astern and ordered his gun-crew to open fire. But even in the moonlight they could not see anything to fire at, probably because they were so much lower than the bridge. One shot might have stopped the U-boat; instead, the chance was missed. There now commenced a taut battle of hide and seek as Captain Irvin swung his ship first this way and then that to confuse the German, always trying to get into a position from which his gun-crew could get in a shot.

The duel in the dark went on for nearly an hour, until, as one particular manoeuvre developed between the two vessels, it suddenly dawned on Captain Irvin that this time *he* was the mouse, having been very neatly lured into a position of attack not from his immediate adversary but from a second U-boat moving in from another direction. Too late the master ordered his ship to swing away, for with the U-boat he had been watching still well visible astern, a torpedo from the other German streaked for *Clintonia*'s port side.

The resultant explosion blew the mainmast clean out of the ship—it came crashing down on the wireless cabin, smashing the cabin and all equipment, making it impossible to send a distress message. The blast swept right across the ship, throwing the breech worker of the four-inch gun, the chief cook, head first into the open breech, his head being forced into the gun barrel and terribly crushed.

The master and chief engineer hurried to the top of the engine-room and on looking down saw that the water was up to the cylinders. There was no other recourse but to abandon ship. The ship's secret papers were dumped overboard and the two lifeboats launched, Chief Officer Buglass taking one boat and the captain the other, the captain including the badly injured cook in his company. They had scarcely got clear of the ship before a second torpedo crashed into her. Again she shivered hugely under an explosion which blew the whole of her bridge high into the air, but still her 3,000 tons remained afloat on her pulpwood cargo. She was doomed, but would take her own time to sink.

Now the first U-boat, the one *Clintonia* had been duelling with, approached and started to shell the ship. It was an incredible scene to the watchers in the lifeboats, like two dogs fighting over a bone; the second U-boat had to retire hurriedly out of the line of fire to escape being hit. So had the lifeboats, for the German gun-crew seemed very erratic with their shooting, three shells whistling a few feet above the boats and sending all hands diving flat to the boards for safety. Grabbing the oars afterwards they pulled hard out of range. The U-boat kept firing away as if determined to shoot off every last bit of the ship's deck cargo. They counted twenty-three shells before its gun was silent.

There was another explosion from *Clintonia*, this time the boiler going up. The mauled ship then began to go down by the stern, rearing up to a vertical position before disappearing from sight in a whirlpool of debris.

The lifeboats had to scatter quickly again as the cargo of pulpwood rushed up to the surface and shot dangerously out of the water over a large area. One hit would have been enough to hole a boat and spill its occupants into the sea.

Lost from each other now, each boat made its separate plans. The captain decided to lay his boat to a sea anchor till daylight. They did what they could for the gravely injured cook, the captain cushioning him gently between his legs to steady him from the rocking motion of the boat, for the sea was getting up. But the cook died as he sat there. Quietly, when the rest of the boat's occupants were lying down trying to get some rest, the captain, helped by the second officer and the chief steward, cast the poor man's mutilated body to the deep.

Clintonia was the last victim of the wolf-pack, but while she was fighting her desperate duel other human dramas were being enacted across the sea to her rear.

Leith, steaming hard in the wake of the scattered convoy, finally arrived at the centrepoint of destruction where the Commodore ship, together with *Soesterberg* and *Empire Brigade*, had gone down. Faced now with the problem of whether to continue at speed after the remnants of the convoy or to stop and save what life he could, Commander Allen decided there was only one reasonable course of action he could take. It was a decision he would amply justify later on the grounds that the remaining ships of the convoy must now be so scattered that the chances of immediately finding any of them were remote, also the U-boats attacking in the area must surely have expended all their torpedoes. Accordingly *Leith* began her mercy work.

Elated survivors of *Assyrian*, seeing with salt stung eyes the glad sight of the sloop ghosting over the debris-strewn sea in the moonlight, raised hoarse cries and cheers as she neared them, but the shouts died away in their throats when she steamed on and deliberately passed them by. The men in the water could not believe their eyes, and on realizing that she was indeed leaving them behind, the night air rang with their desperate yells and vivid curses. Commodore MacKinnon, swimming alone, had also seen the approach of the sloop and, as she steamed on and away, bowed his head over his supporting pitprop. He knew that officially she should not stop but pursue the enemy to the limits, and she was only doing her duty. So this was the end of them.

Then suddenly *Leith* was back and slowing down to save them all from the sea. She had had to make an asdic sweep of the area first, and now her crew worked fast, for when stopped the ship was an easy target for any lurking U-boat. Commander Allen paced agonisingly back and forth on the bridge, frequently stressing the need for speed in forceful language to the first lieutenant supervising operations in the waist. Rescue nets hung down over both sides of the quarter-deck, lifelines were thrown to men swimming, boathooks were busy pulling in anything that floated to see if it held a survivor. When some survivors attempted to climb the nets they found they had lost the use of their legs; *Leith*'s willing sailors climbed down the nets to help the exhausted men up.

From the decks of *Leith* it was a terrible scene made all the more grotesque by the coldly shining light of the moon, the sea littered with wreckage, pitprops, oil, and yelling and screaming men frightened that they might not be seen and left to die.

Steward Daley and his two companions were saved from their raft, but the Greek seaman he had hung on to in the water for so long died soon after being pulled on board, and was returned to the sea. All the men in the waterlogged port lifeboat were saved and several others were picked up out of the sea, including Second Mate Bellas, who was hanging on to a pitprop, and Captain Kearon. There were cheers from the soaking, bedraggled survivors for their popular master as he was helped aboard, but it was a moment of tragedy, too, for Chief Officer King, still lashed to the spar as the master had tried to save him, had died from exposure. His body was left to drift away in the water. Another man who had clung to the same piece of timber had also died just before rescue came, and now slipped away and sank in the sea.

When Engineer Bill Venables, still swimming alone, saw the dark shape of the sloop ahead of him he could hardly believe it was real, and not just a feverish dream. Silhouetted as she was, the searching ship seemed to have come straight out of the moon.

'Ahoy there!' he cried, and an unmistakably live voice immediately answered. He cried out again, and the same voice gave him encouragement—'Keep calling! Keep calling!' They could not see him from the sloop but his voice told them his direction.

When *Leith* drew closer Venables abandoned his life-saving pitprops and threshed through the water like a madman towards her. He saw a lifebelt drop into the sea beside him, thankfully grabbed it and pulled it over his head. Then something snapped inside him and he was pulled on board near senseless.

Five others helped out of the water were injured. One fireman's ribs had been broken by a pounding pitprop, yet he had found the strength to swim on.

Weakly, from some distance away in the sea, the horrified Commodore saw a torpedo speed pointblank for *Leith*. But there was no explosion. The torpedo passed harmlessly underneath her, being set deep for a merchant ship. Minutes later they had found him, but he was totally unable to swim to his rescuers, so they lowered a net and hoisted him up inside it. As he rose into the air, water streaming from him, he was accidentally upended, and even as he swung there he could appreciate the wry humour of the situation. So many times over so many years had he boarded naval ships being accorded the full honours befitting his senior rank; now here he was being hoisted aboard like a sack of potatoes.

More tragic discoveries were made of floating bodies, which were left to drift away in the water. One was the injured fireman who had been sent floating away from *Assyrian* secured on a gangway; when found to be dead he was cast away again on his bizarre funeral craft to go bobbing across the night ocean to eternity.

Now came further horror when the searching sloop came upon a small raft with one man sitting on it. He had a broken arm and was holding on tightly with his sound arm. They tried repeatedly to get near enough to him in the dark to throw him a line, but he would not let go with his good arm to try to get the line, and every time the ship went astern to lose way, the wash from her propellers swept him away out of range. There were no other men in the water near enough to help him, and *Leith* could not remain stopped for too long. Eventually, after many tries, she had to move across to pick up more survivors farther away, leaving the unfortunate man on his raft, alone.

When the count came to be made, nearly half of *Assyrian*'s company had been lost, including one of the Commodore's petty officers and the young ship's carpenter who had worked so hard to build the raft. And of those now rescued, one seaman and the Commodore's yeoman of signals were both critically ill.

Now there were more shouts in the night as the sloop came upon the survivors of *Soesterberg* . . .

The Dutch ship's leaky lifeboat had stayed afloat on its plugging of socks. All the men who were soaking wet had been put in the rear of the boat, where they huddled together under blankets taken from the boat's blanket box. The boat's sail was spread over them, too, so that the body warmth of each man would help the others.

They had first had a good swig of brandy. At first Second Mate Ort had refused because he was a teetotaller. But Captain de Jong told him 'Ort, this is not alcohol, this is medicine which the doctor prescribes.'

'Then I'll take it,' said the mate obediently, 'as medicine I could never refuse.' He took a good swallow—and said afterwards that if all medicine tasted that good he would take it regularly.

After a long time in the boat they suddenly saw white foam from a good distance away, and then something black came out of the darkness at speed towards them. It was *Leith*. The sloop had spotted them from the white sail spread over the wet crew, and when she was near they could hear the sound of the ship's telegraph. The powerful engines were hard in reverse, and her commander worked them so that the rear part, where the climbing nets hung overboard, was exactly at the height of the lifeboat.

'Hurry up!' shouted Commander Allen from the bridge.

His call was unnecessary, for the men who had been unable to bale out the lifeboat to stop it sinking now burst into life and were the first on the warship's deck. Captain de Jong watched them more in sorrow than in anger. He himself climbed aboard carrying the bag with his ship's secret papers, but without the still half full bottle of brandy, which he forgot in the hurry, much to his regret as he had not had time to take a drop himself.

Away went *Leith* to find more survivors. This time they were from the *Empire Brigade*, in various states of exhaustion and some covered in filthy oil. With them was a stoker from *Soesterberg* who had been pitched overboard by the enormous water column thrown up when the ship was torpedoed, but who had managed to keep afloat on two pitprops. Encountering a boat of the British survivors he had clung on to the boat with one arm until it slipped completely out of socket without him noticing it. No sooner had he climbed on to *Leith*'s deck than he dropped unconscious.

Leith continued her systematic search but found only wreckage and bodies. Nothing else living and no sign of the enemy. She now had the survivors of four ships aboard her, including the Estonians from the *Nora*, and resembled a floating casualty station. The wardroom, messdecks and passages were crowded with sprawling bodies, the ship's doctor and his assistant going from one man to another to attend to their medical needs. All the blankets, towels and clothing that could be spared were given to the survivors to keep them warm. For many of them the night ended there, as they slept the sleep of exhaustion. Like Radio Officer Dewar of *Empire Brigade*, who, wet and reeking with oil, fell asleep on the wardroom floor and when he awoke, found he had been covered with Captain de Jong's overcoat. The kindly Dutch master had gone off to look for a warm place to sleep in the engine-room. He found it, but after a few hours bedded down on a metal platform his body really ached and the form of the 'iron toaster' was imprinted on his body.

Engineer Venables, who had collapsed from exposure, was taken to the galley and massaged for an hour before he showed signs of life, after which it took the full strength of two of his rescuers to restrain him as he struggled to get at the galley fire. He was fed hot cocoa, and knew no more till he awoke with a scalded throat, to find himself wrapped in blankets on the messdeck and a friendly Greek sailor lying beside him trying to put a cigarette in his mouth. They were crowded under low lighting and there was the whine of forced ventilation. Eventually someone discovered that Venables was an officer and his uniform was brought from the engine-room where it had been drying. He joined the officer survivors in the wardroom, where the hugely smiling features of Queen Salote looked down on the scene from a photograph on the bulkhead.

Chief Steward Daley, on regaining the use of his legs, went through the crowded alleyways searching for fellow survivors of *Assyrian*, and was glad to find them. Arriving back at the galley he was handed a cup of steaming cocoa and was surprised to see

Assyrian's cooks busy with two huge frying pans, making pancakes. Sailors, probably lookouts and gun-crews, took it in turns to appear and collect a cup of cocoa and a pancake dipped in sugar. They were very tired but showed their genuine appreciation, if it was only to say 'Thanks, scouse,' or 'There's nothing like working your passage, mates . . .'

Commodore MacKinnon had been hauled aboard feeling the certain ill effects of long exposure. They got a hot drink into him, stripped him down and tried to rub him unnumbed, but he could not stop shivering. They wanted to bundle him off to bed, but he refused, saying he would just sleep in a chair. The situation called for a bit of naval strategy. After a quiet word with the ship's doctor Commander Allen insisted that he wanted to turn in but could not do so until the Commodore had done so, at which they finally got the admiral to bed in blankets and there he stayed, in the commander's sleeping cabin.

In the meantime *Fowey* had also been searching for survivors, but without any luck, as she steamed over the route of the convoy. But for *Bluebell*, standing by as dawn came, rescue operations began all over again. First, she found the captain's boat from *Blairspey* with its nineteen occupants, then the two boats from *Beatus*, whose survivors had been drifting for some ten hours since their ship sank. It had been difficult for them to row with all the pitprops and wreckage around, and the best they could do was to get to the windward of the floating mess, in order to avoid damage to the boats. Had help not arrived they would have eventually hoisted sail and tried to make it for home.

Although it was now daylight, the work of getting the survivors aboard *Bluebell* was even trickier than it had been during the night. The wind had freshened and the sea was anything but gentle, requiring great patience and skill to get the corvette alongside the lifeboats. Survivors already aboard willingly helped the sailors with the rescue work, and as before, the boats were emptied of anything useful, from blankets to lifeboat biscuits in tins firmly stamped 'Spillers'. Then the plugs were taken out of the boats and they were left to drift away and sink among the wreckage which still dotted the surface of the ocean as far as the eye could see.

It was 8.25 a.m. when *Bluebell* wirelessed the Commander-in-Chief, Western Approaches, that she had now picked up the captain and eighteen crew of *Blairspey* and the captain and thirty-six crew of *Beatus*, adding the startling message: 'Have now on board 203 survivors. Am rejoining convoy.'

But there was no longer any convoy to rejoin. The surviving ships had all scattered far and wide in a wind-whipped sea growing rougher by the minute.

One of the scattered vessels was the scrap-carrier *Corinthic*, in which Radio Officer Kenneth Howell had been keeping a diary since the start of the voyage. Day by day, for his wife's eyes only, he had entered events in a cheap school exercise book, the kind with arithmetic tables printed at the back. But his entry for the past night was a single paragraph. As *Corinthic*'s pounding engines took her safely away from the scene of slaughter he wrote from the heart.

'Of the events that have taken place during the last few hours of this "Black Friday" I will write again if we are spared to get through this next day and night. Suffice to say at present that I was never so glad and thankful that during these months I have been back at sea I have each day said my prayers as I have been in the habit of at home. I am sure that during the last twenty-four hours only something higher than any good fortune has enabled us to be still sailing on this Saturday morning. For which fact I shall always return thanks.'

10

The Bottomless Bluebell

For five hours after picking up her last survivors, *Leith* steamed at her top speed of sixteen knots over the course of the convoy route, scouring the roughening sea for surviving ships. But depressingly she found none. At 9.30 a.m. on Saturday morning, October 19, the sloop reduced speed to fourteen knots to ease her racing engines.

Commander Allen continued to scan the grey sea through his glasses. He was now painfully aware, from his own observations and such scraps of information as he had been able to glean from survivors, that SC7 had been the victim of a well organized attack by the Germans. From the positions of some of the stricken ships, the times at which they were attacked, and the number of torpedoes known to have been fired, allowing for near misses, it seemed clear that at least two U-boats, perhaps three, had taken part in the assault.

The surprise had been complete and devastating. The three escorts had been rendered powerless by the U-boats' surface tactics, which were entirely unexpected. It had all been a gigantic mess, with each fighting vessel forced instead to take on the role of rescue ship—it had been a case of either doing that or leaving hundreds of men to the mercies of the sea. Now, on this rough morning, some ships at least should still be sailing . . . some must have escaped destruction. But where were they? The empty ocean gave no clue.

The ship's doctor came to the bridge with some bad news. Commodore MacKinnon, suffering acutely from the effects of exposure, had not stopped shivering since his rescue, and his condition had gradually deteriorated. Now the worst had happened. There were signs of pneumonia in his right lung.

The next few hours were a grim challenge for Surgeon-Lieutenant John Robertson, RN, as he struggled to save the admiral's life. A young doctor not long out of Edinburgh University, he tried all he knew to arrest the pneumonia, but the Commodore's condition worsened until he had clearly reached the point of death. There was a gurgling in his throat and he was at his last gasp. At this desperate moment young Robertson took the only gamble left open to him. He had a supply of the new 'M and B 693' tablets, the specially developed drug now being issued to the Services. The tablets were so new that Robertson had not himself used them before, nor knew anybody who had, and he had no idea of the prescribed dose for such a case. Calmly, but with a silent prayer, he administered the tablets to the dying patient, deliberately erring on the side of feeding him too much of the drug rather than too little.

No one, least of all the doctor himself, was quite prepared for what happened next. Only half an hour after being given the tablets the Commodore seemed to rally round, and an hour later he was definitely more peaceful, though still very dangerously ill.

Inspired by the miraculous change in his patient, pulled back from death's door, Robertson began to see a glimmer of hope. 'The Commodore is in a very bad way,' he told the captain, 'but with a little luck we should get him home.'

He would see to it. The young doctor was never more determined.

The good news found its way down among the crew and some of the host of survivors, giving rise to hopes that the other two sick men from *Assyrian* now fighting for their lives might yet be saved.

Among the sailors of *Leith* anger was intense at the slaughter of the convoy, for it seemed obvious to them that the U-boats had worked to a plan and cleverly lain in wait for SC7. The naval men's anger was directed at the continuing situation whereby U-boats appeared to be allowed sanctuary off the southern Irish coast, roaming ready to strike at incoming convoys at will, while the Irish Republic remained stubbornly neutral and over-run with German spies. British warships and planes, denied southern Irish bases, were severely handicapped, yet despite all the carnage at sea the British Government seemed powerless to do anything about it. Why?

Anger was something the survivors themselves were not capable of at this time. They could only feel a numbed relief. Even the thought of the usual remarks from the 'well informed' among the civilian population that would greet them once again when, and if, they reached home, for the present held no bitterness . . . 'Oh, but *you* are all right in the Merchant Navy . . .'

Men sat or lay as they could among clothes hung everywhere to dry, and papers, wallets and paper money also laid out to dry off. They clung to whatever meagre possessions they had managed to save from the sea. There was the mate of one vessel who sat or lay on his sextant, his only saved possession, the whole time, and would not let anyone come near it. All deck officers prized their sextants and the loss was all the greater when, as in one instance, the sextant was new and fitted with micrometer reading and small built-in light. Some other survivors had saved their 'sub bags', but many had only the sea-soaked contents of their pockets. Engineer Bill Venables thought sadly of his own prized possession taken down to the ocean depths by *Assyrian*. The beech and mahogany propeller for his Flying Flea, on which he had lavished so much work, was hanging over his bunk when she sank. It was not unusual for a man to think of his lost belongings at such a time. Down, like everyone else's, had gone

Commodore MacKinnon's precious personal things. In clearer moments he would think of them. Everything gone. The little presents he had been bringing home for his wife and daughter in Britain, the fountain pen he treasured, his pipes, and the comfortable old slippers he had worn for years, steadfastly refusing to allow anyone to buy him new ones . . .

At noon, in worsening weather, *Leith* steamed on following a high easterly course level on an invisible line with the southernmost Hebrides. Commander Allen now wirelessed Western Approaches Command and reported the number of survivors he had picked up, including the Commodore, who was on board in a critical condition. 'Have not found any other ships of the convoy,' the message added. 'Am joining *Fowey* . . .'

But in fact Allen would never sight his fellow escort again.

Commander Aubrey, after searching unsuccessfully for more survivors, had kept *Fowey* steaming on a more southerly course than *Leith*, and at daybreak he was rewarded with the sight of first one ship, then another . . . and another, until excitedly they counted eight scattered vessels in all. Eight ships! Survivors on *Fowey*'s decks gladdened at the cheering sight, waving vigorously at the plodding shapes of vessels they had become familiar with during the long voyage but had never expected to see again.

Commander Aubrey now set about reforming the eight scattered ships into a miniature convoy less than a quarter of the size of the one that had set out from Sydney so long ago. A Commodore ship had to be appointed to lead them, but there was little ceremony attached to this, it was simply a case of choosing either the biggest vessel among them, or the one out ahead. The *Somersby*, the West Hartlepool ship of more than 5,000 tons, fitted the bill admirably. *Fowey*'s morse lamp blinked across the rising seas, and *Somersby*'s radio officer was called to the bridge to help Captain Bill Thompson translate the message and signal their reply by hand torch. And that was that. Captain Thompson, a Cardiff master who had raced *Somersby* to safety by screwing down the safety valves and raising a shuddering ten knots, now took the lead as Commodore ship.

As the weather continued to worsen there was little opportunity for the members of the convoy to take much stock of one another, but it was enough that they were now all together, in fair order, and with *Fowey* to screen them as best she could. Their position was actually some forty miles south-west of *Leith* when close to noon, Commander Aubrey wirelessed Western Approaches Command to report that he had rounded up eight ships of convoy SC7 and was escorting them in at a speed of seven and a half knots. He added that he estimated some ten ships of SC7 had been torpedoed . . .

In fact the full terrible total of ships sunk during the night was sixteen. Together with the four ships lost earlier, SC7 had lost twenty ships; well over half the convoy.

It was at this time that the sloop Scarborough, *coming up in the rear more than eighty miles to the north-west, passed through the area where* Assyrian *and others had gone down. All that remained now was some sea tossed wreckage and an empty, aimlessly drifting lifeboat. There were no signs of survivors.*

In the mid-afternoon, when the black stormy weather was already beginning to merge with evening darkness, the lonesomely steaming *Leith* was relieved to sight the *Heartsease*, still escorting the damaged *Carsbreck*. In all the chaos of the past night, the corvette had stood close by her crippled charge as they steamed through a sea of debris and occasional empty lifeboats, with smoke palls spiralling on the horizon to mark the fate of the convoy ahead of them. *Carsbreck* now was very much down by the bow, but still pushing slowly ahead in ungainly fashion with her mainmast leaning drunkenly in two directions at once, and timber still escaping every now and then from the great hole in her side.

Three other scattered ships of the convoy had come upon the corvette and her charge and were now keeping close company with them. One was the small Norwegian *Inger Elisabeth*, another was the *Corinthic*. A forlorn sight, this small handful of remnants. *Leith* steamed ahead of the five vessels, leading them on into the wild evening seas. The wind had reached gale force, with the darkening sky heavily overcast, and frequent squalls of lashing rain making visibility poor.

In the late afternoon a distant rumbling explosion was clearly heard between decks aboard *Leith*. Half an hour later came the tremors of another explosion. What was happening now? And where?

In his bunk the sick Commodore trembled at the noises. Every time the sloop banged down in the rough weather he thought, in his fever, that it was another torpedo.

Far to the south, as *Fowey*'s convoy of eight ships strove to keep their stations in the ever worsening seas, a familiar nauseating voice came over the ships' radios. 'Jairmany calling, Jairmany calling . . .' Convoy SC7 had been smashed, said Lord Haw-Haw—it was a great and glorious victory for the German U-boats. He went on to describe how the U-boats had beaten the convoy's 'destroyer' escorts and 'pulverized' the merchant ships in a daring night attack . . . But on many of the ships now listening, Haw-Haw's final words were lost in a torrent of jeers and abuse. Aboard the old *Botusk*, such was the richly inventive language used against the English traitor, consigning him to highly imaginative ends, that the like had never been heard before on that ship, nor would be again. Unwittingly, far from being the voice of doom, Haw-Haw was the greatest booster of British morale.

But they steamed on into a dreadful night. The thick squally weather reduced visibility to vanishing point, while a tearing gale whipped ship after ship off her station. For the *Botusk* it was a night of high danger as she nearly ran ashore on the north-west coast of Ireland. Only when they managed to obtain a 'fix' and by dead reckoning retraced their movements did they realize the narrowness of their escape.

Through all the worst of the night *Fowey* managed to keep company with the lead ship of the centre column, but when dawn broke on Sunday, October 20, it disclosed a very changed scene. *Fowey* and her companion found themselves completely alone on a tossing sea, every other vessel of the small convoy having been blown away in the night. It was useless searching for them now. Commander Aubrey decided that his best course of action, with his ship crammed with a hundred and fifty-seven survivors, was to make for an early port; so instead of setting course for Liverpool he planned to steam for the Clyde and try to land the survivors there before darkness. At 10 a.m. he wirelessed these intentions to Western Approaches Command, and *Fowey* sped on her way.

Leith had not been any more fortunate in battling her way through the foul conditions of the night. During the turbulent small hours she lost touch with *Heartsease* and the four merchantmen, and at daylight found herself alone again on a still angry sea. At noon, with still no other ships in sight, Commander Allen wirelessed Western Approaches Command that he was now coming in to land survivors. Unlike *Fowey*, however, he would steam direct to Liverpool.

Late that afternoon aboard *Leith* they witnessed a final sad epitaph to SC7. The two seriously ill men from *Assyrian*, the Commodore's yeoman of signals and a seaman, had both died. Their canvas-wrapped bodies were laid side by side, covered with the red and white ensigns, the burial service was read, the shots fired, and the bodies were slid over the stern.

So many other shipmates who had died had not known these honours. The ceremony, in its way, remembered them all.

The corvette *Bluebell*, after her long hours of rescue work, steamed on but never sighted another ship. Crowded to capacity with survivors, Commander Sherwood decided there was nothing else for it but to get back to the U.K. as soon as possible.

As the corvette did not carry any medical personnel no one knew how to attend to the injured, some of whom ended up swathed in bandages like mummies. But there were no serious cases, and they got by. Of more immediate concern in the cramped conditions prevailing were men who were as sick as a dog for twenty-four hours or more owing to the different, and more violent, motion of the corvette compared with that of a merchantman.

Bluebell was now in the fantastic position of having four

times as many survivors as crew. The naval men gave up every-thing they could to them. Two weary *Empire Miniver* officers were eternally grateful to the sailor who turned over his bunk to them—how they ever managed to climb into it to sleep there together they never knew, but sleep they did. Later, when all ships' officers were requested to move into the wardroom, the two regretfully left their 'comfortable' quarters and moved into the small and overcrowded officers' accommodation where every-one was obliged to spend most of the time sitting on the deck.

All the masters were gathered in the captain's cabin, where Captain Brett of *Beatus* and Captain Weatherill of *Scoresby* tossed up for Commander Sherwood's bunk. Weatherill won. He was the lucky one, the remainder having to share the deck space between them.

But all these were small nuisances against the one great prob-lem: food. The escort corvettes were only stored for ten days, plus a small surplus for emergencies, and with so many mouths to feed the 'winnings' from the lifeboats added little to the general supply. So food had to be strictly rationed, both crew and survivors sharing the same meagre menu. However, it was all done in orderly fashion. In the wardroom it may have been only ship's biscuits and corned beef, but it was correctly served at the table.

Bluebell steamed on through heavily overcast weather. Then she ran into fog, which really placed them in an impossible situation. They had not seen the sun for days, and Commander Sherwood was sailing his ship a little by guess and by God. Every officer survivor aboard—and there were some thirty of them—tried to help by pitching in with his calculations, but none could find the sun to take a sight; except one, Chief Officer Coultas of *Scoresby*, who, to the commander's lasting amuse-ment, swore that he had. However, the blunt truth of their position came out of the murk later when they sighted Tory Island, off north-west Ireland, on the wrong bow. *Bluebell* had been running 'blind' to the south.

But now Commander Sherwood could set course for home at

Bluebell's best speed. Everything would be all right now, he assured his 'guests', and they could all go to sleep, for if they slept they would eat less food. He was not joking, for the rapidly diminishing food supply was his major worry. He decided they would have to make for the nearest point to land the survivors, so headed *Bluebell* for the Clyde instead of trying to make it back to Liverpool, for if fog held them out of Liverpool, as he knew from hard experience it could, they would find themselves in dire straits as the food ran out.

Bluebell responded to the call made on her and sped safely homewards, hour by hour making good passage through still fretful seas. It was blowing a sou-wester as she entered the Firth of Clyde on Sunday, October 20, with some of the masters bent to the task of making out a rough list of the survivors from their ships. At midday, Chief Officer Coultas of *Scoresby* left the bridge and went down into the wardroom to eat. His ration for that meal was a piece of corned beef about one and a half inches square, together with the crumbs at the bottom of a biscuit tin. *Bluebell* was literally down to her last bean.

As the corvette went up to the first buoy of the swept channel she sighted *Fowey*, who signalled her to follow in astern.

At Gourock pier that evening the weary, bedraggled survivors shuffled ashore from the two escort vessels. It was 6 p.m. when *Fowey* landed her survivors, more than a hundred and fifty of them, but if it was an emotional sight to see them pouring from the ship in the half-dark, the scene when *Bluebell* began to discharge was scarcely believable.

Commander Sherwood had no real idea how many men he had aboard until the flow started. As the number rose above two hundred and kept on rising, he exclaimed to the astonished naval officer receiving them, 'Good God, they must be coming up through a hole in the bottom—there was never enough room for all that lot!'

But the ship herself bore testimony enough to the huge number of men she had carried. Inside, all was a shambles. In the men's quarters nearly all the bunks, held by chains, were broken from the weight of exhausted men trying to sit and lie on them.

The survivors from the two ships, more than four hundred of them, waited to be officially checked in by the immigration authorities. They were grateful for cups of tea, sandwiches and cigarettes handed out to them by the WVS and the Church Army. They were questioned by newspaper reporters, but cautioned by officers and masters not to give away any information.

'Aw, come on lads,' pleaded the reporters. 'All the stories will be killed by the censor anyway . . .'

They were packed into a large hall for a meal, it seemed crowded to the roof. Afterwards, sections of them split up and went their separate ways, the seamen to be looked after by the British Sailors' Society and the WVS, the officers to hotel accommodation somehow found for them.

The officers from *Empire Miniver* were taken to a hotel so full that they had to bed down on mattresses placed on the floor of the lounge. But at least they were able to sleep between sheets for the first time since the attack on SC7 began. Those from the *Shekatika* went to a hotel where unbelievably they were not allowed into the dining-room because they were not properly dressed; most of them were in uniform, but with no collar and tie, only a heavy jersey, and wearing seaboots, just as they had gone to their lifeboats. However, they were allowed to go up to their bedrooms and eat there. To add a little cheer to the occasion they managed to buy a bottle of whisky between them by whipping together what cash they had.

In the morning they signed off at the shipping office and went on survivor's leave; they and hundreds of others, almost unnoticed now. The reporters were right, of course; there wasn't a word about it in the newspapers, nor would there ever be.

Bluebell and *Fowey*, after taking aboard some emergency rations, went on to Liverpool. There was another convoy to take out, another convoy to bring in.

But *Bluebell* still carried one survivor, the German Shepherd dog which young Sture Mattsson had saved from the sinking

Gunborg. The kindly sailors had warned the boy that if he took his pet ashore it would have to go into quarantine. Sadly, therefore, he had given the animal a last hug and left it in the safe hands of the corvette's crew.

11

How Do You Feel, Captain?

'October 21, Monday. 8.30 a.m. Berthed along-
side Prince's Pier and disembarked survivors.'

So ran *Leith*'s brief report. All the survivors were up on deck as
she came alongside at Liverpool at that cold hour in the morning.
There were more than a hundred of them, officers and men from
the *Assyrian, Empire Brigade, Soesterberg* and *Nora,* the Estonian ship whose crew she had picked up from their rafts before
SC7's nightmare began.

There to greet them all were a small crowd of dockyard
workers, two WVS tea trolleys, a few naval officers, some waiting
transport lorries, an ambulance and doctor.

They came ashore wearing a weird assortment of clothing;
the lucky ones, that is. Others were half naked, clutching blankets
around them. There was no rank visible among the rescued.
Captain de Jong, the little master of *Soesterberg*, whose survivors had lost their boots, shoes and socks in the leaking lifeboat, now wore shoes several sizes too big for him which he had

scrounged from an ox of an engineer. The old shoes had cracked heels, and the Dutch master shuffled along in them feeling, as he put it, like a Chinese with his first pair of shoes who did not know whether to put his feet or his hands in them. This in addition to a black face, a three-day beard and no cap.

As the survivors walked and limped along the landing stage they passed the stewards of a Cunarder loading meat.

'Which ship?' the loaders called.

'Dozens,' came the laconic reply.

The Cunarder men nearly dropped their load.

It was a grey scene on this early morning, but as always there was a joker to relieve the gloom. He was a rescued seaman aged nearly seventy, married with eight or nine children at home, who had not been able to keep still aboard *Leith*, always busying himself sweeping up and cleaning the messdecks, jawing with the ship's company and telling them how much he longed to get back on the nest. He was an irrepressible character who won the heart of everyone aboard, and got a big cheer as he walked down the gangway.

Then soon all were gone, many to the Seamen's Mission, where some men in tatters, like *Assyrian*'s Radio Officer Stracy and Second Mate Frank Bellas, were served out with Weaver To Wearer suits, plimsolls, and old tweed caps.

The ambulance still waited on the quay. It had come for the sick Commodore. But now two women boarded the sloop.

Commodore Lachlan MacKinnon had recovered consciousness and was weakly dictating a telegram to his wife to tell her that he was still alive when, to his astonishment, she walked into his cabin with their daughter, Ione. They had learned of his critical condition aboard a warship after rescue, and had made the slow and awkward train journey up from their home at Frampton, Dorset, to meet the ship; though it was only by a mixture of good fortune and sympathetic help that they had arrived at the correct port. It was Commander Ughtred James, husband of the Commodore's other daughter in America, who, in his post in the Admiralty, had found out that his father-in-law had been picked up out of the sea seriously ill and the rescue ship was expected to arrive at a 'north-western port' within forty-eight hours. Meeting Mrs. MacKinnon and her daughter from the West Country train, which was terminated outside London in order to escape the bombing, he drove them to Euston to find two expresses drawn up on opposite sides of the same platform; one bound for Liverpool and the other for Glasgow. Which one should they take? He phoned the duty officer in the Admiralty operations room.

'Liverpool is nearer than Glasgow,' came the reply. 'I should take a chance on the former . . .' And so here they were, aboard the sloop. Such were the tensions and dramas of Service families.

The Commodore was still gravely ill. By rights, once pneumonia had set in he should have died within hours, and only the 'M and B' tablets had saved him. Now Surgeon-Lieutenant Robertson refused to allow his patient to be moved from the ship until a pneumonia specialist had been sent from hospital to examine him.

Leith went upstream alongside an oiler to refuel, but no sooner had she connected up than there came a signal ordering her to return forthwith to await the arrival of the specialist. As the very motion of the ship was painful to the Commodore, who had at last found peaceful sleep, Commander Allen signalled back respectfully suggesting that he should continue oiling and return later, as per schedule.

Now Commander Dickinson of *Scarborough* came aboard. SC7's ocean escort had finally arrived at Liverpool after sighting only one lone ship from her once proud convoy; the *Somersby*, heading valiantly for the Clyde. The two escort captains now talked over the unprecedented attack on the convoy.

Another signal was received. *Leith* must return *forthwith*. The specialist had arrived at the quay to find her gone, and he was angry as he left; the senior officer in command of escorts was angry; and the surgeon captain who now met the sloop as she returned to the jetty after oiling up was very, very angry. Bleary-eyed, brusque and impatient, he looked in on the Commodore for one minute, then called out 'Bring in the stretcher!'

The young ship's doctor tried to argue his point that a specialist should examine the Commodore first, but his protests were waved away by the senior man, who also answered the inquiries of the anxious relatives with the merest strained politeness. White faced, Surgeon-Lieutenant Robertson accompanied his patient to the hospital. He had pulled the admiral through so far, and would not leave him now until he knew he was in expert hands.

The abrupt departure of the Commodore dashed the hopes among those of *Leith*'s crew who thought that his inability to be moved would bring them a welcome respite in dock. Instead, *Leith* now moved to her usual berth at Gladstone Dock, the lower deck was cleared and the ship's company mustered on the jetty in an open warehouse to face a forbidding array of top brass. There was the First Lord of the Admiralty, Mr. A. V. Alexander, and other Cabinet Ministers, together with the immaculately dressed Admiral Sir Percy Noble, Commander-in-Chief, Western Approaches, and a number of flag officers. Admiral Noble delivered a 'pep talk' which was hardly music on the ears. As bad a time as they had been through so far, he warned, it was only a taste of what was to come during the following year . . .

But after the bad news, the good. They were to have a few days' leave.

Home!

Home to wives and girl friends. To a flutter on the Unity football pools. To a visit to the pictures: Mickey Rooney in an Andy Hardy film, or Gordon Harker in 'Saloon Bar'. And to the news that men aged thirty-five were to register for military service. . . .

Home, too, for the survivors brought in by *Leith*. Some, like Second Engineer Bill Venables, had not far to go; he lived only across the city in Liverpool.

When he arrived unexpectedly at home his surprised mother said 'What's happened, Bill?'

'Oh, nothing,' he said. 'I've just got some leave.'

Then suddenly he burst into tears and told her that *Assyrian* had gone.

That's how it was. Your feelings on losing a ship in which you had spent seven years of your life were something that could not be explained; but nor could they be bottled up.

Radio Officer Robert Stracy, a man normally most particular about his uniform and appearance, arrived at his home in Manchester in his Weaver To Wearer suit, cloth cap and plimsolls, carrying his few personal belongings wrapped in a newspaper parcel.

'What on earth's the matter?' asked his wife. 'You look a wreck.'

'I've been torpedoed, love.'

Stracy's legs were swollen with a mild dose of 'immersion feet', and he would have to sleep in flannel trousers, or with his legs wrapped up in cloth, for a few days, until the trouble passed off . . .

For the rescued merchant captains as they left *Leith*, there followed the usual questioning at naval headquarters. How had the U-boat attack come about? What was their opinion of it? Were their secret papers saved or destroyed—or could they be still floating?

When the questioning was done, black-faced Captain de Jong shuffled his way through the streets of Liverpool in his oversize shoes, many times having to ask the way to the Dutch Consul. But once there, the wheels began to grind. He was given money to buy necessities for his crew, all of whom had been found accommodation, the injured being taken to hospital.

Captain de Jong sent his chief officer shopping for the men's needs. For himself, being found a room at a hotel, there followed the luxuries of a shave, a bath, a new suit, and some shoes to fit his long suffering feet. Then early to bed, to give himself a 'good farmer's night.' He wrote about that night afterwards, in expressive terms.

'The Hun did not grant me this, however, because as soon as I was sleeping peacefully the first German bombers arrived about ten o'clock over Liverpool, and gave the town the full treatment. It was raining bombs, and behind the hotel stood a large ack-ack gun. When this went into action it shook the whole hotel to its foundations. It was as if you were in a ballast ship in bad weather, when you lie in your bunk and are flung from one side to the other, when the ship comes with its head out of water and then returns with a smack down to the sea, and everything starts creaking and groaning. It was the same feeling here when a bomb landed in the immediate neighbourhood. One explosion followed after the other.

'I thought, "You dirty Hun, you can do what you can but you will have to throw me out of bed because I am too tired." Luckily the raid finished at midnight, and the Germans flew off, leaving behind them a burning town with big rubble heaps. The electric light had gone out, apparently the powerhouse had been hit, and many streets had no water nor gas. A lot of houses were hit round about us, but the hotel fortunately was saved.

'In the morning there were many buildings still burning. When on my way to the office of the Netherlands Shipping Company I met our Dutch Consul, who was looking for another office because his own building had been hit. This is how it went on for a number of nights in Liverpool, and large parts of the city were destroyed. Nevertheless, through all this the people stayed calm. They took it as it came, without grumbling, believing in victory in the end.'

Meanwhile the surviving ships of SC7 had all successfully found their way to the Clyde, either during the same Sunday night that saw the arrival of *Bluebell* and *Fowey*, or the day after.

The *Botusk*, after nearly going aground on the Irish coast, found a warship that escorted her as far as Stranraer. In thick weather later *Botusk* unwittingly steamed straight over a British minefield, but she got safely through to arrive at Gourock the day after *Fowey*.

The aged *Dioni* steamed in, lone survivor of the four Greeks. So did the *Valparaiso*, the only surviving Swede. Fog, a deep, rolling fog, had been Captain Oscar Asplund's good friend.

Then there were five Norwegians: *Karlander, Inger Elisabeth, Havorn, Sneland 1*, and the ancient tanker, the *Thoroy*. Torpedoes had narrowly missed her old plates, but she had thumped on. Born 1893, still going strong.

There was the Danish *Flynderborg*, and the scruffy old British tramp, *Trident*. She had narrowly escaped two torpedoes which crossed her path—God bless her for being so slow! When *Trident* reached Barry Docks later, a generous shipping company would give each of her crew a bonus of £5 and three days' leave, and the officers £10 extra on their wages.

Like *Trident*, the old Hull ship *Corinthic* arrived at anchor during the Sunday night. It rained all that night, and next day there was a heavy mist, but keen eyes looked anxiously for the shapes of familiar vessels, and were relieved to find some of them.

Corinthic moved off first from anchorage, and the crews of each ship came on deck and waved their caps as she passed.

'How do you feel this morning, captain?' sang out *Somersby*'s Captain Bill Thompson. .

'Better than I did on Friday night!' answered fiery little Captain George Nesbitt.

'Good luck . . .' the cry came back through the mist.

Was this all, then—the remains of a thirty-five ship convoy? No, there was one more.

To great cheers, the damaged *Carsbreck* came limping in, shepherded by the faithful *Heartsease*. It was a remarkable achievement by the Glasgow steamer; holed and head down, she went gratefully to anchor.

Heartsease did not stop her engines. Just in to deliver her charge, then straight out again and on to Liverpool. She now carried nine survivors which she had picked up while escorting *Carsbreck*; the men had been adrift in a lifeboat for a day and a half when she spotted them.

Outside Liverpool, 'Heart Disease' had to anchor when she ran into thick fog; the same troublesome fog that had decided *Bluebell*'s Commander Sherwood against taking his crowded ship there. No matter, all the time they were anchored counted towards their next boiler-clean, with its reward of leave.

As the corvette waited for the fog to lift, Commander North, the countryman, took an apple from the box of good Oxford-shire Cox's sent to him by his parents and began a letter to them.

'We shall soon be back in port again after another trip which has lasted a bit longer than usual owing to us having some more incidents . . . This time we had it very fine and it was quite smooth except for one night when it was blowing and raining . . . During our trips we generally have various kinds of birds round the ship. This time we had several starlings, I don't know where they came from. . . .'

You couldn't tell much of the real thing to a family, even should you be allowed to do so. No more than you could give a suitable answer to visitors like the Cabinet Minister he had recently been obliged to show round the ship.

'Well, Commander, I must say you all look *very* comfort-able . . .'

All accounted for, but not quite. There were still more sur-vivors to come in from the cheated Atlantic. And, surprisingly, one more ship.

Back in the disaster area as daylight broke after the night attack, the second lifeboat from *Blairspey*, thankfully intact after narrowly escaping the third torpedo to hit the ship, found itself alone on a freshening sea. Then a vessel was sighted on the horizon. Incredibly it was the *Blairspey*. The big Glasgow ship had drifted some thirty miles south since being hit, and in spite of the heavy damage from the three torpedoes was still afloat on her cargo of timber.

As they gazed at her unbelievingly from a distance, a Sunder-land from Coastal Command broke out of the clouds and began to circle the derelict. They yelled and waved, but the flying boat did not see them. After inspecting the ship it flew off.

Later they found they had company on this desolate morning, when another lifeboat came into sight. In it were the survivors of *Sedgepool*. These men, too, had sighted a ship soon after dawn. It turned out to be . . . *Sedgepool*. With their captain and others lost, they were debating whether to pull across to the badly damaged hulk and climb aboard her to get some dry clothes, when the big vessel suddenly nosed into the water, her stern came up, and she disappeared downwards with the cargo of grain she had been carrying to Manchester. Jokingly they had said earlier in the voyage that it was the only convoy the old *Sedgepool* had ever managed to keep up with. Her first, and her last.

Now the two lifeboats hailed each other and discussed what they should do. The *Sedgepool* boat decided to carry on and try to make the long voyage to the Butt of Lewis, but the *Blairspey* men chose to stay in sight of the derelict, as they felt sure that the Sunderland would have reported her and that a ship would be sent to investigate.

In fact help did come, but from an unexpected quarter. The ocean tug *Salvonia* had sailed out from Campbeltown in answer to the distress messages sent out by *Shekatika*. When she arrived the *Shekatika* had gone, but she then came upon *Blairspey*.

At 5 p.m. in a tossing sea, the fourteen weary occupants of the lifeboat saw the tug appear alongside the ship. The excited waving began again, and this time, thank heaven, they were seen. The tug closed in, and there began the difficult and dangerous business of transferring from the lifeboat to her in the now very high seas. But an hour later all were safely aboard.

Salvonia's shrewd captain was convinced that in spite of the great damage done to her, there was an even chance of the *Blairspey* remaining afloat, and he decided to take her in tow. But in the growing darkness and angry sea it was impossible to connect up. *Salvonia*, it was clear, would have to wait for daylight and a break in the rough weather conditions before she could begin work. As there was also the danger of a U-boat still prowling in the area the tug withdrew at high speed, zigzagging as she went, to pass the night at a safe and wary distance from the derelict.

At dawn the following morning—Sunday, October 20—*Salvonia* returned and, in more favourable weather and seas, made fast the tow. But not only did she salve an empty hulk, her timely reappearance in the area that day also brought rescue for the *Sedgepool* lifeboat, which in the night's heavy seas had not made much distance, and for one of the two boats from *Clintonia*, under Chief Officer Buglass. When she had got all the newcomers safely aboard the 500-ton tug carried survivors from three vessels . . . and still her work was far from finished.

All through Sunday the *Salvonia* towed the reeling, lurching *Blairspey*, and next day she picked up yet more survivors, in one lifeboat but from two ships. They were officers and men from the steamers *Port Gisborne* and *St. Malo*, which had been sunk much earlier on an HX convoy from Halifax. The survivors had spent ten grim days in their boat.

The tug now had more than a hundred grateful survivors on board. One of them was Chief Engineer James Aves of *Sedgepool*. In his pocket was a photograph of his family, practically the only possession he was left with. It had got very tattered while he was swimming after jumping from his abandoned ship, but had dried out quite well. Now, in the warmth of rescue, he got some of his fellow survivors, and members of the crew of *Salvonia,* to autograph the back of it; it became possibly the only personal record of their common drama.

For four more days and nights *Salvonia* hauled the drunken *Blairspey* through the dangerous waters of the Western Approaches, and on Friday, October 25, seven days after surviving the explosions of the three German torpedoes, the battered steamer was towed into the Clyde. When she was put to anchor, some idea of the blast she had suffered could be had from the sight of the engineers' accommodation sticking weirdly six feet out from her side.

Like *Carsbreck*, the other damaged Glasgow steamer which had limped in a few days before her, the *Blairspey* drew some resounding cheers.

There only remained the second lifeboat of survivors from the *Clintonia*. This, under Captain Irvin, had hoisted sail at daybreak to attempt the long journey home, but during the morning they were luckily spotted by the same Sunderland which had circled the derelict *Blairspey*. The sea was far too rough for the flying boat to come down on the water so it dropped them a bag full of food, together with a chart of their position, and a note from the pilot promising to send help.

After the plane flew off they continued slowly on course, scanning the empty sea for hour after dreary hour for any sign of a rescuer. Then, just as the evening dark was gathering on a rising sea, a searching British destroyer came fast over the horizon towards them. They were taken safely aboard and eventually landed at Londonderry.

When, days later, Captain Irvin finally reported to his shipping office on Tyneside, there was one last painful task for him to perform. The member of the crew who, during *Clintonia*'s violent night, had been fatally hurled into the breech of the ship's gun, and later cast to the sea from the lifeboat, had lived just across the river from the office, and the captain was asked to visit the man's sister and break the bad news gently to her.

Such could be the unenviable duties of a master.

The same woman's young son had been *Clintonia*'s cabin boy. As Captain Irvin walked to pay his sad call, he could only thank God that the lad had been spared and he was not having to carry the news of a double tragedy.

12

The Second Assault

The brilliantly executed action against SC7 would have been triumph enough for Admiral Doenitz's 'wolves', but the slaughter did not end there. It continued, only hours later, with huge losses being inflicted on a fast HX convoy coming up in the rear of the slow convoy. The result was a double action which produced the blackest statistics of the war at sea since hostilities had begun.

Just like SC7, the fast convoy HX79, and its unsuspecting escorts, sailed headlong into an assault by a U-boat pack. The attack took place on the night of Saturday, October 19—the night following the assault on SC7—about 250 miles west of the scene of SC7's destruction.

Some of the 'wolves' who had attacked SC7 took part in the new assault. Otto Kretschmer (U-99), Fritz Frauenheim (U-101) and Karl-Heinz Moehle (U-123) had all started home to base following the attack on SC7, having expended all their torpedoes, but the boats of Engelbert Endrass (U-46) and Joachim Schepke (U-100) were still primed for more action and joined in the new ambush. Heinrich Bleichrodt in U-48 also returned to the fray.

Since being chased off by *Scarborough* he had sunk an outward-bound straggler and now had only one usable torpedo. But he was to make it count. . . .

Convoy HX79 had sailed from Halifax days after SC7 at a good eight to nine knots. In addition to being a faster convoy, with many oil-fired ships and tankers, it was also a bigger one, consisting of 49 vessels. It had more escorts, too. Unlike SC7, with its one small escort sloop for the journey across the Atlantic, HX79 was accompanied by two big armed merchant cruisers, one of 14,000 tons and the other of 16,000 tons, while on reaching the outer limits of the Western Approaches it was met by a veritable fighting fleet consisting of two destroyers, four corvettes, a minesweeper, and three anti-submarine trawlers. For additional protection a Dutch submarine sailed in the centre of the convoy, while one of the merchantmen, the 5,000-ton steamer *Loch Lomond*, had been designated rescue ship, to pick up survivors should any vessel be torpedoed.

But although the number of escorts was so much greater, HX79 suffered from precisely the same basic problems as SC7. The escorts from the Western Approaches arrived independently, without any knowledge of the nature of the convoy or any idea who else would be there. The escort commanders did not know each other; they had limited means of communication, especially at night, when they could only talk by dimmed morse lamp; and they had no common plan of defence. Above all, they did not anticipate U-boats attacking on the surface, by night, and in strength.

It was Gunther Prien, patrolling in U-47, who spotted HX79. Prien, the daring ace with the white snorting bull on his conning-tower; the man who, soon after the start of the war, had crept into the British naval stronghold of Scapa Flow and sunk the battleship *Royal Oak*. On sighting HX79, Korvettenkapitan Prien wirelessed the news back to base, and for a second time a wolf-pack gathered and closed in. In the assault Prien, Endrass, Schepke and Bleichrodt were joined by Heinrich Liebe (U-38), the commander who had sunk the *Aenos* and crippled the *Carsbreck*.

As the five U-boats moved in on HX79 the violent pattern of events of the previous night was repeated. Another night of bewilderment, confusion and frustration for the escorts as they searched for an elusive, unseen enemy, their asdics useless against the surfaced raiders, and again the terrible question of whether to stop and pick up survivors or steam on in search of the enemy, for in the event there was far too much rescue work for one ship to handle.

Once again, lookouts on some of the merchant ships could scarcely believe their eyes as they fleetingly glimpsed the shape of a conning-tower speeding close past them in the moonlight. Surely U-boats were *undersea* craft, not meant for racing around like motor torpedo boats? It was all so totally unreal.

On the 6,000-ton motor tanker *Sitala* astonished eyes saw a small dark shape coming up from astern, speed past only about twenty yards away on the starboard beam, unmistakably the conning-tower of a U-boat, the only part of the German visible above the agitated water. Like some great shark's fin it cut away from view. The tanker then had barely twenty minutes to live. The torpedo that hit her sent *Sitala* lurching ablaze into the night, and as her crew abandoned her she was well on fire.

The dismal story of this second night's events is reflected in the experience of one ship, the newest in the convoy, and her crew. The motorship *Wandby*, from Sunderland, was returning from British Columbia on the second leg of her maiden voyage. A splendid looking ship of nearly 5,000 tons, she was in fact the last vessel built on the River Wear to pre-war standards.

Wandby carried a cargo of 1,500 tons of pig-iron and a huge load of timber rising ten or twelve feet high on her decks. She had loaded at Vancouver, sailed down the west coast of America, through the Panama Canal to Bermuda, and there joined a small convoy with instructions to join up with HX79 sailing from Halifax. This they had done, and *Wandby*'s fate was sealed . . .

The attack on HX79 came just sixteen hours after the last unfortunate ship of SC7 was sent beneath the waves. It was still the same day—October 19—though darkness had fallen once again, as the new pack closed in.

At 9 p.m. *Wandby*'s Captain John Kenny saw a sudden glare six miles away on the starboard quarter. It was the explosion from the first ship to be torpedoed, which sank quickly with her captain and a third of her crew.

During the next two hours, as HX79 steamed on under the revealing light of a misty moon, three more ships were sunk. Then it was *Wandby*'s turn.

At about 10.30 p.m. a torpedo struck *Wandby* just forward of the engine-room on the port side, causing a tremendous explosion which blew away the ship's port lifeboat and hurled the ship's fifty-year-old master six feet into the air from where he stood on the port side of the bridge, injuring his leg as he fell. Everyone else escaped either bruised or shaken, but the ship which, only weeks ago, Captain Kenny had stood by as she was proudly completed, had been fatally hit. Her side was leaking badly—she had already started to break up—and the fuel pipe to the donkey boiler was fractured beyond repair. As her auxiliaries were steam driven, the loss of the boiler left them without the use of pumps, steering engine and dynamo, and the ship at the mercy of the incoming sea. Though *Wandby* might float for some time, supported by her timber cargo, her crew could not do a thing to save her.

Captain Kenny ordered abandon ship, and they clambered, all thirty-five of them, into the one remaining lifeboat, the master being the last to leave. They went in orderly fashion, and, due to the master's foresight, prepared as best they could for a long sojourn in the boat. He ensured that each officer was handed a bottle of scotch or brandy, with orders not to open it until instructed to do so, and that tins of cigarettes were distributed among the crew. There was no knowing how long the boat would have to be their refuge.

After two hours, however, the armed trawler HMS *Angle* hove into sight, and eventually closed the boat to take them aboard; 'Angel' they gratefully renamed her later. It was as they were being picked up by *Angle* that the full horror of the night, and the fortunate circumstances of their own escape, was brought home to them.

There was a muffled explosion, and at the same time all the air around them seemed to be sucked away, leaving them in a vacuum. Then, five miles away to the west, a ball of flame erupted to the night sky and a ship's superstructure could be seen passing through the flames high into the air. The sea was ablaze for miles around. So bright was the sky and sea that when Captain Kenny's small case containing his ship's secret papers was accidentally dropped and floated far away from the trawler's side, it was easily spotted and retrieved from the sea by the trawler's boat.

All the men of *Wandby* could think of at their moment of rescue was the appalling way in which the crew of that exploding petrol tanker must have died.

The subsequent events of the night were like the continuation of a bad dream. More explosions, distress calls, and baffled escorts steaming in circles, unable to find the enemy.

Daybreak found *Angle* steaming through a weird sea of sinking ships and half-ships and patches of burning oil, searching for other survivors but finding none. Then into sight came the derelict *Wandby*, still afloat, and she was boarded; but it was found that the engine-room was flooded to the tops of the main engines and she was breaking up fast. The boarding party returned to the trawler and *Angle* continued her search for survivors among the floating wreckage from other ships, but there was no sign of life anywhere. When she swept round again on the completion of her mercy patrol *Wandby* had gone. So had every other derelict but one, an 8,000-ton motor tanker, the *Caprella*. She had been torpedoed for'ard of the bridge, and although her bow was very low in the water she did not appear to be sinking any deeper. When a party climbed aboard to inspect the damage there seemed to be a fair prospect of bringing her in. After all that lost shipping—salvage!

A 'crew' consisting of *Wandby*'s chief engineer, senior third engineer and carpenter, together with eight ratings from *Angle*, including a signalman, now boarded *Caprella* and got to work. The ship's donkey boiler was still warm, and after half an hour on the hand-pump the two engineers had raised enough steam to start the oil-burning equipment. Slowly the Shell tanker began to move off, astern of the trawler.

The approach of darkness, however, brought a turn in the weather, the wind freshened from the east and raised a head-swell which caused the tanker to pitch ominously—and at four a.m. she began to break up. The boarding party, now all gathered aft, could see the foc'sle head rising and falling between the lower and upper bridge for all the world as if the for'ard section was attached to the rest of the vessel by huge hinges. Then the bizarre moment came when the for'ard section broke away. As it sank, the jumper stay between the two masts did not part until it had forced the top part of the mainmast to a crazy angle, and when it did finally part it was like a shot from a four-inch gun.

Now the boarding party were marooned on the still floating half-ship with no means of abandoning it. They sent up a distress flare. *Angle* steamed back to the rescue, but when her boat was launched it sank to the gunwales; excessive use had made it unseaworthy. All that was left now was a Carley raft. *Angle* attempted to fire a line by rifle on the leeward side of the half-ship, so that the boarders could pull the raft across to them. But the wind had risen and this plan proved abortive; the trawler had to steam in circles and could only fire once each time she passed.

Angle's coxswain, a deepsea fisherman, now gave the finest display of ship-handling any man there had witnessed, as he brought the trawler round in the heavy swell dangerously close under the tanker's stern, so that a line could be thrown over to her deck. It was caught amid a shower of fruity language.

But the men were not out of danger yet. The first party to take to the raft in the dark found themselves unable to paddle it away from the tanker, the angry sea nearly washing them into the torn portion of one of the hulk's mid-ship tanks. *Angle* came in close again and passed over another heaving line; they now had a line from the raft to the trawler as well as one back to the tanker; and with one line being heaved on and the other paid out, they were able to get alongside *Angle* and board her, then send the raft back for the remaining men.

Even in these seas the derelict half-ship still remained afloat, apparently the only remaining evidence of the U-boat pack's attack on the convoy. It was a danger to shipping; *Angle* sank the hulk with four shells from her four-inch gun.

Gone were all the hopes of salvage. Gone, too, along with *Wandby* and *Caprella*, were ten other ships of HX79, as they would discover later. The last ship of the convoy to be sunk was the steamer *Loch Lomond*—the designated rescue ship—whose crew themselves, together with survivors they had picked up, had to be rescued by the escort minesweeper. Yet another ship, a big tanker, was damaged but managed to limp into port.

And even then the immediate slaughter by the U-boats was not over. During the same night, an outward-bound convoy also ran foul of surfaced raiders at a cost of seven more merchantmen. All this without loss to Doenitz's 'wolves', who returned jubilantly to base to be greeted by eager war correspondents and photographers. It was a homecoming of heroes.

Official records credited Otto Kretschmer (U-99) with sinking seven ships during the night attack on SC7—nearly half the night's total losses. Karl-Heinz Moehle (U-123) sank four ships, and the remainder were shared between Engelbert Endrass (U-46), Joachim Schepke (U-100) and Fritz Frauenheim (U-101) —it was he who sank the *Assyrian*. Endrass and Schepke enhanced their scores by sinking another three ships each of HX79.

It was a time for medals, justly won and quickly awarded, for Admiral Doenitz believed that none of his commanders should have to wait long for his honours.

One man only on the other side received a medal; for which, in the British order of things, he had to wait. Captain Reginald Sanderson Kearon of the *Assyrian* was awarded the OBE, a tribute to his ship and his men as well as to his own personal courage. His inspiring conduct that night, culminating in his effort to save the life of his elderly chief officer, also brought him another award, that of the Lloyd's War Medal For Bravery At Sea. The medal, with its distinctive blue and silver ribbon, was bestowed upon officers and men of the Merchant Navy and fishing fleets in cases of exceptional gallantry at sea.

And so there it was. The final miserable statistics for the month of October, 1940, recorded the highest tonnage sunk by U-boats since the war began; a total of 352,407 tons. In more human terms this meant the loss of sixty-three merchant ships, almost a third of these from one convoy, SC7. It was the peak achievement of the four-month period, July to October, 1940, which the U-boat commanders called 'the happy time.'

These figures were only disclosed long afterwards. How close to the truth the German claims at the time came, may be seen from this communique issued by the German High Command on October 20, 1940 :

'On the night of October 19th German submarines sank 17 merchant ships with a total tonnage of 110,000 in a British convoy. Other submarines report the sinking of 43,000 tons from other convoys. Thus within two days, by the destruction of two convoys and by single successes, 327,000 tons of enemy merchant shipping has been sunk.'

This enemy communique was, understandably, given little mention in Britain.

So SC7 slipped into naval history as a disaster to be bleakly remembered, its story one of inadequacy, unpreparedness and grim endurance on the part of the British, and cool, rewarding enterprise by the Germans in launching their first big night swoop by a wolf-pack. The enemy had evolved his new style of U-boat warfare by building on the hard lessons learned in the last war; yet, looking at the British state of unpreparedness, it seemed almost as if for the Royal Navy that war had never happened. All the naval escorts of SC7 had been built after the lessons of 1914-18 might have been amply digested, yet their limitations were painfully obvious. And, ostrich-like, secure in its possession of the asdic underwater detector, the Navy had not seemed to realize how naked it was against an enemy submarine operating on the surface. The enemy's surface speed had also been greatly underestimated.

By his own admission, no one was more surprised than Admiral Doenitz himself at the very completeness of the success of his first major assault by night surfaced U-boats operating in unison; he could not believe that the British had not foreseen this eventuality, especially with the knowledge of successes gained by night surfaced U-boats in the latter stages of World War I.

Yet even after the devastating attack on SC7 it was some time before the threat posed by U-boats working together was fully grasped by the British naval command. All Commander Allen of *Leith*, the senior escort of SC7, could report was that he judged at least three U-boats to have taken part in the attack; but he could, and did, stress most strongly the need for better communication between escorts, and for teamwork against attack.

It was all to come. The formation of regular escort groups, skilled at working together. Better communications, with radio-telephony installed in warships. Direction-finding radio, which could quickly locate a talkative U-boat. The 'snowflake' rocket, which lit up the night sky far brighter than starshell, and was free of its flashback and other handicaps. The provision of medically-manned convoy rescue ships. And, most important of all, the installation of ship's radar, to give immediate warning of a surfaced enemy.

Few of the U-boat 'aces' of 1940 would see these changes. Within a year, three of the five 'wolves' who attacked SC7 would be lost; Schepke and Endrass, both killed in action, and Otto Kretschmer, taken prisoner after his boat was sunk.

But that was tomorrow.

13

Last Ship to Die

How do you thank someone for saving your life? It was a question that came up all too often for seamen on the North Atlantic run, but you did your best, as did the survivors of SC7 who later wrote to thank the escorts who had brought them home out of the sea.

Some went further, and one letter that found its way to *Bluebell* took Commander Sherwood and his ship's company 'flat-aback'. It was a thank you letter from Captain Wilfred Brett of the sunken *Beatus*, enclosing a cheque for £7, the proceeds of a 'whip-round' among his grateful crew. The merchant men's generous token of their appreciation was put into *Bluebell*'s kitty.

For most of the survivors of SC7, after a few days' leave, it was a case of another ship and another convoy. And so their war would continue from one voyage to the next, and for some, from one lost ship to another.

Some men would not survive a second time. Like Radio Officer Robert Stracy of *Assyrian*. In 1944 his ship was one of four merchant vessels which missed a convoy and had to sail on together in the Indian Ocean, unescorted. Japanese submarines attacked the four ships and sank them all; there were no survivors.

And Second Mate Ort, the patient, resourceful officer who so greatly helped the captain of the *Soesterberg*. He volunteered for special duties and was parachuted into Holland as a radio operator for 'Radio England', but was taken prisoner and later executed by the Germans.

Most of the surviving ships of SC7 were quickly to vanish. Of the seven British vessels which got away, only two of them were left after another year of war.

The old *Botusk*, the ship with the unlovely name given to her by the Board of Trade when rescued from the scrapheap, sank miserably only three months after SC7, when she struck a mine off the coast of Inverness-shire. At the time, the Commodore of the convoy believed it to be a U-boat attack; two other ships were lost, the remainder of the convoy cracking on at full speed. *Botusk* sank in two minutes with the loss of two men, her survivors being picked up hours later by a Post Office cable ship. It then transpired that the convoy had run into a British minefield. . . .

The Hull scrap carrier *Corinthic*, raised from underwater to fight her war, returned underwater to a deeper grave on April 13, 1941, when torpedoed off the coast of West Africa.

Somersby, the big 5,000-ton Tynesider whose brief glory it had been to lead the remnants of SC7, was torpedoed and sunk on May 13, 1941 at 26 degrees West in the North Atlantic, far west of the SC7 graveyard. All her crew were rescued by a Greek ship.

Trident, the scruffy Tynesider as old as the Kaiser's war, never did fall victim to a torpedo. She died at a buoy off the Tyne on August 2, 1941, when bombed and sunk by enemy aircraft. All her crew, too, got clear.

The damaged *Carsbreck* was repaired and sailed successfully on other convoys until, in October, 1941, almost a year to the day when she limped into the Clyde, a U-boat found her. She was torpedoed and sunk off southern Spain, on the Gibraltar run, with heavy loss of life.

As fate would have it, it was the other, more heavily damaged ship of the convoy, the *Blairspey*, which came through the war. The damage from three torpedoes was so great that she had to be halved amidships and a new forward section built, after which she put to sea again as the *Empire Spey*. At war's end she reverted again to the name of *Blairspey* and went back to her peacetime calling.

The only other British ship of SC7 to survive the war was the redoubtable Laker, *Eaglescliffe Hall*. During her wartime work around Britain's coasts she was 'Mentioned in Despatches' when, on being attacked by enemy aircraft, her crew removed a bomb from the stokehold before it exploded. Two men lost their lives during that attack. After the war *Eaglescliffe Hall* took a fair weather passage back to Canada and resumed her 'sweet water' trade.

Among SC7's eight surviving foreigners the luckiest of all was, surprisingly, the ancient Norwegian tanker *Thoroy*, the oldest ship of the convoy. The ex-British vessel, built in 1893, steamed on unscathed through the war as she had the one before, and in 1947, at the venerable age of fifty-four, was sold to the Turks.

But others of the foreign ships were by no means as fortunate.

The first to go, in particularly distressing circumstances, was the Swedish motor vessel *Valparaiso*. Only two months after surviving SC7, having in the meantime recrossed to Canada, she left Halifax on December 18 with a fast HX convoy. When at 23 degrees West, about 250 miles south of Iceland, the convoy separated in fog and bad weather. *Valparaiso* disappeared with her crew of thirty-three and was never seen or heard of again. She was one of 254 ships (and 1,400 seamen) lost by Sweden in the war.

The Greek *Dioni* went aground in Milford Haven and was subsequently lost. The Danish *Flynderborg* was torpedoed and sunk by a U-boat off Newfoundland in November, 1941. Hardly a year later, in September, 1942, another U-boat torpedoed and sank the Norwegian *Inger Elisabeth* in the Gulf of St. Lawrence.

But the most tragic fate of all was that which befell the Norwegian *Sneland 1*, the little barnacled tramp that had only caught SC7 by the skin of her teeth. Her end came in the dying hours of the war.

It was May 7, 1945. Germany's unconditional surrender had been signed by General Jodl and orders to cease-fire had been given. Up in the Firth of Forth that night, as both merchant ships and warships celebrated by burning flares, firing rockets and exchanging congratulatory messages, *Sneland 1* was one of a number of ships for whom it was duty as usual as they steamed out to form the familiar north-bound convoy. She was captained still by Captain Laegland, as she had been on SC7.

On the convoy this night, for the first time since the war began, the men off-watch would undress to enjoy a peaceful sleep in their bunks; for although the official end to hostilities in Europe was still twenty-four hours away, everyone felt that it was as good as over already.

But for one still active U-boat it was not. At three minutes past 11 p.m. Kapitanleutnant Klusmeier, commander of U-2336, fired his first torpedo. Thirty-five seconds later *Sneland 1* rocked with the explosion. Then another torpedo struck the British *Avondale Park*.

Both ships sank quickly. Aboard *Sneland 1*, Captain Laegland and everyone on the bridge was killed; seven in all lost their lives.

All those years, all those hazardous miles, for this.

The two ships were the last victims of a German U-boat in the Second World War.

SC7's naval escort commanders went on to see the tide turn against the wolf-packs, and indeed the whole of the sea war swing against the enemy.

Commander Dickinson of *Scarborough* gained the DSO, in addition to his DSC, as Captain Dickinson, RN, for bravery and skill in the operations in which the Allied forces were landed in North Africa; afterwards he took command of the aircraft carrier HMS *Victorious*. Lieutenant-Commander North of

Heartsease progressed to take command of the aircraft carrier HMS *Activity*, as Captain North, RNR.

After *Leith*, Commander Allen worked in the Admiralty on the planning of the landings in North Africa, and sailed with the Fleet to Algiers, where he served on General Eisenhower's staff. He later commanded the cruiser HMS *Ceres* in the Normandy landings.

Lieutenant-Commander Aubrey of *Fowey* went on to command the sloop HMS *Wren* in the highly successful 2nd Escort Group of U-boat killers led by Captain F. J. 'Johnny' Walker, RN; and afterwards, as a Commander, Aubrey became senior officer of his own escort group in the fast frigate *Exe*.

From the viewpoint of SC7, perhaps the supreme revenge came for Lieutenant-Commander Sherwood of *Bluebell*. In May, 1943, in the new frigate HMS *Tay*, Sherwood commanded the escort of convoy ONS5 in a pitched battle against a horde of converging U-boats. It proved to be the turning point in the Battle of the Atlantic. Twelve merchant ships of the convoy were lost, but the final cost to the enemy was high: one U-boat sunk or damaged for every British loss. It was a crushing defeat for the Germans.

Sherwood had seen the wheel turn full circle. Three years before, in the *Bluebell*, he had been caught helpless by the first shattering assault by a wolf-pack; now he had been instrumental in dealing a blow from which the demoralized 'wolves' would never recover.

Of SC7's five naval escort vessels, all but one came safely through the war. That one was . . . *Bluebell*. In the months and years after SC7 she rescued many more men from the sea, and helped avenge them, too, on arduous convoy work. She tasted the rigours of the stormy Arctic run to Russia, and it was up there, on the icy rim of the world, that her luck finally ran out. Her commander at the time was the rather raw 'Number One' of SC7 days, now a well seasoned veteran— Lieutenant G. H. Walker, DSC, RNVR.

On February 17, 1945 *Bluebell* was escorting a convoy in the bleak Barents Sea. Shortly after three o'clock in the afternoon of a murky day, she was hit by a torpedo from a U-boat. She blew up and sank at once with the loss of six officers, including her commander, and about eighty ratings. Only one man survived.

14

Your Sixpences, Please

And Commodore Lachlan MacKinnon? He was out of hospital at Liverpool in three weeks. The miracle patient. Soon afterwards, from his home in Dorset, he was ready to report for his next sea duty, fit, well and anxious to get on with the job.

But there followed weeks of waiting, of puzzling, non-committal answers to his enquiries. No matter how he tried or what he did, not one seemed to want anything to do with him.

Eventually the reason for the Navy's embarrassed sidestepping was made clear. Despite his remarkable recovery, and the fact that men years older than he were on Commodore duty, he was judged to be no longer fit for sea physically. SC7 had been his last voyage.

It was a tremendous shock, but MacKinnon was equal to it.

A few months afterwards, in the early summer of 1941, the town of Dorchester held its War Weapons Week. It took a lot of planning, a lot of hard work, for money was short, and the organizers had to go to all sorts of lengths to try to attract it. Fun and games was the order of the day, anything that would cadge a penny. At the entrance to a cinema, for instance, there was a big boarded picture of Hitler sitting in a tin bath. 'Help to drown Hitler!' was the invitation, which you did by throwing pennies in the bath and raising the level of the water.

From stall to stall, giving encouragement to the helpers including his wife and daughter, and to those considering parting with their money, went the organizer of the whole thing; a silvery haired, erect man of about sixty, dressed in a tweedy sports jacket and flannel bags, smoking a pipe and stabbing the air with it occasionally to make his point. One of his best ideas was the sideshow where a toy U-boat was placed in a glass tank set up on the pavement. The customer paid sixpence and was given three marbles which he had to drop down into the water at an angle so as to hit the U-boat and sink it. The organizer was delighted to demonstrate to anyone how to do it, and as they watched him happily 'bomb' the toy in the tank they were not to know that not long ago, in night seas a mile deep, he had clung weakly to a piece of floating timber and fought to stay alive.

'There, you see, it's sunk!'

He joined the voluntary staff of the National Savings movement, speaking at war factories and savings week rallies; he travelled the country, often having to stand for hours in crowded trains despite his rank and age. His talent for the personal touch, his outspokenness and his sense of humour made him welcome everywhere. And he always turned up. You could rely on Mac-Kinnon.

A.B.s and admirals, you did what you could. You did your bit. That's how it was.

Acknowledgments

The authors are grateful to the masters, officers and seamen of the Merchant Navy, and officers and men of the Royal Naval Reserve, Royal Naval Volunteer Reserve, and Royal Navy, whose warm-hearted response and assistance made possible this story of convoy SC7.

THE MERCHANTMEN

Clifford Atkinson of Beverley, Yorks. (Second Radio Officer, ss. *Trident*).

Raymond Baldwin of Whiteparish, Wilts. (Second Radio Officer, ss. *Shekatika*).

Captain Wilfred L. Brett of Cardiff (Master, ss. *Beatus*).

Hilton Brodie of Croftfoot, Glasgow (Chief Cook, ss. *Carsbreck*).

Captain Ronald Coultas of Ravenscar, Yorks. (Chief Officer, ss. *Scoresby*).

John R. Crawford of Wishaw, Lanarkshire (Second Radio Officer, ss. *Blairspey*).

James Daley of Blundellsands, Liverpool (Chief Steward, ss. *Assyrian*).

Captain W. Algwyn Davies of Pen-y-lan, Cardiff (Master, ss. *Botusk*).

William Arthur Dean of Crosby, Liverpool (Fourth Engineer, ss. *Assyrian*).

Captain D. de Jong of Castricum, Holland (Master, ss. *Soesterberg*).

Leonard Dewar of Handsworth, Birmingham (First Radio Officer, ss. *Empire Brigade*).

Gilbert Michael Hing of Pelsall, Staffs. (Third Mate, ss. *Empire Miniver*).

Henry Hotchkiss of Kirkintilloch, Dunbartonshire (Second Radio Officer, ss. *Somersby*).

Kenneth C. R. Howell, MBE, of Overmonnow, Monmouth (First Radio Officer, ss. *Corinthic*).

Captain Thomas H. Irvin of North Shields, Northumberland (Master, ss. *Clintonia*).

Captain Reginald A. Leach of Tonbridge, Kent (Second Mate, ss. *Empire Miniver*).

Charles P. Littleboy of Brisbane, Australia (Radio Officer, ss. *Trevisa*).

Captain Charles R. Madsen of South Shields, Co. Durham (Master, ss. *Eaglescliffe Hall*).

Captain John Mathiesen of Oslo, Norway (Chief Officer, ss. *Sneland 1*).

Sture Mattsson of Stockholm, Sweden (A.B., ss. *Gunborg*).

Bjarne Mjaanes of Auklandshamn, Norway (Steward, ss. *Sneland 1*).

Bernard J. McGovern c/o Marconi Marine (First Radio Officer, ss. *Somersby*).

Inspektor Karl J. Petersen of Gothenburg, Sweden (First Engineer, mv. *Valparaiso*).

Captain Alexander Smith of Findochty, Banffshire (Second Mate, ss. *Shekatika*).

Captain Jack Reardon Smith of Cardiff (Chief Officer, ss. *Botusk*).

Captain Robert Smith of Durham (Master, ss. *Empire Miniver*).

Chief Engineer William H. Venables of Irby, Cheshire (Second Engineer, ss. *Assyrian*).

Captain John Morrison Waters of South Shields, Co. Durham (Second Mate, ss. *Empire Brigade*).

Captain Lawrence Zebedee Weatherill of Llandaff, Cardiff (Master, ss. *Scoresby*).

And from Convoy HX79 :

William J. Edbrooke of Brentwood, Essex (Senior Third Engineer, mv. *Wandby*).

James Griffiths of Rusholme, Manchester (Crew member, mv. *Sitala*).

Captain John Kenny of Arklow, Eire (Master, mv. *Wandby*).

Charles Walker of Pendlebury, Manchester (Crew member, mv. *Sitala*).

The authors thank the following relatives for their generous help and provision of letters and notes:

Mrs. Mary E. Aves, Hartlepool, wife of Chief Engineer James E. Aves, ss. *Sedgepool*; Mrs. Elizabeth Dekonski, Arklow, Eire, daughter of Captain John Kenny, mv. *Wandby*; Miss Sally Green, Belfast, sister of Chief Officer John Green, ss. *Empire Miniver*; Kevin R. Kearon and Roy T. Kearon, Arklow, Eire, brothers of Captain Reginald S. Kearon, OBE, ss. *Assyrian*; Thoralf Laegland, Haugesund, Norway, son of Captain Laegland, ss. *Sneland 1*; Mrs. Constance M. Stracy, Manchester, wife of Radio Officer Robert A. Stracy, ss. *Assyrian*; Mrs. J. W. Thompson, Cardiff, wife of Captain J. William Thompson, ss. *Somersby*.

The authors thank the staff of the General Register Office of Shipping and Seamen, Cardiff, for their patient assistance during three years of research; also the Public Archives of Canada, Montreal; The Marconi International Marine Company Limited, Chelmsford, Essex; and the following shipping companies:

Rich. Amlie & Co., Haugesund, Norway; Andreadis (U.K.) Ltd., London; Billnerbolagen, Gothenburg, Sweden; Cairns, Noble & Co. Ltd., Newcastle upon Tyne; Canada Steamship Lines Ltd., Montreal; Ellerman Lines Ltd., London; Wm. France, Fenwick & Co. Ltd., London; Hall Corporation (Shipping) 1969 Ltd., Montreal; Headlam & Son, Whitby; Johnsonlinjen, Stockholm; Jacob Kjode, Bergen, Norway; Jacob Odland, Haugesund, Norway; Sir R. Ropner & Co. Ltd., Darlington; Christian Salvesen (Managers) Ltd., Leith; Sir William Reardon Smith & Sons Ltd., Cardiff; Stag Line Ltd., North Shields; Vickers Ltd., Barrow-in-Furness; Vinke & Co., Amsterdam; Witherington & Everett, Newcastle upon Tyne.

THE NAVAL ESCORTS

Commander Robert Aubrey, DSC, RN, Ringwood, Hants. (Lieutenant-Commander, HMS *Fowey*).
George S. Boyd, Epsom, Surrey (Chief Stoker, HMS *Leith*).
Lieutenant-Commander Neil K. Boyd, DSC and Bar, RD, RNR, Barton-on-Sea, Hants. (Navigating Officer, HMS *Scarborough*).
Lieutenant Patrick N. Culverwell, RNVR, Leicester (Sub-Lieutenant, HMS *Fowey*).
Rear-Admiral N. Vincent Dickinson, CB, DSO, DSC, Alresford, Hants. (Commander, HMS *Scarborough*).

Lieutenant John D. Hill, RNVR, Ipswich (Navigating Officer, HMS *Heartsease*).

William J. Jenkins, Bramhall, Cheshire (AB/TO, RNR, HMS *Scarborough*).

Eric R. Semmens, Orpington, Kent (Telegraphist, HMS *Leith*).

Captain Robert E. Sherwood, Commander, DSO, RD, RNR, Wendover, Bucks. (Lieutenant-Commander, HMS *Bluebell*).

Commander Anthony S. Tyers, DSC, RN, Aylesbury, Bucks. (Sub-Lieutenant, HMS *Leith*).

The authors thank the following relatives for their very kind assistance :

Miss Enid Allen, London, sister of Commander Roland C. Allen, RN, HMS *Leith* (later Captain Allen, RN); Mrs Ione Carver, Farnham, Surrey, and Mrs Fynvola L. James, Northwood, Middlesex, daughters, and Captain Ughtred H. R. James, CBE, RN, son-in-law, of Vice-Admiral Lachlan Donald Ian MacKinnon, CB, CVO; Miss Cora E. North, Chinnor, Oxon., sister of Lieutenant-Commander Edward J. R. North, RNR, HMS *Heartsease* (later Captain North, RD, RNR).

Also :

R. H. Howard, London (SBA, HMS *Scarborough*).

Dr B. J. Mead, Broadstone, Dorset (Lieutenant, RNVR, HMS *Scarborough*).

Charles H. A. Scott, Dorridge, Warwicks. (Signalman, HMS *Heartsease*).

Stan Stansfield, Manchester (HMS *Scarborough*).

Douglas F. Whittaker, Hereford (Leading Signalman, HMS *Fowey*).

The authors gratefully acknowledge the special contribution made by Korvettenkapitan Heinrich Bleichrodt, Knight's Cross of the Iron Cross, Knight's Cross with Oak Leaves, of Munich, W. Germany (Kapitanleutnant, U-48); and the help of Captain K. T. Raeder, FGN, Naval Attaché, Embassy of the Federal Republic of Germany, London; and Podzun-Verlag, Bad Nauheim, W. Germany.

Also the following kind helpers :

Mrs Ann Baird, Glasgow; Ruth and Eric Bardsley, Bollington, Cheshire; Gordon Duff, St John's, Newfoundland; A. C. Hughes, Hull; Leonard J. McLaughlin, Montreal; Gilbert E. Porteous, Cardiff; Donald Sanderson, Newcastle upon Tyne; A. A. Smith,

Amsterdam; Jeremiah J. Smith, Edinburgh; Theodore Vokos, Piraeus, Greece (Editor 'Naftiliaki'); Mrs. D. Wetterhahn, London.

Finally the authors express their thanks to the many newspapers and magazines which helped in the quest for veterans of SC7, and in particular to the following: *Daily Telegraph*; *Flying Angel*; *Hull Daily Mail*; *Montreal Star*; *The Navy*; *Navy News*; *Newcastle Evening Chronicle*; *Scottish Daily Express*; *Sea Breezes*; *Wexford People*; *Manchester Evening News*; *Liverpool Echo*; *Bridport News*.

Index